TENTH EDITION

Language Awareness

Readings for College Writers

Paul Eschholz

Alfred Rosa

Virginia Clark

UNIVERSITY OF VERMONT

BEDFORD / ST. MARTIN'S   Boston ● New York

For Bedford/St. Martin's

SENIOR DEVELOPMENTAL EDITOR: Alexis P. Walker
PRODUCTION EDITOR: Karen Stocz
PRODUCTION SUPERVISOR: Andrew Ensor
MARKETING MANAGER: Molly Parke
ART DIRECTOR: Lucy Krikorian
TEXT DESIGN: Anna Palchik
COPY EDITOR: Virgina Rubens
PHOTO RESEARCH: Rachel Youdelman
COVER DESIGN: Donna L. Dennison
COVER ART: Ben Allen, "The Words We Leave in the Air"
COMPOSITION: Macmillan Publishing Solutions
PRINTING AND BINDING: Haddon Craftsmen, Inc., an RR Donnelley & Sons Company

PRESIDENT: Joan E. Feinberg
EDITORIAL DIRECTOR: Denise B. Wydra
EDITOR IN CHIEF: Karen S. Henry
DIRECTOR OF DEVELOPMENT: Erica T. Appel
DIRECTOR OF MARKETING: Karen R. Soeltz
DIRECTOR OF EDITING, DESIGN, AND PRODUCTION: Marcia Cohen
ASSISTANT DIRECTOR OF EDITING, DESIGN, AND PRODUCTION: Elise S. Kaiser
MANAGING EDITOR: Shuli Traub

Library of Congress Control Number: 2008940925

Manufactured in the United States of America.

3 2 1 0 9
f e d c b a

For information, write: Bedford/St. Martin's, 75 Arlington Street, Boston, MA 02116   (617-399-4000)

ISBN-10: 0-312-46316-2
ISBN-13: 978-0-312-46316-8

Acknowledgments

PREFACE

Since the first edition of *Language Awareness* appeared in 1974, its purpose has been twofold: to foster an appreciation of the richness, flexibility, and vitality of the English language and to help students to use their language more responsibly and effectively in speech and particularly in writing. These dual aims produced a text that has been used successfully in a variety of courses over the years. Its primary use, however, has been and continues to be in college composition courses. Clearly, many instructors believe as we do—that the study of language and the study of writing go hand in hand.

Because the study of language is so multifaceted, we cover a broad spectrum of topics, including the history of English, the relationship between language and culture, the language of new technologies, and the power of language in influencing advertising, politics, the media, and gender roles. Opening students' eyes to the power of language—its ability to shape and manipulate perceptions and cultural attitudes—is, we believe, one of the worthiest goals a writing class can pursue.

NEW TO THE TENTH EDITION

As in previous editions of *Language Awareness*, the selections in the tenth edition are written primarily in nontechnical language and on topics of current interest. Our questions and introductory material help students to understand those topics, providing clearly defined opportunities for thoughtful writing. Guided by comments and advice from hundreds of colleagues and students across the country who have used the previous editions, we have made some dramatic improvements in this tenth edition.

New Selections

Forty-three selections—over half of the seventy-eight selections in *Language Awareness*—are new to this edition. These selections, chosen for their insight and clear, thought-provoking writing, reflect the language issues of an increasingly complex, multicultural America. Representing a wide variety of ethnic voices, the readings also address the language concerns of other minority groups, with readings on gay rights and deaf culture. New selections include Steven Pinker's "Words Don't Mean What They Mean," Sissela Bok's "The Burden of Deceit in Public Life," Al Gore's "Time to Make Peace with the Planet: 2007 Nobel Prize for Peace Lecture," Andrew Sullivan's "What's So Bad about Hate?," Alleen Pace Nilsen's "From the Dixie Chicks to the St. Louis Rams: What Animal-Based Metaphors Reveal about Sexism," Chang-Rae Lee's "Mute in an English-Only World," Deborah Tannen's "You're Wearing *That*? Under-standing Mothers and Daughters in Conversation," and Naomi Klein's "Barricading the Branded Village."

We believe that the new selections will spark student interest and bring currency to the classic, informative, and well-written essays retained from earlier editions, which include Gordon Allport's "The Language of Prejudice," Helen Keller's "The Day Language Came into My Life," Martin Luther King Jr.'s "I Have a Dream," William Lutz's "The World of Doublespeak," Malcolm X's "Discovering the Power of Language," Gloria Naylor's "The Meanings of a Word," and George Orwell's "Politics and the English Language."

Expanded Introductory Chapters on Reading and Writing

To supplement the study of language with instruction in reading and writing, we have not only expanded the general introduction, but also divided it into two distinct sections so as to focus on and give in-depth coverage to the twin tasks of reading and writing. Based on years of class-room experience, these new chapters provide students with the essentials of college reading and writing. The first chapter, "Reading Critically," provides students with guidelines for critical reading, demonstrates how they can get the most out of their reading by taking advantage of the apparatus accompanying each selection, and shows how they can generate their own writing from the reading they do. The second chapter, "Writing in College," explores the world of academic writing. Here students learn how to master the core elements that all instructors expect in academic essays, starting with an understanding of the writing assignment itself, establishing a thesis, determining an organization, using evidence, and culminating with documenting sources and avoiding plagiarism. Each step in the process is illustrated with a student essay in progress, and the chapter concludes with the complete paper fully documented according to 2009 MLA guidelines.

New Thematic Chapter

Students and teachers, pleased with the relevancy of the thematic chapters in past editions of *Language Awareness*, asked us to provide more material on the speech communities to which we belong as well as new material on language and gender. The result is "Everyday Conversations," a new thematic chapter that offers a collection of readings on each of these important topics, prompting discussion about how we reveal ourselves—where we come from, who we are, and who we'd like to be—in the language we use every day.

New "Language Debates"

The three debates on current language issues—Chapter 7, "Should Learning Be Censored?"; Chapter 8, "Should English Be the Law?"; and Chapter 9, "What's All the Fuss about Natural, Organic, Local Foods?"—are a new feature of this edition. Students will find six articles in each Language Debate chapter, each article offering a different viewpoint on the topic. The debates begin with an introduction of the essential issue, together with an overview of how the multiple perspectives play off one another. The end-of-selection questions and the writing suggestions invite students to bring language concepts and ideas learned in the first six core chapters to bear on the topics of the Language Debates: "Thinking Critically about the Reading" questions at the end of each selection test students on the basic content of each reading, and, at the end of each chapter, a set of Writing Suggestions offers students opportunities to join in the debate by extending their analyses of individual articles and making connections among the various perspectives of the writers.

New Paired Essays in Core Chapters

In each of the first six core chapters, we have included a set of paired essays that offer students different ways of looking at a single issue. The questions following each of the articles in the pair ask students to make connections between the selections and develop their own ideas on the issue. Several of the pairs offer opposing arguments, while others simply present interesting perspectives on a common topic. For example, in Chapter 1 we have paired Henry Louis Gates Jr.'s "What's in a Name?" with Tom Rosenberg's "Changing My Name after Sixty Years," two essays that explore how closely our names are tied to our identities. In Chapter 3, Jonathan Swift's "A Modest Proposal" and George Saunders's "My Amendment" demonstrate how satire can be used for political ends. The use of derogatory language provides the focus for discussion of Gloria Naylor's "The Meanings of a Word" and Andi Zeisler's "The B-Word? You Betcha" in Chapter 4. And in Chapter 6, Andrew Keen's "The Cult of the Amateur" and Annalee Newitz's "What Happens When Blogs Go Mainstream?" explore the significance of the Internet's flood of amateur reporters and ad hoc commentators.

KEY FEATURES OF THE TEXT

Class-Tested Topics

Instructors have told us that "Coming to an Awareness of Language," "Writers on Writing," "Politics, Propaganda, and Doublespeak," "Prejudice, Discrimination, and Stereotypes," and "Media and Advertising" are indispensable in the courses they teach. Not only do the readings in these chapters represent essential areas of language study, but they also teach students useful ways to look at and write about the world around them. Each of these chapters has been updated with new essays that reflect recent trends, but they retain the spirit and purpose of their predecessors.

Chapter Introductions

Brief, one-to two-page chapter introductions discuss the key elements of each chapter's topic and explain why the topic is important to study. In addition, the introductions briefly discuss individual readings, explaining how they connect to larger language issues and how they relate to each other.

Student-Tested Headnotes, Journal Prompts, Questions, Activities, and Writing Suggestions

INFORMATIVE HEADNOTES. Headnotes preceding each selection discuss the content of the essay and provide pertinent information about the author and where and when the selection was first published.

"WRITING TO DISCOVER" JOURNAL PROMPTS. Each selection begins with a journal prompt designed to get students writing—before they start reading—about their own experiences with the language issues discussed in the selection. Students are then more likely to approach the selection with a critical eye. From time to time, class activities or writing assignments ask students to return to these journal writings and to reflect on them before proceeding with more formal writing tasks.

END-OF-SELECTION QUESTIONS. The "Thinking Critically about the Reading" questions at the end of each selection emphasize both content and analysis. Content questions prompt students to develop a deeper understanding of ideas contained in the essay, in some cases by drawing connections to other readings or to their own experiences. Other questions ask students to explore and analyze the writer's strategies, in order to determine how effective writing achieves its aims.

"LANGUAGE IN ACTION" ACTIVITIES.   The Language in Action activities that follow every selection in Chapters 1 through 6 give students a chance to analyze real world examples of the language issues discussed by the essayists, with poems, cartoons, movie reviews, parodies, advertisements, photographs, essay excerpts, letters to the editor, syndicated columns, and more. Designed to be completed either in class or at home in about twenty minutes, these activities ask students to take a hands-on approach to what they are learning from the essays and give them a chance to demonstrate their growing language aptitude.

END-OF-SELECTION WRITING SUGGESTIONS.   To give students more opportunities to practice thinking and writing, we provide several Writing Suggestions at the end of every selection in Chapters 1 through 6 and at the end of each Language Debate. Each suggestion is designed to elicit a three- to five-page paper. Some assignments ask students to use their "Writing to Discover" journal entries as springboards for an extended essay; others ask students to use their analytical skills to make critical connections among articles on the same topic; and some assignments ask students to do library or community-based research in order, for example, to examine the language used in local public documents, the language used in law offices, or campus slang.

Appendix: Finding, Evaluating, and Documenting Sources

This helpful appendix provides greater detail on these sometimes thorny aspects of the research process: conducting research using print and online sources, developing a working bibliography, using subject directories and keyword searches on the Internet, taking notes, and documenting sources using 2009 MLA guidelines for constructing a List of Works Cited.

Glossary of Rhetorical and Linguistic Terms

The Glossary of Rhetorical and Linguistic Terms includes definitions of key language terms and concepts as well as the standard terminology of rhetoric. References to glossary entries appear where needed in the questions that accompany each selection, allowing students to look up unfamiliar terms as they read.

Rhetorical Contents

At the end of the text, an alternate table of contents classifies the selections in *Language Awareness* according to the rhetorical strategies they exemplify, making it easier for instructors to assign readings that parallel the types of writing their students are doing.

HELPFUL SUPPLEMENTS

Free Resources

INSTRUCTOR'S MANUAL   Packed with teaching tips and suggested answers to end-of-selection questions, the Instructor's Manual also offers advice on how to approach the Language in Action activities.

BOOK COMPANION SITE (bedfordstmartins.com/languageaware-ness)   The companion Web site makes *Language Awareness* an even more effective teaching tool. The free site offers resources for both instructors and students, including a PDF version of the Instructor's Manual, comprehension quizzes for every reading, a variety of resources for research and documentation, and links to numerous sites that expand on topics covered in the text.

RE: WRITING: ONLINE COMPOSITION RESOURCES (bedfordstmartins .com/rewriting)   This open-access site collects the best free resources in one convenient location. In addition to a host of useful assignments, activities, exercises, and tutorials, the site offers access to Diana Hacker's invaluable *Research and Documentation Online* material and to *Exercise Central,* where students can practice grammar, punctuation, and mechanics with more than nine thousand self-grading exercises.

Premium Resources

The items below can be packaged with the textbook at a small additional cost to your students. Visit **bedfordstmartins.com/languageawareness/ catalog** to see these and other packaging options.

RE: WRITING PLUS   (bedfordstmartins.com/rewritingplus) neatly gathers our collections of premium digital content into one online library for composition. *Re: Writing Plus* features *Peer Factor,* an online role-playing game introducing students to best practices for giving and receiving peer comments; *icite: visualizing sources* tutorials and hands-on source practice; an online anthology of essays, poems, and stories; hundreds of model documents; and more. Please use ISBN-10: 0-312-56263-2; ISBN-13: 978-0-312-56263-2 when ordering this package.

COMPCLASS   (bedfordstmartins.com/compclass) is the first online course space shaped by the needs of composition students and instructors. In *CompClass,* students can read assignments, do their work, and see their grades all in one place, and instructors can easily monitor student progress and give feedback right away. *CompClass* comes preloaded with the innovative digital content that Bedford/St. Martin's is known for. Please use ISBN-10: 0-312-57524-6; ISBN-13: 978-0-312-57524-3 when ordering this package.

ACKNOWLEDGMENTS

We are grateful to the following reviewers, whose comments helped us shape this edition:

Rosemary Adang, Highline Community College; Thomas Allbaugh, Azusa Pacific University; Beth Bir, Fayetteville State University; Jon W. Brooks, Okaloosa-Walton College; Patricia Donaher, Missouri Western State University; Judith E. Funston, SUNY–Potsdam; Karen K. Gibson, SUNY–Potsdam; Matthew Horn, Kent State University; Philip Hu, Cerritos College; Barbara Hunt, Columbus State University; Joseph Jones, University of Memphis; Cristina Karmas, Graceland University; Beverly R. Lewis, Middle Tennessee State University; Mark Lidman, Metropolitan Community College–Maple Woods; April Middeljans, University of Illinois–Urbana-Champaign; Julie Nichols, Okaloosa-Walton College; Tonia Nikopoulos, University of Illinois–Chicago; Don L.F. Nilsen, Arizona State University; Rayshell E. Palmer, Seminole State College; Matthew Roudané, Georgia State University; Ilene Rubenstein, California State University–Northridge; Tracy Schneider, Solano Community College; Rebecca Shapiro, St. Thomas Aquinas College; Daniel Siddiqi, University of Arizona; Donna Smith-Raymond, SUNY–Potsdam; James D. Suderman, Okaloosa-Walton College; and Matt Willen, Elizabethtown College.

We would like to express our appreciation to the staff at Bedford/ St. Martin's, especially Stephanie Butler and Alexis Walker for supporting us in our efforts to design innovative and engaging Language Debates that provide strong links between language study and real world issues. Cecilia Seiter handled a number of important tasks and facilitated manuscript flow. Thanks go to Karen Stocz, our production editor; to Virginia Rubens, our superlative copyeditor; to Sandy Schechter, Barbara Hernandez, Martha Friedman, and Rachel Youdelman for clearing permissions; to Jan Weber, for her help in developing questions for some of the new selections and for contributing to the Instructor's Manual; and to Sarah Federman for developing reading questions that appear on the book's companion Web site (bedfordstmartins.com/languageawareness). Without our students at the University of Vermont over the years, a book such as *Language Awareness* would not have been possible. Their enthusiasm for language study and writing and their responses to materials included in this book have proved invaluable.

Finally, we thank each other. Beginning in 1971 we have collaborated on many textbooks in language and writing, all of which have gone into multiple editions. With this tenth edition of *Language Awareness*, we enter the thirty-eighth year of working together. Ours must be one of the longest-running and most mutually satisfying writing partnerships in college textbook publishing. The journey has been invigorating and challenging as we have come to understand the complexities and joys of good writing and sought out new ways to help students become better writers.

PAUL ESCHHOLZ
ALFRED ROSA
VIRGINIA CLARK

CONTENTS

    "I saw that the best thing I could do was get hold of a dictionary — to study, to learn some words."

READING CRITICALLY

The readings in *Language Awareness* emphasize the crucial role language plays in virtually every aspect of our lives, and they reveal the essential elements of the writer's craft. As you read and study the selections in this text, you will discover the power of language in our world: You will become more aware of your own language usage and how it affects others, and, at the same time, you will become more sensitive to how the language of others affects you. An additional benefit of close, critical reading is that you will become more familiar with different types of writing and learn how good writers make decisions about writing strategies and techniques. All of these insights will help you become a more thoughtful, discerning reader and, equally important, a better writer.

As the word *critical* suggests, reading critically means questioning what you read in a thoughtful, organized way and with an alert, inquiring mind. Critical reading is a skill you need if you are truly to engage and understand the content of a piece of writing as well as the craft that shapes the writer's ideas into an effective, efficient, and presentable form. Never accept what you read simply because it's in print. Instead, scrutinize it, challenge it, and think about its meaning and significance.

Critical reading is also a skill that takes time and practice to acquire. While most of us learned before we got to college how to read for content and summarize what a writer said, not all of us learned how to analyze what we were reading. Reading critically is like engaging a writer in a conversation—asking for the meaning of a particular statement, questioning the definition of a crucial term, or demanding more evidence to support a generalization. In addition, critical reading requires asking ourselves why we like one piece of writing and not another, or why one argument is more believable or convincing than another.

As you learn more about reading thoughtfully and purposefully, you will come to a better understanding of both the content and the craft of any piece of writing. As an added bonus, learning to read critically will help you read your own work with more insight and, as a result, write more persuasively.

GETTING THE MOST OUT OF YOUR READING

Critical reading requires, first of all, that you commit time and effort. Second, it requires that you apply goodwill and energy to understanding and appreciating what you are reading, even if the subject matter does not immediately appeal to you. Remember, your mission is twofold: You must analyze and comprehend the content of what you are reading; and then, you must understand the writer's methods, to see firsthand the kinds of choices a writer makes in his or her writing.

To help you grow as a critical reader and to get the most out of what you read, use the following classroom-proven steps:

1. Prepare yourself to read a selection.
2. Read the selection to get an overview of it.
3. Annotate the selection with marginal notes.
4. Summarize the selection in your own words.
5. Analyze the selection to come to an understanding of it.

To demonstrate how these steps can work for you, we've applied them to an essay by the popular nonfiction writer Natalie Goldberg. Like the other selections in *Language Awareness,* Goldberg's essay "Be Specific" is accessible and speaks to an important contemporary language issue. She points to the importance of using specific names in speaking and writing, and she demonstrates how we give things their proper dignity and integrity when we name them.

1. Prepare Yourself to Read the Selection

Instead of diving into any given selection in *Language Awareness* or any other book, there are a few things that you can do that will prepare you to get the most out of what you will read. It's helpful, for example, to get a context for what you'll read. What's the essay about? What do you know about the writer's background and reputation? Where was the essay first published? Who was the intended audience for the essay? And, finally, how much do you already know about the subject of the reading selection? We encourage you to consider carefully the materials that precede each selection in this book. Each selection begins with a title, headnote, and journal prompt. From the **title** you often discover the writer's position on an issue or attitude toward the topic. On occasion, the title can give clues about the intended audience and the writer's purpose in writing the piece. The **headnote** contains a biographical note about the author followed by publication information and rhetorical highlights about the selection. In addition to information on the person's life and work, you'll read about his or her reputation and authority to write on the subject of the piece. The **publication information** indicates when the essay was published and in what book or magazine it first appeared. This information, in turn, gives you insight about the intended audience. The **rhetorical highlights** direct your attention to one or more aspects of how the selection was written. Finally, the Writing to Discover **journal prompt** encourages you to collect your thoughts and opinions about the topic or related issues before you commence reading. The journal prompt makes it easy to keep a record of your own knowledge or thinking on a topic before you see what the writer has to offer.

To understand how these context-building materials can work for you, carefully review the following informational materials that accompany Natalie Goldberg's essay "Be Specific."

Be Specific

NATALIE GOLDBERG

Born in 1948, author Natalie Goldberg is a teacher of writing who has conducted writing workshops across the country. In addition to her classes and workshops, Goldberg shares her love of writing in her books; she has made writing about writing her speciality. Her first and best-known work, *Writing Down the Bones: Freeing the Writer Within,* was published in 1986. Goldberg's advice to would-be writers is practical and pithy, on the one hand, and mystical or spiritual in its call to know and become more connected to our environment. In short, as one reviewer observed, "Goldberg teaches us not only how to write better, but how to live better." *Writing Down the Bones* was followed by five more books about writing: *Wild Mind: Living the Writer's Life* (1990), *Living Color: A Writer Paints Her World* (1996), *Thunder and Lightning: Cracking Open the Writer's Craft* (2000), and *Old Friend from Far Away: The Practice of Writing Memoir* (2008). Altogether, more than a million copies of these books are now in print. Goldberg has also written fiction—the novel *Banana Rose* (1995)—and autobiography: *Long Quiet Highway: Waking Up in America* (1993) and *The Great Failure: A Bartender, a Monk, and My Unlikely Path to Truth* (2004).

"Be Specific" is taken from Goldberg's *Writing Down the Bones* and is representative of the book as a whole. Notice the ways in which Goldberg demonstrates her advice to be specific. Which of her many examples resonates best with you?

WRITING TO DISCOVER: *Suppose someone says to you, "I walked in the woods today." What do you envision? Write down what you see in your mind's eye. Now suppose someone says, "I walked in the redwood forest today." Again, write what you see. What's different about your two descriptions, and why?*

Marginal labels:
Title
[Headnote]
Biographical information
Publication information
Rhetorical highlight
Journal prompt

From reading these preliminary materials, what expectations do you have for the selection itself? How does this knowledge equip you to engage the selection before you actually read it? From the *title* you probably inferred that Goldberg will explain what she means by the command "be specific" and what is to be gained by following this advice. Her purpose clearly is to give advice to writers. The *biographical note* reveals that Goldberg has written a number of books detailing her own experiences with writing as well as giving advice to aspiring writers of all ages, and that she has taught writing courses and conducted writing workshops for many years. This experience gives her the knowledge and authority to write on this topic. The *publication information* indicates that the subject of Goldberg's essay is an argument in favor of being specific in writing. Because the selection was first published as part of her book *Writing Down the Bones: Freeing the Writer Within,* Goldberg can anticipate that readers, who we can assume are looking for writing advice, will be open to her argument. The *rhetorical highlight* alerts you to be mindful of how Goldberg practices what she's preaching in her own writing and prompts you to consider her examples. Finally, the *journal prompt*—a hands-on exercise in specificity—asks you to describe in writing the visuals conjured up in your mind by two statements and to draw conclusions about any differences you note in your responses.

It's always a good practice to take several minutes before reading a selection to reflect on what you already know about a particular issue and where you stand on it and why. After reading Goldberg's essay, you can compare your own experiences with being specific—or being unspecific—in writing with those of Goldberg.

2. Read the Selection to Get an Overview of It

Always read the selection at least twice, no matter how long it is. The first reading gives you a chance to get acquainted with the essay and to form first impressions. With the first reading you want to get an overall sense of what the writer is saying, keeping in mind the essay's title and what you learned about the writer in the headnote. The essay will offer you information, ideas, and arguments—some you may have expected; some you may not have. As you read, you may find yourself questioning or modifying your sense of what the writer is saying. Resist the urge to annotate at this point; instead, concentrate on the content, on the main points of what's being said. Now read Natalie Goldberg's essay.

Be Specific

NATALIE GOLDBERG

Be specific. Don't say "fruit." Tell what kind of fruit—"It is a pomegranate." Give things the dignity of their names. Just as with human beings, it is rude to say, "Hey, girl, get in line." That "girl" has a name. (As a matter of fact, if she's at least twenty years old, she's a woman, not a "girl" at all.) Things, too, have names. It is much better to say "the geranium in the window" than "the flower in the window." "Geranium"—that one word gives us a much more specific picture. It penetrates more deeply into the beingness of that flower. It immediately gives us the scene by the window—red petals, green circular leaves, all straining toward sunlight.

About ten years ago I decided I had to learn the names of plants and flowers in my environment. I bought a book on them and walked down the tree-lined streets of Boulder, examining leaf, bark, and seed, trying to match them up with their descriptions and names in the book. Maple, elm, oak, locust. I usually tried to cheat by asking people working in their yards the names of the flowers and trees growing there. I was amazed how few people had any idea of the names of the live beings inhabiting their little plot of land.

When we know the name of something, it brings us closer to the ground. It takes the blur out of our mind; it connects us to the earth. If I walk down the street and see "dogwood," "forsythia," I feel more friendly toward the environment. I am noticing what is around me and can name it. It makes me more awake.

If you read the poems of William Carlos Williams, you will see how specific he is about plants, trees, flowers—chicory, daisy, locust, poplar, quince, primrose, black-eyed Susan, lilacs—each has its own integrity. Williams says, "Write what's in front of your nose." It's good for us to know what is in front of our noses. Not just "daisy," but how the flower is in the season we are looking at it—"The dayseye hugging the earth/in August . . . brownedged,/green and pointed scales/armor his yellow."* Continue to hone your awareness: to the name, to the month, to the day, and finally to the moment.

Williams also says: "No idea, but in things." Study what is "in front of your nose." By saying "geranium" instead of "flower," you are penetrating more deeply into the present and being there. The closer we can get to what's in front of our nose, the more it can teach us everything. "To see the World in a Grain of Sand, and a heaven in a Wild Flower . . . "** 5

In writing groups and classes too, it is good to quickly learn the names of all the other group members. It helps to ground you in the group and make you more attentive to each other's work.

Learn the names of everything: birds, cheese, tractors, cars, buildings. A writer is all at once everything—an architect, French cook, farmer—and at the same time, a writer is none of these things.

---

* William Carlos Williams, "Daisy," in *The Collected Earlier Poems* (New York: New Directions, 1938). [Goldberg's note.]

** William Blake, "The Auguries of Innocence." [Goldberg's note.]

Some students find it valuable to capture their first impressions, thoughts, or reactions immediately after they've finished reading a selection. If you keep a reading journal, record your ideas in a paragraph or two. You are now ready for the second reading of the essay, this time with pencil or pen in hand to annotate the text.

3. Annotate the Selection with Marginal Notes

As you read the essay a second time, engage it—highlight key passages and make marginal annotations. Your second reading will be quite different from your first, because you already know what the essay is about, where it is going, and how it gets there. Now you can relate the parts of the essay more accurately to the whole. Use the second reading to test your first impressions against the words on the page, developing and deepening your sense of the writer's argument. Because you already have a general understanding of the essay's content and structure, you can focus on the writer's purpose and means of achieving it. You can look for features of organization and style that you can learn from and adapt to your own work.

One question that students frequently ask us is "What should I annotate?" When you annotate a text, you should do more than simply underline or highlight what you think are the important points to remember. Instead, as you read, write down your thoughts, reactions, and questions in the margins or on a separate piece of paper. Think of your annotations as an opportunity to have a conversation with the writer of the essay.

Mark what you believe to be the selection's main point when you find it stated directly. Look for the pattern or patterns of development the author uses to explore and support that point, and record the information. If you disagree with a statement or conclusion, object in the margin: "No!" If you're not convinced by the writer's claims or evidence, indicate that response: "Why?" or "Who says?" or "Explain." If you are impressed by an argument or turn of phrase, compliment the writer: "Good point." If there are any words that you do not recognize or that seem to you to be used in a questionable way, circle them so that you can look them up in a dictionary.

Jot down whatever marginal notes come naturally to you. Most readers combine brief responses written in the margins with their own system of underlining, circling, highlighting, stars, vertical lines, and question marks.

Remember that there are no hard-and-fast rules for which elements you annotate. Choose a method of annotation that works best for you and that will make sense to you when you go back to recollect your thoughts and responses to the essay. When annotating a text, don't be timid. Mark up your book as much as you like, or jot down as many responses in your notebook as you think will be helpful. Don't let

---

How to Annotate a Text

Here are some suggestions of elements you may want to mark
to help you keep a record of your responses as you read:

- Memorable statements of important points
- Key terms or concepts
- Central issues or themes
- Examples that support a main point
- Unfamiliar words
- Questions you have about a point or passage
- Your responses to a specific point or passage

---

annotating become burdensome. A word or phrase is usually as good as
a sentence. Notice how one of our students used marginal annotations to
record her responses to Goldberg's text.

Be specific. Don't say "fruit." Tell what kind of
fruit—"It is a pomegranate." Give things the dignity
of their names. Just as with human beings, it is rude to
say, "Hey, girl, get in line." That "girl" has a name.
(As a matter of fact, if she's at least twenty years old,
she's a woman, not a "girl" at all.) Things, too,
have names. It is much better to say "the geranium
in the window" than "the flower in the window."
"Geranium"—that one word gives us a much more
specific picture. It penetrates more deeply into the
beingness of that flower. It immediately gives us the
scene by the window—red petals, green circular leaves,
all straining toward sunlight.

About ten years ago I decided I had to learn
the names of plants and flowers in my environment. I
bought a book on them and walked down the tree-lined
streets of Boulder, examining leaf, bark, and seed, trying
to match them up with their descriptions and names
in the book. Maple, elm, oak, locust. I usually tried to
cheat by asking people working in their yards the names

I agree—tho my grandma calls her friends "the girls"—?

I think I do pay more attn. when people call me by name.

She's practicing what she preaches—but that's a LOT of work....

I doubt I could tell the difference between a maple and an elm.

of the flowers and trees growing there. I was amazed how few people had any idea of the names of the live beings inhabiting their little plot of land.

THESIS → When we know the name of something, it brings us closer to the ground. It takes the blur out of our mind; it connects us to the earth. If I walk down the street and see

Interesting — wonder if it's true. (How could you test it?)

"dogwood," "forsythia," I feel more friendly toward the environment. I am noticing what is around me and can name it. It makes me more awake.

Is Williams a really famous poet? LOOK THIS UP. Why does she keep quoting him?

If you read the poems of William Carlos Williams, you will see how specific he is about plants, trees, flowers—chicory, daisy, locust, poplar, quince, primrose, black-eyed Susan, lilacs—each has its own integrity. Williams says, "Write what's in front of your nose." It's good for us to know what is in front of our noses. Not just "daisy," but how the flower is in the season we are looking at it—"The dayseye hugging the earth/in August . . . brownedged,/green and pointed scales/armor his yellow." Continue to hone your awareness: to the name, to the month, to the day, and finally to the moment.

Williams also says: "No idea, but in things." Study what is "in front of your nose." By saying "geranium" instead of "flower," you are penetrating more deeply into the present and being there. The closer we can get to what's in front of our nose, the more it can teach us everything. "To see the World in a Grain of Sand, and a heaven in a Wild Flower . . . "

I know I couldn't name all the people in my writing class. (Wonder if it would make a difference)

In writing groups and classes too, it is good to quickly learn the names of all the other group members. It helps to ground you in the group and make you more attentive to each other's work.

Not sure what she means here. How can a writer be "all" and "none" of these things??

Learn the names of everything: birds, cheese, tractors, cars, buildings. A writer is all at once everything—an architect, French cook, farmer—and at the same time, a writer is none of these things.

4. Outline the Selection in Your Own Words

After carefully annotating the selection, you will find it worthwhile to summarize what the writer has said, to see how the main points work together to give support to the writer's thesis. An efficient way to do this is to make a simple paragraph-by-paragraph outline of what you've read. Try to capture the essence of each paragraph in a single sentence. Such an outline enables you to understand how the essay works, to see what the writer's position is and how he or she has structured the essay and organized the main ideas.

Consider the following paragraph-by-paragraph outline one of our students made after reading Goldberg's essay:

Paragraph 1: Goldberg announces her topic and demonstrates the power of names with the example of the geranium.

Paragraph 2: She recounts how she went about learning the names of plants and trees in her Colorado neighborhood.

Paragraph 3: She explains how knowing the names of things makes her feel connected to the world around her.

Paragraph 4: She uses the example of poet William Carlos Williams to support her point about the power of names.

Paragraph 5: She continues with the example of Williams to broaden the discussion of what it means to "penetrate more deeply" into the world that is "in front of your nose."

Paragraph 6: She says that knowing the names of people in your writing group or class creates community.

Paragraph 7: She advises writers to "learn the names of everything" as a way of being "at once everything" and "at the same time . . . none of these things."

With your paragraph-by-paragraph outline in hand, you are now ready to analyze the reading.

5. Analyze the Selection to Come to an Understanding of It

After reading the essay a second time and annotating it, you are ready to analyze it, to probe for a deeper understanding of and appreciation for what the writer has done. In analyzing an essay, you will examine its basic parts methodically to see the significance of each part and understand how they relate to one another. One of the best ways to analyze an essay is to answer a basic set of questions—questions that require you to do some critical thinking about the essay's content and form.

Questions to Help You Analyze What You Read

1. What is the writer's main point or thesis?

2. To whom is the essay addressed? To a general audience with little or no background knowledge of the subject? To a specialized group familiar with the topic? To those who are likely to agree or disagree with the argument?

3. What is the writer's purpose in addressing this audience?

4. What is the writer's attitude toward the subject of the essay—positive, critical, objective, ironic, hostile?

5. What assumptions, if any, does the writer make about the subject and/or the audience? Are these assumptions explicit (stated) or implicit (unstated)?

6. What kinds of evidence does the writer use to support his or her thesis—personal experience, expert opinions, statistics? Does the writer supply enough evidence to support his or her position? Is the evidence reliable, specific, and up-to-date?

7. Does the writer address opposing views on the issue?

8. How is the essay organized and developed? Does the writer's strategy of development suit his or her subject and purpose?

9. How effective is the essay? Is the writer convincing about his or her position?

Each essay in *Language Awareness* is followed by a set of "Thinking Critically about the Reading" questions similar to the ones suggested here but more specific to the essay. These questions help you analyze both the content of an essay and the writer's craft. In answering each of these questions, always look for details from the selection itself to support your position.

Having read and reread Goldberg's essay and studied the student annotations to the text, consider the following set of student answers to the key questions listed above. Are there places where you would have answered the questions differently? Explain.

1. What is the writer's main point or thesis?

Goldberg wants to tell her readers why it's important for people, especially writers, to be specific and to learn the names of everything in their part of the world. She states her main point in paragraph 3: "When we know the name of something, it brings us closer to the ground. It takes the blur out of our mind; it connects us to the earth." In short, being specific in what we call things makes us see, think, and write more clearly.

2. *To whom is the essay addressed? To a general audience with little or no background knowledge of the subject? To a specialized group familiar with the topic? To those who are likely to agree or disagree with the argument?*

Goldberg's intended audience seems to be writers who are looking for advice. In paragraph 4, she quotes William Carlos Williams: "Write what's in front of your nose." In paragraph 6, Goldberg stresses the importance of knowing classmates' or group members' names and how this knowledge "helps to ground you in the group and make you more attentive to each other's work." In her final paragraph Goldberg acknowledges her audience of writers by emphasizing the writer's duty to learn the names of everything.

3. *What is the writer's purpose in addressing this audience?*

Goldberg's purpose is to give her readers some direct advice about writing and life: "Be specific." More specifically(!), she advises her readers to give people and things names and to create a specific time context (month, day, moment, etc.) for what they're describing ("Not just 'daisy,' but how the flower is in the season we are looking at it . . .").

4. *What is the writer's attitude toward the subject of the essay — positive, critical, objective, ironic, hostile?*

Goldberg is enthusiastic and extremely positive about the importance of naming things. She believes that "[w]hen we know the name of something, it brings us closer to the ground. It takes the blur out of our mind; it connects us to the earth" and makes us more "awake" to the environment; it allows us to "[penetrate] more deeply" into what is in front of us and to learn from it; and it grounds us and makes us more attentive in a group. She's excited to share her own experiences with learning the names of things.

5. *What assumptions, if any, does the writer make about the subject and/ or the audience? Are these assumptions explicit (stated) or implicit (unstated)?*

Goldberg makes several key assumptions in this essay:
- The title assumes that readers will be comfortable with commands.
- The examples of "pomegranate," "geranium," "maple," "elm," "oak," "locust," "dogwood," and "forsythia" assume that readers have a basic knowledge of fruits, flowers, and trees — or that they'll be motivated enough to look them up.
- The reference to the poet William Carlos Williams assumes that the audience will know who he is and perhaps be familiar with his poetry — or, again, that they will be motivated enough to look him up. Goldberg's footnotes, however, show that she does not assume readers will recognize the poem "Daisy" (paragraph 4) or "The Auguries of Innocence," quoted in paragraph 5.

- Goldberg assumes that readers, after learning the names of the plants, flowers, trees, and people in their environment, will have experiences similar to the ones she has had: "I feel more friendly toward the environment. I am noticing what is around me and can name it. It makes me more awake" (paragraph 3).

6. *What kinds of evidence does the writer use — personal experience, expert opinions, statistics? Does the writer supply enough evidence to support his or her position? Is the evidence reliable, specific, and up-to-date?*

To support her claim that writers need to be specific, Goldberg uses the examples of "fruit/pomegranate," "girl/[name]," and "flower/geranium" in her opening paragraph — hoping that her readers will agree that the specific terms are better than the general ones. She follows these examples with personal experience: She explains how she went about learning the names of plants and flowers in Boulder, Colorado, and shares what she felt as a result. In paragraphs 4 and 5, Goldberg cites the poetry of William Carlos Williams as evidence that specific language creates great poems.

It is difficult to say whether this evidence is enough. Assuming her readers are beginning writers eager to learn, as she seems to have intended, it is probably safe to say that her evidence will be convincing. If a less receptive audience or an audience of nonwriters were reading the essay, though, more evidence or a different kind (maybe examples of how being specific helps in everyday life?) might be needed.

7. *Does the writer address opposing views on the issue?*

While Goldberg does not directly address opposing views, she does discuss what happens when writers or speakers are *not* specific. For example, in paragraph 1 she says that calling someone "girl" instead of calling her by name can be rude, which is another way of saying that it denies that person her dignity — a pretty serious charge. In addition, when she tells us how knowing the names of things brings us closer to our environment, she implies that not knowing these names actually makes us feel disconnected from the world around us — something no one wants to feel.

8. *How is the essay organized and developed? Does the writer's strategy of development suit his or her subject and purpose?*

Goldberg organizes her essay in a straightforward and logical manner. She introduces her topic with her central directive, "Be specific," and then immediately shows through three examples what happens when a writer is specific. She organizes the examples in the body of her essay — paragraphs 2 through 6 — by telling how she learned to be more specific, quoting William Carlos Williams's advice to "Write what's in front of your nose," and advising us that we should learn the names of people in the groups and classes we belong to. Goldberg concludes her essay where she began, by directing us to "Learn the names of everything." In learning the names of everything, she reminds us that "A writer is all at once everything — an architect, French cook, farmer — and at the same time, a writer is none of these things." Although it seems paradoxical at first, this statement, when you stop to think about it, is very empowering — you're not really an architect or a

French cook or a farmer, but, when you write, you get to experience the world the way they do.

9. *How effective is the essay? Is the writer convincing about his or her position?*

Goldberg's essay is effective because it serves her purpose very well. She raises her readers' awareness of the value of names and demonstrates why it is so important to give things their names in order to understand our world and to write effectively about it. Her argument about being specific is convincing — after reading the essay, it's difficult to look at a flower and not wonder, at least, whether it's a tulip, poppy, daffodil, rose, or something else. Goldberg offers practical advice on how each of us can get started learning the names of things, be they the names of the other people in our class or the names of the plants, trees, and flowers on our campus.

READING AS A WRITER

Reading and writing are the two sides of the same coin: Active critical reading is a means to help you become a better writer. By reading we can begin to see how other writers have communicated their experiences, ideas, thoughts, and feelings in their writing. We can study how they have used the various elements of the essay — thesis, unity, organization, beginnings and endings, paragraphs, transitions, effective sentences, word choice, tone, and figurative language — to say what they wanted to say. By studying the style, technique, and rhetorical strategies of other writers we learn how we might effectively do the same. The more we read and write, the more we begin to read as writers and, in turn, to write knowing what readers expect.

What does it mean to read as a writer? Most of us have not been taught to read with a writer's eye, to ask why we like one piece of writing and not another. Likewise, most of us do not ask ourselves why one piece of writing is more believable or convincing than another. When you learn to read with a writer's eye, you begin to answer these important questions and, in the process, come to appreciate what is involved in selecting and focusing a subject as well as the craftsmanship involved in writing — how a writer selects descriptive details, uses an unobtrusive organizational pattern, opts for fresh and lively language, chooses representative and persuasive examples, and emphasizes important points with sentence variety.

On one level, reading stimulates your thinking by providing you with subjects to write about. After reading David Raymond's essay "On Being 17, Bright, and Unable to Read," Helen Keller's "The Day Language Came into My Life," Malcolm X's "Discovering the Power of Language," or Tom Rosenberg's "Changing My Name after Sixty Years," you might, for example, be inspired to write about a powerful language experience you have had and how that experience, in retro-spect, was a "turning point" in your life.

On a second level, reading provides you with information, ideas, and perspectives for developing your own paper. In this way, you respond to what you read, using material from what you've read in an essay. For example, after reading Diane Ravitch's essay on the "language police," you might want to elaborate on what she has written, drawing on your own experiences and either agreeing with her examples or generating bet-ter ones of your own. You could also qualify her argument or take issue with it. The Debates in Chapters 7, 8, and 9 of *Language Awareness* offer you the opportunity to read extensively on focused topics — "Should Learning Be Censored?," "Should English Be the Law?," and "What's All the Fuss about Natural, Organic, Local Foods?" — and to use the information and opinions expressed in these essays as resources for your own thesis-driven paper.

On a third level, active reading can increase your awareness of how others' writing affects you, thus making you more sensitive to how your own writing will affect your readers. For example, if you have been impressed by an author who uses convincing evidence to support each of her claims, you might be more likely to back up your own claims carefully. If you have been impressed by an apt turn of phrase or absorbed by a writer's new idea, you may be less inclined to feed your readers dull, worn out, and trite phrases. More to the point, however, the active reading that you will be encouraged to do in *Language Awareness* will help you to recognize and analyze the essential elements of the essay. When you see, for example, how a writer like Susanne K. Langer uses a strong thesis statement about how language separates humans from the rest of the animal kingdom to control the parts of her essay, you can better appreciate the importance of having a clear thesis statement in your writing. When you see the way Deborah Tannen uses transitions to link key phrases with important ideas so that readers can recognize clearly how the parts of her essay are meant to flow together, you have a better idea of how to achieve such coherence in your own writing. And when you see the way Donna Woolfolk Cross uses a division and classification organizational plan to differentiate clearly the various categories of propaganda, you see a powerful way in which you too can organize an essay using this method of development.

Finally, another important reason to master the skills of critical read-ing is that you will be your own first reader and critic for everything you write. How well you are able to scrutinize your own drafts will powerfully affect how well you revise them, and revising well is crucial to writing well. Reading others' writing with a critical eye is a useful and important practice; the more you read, the more practice you will have in sharpening your skills. The more sensitive you become to the content and style deci-sions made by the writers in *Language Awareness,* the more skilled you will be at making similar decisions in your own writing.

WRITING IN COLLEGE

Whenever you write in college, you are writing as a member of a community of scholars, teachers, and students. By questioning, researching, and writing in company with other members of the college community, you come both to understand college material and to demonstrate your knowledge of it.

Relatively early on in your college career, you will likely begin to focus on a specific discipline—English, history, philosophy, psychology, nutrition, or biology, for example—that belongs to one of several larger curricular groups (traditionally, languages and literature, humanities, social sciences, and natural and applied sciences). You'll notice that writers in your discipline employ particular methods, resources, evidence, language, and stylistic and formatting conventions that differ from those used in other disciplines. Your credibility as a writer in your discipline, as well as the efficiency and effectiveness of your communication, will depend in large part on your adherence to these conventions.

In addition to adhering to the conventions of your discipline, however, you need to meet core standards of well-written academic prose. Most of your instructors will agree, for example, that a good academic paper, regardless of its length, is purposeful and well organized. Writers do not rely on luck or inspiration to produce an effective piece of writing. Instead, good writers plan what they have to say, write a rough draft, revise that draft, edit their work, and proofread the final copy. In short, they follow what is commonly called the writing process.

GETTING YOUR THOUGHTS IN WRITING

The advice below is intended to help you master the core elements that all instructors expect in academic writing, whatever the discipline. As you develop any writing project, be sure that you do all of the following:

1. Understand the writing assignment.
2. Find a subject and topic.
3. Establish your thesis or controlling idea.

4. Determine your organizational plan.
5. Support your thesis with evidence.
6. Be aware of your audience.
7. Acknowledge your sources.
8. Take steps to avoid plagiarism.

1. Understand the Writing Assignment

Much of your college writing will be done in response to specific assignments from your instructors or research questions that you develop in consultation with your teachers. Your environmental studies professor, for example, may ask you to write a report on significant new research on carbon dioxide emissions and global warming; your American history professor may ask you to write an analysis of the long-term effects of Japanese Americans' internment during World War II. From the outset you need to understand precisely what your instructor is asking you to do. The keys to understanding assignments such as these are *subject* words (words that focus on content) and *direction* words (words that indicate your purpose for and method of development in writing). For example, consider what you are being asked to do in each of the following assignments:

> Tell about an experience you have had that dramatically revealed to you the importance of being accurate and precise in your use of language.
>
> Many languages are lost over time because speakers of those languages die. When a language is lost, the particular culture embodied in the language is also lost. Using an extinct language and culture as an example, explain how the language embodies a culture and exactly what is lost when a language becomes extinct.
>
> Advocates of the English-only movement want to see English adopted as our country's official language. Argue for or against the philosophy behind this movement.

In the first example above, the subject words are *experience* and *importance of being accurate and precise in your use of language*. The direction word is *tell,* which means that you must share the details of the experience so that your readers can appreciate them as if they were there, sharing the experience. The content words in the second example are *languages, culture,* and *extinct language and culture*. The direction word is *explain*. In the third example, the content words are *English-only movement* and *our country's official language*. The direction word is *argue*. In each case the subject words limit and focus the content, and the direction words dictate how you will approach this content in writing.

The words *tell, explain,* and *argue* are only a few of the direction words that are commonly found in academic writing assignments. The following list of additional direction words and their meanings will help you better understand your writing assignments and what is expected of you.

Analyze: take apart and examine closely

Categorize: place into meaningful groups

Compare: look for differences, stress similarities

Contrast: look for similarities, stress differences

Critique: point out positive and negative features

Define: provide the meaning for a term or concept

Describe: give detailed sensory perceptions for a person, place, or event

Evaluate: judge according to some established standard

Identify: recognize or single out

Illustrate: show through examples

Interpret: explain the meaning of a document, action, event, or behavior

Prove: demonstrate truth by logic, fact, or example

Synthesize: bring together or make meaningful connections among elements

After reading an assignment several times, check with your instructor if you are still unsure about what is being asked of you. He or she will be glad to clear up any possible confusion before you start writing. Be sure, as well, that you understand any additional requirements of the assignment, such as length or format.

2. Find a Subject and Topic

Although your instructor will sometimes give you specific writing assignments, you will often be asked to choose your own subject and topic. In a course in which you are using *Language Awareness*, you would in this case first select a broad subject within the area of language studies that you think you may enjoy writing about, such as professional jargon, dialects, political speeches, advertising language, or propaganda. A language issue that you have experienced firsthand (discrimination, for example) or something you've read may bring other subjects to mind. You might also consider a language-related issue that involves your career ambitions, such as the areas of business (avoiding exaggerated advertising claims), law (eliminating obscure legal language), nursing (communicating effectively with patients), or journalism (reporting the news objectively). Another option is to list some subjects you enjoy discussing with friends and that you can approach from a language perspective: music (gender bias in hip-hop lyrics), work (decoding insurance policies and medical benefits), and college life (speech codes on campus). In the student essay that concludes this chapter, for example, Tara Ketch combined her interests in children's literature and book banning as she tried to better understand the arguments for and against censorship.

Next, try to narrow your general subject until you arrive at a topic that you think will be both interesting to your readers and appropriate for the length of your paper (and the time you have to write it). The following chart shows how the general areas of jargon, journalism, and television commercials might be narrowed to a specific essay topic. (If you're having trouble coming up with general subjects or specific topics, try some of the discovery techniques discussed in the next section.)

General Subject Area	Narrowed Topic	Specific Essay Topic
Jargon	Medical jargon	Medical jargon used between doctors and terminally ill patients
Journalism	Slanted language in newswriting	Slanted language in newspapers' coverage of international events
Television commercials	Hidden messages in television commercials	Hidden messages in television commercials on children's Saturday morning programs

3. Establish Your Thesis or Controlling Idea

Once you have chosen a subject and topic and generated sufficient ideas and information, you are ready to organize your material and establish a thesis or controlling idea. The *thesis* of an essay is the point you are trying to make. The thesis is often expressed in one or two sentences called a *thesis statement*, such as the following example:

> There is no better place to see language change take place than in the area of student slang.[1]

A thesis statement should be

    a. the most important point you make about your topic;
    b. more general than the ideas and facts used to support it;
    c. focused enough to be covered in the space allotted.

---

1. The thesis statement should not be confused with a *purpose statement*. While a thesis statement makes an assertion about your topic, a purpose statement addresses what you are trying to do in the paper. For example,

    I want to learn how much slang is used on campus and in what areas of student life slang is most prevalent.

Generally speaking, purpose statements should not appear in formal academic essays (though they are appropriate in outlines, in proposals, and in many written reports in the applied and natural sciences).

A thesis statement should not be a question but an assertion. If you find yourself writing a question for a thesis statement, try to answer the question. Your answer will provide the basis for a thesis statement you can use in your essay. An effective strategy for developing a thesis statement is to begin by writing *What I want to say is that* . . . , as in this example:

> What I want to say is that unless language barriers between patients and health-care providers are bridged, many patients' lives will be in potential jeopardy.

Later, you can delete the formulaic opening, and you will be left with the thesis statement:

> Unless language barriers between patients and health-care providers are bridged, many patients' lives will be in potential jeopardy.

The thesis statement usually comes near the beginning of an essay, after a writer offers several sentences that establish a context for the piece. One common strategy is to position the thesis statement as the final sentence of the first paragraph. Occasionally, the thesis is stated elsewhere in an essay, even sometimes at the very end.

Is Your Thesis Solid?

Once you have a possible thesis statement in mind, ask yourself the following questions:

- Does my thesis statement take a clear position on an issue? (Could I imagine someone agreeing or disagreeing with it? If not, it might be a statement of fact, instead of an arguable thesis.)
- Will I be able to find evidence that supports my position? Where? What kinds? (If you're unsure, it wouldn't hurt to take a look at a few secondary sources at this point.)
- Will I be able to make my claim and present sufficient evidence to support it in a paper of the assigned length, and by the due date? (If not, you might need to scale back your claim to something more manageable.)

---

4. Determine Your Organization

There are several organizational patterns you might follow in drafting an essay. Most of you are already familiar with the most common one — *chronological order*. In this pattern, which is often used to narrate a story, explain a process, or relate a series of events, you start with the earliest event or step and move forward in time.

In a comparison-and-contrast essay, you might follow a *block* pattern or a *point-by-point* organization. In a block pattern, a writer provides all the information about one subject, followed by a block of comparable information about the other subject. In a point-by-point comparison, on the other hand, the writer starts by comparing both subjects in terms of a particular point, then compares both on a second point, and so on. In an essay comparing two dialects of American English, for example, you could follow the block pattern, covering all the characteristics of one dialect and then all the characteristics of the other. Alternatively, you could organize your material in terms of defining characteristics (for example, geographical range; characteristics of speakers; linguistic traits), filling in the details for each dialect in turn.

Other patterns of organization include moving from *the general to the specific*, from *smallest to largest*, from *least important to most important*, or from *the usual to the unusual*. In an essay about medical jargon, for instance, you might cover its general characteristics first and then move to specifics, or you might begin with what is most usual (or commonly known) about doctors' language and then discuss what is unusual about it. Whatever order you choose, keep in mind that what you present first and last will probably stay in the reader's mind the longest.

After you choose an organizational pattern, jot down the main ideas in your essay. In other words, make a scratch outline. As you add more information and ideas to your scratch outline, you may want to develop a formal, more detailed outline of your paper. In writing a formal outline, follow these rules:

1. Include the title of your essay, a statement of purpose, and the thesis statement.
2. Write in complete sentences unless your meaning is immediately clear from a phrase. Whether you use sentences or phrases, be sure to use them consistently throughout your outline.
3. If you divide any category, make sure there are at least two subcategories. The reason for this is simple: You cannot divide something into fewer than two parts.
4. Observe the conventions of formal outlining. (See below.)

Notice how each new level of specificity is given a new letter or number designation by student Tara Ketch in the following outline of the essay that appears later in this chapter (pp. 32–38).

Title: "Kids, You Can't Read That Book!"
Purpose: To argue for an approach teachers can use to deal with controversial material
Thesis: A review of the reasons for challenges to books suggests that educators concerned about censorship might forestall outright bans by more attention to

age-appropriateness and to the kinds of guidance given to students who are reading challenging material.

   I. Introduction: censorship
      A. Definition of censorship
      B. Relevant Supreme Court rulings
   II. Reasons books are banned in schools: community, family, and religious values
      A. Offensive language
      B. Sexual explicitness
      C. Gay/lesbian content
      D. Challenges to religious views
      E. Racism and sexism
   III. Considerations for educators in dealing with controversial material
      A. Age-appropriateness and access
      B. Guidance and support for students
   IV. Conclusion

5. Support Your Thesis with Evidence

The types of evidence you use in your academic writing will be determined to some extent by the discipline in which you are working. For example, for a research project in psychology on the prejudice shown toward people with unusual names, you will almost certainly rely heavily on published studies from peer-reviewed journals. Depending on the assignment, however, you might also devise an experiment of your own or interview people with unusual names to gather firsthand accounts of their experiences. For an argument essay on the same topic in a composition course, as in many courses in the humanities, languages, and literatures, you would cite a wide range of sources, perhaps including—but not limited to—peer-reviewed journals. Depending on the assignment, you might also include your own experience and informal observations.

To support her argument on book banning, Tara Ketch derives most of her evidence from an array of experts, as in the following example, where she cites scholar Henry Reichman:

> Henry Reichman writes that in 1990, Frank Mosca's *All-American Boys* (1983) and Nancy Garden's *Annie on My Mind* (1982), two books with gay themes, were donated to high schools in Contra Costa, California; at three of these high schools, the books were seized by administrators and then "lost" (53).

PRIMARY AND SECONDARY SOURCES.   In general, researchers and writers work with two types of evidence: primary sources and secondary sources.

Primary sources in the humanities and languages/literatures are works that grow out of and are close to a time, place, or culture under study. These can include documents such as letters, speeches, interviews, manuscripts, diaries, treaties, maps; creative written works such as novels, plays, poems, songs, and autobiographies; and three-dimensional artifacts such as paintings, sculptures, pottery, weaving, buildings, tools, and furniture. Primary sources in the social, natural, and applied sciences are the factual reports and descriptions of discoveries, experiments, surveys, and clinical trials.

Secondary sources in the humanities and languages/literatures restate, analyze, and interpret primary sources. Common secondary sources include analyses, critiques, histories, and commentaries in the form of books, articles, encyclopedia entries, and documentaries. Secondary sources in the sciences analyze and interpret discoveries and experiments and often comment on the validity of the research models and methods and the value of those discoveries and experiments.

Writing in a specific discipline requires that you use the most authoritative and reliable source materials available for that discipline. Your instructors can help you in this regard by either providing you with a list of resources commonly used in their fields or directing you to such a list in your library or on the Internet. Many academic libraries include helpful subject study guides on their home pages as well.

For a brief guide to finding, evaluating, and documenting sources in print and online, see pages 607–622.

FACTS, STATISTICS, EXAMPLES, AND EXPERT TESTIMONY. The evidence you use in your academic writing should place a high value on facts and statistics, examples and illustrations, and the testimony of experts. You must be accurate in your use of facts and statistics, and you must check and double-check that you have cited them correctly. Be sure that you carefully consider the examples and illustrations you use to support your thesis: Use those that work best with your subject and the audience you have in mind. Finally, be selective in citing the works and comments of experts in your discipline. If you choose wisely, the works of respected scholars and experts will be immediately recognizable to others familiar with the subject area, and your argument will have a much better chance of succeeding.

The following passage illustrates how Tara Ketch uses examples in her paper on banned books in the schools:

> In a debate about Katherine Paterson's 1977 novel *Bridge to Terabithia*, one Lincoln, Nebraska parent protested the use of the words *snotty* and *shut up* along with *Lord* and *damn*, saying, "Freedom of speech was not intended to guarantee schools the right to intrude on traditional family values without warning and regardless of the availability of non-offensive alternatives" (Reichman 47-8).

6. Be Aware of Your Audience

The more effectively you take your audience into consideration, the better your argument will be. You need to anticipate your readers' reactions to your overall point and the kinds of evidence you use to support it, especially if you are presenting controversial or unusual ideas and evidence. You should try to anticipate objections to your argument, take them into account, and either accommodate them (that is, admit their validity) or refute them convincingly. Doing so demonstrates that you are comprehensive, thoughtful, fair, and reasonable—all traits that are required in persuasive academic writing.

Recognizing that not all readers are of the same mind on every issue, Tara Ketch attempts to recognize both sides of the issues she presents:

> Defenders of [*The Adventures of Huckleberry Finn*] point out that such criticism ignores context and intent—Twain was writing specifically to draw negative attention to the South's racist attitudes and practices. Nevertheless, some critics claim that *any* use of such offensive terms, particularly in a text presented as a classic, can do more harm than good.

ESTABLISHING AN APPROPRIATE TONE.   Tone—the degree of formality established between you and your audience—is largely a function of the vocabulary you use and the complexity of your sentences. Formal writing creates a greater distance between you and your readers by using third-person pronouns (*he, she, it, they*). Although it is more customary, and indeed often necessary, to use first-person pronouns (*I, we*) in personal narratives, it is best to avoid them in academic writing where you are aiming to write objectively. By all means, avoid abbreviations and any usage that derives from the informality of e-mail, text messages, and instant messages.

No matter how valid or convincing you think your argument is, you should always write with respect for your audience's intelligence and with appreciation for the time they are spending trying to understand your point of view. Don't attempt to bully the reader with aggressive language or typography (for example, CAPITAL LETTERS or excessive punctuation!!!). Instead, let the strength of your argument and evidence speak for itself.

Tara Ketch assumes a nonstrident, rational attitude toward her subject and a moderate tone that complements her attempt to be understanding about the issues surrounding the frequently contentious subject of censorship. Notice, for example, how she concludes her essay:

> The efforts to censor what children read can generate potentially explosive conflicts within schools and communities. Understanding the reasons that people seek to censor what kids are reading in school will better prepare educators to respond to those efforts in a sensitive and reasonable manner. More importantly, educators will be able to provide the best learning environment for children, one that neither overly restricts the range of their reading nor exposes them, unaided, to material they have neither the experience nor the intellectual maturity to understand.

USING DISCIPLINE-SPECIFIC LANGUAGE.   The point of discipline-specific language, sometimes referred to as professional language or even jargon, is not to make a speaker or writer sound like a scientist, or a humanities scholar, or a geologist. Rather, discipline-specific language provides a kind of "shorthand" means of expressing complex concepts. Its proper use will grow from your knowledge of the discipline, from the reading you have done in the field, and from the hours you have spent in the company of your teachers and peers.

While the meaning of some disciplinary language will become clear to you from context as you read and discuss course material, some of it, left undefined, will present a stumbling block to your understanding of the material. Glossaries of disciplinary terms exist for most disciplines: Make use of them. Also, never be shy about asking your instructor or more experienced classmates for help when you're unsure of the meaning of a term.

CONSIDERING OPPOSING ARGUMENTS.   You will likely not have trouble convincing those who agree with your argument from the outset, but what about those who are skeptical or think differently from you? You need to discover who these people are by talking with them or by reading what they have written. Do your research, be reasonable, and find common ground where possible, but take issue where you must. To refute an opposing argument, you can present evidence showing that the opposition's data or evidence is incomplete or distorted, that its reasoning is faulty, or that its conclusions do not fit the evidence.

For example, notice how Tara Ketch acknowledges an opposing argument and takes issue with it:

> Many would rightly question whether young adults should be exposed to extremely violent novels such as Anthony Burgess's *A Clockwork Orange*, given that they are still too young to put what they read into proper context. Does this mean, however, that such books should be removed altogether from school libraries? Perhaps not.
>
> Libraries and classrooms should be resources for children to broaden their horizons. Students need to learn about the range of human experience in order to make judgments about it; leaving them guessing, or gleaning what information they can from schoolyard conversations, will lead to misunderstood, or perhaps worse, half-understood "facts" of life.

7. Acknowledge Your Sources

Whenever you summarize, paraphrase, or quote a person's thoughts and ideas, and when you use facts or statistics that are not commonly known or believed, you must properly acknowledge the source of your information. If you do not properly acknowledge such ideas and information, you are guilty of plagiarism.

KNOWING WHAT TO DOCUMENT.   You must document the source of your information whenever you do the following:

- quote a source exactly (word for word)
- paraphrase or summarize information or ideas from a source
- cite statistics, tables, charts, or graphs

You do *not* need to document these types of information:

- your own observations, experiences, and ideas
- factual information available in a number of reference works (known as "common knowledge")
- proverbs, sayings, and familiar quotations

QUOTING, PARAPHRASING, AND SUMMARIZING.   **Quotations** from sources are word-for-word transcriptions from an original source. They are ordinarily used when both the idea or information and the precise language of the original are important. If the language is *not* highly distinctive, itself worthy of analysis, or otherwise notable, you should probably paraphrase instead.

Quotations must begin and end with quotation marks. They must be completely accurate, down to the punctuation, and the way in which you integrate them into your paper must not misrepresent their intended meaning. However, if you need to omit some material because it is not relevant to your paper, you may substitute an ellipse (three spaced periods). (Again, be very sure that omitting material does not alter the original source's intended meaning.) Similarly, if you need to make any changes to a quotation—adding a word in order to clarify a reference, or making minor alterations in order to make the quote fit grammatically into your sentence—you may place your added material in brackets ([ ]). Tara Ketch does both in the sentence below:

> As Natalie Goldberg writes, "When we know the name of something . . . [i]t takes the blur out of our mind" (5) — and isn't that the purpose of an education?

A **paraphrase** is a restatement of an idea or information that is roughly the same length as the original. Paraphrase is ordinarily used when the idea or information in the source is important but the language is unremarkable. A paraphrase must be a restatement *in your own words* and in your own style. It does not require quotation marks, but it does require proper citation. Do not substitute synonyms for a handful of words and call it paraphrase—that would be plagiarism (see pp. 27–30).

A **summary** is a restatement of an idea or information that is considerably shorter than the original. Summary is ordinarily used when the original material is too long to reproduce either as a quotation or as a paraphrase. Like a paraphrase, a summary must be in your own words and in your own style; it does not require quotation marks, but it does require full and proper citation. As with paraphrase, do not replace a handful of words with synonyms and call it summary—that would be plagiarism (see pp. 27–31).

CITING CORRECTLY. A reference to the source of borrowed information is called a *citation*. Different disciplines use different systems for presenting citations; in most cases, your instructor will tell you which style to use. In English and the humanities, the documentation style recommended by the Modern Language Association (MLA) is commonly used. In the social sciences, the American Psychological Association (APA) style is generally used. For more information on documentation styles, consult the appropriate manual or handbook. (For MLA style, consult the *MLA Handbook for Writers of Research Papers*, 7th ed. [New York: MLA, 2009]. You may also check MLA guidelines on the Internet at www.mla.org.)

In MLA style, there are two components of documentation: *in-text citations* are placed in the body of your paper; the *list of works cited* provides complete publication data for your in-text citations and is placed at the end of your paper. Both are necessary for complete documentation.

In-Text Citations (MLA Style)

In-text citations, also known as parenthetical citations, give the reader partial citation information immediately, at the point at which it is most meaningful. Rather than having to turn to a footnote or an endnote, the reader sees the citation as a part of the writer's text.

Most in-text citations consist of only the author's last name and a page reference. Usually the author's name is given in an introductory or signal phrase at the beginning of the borrowed material and the page reference is given in parentheses at the end. If the author's name is not given at the beginning, it belongs in parentheses along with the page reference. The parenthetical reference signals the end of the borrowed material and directs your readers to the list of works cited should they want to pursue a particular source. Treat electronic sources as you do print sources, keeping in mind that some electronic sources are not paginated or may use paragraph numbers instead of page numbers. Consider the following examples of in-text citations, followed by the works cited entries to which they refer.

Citation with author's name in the signal phrase

Every day Americans are bombarded with an assortment of advertising for everything from cars, clothing, and vacations to cosmetics, foods, and over-the-counter medicines. Unless people know how advertising language works, they are at the mercy of Madison Avenue. Advertisers, as William Lutz asserts, manipulate us with weasel words, words that "appear to say one thing when in fact they say the opposite, or nothing at all" (443). For example, when

**Citation
with author's
name in
parentheses**

we hear the word *helps* as in "helps relieve pain," we think "relieves pain." Not necessarily true. And to make matters worse, a consumer advocate says, "these unreliable claims require no approval—in practice, that may mean no evidence" (Liebman 594).

Works Cited

Liebman, Bonnie. "Crazy Claims: Which Can You Believe?" *Language Awareness*. Ed. Paul Eschholz, Alfred Rosa, and Virginia Clark. 10th ed. Boston: Bedford/St. Martin's, 2009. 588–594. Print.

Lutz, William. "Weasel Words." *Language Awareness*. Ed. Paul Eschholz, Alfred Rosa, and Virginia Clark. 10th ed. Boston: Bedford/St. Martin's, 2009. 442–451. Print.

List of Works Cited (MLA Style)

Listed below are the general MLA guidelines for creating a works cited list. For a list of commonly used works cited entries, see pp. 617–622. For more specific questions about entry format, consult either the *MLA Handbook* or the Bedford/St.Martin's research Web site: dianahacker.com/resdoc

General Guidelines

- Begin the list on a new page following the last page of text.
- Organize the list alphabetically by author's last name. If the entry has no author name, alphabetize by the first major word of the title.
- Double-space within and between entries.
- Begin each entry at the left margin. If the entry is longer than one line, indent the second and subsequent lines one-half inch.
- Do not number entries.

For a list of works cited for Tara Ketch's student paper, see page 38.

8. Take Steps to Avoid Plagiarism

The importance of honesty and accuracy in doing library research cannot be stressed enough. In working closely with the ideas and words of others, intellectual honesty demands that we distinguish between what we borrow—acknowledging it in a citation—and what is our own. Any material borrowed word for word must be placed within quotation marks and be properly cited. Any idea, explanation, or argument you have paraphrased or summarized must be properly cited, and it must be clear where the paraphrase or summary begins and ends. In short, to use someone else's ideas, whether in their original or altered form, without proper acknowledgment is to be guilty of plagiarism. The Council of Writing Program Administrators offers the following helpful definition of plagiarism in academic settings for administrators, faculty, and students: "In an instructional setting, plagiarism occurs when a writer deliberately uses someone else's language, ideas, or other (not common-knowledge) material without acknowledging its source."

Accusations of plagiarism can be upheld even if plagiarism is unintentional. A little attention and effort can help to eliminate this possibility. While taking notes, check and recheck all direct quotations against the wording of the original, and be sure you've labeled them clearly as quotations. Double-check your paraphrases to be sure that you have not used the writer's wording or sentence structure.

While writing your paper, make sure that you put quotation marks around material taken verbatim, and double-check the text against your note card—or, better yet, against the original—to make sure that the quotation is accurate. When using paraphrases or summaries, be sure to cite the source.

To learn more about how you can avoid plagiarism, go to the "Tutorial on Avoiding Plagiarism" at bedfordstmartins.com/plagiarismtutorial. There you will find information on the consequences of plagiarism, tutorials explaining what sources to acknowledge, how to keep good notes, how to organize your research, and how to appropriately integrate sources. Exercises are included throughout the tutorial to help you practice skills like integrating sources and recognizing acceptable paraphrases and summaries.

The sections that follow provide examples of appropriate use of quotation, paraphrase, and summary.

USING QUOTATION MARKS FOR LANGUAGE BORROWED DIRECTLY.   Again, when you use another person's exact words or sentences, you must enclose the borrowed language in quotation marks. Even if you cite the source, you are guilty of plagiarism if you fail to use quotation marks. The following example demonstrates both plagiarism and a correct citation for a direct quotation.

Original Source

In the last decade, Standards departments have become more tolerant of sex and foul language, but they have cracked down on violence and become more insistent about the politically correct presentation of minorities. Lately, however, they seem to be swinging wildly back and forth between allowing everything and allowing nothing.
> —TAD FRIEND, "You Can't Say That: The Networks Play
> Word Games," *New Yorker* Nov. 19, 2001, page 45.

Plagiarism

In the last decade, Standards departments have become more tolerant of sex and foul language, but, according to social commentator Tad Friend, they have cracked down on violence and become more insistent about the politically correct presentation of minorities. Lately, however, they seem to be swinging wildly back and forth between allowing everything and allowing nothing (45).

Correct Citation of Borrowed Words in Quotation Marks

"In the last decade, Standards departments have become more tolerant of sex and foul language," according to social commentator Tad Friend, "but they have cracked down on violence and become more insistent about the politically correct presentation of minorities. Lately, however, they seem to be swinging wildly back and forth between allowing everything and allowing nothing" (45).

USING YOUR OWN WORDS IN PARAPHRASE AND SUMMARY.   When summarizing or paraphrasing a source, you must use your own language. It is not enough simply to change a word here or there; you must restate the idea(s) from the original *in your own words*, using your own style and sentence structure. In the following example, notice how plagiarism can occur when care is not taken in the wording or sentence structure of a paraphrase.

Original Source

Stereotypes are a kind of gossip about the world, a gossip that makes us prejudge people before we ever lay eyes on them. Hence it is not surprising that stereotypes have something to do with the dark world of prejudice. Explore most prejudices (note that the word means prejudgment) and you will find a cruel stereotype at the core of each one.

> —ROBERT L. HEILBRONER, "Don't Let Stereotypes Warp Your
> Judgment," *Reader's Digest* Jan. 1962, page 254.

Unacceptably Close Wording

According to Heilbroner, we prejudge other people even before we have seen them when we think in stereotypes. That stereotypes are related to the ugly world of prejudice should not surprise anyone. If you explore the heart of most prejudices — beliefs that literally prejudge — you will discover a mean stereotype lurking (254).

Unacceptably Close Sentence Structure

Heilbroner believes that stereotypes are images of people, images that enable people to prejudge other people before they have seen them. Therefore, no one should find it surprising that stereotypes are somehow related to the ugly world of prejudice. Examine most prejudices (the word literally means prejudgment) and you will uncover a vicious stereotype at the center of each (254).

Acceptable Paraphrase

Heilbroner believes that there is a link between stereotypes and the hurtful practice of prejudice. Stereotypes make for easy conversation, a kind of shorthand that enables people to find fault with others before ever meeting them. Most human prejudices, according to Heilbroner, have an ugly stereotype lurking somewhere inside them (254).

Preventing Plagiarism

Questions to Ask about Direct Quotations

- Do quotation marks clearly indicate the language that I borrowed verbatim (word for word)?
- Is the language of the quotation accurate, with no missing or misquoted words or phrases?
- Do the brackets or ellipsis marks clearly indicate any changes or omissions I have introduced?
- Does a signal phrase naming the author introduce each quotation? If not, is the author's name in the parenthetical citation?
- Does a parenthetical page citation follow each quotation?

Questions to Ask about Summaries and Paraphrases

- Is each summary and paraphrase written in my own words and style?
- Does each summary and paraphrase accurately represent the opinion, position, or reasoning of the original writer?
- Does each summary and paraphrase start with a signal phrase so that readers know where my borrowed material begins?
- Does each summary and paraphrase conclude with a parenthetical page citation?

Questions to Ask about Facts and Statistics

- Do I use a signal phrase or some other marker to introduce each fact or statistic that is not common knowledge so that readers know where the borrowed material begins?
- Is each fact or statistic that is not common knowledge clearly documented with a parenthetical page citation?

Finally, as you proofread your final draft, check your citations one last time. If at any time while you are taking notes or writing your paper you have a question about plagiarism, consult your instructor for clarification and guidance before proceeding.

A SAMPLE STUDENT PAPER

As a young adult, Tara Ketch read just about everything that the popular children's writer Judy Blume wrote. While a student at the University of Vermont and a major in elementary education, Ketch took a course in children's literature and was asked to write a term paper on some aspect of the literature she was studying. She thought she might be able to reflect on some of her reading of Blume's books. She also knew that she would soon be looking for a teaching position and realized that any teaching job she accepted would bring her face-to-face with the difficult task of selecting appropriate reading materials.

In her course, Ketch had read both Natalie Goldberg's "Be Specific" (pp. 4–6) and Diane Ravitch's "Language Police" (pp. 506–517), among other essays, and she was generally interested in their discussions of language and how young people learn to read and write. In choosing a specific topic to write about, Ketch decided to delve into the subject of censorship in elementary education. She was interested in learning more about why people want to censor certain books so that she could consider an appropriate response to their efforts. In a way, she wanted to begin to develop her own teaching philosophy with respect to text selection and to argue for a sensible course through what she perceived to be a potentially troublesome area for her as a teacher.

Tara E. Ketch

Professor Rosa

English 111

April 30, 2008

**Title is
centered.**

**Definition of
censorship**

**All lines
double-
spaced.**

**Central
questions**

Kids, You Can't Read That Book!

Censorship is the restriction or suppression of speech or writing.

In schools, debates about censorship arise when school officials,

librarians, parents, or other adults in the community attempt to keep

students from gaining access to particular books. Such attempts

present serious questions for educators. How should educators decide

what materials are fit for American schoolchildren? On what basis

should they decide? A review of the reasons for challenges to books

suggests that educators might forestall outright bans on books by

paying more attention to age-appropriateness and to the kinds of

guidance given to students who are reading challenging material.

The federal government has not set clear limits on censorship

in the schools. In the 1968 case of *Epperson v. Arkansas*, the

Supreme Court stated, "Public education in our Nation is committed

to the control of state and local authorities. Courts do not and

cannot intervene in the resolution of conflicts which arise in the

**In-text
citation—
author
named in
parentheses**

daily operation of school systems and which do not directly and

sharply implicate basic constitutional values" (Reichman 3). Yet in

1982, the Supreme Court ruled that "local school boards may not

remove books from school library shelves simply because they dislike

the ideas contained in those books and seek by their removal to

prescribe what shall be orthodox in politics, nationalism, religion, or

other matters of opinion" (Reichman 4). Different interpretations of

rulings such as these have led to frequent efforts to ban children's

books in school systems for a wide variety of reasons. Generally speaking, most attempts to ban books from school systems stem from the perception that the books offend community, family, or religious values.

Examples of challenges based on language

Challenges based on "offensive" or profane language are especially common in the area of adolescent literature. In the American Library Association's Office for Intellectual Freedom's (OIF) list of the most frequently challenged books from 1990–2000, J. D. Salinger's 1951 novel *Catcher in the Rye*, a perennial target of would-be censors, took the number thirteen slot, largely because of objections to its language, including the "F-word" (Office for Intellectual Freedom). In a debate about Katherine Paterson's 1977 novel *Bridge to Terabithia* (number nine on the OIF's list), one Lincoln, Nebraska, parent protested the use of the words *snotty* and *shut up* along with *Lord* and *damn*, saying, "Freedom of speech was not intended to guarantee schools the right to intrude on traditional family values without warning and regardless of the availability of nonoffensive alternatives" (Reichman 47-8). The school board in this case decided that the book had a value that transcended the use of offensive language.

Examples of challenges based on sexual content

Other challenges come from adults' idea that children should be protected from sexual content. Maya Angelou's 1969 autobiographical novel *I Know Why the Caged Bird Sings* (number three on the OIF's list) portrays rape, among other frankly sexual topics, and has since publication been banned from many school libraries and curricula. On what some would consider the opposite end of the spectrum, Maurice Sendak's 1970 illustrated book *In the Night Kitchen* (number twenty-five on the OIF list) shows a naked little boy, and although there is no explicit sexual content, many people have found the book offensive. According to an online exhibit at the site of the University of Virginia Libraries, "[i]n Springfield,

Ketch 3

Missouri, the book was expurgated by drawing shorts on the nude boy" ("Through the Eyes"). In New York, in 1990, parents tried to have the book removed from an elementary school, and, in Maine, a parent wanted the book removed because she felt it encouraged child molestation (Foerstel 201).

Many of Judy Blume's books have likewise come under fire for their portrayal of sexual themes: In fact, Blume has authored a total of five of the books on the OIF's top 100 list. *Are You There, God? It's Me, Margaret* (number sixty-two) has been banned for its frank discussion of menstruation and adolescent development. *Forever,* which discusses intercourse and abortion, comes in at number eight. These topics are clearly disturbing to many adults who grew up in environments where sex was not openly discussed and who may worry that these books will encourage sexual activity.

Examples of challenges based on gay/lesbian content

A related source of debate is gay and lesbian content. (The OIF categorizes challenges based on homosexual content separately from those based on sexual explicitness.) Two children's books designed to explain gay lifestyles to children, Michael Willhoite's *Daddy's Roommate* and Leslea Newman's *Heather Has Two Mommies*, rank as number two and number eleven, respectively, on the OIF list: Henry Reichman writes

In-text citation— authors named in signal phrase

that in 1990, Frank Mosca's *All-American Boys* (1983) and Nancy Garden's *Annie on My Mind* (1982), two books with gay themes, were donated to high schools in Contra Costa, California; at three of these high schools, the books were seized by administrators and then "lost" (53).

Examples of challenges based on religion

Religion, not surprisingly, has been the focus of many challenges to literature in the schools. The Bible's presence in the classroom has generated criticism from both religious and nonreligious groups: Those arguing from a religious perspective have objected when the Bible has been taught as literature, rather than

Ketch 4

as a sacred text, and those arguing from a secular perspective have objected to its being taught on any basis (Burress 219). Some critics speaking from a religious perspective object to portrayals of the occult in books. The Harry Potter series (collectively number seven on the OIF list) is perhaps the most famous recent target of such objections, the latest of which was leveled by a Gwinnett County, Georgia, parent in 2005, whose lawsuit to have the books removed from county schools was dismissed in 2007 ("Harry Potter").

Examples of challenges based on racism and sexism

Another frequently cited reason for challenges to books is their portrayal of content considered to be racist or sexist. Mark Twain's *Adventures of Huckleberry Finn* (number five on the OIF list), the source of perhaps the most heated controversy of this type, has often been challenged and banned outright because of its use of racist language. Defenders of the text point out that such criticism ignores context and intent—Twain was writing specifically to draw negative attention to the South's racist attitudes and practices. Nevertheless, some critics claim that *any* use of such offensive terms, particularly in a text presented as a classic, can do more harm than good.

Transition

Return to central questions

Return to thesis (age-appropriateness)

This brief review of some of the reasons used to ban children's books leaves us with the questions "How should educators decide what materials are fit for American schoolchildren?" and "On what basis should they decide?" It might be that the issue of age-appropriateness—the third most frequent reason given for challenges to books over the last decade and a half, according to the OIF—requires more attention than it gets from educators. A relatively large number of concerned adults seem interested not in banning books, necessarily, but in ensuring that the right books reach the right audiences in our schools.

Appeals to common ground

   Most educators likely agree that it is possible to identify age-appropriate (and age-inappropriate) themes in many of the books under discussion. Most would probably agree that elementary school children should not be exposed to the issues of rape and abortion present in some young-adult fiction. Many would rightly question whether young adults should be exposed to extremely violent novels such as Anthony Burgess's *A Clockwork Orange*, given that they are still too young to put what they read into proper context. Does this mean, however, that such books should be removed altogether from school libraries? Perhaps not.

Assumption: censorship is contrary to aims of education.

   Libraries and classrooms should be resources for children to broaden their horizons. Students need to learn about the range of human experience in order to make judgments about it; leaving them guessing, or gleaning what information they can from schoolyard conversations, will lead to misunderstood, or perhaps worse, half-understood "facts" of life. As Natalie Goldberg writes, "When we know the name of something . . . [i]t takes the blur out of our mind" (5) — and isn't that the purpose of an education?

Return to thesis (guidance)

Support (expert opinion)

   While outright censorship defeats the purpose of an education, educators must guide children in choosing age-appropriate material and then aid them in understanding material that might prove challenging. As Diane Ravitch writes, "Teachers have a responsibility to choose readings for their students based on their professional judgment of what students are likely to understand and what they need to learn" (506). If a child independently seeks out a controversial novel, educators should oversee the process, in order to give context to what might otherwise be a bewildering experience. In the case of a novel like

Ketch 6

Catcher in the Rye, which most critics agree has literary merit, but whose message is couched in profanity, it is the job of school educators to teach students how to read such literature critically and to understand the distance between the world of the novel and the student's own reality.

Examples of appropriate introduction of controversial literature

Similarly, novels like Maya Angelou's *I Know Why the Caged Bird Sings,* which have strong sexual content, need to be introduced to students old enough to understand something about mature sexual behavior, and discussion needs to focus on the meaning of the content within the world of the novel. Books with content deemed racist or sexist should likewise not automatically be banned: Provided they have intrinsic merit, such books can be useful tools for increasing understanding in our society. Finally, while volatile religious topics are possibly best left outside of classroom discussion, children should have access to religious materials in school libraries in order to allow them to explore various systems of belief.

Conclusion

The efforts to censor what children read can generate potentially explosive conflicts within schools and communities. Understanding the reasons that people seek to censor what kids are reading in school will be better prepare educators to respond to those efforts in a sensitive and reasonable manner. More importantly, educators will be able to provide the best learning environment for children, one that neither overly restricts the range of their reading nor exposes them, unaided, to material they have neither the experience nor the intellectual maturity to understand.

Works Cited

Works Cited begins on new page

Burress, Lee. *Battle of the Books: Literary Censorship in the Public Schools, 1950–1985*. Metuchen, NJ: Scarecrow, 1989. Print.

Foerstel, Herbert N. *Banned in the USA: A Reference Guide to Book Censorship in Schools and Public Libraries*. Revised and expanded edition. London: Greenwood, 2002. Print.

Goldberg, Natalie. "Be Specific." *Language Awareness*. 10th ed. Ed. Paul Eschholz, Alfred Rosa, and Virginia Clark. Boston: Bedford/ St. Martin's, 2009. 4–5. Print.

"Harry Potter to Remain on Gwinnett County School Library Shelves." *School Library Journal* 31 May 2007: n. pag. Web. 23 Apr. 2008.

Office for Intellectual Freedom. "The 100 Most Frequently Challenged Books of 1990–2000 and Challenges by Initiator, Institution, Type, and Year." *ALA*. American Library Association, 2008. Web. 23 Apr. 2008.

Ravitch, Diane. "The Language Police." *Language Awareness*. 10th ed. Ed. Paul Eschholz, Alfred Rosa, and Virginia Clark. Boston: Bedford/St. Martin's, 2009. 506–517. Print.

Reichman, Henry. *Censorship and Selection: Issues and Answers for Schools*. 3rd ed. Chicago: American Library Association, 2001. Print.

"Through the Eyes of a Child." *Censorship: Wielding the Red Pen*. The University of Virginia Libraries, 2000. Web. 23 Apr. 2008.

Second and subsequent lines of entries indented ½" from margin

1

COMING TO AN AWARENESS OF LANGUAGE

Most of us accept language as we accept the air we breathe; we cannot get along without it, and we take it for granted almost all of the time. Many days we find ourselves on language overload, bombarded by a steady stream of verbal and written messages—some invited, others not—but how much do we really know about language? How well do we understand how language works? Few of us are aware of the extent to which language is used to mislead and manipulate. Still fewer of us are fully conscious of the ways, subtle and not, in which our use of language may affect others. And even fewer of us recognize that our very perceptions of the world are influenced, and our thoughts at least partially shaped, by language. However, we are also the beneficiaries of language far more than we are its victims. Language is one of humankind's greatest achievements and most important resources, and it is a subject endlessly fascinating in itself.

If it is true that we are all in some sense prisoners of language, it is equally true that liberation begins with an awareness of that fact. The first section in Chapter 1, "Discovering Language," presents five essays in which individuals tell of their language struggles and their triumphs. In "Discovering the Power of Language," Malcolm X relates how he came to understand the power of words while serving time in the Norfolk Prison Colony. He remembers his frustration and feelings of inadequacy when he recognized the limitations of his slang-filled street talk. Not one to sit around and drown in self-pity, Malcolm X charted a course that empowered and liberated his mind. Next, we read the inspiring story of Helen Keller, a woman who broke the chains of blindness and deafness and connected to the world around her. In "The Day Language Came into My Life," Keller recounts the day she, with the help of her teacher Anne Mansfield Sullivan, discovered "everything had a name, and each name gave birth to a new thought." In the third essay, "On Being 17, Bright, and Unable to Read," David Raymond describes what it is like to be a dyslexic high school student, and how he met his language challenge. The final two readings in this section have been paired because they both explore how closely names are tied to our very identities. In "What's in a Name?," Henry Louis Gates Jr. recounts a childhood experience with his father in which he discovers there's a lot more in a name than he first thought. It's an experience that opens Gates's eyes to racism in America. In "Changing My Name after Sixty Years," Tom Rosenberg offers an insight into what motivated him to return to his original surname—a name his parents changed when they fled Nazi Germany prior to the beginning of World War II.

In the second section of this chapter, "Language Matters," four writers explore some language fundamentals that give us a greater appreciation for the miracle of language that we humans share. In "English Belongs to Everybody," Robert MacNeil celebrates the remarkable resilience and flexibility of the English language. But English can also tie us in knots, as Steven Pinker explains in "Words Don't Mean What They Mean." Pinker's essay is full of examples of how we all participate in an elaborate "linguistic dance" with each other whenever we try to communicate. In "Language and Thought," philosopher Susanne K. Langer explains how language separates humans from the rest of the animal kingdom. She demonstrates the power of language and shows how "without it anything properly called 'thought' is impossible." Finally, in "A Brief History of English," Paul Roberts charts the long and complicated history of the English language from its beginnings around A.D. 600 to the present. He explains how a "minor language, spoken by a few people on a small island" in 1500 evolved into what "is perhaps the greatest language of the world."

Discovering the Power of Language

MALCOLM X

On February 21, 1965, Malcolm X, the Black Muslim leader, was shot to death as he addressed an afternoon rally in Harlem. He was thirty-nine years old. In the course of his brief life, he had risen from a world of thieving, pimping, and drug pushing to become one of the most articulate and powerful African Americans in the United States during the early 1960s. In 1992 his life was reexamined in Spike Lee's film *Malcolm X*. With the assistance of the late Alex Haley, the author of *Roots*, Malcolm X told his story in *The Autobiography of Malcolm X* (1964), a moving account of his search for fulfillment. This selection is taken from the *Autobiography*.

All of us have been in situations in which we have felt somehow betrayed by our language, unable to find just the right words to express ourselves. "Words," as lexicographer Bergen Evans has said, "are the tools for the job of saying what you want to say." As our repertoire of words expands so does our ability to express ourselves—to articulate clearly our thoughts, feelings, hopes, fears, likes, and dislikes. Frustration at not being able to express himself in the letters he wrote drove Malcolm X to the dictionary, where he discovered the power of words.

WRITING TO DISCOVER: *Write about a time when someone told you that it is important to have a good vocabulary. What did you think when you heard this advice? Why do you think people believe that vocabulary is important? How would you assess your own vocabulary?*

I've never been one for inaction. Everything I've ever felt strongly about, I've done something about. I guess that's why, unable to do anything else, I soon began writing to people I had known in the hustling world, such as Sammy the Pimp, John Hughes, the gambling house owner, the thief Jumpsteady, and several dope peddlers. I wrote them all about Allah and Islam and Mr. Elijah Muhammad. I had no idea where most of them lived. I addressed their letters in care of the Harlem or Roxbury bars and clubs where I'd known them.

I never got a single reply. The average hustler and criminal was too uneducated to write a letter. I have known many slick sharp-looking hustlers, who would have you think they had an interest in Wall Street; privately, they would get someone else to read a letter if they received one. Besides, neither would I have replied to anyone writing me something as wild as "the white man is the devil."

What certainly went on the Harlem and Roxbury wires was that Detroit Red was going crazy in stir,[1] or else he was trying some hype to shake up the warden's office.

During the years that I stayed in the Norfolk Prison Colony, never did any official directly say anything to me about those letters, although, of course, they all passed through the prison censorship. I'm sure, however, they monitored what I wrote to add to the files which every state and federal prison keeps on the conversion of Negro inmates by the teachings of Mr. Elijah Muhammad.

But at that time, I felt that the real reason was that the white man   5
knew that he was the devil.

Later on, I even wrote to the Mayor of Boston, to the Governor of Massachusetts, and to Harry S. Truman. They never answered; they probably never even saw my letters. I handscratched to them how the white man's society was responsible for the black man's condition in this wilderness of North America.

It was because of my letters that I happened to stumble upon starting to acquire some kind of homemade education.

I became increasingly frustrated at not being able to express what I wanted to convey in letters that I wrote, especially those to Mr. Elijah Muhammad. In the street, I had been the most articulate hustler out there—I had commanded attention when I said something. But now, trying to write simple English, I not only wasn't articulate, I wasn't even functional. How would I sound writing in slang, the way I would *say* it, something such as, "Look daddy, let me pull your coat about a cat. Elijah Muhammad—"

Many who today hear me somewhere in person, or on television, or those who read something I've said, will think I went to school far beyond the eighth grade. This impression is due entirely to my prison studies.

It had really begun back in the Charlestown Prison, when Bimbi first   10
made me feel envy of his stock of knowledge. Bimbi had always taken charge of any conversation he was in, and I had tried to emulate him. But every book I picked up had few sentences which didn't contain anywhere from one to nearly all of the words that might as well have been in Chinese. When I just skipped those words, of course, I really ended up with little idea of what the book said. So I had come to the Norfolk Prison Colony still going through only book-reading motions. Pretty soon, I would have quit even these motions, unless I had received the motivation that I did.

I saw that the best thing I could do was get hold of a dictionary—to study, to learn some words. I was lucky enough to reason also that I should try to improve my penmanship. It was sad. I couldn't even write in a straight line. It was both ideas together that moved me to request a dictionary along with some tablets and pencils from the Norfolk Prison Colony school.

---

1. Slang for being in jail.

I spent two days just riffling uncertainly through the dictionary's pages. I'd never realized so many words existed! I didn't know *which* words I needed to learn. Finally, just to start some kind of action, I began copying.

In my slow, painstaking, ragged handwriting, I copied into my tablet everything printed on that first page, down to the punctuation marks.

I believe it took me a day. Then, aloud, I read back, to myself, everything I'd written on the tablet. Over and over, aloud, to myself, I read my own handwriting.

I woke up the next morning, thinking about those words—immensely   15
proud to realize that not only had I written so much at one time, but I'd written words that I never knew were in the world. Moreover, with a little effort, I also could remember what many of these words meant. I reviewed the words whose meanings I didn't remember. Funny thing, from the dictionary's first page right now, that "aardvark" springs to my mind. The dictionary had a picture of it, a long-tailed, long-eared, burrowing African mammal, which lives off termites caught by sticking out its tongue as an anteater does for ants.

I was so fascinated that I went on—I copied the dictionary's next page. And the same experience came when I studied that. With every succeeding page, I also learned of people and places and events from history. Actually the dictionary is like a miniature encyclopedia. Finally the dictionary's A section had filled a whole tablet—and I went on into the B's. That was the way I started copying what eventually became the entire dictionary. It went a lot faster after so much practice helped me pick up handwriting speed. Between what I wrote in my tablet, and writing letters, during the rest of my time in prison I would guess I wrote a million words.

I suppose it was inevitable that as my word-base broadened, I could for the first time pick up a book and read and now begin to understand what the book was saying. Anyone who has read a great deal can imagine the new world that opened. Let me tell you something: from then until I left that prison, in every free moment I had, if I was not reading in the library, I was reading on my bunk. You couldn't have gotten me out of books with a wedge. Between Mr. Muhammad's teachings, my correspondence, my visitors . . . and my reading of books, months passed without my even thinking about being imprisoned. In fact, up to then, I never had been so truly free in my life.

THINKING CRITICALLY ABOUT THE READING

1. What motivated Malcolm X "to acquire some kind of homemade education" (7)?

2. Malcolm X narrates his experience as a prisoner using the first-person pronoun *I*. Why is the first person particularly appropriate? What would be lost or gained had he told his story using the third-person pronoun *he*? (Glossary: *Point of View*)

3. For many, *vocabulary building* means learning strange, multisyllabic, difficult-to-spell words. But acquiring an effective vocabulary does not need to be any of these things. What, for you, constitutes an effective vocabulary? How would you characterize Malcolm X's vocabulary in this selection? Do you find his word choice appropriate for his purpose? (Glossary: *Purpose*) Explain.

4. In paragraph 8, Malcolm X remembers thinking how he would "sound writing in slang" and feeling inadequate because he recognized how slang or street talk limited his options. (Glossary: *Slang*) In what kinds of situations is slang useful and appropriate? When is Standard English more appropriate? (Glossary: *Standard English*)

5. In paragraph 8, Malcolm X describes himself as having been "the most articulate hustler out there" but in writing he says he "wasn't even functional." What differences between speaking and writing could account for such a discrepancy? How does the tone of this essay help you understand Malcolm X's dilemma? (Glossary: *Tone*)

6. What is the nature of the freedom that Malcolm X refers to in the final sentence? In what sense is language liberating? Is it possible for people to be "prisoners" of their own language? Explain.

LANGUAGE IN ACTION

Many newspapers carry regular vocabulary-building columns, and the *Reader's Digest* has for many years included a section called "It Pays to Enrich Your Word Power." You might enjoy taking the following quiz, which is excerpted from *Reader's Digest.*

IT PAYS TO ENRICH YOUR WORD POWER

Zeus and his thunderbolts, Thor and his hammer, Medusa and her power to turn flesh into stone: these are all fascinating figures in mythology and folklore. Associated with such legends are words we use today, including the 10 selected below.

1. **panic** *n.*—A: pain. B: relief. C: mess. D: fear.

2. **bacchanal** (*BAK ih NAL*) *n.*— A: drunken party. B: graduation ceremony. C: backache remedy. D: victory parade.

3. **puckish** *adj.*—A: wrinkly. B: quirky. C: quarrelsome. D: mischievous.

4. **cyclopean** (*SIGH klo PEA en*) *adj.*—A: wise. B: gigantic. C: wealthy. D: repetitious.

5. **hector** *v.*—A: to curse. B: bully. C: disown. D: injure.

6. **cupidity** (*kyoo PID ih tee*) *n.*— A: thankfulness. B: ignorance. C: abundance. D: desire.

7. **mnemonic** (*knee MON ik*) *adj.* —pertaining to A: memory. B: speech. C: hearing. D: sight.

8. **stygian** (*STIJ ee an*) *adj.*—A: stingy. B: hellish. C: uncompromising. D: dirty.

9. **narcissistic** *adj.*—A: indecisive. B: very sleepy. C: very vain. D: just.

10. **zephyr** (*ZEF er*) *n.*—A: breeze. B: dog. C: horse. D: tornado.

ANSWERS:

1. **panic**—*[D]* Fear; widespread terror; as, An outbreak of Ebola led to *panic* in the small village. *Pan,* frightening Greek god of nature.

2. **bacchanal**—*[A]* Drunken party; orgy; as, Complaints to the police broke up the *bacchanal. Bacchus,* Roman god of wine.

3. **puckish**—*[D]* Mischievous; prankish. *Puck,* a trick-loving sprite or fairy.

4. **cyclopean**—*[B]* Gigantic; huge; as, the *cyclopean* home runs of Mark McGwire. *Cyclopes,* a race of fierce, one-eyed giants.

5. **hector**—*[B]* To bully; threaten. *Hector,* Trojan leader slain by Achilles and portrayed as a bragging menace in some dramas.

6. **cupidity**—*[D]* Strong desire. *Cupid,* Roman god of love.

7. **mnemonic**—*[A]* Pertaining to memory; as, "Spring forward and fall back" is a *mnemonic* spur to change time twice a year. *Mnemosyne,* Greek goddess of memory.

8. **stygian**—*[B]* Hellish; dark and gloomy. *Styx,* a river in Hades.

9. **narcissistic**—*[C]* Very vain; self-loving; as, The *narcissistic* actress preened for the photographers. *Narcissus,* a youth who fell in love with his own reflection.

10. **zephyr**—*[A]* Soft breeze; as, The storm tapered off to a *zephyr. Zephyrus,* gentle Greek god of the west wind.

Are you familiar with most of the words on the quiz? Did some of the answers surprise you? In your opinion, is the level of difficulty appropriate for the *Reader's Digest* audience? What does the continuing popularity of vocabulary-building features suggest about the attitudes of many Americans toward language?

WRITING SUGGESTIONS

1. All of us have been in situations in which our ability to use language seemed inadequate—for example, when taking an exam; being interviewed for a job; giving directions; or expressing sympathy, anger, or grief. Write a brief essay in which you recount one such frustrating incident in your life. Before beginning to write, review your reactions to Malcolm X's frustrations with his limited vocabulary. Share your experiences with your classmates.

2. Malcolm X solved the problem of his own illiteracy by carefully studying the dictionary. Would this be a viable solution to the national problem of illiteracy? Are there more practical alternatives to Malcolm X's approach? What, for example, is being done in your community to combat illiteracy? What are some of the more successful approaches being used in other parts of the country? Write a brief essay about the problem of illiteracy. In addition to using your library for research, you may want to check out the Internet to see what it has to offer.

The Day Language Came into My Life

HELEN KELLER

Helen Keller (1880–1968) became blind and deaf at the age of eighteen months as a result of a disease. As a child, then, Keller became accustomed to her limited world, for it was all that she knew. She experienced only certain fundamental sensations, such as the warmth of the sun on her face, and few emotions, such as anger and bitterness. It wasn't until she was almost seven years old that her family hired Anne Sullivan, a young woman who would turn out to be an extraordinary teacher, to help her. As Keller learned to communicate and think, the world opened up to her. She recorded her experiences in an autobiography, *The Story of My Life* (1903), from which the following selection is taken.

Helen Keller is in a unique position to remind us of what it is like to pass from the "fog" of prethought into the world where "everything had a name, and each name gave birth to a new thought." Her experiences as a deaf and blind child also raise a number of questions about the relationship between language and thought, emotions, ideas, and memory. Over time, Keller's acquisition of language allowed her to assume all the advantages of her birthright. Her rapid intellectual and emotional growth as a result of language suggests that we, too, have the potential to achieve a greater measure of our humanity by further refining our language abilities.

WRITING TO DISCOVER: *Consider what your life would be like today if you had been born without the ability to understand language or speak or if you had suddenly lost the ability to use language later in life. Write about those aspects of your life that you think would be affected most severely.*

The most important day I remember in all my life is the one on which my teacher, Anne Mansfield Sullivan, came to me. I am filled with wonder when I consider the immeasurable contrast between the two lives which it connects. It was the third of March 1887, three months before I was seven years old.

On the afternoon of that eventful day, I stood on the porch, dumb, expectant. I guessed vaguely from my mother's signs and from the hurrying to and fro in the house that something unusual was about to happen, so I went to the door and waited on the steps. The afternoon sun penetrated the mass of honeysuckle that covered the porch and fell on my upturned face. My fingers lingered almost unconsciously on the familiar leaves and blossoms which had just come forth to greet the sweet southern spring. I did not know what the future held of marvel or surprise for me. Anger and bitterness had preyed upon me continually for weeks and a deep languor had succeeded this passionate struggle.

Have you ever been at sea in a dense fog, when it seemed as if a tangible white darkness shut you in, and the great ship, tense and anxious, groped her way toward the shore with plummet and sounding-line, and you waited with beating heart for something to happen? I was like that ship before my education began, only I was without compass or sounding-line and had no way of knowing how near the harbor was. "Light! give me light!" was the wordless cry of my soul, and the light of love shone on me in that very hour.

I felt approaching footsteps. I stretched out my hand as I supposed to my mother. Someone took it, and I was caught up and held close in the arms of her who had come to reveal all things to me, and, more than all things else, to love me.

The morning after my teacher came she led me into her room and gave me a doll. The little blind children at the Perkins Institution had sent it and Laura Bridgman had dressed it; but I did not know this until afterward. When I had played with it a little while, Miss Sullivan slowly spelled into my hand the word "d-o-l-l." I was at once interested in this finger play and tried to imitate it. When I finally succeeded in making the letters correctly I was flushed with childhood pleasure and pride. Running downstairs to my mother I held up my hand and made the letters for doll. I did not know that I was spelling a word or even that words existed; I was simply making my fingers go in monkeylike imitation. In the days that followed I learned to spell in this uncomprehending way a great many words, among them *pin, hat, cup* and a few verbs like *sit, stand* and *walk*. But my teacher had been with me several weeks before I understood that everything has a name.

One day, while I was playing with my new doll, Miss Sullivan put my big rag doll into my lap also, spelled "d-o-l-l" and tried to make me understand that "d-o-l-l" applied to both. Earlier in the day we had had a tussle over the words "m-u-g" and "w-a-t-e-r." Miss Sullivan had tried to impress it upon me that "m-u-g" is *mug* and that "w-a-t-e-r" is *water,* but I persisted in confounding the two. In despair she had dropped the subject for the time, only to renew it at the first opportunity. I became impatient at her repeated attempts and, seizing the new doll, I dashed it upon the floor. I was keenly delighted when I felt the fragments of the broken doll at my feet. Neither sorrow nor regret followed my passionate outburst. I had not loved the doll. In the still, dark world in which I lived there was no strong sentiment or tenderness. I felt my teacher sweep the fragments to one side of the hearth, and I had a sense of satisfaction that the cause of my discomfort was removed. She brought me my hat, and I knew I was going out into the warm sunshine. This thought, if a wordless sensation may be called a thought, made me hop and skip with pleasure.

We walked down the path to the well-house, attracted by the fragrance of the honeysuckle with which it was covered. Some one was drawing water and my teacher placed my hand under the spout. As the cool stream gushed over one hand she spelled into the other the word *water,* first slowly, then rapidly. I stood still, my whole attention fixed upon the motions of her fingers. Suddenly I felt a misty consciousness as of something forgotten—a thrill of returning thought; and somehow the mystery of language was revealed to me. I knew then that "w-a-t-e-r" meant the wonderful cool something that was flowing over my hand. The living word awakened my soul, gave it light, hope, joy, set it free! There were barriers still, it is true, but barriers that could in time be swept away.

I left the well-house eager to learn. Everything had a name, and each name gave birth to a new thought. As we returned to the house every object which I touched seemed to quiver with life. That was because I saw everything with the strange, new sight that had come to me. On entering the door I remembered the doll I had broken. I felt my way to the hearth and picked up the pieces. I tried vainly to put them together. Then my eyes filled with tears; for I realized what I had done, and for the first time I felt repentance and sorrow.

I learned a great many new words that day. I do not remember what they all were; but I do know that *mother, father, sister, teacher* were among them—words that were to make the world blossom for me, "like Aaron's rod, with flowers." It would have been difficult to find a happier child than I was as I lay in my crib at the close of that eventful day and lived over the joys it had brought me, and for the first time longed for a new day to come.

THINKING CRITICALLY ABOUT THE READING

1. In paragraph 6, Keller writes, "One day, while I was playing with my new doll, Miss Sullivan put my big rag doll into my lap also, spelled 'd-o-l-l' and tried to make me understand that 'd-o-l-l' applied to both." Why do you think Miss Sullivan placed a different doll in her lap? What essential fact about language did the action demonstrate to Keller?

2. In paragraph 6, Keller also tells us that in trying to learn the difference between "m-u-g" and "w-a-t-e-r" she "persisted in confounding the two" terms. In a letter to her home institution, Sullivan elaborated on this confusion, revealing that it was caused by Keller thinking that both words meant "drink." How in paragraph 7 does Keller finally come to understand these words? What does she come to understand about the relationship between them?

3. In paragraph 8, after the experience at the well, Keller comes to believe that "everything had a name, and each name gave birth to a new thought." Reflect on that statement. Does she mean that the process of naming leads to thinking?

4. In paragraph 3, Keller uses the metaphor of being lost in a fog to explain her feeling of helplessness and her frustration at not being able to communicate. Perhaps you have had a similar feeling about an inability to communicate with parents or teachers or of not being able to realize some other longed-for goal. Try using a fresh metaphor to describe feelings you might have had that are similar to Keller's. (Glossary: *Figures of Speech*) Before beginning, however, think about why the fog metaphor works so well.

5. Keller realized that over time words would make her world open up for her. Identify the parts of speech of her first words. In what ways do these parts of speech open up one's world? Explain how these words or parts of speech provide insights into the nature of writing. How does Keller's early language use compare with her use of English in her essay?

6. While it is fairly easy to see how Keller could learn the names of concrete items, it may be more difficult for us to understand how she learned about her emotions. What does her difficulty in coming to terms with abstractions—such as love, bitterness, frustration, repentance, sorrow—tell us as writers about the strategies we need to use to effectively convey emotions and feelings to our readers? In considering your answer, examine the diction Keller uses in her essay. (Glossary: *Diction*)

LANGUAGE IN ACTION

A series of books by Rich Hall "and friends" gives lists of so-called *sniglets,* words for things without names. Notice that *sniglet* is itself a made-up word. Do you know of a person, place, thought, or action that is without a word but needs one? What word would you give it? What does the experience of "naming the unnamed" reveal about the desirability of an extensive vocabulary? What does it reveal about the possibilities and limitations of language? What do the following sniglets reveal about the authors' understanding of the world?

elbonics (*el bon' iks*) n. The actions of two people maneuvering for one armrest in a movie theater.

glackett (*glak' it*) n. The noisy ball inside a spray-paint can.

gription (*grip' shun*) n. The sound of sneakers squeaking against the floor during basketball games.

hangle (*han' gul*) n. A cluster of coat hangers.

lactomangulation (*lak' to man gyu lay' shun*) n. Manhandling the "open here" spout on a milk carton so badly that one has to resort to using the "illegal" side.

motspur (*mot' sper*) n. The pesky fourth wheel on a shopping cart that refuses to cooperate with the other three.

napjerk (*nap' jurk*) n. The sudden convulsion of the body just as one is about to doze off.

optortionist (*op tor' shun ist*) n. The kid in school who can turn his eyelids inside out.

psychophobia (*sy ko fo' be uh*) n. The compulsion, when using a host's bathroom, to peer behind the shower curtain and make sure no one is waiting for you.

xiidigitation (*ksi dij I tay' shun*) n. The practice of trying to determine the year a movie was made by deciphering the roman numerals at the end of the credits.

WRITING SUGGESTIONS

1. It could be said that we process our world in terms of our language. Using a variety of examples from your own experience, write an essay illustrating the validity of this observation. For example, aside from the photographs you took on your last vacation, your trip exists only in the words you use to describe it, whether in conversations or in writing.

2. Helen Keller explains that she felt no remorse when she shattered her doll. "In the still, dark world in which I lived there was no strong sentiment or tenderness" (6) she recalls. However, once she understood that things had names, Keller was able to feel repentance and sorrow. In your own words, try to describe why you think her feelings changed. Before you begin to write, you may want to reread your Writing to Discover entry for the Keller article. You may also want to discuss this issue with classmates or your instructor and do some research of your own into the ways language alters perception among people who are blind or deaf.

On Being 17, Bright, and Unable to Read

Davip Raymond

When the following article appeared in the *New York Times* in 1976, David Raymond was a high school student in Connecticut. In 1981, Raymond graduated from Curry College in Milton, Massachusetts, one of the few colleges with learning-disability programs at the time. He and his family now live in Fairfield, Connecticut, where he works as a builder.

In his essay, Raymond shares his story of being language challenged in a world of readers. Even though testing revealed that Raymond had above-average intelligence, he always felt "dumb" in school. In his plea for understanding for other dyslexic children, he poignantly discusses the emotionally charged difficulties his own dyslexia caused and the many problems he experienced in school as a result.

WRITING TO DISCOVER: *One of the fundamental language arts skills that we are supposed to learn in school is how to read. How do you rate yourself as a reader? How dependent are you on reading in your everyday life? How would your life change if you were unable to read?*

One day a substitute teacher picked me to read aloud from the textbook. When I told her "No, thank you," she came unhinged. She thought I was acting smart, and told me so. I kept calm, and that got her madder and madder. We must have spent 10 minutes trying to solve the problem, and finally she got so red in the face I thought she'd blow up. She told me she'd see me after class.

Maybe someone like me was a new thing for that teacher. But she wasn't new to me. I've been through scenes like that all my life. You see, even though I'm 17 and a junior in high school, I can't read because I have dyslexia. I'm told I read "at a fourth-grade level," but from where I sit, that's not reading. You can't know what that means unless you've been there. It's not easy to tell how it feels when you can't read your homework assignments or the newspaper or a menu in a restaurant or even notes from your own friends.

My family began to suspect I was having problems almost from the first day I started school. My father says my early years in school were the worst years of his life. They weren't so good for me, either. As I look back on it now, I can't find the words to express how bad it really was. I wanted to die. I'd come home from school screaming, "I'm dumb. I'm dumb—I wish I were dead!"

I guess I couldn't read anything at all then—not even my own name—and they tell me I didn't talk as good as other kids. But what I remember about those days is that I couldn't throw a ball where it was supposed to go, I couldn't learn to swim, and I wouldn't learn to ride a bike, because no matter what anyone told me, I knew I'd fail.

Sometimes my teachers would try to be encouraging. When I couldn't   5
read the words on the board they'd say, "Come on, David, you know that
word." Only I didn't. And it was embarrassing. I just felt dumb. And dumb
was how the kids treated me. They'd make fun of me every chance they
got, asking me to spell "cat" or something like that. Even if I knew how
to spell it, I wouldn't; they'd only give me another word. Anyway, it was
awful, because more than anything I wanted friends. On my birthday when
I blew out the candles I didn't wish I could learn to read; what I wished for
was that the kids would like me.

With the bad reports coming from school, and with me moaning
about wanting to die and how everybody hated me, my parents began
looking for help. That's when the testing started. The school tested me,
the child-guidance center tested me, private psychiatrists tested me. Everybody knew something was wrong — especially me.

It didn't help much when they stuck a fancy name onto it. I couldn't
pronounce it then — I was only in second grade — and I was ashamed to
talk about it. Now it rolls off my tongue, because I've been living with it
for a lot of years — dyslexia.

All through elementary school it wasn't easy. I was always having to
do things that were "different," things the other kids didn't have to do. I
had to go to a child psychiatrist, for instance.

One summer my family forced me to go to a camp for children with
reading problems. I hated the idea, but the camp turned out pretty good, and
I had a good time. I met a lot of kids who couldn't read and somehow that
helped. The director of the camp said I had a higher I.Q. than 90 percent of
the population. I didn't believe him.

About the worst thing I had to do in fifth and sixth grade was go to a   10
special education class in another school in our town. A bus picked me up,
and I didn't like that at all. The bus also picked up emotionally disturbed
kids and retarded kids. It was like going to a school for the retarded. I
always worried that someone I knew would see me on that bus. It was a
relief to go to the regular junior high school.

Life began to change a little for me then, because I began to feel better
about myself. I found the teachers cared; they had meetings about me and I
worked harder for them for a while. I began to work on the potter's wheel,
making vases and pots that the teachers said were pretty good. Also, I got a
letter for being on the track team. I could always run pretty fast.

At high school the teachers are good, and everyone is trying to help
me. I've gotten honors some marking periods, and I've won a letter on the
cross-country team. Next quarter I think the school might hold a show of
my pottery. I've got some friends. But there are still some embarrassing
times. For instance, every time there is writing in the class, I get up and go
to the special education room. Kids ask me where I go all the time. Sometimes I say, "to Mars."

Homework is a real problem. During free periods in school I go into the special ed room and staff members read assignments to me. When I get home my mother reads to me. Sometimes she reads an assignment into a tape recorder, and then I go into my room and listen to it. If we have a novel or something like that to read, she reads it out loud to me. Then I sit down with her and we do the assignment. She'll write, while I talk my answers to her. Lately I've taken to dictating into a tape recorder, and then someone—my father, a private tutor, or my mother—types up what I've dictated. Whatever homework I do takes someone else's time, too. That makes me feel bad.

We had a big meeting in school the other day—eight of us, four from the guidance department, my private tutor, my parents, and me. The subject was me. I said I wanted to go to college, and they told me about colleges that have facilities and staff to handle people like me. That's nice to hear.

As for what happens after college, I don't know and I'm worried about that. How can I make a living if I can't read? Who will hire me? How will I fill out the application form? The only thing that gives me any courage is the fact that I've learned about well-known people who couldn't read or had other problems and still made it. Like Albert Einstein, who didn't talk until he was 4 and flunked math. Like Leonardo da Vinci, who everyone seems to think had dyslexia.

I've told this story because maybe some teacher will read it and go easy on a kid in the classroom who has what I've got. Or, maybe some parent will stop nagging his kid, and stop calling him lazy. Maybe he's not lazy or dumb. Maybe he just can't read and doesn't know what's wrong. Maybe he's scared, like I was.

THINKING CRITICALLY ABOUT THE READING

1. What is dyslexia? Is it essential for an understanding of the essay that we know more about dyslexia than Raymond tells us? Explain.

2. Before being diagnosed dyslexic, Raymond remembers feeling "dumb" and the other kids treating him as though he were. How intelligent do you think Raymond is? What evidence did you use to arrive at your conclusion? Explain.

3. What does Raymond's story tell us about the importance of our early childhood experiences, especially within our educational system?

4. Raymond uses many colloquial and idiomatic expressions, such as "she came unhinged" and "she got so red in the face I thought she'd blow up" (1). (Glossary: *Colloquial Expression*) Identify other examples of such diction. How do they affect your reaction to the essay?

5. How has Raymond organized his story? (Glossary: *Organization*)

6. Raymond reveals the purpose of his story in the final paragraph. Why do you suppose he did not announce his intention earlier in the essay? (Glossary: *Purpose*)

LANGUAGE IN ACTION

To help teachers recognize students who might be dyslexic, *Dyslexia Teacher* has posted the following list of dyslexia symptoms on its Web site, www .dyslexia-teacher.com:

- a noticeable difference between the pupil's ability and their actual achievement;
- a family history of learning difficulties;
- difficulties with spelling;
- confusion over left and right;
- writing letters or numbers backwards;
- difficulties with math/science;
- difficulties with organizing themselves;
- difficulty following 2- or 3-step instructions.

Spelling gets singled out as one area that is important to look at when diagnosing dyslexia. According to *Dyslexia Teacher*,

> Spelling is the activity which causes most difficulty for dyslexic children. The observation of spelling errors in short, simple words is the way in which most dyslexic children first come to our attention. Examples of words which cause particular difficulty are: *any, many, island, said, they, because, enough,* and *friend.* Other words will sometimes be spelt in the way that you would expect them to be spelt if our spelling system were rational, for example, *does/dus, please/pleeze, knock/nock, search/serch, journey/jerney,* etc.
>
> Dyslexic children also experience difficulties with "jumbled spellings." These are spelling attempts in which all the correct letters are present, but are written in the wrong order. Examples include *dose/does, freind/friend, siad/said, bule/blue, becuase/because,* and *wores/worse.* "Jumbled spellings" show that the child is experiencing difficulty with visual memory. Non-dyslexic children and adults often use their visual memory when trying to remember a difficult spelling: they write down two or three possible versions of the word on a spare piece of paper and see which spelling "looks right." They are relying on their visual memory to help them, but the visual memory of a dyslexic child may not be adequate for this task.

After hearing of the difficulties that dyslexic children and adults experience, are you better able to empathize with David Raymond's experiences? Imagine you are dyslexic and discuss with your class what it would feel like for you to exhibit some or all of the symptoms described.

WRITING SUGGESTIONS

1. Using your response to the Writing to Discover prompt for the Raymond selection as a starting point, write an essay about the importance of reading and literacy in your life.

2. Imagine that you are away at school. Recently you were caught in a speed trap—you were going seventy miles per hour in a fifty-mile-per-hour zone—and have just lost your license; you will not be able to drive home this coming weekend, as you had planned. Write two letters in which you explain why you will not be able to go home, one to your parents and the other to your best friend. Your audience is different in each case, so be sure to choose your diction accordingly. Try to imitate Raymond's informal yet serious and sincere tone in one of your letters.

What's in a Name?

HENRY LOUIS GATES JR.

The preeminent African American scholar of our time, Henry Louis Gates Jr. is the Alphonse Fletcher University Professor and director of the W. E. B. Du Bois Institute for African and African American Research at Harvard University. Among his impressive list of publications are *Figures in Black: Words, Signs and the "Racial" Self* (1987), *The Signifying Monkey: A Theory of Afro-American Literary Criticism* (1988), *Loose Canons: Notes on Culture Wars* (1992), *The Future of the Race* (1997), and *Thirteen Ways of Looking at a Black Man* (1999). His most recent books are *Mr. Jefferson and Miss Wheatley* (2003) and *Finding Oprah's Roots: Finding Your Own* (2007). His *Colored People: A Memoir* (1994) recollects in a wonderful prose style his youth growing up in Piedmont, West Virginia, and his emerging sexual and racial awareness. Gates first enrolled at Potomac State College and later transferred to Yale, where he studied history. With the assistance of an Andrew W. Mellon Foundation Fellowship and a Ford Foundation Fellowship, he pursued advanced degrees in English at Clare College at the University of Cambridge. He has been honored with a MacArthur Foundation Fellowship, inclusion on *Time* magazine's "25 Most Influential Americans" list, a National Humanities Medal, and election to the American Academy of Arts and Letters.

In "What's in a Name?," excerpted from a longer article published in the fall 1989 issue of *Dissent* magazine, Gates tells the story of an early encounter with the language of prejudice. In learning how one of the "bynames" used by white people to define African Americans robs them of their identity, he feels the sting of racism firsthand. Notice how Gates's use of dialogue gives immediacy and poignancy to his narration.

WRITING TO DISCOVER: *Reflect on racially charged language you have heard. For example, has anyone ever used a racial or ethnic epithet to refer to you? When did you first become aware that such terms existed? How do you feel about being characterized or defined by your race or ethnicity? If you yourself have ever used such terms, what was your intent in using them? What was the response of others?*

The question of color takes up much space in these pages, but the question of color, especially in this country, operates to hide the graver questions of the self.

—JAMES BALDWIN, 1961

...blood, darky, Tar Baby, Kaffir, shine...moor, blackamoor, Jim Crow, spooks....quadroon, meriney, red bone, high yellow...Mammy, porch monkey, home, homeboy, George spearchucker, schwarze, Leroy, Smokey...mouli, buck, Ethiopian, brother, sistah...

—TREY ELLIS, 1989

I had forgotten the incident completely, until I read Trey Ellis's essay, "Remember My Name," in a recent issue of the *Village Voice*[1] (June 13, 1989). But there, in the middle of an extended italicized list of the bynames of "the race" ("the race" or "our people" being the terms my parents used in polite or reverential discourse, "jigaboo" or "nigger" more commonly used in anger, jest, or pure disgust), it was: "George." Now the events of that very brief exchange return to mind so vividly that I wonder why I had forgotten it.

My father and I were walking home at dusk from his second job. He "moonlighted" as a janitor in the evenings for the telephone company. Every day but Saturday, he would come home at 3:30 from his regular job at the paper mill, wash up, eat supper, then at 4:30 head downtown to his second job. He used to make jokes frequently about a union official who moonlighted. I never got the joke, but he and his friends thought it was hilarious. All I knew was that my family always ate well, that my brother and I had new clothes to wear, and that all of the white people in Piedmont, West Virginia, treated my parents with an odd mixture of resentment and respect that even we understood at the time had something directly to do with a small but certain measure of financial security.

He had left a little early that evening because I was with him and I had to be in bed early. I could not have been more than five or six, and we had stopped off at the Cut-Rate Drug Store (where no black person in town but my father could sit down to eat, and eat off real plates with real silverware) so that I could buy some caramel ice cream, two scoops in a wafer cone, please, which I was busy licking when Mr. Wilson walked by.

Mr. Wilson was a very quiet man, whose stony, brooding, silent manner seemed designed to scare off any overtures of friendship, even from white people. He was Irish, as was one-third of our village (another third being Italian), the more affluent among whom sent their children to "Catholic School" across the bridge in Maryland. He had white straight hair, like my Uncle Joe, whom he uncannily resembled, and he carried a black worn metal lunch pail, the kind that Riley[2] carried on the television show. My father always spoke to him, and for reasons that we never did understand, he always spoke to my father.

"Hello, Mr. Wilson," I heard my father say. 5

"Hello, George."

I stopped licking my ice cream cone, and asked my Dad in a loud voice why Mr. Wilson had called him "George."

"Doesn't he know your name, Daddy? Why don't you tell him your name? Your name isn't George."

---

1. *Village Voice:* a nationally distributed weekly newspaper published in New York City.
2. A character on the U.S. television show *The Life of Riley,* a blue-collar, ethnic sitcom popular in the 1950s.

For a moment I tried to think of who Mr. Wilson was mixing Pop up with. But we didn't have any Georges among the colored people in Piedmont; nor were there colored Georges living in the neighboring towns and working at the mill.

"Tell him your name, Daddy."   10

"He knows my name, boy," my father said after a long pause. "He calls all colored people George."

A long silence ensued. It was "one of those things," as my Mom would put it. Even then, that early, I knew when I was in the presence of "one of those things," one of those things that provided a glimpse, through a rent[3] curtain, at another world that we could not affect but that affected us. There would be a painful moment of silence, and you would wait for it to give way to a discussion of a black superstar such as Sugar Ray[4] or Jackie Robinson.[5]

"Nobody hits better in a clutch than Jackie Robinson."

"That's right. Nobody."

I never again looked Mr. Wilson in the eye.   15

THINKING CRITICALLY ABOUT THE READING

1. In the epigraph to this essay, Gates presents two quotations, one by James Baldwin. What do you think Baldwin meant when he wrote "the question of color, especially in this country [America], operates to hide the graver questions of self"? How does this statement relate to the theme of Gates's essay?

2. In his opening paragraph, Gates refers to the other quotation in the epigraph — a list of bynames used to refer to African Americans that appeared in an article by Trey Ellis — and states that his reading of this article triggered a childhood memory for him. How did you first feel after reading Ellis's list of bynames for African Americans? What did you find offensive about these racial slurs? Explain.

3. Later in his opening paragraph Gates reveals that "'the race' or 'our people' [were] the terms my parents used in polite or reverential discourse, 'jigaboo' or 'nigger' more commonly used in anger, jest, or pure disgust." Why does Gates make so much of Mr. Wilson's use of "George" when his own parents used words so much more obviously offensive? What do you see as the essential difference between white people using Trey Ellis's list of terms to refer to people of color and African Americans using the same terms to refer to themselves? Explain.

---

3. torn.

4. Walker Smith Jr. (1921–1989), American professional boxer and six-time world champion.

5. (1919–1972): The first black baseball player in the National League.

4. Gates describes Mr. Wilson and provides some background information about him in paragraph 4. What do you think is Gates's purpose in providing this information? (Glossary: *Description*)

5. Explain what happens in paragraph 12. What is "one of those things," as Gates's mother put it? In what ways is "one of those things" really Gates's purpose in telling his story? Why does Gates say, "I never again looked Mr. Wilson in the eye" (15)?

6. In paragraphs 5 and 6, Gates uses dialogue to capture the key exchange between his father and Mr. Wilson. What does this dialogue add to his narration? (Glossary: *Narration*) What would have been lost if Gates had simply described the conversation between the two men?

LANGUAGE IN ACTION

Comment on the importance of one's name as revealed in the following Ann Landers column.

REFUSAL TO USE NAME IS THE ULTIMATE INSULT

DEAR ANN LANDERS: Boy, when you're wrong, you're really wrong. Apparently, you have never been the victim of a hostile, nasty, passive-aggressive person who refuses to address you by name. Well, I have.

My husband's mother has never called me by my name in the 21 years I've been married to her son. Nor has she ever said "please" or "thank you," unless someone else is within hearing distance. My husband's children by his first wife are the same way. The people they care about are always referred to by name, but the rest of us are not called anything.

If you still think this is a "psychological glitch," as you said in a recent column, try speaking to someone across the room without addressing that person by name. To be nameless and talked at is the ultimate put-down, and I wish you had said so. — "Hey You" in Florida

DEAR FLORIDA: Sorry I let you down. Your mother-in-law's refusal to call you by name is, I am sure, rooted in hostility. Many years ago, Dr. Will Menninger said, "The sweetest sound in any language is the sound of your own name." It can also be a valuable sales tool. My former husband, one of the world's best salesmen, said if you want to make a sale, get the customer's name, use it when you make your pitch, and he will be half sold. His own record as a salesman proved him right.

What is the meaning of Dr. Will Menninger's statement: "The sweetest sound in any language is the sound of your own name"?

WRITING SUGGESTIONS

1. Most people have strong feelings about their names. How do you feel about your name? Do you like it? Does it sound pleasant to you? Do you have a nickname? Do you think your name shapes your self-identity in a positive or

negative way, or do you think it has no effect on your sense of who you are? Write an essay about your name and the way it helps or fails to help you present yourself to the world.

2. Consider the following statement by psychiatrist and author Thomas Szasz taken from his book *The Second Sin*:

> The struggle for definition is veritably the struggle for life itself. In the typical Western two men fight desperately for the possession of a gun that has been thrown to the ground: whoever reaches the weapon first, shoots and lives; his adversary is shot and dies. In ordinary life, the struggle is not for guns but for words: whoever first defines the situation is the victor; his adversary, the victim. . . . In short, he who first seizes the word imposes reality on the other; he who defines thus dominates and lives; and he who is defined is subjugated and may be killed.

In the context of Szasz's words, write an essay in which you explore the power of names to define. Be sure to use the stories of Henry Louis Gates Jr. and Tom Rosenberg ("Changing My Name after Sixty Years," p. 61) as well as stories from your own experience or reading to illustrate your essay.

Changing My Name after Sixty Years

Tom Rosenberg

Tom Rosenberg was born in Berlin, Germany, but in 1938 his family fled Nazi persecution, settling in New York City when Rosenberg was six years old. In an attempt to downplay their Jewish heritage, the Rosenbergs changed their surname to Ross upon arriving in the United States. As Tom Ross, Rosenberg grew up in New York, graduated from the University of Pittsburgh, then joined the Marines and served in the Korean War. He moved to the West Coast upon returning to the United States and served as a political consultant for nearly thirty years, spearheading environmental and outdoor recreation initiatives. He has published a novel, *Phantom on His Wheels* (2000), which draws on his interests in journalism, environmentalism, and politics.

The following essay, which appeared in the July 17, 2000, issue of *Newsweek*, shows how Rosenberg spent most of his life denying his heritage and explains why he has chosen to embrace it now. By choosing to define himself anew he finds pride and hope.

WRITING TO DISCOVER: *Surnames mean a lot in our culture; whether or not we like it, they tell others something about our ethnicity, our heritage, and our possible cultural influences. Not long ago, having a surname that was readily identifiable as "foreign" could be a liability. For the most part, attitudes about names have changed for the better. What do you think of your surname? Have you ever felt hindered or discriminated against because of it? If you could change it, would you? Why or why not?*

My parents left Nazi Germany in 1938, when I was six and my mother was pregnant with my sister. They arrived in America with a lot of baggage—guilt over deserting loved ones, anger over losing their home and business, and a lifelong fear of anti-Semitism.

Shortly thereafter, whether out of fear, a desire to assimilate, or a combination of both, they changed our family name from Rosenberg to Ross. My parents were different from the immigrants who landed on Ellis Island and had their names changed by an immigration bureaucrat. My mother and father voluntarily gave up their identity and a measure of pride for an Anglicized name.

Growing up a German-Jewish kid in the Bronx in the 1940s, a time when Americans were dying in a war fought in part to save Jews from the hated Nazis, was difficult. Even my new name failed to protect me from bigotry; the neighborhood bullies knew a "sheenie" when they saw one.

The bullying only intensified the shame I felt about my family's religious and ethnic background. I spent much of my youth denying my roots and

vying for my peers' acceptance as "Tom Ross." Today I look back and wonder
what kind of life I might have led if my parents had kept our family name.

In the '50s, I doubt Tom Rosenberg would have been accepted as   5
a pledge by Theta Chi, a predominantly Christian fraternity at my college. He probably would have pledged a Jewish fraternity or had the self-
confidence and conviction to ignore the Greek system altogether. Tom
Rosenberg might have married a Jewish woman, stayed in the East, and
maintained closer ties to his Jewish family.

As it was, I moved west to San Francisco. Only after I married and
became a father did I begin to acknowledge my Jewish heritage.

My first wife, a liberal Methodist, insisted that I stop running from
Judaism. For years we attended both a Unitarian church and a Jewish
temple. Her open-minded attitude set the tone in our household and was
passed on to our three kids. As a family, we celebrated Christmas and went
to temple on the High Holidays. But even though my wife and I were
careful to teach our kids tolerance, their exposure to either religion was
minimal. Most weekends, we took the kids on ski trips, rationalizing that
the majesty of the Sierra was enough of a spiritual experience.

So last year, when I decided to tell my children that I was legally changing my name back to Rosenberg, I wondered how they would react. We
were in a restaurant celebrating the publication of my first novel. After they
toasted my tenacity for staying with fiction for some thirty years, I made my
announcement: "I want to be remembered by the name I was born with."

I explained that the kind of discrimination and stereotyping still evident today had made me rethink the years I'd spent denying my family's
history, years that I'd been ashamed to talk about with them. The present
political climate — the initiatives attacking social services for immigrants,
bilingual education, Affirmative Action — made me want to shout "I'm
an immigrant!" My children were silent for a moment before they smiled,
leaned over, and hugged me.

The memories of my years of denial continued to dog me as I told   10
friends and family that I planned to change my name. The rabbi at the
Reform temple that I belong to with my second wife suggested I go a step
further. "Have you thought of taking a Hebrew first name?" he asked.

He must have seen the shocked look on my face. I wondered, is he
suggesting I become more religious, more "Jewish?" "What's involved?"
I asked hesitatingly.

The rabbi explained that the ceremony would be simple and private,
just for family and friends. I would make a few remarks about why I had
selected my name, and then he would say a blessing.

It took me a moment to grasp the significance of what the rabbi was
proposing. He saw my name change as a chance to do more than reclaim
a piece of my family's history; it was an opportunity to renew my commitment to Jewish ideals. I realized it was also a way to give my kids the sense
of pride in their heritage that they had missed out on as children.

A few months later I stood at the pulpit in front of an open, lighted ark, flanked by my wife and the rabbi. Before me stood my children, holding their children. I had scribbled a few notes for my talk, but felt too emotional to use them. I held on to the lectern for support and winged it.

"Every time I step into a temple, I'm reminded that Judaism has survived for 4,000 years. It's survived because it's a positive religion. My parents, your grandparents, changed their name out of fear. I'm changing it back out of pride. I chose the name Tikvah because it means hope."   15

THINKING CRITICALLY ABOUT THE READING

1. Rosenberg's title, along with his name, grabs the reader's attention. What are some of the questions that his title raises? How effectively does he answer them?

2. Why did Rosenberg's parents change their surname soon after arriving in the United States?

3. What advantages did Rosenberg enjoy as Tom Ross? How might his life have been different if he had grown up as a Rosenberg?

4. What is the significance of Rosenberg's not only changing his last name but also taking a Hebrew first name? Why does he do it?

5. Trace the causal chain that begins with the primary cause of Rosenberg's parents changing their name to Ross. What are the effects on their lives and on the life of their son? (Glossary: *Cause and Effect Analysis*)

6. Rosenberg uses a mostly chronological organization for his essay. (Glossary: *Organization*) Why is this organization effective? How does he foreshadow his conclusion?

LANGUAGE IN ACTION

Show business people often change their names to further their careers. Here are the professional names and the original names of a number of celebrities. Discuss with your classmates the significance of the names and the reasons they might have been changed.

Professional Names	*Original Names*
Demi Moore	Demetria Guynes
Mick Jagger	Michael Philip
Marilyn Monroe	Norma Jean Baker
Madonna	Madonna Louise Ciccone
Elle MacPherson	Eleanor Gow
Whoopi Goldberg	Caryn Johnson
Bob Dylan	Robert Zimmerman
Doris Day	Doris von Kappelhoff
Fred Astaire	Frederick Austerlitz

(*continued*)

John Wayne	Marion Michael Morrison
Muhammad Ali	Cassius Marcellus Clay Jr.
Anne Bancroft	Annemaria Italiano
Michael Caine	Maurice J. Micklewhite
Tom Cruise	Thomas Mapother IV
Ringo Starr	Richard Starkey
Cary Grant	Archibald Leach
Chuck Norris	Carlos Ray

WRITING SUGGESTIONS

1. Write a personal essay, using your name, heritage, religion, or some form of inner identification as the primary cause. What effects has it had on your life? How has it enhanced your life? What adverse effects, if any, has it had on you? Without it, how might you be a different person? You may find it helpful to review your response to the Writing to Discover journal prompt for this selection before you begin to write.

2. Choose a grandparent from either your maternal or paternal lineage. Write a narrative history of his or her life. What challenges did he or she face? How did ethnic and cultural heritage affect the way he or she lived? What has this grandparent passed along to you that you are proud of and wish to pass along to your children? What would you just as soon forget?

3. Write an essay in which you compare and contrast the experiences that Henry Louis Gates Jr. ("What's in a Name?," p. 56) and Rosenberg had with names. How did each of them feel when others named and thus defined them? What insights into oppression, namely racial and religious prejudice, do their experiences give you?

English Belongs to Everybody

ROBERT MACNEIL

Born in Montreal, Canada, in 1931, Robert MacNeil graduated from Carleton University in Ottawa in 1955. He is probably best known as the former coanchor of the Public Broadcasting Service's *MacNeil/Lehrer NewsHour*, which was broadcast from 1975 to 1995 and which continues to this day under Jim Lehrer's oversight. During MacNeil's long career in broadcasting and journalism, he covered many major events in American history, including the John F. Kennedy assassination, the 1968 Democratic National Convention, and the 1973 Senate Watergate hearings. MacNeil's publications include *The People Machine: The Influence of Television on American Politics* (1968), which examines the frailties of television news organizations; *The Right Place at the Right Time* (1982), which recounts his experiences as a journalist; *Wordstruck* (1989), an autobiography; and *The Story of English* (1986), which he originally created as a PBS series on the history and development of the English language. In 1998 he published *Breaking News*, a fictional attack on the media's handling of an Oval Office sex scandal, and in 2003, he published a memoir entitled *Looking for My Country: Finding Myself in America*. Most recently, he published *Do You Speak American?* (2005), a book in which he traces the evolution of American English as spoken today.

In the following essay from *Wordstruck*, MacNeil asserts that the supposed demise of English today is actually healthy change. As much as it may disturb grammarians, the ability of English to change keeps it strong and dynamic. English still remains as vital as the many people who speak it.

WRITING TO DISCOVER: *Do you change the way you use language in different situations? If you are like most people, you probably do. Write about how your use of language changes and why. How is your spoken English different from your written English?*

This is a time of widespread anxiety about the language. Some Americans fear that English will be engulfed or diluted by Spanish and want to make it the official language. There is anxiety about a crisis of illiteracy, or a crisis of semiliteracy among high school, even college, graduates.

Anxiety, however, may have a perverse side effect: experts who wish to "save" the language may only discourage pleasure in it. Some are good-humored and tolerant of change, others intolerant and snobbish. Language reinforces feelings of social superiority or inferiority; it creates insiders and outsiders; it is a prop to vanity or a source of anxiety, and on both emotions the language snobs play. Yet the changes and the errors that irritate them are no different in kind from those which have shaped our language for centuries. As Hugh Kenner wrote of certain British critics in *The Sinking Island,* "They took note of language only when it annoyed them." Such people are killjoys: they turn others away from an interest in the language, inhibit their use of it, and turn pleasure off.

Change is inevitable in a living language and is responsible for much of the vitality of English; it has prospered and grown because it was able to accept and absorb change.

As people evolve and do new things, their language will evolve too. They will find ways to describe the new things and their changed perspective will give them new ways of talking about the old things. For example, electric light switches created a brilliant metaphor for the oldest of human experiences, being *turned on* or *turned off.* To language conservatives those expressions still have a slangy, low ring to them; to others they are vivid, fresh-minted currency, very spendable, very "with-it."

That tolerance for change represents not only the dynamism of the   5
English-speaking peoples since the Elizabethans, but their deeply rooted ideas of freedom as well. This was the idea of the Danish scholar Otto Jespersen, one of the great authorities on English. Writing in 1905, Jespersen said in his *Growth and Structure of the English Language*:

> The French language is like the stiff French garden of Louis XIV, while the English is like an English park, which is laid out seemingly without any definite plan, and in which you are allowed to walk everywhere according to your fancy without having to fear a stern keeper enforcing rigorous regulations. The English language would not have been what it is if the English had not been for centuries great respecters of the liberties of each individual and if everybody had not been free to strike out new paths for himself.

I like that idea and do not think it just coincidence. Consider that the same cultural soil, the Celtic-Roman-Saxon-Danish-Norman amalgam, which produced the English language also nourished the great principles of freedom and rights of man in the modern world. The first shoots sprang up in England and they grew stronger in America. Churchill called them "the joint inheritance of the English-speaking world." At the very core of those principles are popular consent and resistance to arbitrary authority; both are fundamental characteristics of our language. The English-speaking peoples have defeated all efforts to build fences around their language, to defer to an academy on what was permissible English and what was not. They'll decide for themselves, thanks just the same.

Nothing better expresses resistance to arbitrary authority than the persistence of what grammarians have denounced for centuries as "errors." In the common speech of English-speaking peoples—Americans, Englishmen, Canadians, Australians, New Zealanders, and others—these usages persist, despite rising literacy and wider education. We hear them every day:

Double negative: "I don't want none of that."

Double comparative: "Don't make that any more heavier!"

Wrong verb: "Will you learn me to read?"

These "errors" have been with us for at least four hundred years, because you can find each of them in Shakespeare.

Double negative: in *Hamlet,* the King says:

Nor what he spake, though it lack'd form a little,
Was not like madness.

Double comparative: In *Othello,* the Duke says:

Yet opinion...throws a more safer voice on you.

Wrong verb: In *Othello,* Desdemona says:

My life and education both do learn me how to respect you.

I find it very interesting that these forms will not go away and lie down. They were vigorous and acceptable in Shakespeare's time; they are far more vigorous today, although not acceptable as standard English. Regarded as error by grammarians, they are nevertheless in daily use all over the world by a hundred times the number of people who lived in Shakespeare's England.

It fascinates me that *axe,* meaning "ask," so common in black Ameri-   10
can English, is standard in Chaucer in all forms—*axe, axen, axed:* "and *axed* him if Troilus were there." Was that transmitted across six hundred years or simply reinvented?

English grew without a formal grammar. After the enormous creativity of Shakespeare and the other Elizabethans, seventeenth- and eighteenth-century critics thought the language was a mess, like an overgrown garden. They weeded it by imposing grammatical rules derived from tidier languages, chiefly Latin, whose precision and predictability they trusted. For three centuries, with some slippage here and there, their rules have held. Educators taught them and written English conformed. Today, English-language newspapers, magazines, and books everywhere broadly agree that correct English obeys these rules. Yet the wild varieties continue to threaten the garden of cultivated English and, by their numbers, actually dominate everyday usage.

Nonstandard English formerly knew its place in the social order. Characters in fiction were allowed to speak it occasionally. Hemingway believed that American literature really did not begin until Mark Twain, who outraged critics by reproducing the vernacular of characters like Huck Finn. Newspapers still clean up the grammar when they quote the ungrammatical, including politicians. The printed word, like Victorian morality, has often constituted a conspiracy of respectability.

People who spoke grammatically could be excused the illusion that their writ held sway, perhaps the way the Normans thought that French had conquered the language of the vanquished Anglo-Saxons. A generation ago, people who considered themselves educated and well-spoken might have had only glancing contact with nonstandard English, usually in a well-understood class, regional, or rural context.

It fascinates me how differently we all speak in different circumstances. We have levels of formality, as in our clothing. There are very formal occasions, often requiring written English: the job application or the letter to the editor—the dark-suit, serious-tie language, with everything pressed and the lint brushed off. There is our less formal out-in-the-world language—a more comfortable suit, but still respectable. There is language for close friends in the evenings, on weekends—blue-jeans-and-sweatshirt language, when it's good to get the tie off. There is family language, even more relaxed, full of grammatical short cuts, family slang, echoes of old jokes that have become intimate shorthand—the language of pajamas and uncombed hair. Finally, there is the language with no clothes on; the talk of couples—murmurs, sighs, grunts—language at its least self-conscious, open, vulnerable, and primitive.

Broadcasting has democratized the publication of language, often at   15
its most informal, even undressed. Now the ears of the educated cannot escape the language of the masses. It surrounds them on the news, weather, sports, commercials, and the ever-proliferating talk and call-in shows.

This wider dissemination of popular speech may easily give purists the idea that the language is suddenly going to hell in this generation, and may explain the new paranoia about it.

It might also be argued that more Americans hear more correct, even beautiful, English on television than was ever heard before. Through television more models of good usage reach more American homes than was ever possible in other times. Television gives them lots of colloquial English, too, some awful, some creative, but that is not new.

Hidden in this is a simple fact: our language is not the special private property of the language police, or grammarians, or teachers, or even great writers. The genius of English is that is has always been the tongue of the common people, literate or not.

English belongs to everybody: the funny turn of phrase that pops into the mind of a farmer telling a story; or the traveling salesman's dirty joke; or the teenager saying, "Gag me with a spoon"; or the pop lyric—all contribute, are all as valid as the tortured image of the academic, or the line the poet sweats over for a week.

Through our collective language sense, some may be thought beauti-   20
ful and some ugly, some may live and some may die; but it is all English and it belongs to everyone—to those of us who wish to be careful with it and those who don't care.

THINKING CRITICALLY ABOUT THE READING

1. Whom does MacNeil describe as "killjoys" (2)? Why does MacNeil believe their influence is destructive to the vitality of the English language?

2. In paragraph 2, MacNeil says the current anxiety about language may lead to a "perverse side effect." What is this side effect? Why does MacNeil describe it as perverse? What other words could he have used to describe it? Explain.

3. In paragraph 4, MacNeil uses the terms *turned on* and *turned off* as examples of how modern influences can contribute to new language metaphors. He characterizes these expressions as being very "with-it." What does he mean? Why do you think he uses one slang term to describe other such terms? Do you find this an effective part of his argument? Why or why not?

4. What simile does Otto Jespersen use in the passage quoted by MacNeil? (Glossary: *Figures of Speech*) Do you find it an effective image? MacNeil adopts the simile and uses it later in the essay. Is it an appropriate simile for MacNeil's argument? Why or why not?

5. Why does MacNeil claim that various examples of "improper" English are not likely to go away soon? Whose work does he cite to reinforce his conclusion? (Glossary: *Examples*)

6. React to MacNeil's statement that English "has always been the tongue of the common people" (18). What does he mean? What does the statement imply to you?

7. What does MacNeil say is the real reason behind the recent perception that American English is undergoing a sudden turn for the worse? What role do television and other forms of mass media play in the modern evolution of the language?

LANGUAGE IN ACTION

English is a dynamic language, but even MacNeil would probably concede that "pushing the envelope" of acceptable speech can be overdone, as the following selection demonstrates. This excerpt is taken from the Web page "Jargon, Weasel Words, and Gobbledygook" by G. Jay Christensen. (You may also want to check Christensen's Web site at www.csun.edu/~vcecn006/jargob.html.) How careful do you think you should be in using the English language? Should there be a balance between dynamic change and consistent, coherent structure and diction? Discuss your answers with your class.

PARAGRAPHS OF BUZZWORDS BUZZ LOUDLY

Dr. Michael Wunsch from Northern Arizona University offered some delightful parodies about how buzzwords are taking over our language. With his permission I quote some of the paragraphs he gave at a recent business communication conference.

Now that we have talked the talk and viably interfaced in a politically correct, huge attempt to jump start, kick start, downsize, rightsize, bash, or showcase something, may I have, my fellow Americans, some of your cutting-edge, walk-the-walk, super input that will hopefully debut and impact somebody's bottom line as we speak while we are on a mission to dig deeper and then move up to the next level, and beyond that, to take care of business on the information superhighway and earn bragging rights?

I knew that you would turn this perceived worst-case scenario around and echo somebody by responding with "Exactly!" Let's be honest, a person doesn't have to be a rocket scientist or heart surgeon to know the big news that you are a happy camper who is cool and great, you know, despite your cautious optimism. No question, you are a warm-and-fuzzy, world-class, wave-of-the-future, state-of-the-art, high-tech, totally awesome, less-than-slow-lane, more-than-happy, user-friendly, outrageously key dude who can and will give much, much more. (In an ad, the point at which the copywriter ran out of hype!) The huge upside is that you are arguably neither a wimp nor a sucker. In my mind, I'm proactively fed up with hanging around; therefore, my agenda is that I am reactively out of here, under condition of anonymity, in an effort to put it all together to bring everybody up to speed. Let's rumble on a big-time roll at a huge 110 percent effort to make things happen at crunch time by advocating zero tolerance! There you go! Have a nice day!

As Bill Maher was fond of saying on *Politically Incorrect*, the previous information has been "satirized" for your protection. Are you persuaded to be careful how you use the English language?

WRITING SUGGESTIONS

1. MacNeil contends that television makes all forms of English accessible to everyone. It does broadcast "bad" English, but it also brings a lot of correct, elegant English into viewers' homes. Think about the language usage on the television shows you watch and the radio stations you listen to. How do they handle slang, dialogue, and other word usage? Also, how does your favorite form of music use language? Are the lyrics poetic or direct? Do they include a lot of slang? Write an essay in which you examine the influence television and radio have had on your own language. Do you and your peers incorporate expressions from these sources into your own speech?

2. MacNeil uses *gag me with a spoon,* the familiar (though now somewhat dated) phrase from Sun-Belt Speak, as an example of a contribution to the English language. Think about other, similar contributions to the language that you have heard—and perhaps even used yourself. Write an essay in which you argue for or against MacNeil's contention that such new phrases or uses of the language contribute to English as a whole. What advantages or features do they offer? What dangers do they pose to the integrity of the language? As a writer, how do you regard such changes?

Words Don't Mean What They Mean

STEVEN PINKER

Internationally recognized language and cognition scholar and researcher Steven Pinker was born in Montreal, Canada, in 1954. He immigrated to the United States shortly after receiving his B.A. from McGill University in 1976. After earning a doctorate from Harvard University in 1979, Pinker taught psychology at Harvard, Stanford University, and the Massachusetts Institute of Technology, where he directed the Center for Cognitive Neuroscience. Currently, he is professor of psychology at Harvard University. Since publishing *Language Learnability and Language Development* in 1984, Pinker has written extensively on language development in children. He has what one critic writing in the *New York Times Book Review* calls "that facility, so rare among scientists, of making the most difficult material...accessible to the average reader." The popularity of Pinker's books *The Language Instinct* (1994), *How the Mind Works* (1997), *Words and Rules: The Ingredients of Language* (1999), *The Blank Slate: The Modern Denial of Human Nature* (2002), and *The Stuff of Thought: Language As a Window into Human Nature* (2007) attests to the public's genuine interest in human language.

In the following article, adapted from *The Stuff of Thought* and first published in the September 6, 2007, issue of *Time,* Pinker discusses how phrases convey different meanings in different contexts and how this flexibility can both help and hinder human communication and relationships. Pinker uses a number of examples from a wide range of endeavors to illustrate his points about words and the ways they work.

WRITING TO DISCOVER: *Have you ever found yourself in a conversation in which the words that were being spoken to you didn't mean what you supposed they meant? For example, if someone were to say "That's really nice" sarcastically, and you missed the sarcastic tone, you'd miss the meaning entirely. Describe such a situation that you've been in, and explain the difference in meaning between the words being spoken and the intended meaning.*

In the movie *Tootsie,* the character played by Dustin Hoffman is disguised as a woman and is speaking to a beautiful young actress played by Jessica Lange. During a session of late-night girl talk, Lange's character says, "You know what I wish? That a guy could be honest enough to walk up to me and say, 'I could lay a big line on you, but the simple truth is I find you very interesting, and I'd really like to make love to you.' Wouldn't that be a relief?"

Later in the movie, a twist of fate throws them together at a cocktail party, this time with Hoffman's character dressed as a man. The actress doesn't recognize him, and he tries out the speech on her. Before he can even finish, she throws a glass of wine in his face and storms away.

When people talk, they lay lines on each other, do a lot of role playing, sidestep, shilly-shally and engage in all manner of vagueness and innuendo. We do this and expect others to do it, yet at the same time we profess to long for the plain truth, for people to say what they mean, simple as that. Such hypocrisy is a human universal.

Sexual come-ons are a classic example. "Would you like to come up and see my etchings?" has been recognized as a double entendre for so long that by 1939, James Thurber could draw a cartoon of a hapless man in an apartment lobby saying to his date, "You wait here, and I'll bring the etchings down."

The veiled threat also has a stereotype: the Mafia wiseguy offering   5
protection with the soft sell, "Nice store you got there. Would be a real shame if something happened to it." Traffic cops sometimes face not-so-innocent questions like, "Gee, Officer, is there some way I could pay the fine right here?" And anyone who has sat through a fund-raising dinner is familiar with euphemistic schnorring like, "We're counting on you to show leadership."

Why don't people just say what they mean? The reason is that conversational partners are not modems downloading information into each other's brains. People are very, very touchy about their relationships. Whenever you speak to someone, you are presuming the two of you have a certain degree of familiarity—which your words might alter. So every sentence has to do two things at once: convey a message and continue to negotiate that relationship.

The clearest example is ordinary politeness. When you are at a dinner party and want the salt, you don't blurt out, "Gimme the salt." Rather, you use what linguists call a whimperative, as in "Do you think you could pass the salt?" or "If you could pass the salt, that would be awesome."

Taken literally, these sentences are inane. The second is an overstatement, and the answer to the first is obvious. Fortunately, the hearer assumes that the speaker is rational and listens between the lines. Yes, your point is to request the salt, but you're doing it in such a way that first takes care to establish what linguists call "felicity conditions," or the prerequisites to making a sensible request. The underlying rationale is that the hearer not be given a command but simply be asked or advised about one of the necessary conditions for passing the salt. Your goal is to have your need satisfied without treating the listener as a flunky who can be bossed around at will.

Warm acquaintances go out of their way not to look as if they are presuming a dominant-subordinate relationship but rather one of equals. It works the other way too. When people are in a subordinate relationship (like a driver with police), they can't sound as if they are presuming anything more than that, so any bribe must be veiled. Fund raisers, simulating an atmosphere of warm friendship with their donors, also can't break the spell with a bald businesslike proposition.

It is in the arena of sexual relationships, however, that the linguistic dance can be its most elaborate. In an episode of *Seinfeld*, George is asked by his date if he would like to come up for coffee. He declines, explaining that caffeine keeps him up at night. Later he slaps his forehead: "'Coffee' doesn't mean coffee! 'Coffee' means sex!" The moment is funny, but it's also a reminder of just how carefully romantic partners must always tread. Make too blatant a request, as in *Tootsie*, and the hearer is offended; too subtle, as in *Seinfeld*, and it can go over the hearer's head.

In the political arena, miscalibrated speech can lead to more serious consequences than wine in the face or a slap on the forehead. In 1980, Wanda Brandstetter, a lobbyist for the National Organization for Women (NOW), tried to get an Illinois state representative to vote for the Equal Rights Amendment (ERA) by handing him a business card on which she had written, "Mr. Swanstrom, the offer for help in your election, plus $1,000 for your campaign for the pro-ERA vote." A prosecutor called the note a "contract for bribery," and the jury agreed.

So how do lobbyists in Gucci Gulch bribe legislators today? They do it with innuendo. If Brandstetter had said, "As you know, Mr. Swanstrom, NOW has a history of contributing to political campaigns. And it has contributed more to candidates with a voting record that is compatible with our goals. These days one of our goals is the ratification of the ERA," she would have avoided a fine, probation and community service.

Indirect speech has a long history in diplomacy, too. In the wake of the Six-Day War in 1967, the U.N. Security Council passed its famous Resolution 242, which called for the "withdrawal of Israeli armed forces from territories occupied in the recent conflict." The wording is ambiguous. Does it mean "some of the territories" or "all of the territories"? In some ways it was best not to ask, since the phrasing was palatable to Israel and its allies only under the former interpretation and to concerned Arab states and their allies only under the latter. Unfortunately, for 40 years partisans have been debating the semantics of Resolution 242, and the Israeli-Arab conflict remains unresolved, to put it mildly.

That's not to say such calculated ambiguity never works for diplomats. After all, the language of an agreement has to be acceptable not just to leaders but to their citizens. Reasonable leaders might thus come to an understanding between themselves, while each exploits the ambiguities of the deal to sell it to their country's more bellicose factions. What's more, diplomats can gamble that times will change and circumstances will bring the two sides together, at which point they can resolve the vagueness amicably.

When all else fails, as it often does, nations can sort out their prob-   15
lems without any words at all—and often without fighting either. In these
cases, they may fall back on communicating through what's known as
authority ranking, also known as power, status, autonomy and dominance.
The logic of authority ranking is "Don't mess with me." Its biological
roots are in the dominance hierarchies that are widespread in the animal
kingdom. One animal claims the right to a contested resource based on
size, strength, seniority or allies, and the other animal cedes it when the
outcome of the battle can be predicted and both sides have a stake in not
getting bloodied in a fight whose winner is a forgone conclusion. Such
sword-rattling gestures as a larger military power's conducting "naval
exercises" in the waters off the coast of a weaker foe are based on just this
kind of preemptive reminder of strength.

People often speak of indirect speech as a means of saving face. What
we're referring to is not just a matter of hurt feelings but a social currency
with real value. The expressive power of words helps us guard this prized
asset, but only as long as we're careful. Words let us say the things we want to
say and also things we would be better off not having said. They let us know
the things we need to know, and also things we wish we didn't. Language is
a window into human nature, but it is also a fistula, an open wound through
which we're exposed to an infectious world. It's not surprising that we sheathe
our words in politeness and innuendo and other forms of doublespeak.

THINKING CRITICALLY ABOUT THE READING

1. Pinker opens his essay with an extended example from the movie *Tootsie*. What point about language does this example illustrate?

2. Pinker creates a number of categories for the ways in which people "lay lines on each other, do a lot of role playing, sidestep, shilly-shally and engage in all manner of vagueness and innuendo" (3). Explain these categories and provide an example of your own for each. In your opinion, do any of the categories overlap?

3. What do you think Pinker means when he says "Such hypocrisy is a human universal" (3)? Do you believe that this hypocrisy is necessary? What would need to change for us to speak the "plain truth" to each other?

4. Why, according to Pinker, do people have so much trouble conversing? How is a conversation between two humans different from a conversation between two modems?

5. What are "felicity conditions" (8)? Describe several situations in which you have used "felicity conditions." Have you ever tried but failed to establish these conditions? Explain what happened.

6. Explain what "indirect speech" (13) is. Why do you think people resort to indirect speech? Why is it not surprising that indirect speech has a long history in the arenas of politics and diplomacy?

LANGUAGE IN ACTION

Read the following English folktale, which is taken from Joseph Jacob's 1890 book *English Fairy Tales*. What do you learn about the nature of words from this story? Explain. How do you think Steven Pinker would respond to this folktale?

FROM "MASTER OF ALL MASTERS"

A girl once went to a fair to be hired as a servant. At last a funny-looking old gentleman engaged her and took her home to his house. When she got there he told her he had something to teach her for in his house he had his own names for things.

He said to her: "What will you call me?"

"Master or Mister or whatever you please, sir."

"You must call me 'Master of Masters.' And what would you call this?" pointing to his bed.

"Bed or couch or whatever you please, sir."

"No, that's my 'barnacle.' And what do you call these?" said he, pointing to his pants.

"Breeches or trousers or whatever you please, sir."

"You must call them 'squibs and crackers.' And what do you call her?" pointing to the cat.

"Kit or cat or whatever you please, sir."

"You must call her 'white-faced simminy.' And this now," showing the fire, "what would you call this?"

"Fire or flame or whatever you please, sir."

"You must call it 'hot cockalorum,' and what this?" he went on, pointing to the water.

"Water or wet or whatever you please, sir."

"No, 'pandalorum' is its name. And what do you call this?" asked he, as he pointed to the house.

"House or cottage or whatever you please, sir."

"You must call it 'high topper mountain.'"

That very night the servant woke her master up in a fright and said: "Master of all masters, get out of your barnacle and put on your squibs and crackers. For white-face simminy has got a spark of hot cockalorum on its tail, and unless you get some pandalorum high topper mountain will be all on hot cockalorum."... That's all.

WRITING SUGGESTIONS

1. According to Pinker, "It is in the arena of sexual relationships...that the linguistic dance can be most elaborate." He supports this claim with examples from an episode of *Seinfeld* and the movie *Tootsie*. What exactly is

the "linguistic dance" to which he refers? Does your own experience or that of your friends with the language used in any dating relationship support or contradict Pinker's claim? How would you characterize conversations in these relationships? Write an essay in which you examine the language between partners in dating relationships. You may find it helpful to compare their language with that of other relationships; for example, is their language as indirect as that of nondating friends?

2. What does Pinker mean when he says, "Language is a window into human nature, but it is also a fistula, an open wound through which we're exposed to an infectious world" (16)? In what ways can language be considered an "open wound"? Why do you suppose that Pinker is not surprised "that we sheathe our words in politeness and innuendo and other forms of doublespeak" (16)? What evidence does he provide to justify his lack of surprise? Are you convinced? Why or why not? Write a paper in which you explore the meaning of Pinker's concluding remarks about language.

Language and Thought

SUSANNE K. LANGER

Susanne K. Langer was born in New York City in 1895 and attended Radcliffe College. There she studied philosophy, an interest she maintained until her death in 1985. She stayed in Cambridge, Massachusetts, as a tutor at Harvard University from 1927 to 1942. Langer then taught at the University of Delaware, Columbia University, and Connecticut College, where she remained from 1954 until the end of her distinguished teaching career. Her books include *Philosophy in a New Key: A Study of the Symbolism of Reason, Rite, and Art* (1942), *Feeling and Form* (1953), and *Mind: An Essay in Human Feeling* (1967).

In the following essay, which originally appeared in *Ms.* magazine, Langer explores how language separates humans from the rest of the animal kingdom. She contends that the use of symbols—in addition to the use of signs that animals also use—frees humans not only to react to their environment but also to think about it. Moreover, symbols allow us to create imagery and ideas not directly related to the real world, so that we can plan, imagine, and communicate abstractions—to do, in essence, the things that make us human.

WRITING TO DISCOVER: *Young children must often communicate—and be communicated to—without the use of language. To a child, for example, a danger sticker on a bottle can mean "don't touch," and a green traffic light might mean "the car will start again." Think back to your own childhood experiences. Write about how communication took place without language. What associations were you able to make?*

A symbol is not the same thing as a sign; that is a fact that psychologists and philosophers often overlook. All intelligent animals use signs; so do we. To them as well as to us sounds and smells and motions are signs of food, danger, the presence of other beings, or of rain or storm. Furthermore, some animals not only attend to signs but produce them for the benefit of others. Dogs bark at the door to be let in; rabbits thump to call each other; the cooing of doves and the growl of a wolf defending his kill are unequivocal signs of feelings and intentions to be reckoned with by other creatures.

We use signs just as animals do, though with considerably more elaboration. We stop at red lights and go on green; we answer calls and bells, watch the sky for coming storms, read trouble or promise or anger in each other's eyes. That is animal intelligence raised to the human level. Those of us who are dog lovers can probably all tell wonderful stories of how high our dogs have sometimes risen in the scale of clever sign interpretation and sign using.

A sign is anything that announces the existence or the imminence of some event, the presence of a thing or a person, or a change in the state of affairs. There are signs of the weather, signs of danger, signs of future good or evil, signs of what the past has been. In every case a sign is closely bound up with something to be noted or expected in experience. It is always a part of the situation to which it refers, though the reference may be remote in space and time. In so far as we are led to note or expect the signified event we are making correct use of a sign. This is the essence of rational behavior, which animals show in varying degrees. It is entirely realistic, being closely bound up with the actual objective course of history—learned by experience, and cashed in or voided by further experience.

If man had kept to the straight and narrow path of sign using, he would be like the other animals, though perhaps a little brighter. He would not talk, but grunt and gesticulate the point. He would make his wishes known, give warnings, perhaps develop a social system like that of bees and ants, with such a wonderful efficiency of communal enterprise that all men would have plenty to eat, warm apartments—all exactly alike and perfectly convenient—to live in, and everybody could and would sit in the sun or by the fire, as the climate demanded, not talking but just basking, with every want satisfied, most of his life. The young would romp and make love, the old would sleep, the middle-aged would do the routine work almost unconsciously and eat a great deal. But that would be the life of a social, superintelligent, purely sign-using animal.

To us who are human, it does not sound very glorious. We want to 5
go places and do things, own all sorts of gadgets that we do not absolutely need, and when we sit down to take it easy we want to talk. Rights and property, social position, special talents and virtues, and above all our ideas, are what we live for. We have gone off on a tangent that takes us far away from the mere biological cycle that animal generations accomplish; and that is because we can use not only signs but symbols.

A symbol differs from a sign in that it does not announce the presence of the object, the being, condition, or whatnot, which is its meaning, but merely *brings this thing to mind*. It is not a mere "substitute sign" to which we react as though it were the object itself. The fact is that our reaction to hearing a person's name is quite different from our reaction to the person himself. There are certain rare cases where a symbol stands directly for its meaning: in religious experience, for instance, the Host is not only a symbol but a Presence. But symbols in the ordinary sense are not mystic. They are the same sort of thing that ordinary signs are; only they do not call our attention to something necessarily present or to be physically dealt with—they call up merely a conception of the thing they "mean."

The difference between a sign and a symbol is, in brief, that a sign causes us to think or act *in face* of the thing signified, whereas a symbol causes us to think *about* the thing symbolized. Therein lies the great importance of symbolism for human life, its power to make this life so different from any other animal biography that generations of men have found it incredible to suppose that they were of purely zoological origin. A sign is always embedded in reality, in a present that emerges from the actual past and stretches to the future; but a symbol may be divorced from reality altogether. It may refer to what is not the case, to a mere idea, a figment, a dream. It serves, therefore, to liberate thought from the immediate stimuli of a physically present world; and that liberation marks the essential difference between human and nonhuman mentality. Animals think, but they think *of* and *at* things; men think primarily *about* things. Words, pictures, and memory images are symbols that may be combined and varied in a thousand ways. The result is a symbolic structure whose meaning is a complex of all their respective meanings, and this kaleidoscope of *ideas* is the typical product of the human brain that we call the "stream of thought."

The process of transforming all direct experience into imagery or into that supreme mode of symbolic expression, language, has so completely taken possession of the human mind that it is not only a special talent but a dominant, organic need. All our sense impressions leave their traces in our memory not only as signs disposing our practical reactions in the future but also as symbols, images representing our *ideas* of things; and the tendency to manipulate ideas, to combine and abstract, mix and extend them by playing with symbols, is man's outstanding characteristic. It seems to be what his brain most naturally and spontaneously does. Therefore his primitive mental function is not judging reality, but *dreaming his desires.*

Dreaming is apparently a basic function of human brains, for it is free and unexhausting like our metabolism, heartbeat, and breath. It is easier to dream than not to dream, as it is easier to breathe than to refrain from breathing. The symbolic character of dreams is fairly well established. Symbol mongering, on this ineffectual, uncritical level, seems to be instinctive, the fulfillment of an elementary need rather than the purposeful exercise of a high and difficult talent.

The special power of man's mind rests on the evolution of this special   10
activity, not on any transcendently high development of animal intelligence. We are not immeasurably higher than other animals; we are different. We have a biological need and with it a biological gift that they do not share.

Because man has not only the ability but the constant need of *conceiving* what has happened to him, what surrounds him, what is demanded of him—in short, of symbolizing nature, himself, and his hopes and fears—he has a constant and crying need of *expression.* What he cannot express, he cannot conceive; what he cannot conceive is chaos, and fills him with terror.

If we bear in mind this all-important craving for expression, we get a new picture of man's behavior; for from this trait spring his powers and his weaknesses. The process of symbolic transformation that all our experiences undergo is nothing more nor less than the process of *conception,* underlying the human faculties of abstraction and imagination.

When we are faced with a strange or difficult situation, we cannot react directly, as other creatures do, with flight, aggression, or any such simple instinctive pattern. Our whole reaction depends on how we manage to conceive the situation—whether we cast it in a definite dramatic form, whether we see it as a disaster, a challenge, a fulfillment of doom, or a fiat of the Divine Will. In words or dreamlike images, in artistic or religious or even in cynical form, we must *construe* the events of life. There is great virtue in the figure of speech, "I can *make* nothing of it," to express a failure to understand something. Thought and memory are processes of *making* the thought content and the memory image; the pattern of our ideas is given by the symbols through which we express them. And in the course of manipulating those symbols we inevitably distort the original experience, as we abstract certain features of it, embroider and reinforce those features with other ideas, until the conception we project on the screen of memory is quite different from anything in our real history.

Conception is a necessary and elementary process; what we do with our conceptions is another story. That is the entire history of human culture—of intelligence and morality, folly and superstition, ritual, language, and the arts—all the phenomena that set man apart from, and above, the rest of the animal kingdom. As the religious mind has to make all human history a drama of sin and salvation in order to define its own moral attitudes, so a scientist wrestles with the mere presentation of "the facts" before he can reason about them. The process of *envisaging* facts, values, hopes, and fears underlies our whole behavior pattern; and this process is reflected in the evolution of an extraordinary phenomenon found always, and only, in human societies—the phenomenon of language.

Language is the highest and most amazing achievement of the symbolistic human mind. The power it bestows is almost inestimable, for without it anything properly called "thought" is impossible. The birth of language is the dawn of humanity. The line between man and beast—between the highest ape and the lowest savage—is the language line. Whether the primitive Neanderthal man was anthropoid or human depends less on his cranial capacity, his upright posture, or even his use of tools and fire, than on one issue we shall probably never be able to settle—whether or not he spoke. 15

In all physical traits and practical responses, such as skills and visual judgments, we can find a certain continuity between animal and human mentality. Sign using is an ever evolving, ever improving function throughout the whole animal kingdom, from the lowly worm that shrinks into his hole at the sound of an approaching foot, to the dog obeying his master's command, and even to the learned scientist who watches the movements of an index needle.

The continuity of the sign-using talent has led psychologists to the belief that language is evolved from the vocal expressions, grunts and coos and cries, whereby animals vent their feelings or signal their fellows; that man has elaborated this sort of communion to the point where it makes a perfect exchange of ideas possible.

I do not believe that this doctrine of the origin of language is correct. The essence of language is symbolic, not signific; we use it first and most vitally to formulate and hold ideas in our own minds. Conception, not social control, is its first and foremost benefit.

Watch a young child that is just learning to speak play with a toy; he says the name of the object, e.g.: "Horsey! horsey! horsey!" over and over again, looks at the object, moves it, always saying the name to himself or to the world at large. It's quite a time before he talks to anyone in particular; he talks first of all to himself. This is his way of forming and fixing the *conception* of the object in his mind, and around this conception all his knowledge of it grows. *Names* are the essence of language; for the *name* is what abstracts the conception of the horse from the horse itself, and lets the mere idea recur at the speaking of the name. This permits the conception gathered from one horse experience to be exemplified again by another instance of a horse, so that the notion embodied in the name is a general notion.

To this end, the baby uses a word long before he *asks* for the object;   20 when he wants his horsey he is likely to cry and fret, because he is reacting to an actual environment, not forming ideas. He uses the animal language of *signs* for his wants; talking is still a purely symbolic process—its practical value has not really impressed him yet.

Language need not be vocal; it may be purely visual, like written language, or even tactual, like the deaf-mute system of speech; but it *must be denotative*. The sounds, intended or unintended, whereby animals communicate do not constitute a language because they are signs, not names. They never fall into an organic pattern, a meaningful syntax of even the most rudimentary sort, as all language seems to do with a sort of driving necessity. That is because signs refer to actual situations, in which things have obvious relations to each other that require only to be noted; but symbols refer to ideas, which are not physically there for inspection, so their connections and features have to be represented. This gives all true language a natural tendency toward growth and development, which seems almost like a life of its own. Languages are not invented; they grow with our need for expression.

In contrast, animal "speech" never has a structure. It is merely an emotional response. Apes may greet their ration of yams with a shout of "Nga!" But they do not say "Nga" between meals. If they could *talk about* their yams instead of just saluting them, they would be the most primitive men instead of the most anthropoid of beasts. They would have ideas, and tell each other things true and false, rational or irrational; they would make plans and invent laws and sing their own praises, as men do.

THINKING CRITICALLY ABOUT THE READING

1. What is Langer's thesis in this essay? Where does she state it? (Glossary: *Thesis*)

2. Define what Langer refers to as a sign. Define symbol. (Glossary: *Definition* and *Symbol*) Why is the distinction between the two so important?

3. What examples of signs and symbols does Langer provide? (Glossary: *Examples*) How effective do you find her examples? What examples of signs and symbols can you provide?

4. What is the essential difference between the way animals "think" and the way humans think? How has that changed human mental function at an organic level? How has the biological change affected our development in relation to animals?

5. In paragraph 11, Langer states: "What [man] cannot express, he cannot conceive; what he cannot conceive is chaos, and fills him with terror." Review the first ten paragraphs of the essay. How does Langer prepare the reader to accept this abstract and bold statement? (Glossary: *Concrete/Abstract* and *Organization*)

6. What does Langer mean when she says, "In words or dreamlike images... we must *construe* the events of life" (13)? How does this claim relate to the process of conception?

LANGUAGE IN ACTION

Review what Langer has to say about signs and symbols, particularly the differences she draws between them in paragraphs 6 and 7. Then examine the following graphics. What does each graphic mean? Which ones are signs, and which are symbols? Be prepared to defend your conclusions in a classroom discussion.

WRITING SUGGESTIONS

1. Using symbols for expression need not involve explicit use of language. Within the framework of a particular society, many methods of symbolic communication are possible. When you walk across campus, for example, what do you want to communicate to others even if you do not speak to anyone? How do you communicate this message? For instance, how does your facial expression, clothing, hairstyle, or jewelry serve as a symbol? Write an essay in which you describe and analyze the nonlanguage symbols you use to communicate.

2. It has often been said that language reveals the character of the person using it. Write an essay in which you analyze the character of a particular writer based on his or her use of language. You may want to comment on a writer in this text whose article you have read, such as Langer. Consider such areas as vocabulary range, sentence variety, slang, correct grammar, technical language, and tone. What do these elements tell you about the character of the person? (Glossary: *Slang, Technical Language,* and *Tone*)

3. Research recent experiments involving animal communication. Some experiments, for example, reveal the gorilla's use of sign language; others show that dolphins have complex communication systems that we are only beginning to understand. Write a paper in which you summarize the research and discuss how it relates to Langer's ideas about human and animal use of signs and symbols. Did you find any evidence that certain animals can use basic symbols? Is there a possibility that gorillas and dolphins can think *about* things rather than simply *of* and *at* them?

A Brief History of English

PAUL ROBERTS

Paul Roberts (1917–1967) was a linguist, teacher, and writer. Born in California, he received his B.A. from San Jose State University and his M.A. and Ph.D. from the University of California at Berkeley. After teaching at San Jose State and then Cornell University, Roberts became director of language at the Center of American Studies in Rome. His books include *Understanding Grammar* (1954), *Patterns of English* (1956), *Understanding English* (1958), *English Sentences* (1962), and *English Syntax* (1964).

In the following selection from *Understanding English*, Roberts recounts the major events in the history of England and discusses their relationship to the development of the English language. He tells how the people who invaded England influenced the language and how, in recent times, the rapid spread of English has resulted in its becoming a major world language.

WRITING TO DISCOVER: *Think about a work you have read that was written in nonmodern English, such as those by Shakespeare, Chaucer, Swift, or their contemporaries. How difficult was it for you to understand the work? Write about what it taught you about the evolution of the English language.*

HISTORICAL BACKGROUNDS

No understanding of the English language can be very satisfactory without a notion of the history of the language. But we shall have to make do with just a notion. The history of English is long and complicated, and we can only hit the high spots.

The history of our language begins a little after A.D. 600. Everything before that is pre-history, which means that we can guess at it but can't prove much. For a thousand years or so before the birth of Christ our linguistic ancestors were savages wandering through the forests of northern Europe. Their language was a part of the Germanic branch of the Indo-European Family.

At the time of the Roman Empire — say, from the beginning of the Christian Era to around A.D. 400 — the speakers of what was to become English were scattered along the northern coast of Europe. They spoke a dialect of Low German. More exactly, they spoke several different dialects, since they were several different tribes. The names given to the tribes who got to England are *Angles, Saxons,* and *Jutes.* For convenience, we can refer to them as Anglo-Saxons.

The first contact with civilization was a rather thin acquaintance with the Roman Empire on whose borders they lived. Probably some of the

Anglo-Saxons wandered into the Empire occasionally, and certainly Roman merchants and traders traveled among the tribes. At any rate, this period was the first of our many borrowings from Latin. Such words as *kettle, wine, cheese, butter, cheap, plum, gem, bishop, church* were borrowed at this time. They show something of the relationship of the Anglo-Saxons with the Romans. The Anglo-Saxons were learning, getting their first taste of civilization.

They still had a long way to go, however, and their first step was to   5
help smash the civilization they were learning from. In the fourth century the Roman power weakened badly. While the Goths were pounding away at the Romans in the Mediterranean countries, their relatives, the Anglo-Saxons, began to attack Britain.

The Romans had been the ruling power in Britain since A.D. 43. They had subjugated the Celts whom they found living there and had succeeded in setting up a Roman administration. The Roman influence did not extend to the outlying parts of the British Isles. In Scotland, Wales, and Ireland the Celts remained free and wild, and they made periodic forays against the Romans in England. Among other defense measures, the Romans built the famous Roman Wall to ward off the tribes in the north.

Even in England the Roman power was thin. Latin did not become the language of the country as it did in Gaul and Spain. The mass of people continued to speak Celtic, with Latin and the Roman civilization it contained in use as a top dressing.

In the fourth century, troubles multiplied for the Romans in Britain. Not only did the untamed tribes of Scotland and Wales grow more and more restive, but the Anglo-Saxons began to make pirate raids on the eastern coast. Furthermore, there was growing difficulty everywhere in the Empire, and the legions in Britain were siphoned off to fight elsewhere. Finally, in A.D. 410, the last Roman ruler in England, bent on becoming emperor, left the islands and took the last of the legions with him. The Celts were left in possession of Britain but almost defenseless against the impending Anglo-Saxon attack.

Not much is surely known about the arrival of the Anglo-Saxons in England. According to the best early source, the eighth-century historian Bede, the Jutes came in 449 in response to a plea from the Celtic king, Vortigern, who wanted their help against the Picts attacking from the north. The Jutes subdued the Picts but then quarreled and fought with Vortigern, and, with reinforcements from the Continent, settled permanently in Kent. Somewhat later the Angles established themselves in eastern England and the Saxons in the south and west. Bede's account is plausible enough, and these were probably the main lines of the invasion.

We do know, however, that the Angles, Saxons, and Jutes were a long   10
time securing themselves in England. Fighting went on for as long as a hundred years before the Celts in England were all killed, driven into Wales, or reduced to slavery. This is the period of King Arthur, who was

not entirely mythological. He was a Romanized Celt, a general, though probably not a king. He had some success against the Anglo-Saxons, but it was only temporary. By 550 or so the Anglo-Saxons were firmly established. English was in England.

OLD ENGLISH

All this is pre-history, so far as the language is concerned. We have no record of the English language until after 600, when the Anglo-Saxons were converted to Christianity and learned the Latin alphabet. The conversion began, to be precise, in the year 597 and was accomplished within thirty or forty years. The conversion was a great advance for the Anglo-Saxons, not only because of the spiritual benefits but because it reestablished contact with what remained of Roman civilization. This civilization didn't amount to much in the year 600, but it was certainly superior to anything in England up to that time.

It is customary to divide the history of the English language into three periods: Old English, Middle English, and Modern English. Old English runs from the earliest records—i.e., seventh century—to about 1100; Middle English from 1100 to 1450 or 1500; Modern English from 1500 to the present day. Sometimes Modern English is further divided into Early Modern, 1500–1700, and Late Modern, 1700 to the present.

When England came into history, it was divided into several more or less autonomous kingdoms, some of which at times exercised a certain amount of control over the others. In the century after the conversion the most advanced kingdom was Northumbria, the area between the Humber River and the Scottish border. By A.D. 700 the Northumbrians had developed a respectable civilization, the finest in Europe. It is sometimes called the Northumbrian Renaissance, and it was the first of the several renaissances through which Europe struggled upward out of the ruins of the Roman Empire. It was in this period that the best of the Old English literature was written, including the epic poem *Beowulf.*

In the eighth century, Northumbrian power declined, and the center of influence moved southward to Mercia, the kingdom of the Midlands. A century later the center shifted again, and Wessex, the country of the West Saxons, became the leading power. The most famous king of the West Saxons was Alfred the Great, who reigned in the second half of the ninth century, dying in 901. He was famous not only as a military man and administrator but also as a champion of learning. He founded and supported schools and translated or caused to be translated many books from Latin into English. At this time also much of the Northumbrian literature of two centuries earlier was copied in West Saxon. Indeed, the great bulk of Old English writing which has come down to us is in the West Saxon dialect of 900 or later.

In the military sphere, Alfred's great accomplishment was his success-   15
ful opposition to the Viking invasions. In the ninth and tenth centuries,
the Norsemen emerged in their ships from their homelands in Denmark
and the Scandinavian peninsula. They traveled far and attacked and plun-
dered at will and almost with impunity. They ravaged Italy and Greece,
settled in France, Russia, and Ireland, colonized Iceland and Greenland,
and discovered America several centuries before Columbus. Nor did they
overlook England.

After many years of hit-and-run raids, the Norsemen landed an army
on the east coast of England in the year 866. There was nothing much to
oppose them except the Wessex power led by Alfred. The long struggle
ended in 877 with a treaty by which a line was drawn roughly from
the northwest of England to the southeast. On the eastern side of the line
Norse rule was to prevail. This was called the Danelaw. The western side was
to be governed by Wessex.

The linguistic result of all this was a considerable injection of Norse
into the English language. Norse was at this time not so different from
English as Norwegian or Danish is now. Probably speakers of English
could understand, more or less, the language of the newcomers who had
moved into eastern England. At any rate, there was considerable inter-
change and word borrowing. Examples of Norse words in the English language are *sky, give, law, egg, outlaw, leg, ugly, scant, sly, crawl, scowl, take,
thrust*. There are hundreds more. We have even borrowed some pronouns
from Norse—*they, their,* and *them*. These words were borrowed first by
the eastern and northern dialects and then in the course of hundreds of
years made their way into English generally.

It is supposed also—indeed, it must be true—that the Norsemen
influenced the sound structure and the grammar of English. But this is
hard to demonstrate in detail.

A SPECIMEN OF OLD ENGLISH

We may now have an example of Old English. The favorite illustration
is the Lord's Prayer, since it needs no translation. This has come to us in
several different versions. Here is one:

Fæder ure,
þu þe eart on heofonum,
si þin nama gehalgod.
Tobecume þin rice.
Gewurþe ðin willa on eorðan swa swa on heofonum.
Urne gedæghwamlican hlaf syle us to dæg.
And forgyf us ure gyltas, swa swa we forgyfaþ urum gyltendum.
And ne gelæd þu us on costnunge,
ac alys us of yfele. Soþlice.

Some of the differences between this and Modern English are merely   20
differences in orthography. For instance, the sign *æ* is what Old English
writers used for a vowel sound like that in modern *hat* or *and*. The *th*
sounds of modern *thin* or *then* are represented in Old English by *þ* or *ð*.
But of course there are many differences in sound too. *Ure* is the ancestor of modern *our*, but the first vowel was like that in *too* or *ooze*. *Hlaf* is
modern *loaf*; we had dropped the *h* sound and changed the vowel, which
in *hlaf* was pronounced something like the vowel in *father*. Old English
had some sounds which we do not have. The sound represented by *y* does
not occur in Modern English. If you pronounce the vowel in *bit* with your
lips rounded, you may approach it.

In grammar, Old English was much more highly inflected than Modern
English is. That is, there were more case endings for nouns, more person and
number endings for verbs, a more complicated pronoun system, various endings for adjectives, and so on. Old English nouns had four cases—nominative,
genitive, dative, accusative. Adjectives had five—all these and an instrumen-
tal case besides. Present-day English has only two cases for nouns—common
case and possessive case. Adjectives now have no case system at all. On the
other hand, we now use a more rigid word order and more structure words
(prepositions, auxiliaries, and the like) to express relationships than Old English did.

Some of this grammar we can see in the Lord's Prayer. *Heofonum*, for
instance, is a dative plural; the nominative singular was *heofon*. *Urne* is an
accusative singular; the nominative is *ure*. In *urum glytendum* both words
are dative plural. *Forgyfaþ* is the first person plural form of the verb. Word
order is different: "urne gedæghwamlican hlaf syle us" in place of "Give us
our daily bread." And so on.

In vocabulary Old English is quite different from Modern English.
Most of the Old English words are what we may call native English: that
is, words which have not been borrowed from other languages but which
have been a part of English ever since English was a part of Indo-European.
Old English did certainly contain borrowed words. We have seen that many
borrowings were coming in from Norse. Rather large numbers had been
borrowed from Latin, too. Some of these were taken while the Anglo-Saxons were still on the Continent (*cheese, butter, bishop, kettle*, etc.); a large
number came into English after the conversion (*angel, candle, priest, mar-
tyr, radish, oyster, purple, school, spend*, etc.). But the great majority of Old
English words were native English.

Now, on the contrary, the majority of words in English are borrowed,
taken mostly from Latin and French. Of the words in *The American College
Dictionary* only about 14 percent are native. Most of these, to be sure, are
common, high-frequency words—*the, of, I, and, because, man, mother, road*,
etc.; of the thousand most common words in English, some 62 percent are
native English. Even so, the modern vocabulary is very much Latinized and
Frenchified. The Old English vocabulary was not.

MIDDLE ENGLISH

Sometime between the years 1000 and 1200 various important
changes took place in the structure of English, and Old English became
Middle English. The political event which facilitated these changes was
the Norman Conquest. The Normans, as the name shows, came originally
from Scandinavia. In the early tenth century they established themselves
in northern France, adopted the French language, and developed a vigorous kingdom and a very passable civilization. In the year 1066, led by
Duke William, they crossed the Channel and made themselves masters of
England. For the next several hundred years, England was ruled by kings
whose first language was French.

One might wonder why, after the Norman Conquest, French did not
become the national language, replacing English entirely. The reason is
that the Conquest was not a national migration, as the earlier Anglo-Saxon
invasion had been. Great numbers of Normans came to England, but they
came as rulers and landlords. French became the language of the court, the
language of the nobility, the language of polite society, the language of literature. But it did not replace English as the language of the people. There
must always have been hundreds of towns and villages in which French was
never heard except when visitors of high station passed through.

But English, though it survived as the national language, was profoundly changed after the Norman Conquest. Some of the changes—in
sound structure and grammar—would no doubt have taken place whether
there had been a Conquest or not. Even before 1066 the case system of
English nouns and adjectives was becoming simplified; people came to rely
more on word order and prepositions than on inflectional endings to communicate their meanings. The process was speeded up by sound changes
which caused many of the endings to sound alike. But no doubt the Conquest facilitated the change. German, which didn't experience a Norman
Conquest, is today rather highly inflected compared to its cousin English.

But it is in vocabulary that the effects of the Conquest are most obvious. French ceased, after a hundred years or so, to be the native language of
very many people in England, but it continued—and continues still—to
be a zealously cultivated second language, the mirror of elegance and civilization. When one spoke English, one introduced not only French ideas
and French things but also their French names. This was not only easy but
socially useful. To pepper one's conversation with French expressions was
to show that one was well-bred, elegant, *au courant*. The last sentence
shows that the process is not yet dead. By using *au courant* instead of, say,
abreast of things, the writer indicates that he is no dull clod who knows
only English but an elegant person aware of how things are done in *le
haut monde*.

Thus French words came into English, all sorts of them. There were
words to do with government: *parliament, majesty, treaty, alliance, tax,*

government; church words: *parson, sermon, baptism, incense, crucifix, religion;* words for foods: *veal, beef, mutton, bacon, jelly, peach, lemon, cream, biscuit;* colors: *blue, scarlet, vermilion;* household words: *curtain, chair, lamp, towel, blanket, parlor;* play words: *dance, chess, music, leisure, conversation;* literary words: *story, romance, poet, literary;* learned words: *study, logic, grammar, noun, surgeon, anatomy, stomach;* just ordinary words of all sorts; *nice, second, very, age, bucket, gentle, final, fault, flower, cry, count, sure, move, surprise, plain.*

All these and thousands more poured into the English vocabulary   30
between 1100 and 1500 until, at the end of that time, many people must have had more French words than English at their command. This is not to say that English became French. English remained English in sound structure and in grammar, though these also felt the ripples of French influence. The very heart of the vocabulary, too, remained English. Most of the high-frequency words—the pronouns, the prepositions, the conjunctions, the auxiliaries, as well as a great many ordinary nouns and verbs and adjectives—were not replaced by borrowings.

Middle English, then, was still a Germanic language, but it differed from Old English in many ways. The sound system and the grammar changed a good deal. Speakers made less use of case systems and other inflectional devices and relied more on word order and structure words to express their meanings. This is often said to be a simplification, but it isn't really. Languages don't become simpler; they merely exchange one kind of complexity for another. Modern English is not a simple language, as any foreign speaker who tries to learn it will hasten to tell you.

For us Middle English is simpler than Old English just because it is closer to Modern English. It takes three or four months at least to learn to read Old English prose and more than that for poetry. But a week of good study should put one in touch with the Middle English poet Chaucer. Indeed, you may be able to make some sense of Chaucer straight off, though you would need instruction in pronunciation to make it sound like poetry. Here is a famous passage from the *General Prologue to the Canterbury Tales,* fourteenth century:

> Ther was also a nonne, a Prioresse,
> That of hir smyling was ful symple and coy,
> Hir gretteste oath was but by Seinte Loy,
> And she was cleped[1] Madame Eglentyne.
> Ful wel she song the service dyvyne,
> Entuned in hir nose ful semely.
> And Frenshe she spak ful faire and fetisly,[2]
> After the scole of Stratford-atte-Bowe,
> For Frenshe of Parys was to hir unknowe.

---

1. named.
2. elegantly.

EARLY MODERN ENGLISH

Sometime between 1400 and 1600 English underwent a couple of sound changes which made the language of Shakespeare quite different from that of Chaucer. Incidentally, these changes contributed much to the chaos in which English spelling now finds itself.

One change was the elimination of a vowel sound in certain unstressed positions at the end of words. For instance, the words *name, stone, wine, dance* were pronounced as two syllables by Chaucer but as just one by Shakespeare. The *e* in these words became, as we say, "silent." But it wasn't silent for Chaucer; it represented a vowel sound. So also the words *laughed, seemed, stored* would have been pronounced by Chaucer as two-syllable words. The change was an important one because it affected thousands of words and gave a different aspect to the whole language.

The other change is what is called the Great Vowel Shift. This was a   35
systematic shifting of half a dozen vowels and diphthongs in stressed syllables. For instance, the word *name* had in Middle English a vowel something like that in the modern word *father; wine* had the vowel of modern *mean; he* was pronounced something like modern *hey; mouse* sounded like *moose; moon* had the vowel of *moan.* Again the shift was thoroughgoing and affected all the words in which these vowel sounds occurred. Since we still keep the Middle English system of spelling these words, the differences between Modern English and Middle English are often more real than apparent.

The vowel shift has meant also that we have come to use an entirely different set of symbols for representing vowel sounds than is used by writers of such languages as French, Italian, or Spanish, in which no such vowel shift occurred. If you come across a strange word—say, *bine*—in an English book, you will pronounce it according to the English system, with the vowel of *wine* or *dine.* But if you read *bine* in a French, Italian, or Spanish book, you pronounce it with the vowel of *mean* or *seen.*

These two changes, then, produced the basic differences between Middle English and Modern English. But there were several other developments that had an effect upon the language. One was the invention of printing, an invention introduced into England by William Caxton in the year 1475. Where before books had been rare and costly, they suddenly became cheap and common. More and more people learned to read and write. This was the first of many advances in communication which have worked to unify languages and to arrest the development of dialect differences, though of course printing affects writing principally rather than speech. Among other things it hastened the standardization of spelling.

The period of Early Modern English—that is, the sixteenth and seventeenth centuries—was also the period of the English Renaissance, when people developed, on the one hand, a keen interest in the past and, on the other, a more daring and imaginative view of the future. New ideas multiplied, and new ideas meant new language. Englishmen had grown accustomed to borrowing words from French as a result of the Norman Conquest; now they borrowed from Latin and Greek. As we have seen, English had been raiding Latin from Old English times and before, but now the floodgates really opened, and thousands of words from the classical languages poured in. *Pedestrian, bonus, anatomy, contradict, climax, dictionary, benefit, multiply, exist, paragraph, initiate, scene, inspire* are random examples. Probably the average educated American today has more words from French in his vocabulary than from native English sources, and more from Latin than from French.

The greatest writer of the Early Modern English period is of course Shakespeare, and the best-known book is the King James Version of the Bible, published in 1611. The Bible (if not Shakespeare) has made many features of Early Modern English perfectly familiar to many people down to the present time, even though we do not use these features in present-day speech and writing. For instance, the old pronouns *thou* and *thee* have dropped out of use now, together with their verb forms, but they are still familiar to us in prayer and in Biblical quotations: "Whither thou goest, I will go." Such forms as *hath* and *doth* have been replaced by *has* and *does;* "Goes he hence tonight?" would now be "Is he going away tonight?"; Shakespeare's "Fie, on't, sirrah" would be "Nuts to that, Mac." Still, all these expressions linger with us because of the power of the works in which they occur.

It is not always realized, however, that considerable sound changes 40 have taken place between Early Modern English and the English of the present day. Shakespearian actors putting on a play speak the words, properly enough, in their modern pronunciation. But it is very doubtful that this pronunciation would be understood at all by Shakespeare. In Shakespeare's time, the word *reason* was pronounced like modern *raisin; face* had the sound of modern *glass;* the *l* in *would, should, palm* was pronounced. In these points and a great many others the English language has moved a long way from what it was in 1600.

RECENT DEVELOPMENTS

The history of English since 1700 is filled with many movements and countermovements, of which we can notice only a couple. One of these is the vigorous attempt made in the eighteenth century, and the rather half-hearted attempts made since, to regulate and control the English language. Many people of the eighteenth century, not understanding very well the forces which govern language, proposed to polish and prune and restrict English, which they felt was proliferating too wildly. There was much talk of an academy which would rule on what people could and could not say and write. The academy never came into being, but the eighteenth century did succeed in establishing certain attitudes which, though they haven't had much effect on the development of the language itself, have certainly changed the native speaker's feeling about the language.

In part, a product of the wish to fix and establish the language was the development of the dictionary. The first English dictionary was published in 1603; it was a list of 2,500 words briefly defined. Many others were published with gradual improvements until Samuel Johnson published his *English Dictionary* in 1755. This, steadily revised, dominated the field in England for nearly a hundred years. Meanwhile in America, Noah Webster published his dictionary in 1828, and before long dictionary publishing was big business in this country. The last century has seen the publication of one great dictionary: the twelve-volume *Oxford English Dictionary,* compiled in the course of seventy-five years through the labors of many scholars. We have also, of course, numerous commercial dictionaries which are as good as the public wants them to be if not, indeed, rather better.

Another product of the eighteenth century was the invention of "English grammar." As English came to replace Latin as the language of scholarship, it was felt that one should also be able to control and dissect it, parse and analyze it, as one could Latin. What happened in practice was that the grammatical description that applied to Latin was removed and superimposed on English. This was silly, because English is an entirely different kind of language, with its own forms and signals and ways of producing meaning. Nevertheless, English grammars on the Latin model were worked out and taught in the schools. In many schools they are still being taught. This activity is not often popular with school children, but it is sometimes an interesting and instructive exercise in logic. The principal harm in it is that it has tended to keep people from being interested in English and has obscured the real features of English structure.

But probably the most important force on the development of English in the modern period has been the tremendous expansion of English-speaking peoples. In 1500 English was a minor language, spoken by a few people on a small island. Now it is perhaps the greatest language of the world, spoken natively by over a quarter of a billion people and as a second language by many millions more. When we speak of English now, we must specify whether we mean American English, British English, Australian English, Indian English, or what, since the differences are considerable. The American cannot go to England or the Englishman to America confident that he will always understand and be understood. The Alabaman in Iowa or the Iowan in Alabama shows himself a foreigner every time he speaks. It is only because communication has become fast and easy that English in this period of its expansion has not broken into a dozen mutually unintelligible languages.

THINKING CRITICALLY ABOUT THE READING

1. What is Roberts's thesis in this essay? (Glossary: *Thesis*) Where does he state it? Does he convince you of his thesis? Why or why not?

2. Why is Roberts careful to describe the relationship between historical events in England and the development of the English language? In what ways did the historical events affect the English language?

3. How would you characterize in social terms the French words that were brought into English by the Norman Conquest? In what areas of life did the French have the greatest influence?

4. Explain what changes the English language underwent as a result of the Great Vowel Shift. What is the importance of this linguistic phenomenon for the history of English?

5. Roberts makes extensive use of examples. (Glossary: *Examples*) Why is his use of examples particularly appropriate for his topic? What did you learn about writing from reading an essay that is so reliant on examples?

6. Roberts wrote this essay in the 1950s, when people were less sensitive to racial and ethnic slurs in writing than they are today. (Glossary: *Biased Language*) Reread the first ten paragraphs, paying particular attention to Roberts's use of such words as *savages, untamed tribes,* and *civilization.* Do you find any of his diction offensive or see how others might find it so? (Glossary: *Diction*) Suggest specific ways to change Roberts's diction in order to improve the impression his writing makes on contemporary readers. How do you as a writer guard against biased writing?

7. Having read Roberts's essay, do you think it is helpful to your education to know something about the history of English? Why or why not?

LANGUAGE IN ACTION

The following passage from Frances Mayes's best-seller *Under the Tuscan Sun: At Home in Italy* (1996) refers to the etymology, or history, of the interesting word *boustrophedon.*

A few summers ago, a friend and I hiked in Majorca above Soller. We climbed across and through miles of dramatic, enormous olives on broad terraces. Up high, we came upon stone huts where the grove tenders sheltered themselves. Although we got lost and encountered a pacing bull in a meadow, we felt this immense peace all day, walking among those trees that looked and may have been a thousand years old. Walking these few curving acres here gives me the same feeling. Unnatural as it is, terracing has a natural feel to it. Some of the earliest methods of writing, called boustrophedon, run from right to left, then from left to right. If we were trained that way, it probably is a more efficient way to read. The etymology of the word reveals Greek roots meaning "to turn like an ox plowing." And that writing is like the rising terraces: The U-turn space required by an ox with plow suddenly loops up a level and you're going in the other direction.

Using your college dictionary, identify the language from which each of the following words was borrowed:

barbecue
buffalo
casino
decoy
ditto
fruit
hustle
marmalade
orangutan
posse
raccoon
veranda

WRITING SUGGESTIONS

1. During its relatively brief four-hundred-year history, American English has consistently been characterized by change. How is American English still changing today? Write about the effects, if any, the war in Iraq, the war on terrorism, the NASA space program, the drug culture, computers and other new technology, the women's movement, the global economy and community, or recent waves of immigration have had on American English.

2. In paragraph 1 Roberts writes, "No understanding of the English language can be very satisfactory without a notion of the history of the language." What exactly does Roberts mean by *understanding*? Write an essay in which you dispute or substantiate his claim.

2

WRITERS ON WRITING

Learning to write well is a demanding and difficult pursuit, but the ability to express exactly what you mean is one of the most enjoyable and rewarding skills you can possess. And, as with any sought-after goal, there is plenty of help available for the aspiring writer. In this chapter, we have gathered some of the best of that advice, offered by professional writers and respected teachers of writing.

The essays included in this chapter are based on current research and thinking on how writers go about their work. In the first section, "Writing in College and Beyond," we offer advice that is in keeping with the demands of writing in both academic settings and beyond. We begin with Maxine Hairston's excellent essay, "What Happens When People Write?" wherein she provides an overview of the writing process and explains how professional writers compose. The rest of the essays in this section look more deeply into the writer's tool bag. Linda Flower analyzes what we mean by audience: "The goal of the writer is to create a momentary common ground between the reader and the writer." She explains that in order to communicate effectively, writers should to know as much about their readers, knowledge, attitudes, and needs as possible. Popular novelist and teacher of writing Anne Lamott recognizes that even though writers may start out with a firm purpose and clear thinking, rough drafts are inevitably very messy affairs. In "The Maker's Eye: Revising Your Own Manuscripts," the late Donald M. Murray recognizes the need to produce a first draft, however messy, so as to move to the real job of writing. For him, as for almost all practicing writers, writing is revising. We conclude the first section with "How to Write an Argument," a brief set of guidelines by Gerald Graff.

"Editing: Getting It Right," the second section in this chapter, offers essays that reflect on some problems encountered in the editing stage of the writing process. We begin with William Zinsser, who makes the case for reducing the clutter that overwhelms contemporary prose and for writing simply. Gregory Pence then offers advice to his students on the use of clichés, always insisting that "clear writing fosters clear thinking." The final two selections function as a pair. In the first piece, "Its Academic, or Is It?" Charles R. Larson wryly explores the ways in which Americans misuse apostrophes. He believes that a decline in reading has led to a lack of knowledge about how to use this important punctuation mark. Further, he laments that few people are even concerned about it. In "Like I Said, Don't Worry," Patricia O'Conner discusses our national attitude toward grammar and usage from a different perspective. O'Conner recognizes that grammar serves a purpose, but she is sympathetic to readers who have been intimidated by it. Although these four writers take different viewpoints, each of them, with humor and without apology, affirms the importance of linguistic rules.

What Happens When People Write?

Maxine Hairston

Maxine Hairston (1922–2005) was Professor Emerita of Rhetoric and Composition at the University of Texas at Austin, where she served as coordinator of advanced expository writing courses, director of first-year English, and associate dean of humanities. She was a chair of the Conference on College Composition and Communication and wrote many articles on rhetoric and teaching writing. She also authored and coauthored several textbooks, including *The Scott, Foresman Handbook for Writers.*

In the following selection, taken from Hairston's textbook *Successful Writing* (2006), now in its eighth edition, she takes the mystery out of writing by giving an overview of the writing process. By looking at the way professional writers work, she shows us how to establish realistic expectations of what should happen each time we sit down to write. Next, Hairston focuses on the differences between two major types of writing—explanatory and exploratory—that writers should master and value equally. She explains how a writer's writing process can change depending on the type of writing someone is doing.

WRITING TO DISCOVER: *Think about what happens when you sit down to write. Do you have one particular pen that you like to use, or do you compose on a personal computer? Where do you like to write? Do you have any special rituals that you go through before settling into your task? Briefly describe in several paragraphs the process you go through from the time you make the decision to put an idea in writing (or are given an assignment) to the time that you submit final copy. Is the process roughly the same for all the different types of writing that you do? Explain.*

Many people who have trouble writing believe that writing is a mysterious process that the average person cannot master. They assume that anyone who writes well does so because of a magic mixture of talent and inspiration, and that people who are not lucky enough to have those gifts can never become writers. Thus they take an "either you have it or you don't" attitude that discourages them before they even start to write.

Like most myths, this one has a grain of truth in it, but only a grain. Admittedly the best writers are people with talent just as the best musicians or athletes or chemists are people with talent. But that qualification does not mean that only talented people can write well any more than it means that only a few gifted people can become good tennis players. Tennis coaches know differently. From experience, they know any reasonably well-coordinated and healthy person can learn to play a fairly good game of tennis if he or she will learn the principles of the game and work at putting them into practice. They help people become tennis players by showing them the strategies that experts use and by giving them criticism and reinforcement as they practice those strategies. In recent years, as we have learned more about the processes of working writers, many teachers have begun to work with their writing students in the same way.

AN OVERVIEW OF THE WRITING PROCESS

How Professional Writers Work

- Most writers don't wait for inspiration. They write whether they feel like it or not. Usually they write on a schedule, putting in regular hours just as they would on a job.
- Professional writers consistently work in the same places with the same tools—pencil, typewriter, or word processor. The physical details of writing are important to them so they take trouble to create a good writing environment for themselves.
- Successful writers work constantly at observing what goes on around them and have a system for gathering and storing material. They collect clippings, keep notebooks, or write in journals.
- Even successful writers need deadlines to make them work, just like everyone else.
- Successful writers make plans before they start to write, but they keep their plans flexible, subject to revision.
- Successful writers usually have some audience in mind and stay aware of that audience as they write and revise.
- Most successful writers work rather slowly; four to six double-spaced pages is considered a good day's work.
- Even successful writers often have trouble getting started; they expect it and don't panic.
- Successful writers seldom know precisely what they are going to write before they start, and they plan on discovering at least part of their content as they work. (See section below on explanatory and exploratory writing.)
- Successful writers stop frequently to reread what they've written and consider such rereading an important part of the writing process.
- Successful writers revise as they write and expect to do two or more drafts of anything they write.
- Like ordinary mortals, successful writers often procrastinate and feel guilty about it; unlike less experienced writers, however, most of them have a good sense of how long they can procrastinate and still avoid disaster.

Explanatory and Exploratory Writing

Several variables affect the method and speed with which writers work—how much time they have, how important their task is, how skilled they are, and so on. The most important variable, however, is the kind of writing they are doing. I am going to focus on two major kinds here: *explanatory* and *exploratory*. To put it briefly, although much too simply, explanatory writing *tends* to be about information; exploratory writing *tends* to be about ideas.

Explanatory writing can take many forms: a movie review, an explanation of new software, an analysis of historical causes, a report on a recent political development, a biographical sketch. These are just a few possibilities. The distinguishing feature of all these examples and other kinds of explanatory writing is that the writer either knows most of what he or she is going to say before starting to write or knows where to find the material needed to get started. A typical explanatory essay might be on some aspect of global warming for an environmental studies course. The material for such a paper already exists—you're not going to create it or discover it within your subconscious. Your job as a writer is to dig out the material, organize it, and shape it into a clearly written, carefully supported essay. Usually you would know who your readers are for an explanatory essay and, from the beginning, shape it for that audience.

Writers usually make plans when they are doing explanatory writing,   5
plans that can range from a page of notes to a full outline. Such plans help them to keep track of their material, put it in some kind of order, and find a pattern for presenting it. For explanatory writing, many writers find that the traditional methods work well; assertion/support, cause and effect, process, compare/contrast, and so on. Much of the writing that students do in college is explanatory, as is much business writing. Many magazine articles and nonfiction books are primarily explanatory writing. It's a crucially important kind of writing, one that we depend on for information and education, one that keeps the machinery of business and government going.

Explanatory writing is not necessarily easy to do nor is it usually formulaic. It takes skill and care to write an accurate, interesting story about the physician who won a Nobel Prize for initiating kidney transplants or an entertaining and informative report on how the movie *Dick Tracy* was made. But the process for explanatory writing is manageable. You identify the task, decide what the purpose and who the audience are, map out a plan for finding and organizing information, then divide the writing itself into doable chunks and start working. Progress may be painful, and you may have to draft and revise several times to clarify points or get the tone just right, but with persistence, you can do it.

Exploratory writing may also take many forms: a reflective personal essay, a profile of a homeless family, an argument in support of funding for multimillion dollar science projects, or a speculative essay about the future of the women's movement. These are only a few possibilities. What distinguishes these examples and exploratory writing in general is that the writer has only a partially formed idea of what he or she is going to write before starting. A typical piece of exploratory writing might be a speculative essay on why movies about the Mafia appeal so much to the American public. You might hit on the idea of writing such a piece after you have seen several mob movies—*Goodfellas, Miller's Crossing,* and *Godfather III*—but not really know what you would say or who your audience would be. The material for such a paper doesn't exist; you would have to begin by reading, talking to people, and by drawing on the ideas and insights you've gleaned from different sources to reach your own point of view. And you would certainly expect some of your most important ideas—your own conclusions—to come to you as you wrote.

Because you don't know ahead of time exactly what you're going to say in exploratory writing, it's hard to make a detailed plan or outline; however, you can and should take copious notes as you prepare to write. You might be able to put down a tentative thesis sentence, for example, "American moviegoers are drawn to movies about the Mafia and mob violence because they appeal to a streak of lawlessness that has always been strong in American character." Such a sentence could be an anchor to get you started writing, but as a main idea, it could change or even disappear as the paper developed.

Many papers you write in college will be exploratory papers, for example, an interpretive paper in a literature course, an essay on the future of an ethnic community for a cultural anthropology course, or an argumentative paper for a government course proposing changes in our election laws. Many magazine articles and books are also exploratory, for example, an article on the roots of violence in American cities or an autobiographical account of being tagged a "slow learner" early in one's school career. Both in and out of college, exploratory writing is as important as explanatory writing because it is the springboard and testing ground for new ideas.

Exploratory writing isn't necessarily harder to do than explanatory   10
writing, but it is harder to plan because it resists any systematic approach. That makes it appeal to some writers, particularly those who have a reflective or speculative turn of mind. They like the freedom of being able just to write to see what is going to develop. But although exploratory writers start out with more freedom, eventually they too have to discipline themselves to organize their writing into clear, readable form. They also have to realize that exploratory writing usually takes longer and requires more drafts.

When you're doing exploratory writing, anticipate that your process will be messy. You have to tolerate uncertainty longer because ideas keep coming as you write and it's not always clear what you're going to do with them and how—or if—you can fit them into your paper. Exploratory writing is also hard to organize—sometimes you'll have to outline *after* you've written your first draft in order to get the paper under control. Finally, you also have to have confidence in your own instincts; now that you are focusing on ideas and reflections more than on facts, you have to believe that you have something worth writing about and that other people are interested in reading it.

Of course, not all writing can be easily classified as either explanatory or exploratory; sometimes you'll be working with information and ideas in the same paper and move from presenting facts to reflecting about their implications. For example, in an economics course you might report on how much Japan has invested in the United States economy over the last decade and where those investments have been made; then you could speculate about the long-range impact on American business. If you were writing a case study of a teenage mother for a social work class, you would use mostly explanatory writing to document the young woman's background, schooling, and important facts about her present situation; then you could go to exploratory writing to suggest how her options for the future can be improved.

In general, readers respond best to writing that thoughtfully connects facts to reflections, explanations to explorations. So don't hesitate to mix the two kinds of writing if it makes your paper stronger and more interesting. At this point, you might ask "Why do these distinctions matter to me?" I think there are several reasons.

First, it helps to realize that there isn't *a* writing process—there are writing *processes,* and some work better than others in specific situations. Although by temperament and habit you may be the "just give me the facts, ma'am," kind of person who prefers to do explanatory writing, you also need to become proficient at exploratory writing in order to write the speculative, reflective papers that are necessary when you have to write about long-range goals or speculate about philosophical issues. If, on the other hand, by temperament you'd rather ignore outlines and prefer to spin theories instead of report on facts, you also need to become proficient at explanatory writing. In almost any profession, you're going to have to write reports, summarize data, or present results of research.

Second, you'll become a more proficient and relaxed writer if you develop the habit of analyzing before you start, whether you are going to be doing primarily explanatory or exploratory writing. Once you decide, you can consciously switch into certain writing patterns and write more efficiently. For instance, when you're writing reports, case studies, research papers, or analyses, take the time to rough out an outline and make a careful list of the main points you need to make. Schedule time for research and checking facts; details are going to be important. Review some of the routine but useful patterns you could use to develop your paper: cause and effect, definition, process, narration, and so forth. They can work well when you have a fairly clear idea of your purpose and what you're going to say.

If you're starting on a less clearly defined, more open-ended paper—for example, a reflective essay about Picasso's portrayal of women for an art history course—allow yourself to be less organized for a while. Be willing to start without knowing where you're going. Look at some paintings to get your ideas flowing, talk to some other students, and then just start writing, confident that you'll find your content and your direction. Don't worry if you can't get the first paragraph right—it will come later. Your first goal with exploratory writing should be to generate a fairly complete first draft in order to give yourself something to work with. Remember to give yourself plenty of time to revise. You'll need it.

Finally, resist the idea that one kind of writing is better than another. It's not. Sometimes there's a tendency, particularly in liberal arts classes, to believe that people who do theoretical or reflective writing are superior; that exploratory writing is loftier and more admirable than writing in which people present facts and argue for concrete causes. That's not really the case. Imaginative, thoughtful writing about theories and opinions is important and interesting, but informative, factual writing is also critically important, and people who can do it well are invaluable. Anyone who hopes to be an effective, confident writer should cultivate the habits that enable him or her to do both kinds of writing well.

THINKING CRITICALLY ABOUT THE READING

1. According to Hairston, in what ways is a writing teacher like a tennis coach? Does this analogy help you to view your writing teacher differently? (Glossary: *Analogy*) Explain.

2. Review the list of items that Hairston provides to explain how professional writers work. How many points on the list are you already doing? What items, if any, surprised you?

3. What are the main differences between explanatory and exploratory writing? Which type do you usually find yourself doing? Is Hairston's essay explanatory, exploratory, or a combination of both types of writing?

4. Discuss how Hairston uses comparison and contrast to explain the differences between explanatory and exploratory writing. (Glossary: *Comparison and Contrast*) What examples does she use to illustrate her points? (Glossary: *Examples*)

5. What transitions does Hairston use to connect the ideas in paragraphs 15 and 16? (Glossary: *Transitions*) Briefly explain how her transitions work.

6. How would you describe Hairston's tone in this essay? (Glossary: *Tone*) Explain how her choice of words helps her create this tone. (Glossary: *Diction*) Use examples from the text to show what you mean. How important is tone to writers? To readers?

7. Carefully examine Hairston's diction or choice of words in this selection. (Glossary: *Diction*) Would you consider any of her words the technical language or jargon of writing teachers? (Glossary: *Technical Language*) Is her language appropriate for her intended audience? Explain.

LANGUAGE IN ACTION

Consider the following cartoon from the *New Yorker.* What insights into the writing process does the cartoon give you? How does humor help people talk about situations that might otherwise be difficult to discuss? Explain.

"No wonder you can't write. You're not plugged in!"

WRITING SUGGESTIONS

1. How well do you know yourself as a writer? Drawing on what you wrote in your Writing to Discover entry for this selection, write an essay in which you describe the process you normally follow in writing a composition. Do you begin by brainstorming for ideas, thinking before you write, or do you simply start writing, hoping that ideas will come to you as you write? How many drafts does it usually take before you have a piece of writing that satisfies you? What part of the process is the most difficult for you? The easiest for you?

2. In list form, describe the processes for writing an explanatory and an exploratory essay. Discuss your lists with others in your class. What are the main differences between the two processes? Write an essay about these differences.

3. How useful do you find outlining? When in the writing process do you usually prepare an outline? Do your outlining practices vary according to the type of writing you are doing? What recommendations about

outlining have your previous teachers made? Consult several texts in the library about outlining. Then, using the preceding questions as a starting point, compose a brief questionnaire about outlining practices and the benefits of outlining, and give the questionnaire to the other students in your writing class. What conclusions can you draw from your tabulated questionnaires? Based on your findings, write an essay arguing for or against the benefits of outlining.

Writing for an Audience

LINDA FLOWER

Linda Flower is professor of rhetoric at Carnegie Mellon University, where she directed the Business Communication program for a number of years. She has been a leading researcher on the composing process, and the results of her investigations have shaped and informed her influential writing texts *Problem-Solving Strategies for Writing* (1993) and *The Construction of Negotiated Meaning* (1994).

In this selection, which is taken from *Problem-Solving Strategies for Writing*, Flower's focus is on audience — the people for whom we write. She believes that writers must establish a "common ground" between themselves and their readers, one that lessens their differences in knowledge, attitudes, and needs. Although we can never be certain who might read what we write, it is nevertheless important for us to have a target audience in mind. Many of the decisions that we make as writers are influenced by that real or imagined reader.

WRITING TO DISCOVER: *Imagine for a moment that you just received a speeding ticket for going sixty-five miles per hour in a thirty-mile-per-hour zone. How would you describe the episode to your best friend? To your parents? To the judge in court? Sketch out the three versions, and then in several paragraphs write about how the three versions of your story differ. How do you account for these differences?*

The goal of the writer is to create a momentary common ground between the reader and the writer. You want the reader to share your knowledge and your attitude toward that knowledge. Even if the reader eventually disagrees, you want him or her to be able for the moment to *see things as you see them.* A good piece of writing closes the gap between you and the reader.

ANALYZE YOUR AUDIENCE

The first step in closing that gap is to gauge the distance between the two of you. Imagine, for example, that you are a student writing your parents, who have always lived in New York City, about a wilderness survival expedition you want to go on over spring break. Sometimes obvious differences such as age or background will be important, but the critical differences for writers usually fall into three areas: the reader's *knowledge* about the topic, his or her *attitude* toward it, and his or her personal or professional *needs*. Because these differences often exist, good writers do more than simply express their meaning; they pinpoint the critical differences between themselves and their reader and design their writing to reduce those differences. Let us look at these areas in more detail.

KNOWLEDGE.   This is usually the easiest difference to handle. What does your reader need to know? What are the main ideas you hope to teach? Does your reader have enough background knowledge to really understand you? If not, what would he or she have to learn?

ATTITUDES.   When we say a person has knowledge, we usually refer to his conscious awareness of explicit facts and clearly defined concepts. This kind of knowledge can be easily written down or told to someone else. However, much of what we "know" is not held in this formal, explicit way. Instead it is held as an attitude or image—as a loose cluster of associations. For instance, my image of lakes includes associations many people would have, including fishing, water skiing, stalled outboards, and lots of kids catching night crawlers with flashlights. However, the most salient or powerful parts of my image, which strongly color my whole attitude toward lakes, are thoughts of cloudy skies, long rainy days, and feeling generally cold and damp. By contrast, one of my best friends has a very different cluster of associations: to him a lake means sun, swimming, sailing, and happily sitting on the end of a dock. Needless to say, our differing images cause us to react quite differently to a proposal that we visit a lake. Likewise, one reason people often find it difficult to discuss religion and politics is that terms such as "capitalism" conjure up radically different images.

As you can see, a reader's image of a subject is often the source of   5
attitudes and feelings that are unexpected and, at times, impervious to mere facts. A simple statement that seems quite persuasive to you, such as "Lake Wampago would be a great place to locate the new music camp," could have little impact on your reader if he or she simply doesn't visualize a lake as a "great place." In fact, many people accept uncritically any statement that fits in with their own attitudes—and reject, just as uncritically, anything that does not.

Whether your purpose is to persuade or simply to present your perspective, it helps to know the image and attitudes that your reader already holds. The more these differ from your own, the more you will have to do to make him or her *see* what you mean.

NEEDS.   When writers discover a large gap between their own knowledge and attitudes and those of the reader, they usually try to change the reader in some way. Needs, however, are different. When you analyze a reader's needs, it is so that you, the writer, can adapt to him. If you ask a friend majoring in biology how to keep your fish tank from clouding, you don't want to hear a textbook recitation on the life processes of algae. You expect a friend to adapt his or her knowledge and tell you exactly how to solve your problem.

The ability to adapt your knowledge to the needs of the reader is often crucial to your success as a writer. This is especially true in writing done on a job. For example, as producer of a public affairs program for a television station, 80 percent of your time may be taken up planning the details of new shows, contacting guests, and scheduling the taping sessions. But when you write a program proposal to the station director, your job is to show how the program will fit into the cost guidelines, the FCC requirements for relevance, and the overall programming plan for the station. When you write that report your role in the organization changes from producer to proposal writer. Why? Because your reader needs that information in order to make a decision. He may be *interested* in your scheduling problems and the specific content of the shows, but he *reads* your report because of his own needs as station director of the organization. He has to act.

In college, where the reader is also a teacher, the reader's needs are a little less concrete but just as important. Most papers are assigned as a way to teach something. So the real purpose of a paper may be for you to make connections between two historical periods, to discover for yourself the principle behind a laboratory experiment, or to develop and support your own interpretation of a novel. A good college paper doesn't just rehash the facts; it demonstrates what your reader, as a teacher, needs to know—that you are learning the thinking skills his or her course is trying to teach.

Effective writers are not simply expressing what they know, like a student madly filling up an examination bluebook. Instead they are *using* their knowledge: reorganizing, maybe even rethinking their ideas to meet the demands of an assignment or the needs of their reader.

THINKING CRITICALLY ABOUT THE READING

1. How, according to Flower, does a competent writer achieve the goal of closing the gap between himself or herself and the reader? How does a writer determine what a reader's "personal or professional needs" (2) are?

2. What, for Flower, is the difference between knowledge and attitude? Why is it important for writers to understand this difference?

3. Flower wrote this selection for college students. How well did she assess your knowledge, attitude, and needs about the subject of a writer's audience? Does Flower's use of language and examples show a sensitivity to her audience? Provide specific examples to support your view. (Glossary: *Examples*)

4. In paragraph 4, Flower discusses the fact that many words have both positive and negative associations. How do you think words come to have associations? (Glossary: *Connotation/Denotation*) Consider, for example, such words as *home, anger, royalty, welfare, politician,* and *strawberry shortcake.*

5. What does Flower believe constitutes a "good college paper" (9)? Do you agree with her assessment? Why or why not?

6. Flower notes in paragraph 4 that many words often have "a loose cluster of associations." Explain how you can use this fact to advantage when writing an argument, a personal essay, or an informative piece.

7. When using technical language in a paper on a subject you have thoroughly researched or are already familiar with, why is it important for you to know your audience? (Glossary: *Audience*) What language strategies might you use to adapt your knowledge to your audience? Explain. How could your classmates, friends, or parents help you?

LANGUAGE IN ACTION

Analyze the language of the Internet home page for Digital Loggers, Inc. Based on your own familiarity with computer language, identify those words that you consider computer jargon. (Glossary: *Technical Language*) Which words are appropriate for a general audience? An expert audience? For what kind of audience do you think this page was written? Explain.

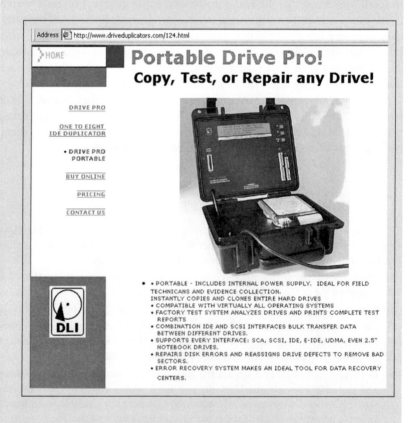

WRITING SUGGESTIONS

1. Write an essay in which you discuss the proposition that honesty is a prerequisite of good writing. Ask yourself what it means to write honestly. What does dishonest writing look and sound like? Do you have a responsibility to be an honest writer? How is honesty in writing related to questions of audience? Be sure to illustrate your essay with examples from your own experiences.

2. In order to write well, a writer has to identify his or her audience. Choose a topic that is important to you and, taking into account what Flower calls your audience's knowledge, attitude, and needs, write a letter about that topic to your best friend. Then write a letter on the same topic to your instructor. How does your message differ from letter to letter? How does your diction change? (Glossary: *Diction*) What conclusions about audience can you draw from your two letters? How successful do you think you were in closing "the gap between you and the reader" in each letter?

Shitty First Drafts

Anne Lamott

Born in San Francisco in 1954, Anne Lamott is a graduate of Goucher College in Baltimore and is the author of six novels, including *Rosie* (1983), *Crooked Little Heart* (1997), *All New People* (2000), and *Blue Shoes* (2002). She has also been the food reviewer for *California* magazine, a book reviewer for *Mademoiselle*, and a regular contributor to *Salon's* "Mothers Who Think." Her nonfiction books include *Operating Instructions: A Journal of My Son's First Year* (1993), in which she describes her adventures as a single parent, *Traveling Mercies: Some Thoughts on Faith* (1999), in which she charts her journey toward faith in God, *Plan B: Further Thoughts on Faith* (2005), and *Grace (Eventually): Thoughts on Faith* (2007).

In the following selection, taken from Lamott's popular book about writing, *Bird by Bird* (1994), she argues for the need to let go and write those "shitty first drafts" that lead to clarity and sometimes brilliance in our second and third drafts.

Writing to Discover: *Many professional writers view first drafts as something they have to do before they can begin the real work of writing—revision. How do you view the writing of your first drafts? What patterns, if any, do you see in your writing behavior when working on first drafts? Is the work liberating? Restricting? Pleasant? Unpleasant? Explain in a paragraph or two.*

Now, practically even better news than that of short assignments is the idea of shitty first drafts. All good writers write them. This is how they end up with good second drafts and terrific third drafts. People tend to look at successful writers, writers who are getting their books published and maybe even doing well financially, and think that they sit down at their desks every morning feeling like a million dollars, feeling great about who they are and how much talent they have and what a great story they have to tell; that they take in a few deep breaths, push back their sleeves, roll their necks a few times to get all the cricks out, and dive in, typing fully formed passages as fast as a court reporter. But this is just the fantasy of the uninitiated. I know some very great writers, writers you love who write beautifully and have made a great deal of money, and not one of them sits down routinely feeling wildly enthusiastic and confident. Not one of them writes elegant first drafts. All right, one of them does, but we do not like her very much. We do not think that she has a rich inner life or that God likes her or can even stand her. (Although when I mentioned this to my priest friend Tom, he said you can safely assume you've created God in your own image when it turns out that God hates all the same people you do.)

Very few writers really know what they are doing until they've done it. Nor do they go about their business feeling dewy and thrilled. They do not type a few stiff warm-up sentences and then find themselves bounding along like huskies across the snow. One writer I know tells me that he sits down every morning and says to himself nicely, "It's not like you don't have a choice, because you do—you can either type or kill yourself." We all often feel like we are pulling teeth, even those writers whose prose ends up being the most natural and fluid. The right words and sentences just do not come pouring out like ticker tape most of the time. Now, Muriel Spark is said to have felt that she was taking dictation from God every morning—sitting there, one supposes, plugged into a Dictaphone, typing away, humming. But this is a very hostile and aggressive position. One might hope for bad things to rain down on a person like this.

For me and most of the other writers I know, writing is not rapturous. In fact, the only way I can get anything written at all is to write really, really shitty first drafts.

The first draft is the child's draft, where you let it all pour out and then let it romp all over the place, knowing that no one is going to see it and that you can shape it later. You just let this childlike part of you channel whatever voices and visions come through and onto the page. If one of the characters wants to say, "Well, so what, Mr. Poopy Pants?," you let her. No one is going to see it. If the kid wants to get into really sentimental, weepy, emotional territory, you let him. Just get it all down on paper, because there may be something great in those six crazy pages that you would never have gotten to by more rational, grown-up means. There may be something in the very last line of the very last paragraph on page six that you just love, that is so beautiful or wild that you now know what you're supposed to be writing about, more or less, or in what direction you might go—but there was no way to get to this without first getting through the first five and a half pages.

I used to write food reviews for *California* magazine before it folded. 5
(My writing food reviews had nothing to do with the magazine folding, although every single review did cause a couple of canceled subscriptions. Some readers took umbrage at my comparing mounds of vegetable puree with various ex-presidents' brains.) These reviews always took two days to write. First I'd go to a restaurant several times with a few opinionated, articulate friends in tow. I'd sit there writing down everything anyone said that was at all interesting or funny. Then on the following Monday I'd sit down at my desk with my notes, and try to write the review. Even after I'd been doing this for years, panic would set in. I'd try to write a lead, but instead I'd write a couple of dreadful sentences, XX them out, try again, XX everything out, and then feel despair and worry settle on my chest like an x-ray apron. It's over, I'd think, calmly. I'm not going to be able to get the magic to work this time. I'm ruined. I'm through. I'm toast. Maybe, I'd think, I can get my old job back as a clerk-typist. But probably not. I'd get up and study my teeth in the mirror for a while. Then I'd stop,

remember to breathe, make a few phone calls, hit the kitchen and chow down. Eventually I'd go back and sit down at my desk, and *sigh* for the next ten minutes. Finally I would pick up my one-inch picture frame, stare into it as if for the answer, and every time the answer would come: all I had to do was to write a really shitty first draft of, say, the opening paragraph. And no one was going to see it.

So I'd start writing without reining myself in. It was almost just typing, just making my fingers move. And the writing would be terrible. I'd write a lead paragraph that was a whole page, even though the entire review could only be three pages long, and then I'd start writing up descriptions of the food, one dish at a time, bird by bird, and the critics would be sitting on my shoulders, commenting like cartoon characters. They'd be pretending to snore, or rolling their eyes at my overwrought descriptions, no matter how hard I tried to tone those descriptions down, no matter how conscious I was of what a friend said to me gently in my early days of restaurant reviewing. "Annie," she said, "it is just a piece of *chicken*. It is just a bit of *cake*."

But because by then I had been writing for so long, I would eventually let myself trust the process—sort of, more or less. I'd write a first draft that was maybe twice as long as it should be, with a self-indulgent and boring beginning, stupefying descriptions of the meal, lots of quotes from my black-humored friends that made them sound more like the Manson girls than food lovers, and no ending to speak of. The whole thing would be so long and incoherent and hideous that for the rest of the day I'd obsess about getting creamed by a car before I could write a decent second draft. I'd worry that people would read what I'd written and believe that the accident had really been a suicide, that I had panicked because my talent was waning and my mind was shot.

The next day, though, I'd sit down, go through it all with a colored pen, take out everything I possibly could, find a new lead somewhere on the second page, figure out a kicky place to end it, and then write a second draft. It always turned out fine, sometimes even funny and weird and helpful. I'd go over it one more time and mail it in.

Then, a month later, when it was time for another review, the whole process would start again, complete with the fears that people would find my first draft before I could rewrite it.

THINKING CRITICALLY ABOUT THE READING

1. What is Lamott's thesis, and where is her statement of the thesis? (Glossary: *Thesis*)

2. Lamott says that the perceptions most people have of how writers work is different from the reality of the work itself. She refers to this in paragraph 1 as "the fantasy of the uninitiated." What does she mean?

3. In paragraph 7 Lamott refers to a time when, through experience, she "eventually let [herself] trust the process—sort of, more or less." She is referring to the writing process, of course, but why "more or less"? Do you think her wariness is personal, or is she speaking for all writers in this regard? Explain.

4. From what Lamott has to say, is writing a first draft more about content or psychology? Do you agree in regard to your own first drafts? Explain.

5. Lamott adds humor to her argument for "shitty first drafts." Give some examples. Do her attempts at humor add or detract from the points she makes? Explain.

6. In paragraph 5, Lamott offers a narrative of her experiences writing a food review in which she refers to an almost ritualistic set of behaviors. What is her purpose in telling her readers this story and the difficulties she has? (Glossary: *Narration*) Is it helpful for us to know this information? Explain.

7. What do you think of Lamott's use of the word *shitty* in her title and in the essay itself? Is it in keeping with the tone of her essay? (Glossary: *Tone*) Are you offended by her use of the word? Why or why not? What would be lost or gained if she used a different word?

LANGUAGE IN ACTION

In his 1990 book *The Play of Words*, Richard Lederer presents the following activity called "Verbs with Verve." What do you learn about the power of verbs from this exercise? Explain.

Researchers showed groups of test subjects a picture of an automobile accident and then asked this question: "How fast were the cars going when they——?" The blank was variously filled in with *bumped, contacted, hit, collided*, or *smashed*. Groups that were asked "How fast were the cars going when they smashed?" responded with the highest estimates of speed.

All of which proves that verbs create specific images in the mind's eye. Because verbs are the words in a sentence that express action and movement, they are the spark plugs of effective style. The more specific the verbs you choose in your speaking and writing, the more sparky will be the images you flash on the minds of your listeners and readers.

Suppose you write, "'No,' she said and left the room." Grammatically there is nothing wrong with this sentence. But because the verbs *say* and *leave* are among the most general and colorless in the English language, you have missed the chance to create a vivid word picture. Consider the alternatives:

SAID		LEFT	
apologized	jabbered	backed	sauntered
asserted	minced	bolted	skipped
blubbered	mumbled	bounced	staggered
blurted	murmured	crawled	stamped

boasted	shrieked	darted	stole
cackled	sighed	flew	strode
commanded	slurred	hobbled	strutted
drawled	snapped	lurched	stumbled
giggled	sobbed	marched	tiptoed
groaned	whispered	plodded	wandered
gurgled	whooped	pranced	whirled

If you had chosen from among these vivid verbs and had crafted the sentence "'No,' she sobbed, and stumbled out of the room," you would have created a powerful picture of someone quite distraught.

Here are brief descriptions of twenty different people. Choosing from the two lists of synonyms for *said* and *left*, fill in the blanks of the sentence "'No,' he/she _____, and _____ out of the room." Select the pair of verbs that best create the most vivid picture of each person described. Throughout your answers try to use as many different verbs as you can:

1. an angry person
2. a baby
3. a braggart
4. a child
5. a clown
6. a confused person
7. a cowboy/cowgirl
8. someone crying
9. a drunkard
10. an embarrassed person
11. an excited person
12. a frightened person
13. a happy person
14. someone in a hurry
15. an injured person
16. a military officer
17. a sneaky person
18. a timid person
19. a tired person
20. a witch

WRITING SUGGESTIONS

1. In order to become a better writer, it is essential to be conscious of what you do as a writer. In other words, you need to reflect on what you are thinking and feeling at each stage of the writing process. Lamott has done just this in writing her essay. Think about what you do at other stages of the writing process—prewriting (gathering information, selecting evidence, checking on the reliability of sources, separating facts from opinions), revising, editing, and proofreading, for example. Write an essay modeled on Lamott's in which you narrate an experience you have had with a particular type of writing or assignment.

2. Lamott's essay is about appearances versus reality. Write an essay in which you set the record straight by exposing the myths or misperceptions people have about a particular job, place, thing, or situation. Naturally, you need to ask yourself how much of an "inside story" you can reveal based on actual experiences you have had. In other words, you know that being a lifeguard is not as romantic as most people think because you have been one. Try to create the same informative but lighthearted tone that Lamott does in her essay by paying particular attention to the language you use.

The Maker's Eye: Revising Your Own Manuscripts

Donald M. Murray

Born in Boston, Massachusetts, Donald M. Murray (1924–2006) taught writing for many years at the University of New Hampshire, his alma mater. He served as an editor at *Time* magazine, and he won the Pulitzer Prize in 1954 for editorials that appeared in the *Boston Globe*. Murray's published works include novels, short stories, poetry, and sourcebooks for teachers of writing, like *A Writer Teaches Writing: A Complete Revision* (1985), *The Craft of Revision* (1991), and *Learning by Teaching* (1982), in which he explores aspects of the writing process. *Write to Learn* (7th ed., 2002), a textbook for college composition courses, is based on Murray's belief that writers learn to write by writing, by taking a piece of writing through the whole process, from invention to revision. In the last decades of his life, Murray produced a weekly column entitled "Now and Then" for the *Boston Globe*.

In the following essay, first published in the *Writer* in October 1973 and later revised for this text, Murray discusses the importance of revision to the work of the writer. Most professional writers live by the maxim that "writing is rewriting." And to rewrite or revise effectively, we need to become better readers of our own work, open to discovering new meanings, and sensitive to our use of language. Murray draws on the experiences of many writers to make a compelling argument for careful revising and editing.

WRITING TO DISCOVER: *Thinking back on your education to date, what did you think you had to do when teachers asked you to revise a piece of your writing? How did the request to revise make you feel? Write about your earliest memories of revising some of your writing. What kinds of changes do you remember making?*

When students complete a first draft, they consider the job of writing done—and their teachers too often agree. When professional writers complete a first draft, they usually feel that they are at the start of the writing process. When a draft is completed, the job of writing can begin.

That difference in attitude is the difference between amateur and professional, inexperience and experience, journeyman and craftsman. Peter F. Drucker, the prolific business writer, calls his first draft "the zero draft"—after that he can start counting. Most writers share the feeling that the first draft, and all of those which follow, are opportunities to discover what they have to say and how best they can say it.

To produce a progression of drafts, each of which says more and says it more clearly, the writer has to develop a special kind of reading skill. In school we are taught to decode what appears on the page as finished writing. Writers, however, face a different category of possibility and responsibility when they read their own drafts. To them the words on the page are never finished. Each can be changed and rearranged, can set off a chain reaction of confusion or clarified meaning. This is a different kind of reading which is possibly more difficult and certainly more exciting.

Writers must learn to be their own best enemy. They must accept the criticism of others and be suspicious of it; they must accept the praise of others and be even more suspicious of it. Writers cannot depend on others. They must detach themselves from their own pages so that they can apply both their caring and their craft to their own work.

Such detachment is not easy. Science-fiction writer Ray Bradbury sup-   5
posedly puts each manuscript away for a year to the day and then rereads it as a stranger. Not many writers have the discipline or the time to do this. We must read when our judgment may be at its worst, when we are close to the euphoric moment of creation.

Then the writer, counsels novelist Nancy Hale, "should be critical of everything that seems to him most delightful in his style. He should excise what he most admires, because he wouldn't thus admire it if he weren't ... in a sense protecting it from criticism." John Ciardi, the poet, adds, "The last act of the writing must be to become one's own reader. It is, I suppose, a schizophrenic process, to begin passionately and to end critically, to begin hot and to end cold; and, more important, to be passion-hot and critic-cold at the same time."

Most people think that the principal problem is that writers are too proud of what they have written. Actually, a greater problem for most professional writers is one shared by the majority of students. They are overly critical, think everything is dreadful, tear up page after page, never complete a draft, see the task as hopeless.

The writer must learn to read critically but constructively, to cut what is bad, to reveal what is good. Eleanor Estes, the children's book author, explains: "The writer must survey his work critically, coolly, as though he were a stranger to it. He must be willing to prune, expertly and hard-heartedly. At the end of each revision, a manuscript may look ... worked over, torn apart, pinned together, added to, deleted from, words changed and words changed back. Yet the book must maintain its original freshness and spontaneity."

Most readers underestimate the amount of rewriting it usually takes to produce spontaneous reading. This is a great disadvantage to the student writer, who sees only a finished product and never watches the craftsman who takes the necessary step back, studies the work carefully, returns to the task, steps back, returns, steps back, again and again. Anthony Burgess, one of the most prolific writers in the English-speaking world, admits, "I might revise a page twenty times." Roald Dahl, the popular children's writer, states, "By the time I'm nearing the end of a story, the first part will have been reread and altered and corrected at least 150 times. . . . Good writing is essentially rewriting. I am positive of this."

Rewriting isn't virtuous. It isn't something that ought to be done. It is simply something that most writers find they have to do to discover what they have to say and how to say it. It is a condition of the writer's life.

There are, however, a few writers who do little formal rewriting, primarily because they have the capacity and experience to create and review a large number of invisible drafts in their minds before they approach the page. And some writers slowly produce finished pages, performing all the tasks of revision simultaneously, page by page, rather than draft by draft. But it is still possible to see the sequence followed by most writers most of the time in rereading their own work.

Most writers scan their drafts first, reading as quickly as possible to catch the larger problems of subject and form, and then move in closer and closer as they read and write, reread and rewrite.

The first thing writers look for in their drafts is *information*. They know that a good piece of writing is built from specific, accurate, and interesting information. The writer must have an abundance of information from which to construct a readable piece of writing.

Next writers look for *meaning* in the information. The specifics must build to a pattern of significance. Each piece of specific information must carry the reader toward meaning.

Writers reading their own drafts are aware of *audience*. They put themselves in the reader's situation and make sure that they deliver information which a reader wants to know or needs to know in a manner which is easily digested. Writers try to be sure that they anticipate and answer the questions a critical reader will ask when reading the piece of writing.

Writers make sure that the *form* is appropriate to the subject and the audience. Form, or genre, is the vehicle which carries meaning to the reader, but form cannot be selected until the writer has adequate information to discover its significance and an audience which needs or wants that meaning.

Once writers are sure the form is appropriate, they must then look at the *structure*, the order of what they have written. Good writing is built on a solid framework of logic, argument, narrative, or motivation which runs through the entire piece of writing and holds it together. This is the time when many writers find it most effective to outline as a way of visualizing the hidden spine by which the piece of writing is supported.

The element on which writers may spend a majority of their time is *development*. Each section of a piece of writing must be adequately developed. It must give readers enough information so that they are satisfied. How much information is enough? That's as difficult as asking how much garlic belongs in a salad. It must be done to taste, but most beginning writers underdevelop, underestimating the reader's hunger for information.

As writers solve development problems, they often have to consider questions of *dimension*. There must be a pleasing and effective proportion among all the parts of the piece of writing. There is a continual process of subtracting and adding to keep the piece of writing in balance.

Finally, writers have to listen to their own voices. *Voice* is the force 20 which drives a piece of writing forward. It is an expression of the writer's authority and concern. It is what is between the words on the page, what glues the piece of writing together. A good piece of writing is always marked by a consistent, individual voice.

As writers read and reread, write and rewrite, they move closer and closer to the page until they are doing line-by-line editing. Writers read their own pages with infinite care. Each sentence, each line, each clause, each phrase, each word, each mark of punctuation, each section of white space between the type has to contribute to the clarification of meaning.

Slowly the writer moves from word to word, looking through language to see the subject. As a word is changed, cut, or added, as a construction is rearranged, all the words used before that moment and all those that follow that moment must be considered and reconsidered.

Writers often read aloud at this stage of the editing process, muttering or whispering to themselves, calling on the ear's experience with language. Does this sound right—or that? Writers edit, shifting back and forth from eye to page to ear to page. I find I must do this careful editing in short runs, no more than fifteen or twenty minutes at a stretch, or I become too kind with myself. I begin to see what I hope is on the page, not what actually is on the page.

This sounds tedious if you haven't done it, but actually it is fun. Making something right is immensely satisfying, for writers begin to learn what they are writing about by writing. Language leads them to meaning, and there is the joy of discovery, of understanding, of making meaning clear as the writer employs the technical skills of language.

Words have double meanings, even triple and quadruple meanings. 25 Each word has its own potential of connotation and denotation. And when writers rub one word against the other, they are often rewarded with a sudden insight, an unexpected clarification.

The maker's eye moves back and forth from word to phrase to sentence to paragraph to sentence to phrase to word. The maker's eye sees the need for variety and balance, for a firmer structure, for a more appropriate form. It peers into the interior of the paragraph, looking for coherence, unity, and emphasis, which make meaning clear.

I learned something about this process when my first bifocals were prescribed. I had ordered a larger section of the reading portion of the glass because of my work, but even so, I could not contain my eyes within this new limit of vision. And I still find myself taking off my glasses and bending my nose toward the page, for my eyes unconsciously flick back and forth across the page, back to another page, forward to still another, as I try to see each evolving line in relation to every other line.

When does this process end? Most writers agree with the great Russian writer Tolstoy, who said, "I scarcely ever reread my published writings, if by chance I come across a page, it always strikes me: all this must be rewritten; this is how I should have written it."

The maker's eye is never satisfied, for each word has the potential to ignite new meaning. This article has been twice written all the way through the writing process. . . . Now it is to be republished in a book. The editors made a few small suggestions, and then I read it with my maker's eye. Now it has been re-edited, re-revised, re-read, and re-re-edited, for each piece of writing to the writer is full of potential and alternatives.

A piece of writing is never finished. It is delivered to a deadline, torn   30
out of the typewriter on demand, sent off with a sense of accomplishment and shame and pride and frustration. If only there were a couple more days, time for just another run at it, perhaps then. . . .

THINKING CRITICALLY ABOUT THE READING

1. What are the essential differences between revising and editing? What types of language concerns are dealt with at each stage? Why is it important to revise before editing?

2. According to Murray, at what point(s) in the writing process do writers become concerned about the individual words they are using? What do you think Murray means when he says in paragraph 24 that "language leads [writers] to meaning"?

3. How does Murray define *information* and *meaning* (13–14)? Why is the distinction between the two terms important?

4. The phrase "the maker's eye" appears in Murray's title and in several places throughout the essay. What do you suppose he means by this? Consider how the maker's eye could be different from the reader's eye.

5. According to Murray, when is a piece of writing finished? What, for him, is the function of deadlines?

6. What does Murray see as the connection between reading and writing? How does reading help the writer? What should writers be looking for in their reading? What kinds of writing techniques or strategies does Murray use in his essay? Why should we read a novel or magazine article differently than we would a draft of one of our own essays?

7. According to Murray, writers look for information, meaning, audience, form, structure, development, dimension, and voice in their drafts. What rationale or logic do you see, if any, in the way Murray has ordered these items? Are these the kinds of concerns you have when reading your drafts? Explain.

8. Murray notes that writers often reach a stage in their editing where they read aloud, "muttering or whispering to themselves, calling on the ear's experience

with language" (23). What exactly do you think writers are listening for when they read aloud? Try reading several paragraphs of Murray's essay aloud. Explain what you learned about his writing. Have you ever read your own writing aloud? If so, what did you discover?

LANGUAGE IN ACTION

Carefully read the opening four paragraphs of Annie Dillard's "Living Like Weasels," which is taken from *Teaching a Stone to Talk* (1982). Using two different color pens, first circle the subject and underline the verb in each main clause in one color, and then circle the subject and underline the verb in each subordinate clause with the other. What does this exercise reveal about Dillard's diction (nouns and verbs) and sentence structure? (Glossary: *Diction*)

A weasel is wild. Who knows what he thinks? He sleeps in his underground den, his tail draped over his nose. Sometimes he lives in his den for two days without leaving. Outside, he stalks rabbits, mice, muskrats, and birds, killing more bodies than he can eat warm, and often dragging the carcasses home. Obedient to instinct, he bites his prey at the neck, either splitting the jugular vein at the throat or crunching the brain at the base of the skull, and he does not let go. One naturalist refused to kill a weasel who was socketed into his hand deeply as a rattlesnake. The man could in no way pry the tiny weasel off, and he had to walk half a mile to water, the weasel dangling from his palm, and soak him off like a stubborn label.

And once, says Ernest Thompson Seton—once, a man shot an eagle out of the sky. He examined the eagle and found the dry skull of a weasel fixed by the jaws to his throat. The supposition is that the eagle had pounced on the weasel and the weasel swiveled and bit as instinct taught him, tooth to neck, and nearly won. I would like to have seen that eagle from the air a few weeks or months before he was shot: was the whole weasel still attached to his feathered throat, a fur pendant? Or did the eagle eat what he could reach, gutting the living weasel with his talons before his breast, bending his beak, cleaning the beautiful airborne bones?

I have been reading about weasels because I saw one last week. I startled a weasel who startled me, and we exchanged a long glance.

Twenty minutes from my house, through the woods by the quarry and across the highway, is Hollins Pond, a remarkable piece of shallowness, where I like to go at sunset and sit on a tree trunk. Hollins Pond is also called Murray's Pond; it covers two acres of bottomland near Tinker Creek with six inches of water and six thousand lily pads. In winter, brown-and-white steers stand in the middle of it, merely dampening their hooves; from the distant shore they look like miracle itself, complete with miracle's nonchalance. Now, in summer, the steers are gone. The water lilies have blossomed and spread to a green horizontal plane that is terra firma to plodding blackbirds, and tremulous ceiling to black leeches, crayfish, and carp.

WRITING SUGGESTIONS

1. Why do you suppose teachers report that revision is the most difficult stage in the writing process for their students? What is it about revision that makes it difficult, or at least makes people perceive it as being difficult? Write an essay in which you explore your own experiences with revision. You may find it helpful to review what you wrote for the Writing to Discover prompt at the beginning of this essay.

2. Writing about pressing social issues usually requires a clear statement of a particular problem and the precise definition of critical terms. For example, if you were writing about the increasing number of people being kept alive by machines, you would need to examine the debate surrounding the legal and medical definitions of the word *death*. Debates continue about the meanings of other controversial terms, such as *morality, minority* (ethnic), *alcoholism, racism, sexual harassment, life* (as in the abortion issue), *pornography, liberal, gay, censorship, conservative, remedial, insanity, literacy, political correctness, assisted suicide, lying, high crimes and misdemeanors,* and *kidnapping* (as in custody disputes). Select one of these words or one of your own. After carefully researching some of the controversial people, situations, and events surrounding your word, write an essay in which you discuss the problems associated with the term and its definition.

How to Write an Argument: What Students and Teachers *Really* Need to Know

GERALD GRAFF

Gerald Graff has taught at the University of New Mexico, Northwestern University, the University of California at Irvine and Berkeley, Ohio State University, Washington University, and the University of Illinois at Chicago, where he is currently a professor of English. He has a strong interest in the teaching of writing on both the graduate and undergraduate levels but is best known for developing the "teach the controversy" approach, a pedagogy that brings the arguments surrounding any issue into the classroom so that students can become involved in the history of the debate, its development, and the various shapes it takes. Graff's books include *Professing Literature* (1987), *Beyond the Culture Wars* (1993), and, most recently, *Clueless in Academe: How Schooling Obscures the Life of the Mind* (2003), a provocative critique of college curricula.

Graff has also been an advocate for clear and purposeful prose, especially in academic settings. In "How to Write an Argument," which is taken from *Clueless in Academe*, Graff practices what he preaches by putting into clear and direct language his directions for writing an argument. Far from simple in content, however, his ideas about research being an ongoing conversation, the need to make a claim, the advice to include a meta-text that comments on the writer's main argument, and the desirability of mixing "Academicspeak" with everyday language are all excellent suggestions worth putting into practice.

WRITING TO DISCOVER: *Write a paragraph in which you reflect on your experiences in writing argumentative essays. What successes have you had? Were you unknowingly following Graff's advice? What problems have you had? Would your efforts have been helped had Graff's suggestions been available to you? Explain.*

1. Enter a conversation just as you do in real life. Begin your text by directly identifying the prior conversation or debate that you are entering. What *you* have to say won't make sense unless your readers know the conversation in which you are saying it.

2. Make a claim, the sooner the better, preferably flagged for the reader by a phrase like "My claim here is that . . . ." You don't actually have to use this exact phrase, but if you couldn't do so you're in trouble.

3. Remind readers of your claim periodically, especially the more you complicate it. If you're writing about a disputed topic—and if you aren't, why write?—you'll also have to stop and tell the reader what you are *not*

saying, what you don't want readers to take you as saying. Some of them will take you to be saying it anyway, but you don't have to make it easy for them.

4. Summarize the objections that you anticipate will be made (or that have in fact been made) against your claim. This is done by using such formulas as "Here you will probably object that . . . ," "To put the point another way . . . ," or "But why, you may ask, am I so emphatic on this point?" Remember that your critics, even when they get mean and nasty, are your friends: you need them to help you to clarify your claim and to indicate why what you're saying is of interest to others besides yourself. Remember, too, that if naysayers didn't exist, you'd have no excuse for saying what you are saying.

5. Say explicitly why you think what you're saying is important and what difference it would make to the world if you are right or wrong. Imagine a reader over your shoulder who asks, "So what?" Or "Who cares about any of this?" Again, you don't actually have to write such questions in, but if you were to do so and couldn't answer them you're in trouble.

6. Write a meta-text into your essay that stands apart from your main text and puts it in perspective. An effective argumentative essay really consists of two texts, one in which you make your argument and a second one in which you tell readers how and how not to read it. This second text is usually signaled by reflexive phrases like "Of course I don't mean to suggest that . . . ," "What I've been trying to say here, then, is that . . . ," etc. When student writing is unclear or lame, the reason often has less to do with jargon, verbal obscurity, or bad grammar than with the absence of this layer of meta-commentary, which explains why the writer thought it was necessary to write the essay in the first place.

7. Remember that readers can process only *one* claim at a time, so resist the temptation to try to squeeze in secondary claims that are better left for another essay or paragraph, or for another section of your essay that's clearly marked off from your main claim. If you're a professional academic, you are probably so anxious to prove that you've left no thought unconsidered that you find it hard to resist the temptation to try to say everything all at once. Remember that giving in to this temptation to say it all at once will result in saying nothing that will be understood while producing horribly overloaded paragraphs and sentences like this one, monster-sized discursive footnotes, and readers who fling your text down and reach for the *TV Guide*.

8. Be bilingual. It is not necessary to avoid Academicspeak—you sometimes need the stuff to say what you want to say. But whenever you do have to say something in Academicspeak, try also to say it in conversational English as well. You'll be surprised to discover that when you restate an academic point in your nonacademic voice, the

point will either sound fresher or you'll see how shallow it is and remove it.

9. Don't kid yourself. If you couldn't explain it to your parents the chances are you don't understand it yourself.

THINKING CRITICALLY ABOUT THE READING

1. What does Graff mean when he suggests, "Enter a conversation just as you do in real life" (1)? Who are the participants in the conversation?

2. In what ways is a debate a conversation? Explain.

3. Why does Graff say that your readers will sometimes assume you are saying something that you are not? Why is that a special liability when writing an argument? Explain.

4. Why are critics of your point of view so important to your argument, according to Graff?

5. What is a "meta-text"? Why is it necessary, according to Graff, to incorporate a meta-text in your argument? Have you ever employed this strategy? If so, how effective has it been for you?

6. Graff says that alternating Academicspeak with conversational English will reveal whether or not you are actually saying something. Explain how that works.

7. What other advice would you add to Graff's list of suggestions for writing an argument? For example, might you say more about audience, tone, organization?

LANGUAGE IN ACTION

The excerpt on p. 127 from *How to Dance the Tango* (1914) literally lists the steps the reader needs to follow in order to perform the dance. Compare these dance instructions to Graff's "How to Write an Argument." As "how to" documents, how are they similar? How are they different? Why do you think Graff chose to write his advice in the form of a numbered list? Was this a good choice, in your opinion?

The Tango

4. HALF GRAPE VINE, DIP, AND PIVOT. The lady steps back with left foot, and passes right foot slightly behind, counting 1, 2. The left foot is dipped to side on count 3, and the feet brought together on count 4, with the weight even on both. The lady now pivots 4 steps around.

The gentleman steps forward with right foot. His remaining steps are the counterpart of the lady's, except that where she uses the right foot, he uses the left.

TANGO TWO.

1. Position and Two-Step ....8 counts
2. Dip, Two-Step, Walk, and Circle Foot................8 counts
   3. Double Scissors
      ....8 counts
   4. Single Scissors
      ....8 counts

Photo by Calder.

Figure III.
Counts 1, 2, in Tango 2.

1. POSITION AND TWO-STEP. Figure III. shows the position for counts 1, 2.

The lady makes a very small step with right foot, putting weight on it, pointing left foot, and looking over her left shoulder, counting 1, 2. She now two-steps straight backward, beginning with left foot, counting 3, 4. The whole movement is repeated.

The gentleman's steps are the counterpart of the lady's except that where she uses the right foot, he uses the left, and that when she two-steps backward, he two-steps forward, his feet following hers directly.

Page six

WRITING SUGGESTIONS

1. It's possible to regard Graff's list of suggestions as an argument in itself. After all, other writers might argue for a different approach to writing an argument. Spend a few minutes studying his list of suggestions and consider whether he has followed his own advice about writing an argument. Provide examples to support your claim.

2. Write an essay on the value of argumentation. Why do so many college instructors place such importance on the skills of argumentation—asserting a claim, finding and selecting evidence to support that claim, considering opposing arguments, finding common ground, being sensitive to one's audience, and establishing a proper tone? Why are these skills important beyond college?

3. Write an argument on a subject and topic of your own choosing. Try putting Graff's advice to work in developing your essay so that you can test the effectiveness of his advice. If you are having trouble coming up with a topic of your own, consider any of the following language-related topics:

   a. A number of languages, spoken by small numbers of people, are becoming extinct. Government should/should not try to save those languages.
   b. Truly offensive song lyrics should/should not be banned.
   c. Campus speech codes should/should not be supported.
   d. Spanglish is/is not a good idea.
   e. Internet censorship is/is not a good idea.

   Once you have completed your argument, append several paragraphs to your essay explaining the degree to which Graff's advice was helpful to you.

Simplicity

WILLIAM ZINSSER

Born in New York City in 1922, William Zinsser was educated at Princeton University. After serving in the Army in World War II, he worked at the *New York Herald Tribune* as an editor, writer, and critic. During the 1970s he taught a popular course in nonfiction at Yale University, and from 1979 to 1987 he was general editor of the Book-of-the-Month Club. Zinsser has written more than a dozen books, including *The City Dwellers* (1962), *Pop Goes America* (1966), and *Spring Training* (1989), and three widely used books on writing: *Writing with a Word Processor* (1983), *Writing to Learn* (1993), and *On Writing Well* (2006). Currently, he teaches journalism at Columbia University, and his freelance writing regularly appears in some of our leading magazines.

The following selection is taken from *On Writing Well*. This book grew out of Zinsser's many years of experience as a professional writer and teacher. In this essay, Zinsser exposes what he believes is the writer's number one problem—"clutter." He sees Americans "strangling in unnecessary words, circular constructions, pompous frills, and meaningless jargon." His solution is simple: Writers must know what they want to say and must be thinking clearly as they start to compose. Then self-discipline and hard work are necessary to achieve clear, simple prose. No matter what your experience as a writer has been, you will find Zinsser's observations sound and his advice practical.

WRITING TO DISCOVER: *Some people view writing as "thinking on paper." They believe that by seeing something written on a page they are better able to "see what they think." Write about the relationship, for you, between writing and thinking. Are you one of those people who likes to "see" ideas on paper while trying to work things out? Or do you like to think through ideas before writing about them?*

Clutter is the disease of American writing. We are a society strangling in unnecessary words, circular constructions, pompous frills and meaningless jargon.

Who can understand the clotted language of everyday American commerce: the memo, the corporation report, the business letter, the notice from the bank explaining its latest "simplified" statement? What member of an insurance or medical plan can decipher the brochure explaining his costs and benefits? What father or mother can put together a child's toy

from the instructions on the box? Our national tendency is to inflate and
thereby sound important. The airline pilot who announces that he is presently anticipating experiencing considerable precipitation wouldn't think
of saying it may rain. The sentence is too simple—there must be something wrong with it.

But the secret of good writing is to strip every sentence to its cleanest components. Every word that serves no function, every long word
that could be a short word, every adverb that carries the same meaning
that's already in the verb, every passive construction that leaves the reader
unsure of who is doing what—these are the thousand and one adulterants
that weaken the strength of a sentence. And they usually occur in proportion to education and rank.

During the 1960s the president of my university wrote a letter to
mollify the alumni after a spell of campus unrest. "You are probably
aware," he began, "that we have been experiencing very considerable
potentially explosive expressions of dissatisfaction on issues only partially
related." He meant that the students had been hassling them about different things. I was far more upset by the president's English than by the
students' potentially explosive expressions of dissatisfaction. I would have
preferred the presidential approach taken by Franklin D. Roosevelt when
he tried to convert into English his own government's memos, such as
this blackout order of 1942:

> Such preparations shall be made as will completely obscure all Fed-
> eral buildings and non-Federal buildings occupied by the Federal gov-
> ernment during an air raid for any period of time from visibility by reason
> of internal or external illumination.

"Tell them," Roosevelt said, "that in buildings where they have to   5
keep the work going to put something across the windows."

Simplify, simplify. Thoreau said it, as we are so often reminded, and
no American writer more consistently practiced what he preached. Open
Walden to any page and you will find a man saying in a plain and orderly
way what is on his mind:

> I went to the woods because I wished to live deliberately, to front
> only the essential facts of life, and see if I could not learn what it had to
> teach, and not, when I came to die, discover that I had not lived.

How can the rest of us achieve such enviable freedom from clutter?
The answer is to clear our heads of clutter. Clear thinking becomes clear
writing; one can't exist without the other. It's impossible for a muddy
thinker to write good English. He may get away with it for a paragraph or
two, but soon the reader will be lost, and there's no sin so grave, for the
reader will not easily be lured back.

Who is this elusive creature, the reader? The reader is someone with
an attention span of about 30 seconds—a person assailed by many forces

competing for attention. At one time those forces were relatively few: newspapers, magazines, radio, spouse, children, pets. Today they also include a galaxy of electronic devices for receiving entertainment and information—television, VCRs, DVDs, CDs, video games, the Internet, e-mail, cell phones, BlackBerries, iPods—as well as a fitness program, a pool, a lawn and that most potent of competitors, sleep. The man or woman snoozing in a chair with a magazine or a book is a person who was being given too much unnecessary trouble by the writer.

It won't do to say that the reader is too dumb or too lazy to keep pace with the train of thought. If the reader is lost, it's usually because the writer hasn't been careful enough. That carelessness can take any number of forms. Perhaps a sentence is so excessively cluttered that the reader, hacking through the verbiage, simply doesn't know what it means. Perhaps a sentence has been so shoddily constructed that the reader could read it in several ways. Perhaps the writer has switched pronouns in mid-sentence, or has switched tenses, so the reader loses track of who is talking or when the action took place. Perhaps Sentence B is not a logical sequel to Sentence A; the writer, in whose head the connection is clear, hasn't bothered to provide the missing link. Perhaps the writer has used a word incorrectly by not taking the trouble to look it up.

Faced with such obstacles, readers are at first tenacious. They blame themselves—they obviously missed something, and they go back over the mystifying sentence, or over the whole paragraph, piecing it out like an ancient rune, making guesses and moving on. But they won't do that for long. The writer is making them work too hard, and they will look for one who is better at the craft.

10

Writers must therefore constantly ask: what am I trying to say? Surprisingly often they don't know. Then they must look at what they have written and ask: have I said it? Is it clear to someone encountering the subject for the first time? If it's not, some fuzz has worked its way into the machinery. The clear writer is someone clearheaded enough to see this stuff for what it is: fuzz.

I don't mean that some people are born clearheaded and are therefore natural writers, whereas others are naturally fuzzy and will never write well. Thinking clearly is a conscious act that writers must force on themselves, as if they were working on any other project that requires logic: making a shopping list or doing an algebra problem. Good writing doesn't come naturally, though most people seem to think it does. Professional writers are constantly bearded by people who say they'd like to "try a little writing sometime"—meaning when they retire from their real profession, like insurance or real estate, which is hard. Or they say, "I could write a book about that." I doubt it.

Writing is hard work. A clear sentence is no accident. Very few sentences come out right the first time, or even the third time. Remember this in moments of despair. If you find that writing is hard, it's because it *is* hard.

THINKING CRITICALLY ABOUT THE READING

1. What exactly is clutter? When do words qualify as clutter, and when do they not?

2. In paragraph 2, Zinsser states that "Our national tendency is to inflate and thereby sound important." What do you think he means by *inflate*? Provide several examples to illustrate how people use language to inflate.

3. In paragraph 9, Zinsser lists some of the language-based obstacles that a reader may encounter in carelessly constructed prose. Which of these problems most tries your patience? Why?

4. One would hope that education would help in the battle against clutter, but, as Zinsser notes, wordiness "usually occur[s] in proportion to education and rank" (3). Do your own experiences or observations support Zinsser's claim? Discuss.

5. What assumptions does Zinsser make about readers? According to Zinsser, what responsibilities do writers have to readers? How do these responsibilities manifest themselves in Zinsser's writing? How do you think Linda Flower (pp. 107–111) would respond to what Zinsser says about audience? (Glossary: *Audience*) Explain.

6. Zinsser believes that writers need to ask themselves two questions—"What am I trying to say?" and "Have I said it?"—constantly as they write (11). How would these questions help you eliminate clutter from your own writing? Give some examples from one of your essays.

7. In order "to strip every sentence to its cleanest components," we need to be sensitive to the words we use and know how they function within our sentences. For each of the "adulterants that weaken the strength of a sentence," which Zinsser identifies in paragraph 3, provide an example from your own writing.

8. Zinsser knows that sentence variety is an important feature of good writing. Locate several examples of the short sentences (seven or fewer words) he uses in this essay, and explain how each relates in length, meaning, and impact to the sentences around it.

LANGUAGE IN ACTION

The following two pages show a passage from Zinsser's final manuscript for this essay as it was published in the first edition of *On Writing Well*. Carefully study the manuscript, and discuss how Zinsser eliminated clutter in his own prose. Then, using Zinsser as a model, judiciously eliminate the clutter from several paragraphs in one of your papers.

5 --

is too dumb or too lazy to keep pace with the ~~writer's~~ train of thought. My sympathies are ~~entirely~~ with him.) ~~He's not so dumb.~~ (If the reader is lost, it is generally because the writer ~~of the article~~ has not been careful enough to keep him on the ~~proper~~ path.

This carelessness can take any number of ~~different~~ forms. Perhaps a sentence is so excessively ~~long and~~ cluttered that the reader, hacking his way through ~~all~~ the verbiage, simply doesn't know what it ~~the writer~~ means. Perhaps a sentence has been so shoddily constructed that the reader could read it in any of several ~~two or three different~~ ways. ~~He thinks he knows what the writer is trying to say, but he's not sure.~~ Perhaps the writer has switched pronouns in mid-sentence, or ~~perhaps he~~ has switched tenses, so the reader loses track of who is talking ~~to whom,~~ or ~~exactly~~ when the action took place. Perhaps Sentence B is not a logical sequel to Sentence A -- the writer, in whose head the connection is ~~perfectly~~ clear, has not bothered to provide ~~given enough thought to providing~~ the missing link. Perhaps the writer has used an important word incorrectly by not taking the trouble to look it up ~~and make sure.~~ He may think that "sanguine" and "sanguinary" mean the same thing, but) ~~I can assure you that~~ (the difference is a bloody big one. ~~to the reader.~~ The reader ~~He~~ can only ~~try to~~ infer ~~what~~ (speaking of big differences) what the writer is trying to imply.

Faced with these ~~such a variety of~~ obstacles, the reader is at first a remarkably tenacious bird. He ~~tends to~~ blames ~~himself.~~ He obviously missed something, ~~he thinks,~~ and he goes back over the mystifying sentence, or over the whole paragraph, piecing it out like an ancient rune, making guesses and moving on. But he won't do this for long. ~~He will soon run out of patience.~~ (The writer is making him work too hard -- harder ~~than he should have to work~~ -- (and the reader will look for ~~a writer~~ one who is better at his craft.

(continued)

6 --

The writer must therefore constantly ask himself: What am
I trying to say? ~~in this sentence?~~ (Surprisingly often, he
doesn't know.) ~~And~~ Then he must look at what he has ~~just~~
written and ask: Have I said it? Is it clear to someone
~~encountering~~ ~~who is coming upon~~ the subject for the first time? If it's
not, ~~clear,~~ it is because some fuzz has worked its way into the
machinery. The clear writer is a person ~~who is~~ clear-headed
enough to see this stuff for what it is: fuzz.

I don't mean ~~to suggest~~ that some people are born
clear-headed and are therefore natural writers, whereas
~~others~~ ~~other people~~ are naturally fuzzy and will ~~therefore~~ never write
well. Thinking clearly is ~~an entirely~~ conscious act that the
writer must ~~force~~ ~~keep forcing~~ upon himself, just as if he were
~~embarking~~ ~~starting out~~ on any other ~~kind of~~ project that ~~requires~~ ~~calls for~~ logic:
adding up a laundry list or doing an algebra problem ~~or playing chess.~~ Good writing doesn't ~~just~~ come naturally, though most
people obviously think ~~it does.~~ ~~it's as easy as walking.~~ The professional

WRITING SUGGESTIONS

1. Each of the essays in Chapter 2, "Writers on Writing," is concerned with the importance of writing well, of using language effectively and responsibly. Write an essay in which you explore one of the common themes (audience, revision, diction, simplicity) that is emphasized in two or more of the selections.

2. Visit your library or local bookstore and examine the reference books offering advice on writing. What kinds of books did you find? What does the large number of such books say to you about Americans' attitudes toward writing? Compare and contrast the approaches several books take and the audiences at which each book is aimed. What conclusions can you draw from your comparisons?

Let's Think Outside the Box of Bad Clichés

GREGORY PENCE

Gregory Pence is an internationally famous expert in the field of bioethics. He is a cum laude graduate of the College of William and Mary and earned his doctorate in philosophy at New York University, writing his dissertation under the direction of the renowned Australian bioethicist Peter Singer. A long-time professor of philosophy in the Medical School of the University of Alabama in Birmingham, Pence has published a number of leading books in the field of cloning and medical ethics, among them *Classic Works in Medical Ethics* (1995), *Who's Afraid of Human Cloning?* (1998), *Flesh of My Flesh: The Ethics of Human Cloning* (1998), *Re-creating Medicine: Ethical Issues at the Frontiers of Medicine* (2000), *Designer Food: Mutant Harvest or Breadbasket of the World?* (2001), *The Ethics of Food: A Reader for the Twenty-First Century* (2002), *The Elements of Bioethics* (2007), and *Classic Cases in Medical Ethics* (2008).

In "Let's Think Outside the Box of Bad Clichés," an essay first published in *Newsweek* on August 6, 2007, Pence focuses on the bad clichés or trite and overused expressions he finds in student writing. He writes, "clear writing fosters clear thinking." We might also consider that the reverse, "clear thinking fosters clear writing," is equally true.

WRITING TO DISCOVER: *In his well-known essay "Politics and the English Language," George Orwell argues that as writers we should avoid using meaningless language. He writes, "prose consists less and less of words chosen for the sake of their meaning, and more and more of phrases tacked together like the sections of a prefabricated henhouse" (p. 165). Would Pence agree with Orwell?*

As a professor of bioethics, I strive to teach my students that clear writing fosters clear thinking. But as I was grading a stack of blue books today, I discovered so many clichés that I couldn't help writing them down. Before I knew it, I had spent the afternoon not grading essays but cataloging the many trite or inaccurate phrases my students rely on to express themselves.

When I grade written work by students, one of the phrases I hate most is "It goes without saying," in response to which I scribble on their essays, "Then why write it?" Another favorite of undergraduates is "It's not for me to say," to which I jot in their blue books, "Then why continue writing?"

I also despise the phrase "Who can say?" to which I reply, "You! That's who! That's the point of writing an essay!"

In teaching bioethics, I constantly hear about "playing God," as in "To allow couples to choose X is to play God." Undergraduates use the phrase constantly as a rhetorical hammer, as if saying it ends all discussion. And I don't even want to get into "opening Pandora's box" or "sliding down the slippery slope."

Sometimes the clichés are simply redundant, as when my students   5 write of a "mass exodus." Can there be a "small" exodus? "Exodus" implies a mass of people.

Other times the expressions defy the rules of logic. A student in a philosophy class writes that philosophy "bores me to tears." But if something brings him to tears, it's certainly not boring.

I also fear that most students don't know what they are saying when they write that a question "boggles the mind." Does every problem in bioethics really boggle the mind? What does this mean?

My students aren't the only ones guilty of cliché abuse. The language of medicine confuses patients' families when physicians write, "On Tuesday the patient was declared brain dead, and on Wednesday life support was removed." So when did the patient really die? Can people die in two ways, once when they are declared brain dead and second when their respirators are removed? Better to write, "Physicians declared the patient dead by neurological criteria and the next day removed his respirator."

All of us repeat trite expressions without thinking. My TV weatherman sometimes says, "It's raining cats and dogs." Should I call the Humane Society? Where did this silly expression come from?

Another common mistake involves "literally." I often hear people on   10 election night say, "He literally won by a landslide." If so, should geologists help us understand how?

Then, of course, there's the criminal who was caught in "broad daylight." I guess he could not have been caught in "narrow" daylight. And are we sure that the sun shone on the day he was caught? I sometimes read about a "bone of contention." I imagine two animals fighting over a bone from a carcass (and not, as students write, from "a dead carcass"). But do writers want to convey that image?

And how can we forget about the "foreseeable future" (versus the "unforeseeable future"?) and the "foregone conclusion" (versus the "non-foregone conclusion"?).

Spare me jargon from sports, such as being "on the bubble" for something. I'd also rather do without other jargon, such as "pushing the [edge of the] envelope." And has writing that we should "think outside the box" become such a cliché that it's now inside the box?

Some of the worst phrases come from the business world. Because of my profession, I read a lot of essays on medicine, ethics and money. So I must endure endless strings of nouns acting as adjectival phrases, such as "health care finance administration official business." Even authors of textbooks on business and hospital administration use such phrases; no wonder that students use them, too.

And in these fields and others, can we do away with "take a leadership role"? These days, can't anyone just lead? 15

Can we also hear more about the short arm of the law (versus its "long" one), about things that sell well besides "hotcakes" and about a quick tour other than a "whirlwind" one?

Beyond the shadow of a doubt, I'd like to leave no stone unturned in grinding such writing to a halt, saving each and every student's essay in the nick of time. But I have a sneaking suspicion that, from time immemorial, that has been an errand of mercy and easier said than done.

THINKING CRITICALLY ABOUT THE READING

1. What is Pence's thesis in this essay? (Glossary: *Thesis*) Does he make his case, as far as you are concerned?

2. What types of clichés does Pence discuss? Are they equally bad, or does Pence consider some worse than others? Explain.

3. Consider whether the expression "bad clichés" is itself a redundancy. Are there good clichés? Explain.

4. Does Pence substantiate his claim in paragraph 14 that "[s]ome of the worst phrases come from the business world"? Would you agree with him? Why or why not?

5. In paragraph 8 Pence gives an example of confusing medical language. Explain how the example he uses contains clichés that are in conflict with each other. Does his rewrite of the example solve the problem he sees? Explain.

6. Pence does not offer any suggestions for avoiding clichés in writing. How do you avoid such usage? How would you advise others to avoid clichés?

LANGUAGE IN ACTION

One way to determine whether or not an expression is a cliché is to begin the phrase and see if the rest of it comes readily to mind. For example, how would you complete the following incomplete expressions?

when push comes to _____
fall between _____ _____
scratch the _____
maintain the _____ _____
takes on a _____ _____ _____ _____
paying lip _____

(*continued*)

put the _____ before the _____

patience of a _____

If you can correctly fill in each of the above examples, you have a good sense of what constitutes a cliché and will be able to detect and eliminate them in your own writing.

WRITING SUGGESTIONS

1. Pence writes, "All of us repeat trite expressions without thinking"[9]. Write an analysis of your own writing with regard to your use of clichés. Begin by reviewing an essay you have written. Scan every sentence looking for clichés and trite expressions you may have used, and determine which ones are necessary and which ones you can eliminate. Finally, make an overall assessment of how much work you need to do to eliminate trite expressions and search for fresh language to use in your writing.

2. Test Pence's statement that "[s]ome of the worst phrases come from the business world"[14]. Find a recent article in a business magazine such as *Forbes, Fortune, Money,* or *Harvard Business Review* and analyze it for the author's use of clichés, empty phrasings, or unnecessary jargon. Write a report on your findings. Is Pence's statement justified, in your opinion?

Its Academic, or Is it?

CHARLES R. LARSON

A professor of literature at American University in Washington, D.C., since 1965, Charles R. Larson received both his B.A. and M.A. from the University of Colorado and his Ph.D. from Indiana University. After graduating from Colorado, he was among the first generation of Americans to join the Peace Corps, serving in Nigeria for two years. Larson has written several critical studies, including *The Novel in the Third World* (1976), *American Indian Fiction* (1978), and *The Ordeal of the African Writer* (2001), and two works of fiction, *Academia Nuts* (1977) and *Arthur Dimmesdale* (1983). His articles, essays, and stories appear regularly in major magazines and newspapers.

In the following essay, which first appeared in *Newsweek* on November 6, 1995, Larson takes a stand for correct usage. He asks, "Does punctuation count any longer? Are my complaints the ramblings of an old goat who's taught English for too many years?" Larson's essay is the first of a pair of essays on the same topic: the importance of grammar and how to respond to the requirement that we write correctly. You can get a somewhat different take on the subject by reading the essay by Patricia T. O'Conner on pages 143–146.

WRITING TO DISCOVER: *Write about your experiences in using the apostrophe. Do you usually use this mark of punctuation correctly, or do you make frequent mistakes? Do the words* it's *and* its *give you trouble? If so, to what do you attribute your trouble in determining which form of the word to use?*

If you're 35 years or older, you probably identify a common grammatical error in the heading on this page. Younger than that and, well, you likely have another opinion: "Its all relative"—except, of course, for the apostrophe. Unfortunately, age appears to be the demarcation here. For those in the older group, youth has already won the battle. I've been keeping a list of places where its is misused: newspapers, magazines, op-eds in major publications and, more recently, wall texts in museums. A few weeks ago I encountered the error in a book title: *St. Simons: A. Summary of It's History*, by R. Edwin and Mary A. Green. My list is getting longer and longer.

Does it even matter that the apostrophe is going the way of the stop sign and the directional signal in our society? Does punctuation count any longer? Are my complaints the ramblings of an old goat who's taught English for too many years?

What's the big deal, anyway? Who cares whether it's its or it's? Editors don't seem to know when the apostrophe's necessary. (One of them confessed to me that people have always been confused about the apostrophe—better just get rid of it.) My university undergraduates are

clearly befuddled by the correct usage. Too many graduate applications—
especially those of students aspiring to be creative writers—provide no
clue that the writer understands when an apostrophe is required. Even
some of my colleagues are confused by this ugglesome contraction.

How can a three-letter word be so disarming, so capable of separating
the men from the boys? Or the women from the girls? When in doubt use
it both ways, as in a recent advertisement hyping improved SAT, GRE,
and LSAT scores: "Kaplan locations all over the U.S. are offering full-
length exams just like the actual tests. It's a great way to test your skills
and get a practice score without the risk of your score being reported to
schools. And now, for a limited time only, its absolutely free!"

And now, students, which one of the above spellings of the I word is   5
correct: (a) the first, (b) the second, (c) both, or (d) neither? Any wonder
why Educational Testing Services had to add 100 points to the revised
SAT exams?

It's been my recent experience that the apostrophe hasn't actually
exited common usage; it's simply migrated somewhere later in the sentence. Hence, "Shes lost her marble's" has become the preferred use of
this irritating snippet of punctuation in current American writing. "Hes
not lost his hat; hes lost his brains'." "Theres gold in them there hill's." Or
"It was the best of times' and the worst of time's." The latter, of course, is
from Charles Dickens *A Tale of Two Cities'*. Or is it Charle's Dickens?

Where will this end? Virtual apostrophe's? At times I wonder if all
those missing apostrophes are floating somewhere in outer space. Don't
they have to be somewhere, if—as some philosophers tell us—nothing is
ever lost? Lately, I've seen the dirty three-letter word even punctuated as
its'. What's next?

I'ts? 'Its?

How complicated can this be? How difficult is it to teach a sixth grader
how to punctuate correctly?

Heaven knows I've tried to figure it out, agonized about it for years. I   10
remember being dismayed nearly 20 years ago when I was walking around
the neighborhood and discovered an enormous stack of books that someone had put out on the curb, free for the taking. Most of the titles were for-
gettable; hence the reason they'd been left for scavengers or the next trash
pickup. However, mixed among the flotsam and jetsam was a brand-new
hardback collegiate dictionary. How could this be, I asked myself? Could
someone have too many dictionaries? I think the ideal would be one in
every room.

Someone was sending me a signal. If words are unimportant, punctuation is something even more lowly. Why worry about such quodlibets?
When was the last time anyone even noticed? Certainly, no one at Touch-
stone Books caught the errors in a recent ad for *Failing at Fairness: How
Our Schools Cheat Girls*, by Myra and David Sadker. A testimonial for the
book reads as follows: "Reader's will be stunned at the overwhelming

evidence of sexism the author's provide." You bet, and the blurb writers' lack of grammatical correctness.

If editors at publishing houses can't catch these errors, who can? Errors common to advertising copy have already spread into the books themselves. I dread walking into a bookstore a decade from now and encountering the covers of classics edited by a new generation of apostrophe-challenged editors: *Father's and Sons', The Brothers' Karamazov, The Adventure's of Huckleberry Finn, The Postman Alway's Ring's Twice, A Mid-summers' Night Dream.* (Who's wood's these are I think I know . . .)

The apostrophe is dead because reading is dead. Notice that I didn't say "The apostrophe's dead because reading's dead." That's far too complex an alteration. When in doubt simply write out the full sentence, carefully avoiding all possessives and contradictions. Soon, no one will be certain about grammatical usage anyway. Computers will come without an apostrophe key. Why bother about errors on the Internet? E-mail messages are often so badly written they make no sense. Fortunately, they get erased almost immediately. Everything pass'es too quickly.

Last week I went to a lamp store to purchase two new floor lamps for our living room: five rooms of lamps and hundreds of styles—except for one minor problem. Not one lamp was designed for reading. Virtually all the lamps illuminated the ceiling; all were designed for television addicts, not readers. So how is one supposed to read *TV Guide*? The place was so dark (was I expected to hold my book up to the ceiling?) I could hardly find my way out. And speaking of TV, what's the plural: TVs or TV's?

Time to stop this grumbling. Thing's fall apart. If I start making a list 15 only of the times the apostrophe is used properly, I won't even have to worry about it. I can already hear you say, "Your kidding."

THINKING CRITICALLY ABOUT THE READING

1. Is Larson exaggerating about the misuse of the apostrophe? Do you agree that problems with proper punctuation in general are widespread?

2. To what does Larson attribute the so-called death of the apostrophe? What evidence does he have for the cause he identifies? Is this evidence convincing? Explain.

3. Larson asks in paragraph 3 about the misuse of the apostrophe, "What's the big deal, anyway? Who cares whether it's *its* or *it's*?" How does Larson answer this question? How would you answer it?

4. In paragraph 14 Larson talks about his experience in attempting to buy two reading lamps. Do you agree with him that the experience is revealing with respect to misuse of the apostrophe? Why or why not?

5. What is Larson's attitude toward the apostrophe problem? Is he resigned? Angry? Amused? Hopeful? How do you know? (Glossary: *Tone*)

6. What solutions, if any, does Larson offer for stemming the tide of the apostrophe problem? What solutions can you offer?

LANGUAGE IN ACTION

Correct any of the following sentences for apostrophe use, if necessary:
  a. Its not a matter of whether or not the residents in the area need the cities help.
  b. They're planning to build a new school but it needs to be approved by the districts voters.
  c. What's planned is a new elementary school in the old ones' location.
  d. Wait'll they see how hard it is to get the votes they'll need.
  e. The school system's not hearing voters wishes; it's simply not open to suggestions.

WRITING SUGGESTIONS

1. Larson has focused on problems with the proper use of apostrophes. Write an essay modeled on Larson's in which you look at the way commas are used today in both published and unpublished writing. You might want to begin by examining your own work and the work of others in your writing class before moving on to published samples. Does the use of the comma seem to exhibit the same lapses in correctness that Larson finds in the use of the apostrophe? If so, do these lapses occur as often or less often? If they occur often, why do you think they do? Larson contends that errors in the use of the apostrophe are attributable to a decline in reading; might the same be true of errors in the use of commas?

2. Is punctuation merely a matter of appearances—of following the rules so you don't look dumb? Or might there be other, deeper reasons that proper punctuation use is important? Write an essay in which you discuss the importance of the use of punctuation. You may want to start this assignment by reading appropriate chapters in Lynne Truss's *Eats, Shoots, & Leaves: The Zero Tolerance Approach to Punctuation* (2003), a popular and entertaining book on the subject.

Like I Said, Don't Worry

PATRICIA T. O'CONNER

A former *New York Times Book Review* editor, Patricia T. O'Conner has reviewed for the *Book Review* and written "On Language" guest columns for William Safire in the *New York Times Magazine*. She has also conducted a grammar course for *Times* employees. In her two books, *Woe Is I: The Grammarphobe's Guide to Better English in Plain English* (1996) and *Words Fail Me: What Everyone Who Writes Should Know about Writing* (1999), O'Conner strives to demystify the realms of grammar, usage, and writing.

In the following article, which first appeared in *Newsweek* on December 9, 1996, O'Conner suggests that we lighten up about grammar and usage because we are all prone to occasional lapses. She believes that rather than being obsessed by error, we should nurture our "love [of] talking about words, about language." O'Conner's essay is the second of a pair of essays on the same subject. If you haven't already done so, you may want to read Charles R. Larson's "Its Academic, or Is It?" (pp. 139–141).

WRITING TO DISCOVER: *Does grammar cause you anxiety? If so, why do you suppose that is? Were you made anxious by your teachers or others who read what you have written? Or is your anxiety caused by something more abstract — say, the unusual terms that grammarians use, or the number of rules that you need to memorize in order to speak and write correctly? Whatever the cause, if you do have grammar anxiety, what do you think you might do to help the situation? If, on the other hand, you think you speak and write grammatically and have no fear of grammar, what has given you confidence?*

Now that I'm a grammar maven, everyone's afraid to talk to me. Well, not everyone. Since my grammar book was published [in 1996], my friends have discovered a new sport: gotcha! The object is to correct my speech, to catch me in the occasional "between you and I" (OK, I admit it). The winner gets to interrupt with a satisfied "aha!"

But people I meet for the first time often confess that speaking with an "authority" on language gives them the willies. Grammar, they say apologetically, was not their best subject. And they still don't get it: the subjunctives, the dependent clauses, the coordinating conjunctions. So their English is bound to be flawed, they warn, and I should make allowances. They relax when I tell them that I'm not perfect either, and that I don't use technical jargon when I write about grammar. You don't have to scare readers off with terms like *gerund* and *participle* to explain why an *-ing* word like *bowling* can play so many different roles in a sentence. With the intimidating terminology out of the way, most people express a lively, even passionate, interest in English and how it works. As a reader recently told me, "I don't need to know all the parts of a car to be a good driver."

Grammarians and hairsplitting wannabes have always loved to argue over the fine points of language. What surprises me these days is the number of grammatically insecure people who are discussing English with just as much fervor, though without the pedantry. As a guest author on radio call-in shows and online chats, I've found that the chance to air a linguistic grievance or pose a question in a nonjudgmental atmosphere often proves irresistible. "Is *irregardless* OK?" a caller hesitantly asks. "I hear it so much these days." (No.) Or, "Is *sprang* a word?" (Yes.) "Media *is* or media *are*?" (*Are*, for the time being.) I saw an ad with the word *alright*, spelled A-L-R-I-G-H-T. It is correct? (No, it's not all right.) "If I *was*? Or if I *were*'?" (It depends.) I love it when people who say they hated grammar in school get all worked up over *like* versus *as*, or *convince* versus *persuade*, or *who* versus *whom*. Obviously it wasn't grammar per se that once turned them off. It was the needless pedagoguery — the tyranny of the pluperfects, the intransitives, and all the rest. The truth is that people love talking about words, about language. After years as an editor at *The New York Times Book Review*, I can vouch that almost everybody gets something wrong now and then — a dangler here, a spelling problem there, a runaway sentence, beastly punctuation. Those who regularly screw up would like to do better, and even the whizzes admit they'd like to get rid of a weakness or two.

So, is grammar back? Has good English become . . . cool?

Before you laugh, download this. Thanks to the computer, Americans   5
are communicating with one another at a rate undreamed of a generation ago—and *in writing*. People who seldom wrote more than a memo or a shopping list are producing blizzards of words. Teenagers who once might have spent the evening on the phone are hunched over their computers, gossiping by e-mail and meeting in chat rooms. Wired college students are conferring with professors, carrying on romances, and writing home for money, all from computer terminals in their dorm rooms. Many executives who once depended on secretaries to "put it in English" are now clicking on REPLY and winging it.

The downside of all this techno-wizardry is that our grammar isn't quite up to the mark. We're writing more, and worse, than ever before. (If you don't believe this, check out a chat room or an electronic bulletin board. It's not a pretty sight.) The ease and immediacy of electronic communication are forcing the computer-literate to think about their grammar for the first time in years, if ever. It's ironic that this back-to-basics message should come from cyberspace. Or is it? Amid the din of the information revolution, bombarded on all sides by technological wonders, we can hardly be blamed for finding in grammar one small sign of order amid the chaos.

There is evidence of this return to order elsewhere in our society, too. Perhaps the "family values" mantra, for better or worse, is nothing more than a call for order in a culture that seems to have lost its moral bearings. At any rate, laissez-faire grammar bashers who used to regard good English as an impediment to spontaneity and creativity are seeing the light—and it's not spelled L-I-T-E.

But what about those of us whose "lex" education is a dim memory? The very word *grammar* evokes a visceral response—usually fear. If it makes your hair stand on end, you're part of a proud tradition. The earliest grammarians, bless their shriveled hearts, did English a disservice by appealing more to our feelings of inferiority than to our natural love of words. They could never quite forgive our mongrel tongue for not being Latin, but felt that English could redeem itself somewhat by conforming to the rules of Latin grammar. The word *grammar*, in fact, originally meant "the study of Latin." All this may help explain a couple of silly no-nos from the past, discredited by the most respected twentieth-century grammarians: those inflexible rules against splitting an infinitive and ending a sentence with a preposition.

Surely no school subject has been more detested and reviled by its victims than grammar. Some people would rather have a root canal than define the uninflected root of a word. At the same time, the ability to use language well appeals to our need to be understood, to participate, to be one of the tribe. It's no wonder so many of the people I meet confess to being grammatically inadequate, yet fascinated by words.

My message to these people, delivered from the lofty heights of my newly acquired mavenhood, is this: stop beating up on yourselves. It's only a grammatical error, not a drive-by shooting. Words are wonderful, but they're not sacred. And between you and I (aha!), nobody's perfect.
10

THINKING CRITICALLY ABOUT THE READING

1. O'Conner thinks we should relax about grammar. Does she believe that we can therefore ignore the rules of grammar? Explain.

2. What does O'Conner believe gets lost in the overly strict concern for the rules of grammar?

3. What is ironic, according to O'Conner, about the fact that we are writing more than ever before in history? (Glossary: *Irony*)

4. According to O'Conner, what happens to grammar when people are in a non-judgmental environment?

5. O'Conner writes in paragraph 6, "Amid the din of the information revolution, bombarded on all sides by technological wonders, we can hardly be blamed for finding in grammar one small sign of order amid chaos." What does she mean?

6. What is O'Conner's overall tone in this essay? (Glossary: *Tone*) In your opinion, how does her tone fit her subject and her attitude toward grammar?

7. What humor does O'Conner inject into her last sentence? To what does her "aha!" link in the essay?

LANGUAGE IN ACTION

How would you correct the usage errors in each of the following sentences?

Voting data was collected after the election.

The ending of the movie was climatic.

Sophia's lyrics complimented his music.

We could of gone to the football game but it was too cold.

A huge amount of students were gathered in the courtyard.

Liz's teacher made an illusion to one of Shakespeare's sonnets.

Jordan liked to reverse the old proverb by saying "It's not the principal but the money."

The consensus of opinion was that the exam was very easy.

Whose to say if it's the right answer.

Gasoline prices are very expensive now.

WRITING SUGGESTIONS

1. Compare and contrast O'Conner's essay with the one written by Charles R. Larson on pages 139–141. In what do the two authors agree and disagree? Is there more to be said on the topic of grammar? Which author's philosophy do you prefer, and why?

2. O'Conner writes: "The truth is that people love talking about words, about language" (3). Write an essay in which you explore this topic. Begin by conducting an informal study among your friends and relatives. When you ask them directly whether they "love language," what do they say? In what ways, if any, do they exhibit a love of language? Do they enjoy reading? Do they like to write anything? If so, what do they write? Do they prefer talking to writing or reading? What, if anything, fascinates them about language—vocabulary, pronunciation, grammar? Something else?

3

Politics, Propaganda, and Doublespeak

Political language is powerful; it is persuasive. At its best political language inspires people and challenges them to make a difference, offering the hope that in working together, we can create a better world. Over forty years ago President John F. Kennedy energized a nation by exhorting its citizens to "ask not what your country can do for you—ask what you can do for your country." And we have heard stories of how, with powerful words, Franklin D. Roosevelt and Winston Churchill rallied their nations to defeat Nazi Germany during World War II and how Mahatma Gandhi, Martin Luther King Jr., and Nelson Mandela championed nonviolence in leading the fight against oppression and racism in India, America, and South Africa.

But political language can be abused. At its worst, political language can be deliberately manipulated to mislead, deceive, or cover up. In the wake of the war in Vietnam, the Watergate scandal and the subsequent resignation of President Nixon, the Iran-Contra affair, the Clinton-Lewinsky scandal, and the wars in Iraq and Afghanistan, Americans have grown cynical about their political leaders' promises and programs. As presidential campaigns seem to get started earlier and earlier, we are fed a daily diet of political language. Political speech saturates the American media. In daily newspapers and on the evening news we listen to fiery sound bites and seemingly spontaneous one-liners—presented as though they contained an entire argument or philosophy. Our politicians are savvy about the time constraints in news media, and their speechwriters make sure that long speeches have at least a few headline-grabbing quotes that might win them wide, albeit brief, coverage. But in the end, we are left wondering what we can believe and who we can trust.

In the opening section of this chapter, "Language That Manipulates," we begin with four essays to help you think critically about the political language that you hear every day so that you can function as a responsible citizen. In the first essay, "Propaganda: How Not to Be Bamboozled," Donna Woolfolk Cross takes the mystery out of the oft-misunderstood word *propaganda* as she identifies and defines thirteen of the rhetorical devices the propagandist uses to manipulate language for political purposes. Her examples and advice, in turn, will help you to detect these nasty "tricks" and not to be misled by the silver tongues of politicians. George Orwell, in his classic essay "Politics and the English Language," picks up where Cross leaves off. Orwell knows that language is power, and he argues for a clear, simplified English that everyone can understand. He takes politicians to task for language that he claims is "designed to make lies sound truthful and murder respectable, and to give an appearance of solidity to pure wind." In "The World of Doublespeak," political watchdog William Lutz examines the language of government and corporate bureaucrats, "language which pretends to communicate but doesn't." His examples illustrate how language can be used to deliberately "mislead, distort, deceive, inflate, circumvent, obfuscate." Finally, Sissela Bok, in "The Burden of Deceit in Public Life," examines the presence of deceit, lying, and secrecy in our communities and nation, assesses the impact that this behavior has on public life, and calls for reasoned, civil, and responsible public debate of the issue. She is quick to caution that "when the definitions and distinctions are blurred together in the public debate, it becomes easier to short-circuit reflection about the underlying moral questions regarding when deceit might be considered excusable or even justifiable."

In the second section of this chapter, "Making a Difference: Using Language Responsibly," we include six selections from very different eras. Despite the widely divergent contexts and issues they address, these writers rely on many of the same rhetorical techniques and strategies to give depth and resonance to their messages. Martin Luther King Jr.'s "I Have a Dream" speech uses brilliant, rich images and compelling logic to insist on equality for all Americans. Delivered on the steps of the Lincoln Memorial in 1963 during the height of the civil rights movement, this speech is considered by many to be one of the greatest speeches of the last century. In a remarkable speech delivered in the years leading up to the Civil War, the illiterate preacher and abolitionist Sojourner Truth shows great rhetorical skill in fighting oppression on two fronts, demanding the emancipation of African Americans and rights for women. Expressing equal passion for a different cause, Al Gore delivered a call for action to confront the inconvenient truth of climate change in "Time to Make Peace with the Planet," his acceptance speech for the 2007 Nobel Prize for Peace. In the speech, Gore, asks the global community to act responsibly even though "[t]he way ahead is difficult. The outer boundary of what we currently believe is feasible is still far short of what we actually must do." When she won the Nobel Prize for Literature in 1993, novelist Toni Morrison used the platform to deliver "When Language Dies," a lecture in which she reminds us all reminds us of the centrality of language to our lives and of our responsibility to use language creatively and well. This section of the chapter concludes with two readings that use similarly sharp satire to make very different arguments. In "A Modest Proposal," Jonathan Swift uses his wit to attack the wealthy English landlords who were, in his eyes, responsible for the widespread homelessness among sharecroppers in Ireland. In this classic essay, Swift's narrator uses a logical argument to propose infanticide and cannibalism as the solution to Ireland's problem. Finally, in "My Amendment," George Saunders takes a satiric look at the current debate in the United States over same-sex unions. His proposal for a "supplementary" constitutional amendment to ban "samish-sex marriage" is as outrageous—and as trenchant—as Swift's for dealing with drought and famine in Ireland.

Propaganda: How Not to Be Bamboozled

DONNA WOOLFOLK CROSS

Donna Woolfolk Cross graduated from the University of Pennsylvania in 1969 and went on to receive her M.A. from the University of California, Los Angeles. A professor of English at Onondaga Community College in Syracuse, New York, Cross has written extensively about language that manipulates, including the books *Mediaspeak: How Television Makes Up Your Mind* (1981) and *Word Abuse: How the Words We Use Use Us* (1979), which won an award from the National Council of Teachers of English. Her early work as a writer of advertising copy influences her teaching and writing. In an interview she remarked, "I was horrified to discover that first-year college students were completely unaware of—and, therefore, unable to defend themselves against—the most obvious ploys of admen and politicians. . . . We tend to think of language as something we use; we are much less often aware of the way we are used by language. The only defense is to become wise to the ways of words."

Although most people are against propaganda in principle, few know exactly what it is and how it works. In the following essay, which first appeared in *Speaking of Words: A Language Reader* (1977), Cross takes the mystery out of propaganda. She starts by providing a definition of it, and then she classifies the tricks of the propagandist into thirteen major categories. Cross's essay is chock-full of useful advice on how not to be manipulated by propaganda.

WRITING TO DISCOVER: *What do you think of when you hear the word* propaganda? *What kinds of people, organizations, or issues do you associate with it? Write about why you think people use propaganda.*

Propaganda. If an opinion poll were taken tomorrow, we can be sure that nearly everyone would be against it because it *sounds* so bad. When we say, "Oh, that's just propaganda," it means, to most people, "That's a pack of lies." But really, propaganda is simply a means of persuasion and so it can be put to work for good causes as well as bad—to persuade people to give to charity, for example, or to love their neighbors, or to stop polluting the environment.

For good or evil, propaganda pervades our daily lives, helping to shape our attitudes on a thousand subjects. Propaganda probably determines the brand of toothpaste you use, the movies you see, the candidates you elect when you get to the polls. Propaganda works by tricking us, by

momentarily distracting the eye while the rabbit pops out from beneath
the cloth. Propaganda works best with an uncritical audience. Joseph
Goebbels, propaganda minister in Nazi Germany, once defined his work
as "the conquest of the masses." The masses would not have been conquered, however, if they had known how to challenge and to question,
how to make distinctions between propaganda and reasonable argument.

People are bamboozled mainly because they don't recognize propaganda when they see it. They need to be informed about the various
devices that can be used to mislead and deceive—about the propagandist's overflowing bag of tricks. The following, then, are some common
pitfalls for the unwary.

1. NAME-CALLING

As its title suggests, this device consists of labeling people or ideas
with words of bad connotation, literally, "calling them names." Here the
propagandist tries to arouse our contempt so we will dismiss the "bad
name" person or idea without examining its merits.

Bad names have played a tremendously important role in the history of   5
the world. They have ruined reputations and ended lives, sent people to prison
and to war, and just generally made us mad at each other for centuries.

Name-calling can be used against policies, practices, beliefs and ideals,
as well as against individuals, groups, races, nations. Name-calling is at work
when we hear a candidate for office described as a "foolish idealist" or a
"two-faced liar" or when an incumbent's policies are denounced as "reck-
less," "reactionary," or just plain "stupid." Some of the most effective names
a public figure can be called are ones that may not denote anything specific:
"Congresswoman Jane Doe is a *bleeding heart!*" (Did she vote for funds to
help paraplegics?) or "The senator is a *tool of Washington!*" (Did he happen to agree with the president?) Senator Yakalot uses name-calling when
he denounces his opponent's "radical policies" and calls them (and him)
"socialist," "pinko," and part of a "heartless plot." He also uses it when he
calls cars "puddle-jumpers," "can openers," and "motorized baby buggies."

The point here is that when the propagandist uses name-calling, he
doesn't want us to think—merely to react, blindly, unquestioningly. So
the best defense against being taken in by name-calling is to stop and ask,
"Forgetting the bad name attached to it, what are the merits of the idea
itself? What does this name really mean, anyway?"

2. GLITTERING GENERALITIES

Glittering generalities are really name-calling in reverse. Name-calling
uses words with bad connotations; glittering generalities are words with
good connotations—"virtue words," as the Institute for Propaganda

Analysis has called them. The Institute explains that while name-calling tries to get us to *reject* and *condemn* someone or something without examining the evidence, glittering generalities try to get us to *accept* and *agree* without examining the evidence.

We believe in, fight for, live by "virtue words" which we feel deeply about: "justice," "motherhood," "the American way," "our Constitutional rights," "our Christian heritage." These sound good, but when we examine them closely, they turn out to have no specific, definable meaning. They just make us feel good. Senator Yakalot uses glittering generalities when he says, "I stand for all that is good in America, for our American way and our American birthright." But what exactly *is* "good for America"? How can we define our "American birthright"? Just what parts of the American society and culture does "our American way" refer to?

We often make the mistake of assuming we are personally unaffected   10
by glittering generalities. The next time you find yourself assuming that, listen to a political candidate's speech on TV and see how often the use of glittering generalities elicits cheers and applause. That's the danger of propaganda; it *works*. Once again, our defense against it is to ask questions: Forgetting the virtue words attached to it, what are the merits of the idea itself? What does "Americanism" (or "freedom" or "truth") really *mean* here? ...

Both name-calling and glittering generalities work by stirring our emotions in the hope that this will cloud our thinking. Another approach that propaganda uses is to create a distraction, a "red herring," that will make people forget or ignore the real issues. There are several different kinds of "red herrings" that can be used to distract attention.

3. PLAIN-FOLKS APPEAL

"Plain folks" is the device by which a speaker tries to win our confidence and support by appearing to be a person like ourselves—"just one of the plain folks." The plain-folks appeal is at work when candidates go around shaking hands with factory workers, kissing babies in supermarkets, and sampling pasta with Italians, fried chicken with Southerners, bagels and blintzes with Jews. "Now I'm a businessman like yourselves" is a plain-folks appeal, as is "I've been a farm boy all my life." Senator Yakalot tries the plain-folks appeal when he says, "I'm just a small-town boy like you fine people." The use of such expressions once prompted Lyndon Johnson to quip, "Whenever I hear someone say, 'I'm just an old country lawyer,' the first thing I reach for is my wallet to make sure it's still there."

The irrelevancy of the plain-folks appeal is obvious: even if the man *is* "one of us" (which may not be true at all), that doesn't mean that his ideas and programs are sound—or even that he honestly has our best interests at heart. As with glittering generalities, the danger here is that we may mistakenly assume we are immune to this appeal. But propagandists wouldn't use it unless it had been proved to work. You can protect yourself by asking, "Aside from his 'nice guy next door' image, what does this man stand for? Are his ideas and his past record really supportive of my best interests?"

4. *ARGUMENTUM AD POPULUM* (STROKING)

Argumentum ad populum means "argument to the people" or "telling the people what they want to hear." The colloquial term from the Watergate era is "stroking," which conjures up pictures of small animals or children being stroked or soothed with compliments until they come to like the person doing the complimenting—and, by extension, his or her ideas.

We all like to hear nice things about ourselves and the group we   15
belong to—we like to be liked—so it stands to reason that we will respond warmly to a person who tells us we are "hard-working taxpayers" or "the most generous, free-spirited nation in the world." Politicians tell farmers they are the "backbone of the American economy" and college students that they are the "leaders and policy makers of tomorrow." Commercial advertisers use stroking more insidiously by asking a question which invites a flattering answer: "What kind of a man reads *Playboy?*" (Does he really drive a Porsche and own $10,000 worth of sound equipment?) Senator Yakalot is stroking his audience when he calls them the "decent law-abiding citizens that are the great pulsing heart and the life blood of this, our beloved country," and when he repeatedly refers to them as "you fine people," "you wonderful folks."

Obviously, the intent here is to sidetrack us from thinking critically about the man and his ideas. Our own good qualities have nothing to do with the issue at hand. Ask yourself, "Apart from the nice things he has to say about me (and my church, my nation, my ethnic group, my neighbors), what does the candidate stand for? Are his or her ideas in my best interests?"

5. *ARGUMENTUM AD HOMINEM*

Argumentum ad hominem means "argument to the man" and that's exactly what it is. When a propagandist uses *argumentum ad hominem*, he wants to distract our attention from the issue under consideration with personal attacks on the people involved. For example, when Lincoln issued the Emancipation Proclamation, some people responded by calling him the "baboon." But Lincoln's long arms and awkward carriage had nothing to do with the merits of the Proclamation or the question of whether or not slavery should be abolished.

Today *argumentum ad hominem* is still widely used and very effective. You may or may not support the Equal Rights Amendment, but you should be sure your judgment is based on the merits of the idea itself, and not the result of someone's denunciation of the people who support the ERA as "fanatics" or "lesbians" or "frustrated old maids." Senator Yakalot is using *argumentum ad hominem* when he dismisses the idea of using smaller automobiles with a reference to the personal appearance of one of its supporters, Congresswoman Doris Schlepp. Refuse to be waylaid by *argumentum ad hominem* and ask, "Do the personal qualities of the person being discussed have anything to do with the issue at hand? Leaving him or her aside, how good is the idea itself?"

6. TRANSFER (GUILT OR GLORY BY ASSOCIATION)

In *argumentum ad hominem*, an attempt is made to associate negative aspects of a person's character or personal appearance with an issue or idea he supports. The transfer device uses this same process of association to make us accept or condemn a given person or idea.

A better name for the transfer device is guilt (or glory) by association.   20 In glory by association, the propagandist tries to transfer the positive feelings of something we love and respect to the group or idea he wants us to accept. "This bill for a new dam is in the best tradition of this country, the land of Lincoln, Jefferson, and Washington," is glory by association at work. Lincoln, Jefferson, and Washington were great leaders that most of us revere and respect, but they have no logical connection to the proposal under consideration—the bill to build a new dam. Senator Yakalot uses glory by association when he says full-sized cars "have always been as American as Mom's apple pie or a Sunday drive in the country."

The process works equally well in reverse, when guilt by association is used to transfer our dislike or disapproval of one idea or group to some other idea or group that the propagandist wants us to reject and condemn. "John Doe says we need to make some changes in the way our government operates; well, that's exactly what the Ku Klux Klan has said, so there's a meeting of great minds!" That's guilt by association for you; there's no logical connection between John Doe and the Ku Klux Klan apart from the one the propagandist is trying to create in our minds. He wants to distract our attention from John Doe and get us thinking (and worrying) about the Ku Klux Klan and its politics of violence. (Of course, there are sometimes legitimate associations between the two things; if John Doe had been a *member* of the Ku Klux Klan, it would be reasonable and fair to draw a connection between the man and his group.) Senator Yakalot tries to trick his audience with guilt by association when he remarks that "the words 'community' and 'communism' look an awful lot alike!" He does it again when he mentions that Mr. Stu Pott "sports a Fidel Castro beard."

How can we learn to spot the transfer device and distinguish between fair and unfair associations? We can teach ourselves to *suspend judgment* until we have answered these questions: "Is there any legitimate connection between the idea under discussion and the thing it is associated with? Leaving the transfer device out of the picture, what are the merits of the idea by itself?"

7. BANDWAGON

Ever hear of the small, ratlike animal called the lemming? Lemmings are arctic rodents with a very odd habit: periodically, for reasons no one entirely knows, they mass together in a large herd and commit suicide by rushing into deep water and drowning themselves. They all run in together, blindly, and not one of them ever seems to stop and ask, "*Why* am I doing this? Is this really what I want to do?" and thus save itself from destruction. Obviously, lemmings are driven to perform their strange mass suicide rites by common instinct. People choose to "follow the herd" for more complex reasons, yet we are still all too often the unwitting victims of the bandwagon appeal.

Essentially, the bandwagon urges us to support an action or an opinion because it is popular—because "everyone else is doing it." This call to "get on the bandwagon" appeals to the strong desire in most of us to be one of the crowd, not to be left out or alone. Advertising makes extensive use of the bandwagon appeal ("join the Pepsi people"), but so do politicians ("Let us join together in this great cause"). Senator Yakalot uses the bandwagon appeal when he says that "More and more citizens are rallying to my cause every day," and asks his audience to "join them—and me—in our fight for America."

One of the ways we can see the bandwagon appeal at work is in the   25
overwhelming success of various fashions and trends which capture the interest (and the money) of thousands of people for a short time, then disappear suddenly and completely. For a year or two in the fifties, every child in North America wanted a coonskin cap so they could be like Davy Crockett; no one wanted to be left out. After that there was the hula-hoop craze that helped to dislocate the hips of thousands of Americans. [In the 1970s], what made millions of people rush out to buy their very own "pet rocks"?

The problem here is obvious: just because everyone's doing it doesn't mean that *we* should too. Group approval does not prove that something is true or is worth doing. Large numbers of people have supported actions we now condemn. [Within the last century], Hitler and Mussolini rose to absolute and catastrophically repressive rule in two of the most sophisticated and cultured countries of Europe. When they came into power they were welled up by massive popular support from millions of people who didn't want to be "left out" at a great historical moment.

Once the mass begins to move—on the bandwagon—it becomes harder and harder to perceive the leader *riding* the bandwagon. So don't be a lemming, rushing blindly on to destruction because "everyone else is doing it." Stop and ask, "Where is this bandwagon headed? Never mind about everybody else, is this what is best for *me*?" . . .

As we have seen, propaganda can appeal to us by arousing our emotions or distracting our attention from the real issues at hand. But there's a third way that propaganda can be put to work against us—by the use of faulty logic. This approach is really more insidious than the other two because it gives the appearance of reasonable, fair argument. It is only when we look more closely that the holes in the logical fiber show up. The following are some of the devices that make use of faulty logic to distort and mislead.

8. FAULTY CAUSE AND EFFECT

As the name suggests, this device sets up a cause-and-effect relationship that may not be true. The Latin name for this logical fallacy is *post hoc ergo propter hoc,* which means "after this, therefore because of this." But just because one thing happened after another doesn't mean that one *caused* the other.

An example of false cause-and-effect reasoning is offered by the story 30 (probably invented) of the woman aboard the ship *Titanic.* She woke up from a nap and, feeling seasick, looked around for a call button to summon the steward to bring her some medication. She finally located a small button on one of the walls of her cabin and pushed it. A split second later, the *Titanic* grazed an iceberg in the terrible crash that was to send the entire ship to its destruction. The woman screamed and said, "Oh, God, what have I done? What have I done?" The humor of that anecdote comes from the absurdity of the woman's assumption that pushing the small red button resulted in the destruction of a ship weighing several hundred tons: "It happened after I pushed it, therefore it must be *because* I pushed it"—*post hoc ergo propter hoc* reasoning. There is, of course, no cause-and-effect relationship there.

The false cause-and-effect fallacy is used very often by political candidates. "After I came to office, the rate of inflation dropped to 6 percent." But did the person do anything to cause the lower rate of inflation or was it the result of other conditions? Would the rate of inflation have dropped anyway, even if he hadn't come to office? Senator Yakalot uses false cause and effect when he says "our forefathers who made this country great never had free hot meal handouts! And look what they did for our country!" He does it again when he concludes that "driving full-sized cars means a better car safety record on our American roads today."

False cause-and-effect reasoning is terribly persuasive because it seems so logical. Its appeal is apparently to experience. We swallowed X product—and the headache went away. We elected Y official and unemployment went down. Many people think, "There *must* be a connection." But causality is an immensely complex phenomenon; you need a good deal of evidence to prove that an event that follows another in time was "therefore" caused by the first event.

Don't be taken in by false cause and effect; be sure to ask, "Is there enough evidence to prove that this cause led to that effect? Could there have been any *other* causes?"

9. FALSE ANALOGY

An analogy is a comparison between two ideas, events, or things. But comparisons can be fairly made only when the things being compared are alike in significant ways. When they are not, false analogy is the result.

A famous example of this is the old proverb "Don't change horses in   35
the middle of a stream," often used as an analogy to convince voters not to change administrations in the middle of a war or other crisis. But the analogy is misleading because there are so many differences between the things compared. In what ways is a war or political crisis like a stream? Is the president or head of state really very much like a horse? And is a nation of millions of people comparable to a man trying to get across a stream? Analogy is false and unfair when it compares two things that have little in common and assumes that they are identical. Senator Yakalot tries to hoodwink his listeners with false analogy when he says, "Trying to take Americans out of the kind of cars they love is as undemocratic as trying to deprive them of the right to vote."

Of course, analogies can be drawn that are reasonable and fair. It would be reasonable, for example, to compare the results of busing in one small Southern city with the possible results in another, *if* the towns have the same kind of history, population, and school policy. We can decide for ourselves whether an analogy is false or fair by asking, "Are the things being compared truly alike in significant ways? Do the differences between them affect the comparison?"

10. BEGGING THE QUESTION

Actually, the name of this device is rather misleading, because it does not appear in the form of a question. Begging the question occurs when, in discussing a questionable or debatable point, a person assumes as already established the very point that he is trying to prove. For example, "No thinking citizen could approve such a completely unacceptable policy as this one." But isn't the question of whether or not the policy *is* acceptable the very point to be established? Senator Yakalot begs the question when he announces that his opponent's plan won't work "because it is unworkable."

We can protect ourselves against this kind of faulty logic by asking, "What is assumed in this statement? Is the assumption reasonable, or does it need more proof?"

11. THE TWO-EXTREMES FALLACY (FALSE DILEMMA)

Linguists have long noted that the English language tends to view reality in sets of two extremes or polar opposites. In English, things are either black or white, tall or short, up or down, front or back, left or right, good or bad, guilty or not guilty. We can ask for a "straightforward yes-or-no answer" to a question, the understanding being that we will not accept or consider anything in between. In fact, reality cannot always be dissected along such strict lines. There may be (usually are) *more* than just two possibilities or extremes to consider. We are often told to "listen to both sides of the argument." But who's to say that every argument has only two sides? Can't there be a third—even a fourth or fifth—point of view?

The two-extremes fallacy is at work in this statement by Lenin, the   40 great Marxist leader: "You cannot eliminate *one* basic assumption, one substantial part of this philosophy of Marxism (it is as if it were a block of steel), without abandoning truth, without falling into the arms of bourgeois-reactionary falsehood." In other words, if we don't agree 100 percent with every premise of Marxism, we must be placed at the opposite end of the political-economic spectrum—for Lenin, "bourgeois-reactionary falsehood." If we are not entirely *with* him, we must be against him; those are the only two possibilities open to us. Of course, this is a logical fallacy; in real life there are any number of political positions one can maintain *between* the two extremes of Marxism and capitalism. Senator Yakalot uses the two-extremes fallacy in the same way as Lenin when he tells his audience that "in this world a man's either for private enterprise or he's for socialism."

One of the most famous examples of the two-extremes fallacy in recent history is the slogan, "America: Love it or leave it," with its implicit suggestion that we either accept everything just as it is in America today without complaint—or get out. Again, it should be obvious that there is a whole range of action and belief between those two extremes.

Don't be duped; stop and ask, "Are those really the only two options I can choose from? Are there other alternatives not mentioned that deserve consideration?"

12. CARD STACKING

Some questions are so multifaceted and complex that no one can make an intelligent decision about them without considering a wide variety of evidence. One selection of facts could make us feel one way and another selection could make us feel just the opposite. Card stacking is a device of propaganda which selects only the facts that support the propagandist's point of view, and ignores all the others. For example, a candidate could be made to look like a legislative dynamo if you say, "Representative McNerd introduced more new bills than any other member of the Congress," and neglect to mention that most of them were so preposterous that they were laughed off the floor.

Senator Yakalot engages in card stacking when he talks about the proposal to use smaller cars. He talks only about jobs without mentioning the cost to the taxpayers or the very real—though still denied—threat of depletion of resources. He says he wants to help his countrymen keep their jobs, but doesn't mention that the corporations that offer the jobs will also make large profits. He praises the "American chrome industry," overlooking the fact that most chrome is imported. And so on.

The best protection against card stacking is to take the "Yes, but ..." 45
attitude. This device of propaganda is not untrue, but then again it is not the *whole* truth. So ask yourself, "Is this person leaving something out that I should know about? Is there some other information that should be brought to bear on this question?" ...

So far, we have considered three approaches that the propagandist can use to influence our thinking: appealing to our emotions, distracting our attention, and misleading us with logic that may appear to be reasonable but is in fact faulty and deceiving. But there is a fourth approach that is probably the most common propaganda trick of them all.

13. TESTIMONIAL

The testimonial device consists in having some loved or respected person give a statement of support (testimonial) for a given product or idea. The problem is that the person being quoted may *not* be an expert in the field; in fact, he may know nothing at all about it. Using the name of a man who is skilled and famous in one field to give a testimonial for something in another field is unfair and unreasonable.

Senator Yakalot tries to mislead his audience with testimonial when he tells them that "full-sized cars have been praised by great Americans like John Wayne and Jack Jones, as well as by leading experts on car safety and comfort."

Testimonial is used extensively in TV ads, where it often appears in such bizarre forms as Joe Namath's endorsement of a pantyhose brand.

Here, of course, the "authority" giving the testimonial not only is no expert about pantyhose, but obviously stands to gain something (money!) by making the testimonial.

When celebrities endorse a political candidate, they may not be making money by doing so, but we should still question whether they are in any better position to judge than we ourselves. Too often we are willing to let others we like or respect make our decisions *for us,* while we follow along acquiescently. And this is the purpose of testimonial—to get us to agree and accept *without* stopping to think. Be sure to ask, "Is there any reason to believe that this person (or organization or publication or whatever) has any more knowledge or information than I do on this subject? What does the idea amount to on its own merits, without the benefit of testimonial?" 50

The cornerstone of democratic society is reliance upon an informed and educated electorate. To be fully effective citizens we need to be able to challenge and to question wisely. A dangerous feeling of indifference toward our political processes exists today. We often abandon our right, our duty, to criticize and evaluate by dismissing *all* politicians as "crooked," *all* new bills and proposals as "just more government bureaucracy." But there are important distinctions to be made, and this kind of apathy can be fatal to democracy.

If we are to be led, let us not be led blindly, but critically, intelligently, with our eyes open. If we are to continue to be a government "by the people," let us become informed about the methods and purposes of propaganda, so we can be the masters, not the slaves of our destiny.

THINKING CRITICALLY ABOUT THE READING

1. According to Cross, what is propaganda? Who uses propaganda? Why is it used? (Glossary: *Propaganda*)

2. Why does Cross believe that it is necessary for people in a democratic society to become informed about the methods and practices of propaganda? What is her advice for dealing with propaganda?

3. What is a "red herring," and why do people use this technique? What is "begging the question"? (Glossary: *Logical Fallacies*)

4. What, according to Cross, is the most common propaganda trick? Provide some examples of it from your own experience.

5. How does Cross use examples in her essay? (Glossary: *Examples*) What do you think of the examples from Senator Yakalot? What, if anything, does this hypothetical senator add to the essay? Which other examples do you find most effective? Least effective? Explain why.

6. In her discussion of the bandwagon appeal (23–28), Cross uses the analogy of the lemmings. How does the analogy work? Why is it not a false analogy? (Glossary: *Analogy*) How do analogies help you, as a writer, explain your subject to readers?

LANGUAGE IN ACTION

At the beginning of her essay, Cross claims that propaganda "can be put to work for good causes as well as bad." Consider the following advertisements for the U.S. Postal Service's breast-cancer-stamp campaign and for the University of Vermont's Direct Service Programs. How would you characterize the appeal of each? What propaganda techniques does each use? Do you ever find appeals such as these objectionable? Why or why not? In what situations do you think it would be acceptable for you to use propaganda devices in your own writing?

Women Helping Battered Women

Summer or Fall Semester

Internships

Join the fight against domestic violence! You will work in a friendly, supportive environment. You will do challenging work for a worthwile cause. You will have lots of learning opportunities. We need reliable people who are committed to social justice. You will need good communication skills, an open mind, and the ability to work somewhat independently.

We are now accepting Applications.

Internships will be offered in the following programs:

Shelter Services
Hotline Program
Children's Shelter Services
Children's Playgroup Program
Development and Fundraising

Work Study Positions available in all the above programs as well as in the financial and administrative programs.

All interns in Direct Service Programs have to complete the full Volunteer Training. The next trainings will be in May and September 2008. Call now for more information: 658-3131.

WRITING SUGGESTIONS

1. Using several of the devices described by Cross, write a piece of propaganda. You may want to persuade your classmates to join a particular campus organization, support a controversial movement or issue, or vote for a particular candidate in an election.

2. Cross acknowledges in paragraph 1 that propaganda is "simply a means of persuasion," but she quickly cautions that people need to recognize propaganda and be alert to its potential to mislead or deceive. Write an essay for your campus newspaper arguing for a "short course" on propaganda recognition at your school. You might want to consider the following questions in your essay: How do propaganda and argumentation differ? Do both always

have the same intended effect? What could happen to people who don't recognize or understand propaganda when they encounter it?

3. Using Cross's list of propaganda devices, write an essay analyzing several
   newspaper editorials, political speeches, public-service advertising campaigns,
   or comparable examples of contemporary prose. What did you learn about
   the people or organizations as a result of your analysis? How were their positions on issues or their purposes expressed? Which propaganda devices did
   they use? After reading Cross's essay, did you find yourself "buying" the propaganda or recognizing and questioning it? Submit the original editorials,
   speeches, or advertisements with your essay.

Politics and the English Language

GEORGE ORWELL

George Orwell (1903–1950), one of the most brilliant social critics of the twentieth century, grew up in England and received a traditional education at Eton. Instead of going on to a university, he joined the civil service and was sent to Burma at the age of nineteen as an assistant superintendent of police. Disillusioned with British imperialism, Orwell resigned in 1929 and began a decade of studying social and political issues firsthand and then writing about them in such works as *Down and Out in Paris and London* (1933) and *The Road to Wigan Pier* (1937). His most famous books are *Animal Farm* (1945), a satire of the Russian Revolution, and *1984* (1949), a chilling novel set in an imagined totalitarian state of the future.

In *1984*, the government has imposed on its subjects a simplified language, Newspeak, which is continually revised to give them fewer words with which to express themselves. Words like *terrible, abhorrent,* and *evil*, for example, have been replaced by the single expression *doubleplus-ungood*. The way people use language, Orwell maintains, is a result of the way they think as well as an important influence on their thought. This is also the point of his classic essay "Politics and the English Language." Even though it was published in 1946, the essay is as accurate and relevant now as it was more than sixty years ago. Indeed, during the wars in Vietnam, Kosovo, and Iraq, various American officials were still using euphemisms such as *pacification, transfer of population,* and *ethnic cleansing*—words and phrases Orwell had exposed as doubletalk. Orwell, however, goes beyond exposé in this essay. He holds up to public view and ridicule some choice examples of political language at its worst, but he also offers a few short and effective rules for those who want to write more clearly.

WRITING TO DISCOVER: *Have you ever stopped to think about what clichéd phrases like* toe the line, walk the straight and narrow, sharp as a tack, *and* fly off the handle *really mean? Jot down the clichés that you find yourself or hear others using. What images come to mind when you hear them? Are these words and phrases effective expressions, or are they a kind of verbal shorthand that we automatically depend on? Explain.*

Most people who bother with the matter at all would admit that the English language is in a bad way, but it is generally assumed that we cannot by conscious action do anything about it. Our civilization is decadent and our language—so the argument runs—must inevitably share in the general collapse. It follows that any struggle against the abuse of language is a sentimental archaism, like preferring candles to electric light or hansom cabs to aeroplanes. Underneath this lies the half-conscious belief that language is a natural growth and not an instrument which we shape for our own purposes.

Now, it is clear that the decline of a language must ultimately have political and economic causes: it is not due simply to the bad influence of this or that individual writer. But an effect can become a cause, reinforcing the original cause and producing the same effect in an intensified form, and so on indefinitely. A man may take to drink because he feels himself to be a failure, and then fail all the more completely because he drinks. It is rather the same thing that is happening to the English language. It becomes ugly and inaccurate because our thoughts are foolish, but the slovenliness of our language makes it easier for us to have foolish thoughts. The point is that the process is reversible. Modern English, especially written English, is full of bad habits which spread by imitation and which can be avoided if one is willing to take the necessary trouble. If one gets rid of these habits one can think more clearly, and to think clearly is a necessary first step towards political regeneration: so that the fight against bad English is not frivolous and is not the exclusive concern of professional writers. I will come back to this presently, and I hope that by that time the meaning of what I have said here will have become clearer. Meanwhile here are five specimens of the English language as it is now habitually written.

These five passages have not been picked out because they are especially bad—I could have quoted far worse if I had chosen—but because they illustrate various of the mental vices from which we now suffer. They are a little below the average, but are fairly representative samples. I number them so that I can refer back to them when necessary:

(1) I am not, indeed, sure whether it is not true to say that the Milton who once seemed not unlike a seventeenth-century Shelley had not become, out of an experience ever more bitter in each year, more alien [*sic*] to the founder of that Jesuit sect which nothing could induce him to tolerate.

—PROFESSOR HAROLD LASKI (Essay in *Freedom of Expression*)

(2) Above all, we cannot play ducks and drakes with a native battery of idioms which prescribes such egregious collocations of vocables as the Basic *put up with* for *tolerate* or *put at a loss* for *bewilder*.

—PROFESSOR LANCELOT HOGBEN (*Interglossa*)

(3) On the one side we have the free personality: by definition it is not neurotic, for it has neither conflict nor dream. Its desires, such as they are, are transparent, for they are just what institutional approval keeps in the forefront of consciousness; another institutional pattern would alter their number and intensity; there is little in them that is natural, irreducible, or culturally dangerous. But *on the other side,* the social bond

itself is nothing but the mutual reflection of these self-secure integrities. Recall the definition of love. Is not this the very picture of a small academic? Where is there a place in this hall of mirrors for either personality or fraternity?

—Essay on psychology in *Politics* (New York)

(4) All the "best people" from the gentlemen's clubs, and all the frantic fascist captains, united in common hatred of Socialism and bestial horror of the rising tide of the mass revolutionary movement, have turned to acts of provocation, to foul incendiarism, to medieval legends of poisoned wells, to legalize their own destruction of proletarian organizations, and rouse the agitated petty-bourgeoisie to chauvinistic fervor on behalf of the fight against the revolutionary way out of the crisis.

—Communist pamphlet

(5) If a new spirit *is* to be infused into this old country, there is one thorny and contentious reform which must be tackled, and that is the humanization and galvanization of the B.B.C. Timidity here will bespeak canker and atrophy of the soul. The heart of Britain may be sound and of strong beat, for instance, but the British lion's roar at present is like that of Bottom in Shakespeare's *Midsummer Night's Dream*—as gentle as any sucking dove. A virile new Britain cannot continue indefinitely to be traduced in the eyes or rather ears, of the world by the effete languors of Langham Place, brazenly masquerading as "standard English." When the voice of Britain is heard at nine o'clock, better far and infinitely less ludicrous to hear aitches honestly dropped than the present priggish, inflated, inhibited, schoolma'amish arch braying of blameless bashful mewing maidens!

—Letter in *Tribune*

Each of these passages has faults of its own, but, quite apart from avoidable ugliness, two qualities are common to all of them. The first is staleness of imagery; the other is lack of precision. The writer either has a meaning and cannot express it, or he inadvertently says something else, or he is almost indifferent as to whether his words mean anything or not. This mixture of vagueness and sheer incompetence is the most marked characteristic of modern English prose, and especially of any kind of political writing. As soon as certain topics are raised, the concrete melts into the abstract and no one seems able to think of turns of speech that are not hackneyed: prose consists less and less of *words* chosen for the sake of their meaning, and more and more of *phrases* tacked together like the sections of a prefabricated henhouse. I list below, with notes and examples, various of the tricks by means of which the work of prose-construction is habitually dodged:

DYING METAPHORS.   A newly invented metaphor assists thought by   5
evoking a visual image, while on the other hand a metaphor which is technically "dead" (e.g., *iron resolution*) has in effect reverted to being an ordinary word and can generally be used without loss of vividness. But in

between these two classes there is a huge dump of worn-out metaphors which have lost all evocative power and are merely used because they save people the trouble of inventing phrases for themselves. Examples are: *ring the changes on, take up the cudgels for, toe the line, ride roughshod over, stand shoulder to shoulder with, play into the hands of, no axe to grind, grist to the mill, fishing in troubled waters, on the order of the day, Achilles' heel, swan song, hotbed.* Many of these are used without knowledge of their meaning (what is a "rift," for instance?), and incompatible metaphors are frequently mixed, a sure sign that the writer is not interested in what he is saying. Some metaphors now current have been twisted out of their original meaning without those who use them even being aware of the fact. For example, *toe the line* is sometimes written *tow the line.* Another example is the *hammer and the anvil,* now always used with the implication that the anvil gets the worst of it. In real life it is always the anvil that breaks the hammer, never the other way about: a writer who stopped to think what he was saying would be aware of this, and would avoid perverting the original phrase.

OPERATORS OR VERBAL FALSE LIMBS. These save the trouble of picking out appropriate verbs and nouns, and at the same time pad each sentence with extra syllables which give it an appearance of symmetry. Characteristic phrases are *render inoperative, militate against, make contact with, be subjected to, give rise to, give grounds for, have the effect of, play a leading part (role) in, make itself felt, take effect, exhibit a tendency to, serve the purpose of,* etc., etc. The keynote is the elimination of simple verbs. Instead of being a single word, such as *break, stop, spoil, mend, kill,* a verb becomes a *phrase,* made up of a noun or adjective tacked on to some general-purpose verb such as *prove, serve, form, play, render.* In addition, the passive voice is wherever possible used in preference to the active, and noun constructions are used instead of gerunds (*by examination of* instead of *by examining*). The range of verbs is further cut down by means of the *-ize* and *de-* formations, and the banal statements are given an appearance of profundity by means of the *not un-* formation. Simple conjunctions and prepositions are replaced by such phrases as *with respect to, having regard to, the fact that, by dint of, in view of, in the interests of, on the hypothesis that;* and the ends of sentences are saved from anticlimax by such resounding common-places as *greatly to be desired, cannot be left out of account, a development to be expected in the near future, deserving of serious consideration, brought to a satisfactory conclusion,* and so on and so forth.

PRETENTIOUS DICTION. Words like *phenomenon, element, individual* (as noun), *objective, categorical, effective, virtual, basic, primary, promote, constitute, exhibit, exploit, utilize, eliminate, liquidate,* are used to dress up simple statements and give an air of scientific impartiality to biased judgments. Adjectives like *epoch-making, epic, historic, unforgettable, triumphant, age-old, inevitable, inexorable, veritable,* are used to dignify the sordid processes of international politics, while writing that aims at glorifying war usually takes on an archaic color, its characteristic words being: *realm, throne, chariot, mailed fist, trident, sword, shield, buckler, banner, jackboot, clarion.* Foreign words and expressions such as *cul de sac, ancien régime, deus ex machina, mutatis mutandis, status quo, gleichschaltung, weltanschauung,* are used to give an air of culture and elegance. Except for the useful abbreviations *i.e., e.g.,* and *etc.,* there is no real need for any of the hundreds of foreign phrases now current in English. Bad writers, and especially scientific, political, and sociological writers, are nearly always haunted by the notion that Latin or Greek words are grander than Saxon ones, and unnecessary words like *expedite, ameliorate, predict, extraneous, deracinated, clandestine, subaqueous* and hundreds of others constantly gain ground from their Anglo-Saxon opposite numbers.[1] The jargon peculiar to Marxist writing (*hyena, hangman, cannibal, petty bourgeois, these gentry, lacquey, flunkey, mad dog, White Guard,* etc.) consists largely of words and phrases translated from Russian, German, or French; but the normal way of coining a new word is to use a Latin or Greek root with the appropriate affix and, where necessary, the *-ize* formation. It is often easier to make up words of this kind (*deregionalize, impermissible, extramarital, non-fragmentary,* and so forth) than to think up the English words that will cover one's meaning. The result, in general, is an increase in slovenliness and vagueness.

MEANINGLESS WORDS.   In certain kinds of writing, particularly in art criticism and literary criticism, it is normal to come across long passages which are almost completely lacking in meaning.[2] Words like *romantic, plastic, values, human, dead, sentimental, natural, vitality,* as used in art criticism, are strictly meaningless, in the sense that they not only do not point to any discoverable object, but are hardly ever expected to do so by the reader. When one critic writes, "The outstanding feature of Mr. X's work is its living quality," while another writes, "The immediately striking thing about Mr. X's work is its peculiar deadness," the reader accepts this as a simple difference of opinion. If words like *black* and *white* were

---

1. An interesting illustration of this is the way in which the English flower names which were in use till very recently are being ousted by Greek ones, *snapdragon* becoming *antirrhinum, forget-me-not* becoming *myosotis,* etc. It is hard to see any practical reason for this change of fashion: it is probably due to an instinctive turning-away from the more homely word and a vague feeling that the Greek word is scientific.

2. Example: "Comfort's catholicity of perception and image, strangely Whitmanesque in range, almost the exact opposite in esthetic compulsion, continues to evoke that trembling atmospheric accumulative hinting at a cruel, an inexorably serene timelessness....Wrey Gardiner scores by aiming at simple bull's-eyes with precision. Only they are not so simple, and through this contented sadness runs more than the surface bittersweet of resignation." (*Poetry Quarterly*)

involved, instead of the jargon words *dead* and *living,* he would see at
once that language was being used in an improper way. Many political
words are similarly abused. The word *Fascism* has now no meaning except
in so far as it signifies "something not desirable." The words *democracy,*
freedom, patriotic, realistic, justice, have each of them several different
meanings which cannot be reconciled with one another. In the case of
a word like *democracy,* not only is there no agreed definition, but the
attempt to make one is resisted from all sides. It is almost universally felt
that when we call a country democratic we are praising it: consequently
the defenders of every kind of regime claim that it is a democracy, and fear
that they might have to stop using the word if it were tied down to any
one meaning. Words of this kind are often used in a consciously dishonest
way. That is, the person who uses them has his own private definition, but
allows his hearer to think he means something quite different. Statements
like, *Marshal Pétain was a true patriot, The Soviet Press is the freest in the*
world, the Catholic Church is opposed to persecution, are almost always made
with intent to deceive. Other words used in variable meanings, in most
cases more or less dishonestly, are: *class, totalitarian, science, progressive,*
reactionary, bourgeois, equality.

Now that I have made this catalogue of swindles and perversions, let
me give another example of the kind of writing that they lead to. This
time it must of its nature be an imaginary one. I am going to translate a
passage of good English into modern English of the worst sort. Here is a
well-known verse from *Ecclesiastes:*

> I returned and saw under the sun, that the race is not to the swift, nor the
> battle to the strong, neither yet bread to the wise, nor yet riches to men
> of understanding, nor yet favour to men of skill; but time and chance
> happeneth to them all.

Here it is in modern English: 10

> Objective consideration of contemporary phenomena compels the
> conclusion that success or failure in competitive activities exhibits no
> tendency to be commensurate with innate capacity, but that a con-
> siderable element of the unpredictable must invariably be taken into
> account.

This is a parody, but a very gross one. Exhibit (3), above, for instance,
contains several patches of the same kind of English. It will be seen that I
have not made a full translation. The beginning and ending of the sentence
follow the original meaning fairly closely, but in the middle the concrete
illustrations—race, battle, bread—dissolve into the vague phrase "success
or failure in competitive activities." This had to be so, because no modern writer of the kind I am discussing—no one capable of using phrases
like "objective consideration of contemporary phenomena"—would ever

tabulate his thoughts in that precise and detailed way. The whole tendency of modern prose is away from concreteness. Now analyze these two sentences a little more closely. The first contains forty-nine words but only sixty syllables, and all its words are those of everyday life. The second contains thirty-eight words of ninety syllables: eighteen of its words are from Latin roots, and one from Greek. The first sentence contains six vivid images, and only one phrase ("time and chance") that could be called vague. The second contains not a single fresh, arresting phrase, and in spite of its ninety syllables it gives only a shortened version of the meaning contained in the first. Yet without a doubt it is the second kind of sentence that is gaining ground in modern English. I do not want to exaggerate. This kind of writing is not yet universal, and outcrops of simplicity will occur here and there in the worst-written page. Still, if you or I were told to write a few lines on the uncertainty of human fortunes, we should probably come much nearer to my imaginary sentence than to the one from *Ecclesiastes*.

As I have tried to show, modern writing at its worst does not consist in picking out words for the sake of their meaning and inventing images in order to make the meaning clearer. It consists in gumming together long strips of words which have already been set in order by someone else, and making the results presentable by sheer humbug. The attraction of this way of writing is that it is easy. It is easier—even quicker, once you have the habit—to say *In my opinion it is not an unjustifiable assumption that* than to say *I think*. If you use ready-made phrases, you not only don't have to hunt about for words; you also don't have to bother with the rhythms of your sentences, since these phrases are generally so arranged as to be more or less euphonious. When you are composing in a hurry—when you are dictating to a stenographer, for instance, or making a public speech—it is natural to fall into a pretentious, Latinized style. Tags like *a consideration which we should do well to bear in mind* or *a conclusion to which all of us would readily assent* will save many a sentence from coming down with a bump. By using stale metaphors, similes, and idioms, you save much mental effort, at the cost of leaving your meaning vague, not only for your reader but for yourself. This is the significance of mixed metaphors. The sole aim of a metaphor is to call up a visual image. When these images clash—as in *The Fascist octopus has sung its swan song, the jackboot is thrown into the melting pot*—it can be taken as certain that the writer is not seeing a mental image of the objects he is naming; in other words he is not really thinking. Look again at the examples I gave at the beginning of this essay. Professor Laski (1) uses five negatives in fifty-three words. One of these is superfluous, making nonsense of the whole passage, and in addition there is the slip *alien* for *akin*, making further nonsense, and several avoidable pieces of clumsiness which increase the general vagueness. Professor Hogben (2) plays ducks and drakes with a battery which is able to write prescriptions, and, while disapproving of the everyday phrase *put up with*, is unwilling to look *egregious* up in the dictionary and see what it means;

(3), if one takes an uncharitable attitude towards it, is simply meaning-less: probably one could work out its intended meaning by reading the whole of the article in which it occurs. In (4), the writer knows more or less what he wants to say, but an accumulation of stale phrases chokes him like tea leaves blocking a sink. In (5), words and meaning have almost parted company. People who write in this manner usually have a general emotional meaning—they dislike one thing and want to express solidar-ity with another—but they are not interested in the detail of what they are saying. A scrupulous writer, in every sentence that he writes, will ask himself at least four questions, thus: What am I trying to say? What words will express it? What image or idiom will make it clearer? Is this image fresh enough to have an effect? And he will probably ask himself two more: Could I put it more shortly? Have I said anything that is avoidably ugly? But you are not obliged to go to all this trouble. You can shirk it by simply throwing your mind open and letting the ready-made phrases come crowding in. They will construct your sentences for you—even think your thoughts for you, to a certain extent—and at need they will perform the important service of partially concealing your meaning even from your-self. It is at this point that the special connection between politics and the debasement of language becomes clear.

In our time it is broadly true that political writing is bad writing. Where it is not true, it will generally be found that the writer is some kind of rebel, expressing his private opinions and not a "party line." Orthodoxy, of whatever color, seems to demand a lifeless, imitative style. The politi-cal dialects to be found in pamphlets, leading articles, manifestos, White Papers, and the speeches of under-secretaries do, of course, vary from party to party, but they are all alike in that one almost never finds in them a fresh, vivid, homemade turn of speech. When one watches some tired hack on the platform mechanically repeating the familiar phrases—*bestial atroci-ties, iron heel, bloodstained tyranny, free peoples of the world, stand shoulder to shoulder*—one often has a curious feeling that one is not watching a live human being but some kind of dummy: a feeling which suddenly becomes stronger at moments when the light catches the speaker's spectacles and turns them into blank discs which seem to have no eyes behind them. And this is not altogether fanciful. A speaker who uses that kind of phraseol-ogy has gone some distance towards turning himself into a machine. The appropriate noises are coming out of his larynx, but his brain is not involved as it would be if he were choosing his words for himself. If the speech he is making is one that he is accustomed to make over and over again, he may be almost unconscious of what he is saying, as one is when one utters the responses in church. And this reduced state of consciousness, if not indis-pensable, is at any rate favorable to political conformity.

In our time, political speech and writing are largely the defense of the indefensible. Things like the continuance of British rule in India, the Russian purges and deportations, the dropping of the atom bombs on Japan, can indeed be defended, but only by arguments which are too brutal for most people to face, and which do not square with the professed aims of political parties. Thus political language has to consist largely of euphemism, question-begging, and sheer cloudy vagueness. Defenseless villages are bombarded from the air, the inhabitants driven out into the countryside, the cattle machine-gunned, the huts set on fire with incendiary bullets: this is called *pacification*. Millions of peasants are robbed of their farms and sent trudging along the roads with no more than they can carry: this is called *transfer of population* or *rectification of frontiers*. People are imprisoned for years without trial, or shot in the back of the neck or sent to die of scurvy in Arctic lumber camps: this is called *elimination of unreliable elements*. Such phraseology is needed if one wants to name things without calling up mental pictures of them. Consider for instance some comfortable English professor defending Russian totalitarianism. He cannot say outright, "I believe in killing off your opponents when you can get good results by doing so." Probably, therefore, he will say something like this:

> While freely conceding that the Soviet régime exhibits certain features which the humanitarian may be inclined to deplore, we must, I think, agree that a certain curtailment of the right to political opposition is an unavoidable concomitant of transitional periods, and that the rigors which the Russian people have been called upon to undergo have been amply justified in the sphere of concrete achievement.

The inflated style is itself a kind of euphemism. A mass of Latin words   15
falls upon the facts like soft snow, blurring the outlines and covering up all the details. The great enemy of clear language is insincerity. When there is a gap between one's real and one's declared aims, one turns as it were instinctively to long words and exhausted idioms, like a cuttlefish squirting out ink. In our age there is no such thing as "keeping out of politics." All issues are political issues, and politics itself is a mass of lies, evasions, folly, hatred, and schizophrenia. When the general atmosphere is bad, language must suffer. I should expect to find—this is a guess which I have not sufficient knowledge to verify—that the German, Russian, and Italian languages have all deteriorated in the last ten or fifteen years, as a result of dictatorship.

But if thought corrupts language, language can also corrupt thought. A bad usage can spread by tradition and imitation, even among people who should and do know better. The debased language that I have been discussing is in some ways very convenient. Phrases like *a not unjustifiable assumption, leaves much to be desired, would serve no good purpose, a consideration which we should do well to bear in mind,* are a continuous temptation, a packet of aspirins always at one's elbow. Look back through this essay, and for certain you will find that I have again and again committed the very faults I am protesting against. By this morning's post I have received a pamphlet dealing with conditions in Germany. The author tells me that he "felt impelled" to write it. I open it at random, and here is almost the first sentence that I see: "[The Allies] have an opportunity not only of achieving a radical transformation of Germany's social and political structure in such a way as to avoid a nationalistic reaction in Germany itself, but at the same time of laying the foundations of a cooperative and unified Europe." You see, he "feels impelled" to write—feels, presumably, that he has something new to say—and yet his words, like cavalry horses answering the bugle, group themselves automatically into the familiar dreary pattern. The invasion of one's mind by ready-made phrases (*lay the foundations, achieve a radical transformation*) can only be prevented if one is constantly on guard against them, and every such phrase anesthetizes a portion of one's brain.

I said earlier that the decadence of our language is probably curable. Those who deny this would argue, if they produced an argument at all, that language merely reflects existing social conditions, and that we cannot influence its development by any direct tinkering with words and constructions. So far as the general tone or spirit of a language goes, this may be true, but it is not true in detail. Silly words and expressions have often disappeared, not through any evolutionary process but owing to the conscious action of a minority. Two recent examples were *explore every avenue* and *leave no stone unturned*, which were killed by the jeers of a few journalists. There is a long list of fly-blown metaphors which could similarly be got rid of if enough people would interest themselves in the job; and it should also be possible to laugh the *not un-* formation out of existence,[3] to reduce the amount of Latin and Greek in the average sentence, to drive out foreign phrases and strayed scientific words, and, in general, to make pretentiousness unfashionable. But all these are minor points. The defense of the English language implies more than this, and perhaps it is best to start by saying what it does *not* imply.

To begin with, it has nothing to do with archaism, with the salvaging of obsolete words and turns of speech, or with the setting up of a "standard English" which must never be departed from. On the contrary, it is especially concerned with the scrapping of every word or idiom which has outworn its usefulness. It has nothing to do with correct grammar and syntax, which are of no importance so long as one makes one's meaning clear, or with the avoidance of Americanisms, or with having what is called a "good prose style." On the other hand it is not concerned with fake simplicity and the attempt to make written English colloquial. Nor does it even imply in every case preferring the Saxon word to the Latin one, though it does imply using the fewest and shortest words that will cover one's meaning. What is above all needed is to let the meaning choose the word, and not the other way about. In prose, the worst thing one can do with words is to surrender to them. When you think of a concrete object, you think wordlessly, and then, if you want to describe the thing you have

---

3. One can cure oneself of the *not un-* formation by memorizing this sentence: *A not unblack dog was chasing a not unsmall rabbit across a not ungreen field.*

been visualizing you probably hunt about till you find the exact words that seem to fit it. When you think of something abstract you are more inclined to use words from the start, and unless you make a conscious effort to prevent it, the existing dialect will come rushing in and do the job for you, at the expense of blurring or even changing your meaning. Probably it is better to put off using words as long as possible and get one's meaning as clear as one can through pictures or sensations. Afterwards one can choose—not simply *accept*—the phrases that will best cover the meaning, and then switch round and decide what impression one's words are likely to make on another person. This last effort of the mind cuts out all stale or mixed images, all prefabricated phrases, needless repetitions, and humbug and vagueness generally. But one can often be in doubt about the effect of a word or a phrase, and one needs rules that one can rely on when instinct fails. I think the following rules will cover most cases:

1. Never use a metaphor, simile, or other figure of speech which you are used to seeing in print.
2. Never use a long word where a short one will do.
3. If it is possible to cut a word out, always cut it out.
4. Never use the passive where you can use the active.
5. Never use a foreign phrase, a scientific word, or a jargon word if you can think of an everyday English equivalent.
6. Break any of these rules sooner than say anything outright barbarous.

These rules sound elementary, and so they are, but they demand a deep change of attitude in anyone who has grown used to writing in the style now fashionable. One could keep all of them and still write bad English, but one could not write the kind of stuff that I quoted in those five specimens at the beginning of this article.

I have not here been considering the literary use of language, but merely language as an instrument for expressing and not for concealing or preventing thought. Stuart Chase and others have come near to claiming that all abstract words are meaningless, and have used this as a pretext for advocating a kind of political quietism. Since you don't know what Fascism is, how can you struggle against Fascism? One need not swallow such absurdities as this, but one ought to recognize that the present political chaos is connected with the decay of language, and that one can probably bring about some improvement by starting at the verbal end. If you simplify your English, you are freed from the worst follies of orthodoxy. You cannot speak any of the necessary dialects, and when you make a stupid remark its stupidity will be obvious, even to yourself. Political language—and with variations this is true of all political parties, from Conservatives to Anarchists—is designed to make lies sound truthful and murder respectable, and to give an appearance of solidity to pure wind. One cannot change this all in a moment, but one can at least change one's own habits, and from time to time one can even, if one jeers loudly enough, send some worn-out and useless phrase—some *jackboot, Achilles' heel, hotbed, melting pot, acid test, veritable inferno,* or other lump of verbal refuse—into the dustbin where it belongs.

THINKING CRITICALLY ABOUT THE READING

1. In your own words, summarize Orwell's argument in this essay. (Glossary: *Argument*) Do you agree or disagree with him? Explain why.

2. For what audience do you think Orwell wrote this essay? (Glossary: *Audience*) What in his diction leads you to this conclusion? (Glossary: *Diction*)

3. Grammarians and usage experts have long objected to mixed metaphors (for example, "Politicians who have their heads in the sand are leading the country over the precipice") because they are inaccurate. For Orwell, a mixed metaphor is symptomatic of a greater problem (12). What is that problem?

4. What are dead and dying metaphors (5)? (Glossary: *Figures of Speech*) Why do dying metaphors disgust Orwell?

5. Following are some of the metaphors and similes that Orwell uses in his essay. (Glossary: *Figures of Speech*) Explain how each one works and comment on its effectiveness.

   a. "Prose consists less and less of *words* chosen for the sake of their meaning, and more and more of *phrases* tacked together like the sections of a prefabricated henhouse" (4).

   b. "But in between these two classes there is a huge dump of worn-out metaphors which have lost all evocative power" (5).

   c. "The writer knows more or less what he wants to say, but an accumulation of stale phrases chokes him like tea leaves blocking a sink" (12).

   d. "A mass of Latin words falls upon the facts like soft snow, blurring the outlines and covering up all the details" (15).

   e. "When there is a gap between one's real and one's declared aims, one turns ... instinctively to long words and exhausted idioms, like a cuttlefish squirting out ink" (15).

   f. "He ... feels, presumably, that he has something new to say—and yet his words, like cavalry horses answering the bugle, group themselves automatically into the familiar dreary pattern" (16).

6. According to Orwell, what are four important questions scrupulous writers ask themselves before they begin to write (12)?

7. Orwell says that one of the evils of political language is question-begging (14). What does he mean? Why, according to Orwell, has political language deteriorated? Do you agree with him that "the decadence of our language is probably curable" (17)? Why or why not?

8. In this essay, Orwell moves from negative arguments (criticisms) to positive ones (proposals). Where does he make the transition from criticisms to proposals? (Glossary: *Transitions*) Do you find the organization of his argument effective? (Glossary: *Organization*) Explain.

LANGUAGE IN ACTION

Read Robert Yoakum's "Everyspeech," a parody that first appeared in the *New York Times* in November 1994. Yoakum was a speechwriter for John F. Kennedy's successful 1960 campaign. As you read, identify the features of political speech that are the butt of Yoakum's humor. Does he point out the same language abuses that Orwell criticizes in his essay? What propaganda devices does Yoakum use (see Cross's essay on pp. 149–159)?

EVERYSPEECH

Ladies and gentlemen. I am delighted to see so many friends from the Third Congressional District. And what better site for some straight talk than at this greatest of all state fairs, where ribbons reward American individual enterprise, whether for the biggest beets or the best bull?

Speaking of bull, my opponent has said some mighty dishonest things about me. But what can you expect from a typical politician? I want to address some fundamental issues that set me apart from my opponent and his failed party—the party of gutlessness and gridlock.

The American people are ready for straight talk, although don't count on the press to report it straight. The press, like my opponent, has no respect for the public.

This democracy must return to its roots or it will perish, and its roots are you—the honest, hard-working, God-fearing people who made this the greatest nation on earth. Yes, we have problems. But what problems would not be solved if the press and politicians had faith in the people?

Take crime, for example. Rampant, brutal crime. My rival in this race believes that redemption and rehabilitation are the answers to the lawlessness that is tearing our society apart.

Well, if R and R is what you want for those robbers and rapists, don't vote for me. If pampering the punks is what you want, vote for my opponent.

Do I believe in the death penalty? You bet! Do I believe in three strikes and you're out? No, I believe in *two* strikes and you're out! I believe in three strikes and you're *dead*!

You can count on me to crack down on crime, but I won't ignore the other big C word: character. Character made our nation great. Character, and respect for family values. A belief in children and parents. In brothers and sisters and grandparents.

Oh, sure, that sounds corny. Those cynical inside-the-Beltway journalists will ridicule me tomorrow, but I would rather be guilty of a corny defense of family values than of coddling criminals.

While I'm making myself unpopular with the press and a lot of politicians, I might as well alienate even more Washington wimps by telling you frankly how I feel about taxes. I'm against them! Not just in an election year, like my adversary, but every year!

I'm in favor of slashing wasteful welfare, which is where a lot of your hard-earned tax dollars go. The American people have said "enough!" to welfare, but inside the Beltway they don't give a hoot about the industrious folks I see

(continued)

before me today. They're too busy with their cocktail parties, diplomatic functions, and society balls.

My opponent loves those affairs, but I'd rather be with my good friends here than with those fork-tongued lawyers, cookie-pushing State Department fops, and high-priced lobbyists. I promise that when elected, my main office will be right here in the Third District. My branch office will be in D.C. And I promise you this: I shall serve only two terms and then return to live with the folks I love.

So on Nov. 8, if you want someone with an independent mind and the courage to change—*to change back to good old American values*—if you've had enough and want someone tough, vote for me. Thank you, and God bless America.

WRITING SUGGESTIONS

1. Orwell claims that political speech is filled with such words as *patriotism, democracy, freedom, realistic,* and *justice,* words that have "several different meanings which cannot be reconciled with one another" (8). Why is Orwell so uneasy about these words? What do these words mean to you? How do your meanings differ from those of others? For example, someone who has served in the armed forces, been a political prisoner, or served as a juror may attach distinct meanings to the words *patriotism, freedom,* or *justice.* In a brief essay, recount an experience that gave you real insight into the meaning of one of these words or a word similar to them.

2. Collect examples of bureaucratic writing on your campus. How would you characterize most of this writing? Who on your campus seems to be prone to manipulative language—college administrators, student leaders, or faculty? Use information from the Orwell and Cross articles in this chapter and from Birk and Birk's article "Selection, Slanting, and Charged Language" (pp. 394–402) to analyze the writing you collect. Then write an essay in which you assess the health of the English language at your school.

The World of Doublespeak

WILLIAM LUTZ

Born in Racine, Wisconsin, in 1940, William Lutz has been a professor of English at Rutgers University since 1991 and was editor of the *Quarterly Review of Doublespeak* for fourteen years. Through his book *Doublespeak: From Revenue Enhancement to Terminal Living* (1980), Lutz first awakened Americans to how people in important positions were manipulating language. As chair of the National Council of Teachers of English's Committee on Public Doublespeak, Lutz has been a watchdog of public officials who use language to "mislead, distort, deceive, inflate, circumvent, obfuscate." Each year the committee presents the Orwell Awards, recognizing the most outrageous uses of public doublespeak in the worlds of government and business. Lutz's recent books are *The New Doublespeak: Why No One Knows What Anyone's Saying Anymore* (1997) and *Doublespeak Defined: Cut through the Bull**** and Get to the Point* (1999).

In the following essay, which first appeared in Christopher Ricks's and Leonard Michaels's anthology *State of the Language* (1990), Lutz examines doublespeak, "language which pretends to communicate but doesn't, language which makes the bad seem good, the negative appear positive, the unpleasant attractive, or at least tolerable." He identifies the various types of doublespeak and cautions us about the possible serious effects that doublespeak can have on our thinking.

WRITING TO DISCOVER: *Have you ever heard or read language that you thought was deliberately evasive, language that manipulated your perception of reality, or, worse yet, language that communicated nothing? Jot down your thoughts about such language. For example, what kinds of language do people use to talk about death, cancer, mental illness, firing a person, killing someone, or ending a relationship? Do you think evasive or manipulative language is ever justified? Explain.*

Farmers no longer have cows, pigs, chickens, or other animals on their farms; according to the U.S. Department of Agriculture, farmers have "grain-consuming animal units" (which, according to the Tax Reform Act of 1986, are kept in "single-purpose agricultural structures," not pig pens and chicken coops). Attentive observers of the English language also learned recently that the multibillion dollar stock market crash of 1987 was simply a "fourth quarter equity retreat"; that airplanes don't crash, they just have "uncontrolled contact with the ground"; that janitors are really "environmental technicians"; that it was a "diagnostic misadventure of a high magnitude" which caused the death of a patient in a Philadelphia hospital, not medical malpractice; and that President Reagan wasn't really unconscious while he underwent minor surgery, he was just in a "non-decision-making form." In other words, doublespeak continues to spread as the official language of public discourse.

Doublespeak is a blanket term for language which pretends to communicate but doesn't, language which makes the bad seem good, the negative appear positive, the unpleasant attractive, or at least tolerable. It is language which avoids, shifts, or denies responsibility, language which is at variance with its real or its purported meaning. It is language which conceals or prevents thought. Basic to doublespeak is incongruity, the incongruity between what is said, or left unsaid, and what really is: between the word and the referent, between seem and be, between the essential function of language, communication, and what doublespeak does—mislead, distort, deceive, inflate, circumvent, obfuscate.

When shopping, we are asked to check our packages at the desk "for our convenience," when it's not for our convenience at all but for the store's "program to reduce inventory shrinkage." We see advertisements for "preowned," "experienced," or "previously distinguished" cars, for "genuine imitation leather," "virgin vinyl," or "real counterfeit diamonds." Television offers not reruns but "encore telecasts." There are no slums or ghettos, just the "inner city" or "substandard housing" where the "disadvantaged," "economically nonaffluent," or "fiscal underachievers" live. Nonprofit organizations don't make a profit, they have "negative deficits" or "revenue excesses." In the world of doublespeak dying is "terminal living."

We know that a toothbrush is still a toothbrush even if the advertisements on television call it a "home plaque removal instrument," and even that "nutritional avoidance therapy" means a diet. But who would guess that a "volume-related production schedule adjustment" means closing an entire factory in the doublespeak of General Motors, or that "advanced downward adjustments" means budget cuts in the doublespeak of Caspar Weinberger, or that "energetic disassembly" means an explosion in a nuclear power plant in the doublespeak of the nuclear power industry?

The euphemism, an inoffensive or positive word or phrase designed 5
to avoid a harsh, unpleasant, or distasteful reality, can at times be doublespeak. But the euphemism can also be a tactful word or phrase; for example, "passed away" functions not just to protect the feelings of another person but also to express our concern for another's grief. This use of the euphemism is not doublespeak but the language of courtesy. A euphemism used to mislead or deceive, however, becomes doublespeak. In 1984, the U.S. State Department announced that in its annual reports on the status of human rights in countries around the world it would no longer use the word "killing." Instead, it would use the phrase "unlawful or arbitrary deprivation of life." Thus the State Department avoids discussing government-sanctioned killings in countries that the United States supports and has certified as respecting human rights.

The Pentagon also avoids unpleasant realities when it refers to bombs and artillery shells which fall on civilian targets as "incontinent ordnance" or killing the enemy as "servicing the target." In 1977 the Pentagon tried to slip funding for the neutron bomb unnoticed into an appropriations bill by calling it an "enhanced radiation device." And in 1971 the CIA gave us that most famous of examples of doublespeak when it used the phrase "eliminate with extreme prejudice" to refer to the execution of a suspected double agent in Vietnam.

Jargon, the specialized language of a trade or profession, allows colleagues to communicate with each other clearly, efficiently, and quickly. Indeed, it is a mark of membership to be able to use and understand the group's jargon. But it can also be doublespeak—pretentious, obscure, and esoteric terminology used to make the simple appear complex, and not to express but impress. In the doublespeak of jargon, smelling something becomes "organoleptic analysis," glass becomes "fused silicate," a crack in a metal support beam becomes a "discontinuity," conservative economic policies become "distributionally conservative notions."

Lawyers and tax accountants speak of an "involuntary conversion" of property when discussing the loss or destruction of property through theft, accident, or condemnation. So if your house burns down, or your car is stolen or destroyed in an accident, you have, in legal jargon, suffered an "involuntary conversion" of your property. This is a legal term with a specific meaning in law and all lawyers can be expected to understand it. But when it is used to communicate with a person outside the group who does not understand such language, it is doublespeak. In 1978 a National Airlines 727 airplane crashed while attempting to land at the Pensacola, Florida, airport, killing three passengers, injuring twenty-one others, and destroying the airplane. Since the insured value of the airplane was greater than its book value, National made an after-tax insurance benefit of $1.7 million on the destroyed airplane, or an extra eighteen cents a share. In its annual report, National reported that this $1.7 million was due to "the involuntary conversion of a 727," thus explaining the profit without even hinting at the crash and the deaths of three passengers.

Gobbledygook or bureaucratese is another kind of doublespeak. Such doublespeak is simply a matter of overwhelming the audience with technical, unfamiliar words. When asked why U.S. forces lacked intelligence information on Grenada before they invaded the island in 1983, Admiral Wesley L. McDonald told reporters that "We were not micromanaging Grenada intelligence-wise until about that time frame."

Some gobbledygook, however impressive it may sound, doesn't even make sense. During the 1988 presidential campaign, vice presidential candidate Senator Dan Quayle explained the need for a strategic defense initiative by saying: "Why wouldn't an enhanced deterrent, a more stable peace, a better prospect to denying the ones who enter conflict in the first place to have a reduction of offensive systems and an introduction to defensive capability. I believe this is the route the country will eventually go."

10

In 1974, Alan Greenspan, then chairman of the President's Council of Economic Advisors, was testifying before a Senate Committee and was in the difficult position of trying to explain why President Nixon's economic policies weren't effective in fighting inflation: "It is a tricky problem to find the particular calibration in timing that would be appropriate to stem the acceleration in risk premiums created by falling incomes without prematurely aborting the decline in the inflation-generated risk premiums." In 1988, when speaking to a meeting of the Economic Club of New York, Mr. Greenspan, now Federal Reserve chairman, said, "I guess I should warn you, if I turn out to be particularly clear, you've probably misunderstood what I've said."

The investigation into the *Challenger* disaster in 1986 revealed the gobbledygook and bureaucratese used by many involved in the shuttle program. When Jesse Moore, NASA's associate administrator, was asked if the performance of the shuttle program had improved with each launch or if it had remained the same, he answered, "I think our performance in terms of the liftoff performance and in terms of the orbital performance, we knew more about the envelope we were operating under, and we have been pretty accurately staying in that. And so I would say the performance has not by design drastically improved. I think we have been able to characterize the performance more as a function of our launch experience as opposed to it improving as a function of time."

A final kind of doublespeak is simply inflated language. Car mechanics may be called "automotive internists," elevator operators "members of the vertical transportation corps," and grocery store checkout clerks "career associate scanning professionals," while television sets are proclaimed to have "nonmulticolor capability." When a company "initiates a career alternative enhancement program" it is really laying off five thousand workers; "negative patient care outcome" means that the patient died; and "rapid oxidation" means a fire in a nuclear power plant.

The doublespeak of inflated language can have serious consequences. The U.S. Navy didn't pay $2,043 a piece for steel nuts; it paid all that money for "hexiform rotatable surface compression units," which, by the way, "underwent catastrophic stress-related shaft detachment." Not to be outdone, the U.S. Air Force paid $214 apiece for Emergency Exit Lights, or flashlights. This doublespeak is in keeping with such military doublespeak as "preemptive counterattack" for first strike, "engage the enemy on all sides" for ambush, "tactical redeployment" for retreat, and "air support" for bombing. In the doublespeak of the military, the 1983 invasion of Grenada was conducted not by the U.S. Army, Navy, Air Force, and Marines but by the "Caribbean Peace Keeping Forces." But then according to the Pentagon it wasn't an invasion, it was a "predawn vertical insertion."

These last examples of doublespeak should make it clear that doublespeak is not the product of careless language or sloppy thinking. Indeed,   15 serious doublespeak is the product of clear thinking and is carefully designed and constructed to appear to communicate but in fact to mislead. Thus, it's not a tax increase but "revenue enhancement," "tax base broadening," or "user fees," so how can you complain about higher taxes? It's not acid rain, it's just "poorly buffered precipitation," so don't worry about all those dead trees. That isn't the Mafia in Atlantic City, those are just "members of a career-offender cartel," so don't worry about the influence of organized crime in the city. The Supreme Court justice wasn't addicted to the painkilling drug he was taking, it's just that the drug had simply "established an interrelationship with the body, such that if the drug is removed precipitously, there is a reaction," so don't worry that his decisions might have been influenced by his drug addition. It's not a Titan II nuclear-armed, intercontinental, ballistic missile 630 times more powerful than the atomic bomb dropped on Hiroshima, it's just a "very large, potentially disruptive reentry system," so don't worry about the threat of nuclear destruction. Serious doublespeak is highly strategic, and it breeds suspicion, cynicism, distrust, and, ultimately, hostility.

In his famous and now-classic essay "Politics and the English Language," which was published in 1946, George Orwell wrote that the "great enemy of clear language is insincerity. When there is a gap between one's real and one's declared aims, one turns as it were instinctively to long words and exhausted idioms, like a cuttlefish squirting out ink." For Orwell, language was an instrument for "expressing and not for concealing or preventing thought." In his most biting comment, Orwell observes that "in our time, political speech and writing are largely the defense of the indefensible.... Political language has to consist largely of euphemism, question-begging, and sheer cloudy vagueness.... Political language... is designed to make lies sound truthful and murder respectable, and to give an appearance of solidity to pure wind."

Orwell understood well the power of language as both a tool and a weapon. In the nightmare world of his novel *1984,* he depicted language as one of the most important tools of the totalitarian state. Newspeak, the official state language in *1984,* was designed not to extend but to *diminish* the range of human thought, to make only "correct" thought possible and all other modes of thought impossible. It was, in short, a language designed to create a reality which the state wanted.

Newspeak had another important function in Orwell's world of *1984.* It provided the means of expression for doublethink, which Orwell described in his novel as "the power of holding two contradictory beliefs in one's mind simultaneously, and accepting both of them." The classic example of doublethink in Orwell's novel is the slogan "War is Peace." And lest you think doublethink is confined only to Orwell's novel, you need only recall the words of Secretary of State Alexander Haig when he testified before a Congressional Committee in 1982 that a continued weapons build-up by the United States is "absolutely essential to our hopes for meaningful arms reduction." Or the words of Senator Orrin Hatch in 1988: "Capital punishment is our society's recognition of the sanctity of human life."

The more sophisticated and powerful uses of doublespeak can at times be difficult to identify. On 27 July 1981, President Ronald Reagan said in a television speech: "I will not stand by and see those of you who are dependent on Social Security deprived of the benefits you've worked so hard to earn. You will continue to receive your checks in the full amount due you." This speech had been billed as President Reagan's position on Social Security, a subject of much debate at the time. After the speech, public opinion polls recorded the great majority of the public as believing that President Reagan had affirmed his support for Social Security and that he would not support cuts in benefits. Five days after the speech, however, White House spokesperson David Gergen was quoted in the press as saying that President Reagan's words had been "carefully chosen." What President Reagan did mean, according to Gergen, was that he was reserving the right to decide who was "dependent" on those benefits, who had "earned" them, and who, therefore, was "due" them.

During the 1982 Congressional election campaign, the Republican   20
National Committee sponsored a television advertisement which pictured an elderly, folksy postman delivering Social Security checks "with the 7.4 percent cost-of-living raise that President Reagan promised." Looking directly at his audience, the postman then adds that Reagan "promised that raise and he kept his promise, in spite of those sticks-in-the-mud who tried to keep him from doing what we elected him to do."

The commercial was deliberately misleading. The cost-of-living increases had been provided automatically by law since 1975, and President Reagan had tried three times to roll them back or delay them but was overruled by congressional opposition. When these discrepancies were pointed out to an official of the Republican National Committee, he called the commercial "inoffensive" and added, "Since when is a commercial supposed to be accurate? Do women really smile when they clean their ovens?"

In 1986, with the *Challenger* tragedy and subsequent investigation, we discovered that doublespeak seemed to be the official language of NASA, the National Aeronautics and Space Administration, and of the contractors engaged in the space shuttle program. The first thing we learned is that the *Challenger* tragedy wasn't an accident. As Kay Parker of NASA said, experts were "working in the anomaly investigation." The "anomaly" was the explosion of the *Challenger*.

When NASA reported that it was having difficulty determining how or exactly when the *Challenger* astronauts died, Rear Admiral Richard Truly reported that "whether or not a cabin rupture occurred prior to water impact has not yet been determined by a superficial examination of the recovered components." The "recovered components" were the bodies of the astronauts. Admiral Truly also said that "extremely large forces were imposed on the vehicle as evidenced by the immediate breakup into many pieces." He went on to say that "once these forces have been accurately determined, if in fact they can be, the structural analysts will attempt to estimate the effect on the structural and pressure integrity of the crew module." NASA referred to the coffins of the astronauts as "crew transfer containers."

Arnold Aldrich, manager of the national space transportation systems program at Johnson Space Center, said that "the normal process during the countdown is that the countdown proceeds, assuming we are in a go posture, and at various points during the countdown we tag up on the operational loops and face to face in the firing room to ascertain the facts that project elements that are monitoring the data and that are understanding the situation as we proceed are still in the go condition."

In testimony before the commission investigating the *Challenger* accident, Allen McDonald, an engineer for Morton Thiokol (the maker of the rocket), said he had expressed concern about the possible effect of cold weather on the booster rocker's O-ring seals the night before the launch: "I made the comment that lower temperatures are in the direction of badness for both O-rings, because it slows down the timing function."   25

Larry Mulloy, manager of the space shuttle solid rocket booster program at Marshall Space Flight Center, responded to a question assessing whether problems with the O-rings or with the insulation of the liner of the nozzle posed a greater threat to the shuttle by saying, "The criticality in answering your question, sir, it would be a real foot race as to which one would be considered more critical, depending on the particular time that you looked at your experience with that."

After several executives of Rockwell International, the main contractor to build the shuttle, had testified that Rockwell had been opposed to launching the shuttle because of the danger posed by ice formation on the launch platform, Martin Cioffoletti, vice president for space transportation at Rockwell, said: "I felt that by telling them we did not have a sufficient data base and could not analyze the trajectory of the ice, I felt he understood that Rockwell was not giving a positive indication that we were for the launch."

Officials at Morton Thiokol, when asked why they reversed earlier decisions not to launch the shuttle, said the reversal was "based on the re-evaluation of those discussions." The Presidential commission investigating the accident suggested that this statement could be translated to mean there was pressure from NASA.

One of the most chilling uses of doublespeak occurred in 1981 when then Secretary of State Alexander Haig was testifying before congressional committees about the murder of three American nuns and a Catholic lay worker in El Salvador. The four women had been raped and then shot at close range, and there was clear evidence that the crime had been committed by soldiers of the Salvadoran government. Before the House Foreign Affairs Committee, Secretary Haig said, "I'd like to suggest to you that some of the investigations would lead one to believe that perhaps the vehicle the nuns were riding in may have tried to run a roadblock, or may accidentally have been perceived to have been doing so, and there'd been an exchange of fire and then perhaps those who inflicted the casualties sought to cover it up. And this could have been at a very low level of both competence and motivation in the context of the issue itself. But the facts on this are not clear enough for anyone to draw a definitive conclusion."

The next day, before the Senate Foreign Relations Committee, Secretary Haig claimed that press reports on his previous testimony were inaccurate. When Senator Claiborne Pell asked whether Secretary Haig was suggesting the possibility that "the nuns may have run through a roadblock," Secretary Haig replied, "You mean that they tried to violate ... ? Not at all, no, not at all. My heavens! The dear nuns who raised me in my parochial schooling would forever isolate me from their affections and respect." When Senator Pell asked Secretary Haig, "Did you mean that the nuns were firing at the people, or what did 'an exchange of fire' mean?" Secretary Haig replied, "I haven't met any pistol-packing nuns in my day, Senator. What I meant was that if one fellow starts shooting, then the next thing you know they all panic." Thus did the Secretary of State of the United States explain official government policy on the murder of four American citizens in a foreign land. 30

The congressional hearings for the IranContra affair produced more doublespeak. During his second day of testimony before the Select Committee on Secret Military Assistance to Iran and the Nicaraguan Opposition, Oliver North admitted that he had on different occasions lied to the Iranians, his colleague Maj. Gen. Richard Secord, congressional investigators, and the Congress, and that he had destroyed evidence and created false documents. North then asserted to the committee that everything he was about to say would be the truth.

North used the words "residuals" and "diversions" to refer to the millions of dollars which were raised for the contras by overcharging Iran for arms. North also said that he "cleaned" and "fixed" things up, that he was "cleaning up the historical record," and that he "took steps to ensure" that things never "came out"—meaning he lied, destroyed official government documents, and created false documents. Some documents weren't destroyed; they were "non-log[ged]" or kept "out of the system so that outside knowledge would not necessarily be derived from having the documents themselves."

North was also careful not to "infect other people with unnecessary knowledge." He explained that the Nicaraguan Humanitarian Assistance Office provided humanitarian aid in "mixed loads," which, according to North, "meant...beans and Band-Aids and boots and bullets." For North, people in other countries who helped him were "assets." "Project

Democracy" was a "euphemism" he used at the time to refer to the organization that was building an airfield for the contras.

In speaking of a false chronology of events which he helped construct, North said that he "was provided with additional input that was radically different from the truth. I assisted in furthering that version." He mentions "a different version from the facts" and calls the chronology "inaccurate." North also testified that he and William Casey, then head of the C.I.A., together falsified the testimony that Casey was to give to Congress. "Director Casey and I fixed that testimony and removed the offensive portions. We fixed it by omission. We left out — it wasn't made accurate, it wasn't made fulsome, it was fixed by omission." Official lies were "plausible deniability."

While North admitted that he had shredded documents after being   35
informed that officials from the Attorney General's office wanted to inspect some of the documents in his office, he said, "I would prefer to say that I shredded documents that day like I did on all other days, but perhaps with increased intensity."

North also preferred to use the passive to avoid responsibility. When asked "Where are the non-logged documents?" he replied, "I think they were shredded." Again, when asked on what authority he agreed to allow Secord to make a personal profit off the arms sale to Iran, North replied with a long, wordy response filled with such passive constructions as "it was clearly indicated," "it was already known," and "it was recognized." But he never answered the question.

For North, the whole investigation by Congress was just an attempt "to criminalize policy differences between coequal branches of government and the Executive's conduct of foreign affairs." Lying to Congress, shredding official documents, violating laws, conducting unauthorized activities were all just "policy differences" to North. But North was generous with the committee: "I think there's fault to go on both sides. I've said that repeatedly throughout my testimony. And I have accepted the responsibility for my role in it." While North accepts responsibility, he does not accept accountability.

This final statement of North's bears close reading for it reveals the subtlety of his language. North states as fact that Congress was at fault, but at fault for what he doesn't specify. Furthermore, he does not accept responsibility for any specific action, only for his "role," whatever that may have been, in "it." In short, while he may be "responsible" (not guilty) for violating the law, Congress shares in that responsibility for having passed the law.

In Oliver North's doublespeak, then, defying a law is complying with it, noncompliance is compliance. North's doublespeak allowed him to help draft a letter to Congress saying that "we are complying with the letter and spirit" of the Boland Amendment, when what the letter really meant, North later admitted, was that "Boland doesn't apply to us and so we're complying with its letter and spirit."

Contrary to his claim that he was a "stand up guy" who would tell all   40
and take whatever was coming to him, North disclaimed all responsibility
for his actions: "I was authorized to do everything that I did." Yet when
he was asked who gave him authorization, North replied, "My superiors."
When asked which superior, he replied: "Well, who—look who sign—I
didn't sign those letters to the—to this body." And North's renowned
steel-trap memory went vague or forgetful again.

After North had testified, Admiral John Poindexter, North's superior,
testified before the committee. Once again, doublespeak flourished. In
the world of Admiral John Poindexter, one does not lie but "misleads"
or "withholds information." Likewise, one engages in "secret activities"
which are not the same as covert actions. In Poindexter's world, one can
"acquiesce" in a shipment of weapons while at the same time not authorize
the shipment. One can transfer millions of dollars of government money
as a "technical implementation" without making a "substantive decision."
One can also send subordinates to lie to congressional committees if one
does not "micromanage" them. In Poindexter's world, "outside interference" occurs when Congress attempts to fulfill its constitutional function
of passing legislation.

For Poindexter, withholding information was not lying. When asked
about Col. North's testimony that he had lied to a congressional committee and that Poindexter had known that North intended to lie, Poindexter
replied, "there was a general understanding that he [North] was to withhold
information.... I...did not expect him to lie to the committee. I expected
him to be evasive....I'm sure they [North's answers] were very carefully
crafted, nuanced. The total impact, I am sure, was one of withholding information from the Congress, but I'm still not convinced...that he lied."

Yet Poindexter protested that it is not "fair to say that I have mis-
informed Congress or other Cabinet officers. I haven't testified to that.
I've testified that I withheld information from Congress. And with regard
to the Cabinet officers, I didn't withhold anything from them that they
didn't want withheld from them." Poindexter did not explain how it is
possible to withhold information that a person wants withheld.

The doublespeak of Alexander Haig, Oliver North, and John Poindexter occurred during their testimony before congressional committees.
Perhaps their doublespeak was not premeditated but just happened to be
the way they spoke, and thought. President Jimmy Carter in 1980 could
call the aborted raid to free the American hostages in Tehran an "incomplete success" and really believe that he had made a statement that clearly
communicated with the American public. So too could President Ronald
Reagan say in 1985 that "ultimately our security and our hopes for success
at the arms reduction talks hinge on the determination that we show here
to continue our program to rebuild and refortify our defenses" and really
believe that greatly increasing the amount of money spent building new
weapons will lead to a reduction in the number of weapons in the world. If

we really believe that we understand such language and that such language communicates and promotes clear thought, then the world of *1984* with its control of reality through language is upon us.

THINKING CRITICALLY ABOUT THE READING

1. What, according to Lutz, is doublespeak? What are its essential characteristics?

2. What is a euphemism? Are all euphemisms examples of doublespeak? Explain.

3. In his discussion of Oliver North's testimony during the Irancontra hearings, Lutz states, "While North accepts responsibility, he does not accept accountability" (37). Explain what Lutz means here. What differences do you draw between responsibility and accountability?

4. Why, according to Lutz, does "doublespeak continue to spread as the official language of public discourse" (1)? In your opinion, is doublespeak as widespread today as it was when Lutz wrote his article? What examples can you provide to back up your opinion?

5. Lutz discusses four basic types or categories of doublespeak—euphemism, jargon, gobbledygook, and inflated language. In what ways does this classification serve to clarify not only the concept of doublespeak but also its many uses? (Glossary: *Classification*)

6. Lutz is careful to illustrate each of the basic types of doublespeak with examples. Why is it important to use plenty of examples in an essay like this? (Glossary: *Examples*) What do his many examples reveal about Lutz's expertise on the subject?

7. Why does Lutz believe that we must recognize doublespeak for what it is and voice our dissatisfaction with those who use it?

LANGUAGE IN ACTION

In an article called "Public Doublespeak," Terence Moran presents the following list of recommended language, which school administrators in Brooklyn gave their elementary school teachers to use when discussing students with their parents.

FOR PARENT INTERVIEWS AND REPORT CARDS

Harsh Expression (Avoid)	Acceptable Expression (Use)
Does all right if pushed	Accomplishes tasks when interest is stimulated.
Too free with fists	Resorts to physical means of winning his point or attracting attention.
Lies (Dishonest)	Shows difficulty in distinguishing between imaginary and factual material.

(**continued**)

Cheats	Needs help in learning to adhere to rules and standards of fair play.
Steals	Needs help in learning to respect the property rights of others.
Noisy	Needs to develop quieter habits of communication.
Lazy	Needs ample supervision in order to work well.
Is a bully	Has qualities of leadership but needs help in learning to use them democratically.
Associates with "gangs"	Seems to feel secure only in group situations; needs to develop sense of independence.
Disliked by other children	Needs help in learning to form lasting friendships.

What are your reactions to these recommendations? Why do you suppose the school administrators made up this list? What purpose does such language serve? Do you believe the "acceptable" language belongs in our nation's schools? Why or why not?

WRITING SUGGESTIONS

1. Think of the ways that you encounter doublespeak every day, whether in school or at work, or while reading a newspaper or watching television. How does it affect you? What do you suppose the speakers' or writers' motives are in using doublespeak? Using your own experiences and observations, write an essay in which you explore the reasons why people use doublespeak. Before starting to write, you may find it helpful to review your Writing to Discover response to the Lutz essay.

2. In his concluding paragraph Lutz states, "If we really believe that we understand [doublespeak] and that such language communicates and promotes clear thought, then the world of *1984* with its control of reality through language is upon us." In an essay, discuss whether or not Lutz is overstating the case and being too pessimistic and whether or not the American public is really unaware of—or apathetic about—how doublespeak manipulates and deceives. Consider also whether or not the American public has reacted to doublespeak with, as Lutz suggests, "suspicion, cynicism, distrust, and, ultimately, hostility."

3. Using resources in your library or on the Internet, write a paper about the language of funeral directors, stockbrokers, college professors, health-care professionals, or some other occupation of your choice. How pervasive is doublespeak in the occupation you selected? Based on the results of your research, why do you think people with this type of job use such language? Do you find this language troublesome? If so, what can be done to change the situation? If not, why not?

The Burden of Deceit in Public Life

SISSELA BOK

Sissela Bok was born in 1934 in Sweden and grew up in Switzerland, France, and the United States. After studying at the Sorbonne, University of Paris, Bok earned both her B.A. and M.A. in psychology from George Washington University in 1957 and 1958, respectively, and a Ph.D. in philosophy from Harvard University in 1970. Her interest in human values and ethics first manifested itself in her book *Lying: Moral Choice in Public and Private Life* (1978). Here Bok considers many aspects of lying, from "little white lies" to those told "in the national interest," in an effort to discover when and why people deceive and whether it is ever morally right to do so. She discovered that while the Ten Commandments forbid perjury in a court of law but do not otherwise mention lying and that our contemporary laws generally do the same, truthfulness is universally regarded as one of the chief moral virtues, and its absence as a defect is not easily forgiven. Her book on lying was followed by *Secrets: On the Ethics of Concealment and Revelation* (1983), *A Strategy for Peace: Human Values* (1989), *Common Values* (1995), and *Mayhem: Violence as Public Entertainment* (1998). Bok has served on committees for Amnesty International and the Pulitzer Prize Board and as an advisor to various hospitals and the Department of Health and Human Services in Washington, D.C. Currently she teaches courses in ethics and decision-making at Brandeis University, where she is professor of philosophy.

In 2006 the Massachusetts Institute for a New Commonwealth and the Massachusetts Foundation for the Humanities invited Bok to deliver the Commonwealth Humanities Lecture. Bok responded with "The Burden of Deceit in Public Life." In this shortened version of her lecture, she tells us why it is so important in a democracy to foster a thoughtful, responsible debate about deceit, lying, and secrecy and their impact on individuals and society as a whole. Notice how careful she is to define the key terms clearly and precisely.

WRITING TO DISCOVER: *Lying happens every day in our society, whether it is a politician hiding behind a subtly worded statement or a guest fibbing to a host about the quality of a meal. What, for you, constitutes lying? Are all lies the same? In other words, are there different degrees or types of lying?*

I want to ask . . . what we can do to bring about a more thoughtful debate on deceit, lying, and secrecy, instead of what has come to resemble, too often, shouting matches about lying and cheating between adversaries in politics and many other walks of life. . . . I see both the concept of "commonwealth" and that of "humanities" as centrally related to my topic, "The Burden of Deceit in Public Life."

It is crucial to think of that burden as imposed not just on individuals but on a commonwealth, a community. Practices of deceit in public life do affect us collectively and, in so doing, they place a great burden on "the common weal"—the common good. . . .

I want also to draw on the perspective of public health, and to refer to the "burden of disease," a concept that has become central to that field in recent decades. . . . I want to suggest ways in which we might use that public health perspective and that concept of a burden of disease in thinking about the societal risks from practices of deceit and excessive secrecy. . . .

As we are all aware, charges of lying, cheating, even treason [are] commonplace, whether in connection with practices of deceit in business, the arts, journalism, or, especially, in politics and government. Mutual accusations—shouting matches, too often,—resonate, with adversaries showing little hesitation to impute lies to one another.

I am convinced that this spiraling of vast accusations about lying   5 contributes in its own right to the collective burden of deceit, by making it easier for people to conclude there is lying everywhere. What gets lost in the way many books and articles and blogs attribute words such as "lie," "lying," and "liar" to adversaries are important differences between simple errors, on the one hand, and, on the other, a variety of ways of misleading people, including duplicity, mendacity, deception, deceit, lying, exaggerations, and euphemisms.

Blurring together all such concepts hampers the thoughtful national debate we ought to be having on the role of deceit in public life and the burden it imposes. Americans, deeply divided over the war in Iraq, disagree sharply over whether President Bush and his administration misled the nation during the build-up to the war, much as citizens disagreed during the Johnson administration regarding the escalation of the war in Vietnam, and about the role of deceit and secrecy in each case. Not only is it crucial to consider the role of deceit and secrecy in public life at a time when the nation is at war; we need to ask, as well, whether the burden that practices of deceit impose is especially likely to contribute to the other burden I mentioned: the burden of disease, adding to the toll of disability and death. It is a burden that grows in war time as well as at other times of national emergency, as caused by hurricanes, floods, earthquakes, and epidemics.

We can look back to September 1918, for a particularly tragic compounding of the burden of deceit and that of disease. It was when America was in the "war to end all wars" under President Woodrow Wilson that the influenza pandemic struck with all its force, ravaging military encampments and civilian populations alike. The pandemic would end up taking far more lives, in the course of a few months, than World War I itself— estimates of deaths now range between 50 and 100 million people, worldwide, mostly young adults in the prime of life: possibly 8 to 10 percent of all living adults.

In hindsight, it is almost incomprehensible that President Wilson, preoccupied with the war in Europe, took next to no public notice of the threat posed by the pandemic. It is as if he had become the prisoner of his own single-minded focus on the war. According to John M. Barry, in *The Great Influenza,* "no national official ever publicly acknowledged the danger of influenza." So far as I can tell, the president himself did not lie outright about the epidemic; but in offering no leadership in the crisis, he failed utterly in his duty to the public.

Secrecy contributed to President Wilson's failure in this regard. He had spoken most forcefully against secrecy during the 1912 presidential campaign, holding that "everybody knows that corruption thrives in secret places" and that "secrecy means impropriety." By 1918, he instituted laws to stifle dissent and to enforce "voluntary" self-censorship for the press. The Espionage Act of 1917 made it a crime for a person to convey information with intent to interfere with the operation or success of the armed forces. The Sedition Act of 1918, making it illegal to speak out against the government, was invoked to send critics of the war to prison. The euphemistically named "Committee on Public Information" helped to stifle dissent in order to promote the war and keep public morale high. As a result, critics kept quiet and American newspapers remained incongruously upbeat even as the nation was overwhelmed by the pandemic. Many papers simply reiterated the official phrases about there being no need to fear illness so long as you washed your hands and took other reasonable precautions.

If critics had been free to challenge the government—not only its   10
conduct of the war but also its response to the pandemic—it might have been possible to save thousands of lives. Instead, as the death toll mounted, citizens were left bewildered, finding no guidance from the press and increasingly skeptical of official pronouncements. The pervasive distrust contributed to the burden of deceit and compounded the burden of disease, disability, and death.

As we seek to engage a more thoughtful debate about deceit in public life today, it is worth keeping in mind the compounding of the burdens of deceit and of disease in 1918 and during later national crises such as that of the war in Vietnam. In each case, it matters to think through the differences between ways of misleading people, and crucial distinctions without which it becomes well-nigh impossible to consider the moral questions deceit raises. I shall mention, in turn, what I see as some of the most important definitions, distinctions, and the moral questions.

With respect to definitions, there is no one way to define "lie" or "deceit," any more than "promise," "violence," "happiness," or most nontechnical concepts, as the philosopher John Searle has shown, in *Speech Acts.* What matters, therefore, is to be clear about the definitions one is using, and to make sure they do not confuse important distinctions and moral questions. I have found the following helpful while discussing alternative definitions in my books *Lying* and *Secrets.*

Secrecy, to begin with, involves concealment but need not involve any intention to mislead. While all forms of deceit, all lies, involve keeping something secret, the reverse is not true. Keeping something secret, such as one's private hopes or fears, need not at all be meant to mislead others. But withholding part of the information needed by those to whom one speaks can be as deceptive as any lie. For a public official to fail to reveal what citizens have every right to know is as deceptive as for a physician to keep patients in the dark about a diagnosis of, say, cancer.

Deception can be either intended or wholly unintended, as when we end up deceived by mirages, dreams, or illusions without anyone who intends to mislead us. When we deceive others intentionally, we communicate messages meant to mislead them, to make them believe what we do not ourselves believe.

Self-deception includes the many forms of avoidance, such as denial,   15
psychic numbing, and compartmentalization, by which people seem to take part in shielding themselves from perceiving knowledge.

Deceit is limited to intentional deception of others. It can take place through words or acts: anything people do or say in order to mislead others constitutes such intentional deception, as when disguises are used for such a purpose, or false passports, as well as in all cases of lying or of secrecy meant to mislead.

Lies are statements meant to mislead listeners and believed to be false by those who make them. But just as false statements need not be deceitful, so true statements can sometimes be meant to deceive. An isolated true statement told by someone known to be a habitual liar can be intended to mislead listeners, and succeed in doing so, as much as lies by persons thought honest. Persons adept at producing "information overload," moreover, as in lengthy, confusing sales agreements or insurance documents, can aim to deceive others without telling actual lies.

Mendacity characterizes someone given to different forms of deceit, including lies, and frequently including, too, self-deception.

Among the most common failures to draw distinctions in the public debates over deceit are those of conflating or confusing lies and honest mistakes; deception through outright lies, half-truths, and silence; foolish promises or predictions and knowingly false ones; telling what one knows are lies and refusing to acknowledge that what one once believed to be true has been shown to be false; and slipping into a lie and undertaking a policy of deceit—something that can happen to anyone and that is quite different from choosing to be someone who deals with others through deceit.

In turn, when the definitions and distinctions are blurred together in   20
the public debate, it becomes easier to short-circuit reflection about the underlying moral questions regarding when deceit might be considered excusable or even justifiable. In my book *Lying*, I suggested a three-step procedure for weighing a lie one takes to be needed to achieve a good purpose: first, to ask whether there are alternative courses of action that

will bring about the same aim without requiring deception; second, to set forth with care the moral reasons thought to excuse or justify the lie, and the possible counterarguments; and third, as a test of these two steps, to ask how a public of reasonable persons would respond to such arguments.

People tend to have starkly diverging perspectives on what they see as defining lies and other forms of deceit, on the distinctions I have mentioned, as well as on the underlying moral questions, depending on whether they are thinking about engaging in deceit or believe they have been deceived. Most people value truthfulness more highly in others than when it comes to their own choices. When they find themselves on the receiving end of other people's lies, they are far more suspicious of the underlying motives than when they consider possible lies of their own. When they do consider lying, they often take for granted that they have good reason to lie without stopping to consider the moral arguments for and against their action, much less to ask whether they could be defended in public.

The most serious mistake they make is to evaluate the costs and benefits of a particular lie or group of lies in an isolated case, and then to favor the lies if the benefits seem to outweigh the costs. Least of all do they take into account what I call three "hidden risks"—apart from immediate costs to the persons deceived and others affected—that ought also to enter into any serious weighing of pros and cons: risks to themselves; to their colleagues, profession, or line of work; and to trust.

The first hidden risk is the most difficult one of all for persons involved in deceit to perceive: the costs to themselves. Because liars tend to overestimate their own good will and their chances of escaping detection, they underestimate the damage to their reputation and their credibility once they are found to have lied. And if they do get away with lies at first, further psychological and moral barriers may wear down: they may come to see more and more lies to be needed and find fewer among them morally problematic. In the end, they may find it harder and harder to distinguish lies from half-truths or to confront the likelihood that the cobbled-together edifice will crumble.

The second hidden risk is to the institution or profession one represents. When journalists or social scientists or public officials are found to engage in deceit, they contribute to the public's distrust of their colleagues and their profession. Politicians who resort to smears and deceptive campaign ads have contributed to public distaste for politics and to declining numbers of voters, with many staying home at election time, declaring a "pox on both your houses."

Most remote of all, as people calculate the pros and cons of particular lies, is the third risk: that of the corrosive and cumulative effects that their lies, once suspected, may have not only on their own credibility or that of their profession, but on trust more generally. Lies invite imitation, preventive duplicity, and retaliation after the fact. As they spread, suspicions mount and trust erodes. Naive trust invites abuses all its own; but when distrust becomes too overpowering within a family, a community, or a nation, it becomes impossible to meet joint needs—to serve the public weal.

Everyone has reason to think through how their lies may add to the burden of deceit; but public servants, doctors, clergy, lawyers, bankers, journalists, and other professionals have a special responsibility in this regard, given the privileges they have been granted. Public officials, above all, can have a uniquely deleterious effect on trust. When they act so as to undermine trust, this cuts at the roots of democracy. To the extent that citizens lose confidence in what leaders say, they are disempowered: they cannot know enough about the facts to form an intelligent opinion without relying on the information provided to them. Once disenchanted on that score, citizens may suspect even the most honest officials. As James Madison wrote, "a popular government, without popular information, or the means of acquiring it, is but a prologue to a Farce or a Tragedy; or perhaps both."

To illustrate how questions arise about whether certain forms of deceit are more excusable than others, let me mention three examples. The first concerns Russia's President Boris Yeltsin's campaign for reelection ten years ago. On June 16, 1996, he won the first round of the elections with about 35 percent of the votes. The runoff election, in which he faced Communist Party Leader Gennady Zuyganov, was scheduled for July 3. Between the two election dates, it was later discovered, Yeltsin had suffered a severe heart attack. Here was information that would have been crucial for voters considering his fitness for office. Instead, they saw videos of him dancing with vigor and apparent glee, and Yeltsin appeared on television to declare that he knew exactly what to do and that he had "the strength and will and decisiveness for that." With the help of his doctors and his inner circle, he let it be known that he had a cold and would shortly return to work.

My second example is one we're all familiar with. In a televised speech to the nation on August 17, 1998, President Bill Clinton admitted that he had misled his family, his colleagues, and the public about his relationship with Monica Lewinsky. Split screens showed the president acknowledging in August what he had denied in his earlier, finger-pointing speech January 26. Both Presidents Yeltsin and Clinton may have taken for granted that it was legitimate to lie to citizens to protect what they saw as private matters. In retrospect, few would claim that privacy automatically justifies not only silence but falsehood on such scores; much less that anyone should go so far as to present deceptive or perjurious testimony in election campaigns or in court. When public officials lie to citizens they turn whatever is being lied about into a matter of public concern, bringing into play the three hidden risks, no matter how rightfully private the subject of the lie may have been in itself.

My third example is that of a young English orphan, Margaret Armstrong. She was the daughter of one of England's most notorious alleged murderers, Major Herbert Armstrong, who was hanged in 1922 for poisoning her mother. Margaret was seven years old at the time of his trial and was sent to live with a family in a different part of the country. She lived for 73 years in fear of being branded as a murderer's daughter. She chose to shield herself, not exactly by lying but by telling a very partial truth to anyone who asked about her parents: "I always used to say that my mother had died of food poisoning and my father had fallen and broken his neck."

Margaret Armstrong's dissimulation was surely excusable, considering that it began when she was a young child, trying to survive emotionally and to protect information which the public had no right to learn about. But it was a heavy burden for her to bear, since it forced her to continue to live a lie regarding her past. It was only when she was 80 years old, and had lived through the anguish of a BBC "Mystery" TV series about her parents, that she could at last acknowledge publicly her parents, discuss the doubts that had arisen about her father's guilt, and disclose the stratagem she used in self-defense—without the slightest fear of being stigmatized.

What about the question of whether some practices of deceit are not only more excusable but more justifiable, say on grounds of self-defense or national security? On this score, there is great disagreement; but I see no problem in defending openly a policy such as that of lying to persecutors searching for their victims. Likewise, in times of war, there clearly is a place for stratagems and deceits, just as violence may be called for, most legitimately in cases of national self-defense. But the rationale of self-defense, individual as well as collective, and the broader one of national security has been invoked for a vast panoply of lies and other forms of deceit that, because they cannot be openly defended, tend to be shrouded in secrecy.

When official lies intended to deceive adversaries on grounds of national security are found to have misled the domestic public as well, the damage to trust can be especially great. For example, take what President Dwight D. Eisenhower spoke of as his greatest regret, in looking back at his years in office—"the lie we told about the U-2 in May 1960" as quoted by David Wise in *The Politics of Lying: Government Deception, Secrecy, and Power.*

At first, when an American U-2 plane was shot down 1,300 miles inside the Soviet Union, while on an intelligence mission, Eisenhower authorized a State Department spokesman to insist that the plane had been on a weather mission; but when Nikita Khruschev made public the photo of the CIA pilot, Francis Gary Powers, Eisenhower had to admit that this claim had been false, and that the United States had been conducting spy flights over the Soviet Union.

As the country reeled from this exposure, President Eisenhower considered resigning. His sense of burden was both personal—of having been shamed publicly—and for his administration, seeing the Paris Summit Conference that he had worked so hard to bring about break up as Khruschev dramatically stormed out after lacerating the United States. Looking back, the president later said that he had "not realized how high a price we would pay for that lie." After that, according to Tom Wicker's book *Dwight D. Eisenhower*, he saw nothing worthwhile left for him to do as president:

> Thus passed the best hope and opportunity, until then, for a comprehensive test ban treaty as the centerpiece of disarmament between hostile superpowers. . . . The nuclear arms race and the Cold War, the vast expenditures to sustain both with tensions only occasionally lessened and never removed would continue for nearly thirty years, through seven more administrations, into the 1980s.

The war in Vietnam offers another example for which national security   35 was invoked in defense of a multitude of deceitful actions and practices, as when President Lyndon Johnson concealed plans to escalate the war in Vietnam during the election campaign of 1964, pointing to the risks that Senator Barry Goldwater might bomb North Vietnam if elected—actions that Johnson himself undertook after he had been reelected. The thorough historical documentation of these practices, beginning with the Pentagon Papers, offers unique insight into the practices themselves, and their interaction with ignorance, self-deception, and secrecy. In turn, there is much to be learned from this documentation about the ways in which what I have called the burden of deceit can compound the burden of death and disability.

When it comes to the war in Iraq, the questions of whether there were lies in the first place or of whether, and if so when, other forms of deceit were used, are precisely what is under dispute today. Defenders of the administration's war policies reject all imputations of deceit. True, some among them acknowledge, their predictions turned out to be wrong; true, they may have relied on faulty intelligence or untrustworthy informants. But they spoke in error, they insist, never intending to mislead.

A great many people have concluded, however, that the Administration misled them intentionally. By what means, if not through deceit, they ask, did we find ourselves mired in this war that has come to exact such great human sacrifice and such vast financial outlays? Increasing numbers now question whether intelligence was simply erroneous or whether it was twisted, "cherry-picked," to mislead the public. They are skeptical about the sincerity of those who claimed that Iraq had weapons of mass destruction and who issued warnings such as that "the smoking gun that could turn into a mushroom cloud" or who claimed to know that Saddam Hussein was in league with Al-Qaeda.

Even among those who hold such sharply discordant views, however, there are two areas of agreement. First, most people now agree that the president and other public officials presented arguments to support going to war that relied on evidence later found to be false. Second, most also agree that the burden of death, disability, and suffering resulting from the invasion is far greater than the proponents of going to war had predicted.

Such agreement can serve as the beginning of a careful sorting through — one that will surely take time — of the different statements made on all sides during the period leading up to the invasion of Iraq. This process will require inquiring into which claims might have been based on error, at least at first; which ones stemmed from overconfidence in poor documentation and unreliable sources; on ignorance or sheer naïveté; and which other ones give every indication of having been intended to mislead the public.

For this purpose, it will be indispensable to look back at past experi-   40
ence, as in the examples I have cited from earlier presidencies, in the light of the burden that practices of deceit impose on public life. It will also be helpful to ask what we can learn from public health efforts to combat and overcome the burden of disease, by assessing risk factors, comparing preventive measures, and stressing rehabilitative measures, and to consider how the two burdens can interact, in order to determine what choices are open to government officials, journalists, and all of us as members of the public to work together to alleviate both burdens.

But it is important for people on all sides of this as of other contro-versies involving charges of deceit not to rush to judgment, to give oppo-nents the benefit of the doubt. For false accusations of lying and cheating can add to the burden of deceit in a society as well, and to the loss of trust, as can claims that critics lack patriotism and the general free-for-alls about lying that I have qualified as shouting-matches.

Here again, it helps to compare our present challenges with those of public health and assessing the burden of disease. We are surely aware of all the damage done when false rumors are spread about what causes diseases and what protects from them — as when fears of vaccination risk delay in the eradication of polio or when warnings about contaminated drinking water are dismissed as propaganda.

Few decisions in a democracy can be more crucial than that of whether or not to go to war. The burden of disease — of death and disability — for a democracy of having done so based on mistakes, misjudgments, and faulty information is already great; but if deceit was involved in presenting it or in exaggerating the need for haste in acting before the information could be checked, it endangers the very essence of democracy — the informed consent of the governed.

As Thomas Jefferson said, insisting that citizens have a right to full information about the possibility of a war, "It is their sweat which is to earn all the expenses of the war, and their blood which is to flow in expia-tion of the causes of it."

THINKING CRITICALLY ABOUT THE READING

1. What is deceit? How is it different from secrecy and lies? Illustrate the differences with examples of your own. (Glossary: *Examples*)

2. Why do you suppose Bok introduces the concept of "burden of disease" into her discussion of the "burden of deceit"? What point is Bok making with her example of World War I and the influenza pandemic of 1918?

3. According to Bok, why is it important for each of us to make clear distinctions in public debates over deceit? What happens when we fail to make clear distinctions, when we conflate and confuse terms?

4. In what situations might lying be considered excusable or even justifiable? What three-step procedure does Bok recommend for weighing the potential impact of a lie? Explain.

5. According to Bok, what role does trust play in the workings of a democracy? What happens when public trust turns to distrust? Explain.

6. Bok claims that as people calculate the pros and cons of a particular lie they often do not take into account what she calls "hidden risks." What are these risks, and why do people generally fail to take account of them?

7. Bok believes that when charges of deceit have been leveled it is important for us "not to rush to judgment, to give opponents the benefit of the doubt. For false accusations of lying and cheating can add to the burden of deceit in a society as well, and to the loss of trust, as can claims that critics lack patriotism and the general free-for-alls about lying that I have qualified as shouting-matches" (41). In what ways do false accusations and claims add to the burden of deceit?

8. What happens when we let debates slip into shouting matches? Who wins? Who loses? What can be done to avert a shouting match when a debate seems to be headed in that direction?

LANGUAGE IN ACTION

Consider each of the following situations in light of what Bok counsels about deceit. In each instance, how far could you justify keeping someone else's secret? Would you lie for the other person? If you felt it necessary not to keep silent, what would you do? Why? Share your responses with your classmates.

a. After having been out of work for a long time and with a large family to feed, you have just been hired as a truck driver for a toxic waste disposal company. Before long you learn that the company is dumping the waste illegally, without the proper safeguards. State investigators have so far been unsuccessful in identifying the company or companies that have been doing this. If you come forward with the information, you will lose your job.

b. A classmate who is a close friend tells you that he/she intends to buy a term paper for a course you are both taking. You learn that your friend did so and received an A grade for the paper, while yours, on which you worked for three weeks, was graded B−.

Discuss any differences you and your classmates see in how you would handle the two situations.

WRITING SUGGESTIONS

1. Write an essay in which you agree or disagree with Bok's statement: "[W]hen distrust becomes too overpowering within a family, a community, or a nation, it becomes impossible to meet joint needs—to serve the public weal" (25). Use examples from your own experience, observation, or reading to support your position.

2. Who or what has had the greatest influence in the development of your ethical/ moral standards or values? Has it been an individual or an institution—family, church, school, local community—or some other source? Write an essay in which you describe your core values and the individual or institution that has influenced you most in developing these values.

3. Consider the following moral dilemma:

   > Your are the chief executive officer of a cosmetics company whose only profitable product is a heavily advertised facial cream. Several women in a single city have suffered acid burns from the cream, but the news has not gotten into the newspapers. Nobody knows whether the cream was contaminated in your plant or tampered with at a later point. If you recall the cream, or even if the news gets out and women stop buying it, your company will go bankrupt.

   In an essay answer the central question: What should you do? What options do you have to resolve the problem? In your answer, explain why you adopted one solution instead of another. Can you arrive at a general principle that would guide you in deciding other, similar situations? Before starting to write, you may find it helpful to revisit the discussions you and your classmates had about the two situations described in the Language in Action activity.

I Have a Dream

MARTIN LUTHER KING JR.

Martin Luther King Jr., son of a Baptist minister, was born in 1929 and
ordained at the age of eighteen. King went on to study at Morehouse
College, Crozer Theological Seminary, Boston University, and Chicago
Theological Seminary. He first came to prominence in 1955 when he led
a successful boycott against the segregated bus system of Montgomery,
Alabama. As the first president of the Southern Christian Leadership
Conference, King promoted a policy of massive but nonviolent resistance
to racial injustice. The leading spokesman for the civil rights movement
during the 1950s and 1960s, he also championed women's rights and
protested the Vietnam War. In 1964 his efforts won him the Nobel Peace
Prize. King was assassinated in April 1968 after he spoke at a rally in
Memphis, Tennessee.

King delivered "I Have a Dream" in 1963 from the steps of the
Lincoln Memorial to more than two hundred thousand people who had
come to Washington, D.C., to demonstrate for civil rights. In this mighty
sermon—replete with allusions to the Bible, the Negro spiritual tradition, and great documents and speeches of the past—King presented his
indictment of the present and his vision of the future.

WRITING TO DISCOVER: *Have you ever heard a speech that you found
particularly inspiring or moving? Make some notes about why the speech or
the speaker was so effective. How did the speech affect the way you now think
about the speaker's subject?*

I am happy to join with you today in what will go down in history as
the greatest demonstration for freedom in the history of our nation.

Five score years ago, a great American, in whose symbolic shadow
we stand today, signed the Emancipation Proclamation. This momen-
tous decree came as a great beacon light of hope to millions of Negro
slaves who had been seared in the flames of withering injustice. It came
as a joyous daybreak to end the long night of their captivity. But one
hundred years later, the Negro still is not free. One hundred years
later, the life of the Negro is still sadly crippled by the manacles of
segregation and the chains of discrimination. One hundred years later,
the Negro lives on a lonely island of poverty in the midst of a vast
ocean of material prosperity. One hundred years later, the Negro is

still anguished in the corners of American society and finds himself in exile in his own land. And so we have come here today to dramatize a shameful condition.

In a sense we have come to our nation's capital to cash a check. When the architects of our republic wrote the magnificent words of the Constitution and the Declaration of Independence, they were signing a promissory note to which every American was to fall heir. This note was the promise that all men — yes, Black men as well as white men — would be guaranteed the inalienable rights of life, liberty, and the pursuit of happiness.

It is obvious today that America has defaulted on this promissory note insofar as her citizens of color are concerned. Instead of honoring this sacred obligation, America has given the Negro people a bad check, a check which has come back marked "insufficient funds." But we refuse to believe that the bank of justice is bankrupt. We refuse to believe that there are insufficient funds in the great vaults of opportunity of this nation; and so we have come to cash this check, a check that will give us upon demand the riches of freedom and the security of justice.

We have also come to this hallowed spot to remind America of the fierce urgency of *now*. This is no time to engage in the luxury of cooling off or to take the tranquilizing drug of gradualism. *Now* is the time to make real the promises of democracy. *Now* is the time to rise from the dark and desolate valley of segregation to the sunlit path of racial justice. Now is the time to lift our nation from the quicksands of racial injustice to the solid rock of brotherhood. *Now* is the time to make justice a reality for all of God's children.

It would be fatal for the nation to overlook the urgency of the moment. This sweltering summer of the Negro's legitimate discontent will not pass until there is an invigorating autumn of freedom and equality. Nineteen sixty-three is not an end, but a beginning. And those who hope that the Negro needed to blow off steam and will now be content will have a rude awakening if the nation returns to business as usual. There will be neither rest nor tranquility in America until the Negro is granted his citizenship rights. The whirlwinds of revolt will continue to shake the foundations of our nation until the bright day of justice emerges.

But there is something that I must say to my people who stand on the warm threshold which leads into the palace of justice. In the process of gaining our rightful place, we must not be guilty of wrongful deeds. Let us not seek to satisfy our thirst for freedom by drinking from the cup of bitterness and hatred. We must forever conduct our struggle on the high plane of dignity and discipline. We must not allow our creative protest to degenerate into physical violence. Again and again we must rise to the majestic heights of meeting physical force with soul force. And the marvelous new militancy which has engulfed the Negro community must not lead us to a distrust of all white people; for many of our white brothers, as evidenced by their presence here today, have come to realize that their destiny is tied up with our destiny, and they have come to realize that their freedom is inextricably bound to our freedom.

We cannot walk alone. And as we walk we must make the pledge that we shall always march ahead. We cannot turn back. There are those who are asking the devotees of civil rights, "When will you be satisfied?" We can never be satisfied as long as the Negro is the victim of the unspeakable horrors of police brutality. We can never be satisfied as long as our bodies, heavy with the fatigue of travel, cannot gain lodging in the motels of the highways and the hotels of the cities. We cannot be satisfied as long as the Negro's basic mobility is from a smaller ghetto to a larger one. We can never be satisfied as long as our children are stripped of their selfhood and robbed of their dignity by signs stating "For Whites Only." We cannot be satisfied as long as the Negro in Mississippi cannot vote and a Negro in New York believes he has nothing for which to vote. No, no, we are not satisfied, and we will not be satisfied until justice rolls down like waters and righteousness like a mighty stream.

I am not unmindful that some of you have come here out of great trials and tribulations. Some of you have come fresh from narrow jail cells. Some of you have come from areas where your quest for freedom left you battered by the storms of persecution and staggered by the winds of police brutality. You have been the veterans of creative suffering. Continue to work with the faith that unearned suffering is redemptive.

Go back to Mississippi, and go back to Alabama. Go back to South   10
Carolina. Go back to Georgia. Go back to Louisiana. Go back to the slums and ghettos of our Northern cities, knowing that somehow this situation can and will be changed. Let us not wallow in the valley of despair.

I say to you today, my friends, even though we face the difficulties of today and tomorrow, I still have a dream. It is a dream deeply rooted in the American dream. I have a dream that one day this nation will rise up and live out the true meaning of its creed: "We hold these truths to be self-evident, that all men are created equal." I have a dream that one day, on the red hills of Georgia, sons of former slaves and the sons of former slave owners will be able to sit down together at the table of brotherhood. I have a dream that one day even the state of Mississippi, a state sweltering with the heat of injustice, sweltering with the heat of oppression, will be transformed into an oasis of freedom and justice. I have a dream that my four little children will one day live in a nation where they will not be judged by the color of their skin, but by the content of their character.

I have a dream today. I have a dream that one day down in Alabama—with its vicious racists, with its governor's lips dripping with the words of interposition and nullification—one day right there in Alabama, little Black boys and Black girls will be able to join hands with little white boys and white girls as sisters and brothers.

I have a dream today. I have a dream that one day every valley shall be exalted and every hill and mountain shall be made low, the rough places will be made plain and the crooked places will be made straight, and the glory of the Lord shall be revealed, and all flesh shall see it together.

This is our hope. This is the faith that I go back to the South with. And with this faith we will be able to hew out of the mountain of despair a stone of hope. With this faith we will be able to transform the jangling discords of our nation into a beautiful symphony of brotherhood. With this faith we will be able to work together, to play together, to struggle together, to go to jail together, to stand up for freedom together, knowing that we will be free one day.

And this will be the day—this will be the day when all of God's chil-   15
dren will be able to sing with new meaning:

> My country, 'tis of thee,
> Sweet land of liberty,
>   Of thee I sing;
> Land where my fathers died,
> Land of the Pilgrims' pride,
> From every mountainside
>   Let freedom ring.

And if America is to be a great nation, this must become true.

And so let freedom ring from the prodigious hilltops of New Hampshire. Let freedom ring from the mighty mountains of New York. Let freedom ring from the heightening Alleghenies of Pennsylvania. Let freedom ring from the snow-capped Rockies of Colorado. Let freedom ring from the curvaceous slopes of California.

But not only that. Let freedom ring from Stone Mountain of Georgia. Let freedom ring from Lookout Mountain of Tennessee. Let freedom ring from every hill and molehill of Mississippi. "From every mountainside let freedom ring."

And when this happens—when we allow freedom to ring, when we let it ring from every village and every hamlet, from every state and every city—we will be able to speed up that day when all of God's children, Black men and white men, Jews and Gentiles, Protestants and Catholics, will be able to join hands and sing in the words of the old Negro spiritual: "Free at last! Free at last! Thank God Almighty. We are free at last!"

THINKING CRITICALLY ABOUT THE READING

1. Why does King say that the Constitution and the Declaration of Independence act as a "promissory note" (3) to the American people? In what way has America "defaulted" (4) on its promise?

2. King delivered his address to two audiences: the huge audience that listened to him in person, and another, even larger audience. (Glossary: *Audience*) What is that larger audience? What did King do in his speech to catch its attention and to deliver his point?

3. What does King mean when he says that in gaining a rightful place in society "we must not be guilty of wrongful deeds" (7)? Why is the issue so important to him?

4. King uses parallel constructions and repetition throughout his speech. Identify the phrases and words that he particularly emphasizes. Explain what these techniques add to the persuasiveness of his argument.

5. King makes liberal use of metaphor—and metaphorical imagery—in his speech. (Glossary: *Figures of Speech*) Choose a few examples, and examine what they add to the speech. How do they help King engage his listeners' feelings of injustice and give them hope for a better future?

6. When *will* King be satisfied in his quest for civil rights?

7. What, in a nutshell, is King's dream? What vision does he have for the future?

LANGUAGE IN ACTION

In using the photograph on the facing page of Martin Luther King Jr. in its "Think Different" advertising campaign, the Apple Computer company is relying on our cultural memory of King's "I Have a Dream" speech and of King as a person who was creative in his efforts to promote racial justice. To what extent does achieving racial equality depend on "thinking differently"?

WRITING SUGGESTIONS

1. King's language is powerful and his imagery is vivid, but the effectiveness of any speech depends partially upon its delivery. If read in monotone, King's use of repetition and parallel language would sound almost redundant rather than inspiring. Keeping presentation in mind, write a short speech that argues a point of view about which you feel strongly. Use King's speech as a model, and incorporate imagery, repetition, and metaphor to communicate your point. Read your speech aloud to a friend to see how it flows and how effective your use of language is. Refine your presentation—both your text and how you deliver it—and then present your speech to your class.

2. King uses a variety of metaphors in his speech, but sometimes a single encompassing metaphor can be useful to establish the tone and purpose of an essay. Write a description based on a metaphor that conveys a dominant impression from the beginning. Try to avoid clichés ("My dorm is a beehive," "My life is an empty glass"), but make your metaphor readily understandable. For example, you could say, "A police siren is a lullaby in my neighborhood," or "My town is a car that has gone 15,000 miles since its last oil change." Carry the metaphor through the entire description.

And Ain't I a Woman?

SOJOURNER TRUTH

Sojourner Truth was born a slave named Isabella in Ulster County, New York, in 1797. Freed by the New York State Emancipation Act of 1827, she went to New York City and underwent a profound religious transformation. She worked as a domestic servant and, in her active evangelism, tried to reform prostitutes. Adopting the name Sojourner Truth in 1843, she became a traveling preacher and abolitionist.

Although she remained illiterate, Truth's compelling presence gripped her audience as she spoke eloquently about emancipation and women's rights at conventions throughout the Northeast. Truth dictated her memoirs to Olive Gilbert and they were published as *The Narative of Sojourner Truth: A Northern Slave* (1850). After the Civil War, she worked to provide education and employment for emancipated slaves until her death in 1883.

WRITING TO DISCOVER: *What comes to mind when you hear the word* speech? *What are the speaking styles you respond to most, the ones that captivate you as a listener? Do you like speeches that sound reasoned and logical, or do you like ones that appeal to your emotions? Explain.*

Well, children, where there is so much racket there must be something out of kilter. I think that 'twixt the Negroes of the South and the women at the North, all talking about rights, the white men will be in a fix pretty soon. But what's all this here talking about?

That man over there says that women need to be helped into carriages, and lifted over ditches, and to have the best place everywhere. Nobody ever helps me into carriages, or over mud puddles, or gives me any best place! And ain't I a woman? Look at me! Look at my arm. I have plowed and planted, and gathered into barns, and no man could head me! And ain't I a woman? I could work as much and eat as much as a man — when I could get it — and bear the lash as well! And ain't I a woman? I have borne thirteen children, and seen them most all sold off to slavery, and when I cried out with my mother's grief, none but Jesus heard me! And ain't I a woman?

Then they talk about this thing in the head; what's this they call it? [Intellect, someone whispers.] That's it, honey. What's that got to do with women's rights or Negro's rights? If my cup won't hold but a pint, and yours holds a quart, wouldn't you be mean not to let me have my little half-measure full?

Then that little man in black there, he says women can't have as much rights as men, 'cause Christ wasn't a woman! Where did your Christ come from? Where did your Christ come from? From God and a woman! Man had nothing to do with him.

If the first woman God ever made was strong enough to turn the   5
world upside down all alone, these women together ought to be able to
turn it back, and get it right side up again! And now they is asking to do
it, the men better let them.

Obliged to you for hearing me, and now old Sojourner ain't got nothing more to say.

THINKING CRITICALLY ABOUT THE READING

1. What does Truth mean when she says, "Where there is so much racket there
   must be something out of kilter" (1)? Why does Truth believe that white men
   are going to find themselves in a "fix" (1)?

2. What does Truth put forth as her "credentials" as a woman? Why is it important for her to define what a woman is for her audience?

3. How does Truth use the comments of "that man over there" (2) and "that
   little man in black" (4) to help her establish her definition of woman?

4. What is the effect of Truth's repetition of the question "And ain't I a woman?"
   four times? What other questions does she ask? Why do you suppose Truth
   doesn't provide answers to questions in paragraph 3, but does for the question in paragraph 4?

5. How would you characterize Truth's tone in this speech? What phrases in the
   speech suggest that tone to you? (Glossary: *Tone*)

6. How does Truth counter the argument that "women can't have as much
   rights as men, 'cause Christ wasn't a woman" (4)?

LANGUAGE IN ACTION

Carefully read the following letter to the editor of the *New York Times*. In
it Nancy Stevens, president of a small Manhattan advertising agency, argues
against using the word *guys* to address women. How do you think Truth
would react to the use of the word *guys* to refer to women? Do you find
such usage objectionable?

WOMEN AREN'T GUYS

A young woman, a lawyer, strides into a conference room. Already in
attendance, at what looks to be the start of a high-level meeting, are four
smartly dressed women in their 20's and 30's. The arriving woman plunks her
briefcase down at the head of the polished table and announces, "O.K., guys,
let's get started."

On "Kate and Allie," a television show about two women living together
with Kate's daughter and Allie's daughter and son, the dialogue often runs to
such phrases as, "Hey, you guys, who wants pizza?" All of the people addressed

are female, except for Chip, the young son. "Come on, you guys, quit fighting," pleads one of the daughters when there is a tiff between the two women.

Just when we were starting to be aware of the degree to which language affects people's perceptions of women and substitute "people working" for "men working" and "humankind" for "mankind," this "guy" thing happened. Just when people have started becoming aware that a 40-year-old woman shouldn't be called a girl, this "guy" thing has crept in.

Use of "guy" to mean "person" is so insidious that I'll bet most women don't notice they are being called "guys," or, if they do, find it somehow flattering to be one of them.

Sometimes, I find the courage to pipe up when a bunch of us are assembled and are called "guys" by someone of either gender. "We're not guys," I say. Then everyone looks at me funny.

One day, arriving at a business meeting where there were five women and one man, I couldn't resist. "Hello, ladies," I said. Everyone laughed embarrassedly for the blushing man until I added, "and gent." Big sigh of relief. Wouldn't want to call a guy a "gal" now, would we?

Why is it not embarrassing for a woman to be called "guy"? We know why. It's the same logic that says women look sexy and cute in a man's shirt, but did you ever try your silk blouse on your husband and send him to the deli? It's the same mentality that holds that anything male is worthy (and to be aspired toward) and anything female is trivial.

We all sit around responding, without blinking, "black with one sugar, please," when anyone asks, "How do you guys like your coffee?"

What's all that murmuring I hear?

"Come on, lighten up."

"Be a good guy."

"Nobody means anything by it."

Nonsense.

WRITING SUGGESTIONS

1. Truth spoke out against the injustice she saw around her. In arguing for the rights of women, she found it helpful to define *woman* in order to make her point. What social cause do you find most compelling today? Human rights? AIDS awareness? Domestic abuse? Alcoholism? Gay marriage? Racism? Select an issue about which you have strong feelings. Now carefully identify all key terms that you must define before arguing your position. Write an essay in which you use definition to make your point convincingly.

2. Truth's speech holds out hope for the future. She envisioned a future in which women join together to take charge and "turn [the world] back, and get it right side up again" (5). What she envisioned has, to some extent, come to pass. Write an essay in which you speculate about how Truth would react to the world as we know it. What do you think would please her? What would disappoint her? What do you think she would want to change about our society? Explain your reasoning.

Time to Make Peace with the Planet: 2007 Nobel Prize for Peace Lecture

AL GORE

Albert Gore Jr., the forty-fifth vice president of the United States, was born in Washington, D.C., on March 31, 1948. The son of a U.S. congressman, Gore grew up in Washington and graduated from St. Albans Episcopal School for Boys in 1965. He majored in government at Harvard University, where he first developed an interest in becoming a writer. After graduation in 1969, he enlisted in the army and was stationed as a reporter in Vietnam. When he returned home in 1971, he was hired on as an investigative reporter for the Nashville *Tennessean*. After a year in the Graduate School of Religion at Vanderbilt University and two years in Vanderbilt's law school, Gore successfully ran for a seat in the U.S. House of Representatives in 1976. Gore served four terms in the House before being elected U.S. senator from Tennessee. In Congress he championed health issues, nuclear arms control, and what was to become his signature issue, the environment. At age thirty-nine, Gore tried unsuccessfully to gain the 1988 Democratic nomination for president, and in 1992 Bill Clinton selected him as his running mate for that year's winning ticket. The Clinton-Gore team was reelected in 1996. Gore lost his own bid for the presidency in 2000, after a controversial U.S. Supreme Court ruling halting a recount of Florida's popular vote.

For several decades now Gore has been a strong advocate of protecting the environment. In his book *Earth in the Balance: Ecology and the Human Spirit,* he states that "we must make the rescue of the environment the central organizing principle for civilization." In January 2006 Gore's environmental documentary *An Inconvenient Truth* made a splash at the Sundance Film Festival. A book by the same name appeared later in 2006, and the movie won an Academy Award in 2007. Gore's third book, *The Assault on Reason,* appeared in 2007.

On October 12, 2007, the Nobel committee announced that Gore, together with the United Nations Intergovernmental Panel on Climate Change, had been awarded the 2007 Nobel Peace Prize for their efforts to raise awareness about the potentially catastrophic effects of global warming. On December 10, 2007, in Oslo, Norway, Gore delivered "Time to Make Peace with the Planet," an impassioned call to action for the global community to stem the tide of climate change.

WRITING TO DISCOVER: *What do you know about global warming? On a scale of one to ten, ten being extremely important, how important do you believe it is that the global community address this issue? Are there other equally important issues facing the world today? What do you think individuals can do to help reverse global climate change?*

Your Majesties, Your Royal Highnesses, Honorable members of the Norwegian Nobel Committee, Excellencies, Ladies and gentlemen.

I have a purpose here today. It is a purpose I have tried to serve for many years. I have prayed that God would show me a way to accomplish it.

Sometimes, without warning, the future knocks on our door with a precious and painful vision of what might be. One hundred and nineteen years ago, a wealthy inventor read his own obituary, mistakenly published years before his death. Wrongly believing the inventor had just died, a newspaper printed a harsh judgment of his life's work, unfairly labeling him "The Merchant of Death" because of his invention — dynamite. Shaken by this condemnation, the inventor made a fateful choice to serve the cause of peace.

Seven years later, Alfred Nobel created this prize and the others that bear his name.

Seven years ago tomorrow, I read my own political obituary in a judg- 5 ment that seemed to me harsh and mistaken — if not premature. But that unwelcome verdict also brought a precious if painful gift: an opportunity to search for fresh new ways to serve my purpose.

Unexpectedly, that quest has brought me here. Even though I fear my words cannot match this moment, I pray what I am feeling in my heart will be communicated clearly enough that those who hear me will say, "We must act."

The distinguished scientists with whom it is the greatest honor of my life to share this award have laid before us a choice between two different futures — a choice that to my ears echoes the words of an ancient prophet: "Life or death, blessings or curses. Therefore, choose life, that both thou and thy seed may live."

We, the human species, are confronting a planetary emergency — a threat to the survival of our civilization that is gathering ominous and destructive potential even as we gather here. But there is hopeful news as well: we have the ability to solve this crisis and avoid the worst — though not all — of its consequences, if we act boldly, decisively and quickly.

However, despite a growing number of honorable exceptions, too many of the world's leaders are still best described in the words Winston Churchill applied to those who ignored Adolf Hitler's threat: "They go on in strange paradox, decided only to be undecided, resolved to be irresolute, adamant for drift, solid for fluidity, all powerful to be impotent."

So today, we dumped another 70 million tons of global-warming pollu- 10 tion into the thin shell of atmosphere surrounding our planet, as if it were an open sewer. And tomorrow, we will dump a slightly larger amount, with the cumulative concentrations now trapping more and more heat from the sun.

As a result, the earth has a fever. And the fever is rising. The experts have told us it is not a passing affliction that will heal by itself. We asked for a second opinion. And a third. And a fourth. And the consistent conclusion, restated with increasing alarm, is that something basic is wrong.

We are what is wrong, and we must make it right.

Last September 21, as the Northern Hemisphere tilted away from the sun, scientists reported with unprecedented distress that the North Polar ice cap is "falling off a cliff." One study estimated that it could be completely gone during summer in less than twenty-two years. Another new study, to be presented by U.S. Navy researchers later this week, warns it could happen in as little as seven years.

Seven years from now.

In the last few months, it has been harder and harder to misinterpret the   15
signs that our world is spinning out of kilter. Major cities in North and South America, Asia and Australia are nearly out of water due to massive droughts and melting glaciers. Desperate farmers are losing their livelihoods. Peoples in the frozen Arctic and on low-lying Pacific Islands are planning evacuations of places they have long called home. Unprecedented wildfires have forced a half million people from their homes in one country and caused a national emergency that almost brought down the government in another. Climate refugees have migrated into areas already inhabited by people with different cultures, religions, and traditions, increasing the potential for conflict. Stronger storms in the Pacific and Atlantic have threatened whole cities. Millions have been displaced by massive flooding in South Asia, Mexico, and eighteen countries in Africa. As temperature extremes have increased, tens of thousands have lost their lives. We are recklessly burning and clearing our forests and driving more and more species into extinction. The very web of life on which we depend is being ripped and frayed.

We never intended to cause all this destruction, just as Alfred Nobel never intended that dynamite be used for waging war. He had hoped his invention would promote human progress. We shared that same worthy goal when we began burning massive quantities of coal, then oil and methane.

Even in Nobel's time, there were a few warnings of the likely consequences. One of the very first winners of the Prize in Chemistry worried that, "We are evaporating our coal mines into the air." After performing 10,000 equations by hand, Svante Arrhenius calculated that the earth's average temperature would increase by many degrees if we doubled the amount of CO_2 in the atmosphere.

Seventy years later, my teacher, Roger Revelle, and his colleague, Dave Keeling, began to precisely document the increasing CO_2 levels day by day.

But unlike most other forms of pollution, CO_2 is invisible, tasteless, and odorless—which has helped keep the truth about what it is doing to our climate out of sight and out of mind. Moreover, the catastrophe now threatening us is unprecedented—and we often confuse the unprecedented with the improbable.

We also find it hard to imagine making the massive changes that are   20
now necessary to solve the crisis. And when large truths are genuinely

inconvenient, whole societies can, at least for a time, ignore them. Yet as George Orwell reminds us: "Sooner or later a false belief bumps up against solid reality, usually on a battlefield."

In the years since this prize was first awarded, the entire relationship between humankind and the earth has been radically transformed. And still, we have remained largely oblivious to the impact of our cumulative actions.

Indeed, without realizing it, we have begun to wage war on the earth itself. Now, we and the earth's climate are locked in a relationship familiar to war planners: "Mutually assured destruction."

More than two decades ago, scientists calculated that nuclear war could throw so much debris and smoke into the air that it would block life-giving sunlight from our atmosphere, causing a "nuclear winter." Their eloquent warnings here in Oslo helped galvanize the world's resolve to halt the nuclear arms race.

Now science is warning us that if we do not quickly reduce the global warming pollution that is trapping so much of the heat our planet normally radiates back out of the atmosphere, we are in danger of creating a permanent "carbon summer."

As the American poet Robert Frost wrote, "Some say the world will   25
end in fire; some say in ice." Either, he notes, "would suffice."

But neither need be our fate. It is time to make peace with the planet.

We must quickly mobilize our civilization with the urgency and resolve that has previously been seen only when nations mobilized for war. These prior struggles for survival were won when leaders found words at the eleventh hour that released a mighty surge of courage, hope and readiness to sacrifice for a protracted and mortal challenge.

These were not comforting and misleading assurances that the threat was not real or imminent; that it would affect others but not ourselves; that ordinary life might be lived even in the presence of extraordinary threat; that Providence could be trusted to do for us what we would not do for ourselves.

No, these were calls to come to the defense of the common future. They were calls upon the courage, generosity and strength of entire peoples, citizens of every class and condition who were ready to stand against the threat once asked to do so. Our enemies in those times calculated that free people would not rise to the challenge; they were, of course, catastrophically wrong.

Now comes the threat of climate crisis—a threat that is real, rising,   30
imminent, and universal. Once again, it is the eleventh hour. The penalties for ignoring this challenge are immense and growing, and at some near point would be unsustainable and unrecoverable. For now we still have the power to choose our fate, and the remaining question is only this: Have we the will to act vigorously and in time, or will we remain imprisoned by a dangerous illusion?

Mahatma Gandhi awakened the largest democracy on earth and forged a shared resolve with what he called "Satyagraha" — or "truth force."

In every land, the truth — once known — has the power to set us free.

Truth also has the power to unite us and bridge the distance between "me" and "we," creating the basis for common effort and shared responsibility.

There is an African proverb that says, "If you want to go quickly, go alone. If you want to go far, go together." We need to go far, quickly.

We must abandon the conceit that individual, isolated, private actions   35
are the answer. They can and do help. But they will not take us far enough without collective action. At the same time, we must ensure that in mobilizing globally, we do not invite the establishment of ideological conformity and a new lock-step "ism."

That means adopting principles, values, laws, and treaties that release creativity and initiative at every level of society in multifold responses originating concurrently and spontaneously.

This new consciousness requires expanding the possibilities inherent in all humanity. The innovators who will devise a new way to harness the sun's energy for pennies or invent an engine that's carbon negative may live in Lagos or Mumbai or Montevideo. We must ensure that entrepreneurs and inventors everywhere on the globe have the chance to change the world.

When we unite for a moral purpose that is manifestly good and true, the spiritual energy unleashed can transform us. The generation that defeated fascism throughout the world in the 1940s found, in rising to meet their awesome challenge, that they had gained the moral authority and long-term vision to launch the Marshall Plan, the United Nations, and a new level of global cooperation and foresight that unified Europe and facilitated the emergence of democracy and prosperity in Germany, Japan, Italy and much of the world. One of their visionary leaders said, "It is time we steered by the stars and not by the lights of every passing ship."

In the last year of that war, you gave the Peace Prize to a man from my hometown of 2,000 people, Carthage, Tennessee. Cordell Hull was described by Franklin Roosevelt as the "Father of the United Nations." He was an inspiration and hero to my own father, who followed Hull in the Congress and the U.S. Senate and in his commitment to world peace and global cooperation.

My parents spoke often of Hull, always in tones of reverence and   40
admiration. Eight weeks ago, when you announced this prize, the deepest emotion I felt was when I saw the headline in my hometown paper that simply noted I had won the same prize that Cordell Hull had won. In that moment, I knew what my father and mother would have felt were they alive.

Just as Hull's generation found moral authority in rising to solve the world crisis caused by fascism, so too can we find our greatest opportunity in rising to solve the climate crisis. In the Kanji characters used in both

Chinese and Japanese, "crisis" is written with two symbols, the first meaning "danger," the second "opportunity." By facing and removing the danger of the climate crisis, we have the opportunity to gain the moral authority and vision to vastly increase our own capacity to solve other crises that have been too long ignored.

We must understand the connections between the climate crisis and the afflictions of poverty, hunger, HIV-AIDS and other pandemics. As these problems are linked, so too must be their solutions. We must begin by making the common rescue of the global environment the central organizing principle of the world community.

Fifteen years ago, I made that case at the "Earth Summit" in Rio de Janeiro. Ten years ago, I presented it in Kyoto. This week, I will urge the delegates in Bali to adopt a bold mandate for a treaty that establishes a universal global cap on emissions and uses the market in emissions trading to efficiently allocate resources to the most effective opportunities for speedy reductions.

This treaty should be ratified and brought into effect everywhere in the world by the beginning of 2010—two years sooner than presently contemplated. The pace of our response must be accelerated to match the accelerating pace of the crisis itself.

Heads of state should meet early next year to review what was accomplished in Bali and take personal responsibility for addressing this crisis. It is not unreasonable to ask, given the gravity of our circumstances, that these heads of state meet every three months until the treaty is completed. 45

We also need a moratorium on the construction of any new generating facility that burns coal without the capacity to safely trap and store carbon dioxide.

And most important of all, we need to put a *price* on carbon—with a CO_2 tax that is then rebated back to the people, progressively, according to the laws of each nation, in ways that shift the burden of taxation from employment to pollution. This is by far the most effective and simplest way to accelerate solutions to this crisis.

The world needs an alliance—especially of those nations that weigh heaviest in the scales where earth is in the balance. I salute Europe and Japan for the steps they've taken in recent years to meet the challenge, and the new government in Australia, which has made solving the climate crisis its first priority.

But the outcome will be decisively influenced by two nations that are now failing to do enough: the United States and China. While India is also growing fast in importance, it should be absolutely clear that it is the two largest CO_2 emitters—most of all, my own country—that will need to make the boldest moves, or stand accountable before history for their failure to act.

Both countries should stop using the other's behavior as an excuse for stalemate and instead develop an agenda for mutual survival in a shared global environment. 50

These are the last few years of decision, but they can be the first years of a bright and hopeful future if we do what we must. No one should believe a solution will be found without effort, without cost, without change. Let us acknowledge that if we wish to redeem squandered time and speak again with moral authority, then these are the hard truths:

The way ahead is difficult. The outer boundary of what we currently believe is feasible is still far short of what we actually must do. Moreover, between here and there, across the unknown, falls the shadow.

That is just another way of saying that we have to expand the boundaries of what is possible. In the words of the Spanish poet Antonio Machado, "Pathwalker, there is no path. You must make the path as you walk."

We are standing at the most fateful fork in that path. So I want to end as I began, with a vision of two futures—each a palpable possibility—and with a prayer that we will see with vivid clarity the necessity of choosing between those two futures, and the urgency of making the right choice now.

The great Norwegian playwright, Henrik Ibsen, wrote, "One of these days, the younger generation will come knocking at my door."   55

The future is knocking at our door right now. Make no mistake, the next generation *will* ask us one of two questions. Either they will ask: "What were you thinking; why didn't you act?"

Or they will ask instead: "How did you find the moral courage to rise and successfully resolve a crisis that so many said was impossible to solve?"

We have everything we need to get started, save perhaps political will, but political will is a renewable resource.

So let us renew it, and say together: "We have a purpose. We are many. For this purpose we will rise, and we will act."

THINKING CRITICALLY ABOUT THE READING

1. What is Gore's point in opening his lecture with the story of Alfred Nobel and his invention of dynamite? How does Nobel's story serve to introduce Gore's own story? (Glossary: *Beginnings and Endings*)

2. In paragraph 8, Gore announces that humans are facing a "planetary emergency." What, for Gore, are the unmistakable signs that a problem exists? In paragraph 12, Gore tells us that "[W]e are what is wrong." In what ways are "we" the cause of the our environmental problem?

3. What assumptions does Gore make about his audience's knowledge of global warming?

4. Gore is quick to point his finger at rising levels of CO_2 in the atmosphere. Why is CO_2 a culprit? Why, according to Gore, is it so easy to ignore CO_2?

5. In paragraph 20, Gore states that "when large truths are genuinely inconvenient, whole societies can, at least for a time, ignore them." What does he

mean? In what sense can a large truth be inconvenient? In what ways is climate change an inconvenient truth? Explain.

6. At various points throughout his speech Gore quotes Winston Churchill, Henrik Ibsen, Antonio Machado, Robert Frost, Mahatma Gandhi, and an African proverb. What does each quotation add to his speech? Why do you suppose Gore chose to quote them? Explain.

7. What does Gore mean when he says "It is time to make peace with the planet" (26)? What do you think it will take for the global community to accomplish this? What "hard truths" must we all accept in order to meet the challenges of climate change?

8. In your opinion, is Gore optimistic or pessimistic about the global community's chances of meeting and resolving the climate crisis? Point to places in the text that led you to your answer. Does Gore's argument convince you about the seriousness of the problem and move you to action? Explain why or why not.

LANGUAGE IN ACTION

For the April 16, 2007, issue of *Newsweek*, Jerry Adler wrote a cover story about the debate over what to call the climate issue that Al Gore champions. Consider these paragraphs from Adler's article:

What is the most pressing environmental issue we face today? "Global warming"? The "greenhouse effect"? At the [2007] Oscar ceremonies, Al Gore referred to a "climate crisis," but in his [2007] State of the Union address President Bush chose the comparatively anodyne phrase "climate change." They all refer to the same thing, but the first rule of modern political discourse is that before addressing any empirical problem each side must "frame the debate" in the most favorable way. . . . Behind the overt campaign to head off whatever it is—environmental heating? thermal catastrophe?—is a covert struggle over what we should even call it. . . .

"[G]lobal warming" seems to have won out over its rivals, if one can judge by the *New York Times*, where for each of the last three years "global warming" has outpaced references to "climate change" by almost exactly two to one—or an even bigger margin if you throw out articles that are actually about changes in the economic or cultural climate. Both of these phrases have triumphed over "greenhouse effect," which was the most common term in the early 1980s, when the phenomenon of atmospheric pyrogenesis first came to public attention. Arguably, if your goal is to affect public attitudes and policies, "greenhouse effect," which refers to the buildup of heat-trapping gases in the atmosphere, puts the emphasis in the wrong place, on the mechanism rather than the outcome. George Lakoff, the Berkeley professor of linguistics and cognitive science, is a strong backer of the dark horse "climate crisis," which is also favored by Gore (along with the rather more cumbersome term he used in his congressional testimony last month, "planetary emergency"). "'Climate change' doesn't suggest immediate action," says Lakoff. "'Climate crisis' says immediate action is needed. The framing is not just a matter of labels, it's modes of thought. In Europe they use 'climate chaos.'"

Discuss the language debate that Adler describes. How does each of the labels he discusses—"global warming," "greenhouse effect," "climate change," "climate crisis," or "climate chaos"—serve to "frame the debate"? Which label best describes the way you view the issue of our changing climate? Explain.

WRITING SUGGESTIONS

1. In paragraph 30, Gore asks the key question that is on everyone's mind: "Have we the will to act vigorously and in time, or will we remain imprisoned by a dangerous illusion?" Write an essay in which you answer Gore's question. Before beginning to write, you may find it helpful to consider some of the following questions: What is the "dangerous illusion" that Gore believes imprisons us? When Gore tells us that "we must act" and that "we will act," what specifically do you think he wants us to do? Do you think Americans are ready to make the sacrifices needed to turn the tide of climate change?

2. What can you and your fellow students do that will have a positive impact on our shared environment? Write an action plan for making your dormitory, classroom building, or some other campus facility a "green facility." Start by inspecting the building itself and surveying people who live or work there and then note opportunities to recycle materials, to conserve energy, to replace equipment, to purchase energy-saving equipment, and/or to schedule/utilize the facility differently. Present the details of your findings in an action plan for the residents of your dormitory or for the student body at large to consider.

When Language Dies: 1993 Nobel Prize for Literature Lecture

Toni Morrison

The African American novelist Toni Morrison was born Chloe Anthony Wofford near Lake Erie in Lorain, Ohio, in 1931. She received her B.A. in English from Howard University in 1953 and an M.A. from Cornell University in 1955. After teaching English at Texas Southern University and at Howard, Morrison worked in New York City as an editor for Random House. She published her first novel, *The Bluest Eye*, in 1970; it was followed by *Sula* in 1973, *Song of Solomon* in 1977, *Tar Baby* in 1981, *Beloved* in 1987, and *Jazz* in 1992. Morrison's most recent work includes *Paradise* in 1999, *Love* in 2003, and *A Mercy* in 2008. Her novels have won her both popular and critical acclaim as a talented storyteller whose characters struggle for their identity and dignity in a society that seems all too ready to stand in their way. As a novelist she has risen to a preeminent position in American letters for her portrayals of the black experience. In 1984 she was appointed to the Albert Schweitzer chair at the University of Albany, and from 1989 until her retirement in 2006, she taught at Princeton University.

It came as no surprise to her critics and fans alike when, in accepting the 1993 Nobel Prize for Literature, Morrison turned to language as her subject. As Caroline Morehead wrote in the *Spectator,* Morrison "writes energetically and richly, using words in a way very much her own. The effect is one of exoticism, and exciting curiousness in the language, a balanced sense of the possible that stops, always, short of the absurd." Other critics have called her style "elegant," "lyrical," "evocative," and "impressionistic." In "When Language Dies," Morrison speaks to us of our responsibility not to violate the power and beauty of our language but to maximize its magical and generative properties.

WRITING TO DISCOVER: *What does it mean to you to have language? How would you define* language *in a sentence or two? What would your world be like without language?*

"Once upon a time there was an old woman. Blind but wise." Or was it an old man? A guru, perhaps. Or a griot soothing restless children. I have heard this story, or one exactly like it, in the lore of several cultures.

"Once upon a time there was an old woman. Blind. Wise."

In the version I know the woman is the daughter of slaves, black, American, and lives alone in a small house outside of town. Her reputation for wisdom is without peer and without question. Among her people she is both the law and its transgression. The honor she is paid and the awe in which she is held reach beyond her neighborhood to places far away; to the city where the intelligence of rural prophets is the source of much amusement.

One day the woman is visited by some young people who seem to be bent on disproving her clairvoyance and showing her up for the fraud they believe she is. Their plan is simple: they enter her house and ask the one question the answer to which rides solely on her difference from them, a difference they regard as a profound disability: her blindness. They stand before her, and one of them says, "Old woman, I hold in my hand a bird. Tell me whether it is living or dead."

She does not answer, and the question is repeated. "Is the bird I am   5 holding living or dead?"

Still she doesn't answer. She is blind and cannot see her visitors, let alone what is in their hands. She does not know their color, gender or homeland. She only knows their motive.

The old woman's silence is so long, the young people have trouble holding their laughter.

Finally she speaks and her voice is soft but stern. "I don't know," she says. "I don't know whether the bird you are holding is dead or alive, but what I do know is that it is in your hands. It is in your hands."

Her answer can be taken to mean: if it is dead, you have either found it that way or you have killed it. If it is alive, you can still kill it. Whether it is to stay alive, it is your decision. Whatever the case, it is your responsibility.

For parading their power and her helplessness, the young visitors are   10 reprimanded, told they are responsible not only for the act of mockery but also for the small bundle of life sacrificed to achieve its aims. The blind woman shifts attention away from assertions of power to the instrument through which that power is exercised.

Speculation on what (other than its own frail body) that bird-in-the-hand might signify has always been attractive to me, but especially so now, thinking as I have been, about the work I do that has brought me to this company. So I choose to read the bird as language and the woman as a practiced writer. She is worried about how the language she dreams in, given to her at birth, is handled, put into service, even withheld from her for certain nefarious purposes. Being a writer she thinks of language partly as a system, partly as a living thing over which one has control, but mostly as agency—as an act with consequences. So the question the children put to her: "Is it living or dead?" is not unreal because she thinks of language as susceptible to death, erasure; certainly imperiled and sal-vageable only by an effort of the will. She believes that if the bird in the hands of her visitors is dead the custodians are responsible for the corpse. For her a dead language is not only one no longer spoken or written, it is unyielding language content to admire its own paralysis. Like statist language, censored and censoring. Ruthless in its policing duties, it has no desire or purpose other than maintaining the free range of its own narcotic narcissism, its own exclusivity and dominance. However moribund, it is not without effect for it actively thwarts the intellect, stalls conscience, suppresses human potential. Unreceptive to interrogation, it cannot form or tolerate new ideas, shape other thoughts, tell another story, fill baffling silences. Official language smitheryed to sanction ignorance and preserve privilege is a suit of armor, polished to shocking glitter, a husk from which the knight departed long ago. Yet there it is: dumb, predatory, sentimental. Exciting reverence in schoolchildren, providing shelter for despots, summoning false memories of stability, harmony among the public.

She is convinced that when language dies, out of carelessness, disuse, and absence of esteem, indifference or killed by fiat, not only she herself, but all users and makers are accountable for its demise. In her country children have bitten their tongues off and use bullets instead to iterate the voice of speechlessness, of disabled and disabling language, of language adults have abandoned altogether as a device for grappling with meaning, providing guidance, or expressing love. But she knows tongue-suicide is not only the choice of children. It is common among the infantile heads of state and power merchants whose evacuated language leaves them with no access to what is left of their human instincts for they speak only to those who obey, or in order to force obedience.

The systematic looting of language can be recognized by the tendency of its users to forgo its nuanced, complex, mid-wifery properties for menace and subjugation. Oppressive language does more than represent violence; it is violence; does more than represent the limits of knowledge; it limits knowledge. Whether it is obscuring state language or the faux-language of mindless media; whether it is the proud but calcified language of the academy or the commodity-driven language of science; whether it is the malign language of law-without-ethics, or language designed for the estrangement of minorities, hiding its racist plunder in its literary cheek—it must be rejected, altered and exposed. It is the language that drinks blood, laps vulnerability, tucks its fascist boots under crinolines of respectability and patriotism as it moves relentlessly toward the bottom line and the bottomed-out mind. Sexist language, racist language, theistic language—all are typical of the policing languages of mastery, and cannot, do not permit new knowledge or encourage the mutual exchange of ideas.

The old woman is keenly aware that no intellectual mercenary, nor insatiable dictator, no paid-for politician or demagogue, no counterfeit journalist would be persuaded by her thoughts. There is and will be rousing language to keep citizens armed and arming; slaughtered and slaughtering in the malls, courthouses, post offices, playgrounds, bedrooms and boulevards; stirring, memorializing language to mask the pity and waste of needless death. There will be more diplomatic language to countenance rape, torture, assassination. There is and will be more seductive, mutant language designed to throttle women, to pack their throats like paté-producing geese with their own unsayable, transgressive words; there will be more of the language of surveillance disguised as research; of politics and history calculated to render the suffering of millions mute; language glamorized to thrill the dissatisfied and bereft into assaulting their neighbors; arrogant pseudo-empirical language crafted to lock creative people into cages of inferiority and hopelessness.

Underneath the eloquence, the glamour, the scholarly associations,   15
however stirring or seductive, the heart of such language is languishing, or perhaps not beating at all—if the bird is already dead.

She has thought about what could have been the intellectual history of any discipline if it had not insisted upon, or been forced into, the waste of time and life that rationalizations for and representations of dominance required—lethal discourses of exclusion blocking access to cognition for both the excluder and the excluded.

The conventional wisdom of the Tower of Babel story is that the collapse was a misfortune. That it was the distraction, or the weight of many languages that precipitated the tower's failed architecture. That one monolithic language would have expedited the building and heaven would have been reached. Whose heaven, she wonders? And what kind? Perhaps the achievement of Paradise was premature, a little hasty if no one could take the time to understand other languages, other views, other narratives. Had they, the heaven they imagined might have been found at their feet. Complicated, demanding yes, but a view of heaven as life; not heaven as post-life.

She would not want to leave her young visitors with the impression that language should be forced to stay alive merely to be. The vitality of language lies in its ability to limn the actual, imagined and possible lives of its speakers, readers, writers. Although its poise is sometimes in displacing experience it is not a substitute for it. It arcs toward the place where meaning may lie. When a President of the United States thought about the graveyard his country had become, and said "The world will little note nor long remember what we say here. But it will never forget what they did here," his simple words are exhilarating in their life-sustaining properties because they refused to encapsulate the reality of 600,000 dead men in a cataclysmic race war. Refusing to monumentalize, disdaining the "final word," the precise "summing up," acknowledging their "poor power to add or detract," his words signal deference to the uncapturability of the life it mourns. It is the deference that moves her, that recognition that language can never live up to life once and for all. Nor should it. Language can never "pin down" slavery, genocide, war. Nor should it yearn for the arrogance to be able to do so. Its force, its felicity is in its reach toward the ineffable.

Be it grand or slender, burrowing, blasting, or refusing to sanctify; whether it laughs out loud or is a cry without an alphabet, the choice word, the chosen silence, unmolested language surges toward knowledge, not its destruction. But who does not know of literature banned because it is interrogative; discredited because it is critical; erased because alternate? And how many are outraged by the thought of a self-ravaged tongue?

Word-work is sublime, she thinks, because it is generative; it makes   20
meaning that secures our difference, our human difference—the way in which we are like no other life.

We die. That may be the meaning of life. But we do language. That may be the measure of our lives.

"Once upon a time, . . ." visitors ask an old woman a question. Who are they, these children? What did they make of that encounter? What did they hear in those final words: "The bird is in your hands"? A sentence that gestures toward possibility or one that drops a latch? Perhaps what the children heard was "It's not my problem. I am old, female, black, blind. What wisdom I have now is in knowing I can not help you. The future of language is yours."

They stand there. Suppose nothing was in their hands? Suppose the visit was only a ruse, a trick to get to be spoken to, taken seriously as they have not been before? A chance to interrupt, to violate the adult world, its miasma of discourse about them, for them, but never to them? Urgent questions are at stake, including the one they have asked: "Is the bird we hold living or dead?" Perhaps the question meant: "Could someone tell us what is life? What is death?" No trick at all; no silliness. A straightforward question worthy of the attention of a wise one. An old one. And if the old and wise who have lived life and faced death cannot describe either, who can?

But she does not; she keeps her secret; her good opinion of herself; her gnomic pronouncements; her art without commitment. She keeps her distance, enforces it and retreats into the singularity of isolation, in sophisticated, privileged space.

Nothing, no word follows her declarations of transfer. That silence   25
is deep, deeper than the meaning available in the words she has spoken. It shivers, this silence, and the children, annoyed, fill it with language invented on the spot.

"Is there no speech," they ask her, "no words you can give us that helps us break through your dossier of failures? Through the education you have just given us that is no education at all because we are paying close attention to what you have done as well as to what you have said? To the barrier you have erected between generosity and wisdom?

"We have no bird in our hands, living or dead. We have only you and our important question. Is the nothing in our hands something you could not bear to contemplate, to even guess? Don't you remember being young when language was magic without meaning? When what you could say, could not mean? When the invisible was what imagination strove to see? When questions and demands for answers burned so brightly you trembled with fury at not knowing?

"Do we have to begin consciousness with a battle heroines and heroes like you have already fought and lost leaving us with nothing in our hands

except what you have imagined is there? Your answer is artful, but its arti-
ness embarrasses us and ought to embarrass you. Your answer is indecent
in its self-congratulation. A made-for-television script that makes no sense
if there is nothing in our hands.

"Why didn't you reach out, touch us with your soft fingers, delay the
sound bite, the lesson, until you knew who we were? Did you so despise
our trick, our modus operandi you could not see that we were baffled about
how to get your attention? We are young. Unripe. We have heard all our
short lives that we have to be responsible. What could that possibly mean
in the catastrophe this word has become; where, as a poet said, "nothing
needs to be exposed since it is already barefaced." Our inheritance is an
affront. You want us to have your old, blank eyes and see only cruelty and
mediocrity. Do you think we are stupid enough to perjure ourselves again
and again with the fiction of nationhood? How dare you talk to us of duty
when we stand waist deep in the toxin of your past?

"You trivialize us and trivialize the bird that is not in our hands. Is   30
there no context for our lives? No song, no literature, no poem full of vitamins, no history connected to experience that you can pass along to help
us start strong? You are an adult. The old one, the wise one. Stop thinking
about saving your face. Think of our lives and tell us your particularized
world. Make up a story. Narrative is radical, creating us at the very moment
it is being created. We will not blame you if your reach exceeds your grasp;
if love so ignites your words they go down in flames and nothing is left
but their scald. Or if, with the reticence of a surgeon's hands, your words
suture only the places where blood might flow. We know you can never
do it properly—once and for all. Passion is never enough; neither is skill.
But try. For our sake and yours forget your name in the street; tell us what
the world has been to you in the dark places and in the light. Don't tell us
what to believe, what to fear. Show us belief's wide skirt and the stitch that
unravels fear's caul. You, old woman, blessed with blindness, can speak the
language that tells us what only language can: how to see without pictures.
Language alone protects us from the scariness of things with no names.
Language alone is meditation.

"Tell us what it is to be a woman so that we may know what it is to
be a man. What moves at the margin. What it is to have no home on this
place. To be set adrift from the one you knew. What it is to live at the edge
of towns that cannot bear your company.

"Tell us about ships turned away from shorelines at Easter, placenta
in a field. Tell us about a wagonload of slaves, how they sang so softly
their breath was indistinguishable from the falling snow. How they knew
from the hunch of the nearest shoulder that the next stop would be their
last. How, with hands prayered in their sex, they thought of heat, then
suns. Lifting their faces, as though is was there for the taking. Turning as
though there for the taking. They stop at an inn. The driver and his mate
go in with the lamp leaving them humming in the dark. The horse's void

steams into the snow beneath its hooves and its hiss and melt is the envy of the freezing slaves.

"The inn door opens: a girl and a boy step away from its light. They climb into the wagon bed. The boy will have a gun in three years, but now he carries a lamp and a jug of warm cider. They pass it from mouth to mouth. The girl offers bread, pieces of meat and something more: a glance into the eyes of the one she serves. One helping for each man, two for each woman. And a look. They look back. The next stop will be their last. But not this one. This one is warmed."

It's quiet again when the children finish speaking, until the woman breaks into the silence.

"Finally," she says, "I trust you now. I trust you with the bird that is   35 not in your hands because you have truly caught it. Look. How lovely it is, this thing we have done—together."

THINKING CRITICALLY ABOUT THE READING

1. What significance does Morrison give her story of the old blind woman and the young people who visit her?

2. In paragraph 11, Morrison refers to the deadening qualities of "statist language." To what is she referring? Why is such language abhorrent to her?

3. Who is responsible for the "looting of language" to which she refers in paragraph 13?

4. What is the story of the Tower of Babel? What significance does Morrison see in the story? Does she see the alternative of a single language as good or bad? Explain.

5. Morrison claims that language should never be a substitute for life itself. She writes, "Its force, its felicity is in its reach toward the ineffable"(18). What does she mean by this statement?

6. The questions that Morrison asks through the young people turn slowly into a narrative about slaves in a wagon. What does this story signify for the old blind woman? At the end, why does she feel she can trust the young people? What have they "done—together"(35)?

LANGUAGE IN ACTION

In small groups, discuss the proposition that honesty, while it does not guarantee good writing, is a prerequisite to good writing. What does it mean to you to be honest in your writing? What kind of language is honest language? At the end of fifteen or twenty minutes share your group's thinking with the other groups.

WRITING SUGGESTIONS

1. It has often been said that what separates humans from other creatures is our ability to use language to convey highly sophisticated and complex emotions and knowledge, feelings and ideas. Perhaps one of the greatest benefits of language, however, is our ability to imagine, to envision what might be, what could be achieved—in short, language gives us the power to imagine new possibilities, a different world. Write an essay in which you explore further this extraordinary power and the special demands it places on us as humans.

2. The young people in Morrison's speech ask the old woman, "Don't you remember being young when language was magic without meaning? When what you could say, could not mean? When the invisible was what imagination strove to see? When questions and demands for answers burned so brightly you trembled with fury at not knowing?"(27). Does that description of the sense of language for young people sound familiar to you? What was language like for you as a child? What was lost as you grew? What was gained? Write an essay describing your experiences with the different faces of language, with the magic of language. In preparation for writing, think of the nursery rhymes you knew and the stories that you heard, that you read, or that were read to you. Think of the songs you sang, the secret words you knew, the taunts and cheers you offered and received.

A Modest Proposal

JONATHAN SWIFT

One of the world's greatest satirists, Jonathan Swift was born in 1667 to English parents in Dublin, Ireland, and was educated at Trinity College. When his early efforts at a literary career in England met no success, he returned to Ireland in 1694 and was ordained an Anglican clergyman. From 1713 until his death in 1745, he was dean of St. Patrick's Cathedral in Dublin. A prolific chronicler of human folly, Swift is best known as the author of *Gulliver's Travels* and of the work included here, "A Modest Proposal."

In the 1720s Ireland had suffered several famines, but the English gentry, who owned most of the land, did nothing to alleviate the suffering of tenant farmers and their families; nor would the English government intervene. A number of pamphlets were circulated proposing solutions to the so-called "Irish problem." "A Modest Proposal," published anonymously in 1729, was Swift's ironic contribution to the discussion.

WRITING TO DISCOVER: *Satire is a dramatic literary art form wherein the shortcomings, foibles, abuses, and idiocies of both people and institutions are accentuated and held up for ridicule in order to shame these perpetrators into reforming themselves. Perhaps the very easiest way to see satire around us today is in the work of our political cartoonists. Make a list of individuals and institutions both here and abroad who today might make good subjects for satire. For each individual and institution on your list provide one or two traits or characteristics that might be held up for ridicule.*

> *A Modest Proposal for Preventing the Children of Poor People in Ireland from Being a Burden to Their Parents or Country, and for Making Them Beneficial to the Public*

It is a melancholy object to those who walk through this great town, or travel in the country, when they see the streets, the roads and cabin-doors crowded with beggars of the female sex, followed by three, four, or six children, all in rags, and importuning every passenger for an alms. These mothers, instead of being able to work for their honest livelihood, are forced to employ all their time in strolling, to beg sustenance for their helpless infants, who, as they grow up, either turn thieves for want of work, or leave their dear native country to fight for the Pretender in Spain, or sell themselves to the Barbadoes.

I think it is agreed by all parties that this prodigious number of children, in the arms, or on the backs, or at the heels of their mothers, and frequently of their fathers, is in the present deplorable state of the kingdom a very great additional grievance; and therefore whoever could find out a fair, cheap, and easy method of making these children sound and useful members of the commonwealth would deserve so well of the public as to have his statue set up for a preserver of the nation.

But my intention is very far from being confined to provide only for the children of professed beggars; it is of a much greater extent, and shall take in the whole number of infants at a certain age who are born of parents in effect as little able to support them as those who demand our charity in the streets.

As to my own part, having turned my thoughts for many years upon this important subject, and maturely weighed the several schemes of other projectors, I have always found them grossly mistaken in their computation. It is true a child just dropped from its dam may be supported by her milk for a solar year with little other nourishment, at most not above the value of two shillings, which the mother may certainly get, or the value in scraps, by her lawful occupation of begging, and it is exactly at one year old that I propose to provide for them, in such a manner as, instead of being a charge upon their parents, or the parish, or wanting food and raiment for the rest of their lives, they shall, on the contrary, contribute to the feeding and partly to the clothing of many thousands.

There is likewise another great advantage in my scheme, that it will   5
prevent those voluntary abortions, and that horrid practice of women murdering their bastard children, alas, too frequent among us, sacrificing the poor innocent babes, I doubt, more to avoid the expense than the shame, which would move tears and pity in the most savage and inhuman breast.

The number of souls in Ireland being usually reckoned one million and a half, of these I calculate there may be about two hundred thousand couples whose wives are breeders, from which number I subtract thirty thousand couples who are able to maintain their own children, although I apprehend there cannot be so many under the present distresses of the kingdom; but this being granted, there will remain an hundred and seventy thousand breeders. I again subtract fifty thousand for those women who miscarry, or whose children die by accident or disease within the year. There only remain an hundred and twenty thousand children of poor parents annually born: the question therefore is, how this number shall be reared, and provided for, which as I have already said, under the present situation of affairs is utterly impossible by all the methods hitherto proposed, for we can neither employ them in handicraft or agriculture; we neither build houses (I mean in the country), nor cultivate land: they can very seldom pick up a livelihood by stealing until they arrive at six years old, except where they are of towardly parts, although I confess they learn the rudiments much earlier, during which time they can however be properly looked upon only as probationers, as I have been informed by a principal gentleman in the County of Cavan, who protested to me that he

never knew above one or two instances under the age of six, even in a part
of the kingdom so renowned for the quickest proficiency in that art.

I am assured by our merchants that a boy or girl before twelve years old
is no salable commodity, and even when they come to this age, they will not
yield above three pounds, or three pounds and half-a-crown at most on the
Exchange, which cannot turn to account either to the parents or the kingdom,
the charge of nutriment and rags having been at least four times that value.

I shall now therefore humbly propose my own thoughts, which I hope
will not be liable to the least objection.

I have been assured by a very knowing American of my acquaintance in
London, that a young healthy child well nursed is at a year old a most delicious,
nourishing and wholesome food, whether stewed, roasted, baked, or boiled,
and I make no doubt that it will equally serve in a fricassee, or a ragout.

I do therefore humbly offer it to public consideration, that of the hun-   10
dred and twenty thousand children already computed, twenty thousand
may be reserved for breed, whereof only one fourth part to be males, which
is more than we allow to sheep, black-cattle, or swine, and my reason is that
these children are seldom the fruits of marriage, a circumstance not much
regarded by our savages, therefore one male will be sufficient to serve four
females. That the remaining hundred thousand may at a year old be offered
in sale to the persons of quality, and fortune, through the kingdom, always
advising the mother to let them suck plentifully in the last month, so as to
render them plump, and fat for a good table. A child will make two dishes
at an entertainment for friends, and when the family dines alone, the fore or
hind quarter will make a reasonable dish, and seasoned with a little pepper
or salt will be very good boiled on the fourth day, especially in winter.

I have reckoned upon a medium, that a child just born will weigh
twelve pounds, and in a solar year if tolerably nursed increaseth to twenty-
eight pounds.

I grant this food will be somewhat dear, and therefore very proper for
landlords, who, as they have already devoured most of the parents, seem
to have the best title to the children.

Infant's flesh will be in season throughout the year, but more plentiful
in March, and a little before and after, for we are told by a grave author,
an eminent French physician, that fish being a prolific diet, there are more
children born in Roman Catholic countries about nine months after Lent
than at any other season; therefore reckoning a year after Lent, the markets will be more glutted than usual, because the number of Popish infants
is at least three to one in this kingdom, and therefore it will have one other
collateral advantage by lessening the number of Papists among us.

I have already computed the charge of nursing a beggar's child (in
which list I reckon all cottagers, laborers, and four-fifths of the farmers) to
be about two shillings *per annum*, rags included, and I believe no gentleman would repine to give ten shillings for the carcass of a good fat child,
which, as I have said, will make four dishes of excellent nutritive meat,

when he hath only some particular friend of his own family to dine with him. Thus the Squire will learn to be a good landlord and grow popular among his tenants, the mother will have eight shillings net profit, and be fit for work until she produces another child.

Those who are more thrifty (as I must confess the times require) may 15 flay the carcass; the skin of which artificially dressed, will make admirable gloves for ladies, and summer boots for fine gentlemen.

As to our city of Dublin, shambles may be appointed for this purpose, in the most convenient parts of it, and butchers we may be assured will not be wanting, although I rather recommend buying the children alive, and dressing them hot from the knife, as we do roasting pigs.

A very worthy person, a true lover of his country, and whose virtues I highly esteem, was lately pleased in discoursing on this matter to offer a refinement upon my scheme. He said that many gentlemen of this kingdom having of late destroyed their deer, he conceived that the want of venison might be well supplied by the bodies of young lads and maidens, not exceeding fourteen years of age, nor under twelve, so great a number of both sexes in every county being now ready to starve, for want of work and service: and these to be disposed of by their parents if alive, or otherwise by their nearest relations. But with due deference to so excellent a friend, and so deserving a patriot, I cannot be altogether in his sentiments. For as to the males, my American acquaintance assured me from frequent experience that their flesh was generally tough and lean, like that of our schoolboys, by continual exercise, and their taste disagreeable, and to fatten them would not answer the charge. Then as to the females, it would, I think with humble submission, be a loss to the public, because they soon would become breeders themselves: and besides, it is not improbable that some scrupulous people might be apt to censure such a practice (although indeed very unjustly) as a little bordering upon cruelty, which I confess, hath always been with me the strongest objection against any project, howsoever well intended.

But in order to justify my friend, he confessed that this expedient was put into his head by the famous Psalmanazar, a native of the island Formosa, who came from thence to London, above twenty years ago, and in conversation told my friend that in his country when any young person happened to be put to death, the executioner sold the carcass to persons of quality, as a prime dainty, and that, in his time, the body of a plump girl of fifteen, who was crucified for an attempt to poison the emperor, was sold to his Imperial Majesty's Prime Minister of State, and other great Mandarins of the Court, in joints from the gibbet, at four hundred crowns. Neither indeed can I deny that if the same use were made of several plump young girls in this town who, without one single groat to their fortunes, cannot stir abroad without a chair, and appear at the playhouse and assemblies in foreign fineries which they never will pay for, the kingdom would not be the worse.

Some persons of a desponding spirit are in great concern about that vast number of poor people, who are aged, diseased, or maimed, and I have been desired to employ my thoughts what course may be taken to ease the nation of so grievous an encumbrance. But I am not in the least pain upon that matter, because it is very well known that they are every day dying, and rotting, by cold, and famine, and filth, and vermin, as fast as can be reasonably expected. And as to the younger laborers, they are now in almost as hopeful a condition. They cannot get work, and consequently pine away from want of nourishment, to a degree that if at any time they are accidentally hired to common labor, they have not strength to perform it; and thus the country and themselves are in a fair way of being soon delivered from the evils to come.

I have too long digressed, and therefore shall return to my subject. I think the advantages by the proposal which I have made are obvious and many, as well as of the highest importance.   20

For first, as I have already observed, it would greatly lessen the number of Papists, with whom we are yearly over-run, being the principal breeders of the nation, as well as our most dangerous enemies, and who stay at home on purpose with a design to deliver the kingdom to the Pretender, hoping to take their advantage by the absence of so many good Protestants, who have chosen rather to leave their country than stay at home and pay tithes against their conscience to an idolatrous Episcopal curate.

Secondly, the poorer tenants will have something valuable of their own, which by law may be made liable to distress, and help to pay their landlord's rent, their corn and cattle being already seized, and money a thing unknown.

Thirdly, whereas the maintenance of an hundred thousand children, from two years old, and upwards, cannot be computed at less than ten shillings a piece *per annum,* the nation's stock will be thereby increased fifty thousand pounds *per annum,* besides the profit of a new dish, introduced to the tables of all gentlemen of fortune in the kingdom, who have any refinement in taste, and the money will circulate among ourselves, the goods being entirely of our own growth and manufacture.

Fourthly, the constant breeders, besides the gain of eight shillings sterling *per annum,* by the sale of their children, will be rid of the charge of maintaining them after the first year.

Fifthly, this food would likewise bring great custom to taverns, where   25
the vintners will certainly be so prudent as to procure the best receipts for dressing it to perfection, and consequently have their houses frequented by all the fine gentlemen, who justly value themselves upon their knowledge in good eating; and a skillful cook, who understands how to oblige his guests, will contrive to make it as expensive as they please.

Sixthly, this would be a great inducement to marriage, which all wise nations have either encouraged by rewards, or enforced by laws and penalties. It would increase the care and tenderness of mothers towards their children, when they were sure of a settlement for life, to the poor babes, provided in some sort by the public to their annual profit instead of expense. We should soon see an honest emulation among the married women, which of them could bring the fattest child to the market. Men would become as fond of their wives, during the time of their pregnancy, as they are now of their mares in foal, their cows in calf, or sows when they are ready to farrow, nor offer to beat or kick them (as it is too frequent a practice) for fear of a miscarriage.

Many other advantages might be enumerated. For instance, the addition of some thousand carcasses in our exportation of barrelled beef; the propagation of swine's flesh, and improvement in the art of making good bacon, so much wanted among us by the great destruction of pigs, too frequent at our tables; which are no way comparable in taste or magnificance to a well-grown, fat yearling child, which roasted whole will make a considerable figure at a Lord Mayor's feast, or any other public entertainment. But this and many others I omit, being studious of brevity.

Supposing that one thousand families in this city would be constant customers for infants' flesh, besides others who might have it at merry meetings, particularly weddings and christenings; I compute that Dublin would take off annually about twenty thousand carcasses, and the rest of the kingdom (where probably they will be sold somewhat cheaper) the remaining eighty thousand.

I can think of no one objection that will possibly be raised against this proposal, unless it should be urged that the number of people will be thereby much lessened in the kingdom. This I freely own, and it was indeed one principal design in offering it to the world. I desire the reader will observe, that I calculate my remedy *for this one individual Kingdom of* Ireland, *and for no other that ever was, is, or, I think, ever can be upon earth.* Therefore let no man talk to me of other expedients: *Of taxing our absentees at five shillings a pound: Of using neither clothes, nor household furniture except what is of our own growth and manufacture: Of utterly rejecting the materials and instruments that promote foreign luxury: Of curing the expensiveness of pride, vanity, idleness, and gaming in our women: Of introducing a vein of parsimony, prudence, and temperance: Of learning to love our country, wherein we differ even from* Laplanders, *and the inhabitants of* Topinamboo: *Of quitting our animosities and factions, nor act any longer like the* Jews, *who were murdering one another at the very moment their city was taken: Of being a little cautious not to sell our country and consciences for nothing: Of teaching landlords to have at least one degree of mercy towards their tenants.* Lastly, *of putting a spirit of honesty, industry, and skill into our shopkeepers, who, if a resolution could now be taken to buy only our native goods, would immediately unite to cheat and exact upon us in the price, the measure and the goodness, nor could ever yet be brought to make one fair proposal of just dealing, though often and earnestly invited to it.*

Therefore I repeat, let no man talk to me of these and the like expedients, till he hath at least a glimpse of hope that there will ever be some hearty and sincere attempt to put them in practice.

30

But as to myself, having been wearied out for many years with offering vain, idle, visionary thoughts, and at length utterly despairing of success, I fortunately fell upon this proposal, which as it is wholly new, so it hath something solid and real, of no expense and little trouble, full in our own power, and whereby we can incur no danger in disobliging England. For this kind of commodity will not bear exportation, the flesh being of too tender a consistence to admit a long continuance in salt, *although perhaps I could name a country which would be glad to eat up our whole nation without it.*

After all I am not so violently bent upon my own opinion as to reject any offer, proposed by wise men, which shall be found equally innocent, cheap, easy and effectual. But before some thing of that kind shall be advanced in contradiction to my scheme, and offering a better, I desire the author, or authors, will be pleased maturely to consider two points. First, as things now stand, how they will be able to find food and raiment for a hundred thousand useless mouths and backs? And secondly, there being a round million of creatures in human figure, throughout this kingdom, whose whole subsistence put into a common stock would leave them in debt two millions of pounds sterling; adding those who are beggars by profession, to the bulk of farmers, cottagers, and laborers with their wives and children, who are beggars in effect; I desire those politicians who dislike my overture, and may perhaps be so bold to attempt an answer, that they will first ask the parents of these mortals whether they would not at this day think it a great happiness to have been sold for food at a year old, in the manner I prescribe, and thereby have avoided such a perpetual scene of misfortunes as they have since gone through, by the oppression of landlords, the impossibility of paying rent without money or trade, the want of common sustenance, with neither house nor clothes to cover them from the inclemencies of weather, and the most inevitable prospect of entailing the like, or greater miseries upon their breed for ever.

I profess in the sincerity of my heart that I have not the least personal interest in endeavoring to promote this necessary work, having no other motive than the *public good of my country, by advancing our trade, providing for infants, relieving the poor, and giving some pleasure to the rich.* I have no children by which I can propose to get a single penny; the youngest being nine years old, and my wife past child-bearing.

THINKING CRITICALLY ABOUT THE READING

1. What problem does Swift address in his proposal? What are some of the solutions that he offers? What does Swift see as the "advantages" (20) of his proposal?

2. What "other expedients" (29) are dismissed as "vain, idle, visionary thoughts" (31)? What can you infer about Swift's purpose from paragraphs 29 through 31? (Glossary: *Purpose*) Explain.

3. Describe the "author" of the proposal. Why do you suppose Swift chose such a character or persona to present this plan? At what points in the essay can you detect Swift's own voice coming through?

4. Swift entitles his essay "A Modest Proposal," and in paragraph 2 he talks of making Ireland's "children sound and useful members of the commonwealth." In what ways are Swift's title and statement ironic? Cite several other examples of Swift's irony. (Glossary: *Irony*)

5. In what ways, if any, can the argument presented in this essay be seen as logical? What is the effect, for example, of the complicated calculations in paragraph 6?

6. Satire often has a "stealth quality" about it; that is, the audience for whom it is intended often does not realize at first that the author of the satire is not being serious. At some point in the satire the audience usually catches on and then begins to see the larger issue at the center of the satire. At what point in your reading of "A Modest Proposal" did you begin to catch on to Swift's technique and larger, more important, message?

7. Toward what belief and/or action is Swift attempting to persuade his readers? How does he go about doing so? For example, did you feel a sense of outrage at any point in the essay? Did you feel that the essay was humorous at any point? If so, where and why?

LANGUAGE IN ACTION

Consider the following news item, "Global Food Summit in Rome," by P. P. Rega. The piece, which first appeared on <TheSpoof.com> on June 8, 2008, reports on a meeting of world leaders to "resolve the present worldwide food crisis."

GLOBAL FOOD SUMMIT IN ROME
P. P. Rega

The Global Food Crisis Summit was held in Rome, Italy, this past week. Agricultural ministers, medical experts, and political activists from around the world convened in the Eternal City to resolve the present worldwide food crisis. Below is a copy of the first day's schedule of lectures and activities that have been sponsored by the United Nation's Food and Agriculture Organization.

Program

0730–0830: Registration at the southwest entrance to The Colosseum

Cappuccino, caffè latte, biscotti anginetti, cenci alla fiorentina e cornetti a piacere

0830–0900: Introduction

0900–0930: Uganda: Dehydration, Diarrhea and Death

0930–1000: Malnutrition in Myanmar

1000–1030: Break

Gelati assortiti da Giolitti (cioccolato, nocciole, e crema) con biscotti ed acqua minerale o caffè

1030–1100: Small Farmers in Indonesia: Source of Global Salvation

1100–1200: Introduction of Rice Farming in Haiti: Is It Enough?

1200–1300: Global Epidemic: Drop in Life Expectancy among the Poor and Starving

1300–1500: Lunch at Da Piperno

L'antipasto: Carciofi alla giudia

Vino: Verdicchio di Matelica Terre di Valbona 2006

Il Primo: Risotto alla pescatore oppure zuppa napoletana

 Vino: Tommaso Bussola Amarone di Valpolicella 2002

Il Secondo: Coda alla Vaccinara

Il Contorno: Vignarola

 Vino: Cantina Nobile di Montepulciano 1999

Formaggi: Fontina Val d'Aosta, bocconcini alla panna di bufala, pecorino romano

Il Dolce: Aranci in salsa di marsala

Caffè

Sambuca siciliana con tre mosche

1500–1600: Improving Crop Production in Zimbabwe: A Lesson To Us All.

1600–1700: Fertilizer or Seeds?

1700–1730: Break

Pizza alla quattro stagione

 Birra: Nastro Azzurro alla spina

1800–1900: Keynote Speaker: Al Gore

 Topic: Doubling Global Food Production in the 21st Century

1900– 2100: Dinner at La Pergola

L'antipasto: Mozzarella in carrozza

 Vino: Prosecco Superiore di Locarno 2001

Il Primo: Gnocchetti all'amatriciana

 Vino: Recioto di Soave da Anselmi 2003

Il Secondo: Stufato di manzo con cipolline

(continued)

Il Contorno: Fritto misto vegetariano

  Vino: Brunello di Montalcino 2001

Formaggi: Gorgonzola, mascarpone di bufala di Battipaglia, Parmigiano-Reggiano

Il Dolce: Cassata alla siciliana

  Caffè
  Limoncello amalfitana

What were your first impressions of Rega's story? What, for you, is Rega's point in presenting "the first day's schedule of lectures and activities"? Do you need to know Italian in order to grasp Rega's message? How do you think Swift would respond to such a meeting? What similarities do you see in the messages of Swift and Rega? Explain.

WRITING SUGGESTIONS

1. Write a modest proposal of your own to solve a difficult social or political problem of the present day or, on a smaller scale, a problem you see facing your school or community.

2. What do you think is the most effective way to bring about social change and to influence societal attitudes? Would Swift's methods work today, or would they have to be significantly modified as Rega has done in "Global Food Summit in Rome"? Write an essay in which you compare and contrast Swift's, Rega's, and George Saunders's ("My Amendment," pp. 237–241) tactics in an effort to determine how a writer can best influence public opinion today.

My Amendment

GEORGE SAUNDERS

George Saunders, born in Amarillo, Texas, in 1958 and raised in Chicago, seems to have avoided the left-brain/right-brain "tracking" many of us are subject to early on. After earning a B.S. in geophysical engineering from the Colorado School of Mines in 1981, Saunders went on to earn an M.A. in creative writing from Syracuse University in 1988. From 1989 to 1996, after spending some time exploring for oil in Sumatra, Saunders worked as a technical writer and geophysical engineer at an environmental engineering firm in Rochester, New York. In 1997 he joined the faculty of the MFA program in creative writing at Syracuse University. Saunders has been awarded a number of important prizes for his writing, most notably a MacArthur Foundation Fellowship, commonly referred to as the "genius grant," and a Guggenheim Fellowship, both in 2006.

Saunders has published three collections of stories—*In Persuasion Nation, Pastoralia,* and *CivilWarLand in Bad Decline;* a novella, *The Brief and Frightening Reign of Phil;* a book of essays, *The Braindead Megaphone;* and a children's story, *The Very Persistent Gappers of Frip.* His work has appeared in the *New Yorker, Harper's, Slate, McSweeney's,* and *GQ,* among other places, and he writes a weekly column, "American Psyche," for Britain's newspaper *The Guardian.* Saunders's inventive, witty, and often darkly disturbing fiction takes as its most frequent subject the excesses of modern American culture. The satirical bent, tragicomic tone, and serious moral underpinning of his work invite frequent comparisons to American authors Mark Twain, Kurt Vonnegut, and Thomas Pynchon. In "My Amendment," which first appeared in the *New Yorker* on March 8, 2004, Saunders offers his perspective on the debate in the United States over same-sex unions.

WRITING TO DISCOVER: *Do you have a position on the debate over same-sex unions? On what principles or other grounds do you base this position? Could you imagine someone persuading you that your position was wrong? If so, what would it take?*

As an obscure, middle-aged, heterosexual short-story writer, I am often asked, George, do you have any feelings about Same-Sex Marriage?

To which I answer, Actually, yes, I do.

Like any sane person, I am against Same-Sex Marriage, and in favor of a constitutional amendment to ban it.

To tell the truth, I feel that, in the interest of moral rigor, it is necessary for us to go a step further, which is why I would like to propose a supplementary constitutional amendment.

237

In the town where I live, I have frequently observed a phenomenon I   5
have come to think of as Samish-Sex Marriage. Take, for example, K, a male
friend of mine, of slight build, with a ponytail. K is married to S, a tall, stocky
female with extremely short hair, almost a crewcut. Often, while watching
K play with his own ponytail as S towers over him, I have wondered, Isn't it
odd that this somewhat effeminate man should be married to this somewhat
masculine woman? Is K not, on some level, imperfectly expressing a slight
latent desire to be married to a man? And is not S, on some level, imperfectly
expressing a slight latent desire to be married to a woman?

Then I ask myself, Is this truly what God had in mind?

Take the case of L, a female friend with a deep, booming voice. I
have often found myself looking askance at her husband, H. Though H is
basically pretty masculine, having neither a ponytail nor a tight feminine
derrière like K, still I wonder: H, when you are having marital relations
with L, and she calls out your name in that deep, booming, nearly male
voice, and you continue having marital relations with her (i.e., you are not
"turned off"), does this not imply that you, H, are, in fact, still "turned
on"? And doesn't this indicate that, on some level, you, H, have a slight
latent desire to make love to a man?

Or consider the case of T, a male friend with an extremely small penis.
(We attend the same gym.) He is married to O, an average-looking woman
who knows how to fix cars. I wonder about O. How does she know so
much about cars? Is she not, by tolerating this non-car-fixing, short-penised
friend of mine, indicating that, on some level, she wouldn't mind being
married to a woman, and is therefore, perhaps, a tiny bit functionally gay?

And what about T? Doesn't the fact that T can stand there in the
shower room at our gym, confidently towelling off his tiny unit, while O
is at home changing their sparkplugs with alacrity, indicate that it is only a
short stroll down a slippery slope before he is completely happy being the
"girl" in their relationship, from which it is only a small fey hop down the
same slope before T is happily married to another man, perhaps my car
mechanic, a handsome Portuguese fellow I shall refer to as J?

Because my feeling is, when God made man and woman He had   10
something very specific in mind. It goes without saying that He did not
want men marrying men, or women marrying women, but also what He
did not want, in my view, was feminine men marrying masculine women.

Which is why I developed my Manly Scale of Absolute Gender.

Using my Scale, which assigns numerical values according to a set of
masculine and feminine characteristics, it is now easy to determine how
Manly a man is and how Fem a woman is, and therefore how close to a
Samish-Sex Marriage a given marriage is.

Here's how it works. Say we determine that a man is an 8 on the
Manly Scale, with 10 being the most Manly of all and 0 basically a Neuter.
And say we determine that his fiancée is a −6 on the Manly Scale, with
a −10 being the most Fem of all. Calculating the difference between the

man's rating and the woman's rating—the Gender Differential—we see that this proposed union is not, in fact, a Samish-Sex Marriage, which I have defined as "any marriage for which the Gender Differential is less than or equal to 10 points."

Friends whom I have identified as being in Samish-Sex Marriages often ask me, George, given that we have scored poorly, what exactly would you have us do about it?

Well, one solution I have proposed is divorce—divorce followed   15 by remarriage to a more suitable partner. K, for example, could marry a voluptuous high-voiced N.F.L. cheerleader, who would more than offset his tight feminine derrière, while his ex-wife, S, might choose to become involved with a lumberjack with very large arms, thereby neutralizing her thick calves and faint mustache.

Another, and of course preferable, solution would be to repair the existing marriage, converting it from a Samish-Sex Marriage to a healthy Normal Marriage, by having the feminine man become more masculine and/or the masculine woman become more feminine.

Often, when I propose this, my friends become surly. How dare I, they ask. What business is it of mine? Do I think it is easy to change in such a profound way?

To which I say, It is not easy to change, but it is possible.

I know, because I have done it.

When young, I had a tendency to speak too quickly, while gesturing   20 too much with my hands. Also, my opinions were unfirm. I was constantly contradicting myself in that fast voice, while gesturing like a girl. Also, I cried often. Things seemed so sad. I had long blond hair, and liked it. My hair was layered and fell down across my shoulders, and, I admit it, I would sometimes slow down when passing a shopwindow to look at it, to look at my hair! I had a strange constant feeling of being happy to be alive. This feeling of infinite possibility sometimes caused me to laugh when alone, or even, on occasion, to literally skip down the street, before pausing in front of a shopwindow and giving my beautiful hair a cavalier toss.

To tell the truth, I do not think I would have scored very high on my Manly Scale, if the Scale had been invented at that time, by me. I suspect I would have scored so Fem on the test that I would have been prohibited from marrying my wife, P, the love of my life. And I think, somewhere in my heart, I knew that.

I knew I was too Fem.

So what did I do about it? Did I complain? Did I whine? Did I expect activist judges to step in on my behalf, manipulating the system to accommodate my peculiarity?

No, I did not.

What I did was I changed. I undertook what I like to think of as a clas-   25 sic American project of self-improvement. I made videos of myself talking, and studied these, and in time succeeded in training myself to speak more slowly, while almost never moving my hands. Now, if you ever meet me, you will observe that I always speak in an extremely slow and manly and almost painfully deliberate way, with my hands either driven deep into my pockets or held stock-still at the ends of my arms, which are bent slightly at the elbows, as if I were ready to respond to the slightest provocation by punching you in the face. As for my opinions, they are very firm. I rarely change them. When I feel like skipping, I absolutely do not skip. As for my long beautiful hair—well, I am lucky, in that I am rapidly going bald. Every month, when I recalculate my ranking on the Manly Scale, I find myself becoming more and more Manly, as my hair gets thinner and my girth increases, thickening my once lithe, almost girlish physique, thus insuring the continuing morality and legality of my marriage to P.

My point is simply this: If I was able to effect these tremendous positive changes in my life, to avoid finding myself in the moral/legal quagmire of a Samish-Sex Marriage, why can't K, S, L, H, T, and O do the same?

I implore any of my readers who find themselves in a Samish-Sex Marriage: Change. If you are a feminine man, become more manly. If you are a masculine woman, become more feminine. If you are a woman and are thick-necked or lumbering, or have ever had the slightest feeling of attraction to a man who is somewhat pale and fey, deny these feelings and, in a spirit of self-correction, try to become more thin-necked and light-footed, while, if you find it helpful, watching videos of naked masculine men, to sort of retrain yourself in the proper mode of attraction. If you are a man and, upon seeing a thick-waisted, athletic young woman walking with a quasi-mannish gait through your local grocery, you imagine yourself in a passionate embrace with her, in your car, a car that is parked just outside, and which is suddenly, in your imagination, full of the smell of her fresh young breath—well, stop thinking that! Are you a man or not?

I, for one, am sick and tired of this creeping national tendency to let certain types of people take advantage of our national good nature by marrying individuals who are essentially of their own gender. If this trend continues, before long our towns and cities will be full of people like K, S, L, H, T, and O, people "asserting their rights" by dating, falling in love with, marrying, and spending the rest of their lives with whomever they please.

I, for one, am not about to stand by and let that happen.

Because then what will we have? A nation ruled by the anarchy of unconstrained desire. A nation of willful human hearts, each lurching this way and that and reaching out for whatever it spontaneously desires, trying desperately to find some comforting temporary shred of warmth in a mostly cold world, totally unconcerned about the external form in which that other, long-desired heart is embodied. 30

That is not the kind of world in which I wish to live.

I, for one, intend to become ever more firmly male, enjoying my golden years, while watching P become ever more female, each of us vigilant for any hint of ambiguity in the other.

And as our children grow, should they begin to show the slightest hint of some lingering residue of the opposite gender, P and I will lovingly pull them aside and list all the particulars by which we were able to identify their unintentional deficiency.

Then, together, we will devise a suitable correction.

And, in this way, the race will go on.   35

THINKING CRITICALLY ABOUT THE READING

1. Are the "George" of the piece and the author George Saunders the same person? On what do you base your conclusion?

2. Who or what is the precise target of the author's satire? How do you know?

3. Who is the author's intended audience? (Glossary: *Audience*) What in this essay led you to this conclusion?

4. Explain the pheonomenon the narrator identifies as "Samish-Sex Marriage." How does it relate to "same-sex marriage"? What is the effect of the "-ish" that the narrator uses to distinguish them?

5. In paragraph 10, the narrator of the piece says, "Because my feeling is, when God made man and woman He had something very specific in mind." How does his insistence on knowing God's "very specific" intentions fuel the satire?

6. What is the "Manly Scale of Absolute Gender" (11)? Why do you think the narrator terms it a "Manly" scale, rather than simply a "Scale of Absolute Gender"? What tendency or tendencies does the scale satirize?

7. What happens in the piece when, in paragraphs 18 and 19, the narrator announces: "To which I say, It is not easy to change, but it is possible. I know, because I have done it"? Were there hints of his own likely "gender rating" earlier in the piece? What importance do his revelations about his "unfirm" past have?

8. What, in the end, does the author seem to suggest about the future his narrator depicts with dread: "A nation of willful human hearts, each lurching this way and that and reaching out for whatever it spontaneously desires, trying desperately to find some comforting temporary shred of warmth in a mostly cold world, totally unconcerned about the external form in which that other, long-desired heart is embodied" (30)?

LANGUAGE IN ACTION

As you read the following story that first appeared in a Sierra Club newsletter under the title "A Fable for Our Times," carefully consider the writer's choice of words. Circle or underline words or phrases that seem particularly well chosen to you.

Once upon a time there was a small, beautiful, green, and graceful country called Vietnam. It needed to be saved. (In later years no one could remember exactly what it needed to be saved from, but that is another story.) For many years Vietnam was in the process of being saved by France, but the French eventually tired of their labors and left. Then America took on the job. America was well-equipped for country-saving. It was the richest and most powerful nation on earth. It had, for example, nuclear explosives on hand and ready to use equal to six tons of TNT for every man, woman, and child in the world. It had huge and very efficient factories, brilliant and dedicated scientists, and most (but not every-body) would agree, it had good intentions. Sadly, America had one fatal flaw—its inhabitants were in love with technology and thought it could do no wrong. A visitor to America during the time of this story would probably have guessed its outcome after seeing how its inhabitants were treating their own country. The air was mostly foul, the water putrid, and most of the land was either covered with concrete or garbage. But Americans were never much on introspection, and they didn't foresee the result of their loving embrace on the small country. They set out to save Vietnam with the same enthusiasm and determination their forefathers had displayed in conquering the frontier. They bombed. More than 3 million tons of explosives were dropped—50 per cent more than the total bomb tonnage dropped in both theaters of World War II. Technologists looked on in awe and spoke of a ditch 30 feet deep, 45 feet wide, and 30 thousand miles long if all the craters were placed in a row. What the Vietnam peasant spoke of was never recorded. Entire villages were destroyed by bombing, napalm fires, and artillery. After one such mission an American officer made the prophetic explana-tion that it was necessary to destroy the village in order to save it. Unquestioned, the logic of such a statement became sanctified. They bombed with chemicals as well as explosives, and trees, bushes, plants died by the millions of acres in a program with the Orwellian name of "operation Ranch Hand," whose macabre motto was "only we can prevent forests." The consequences of such a deliberate and massive ecological attack were unknown and unknowable, but there was no deterrent. Thousands of herbicide and defoliant missions were flown before anyone seriously questioned their long-range effects on humans and animals, as well as on plants. By the time deformed fetuses began appearing and signs of last-ing ecological damage were becoming increasingly apparent, success had been achieved. Vietnam had been saved. But the country was dead.

In your opinion, what is the writer's tone in this selection? (Glossary: *Tone*) Point to specific words or phrases that the writer uses that led you to this conclusion. How appropriate is this tone in light of the writer's thesis and purpose in this fable? (Glossary: *Thesis, Purpose*) What light, if any, does this fable shed on America in the twenty-first century? Explain.

WRITING SUGGESTIONS

1. The narrator of "My Amendment" concludes by stating the presumed effects of his vigilance against "samish-sex" unions: "And, in this way, the race will go on." The narrator's position is deliberately made to seem extreme, but it

reflects a geniune fear on the part of those opposed to same-sex unions: the end, if not of the race itself, at least of cherished cultural traditions and a time-honored way of life. Where do you stand? Write an essay in which you argue either for or against the official recognition of same-sex unions. In supporting your position, explain specifically what you think the consequences of allowing such unions would be, for better or for worse.

2. Saunders's "My Amendment," like Jonathan Swift's "A Modest Proposal" (pp. 227–233), is an example of satire designed to express the author's point of view about an important issue of the day. Choose an issue that's currently debated and of interest to you—U.S. immigration policy; off-shore exploration and drilling for oil; stem cell research; public financing for political campaigns—and write a satirical piece in which you argue for the opposite of what you actually believe. When you've finished, write a short piece reflecting on how successful you think you were. Would a straightforward argument have been easier to write? Which do you think would be more effective in persuading an audience? Why?

4

PREJUDICE, DISCRIMINATION, AND STEREOTYPES

No single issue has absorbed our national consciousness more than prejudice and discrimination. That we are defined by and define others is an inevitability of our human condition, but the manner in which we relate to each other is a measure of our progress as a multiracial, multiethnic, and multicultural society. In a larger sense, it is a measure of our growth as a civilization. Not even the most optimistic observers of our society believe that equality is within sight or perhaps even ultimately possible, but implicit in all views of the subject is the notion that we can and must improve our appreciation of each other if we are to better our lives.

Our purpose in the first section of this chapter, "Where Does Prejudice Come From?," is to introduce you to some ideas on the sources of prejudice and to illustrate the role that language plays in the origin and perpetuation of prejudice and discrimination. We begin with Andrew Sullivan's "What's So Bad about Hate?," an in-depth inquiry into the nature of hatred and its relationship to prejudice, bias, bigotry, malice, anger, and all the emotions in between. Next we present Gordon Allport's classic essay "The Language of Prejudice," acknowledged by scholars for the past fifty years as the definitive word on the subject. Allport's concepts of "nouns that cut slices" and "verbal realism and symbol phobia" demonstrate not only how language encodes prejudice but also how we can use language to escape bias and bigotry. In "Signs of Infection," *New York Times* writer Bob Herbert reflects on the implications of Don Imus's attack on members of the Rutgers women's basketball team. He writes, "The attention surrounding Mr. Imus's very public self-immolation is an opportunity for Americans to acknowledge that we have a problem. Not only is the society still permeated by racism and sexism and the stereotypes they spawn, but we have allowed a debased and profoundly immature culture to emerge in which the coarsest, most socially destructive images and language are an integral part of the everyday discourse." Alleen Pace Nilsen's "From the Dixie Chicks to the St. Louis Rams: What Animal-Based Metaphors Reveal about Sexism," which concludes this section, demonstrates the ways that sexist terms tell the story of how we view women in our culture.

The second section of this chapter on prejudice, "Prejudice, Stereotypes, and the Minority Experience," takes a closer look at how language, culture, and prejudice interact in our society. In her essay illustrating her family and friends' repurposing of the racially charged term *nigger,* Gloria Naylor reminds us that words themselves do not exist in isolation, but are rather the product of the minds and hearts that use them. In "The B-Word? You Betcha," a provocative essay by Andi Zeisler, the author tells us why she and her copublisher Lisa Jervis named their magazine *Bitch* and lets us in on both the criticism and the support that edgy title has attracted. Next, noted women's rights advocate and writer Gloria Steinem deconstructs the term "chick flick," and Grace Hsiang, just starting out on her writing career, casts light on intraracial discrimination, a type of prejudice that is little known and even less talked about. We move next to Brent Staples's essay entitled "Black Men and Public Space" as he reflects on the way his presence as an African American alters public spaces and shapes the attitudes and actions of those around him. His analysis reaches into the world of body language and spatial relationships—that is, the messages we send and receive through nonverbal means. Finally, in a poignant essay, the late Audre Lorde tells of her family's dismay and silence when they came face-to-face with the bitterness of racism in our nation's capital.

What's So Bad about Hate?

ANDREW SULLIVAN

Andrew Sullivan was born in 1963 in South Godstone, Surrey, England, to Irish parents. He earned his B.A. degree in modern history at Magdalene College, Oxford, and his masters degree and Ph.D. in government at Harvard University. Sullivan began his career in journalism at the *New Republic* and later wrote for the *New York Times Magazine*. A gay, Catholic, conservative, and often controversial commentator, Sullivan is perhaps best known for his blog *The Daily Dish*, which became very popular post-9/11 and was by 2005 receiving over 50,000 hits a day. In 2007, Sullivan accepted an editorial position with *The Atlantic*. He has written several books: *Virtually Normal: An Argument about Homosexuality* (1995); *Love Undetectable: Notes on Friendship, Sex and Survival* (1998); and *The Conservative Soul: How We Lost It, How to Get It Back* (2006).

In "What's So Bad about Hate?," first published in the *New York Times Magazine* on September 26, 1999, Sullivan reveals how little we actually know about the emotion that lies at the base of prejudice. As he writes, "For all its emotional punch, 'hate' is far less nuanced an idea than prejudice, or bigotry, or bias, or anger, or even aversion to others."

WRITING TO DISCOVER: *Have you ever been so upset by someone that you could say that you hated the person? If so, what prompted your reaction? How would you characterize the nature of the hatred you felt? Do you think it was an uncontrollable response or a conscious one? Do you think you had your reasons and would react the same way again in similar circumstances?*

I.

I wonder what was going on in John William King's head [in 1997] when he tied James Byrd Jr.'s feet to the back of a pickup truck and dragged him three miles down a road in rural Texas. King and two friends had picked up Byrd, who was black, when he was walking home, half-drunk, from a party. As part of a bonding ritual in their fledgling white supremacist group, the three men took Byrd to a remote part of town, beat him and chained his legs together before attaching them to the truck. Pathologists at King's trial testified that Byrd was probably alive and conscious until his body finally hit a culvert and split in two. When King was offered a chance to say something to Byrd's family at the trial, he smirked and uttered an obscenity.

We know all these details now, many months later. We know quite a large amount about what happened before and after. But I am still drawn, again and again, to the flash of ignition, the moment when fear and loathing became hate, the instant of transformation when King became hunter and Byrd became prey.

What was that? And what was it when Buford Furrow Jr., long-time member of the Aryan Nations, calmly walked up to a Filipino-American mailman he happened to spot, asked him to mail a letter and then shot him at point-blank range? Or when Russell Henderson beat Matthew Shepard, a young gay man, to a pulp, removed his shoes and then, with the help of a friend, tied him to a post like a dead coyote to warn off others?

For all our documentation of these crimes and others, our political and moral disgust at them, our morbid fascination with them, our sensitivity to their social meaning, we seem at times to have no better idea now than we ever had of what exactly they were about. About what that moment means when, for some reason or other, one human being asserts absolute, immutable superiority over another. About not the violence, but what the violence expresses. About what—exactly—hate is. And what our own part in it may be.

I find myself wondering what hate actually is in part because we have created an entirely new offense in American criminal law—a "hate crime"—to combat it. And barely a day goes by without someone somewhere declaring war against it. Last month President Clinton called for an expansion of hate-crime laws as "what America needs in our battle against hate." A couple of weeks later, Senator John McCain used a campaign speech to denounce the "hate" he said poisoned the land. New York's mayor, Rudolph Giuliani, recently tried to stop the Million Youth March in Harlem on the grounds that the event was organized by people "involved in hate marches and hate rhetoric."

The media concurs in its emphasis. In 1985, there were 11 mentions of "hate crimes" in the national media database Nexis. By 1990, there were more than a thousand. In the first six months of 1999, there were 7,000. "Sexy fun is one thing," wrote a *New York Times* reporter about sexual assaults in Woodstock '99's mosh pit. "But this was an orgy of lewdness tinged with hate." And when Benjamin Smith marked the Fourth of July this year by targeting blacks, Asians, and Jews for murder in Indiana and Illinois, the story wasn't merely about a twisted young man who had emerged on the scene. As the *Times* put it, "Hate arrived in the neighborhoods of Indiana University, in Bloomington, in the early-morning darkness."

But what exactly was this thing that arrived in the early-morning darkness? For all our zeal to attack hate, we still have a remarkably vague idea of what it actually is. A single word, after all, tells us less, not more. For all its emotional punch, "hate" is far less nuanced an idea than prejudice, or bigotry, or bias, or anger, or even mere aversion to others. Is it to stand in

5

for all these varieties of human experience—and everything in between? If so, then the war against it will be so vast as to be quixotic. Or is "hate" to stand for a very specific idea or belief, or set of beliefs, with a very specific object or group of objects? Then waging war against it is almost certainly unconstitutional. Perhaps these kinds of questions are of no concern to those waging war on hate. Perhaps it is enough for them that they share a sentiment that there is too much hate and never enough vigilance in combating it. But sentiment is a poor basis for law, and a dangerous tool in politics. It is better to leave some unwinnable wars unfought.

II.

Hate is everywhere. Human beings generalize all the time, ahead of time, about everyone and everything. A large part of it may even be hard-wired. At some point in our evolution, being able to know beforehand who was friend or foe was not merely a matter of philosophical reflection. It was a matter of survival. And even today it seems impossible to feel a loyalty without also feeling a disloyalty, a sense of belonging without an equal sense of unbelonging. We're social beings. We associate. Therefore we disassociate. And although it would be comforting to think that the one could happen without the other, we know in reality that it doesn't. How many patriots are there who have never felt a twinge of xenophobia?

Of course, by hate we mean something graver and darker than this kind of lazy prejudice. But the closer you look at this distinction, the fuzzier it gets. Much of the time, we harbor little or no malice toward people of other backgrounds or places or ethnicities or ways of life. But then a car cuts you off at an intersection and you find yourself noticing immediately that the driver is a woman, or black, or old, or fat, or white, or male. Or you are walking down a city street at night and hear footsteps quickening behind you. You look around and see that it is a white woman and not a black man, and you are instantly relieved. These impulses are so spontaneous they are almost involuntary. But where did they come from? The mindless need to be mad at someone—anyone—or the unconscious eruption of a darker prejudice festering within?

In 1993, in San Jose, Calif., two neighbors—one heterosexual, one 　10 homosexual—were engaged in a protracted squabble over grass clippings. (The full case is recounted in *Hate Crimes,* by James B. Jacobs and Kimberly Potter.) The gay man regularly mowed his lawn without a grass catcher, which prompted his neighbor to complain on many occasions that grass clippings spilled over onto his driveway. Tensions grew until one day, the gay man mowed his front yard, spilling clippings onto his neighbor's driveway, prompting the straight man to yell an obscene and common anti-gay insult. The wrangling escalated. At one point, the gay man agreed to collect the clippings from his neighbor's driveway but then later found them dumped on his own porch. A fracas ensued with the gay man spraying the straight man's son with a garden hose, and the son hitting and kicking the gay man several times, yelling anti-gay slurs. The police were called, and the son was eventually convicted of a hate-motivated assault, a felony. But what was the nature of the hate: anti-gay bias, or suburban property-owner madness?

Or take the Labor Day parade last year in Broad Channel, a small island in Jamaica Bay, Queens. Almost everyone there is white, and in recent years a group of local volunteer firefighters has taken to decorating a pickup truck for the parade in order to win the prize for "funniest float." Their themes have tended toward the outrageously provocative. Beginning in 1995, they won prizes for floats depicting "Hasidic Park," "Gooks of Hazzard" and "Happy Gays." Last year, they called their float "Black to the Future, Broad Channel 2098." They imagined their community a century hence as a largely black enclave, with every stereotype imaginable: watermelons, basketballs and so on. At one point during the parade, one of them mimicked the dragging death of James Byrd. It was caught on videotape, and before long the entire community was depicted as a caldron of hate.

It's an interesting case, because the float was indisputably in bad taste and the improvisation on the Byrd killing was grotesque. But was it hate? The men on the float were local heroes for their volunteer work; they had no record of bigoted activity, and were not members of any racist organizations. In previous years, they had made fun of many other groups and saw themselves more as provocateurs than bigots. When they were described as racists, it came as a shock to them. They apologized for poor taste but refused to confess to bigotry. "The people involved aren't horrible people," protested a local woman. "Was it a racist act? I don't know. Are they racists? I don't think so."

If hate is a self-conscious activity, she has a point. The men were primarily motivated by the desire to shock and to reflect what they thought was their community's culture. Their display was not aimed at any particular black people, or at any blacks who lived in Broad Channel—almost none do. But if hate is primarily an unconscious activity, then the matter is obviously murkier. And by taking the horrific lynching of a black man as a spontaneous object of humor, the men were clearly advocating indifference to it. Was this an aberrant excess? Or the real truth about the men's feelings toward African-Americans? Hate or tastelessness? And how on earth is anyone, even perhaps the firefighters themselves, going to know for sure?

Or recall H. L. Mencken. He shared in the anti-Semitism of his time with more alacrity than most and was an indefatigable racist. "It is impossible," he wrote in his diary, "to talk anything resembling discretion or judgment into a colored woman. They are all essentially childlike, and even hard experience does not teach them anything." He wrote at another time of the "psychological stigmata" of the "Afro-American race." But it is also true that, during much of his life, day to day, Mencken conducted himself with no regard to race, and supported a politics that was clearly integrationist. As the editor of his diary has pointed out, Mencken published many black authors in his magazine, *The Mercury,* and lobbied on their behalf with his publisher, Alfred A. Knopf. The last thing Mencken ever wrote was a diatribe against racial segregation in Baltimore's public parks. He was good friends with leading black writers and journalists, including James Weldon Johnson, Walter White, and George S. Schuyler, and played an underappreciated role in promoting the Harlem Renaissance.

What would our modern view of hate do with Mencken? Probably ignore him, or change the subject. But, with regard to hate, I know lots of people like Mencken. He reminds me of conservative friends who oppose almost every measure for homosexual equality yet genuinely delight in the company of their gay friends. It would be easier for me to think of them as haters, and on paper, perhaps, there is a good case that they are. But in real life, I know they are not. Some of them clearly harbor no real malice toward me or other homosexuals whatsoever. 15

They are as hard to figure out as those liberal friends who support every gay rights measure they have ever heard of but do anything to avoid going into a gay bar with me. I have to ask myself in the same, frustrating kind of way: are they liberal bigots or bigoted liberals? Or are they neither bigots nor liberals, but merely people?

III.

Hate used to be easier to understand. When Sartre described anti-Semitism in his 1946 essay "Anti-Semite and Jew," he meant a very specific array of firmly held prejudices, with a history, an ideology and even a pseudoscience to back them up. He meant a systematic attempt to demonize and eradicate an entire race. If you go to the Web site of the World Church of the Creator, the organization that inspired young Benjamin Smith to murder in Illinois earlier this year, you will find a similarly bizarre, pseudorational ideology. The kind of literature read by Buford Furrow before he rained terror on a Jewish kindergarten last month and then killed a mailman because of his color is full of the same paranoid loopiness. And when we talk about hate, we often mean this kind of phenomenon.

But this brand of hatred is mercifully rare in the United States. These professional maniacs are to hate what serial killers are to murder. They should certainly not be ignored; but they represent what Harold Meyerson, writing in *Salon,* called "niche haters": cold blooded, somewhat deranged, often poorly socialized psychopaths. In a free society with relatively easy access to guns, they will always pose a menace.

But their menace is a limited one, and their hatred is hardly typical of anything very widespread. Take Buford Furrow. He famously issued a "wake-up call" to "kill Jews" in Los Angeles, before he peppered a Jewish community center with gunfire. He did this in a state with two Jewish female senators, in a city with a large, prosperous Jewish population, in a country where out of several million Jewish Americans, a total of 66 were reported by the F.B.I. as the targets of hate-crime assaults in 1997. However despicable Furrow's actions were, it would require a very large stretch to describe them as representative of anything but the deranged fringe of an American subculture.

Most hate is more common and more complicated, with as many varieties as there are varieties of love. Just as there is possessive love and needy love; family love and friendship; romantic love and unrequited love; passion and respect, affection and obsession, so hatred has its shadings. There is hate that fears, and hate that merely feels contempt; there is hate that expresses power, and hate that comes from powerlessness; there is revenge, and there is hate that comes from envy. There is hate that was love, and hate that is a curious expression of love. There is hate of the other, and hate of something that reminds us too much of ourselves. There is the oppressor's hate, and the victim's hate. There is hate that burns slowly, and hate that fades. And there is hate that explodes, and hate that never catches fire. 20

The modern words that we have created to describe the varieties of hate — "sexism," "racism," "anti-Semitism," "homophobia" — tell us very little about any of this. They tell us merely the identities of the victims; they don't reveal the identities of the perpetrators, or what they think, or how they feel. They don't even tell us how the victims feel. And this simplicity is no accident. Coming from the theories of Marxist and post-Marxist academics, these "isms" are far better at alleging structures of power than at delineating the workings of the individual heart or mind. In fact, these "isms" can exist without mentioning individuals at all.

We speak of institutional racism, for example, as if an institution can feel anything. We talk of "hate" as an impersonal noun, with no hater specified. But when these abstractions are actually incarnated, when someone feels something as a result of them, when a hater actually interacts with a victim, the picture changes. We find that hates are often very different phenomena one from another, that they have very different psychological dynamics, that they might even be better understood by not seeing them as varieties of the same thing at all.

There is, for example, the now unfashionable distinction between reasonable hate and unreasonable hate. In recent years, we have become accustomed to talking about hates as if they were all equally indefensible, as if it could never be the case that some hates might be legitimate, even necessary. But when some 800,000 Tutsis are murdered under the auspices of a Hutu regime in Rwanda, and when a few thousand Hutus are killed in revenge, the hates are not commensurate. Genocide is not an event like a hurricane, in which damage is random and universal; it is a planned and often merciless attack of one group upon another. The hate of the perpetrators is a monstrosity. The hate of the victims, and their survivors, is justified. What else, one wonders, were surviving Jews supposed to feel toward Germans after the Holocaust? Or, to a different degree, South African blacks after apartheid? If the victims overcome this hate, it is a supreme moral achievement. But if they don't, the victims are not as culpable as the perpetrators. So the hatred of Serbs for Kosovars today can never be equated with the hatred of Kosovars for Serbs.

Hate, like much of human feeling, is not rational, but it usually has its reasons. And it cannot be understood, let alone condemned, without knowing them. Similarly, the hate that comes from knowledge is always different from the hate that comes from ignorance. It is one of the most foolish clichés of our time that prejudice is always rooted in ignorance, and can usually be overcome by familiarity with the objects of our loathing. The racism of many Southern whites under segregation was not appeased by familiarity with Southern blacks; the virulent loathing of Tutsis by many Hutus was not undermined by living next door to them for centuries. Theirs was a hatred that sprang, for whatever reasons, from experience. It cannot easily be compared with, for example, the resilience of anti-Semitism in Japan, or hostility to immigration in areas where immigrants are unknown, or fear of homosexuals by people who have never knowingly met one.

The same familiarity is an integral part of what has become known as "sexism." Sexism isn't, properly speaking, a prejudice at all. Few men live without knowledge or constant awareness of women. Every single sexist man was born of a woman, and is likely to be sexually attracted to women. His hostility is going to be very different than that of, say, a reclusive member of the Aryan Nations toward Jews he has never met. 　　25

In her book *The Anatomy of Prejudices,* the psychotherapist Elisabeth Young-Bruehl proposes a typology of three distinct kinds of hate: obsessive, hysterical, and narcissistic. It's not an exhaustive analysis, but it's a beginning in any serious attempt to understand hate rather than merely declaring war on it. The obsessives, for Young-Bruehl, are those, like the Nazis or Hutus, who fantasize a threat from a minority, and obsessively try to rid themselves of it. For them, the very existence of the hated group is threatening. They often describe their loathing in almost physical terms: they experience what Patrick Buchanan, in reference to homosexuals, once described as a "visceral recoil" from the objects of their detestation. They often describe those they hate as diseased or sick, in need of a cure. Or they talk of "cleansing" them, as the Hutus talked of the Tutsis, or call them "cockroaches," as Yitzhak Shamir called the Palestinians. If you read material from the Family Research Council, it is clear that the group regards homosexuals as similar contaminants. A recent posting on its Web site about syphilis among gay men was headlined, "Unclean."

Hysterical haters have a more complicated relationship with the objects of their aversion. In Young-Bruehl's words, hysterical prejudice is a prejudice that "a person uses unconsciously to appoint a group to act out in the world forbidden sexual and sexually aggressive desires that the person has repressed." Certain kinds of racists fit this pattern. White loathing of blacks is, for some people, at least partly about sexual and physical envy. A certain kind of white racist sees in black America all those impulses he wishes most to express himself but cannot. He idealizes in "blackness" a sexual freedom, a physical power, a Dionysian release that he detests but also longs for. His fantasy may not have any basis in reality, but it is powerful nonetheless. It is a form of love-hate, and it is impossible to understand the nuances of racism in, say, the American South, or in British Imperial India, without it.

Unlike the obsessives, the hysterical haters do not want to eradicate the objects of their loathing; rather they want to keep them in some kind of permanent and safe subjugation in order to indulge the attraction of their repulsion. A recent study, for example, found that the men most likely to be opposed to equal rights for homosexuals were those most likely to be aroused by homoerotic imagery. This makes little rational sense, but it has a certain psychological plausibility. If homosexuals were granted equality, then the hysterical gay-hater might panic that his repressed passions would run out of control, overwhelming him and the world he inhabits.

A narcissistic hate, according to Young-Bruehl's definition, is sexism. In its most common form, it is rooted in many men's inability even to imagine what it is to be a woman, a failing rarely challenged by men's control of our most powerful public social institutions. Women are not so much hated by most men as simply ignored in non-sexual contexts, or never conceived of as true equals. The implicit condescension is mixed, in many cases, with repressed and sublimated erotic desire. So the unawareness of women is sometimes commingled with a deep longing or contempt for them.

Each hate, of course, is more complicated than this, and in any one person hate can assume a uniquely configured combination of these types. So there are hysterical sexists who hate women because they need them so much, and narcissistic sexists who hardly notice that women exist, and sexists who oscillate between one of these positions and another. And there are gay-bashers who are threatened by masculine gay men and gay-haters who feel repulsed by effeminate ones. The soldier who beat his fellow soldier Barry Winchell to death with a baseball bat in July had earlier lost a fight to him. It was the image of a macho gay man—and the shame of being bested by him—that the vengeful soldier had to obliterate, even if he needed a gang of accomplices and a weapon to do so. But the murderers of Matthew Shepard seem to have had a different impulse: a visceral disgust at the thought of any sexual contact with an effeminate homosexual. Their anger was mixed with mockery, as the cruel spectacle at the side of the road suggested.

In the same way, the pathological anti-Semitism of Nazi Germany was obsessive, inasmuch as it tried to cleanse the world of Jews; but also, as Daniel Jonah Goldhagen shows in his book, *Hitler's Willing Executioners*, hysterical. The Germans were mysteriously compelled as well as repelled by Jews, devising elaborate ways, like death camps and death marches, to keep them alive even as they killed them. And the early Nazi phobia of interracial sex suggests as well a lingering erotic quality to the relationship, partaking of exactly the kind of sexual panic that persists among some homosexual-haters and antimiscegenation racists. So the concept of "homophobia," like that of "sexism" and "racism," is often a crude one. All three are essentially cookie-cutter formulas that try to understand human impulses merely through the one-dimensional identity of the victims, rather than through the thoughts and feelings of the haters and hated.

This is deliberate. The theorists behind these "isms" want to ascribe all blame to one group in society—the "oppressors"—and render specific others—the "victims"—completely blameless. And they want to do this in order in part to side unequivocally with the underdog. But it doesn't take a genius to see how this approach, too, can generate its own form of bias. It can justify blanket condemnations of whole groups of people—white straight males, for example—purely because of the color of their skin or the nature of their sexual orientation. And it can condescendingly ascribe innocence to whole groups of others. It does exactly what hate does: it hammers the uniqueness of each individual into the anvil of group identity. And it postures morally over the result.

In reality, human beings and human acts are far more complex, which is why these isms and the laws they have fomented are continually coming under strain and challenge. Once again, hate wriggles free of its definers. It knows no monolithic groups of haters and hated. Like a river, it has many eddies, backwaters, and rapids. So there are anti-Semites who actually admire what they think of as Jewish power, and there are gay-haters who look up to homosexuals and some who want to sleep with them. And there are black racists, racist Jews, sexist women, and anti-Semitic homosexuals. Of course there are.

IV.

Once you start thinking of these phenomena less as the "isms" of sexism/racism and "homophobia," once you think of them as independent psychological responses, it's also possible to see how they can work in a bewildering variety of ways in a bewildering number of people. To take one obvious and sad oddity: people who are demeaned and objectified in society may develop an aversion to their tormentors that is more hateful in its expression than the prejudice they have been subjected to. The F.B.I. statistics on hate crimes throws up an interesting point. In America in the 1990s, blacks were up to three times as likely as whites to commit a hate crime, to express their hate by physically attacking their targets or their property. Just as sexual abusers have often been victims of sexual abuse, and wife-beaters often grew up in violent households, so hate criminals may often be members of hated groups.

Even the Columbine murderers were in some sense victims of hate   35
before they were purveyors of it. Their classmates later admitted that Dylan Klebold and Eric Harris were regularly called "faggots" in the corridors and classrooms of Columbine High and that nothing was done to prevent or stop the harassment. This climate of hostility doesn't excuse the actions of Klebold and Harris, but it does provide a more plausible context. If they had been black, had routinely been called "nigger" in the school and had then exploded into a shooting spree against white students, the response to the matter might well have been different. But the hate would have been the same. In other words, hate-victims are often hate-victimizers as well. This doesn't mean that all hates are equivalent, or that some are not more justified than others. It means merely that hate goes both ways; and if you try to regulate it among some, you will find yourself forced to regulate it among others.

It is no secret, for example, that some of the most vicious anti-Semites in America are black, and that some of the most virulent anti-Catholic bigots in America are gay. At what point, we are increasingly forced to ask, do these phenomena become as indefensible as white racism or religious toleration of anti-gay bigotry? That question becomes all the more difficult when we notice that it is often minorities who commit some of the most hate-filled offenses against what they see as their oppressors. It was the mainly gay AIDS activist group Act Up that perpetrated the hateful act of desecrating Communion hosts at a Mass at St. Patrick's Cathedral in New York. And here is the playwright Tony Kushner, who is gay, responding to the Matthew Shepard beating in *The Nation* magazine: "Pope John Paul II endorses murder. He, too, knows the price of discrimination, having declared anti-Semitism a sin. . . . He knows that discrimination kills. But when the Pope heard the news about Matthew Shepard, he, too, worried about spin. And so, on the subject of gay-bashing, the Pope and his cardinals and his bishops and priests maintain their cynical political silence. . . . To remain silent is to endorse murder." Kushner went on to describe the Pope as a "homicidal liar."

Maybe the passion behind these words is justified. But it seems clear enough to me that Kushner is expressing hate toward the institution of the Catholic Church, and all those who perpetuate its doctrines. How else to interpret the way in which he accuses the Pope of cynicism, lying, and murder? And how else either to understand the brutal parody of religious vocations expressed by the Sisters of Perpetual Indulgence, a group of gay men who dress in drag as nuns and engage in sexually explicit performances in public? Or T-shirts with the words "Recovering Catholic" on them, hot items among some gay and lesbian activists? The implication that someone's religious faith is a mental illness is clearly an expression of contempt. If that isn't covered under the definition of hate speech, what is?

Or take the following sentence: "The act male homosexuals commit is ugly and repugnant and afterwards they are disgusted with themselves. They drink and take drugs to palliate this, but they are disgusted with the act and they are always changing partners and cannot be really happy." The thoughts of Pat Robertson or Patrick Buchanan? Actually that sentence was written by Gertrude Stein, one of the century's most notable lesbians. Or take the following, about how beating up "black boys like that made us feel good inside. . . . Every time I drove my foot into his [expletive], I felt better." It was written to describe the brutal assault of an innocent bystander for the sole reason of his race. By the end of the attack, the victim had blood gushing from his mouth as his attackers stomped on his genitals. Are we less appalled when we learn that the actual sentence was how beating up "white boys like that made us feel good inside. . . . Every time I drove my foot into his [expletive], I felt better?" It was written by Nathan McCall, an African-American who later in life became a successful journalist at the *Washington Post* and published his memoir of this "hate crime" to much acclaim.

In fact, one of the stranger aspects of hate is that the prejudice expressed by a group in power may often be milder in expression than the prejudice felt by the marginalized. After all, if you already enjoy privilege, you may not feel the anger that turns bias into hate. You may not need to. For this reason, most white racism may be more influential in society than most black racism—but also more calmly expressed.

So may other forms of minority loathing—especially hatred within 40 minorities. I'm sure that black conservatives like Clarence Thomas or Thomas Sowell have experienced their fair share of white racism. But I wonder whether it has ever reached the level of intensity of the hatred directed toward them by other blacks? In several years of being an openly gay writer and editor, I have experienced the gamut of responses to my sexual orientation. But I have only directly experienced articulated, passionate hate from other homosexuals. I have been accused over the years by other homosexuals of being a sellout, a hypocrite, a traitor, a sexist, a racist, a narcissist, a snob. I've been called selfish, callous, hateful, self-hating, and malevolent. At a reading, a group of lesbian activists portrayed my face on a poster within the crossfires of a gun. Nothing from the religious right has come close to such vehemence.

I am not complaining. No harm has ever come to me or my property, and much of the criticism is rooted in the legitimate expression of political differences. But the visceral tone and style of the gay criticism can only be described as hateful. It is designed to wound personally, and it often does. But its intensity comes in part, one senses, from the pain of being excluded for so long, of anger long restrained bubbling up and directing itself more aggressively toward an alleged traitor than an alleged enemy. It is the hate of the hated. And it can be the most hateful hate of all. For this reason, hate-crime laws may themselves be an oddly

biased category—biased against the victims of hate. Racism is everywhere, but the already victimized might be more desperate, more willing
to express it violently. And so more prone to come under the suspicious
eye of the law.

V.

And why is hate for a group worse than hate for a person? In Laramie,
Wyoming, the now-famous epicenter of "homophobia," where Matthew
Shepard was brutally beaten to death, vicious murders are not unknown.
In the previous 12 months, a 15-year-old pregnant girl was found east
of the town with 17 stab wounds. Her 38-year-old boyfriend was apparently angry that she had refused an abortion and left her in the Wyoming
foothills to bleed to death. In the summer of 1998, an 8-year-old Laramie
girl was abducted, raped and murdered by a pedophile, who disposed of
her young body in a garbage dump. Neither of these killings was deemed
a hate crime, and neither would be designated as such under any existing
hate-crime law. Perhaps because of this, one crime is an international leg-
end; the other two are virtually unheard of.

But which crime was more filled with hate? Once you ask the question, you realize how difficult it is to answer. Is it more hateful to kill a
stranger or a lover? Is it more hateful to kill a child than an adult? Is it
more hateful to kill your own child than another's? Under the law before
the invention of hate crimes, these decisions didn't have to be taken. But
under the law after hate crimes, a decision is essential. A decade ago, a
murder was a murder. Now, in the era when group hate has emerged as
our cardinal social sin, it all depends.

The supporters of laws against hate crimes argue that such crimes
should be disproportionately punished because they victimize more than
the victim. Such crimes, these advocates argue, spread fear, hatred and
panic among whole populations, and therefore merit more concern. But,
of course, all crimes victimize more than the victim, and spread alarm in
the society at large. Just think of the terrifying church shooting in Texas
only two weeks ago. In fact, a purely random murder may be even more
terrifying than a targeted one, since the entire community, and not just
a part of it, feels threatened. High rates of murder, robbery, assault, and
burglary victimize everyone, by spreading fear, suspicion, and distress
everywhere. Which crime was more frightening to more people this summer: the mentally ill Buford Furrow's crazed attacks in Los Angeles, killing one, or Mark Barton's murder of his own family and several random
day-traders in Atlanta, killing 12? Almost certainly the latter. But only Furrow was guilty of "hate."

One response to this objection is that certain groups feel fear more   45
intensely than others because of a history of persecution or intimidation.

But doesn't this smack of a certain condescension toward minorities? Why, after all, should it be assumed that gay men or black women or Jews, for example, are as a group more easily intimidated than others? Surely in any of these communities there will be a vast range of responses, from panic to concern to complete indifference. The assumption otherwise is the kind of crude generalization the law is supposed to uproot in the first place. And among these groups, there are also likely to be vast differences. To equate a population once subjected to slavery with a population of Mexican immigrants or third-generation Holocaust survivors is to equate the unequatable. In fact, it is to set up a contest of vulnerability in which one group vies with another to establish its particular variety of suffering, a contest that can have no dignified solution.

Rape, for example, is not classified as a "hate crime" under most existing laws, pitting feminists against ethnic groups in a battle for recognition. If, as a solution to this problem, everyone, except the white straight able-bodied male, is regarded as a possible victim of a hate crime, then we have simply created a two-tier system of justice in which racial profiling is reversed, and white straight men are presumed guilty before being proven innocent, and members of minorities are free to hate them as gleefully as they like. But if we include the white straight male in the litany of potential victims, then we have effectively abolished the notion of a hate crime altogether. For if every crime is possibly a hate crime, then it is simply another name for crime. All we will have done is widened the search for possible bigotry, ratcheted up the sentences for everyone and filled the jails up even further.

Hate-crime-law advocates counter that extra penalties should be imposed on hate crimes because our society is experiencing an "epidemic" of such crimes. Mercifully, there is no hard evidence to support this notion. The Federal Government has only been recording the incidence of hate crimes in this decade, and the statistics tell a simple story. In 1992, there were 6,623 hate-crime incidents reported to the F.B.I, by a total of 6,181 agencies, covering 51 percent of the population. In 1996, there were 8,734 incidents reported by 11,355 agencies, covering 84 percent of the population. That number dropped to 8,049 in 1997. These numbers are, of course, hazardous. They probably underreport the incidence of such crimes, but they are the only reliable figures we have. Yet even if they are faulty as an absolute number, they do not show an epidemic of "hate crimes" in the 1990s.

Is there evidence that the crimes themselves are becoming more vicious? None. More than 60 percent of recorded hate crimes in America involve no violent, physical assault against another human being at all, and, again, according to the F.B.I., that proportion has not budged much in the 1990s. These impersonal attacks are crimes against property or crimes of "intimidation." Murder, which dominates media coverage of hate crimes, is a tiny proportion of the total. Of the 8,049 hate crimes reported to the F.B.I. in 1997, a total of eight were murders. Eight. The number of hate crimes that were aggravated assaults (generally involving a weapon) in 1997 is less than 15 percent of the total. That's 1,237 assaults too many, of course, but to put it in perspective, compare it with a reported 1,022,492 "equal opportunity" aggravated assaults in America in the same year. The number of hate crimes that were physical assaults is half the total. That's 4,000 assaults too many, of course, but to put it in perspective, it compares with around 3.8 million "equal opportunity" assaults in America annually.

The truth is, the distinction between a crime filled with personal hate and a crime filled with group hate is an essentially arbitrary one. It tells us nothing interesting about the psychological contours of the specific actor or his specific victim. It is a function primarily of politics, of special interest groups carving out particular protections for themselves, rather than a serious response to a serious criminal concern. In such an endeavor, hate-crime-law advocates cram an entire world of human motivations into an immutable, tiny box called hate, and hope to have solved a problem. But nothing has been solved; and some harm may even have been done.

In an attempt to repudiate a past that treated people differently 50 because of the color of their skin, or their sex, or religion or sexual orientation, we may merely create a future that permanently treats people differently because of the color of their skin, or their sex, religion, or sexual orientation. This notion of a hate crime, and the concept of hate that lies behind it, takes a psychological mystery and turns it into a facile political artifact. Rather than compounding this error and extending even further, we should seriously consider repealing the concept altogether.

To put it another way: violence can and should be stopped by the government. In a free society, hate can't and shouldn't be. The boundaries between hate and prejudice and between prejudice and opinion and between opinion and truth are so complicated and blurred that any attempt to construct legal and political fire walls is a doomed and illiberal venture. We know by now that hate will never disappear from human consciousness; in fact, it is probably, at some level, definitive of it. We know after decades of education measures that hate is not caused merely by ignorance; and after decades of legislation, that it isn't caused entirely by law.

To be sure, we have made much progress. Anyone who argues that America is as inhospitable to minorities and to women today as it has been in the past has not read much history. And we should, of course, be vigilant that our most powerful institutions, most notably the government, do not actively or formally propagate hatred; and insure that the violent expression of hate is curtailed by the same rules that punish all violent expression.

But after that, in an increasingly diverse culture, it is crazy to expect that hate, in all its variety, can be eradicated. A free country will always mean a hateful country. This may not be fair, or perfect, or admirable, but it is reality, and while we need not endorse it, we should not delude ourselves into thinking we can prevent it. That is surely the distinction between toleration and tolerance. Tolerance is the eradication of hate; toleration is co-existence despite it. We might do better as a culture and as a polity if we concentrated more on achieving the latter rather than the former. We would certainly be less frustrated.

And by aiming lower, we might actually reach higher. In some ways, some expression of prejudice serves a useful social purpose. It lets off steam; it allows natural tensions to express themselves incrementally; it can siphon off conflict through words, rather than actions. Anyone who has lived in the ethnic shouting match that is New York City knows exactly what I mean. If New Yorkers disliked each other less, they wouldn't be able to get on so well. We may not all be able to pull off a Mencken—bigoted in words, egalitarian in action—but we might achieve a lesser form of virtue: a human acceptance of our need for differentiation, without a total capitulation to it.

Do we not owe something more to the victims of hate? Perhaps we do. But it is also true that there is nothing that government can do for the hated that the hated cannot better do for themselves. After all, most bigots are not foiled when they are punished specifically for their beliefs. In fact, many of the worst haters crave such attention and find vindication in such rebukes. Indeed, our media's obsession with "hate," our elevation of it above other social misdemeanors and crimes, may even play into the hands of the pathetic and the evil, may breathe air into the smoldering embers of their paranoid loathing. Sure, we can help create a climate in which such hate is disapproved of—and we should. But there is a danger that if we go too far, if we punish it too much, if we try to abolish it altogether, we may merely increase its mystique, and entrench the very categories of human difference that we are trying to erase.

For hate is only foiled not when the haters are punished but when the hated are immune to the bigot's power. A hater cannot psychologically wound if a victim cannot psychologically be wounded. And that immunity to hurt can never be given; it can merely be achieved. The racial epithet only strikes at someone's core if he lets it, if he allows the bigot's definition of him to be the final description of his life and his person—if somewhere in his heart of hearts, he believes the hateful slur to be true. The only final answer to this form of racism, then, is not majority persecution of it, but minority indifference to it. The only permanent rebuke to homophobia is not the enforcement of tolerance, but gay equanimity in the face of prejudice. The only effective answer to sexism is not a morass of legal proscriptions, but the simple fact of female success. In this, as in so many other things, there is no solution to the problem. There is only a transcendence of it. For all our rhetoric, hate will never be destroyed. Hate, as our predecessors knew better, can merely be overcome.

55

THINKING CRITICALLY ABOUT THE READING

1. What does Sullivan mean when he writes in paragraph 8, "A large part of [hate] may even be hard-wired"? If he is correct, what might one conclude about attempts to legislate against hate crimes?

2. In paragraph 21, Sullivan writes that the "modern words we have created to describe the varieties of hate — 'sexism,' 'racism,' 'anti-Semitism,' 'homophobia' — tell us very little" about the different kinds of hate he delineates in the paragraph above. What does he mean by this?

3. Some argue that hatred is a result of ignorance. How does Sullivan respond to this argument?

4. What does Sullivan see as the difference between the hatred of the perpetrator and the hatred of the victim in return (24)?

5. Sullivan cites Elisabeth Young-Bruehl's typology of hate in paragraph 26. What three kinds of hate does she identify, and what characterizes each type? How helpful do you find her classification in understanding hate? (Glossary: *Classification*)

6. What problems does Sullivan see with respect to hate-crime legislation (42–56)? What arguments does he present in favor of repealing hate-crime legislation? Do you agree or disagree with his reasons?

7. What does Sullivan find interesting about the hate that has been directed at him by other gay people? How does he explain it?

LANGUAGE IN ACTION

In preparation for a classroom discussion, search the Web for hate-crime legislation in the state where you are attending college. If your state is one that does not have a hate-crime law, examine a state that does. What does the law stipulate as a hate crime? Is the law necessary, in your opinion? Why or why not? Compare your comments with those of others in your class.

WRITING SUGGESTIONS

1. Write an essay in which you examine the various terms for hate that Sullivan uses in his essay. How might an examination of these terms help us to understand both the dynamics of prejudice and how we, as individuals and as a society, respond to these dynamics?

2. In paragraph 56, Sullivan writes: "For hate is only foiled not when the haters are punished but when the hated are immune to the bigot's power. A hater cannot psychologically wound if a victim cannot psychologically be wounded. And that immunity to hurt can never be given; it can merely be achieved." Write an essay in which you explore the implications of Sullivan's comments here. Consider in particular how what Sullivan writes here relates to the establishment of hate-crime laws.

The Language of Prejudice

GORDON ALLPORT

Gordon Allport was born in Montezuma, Indiana, in 1897. He attended Harvard College and graduated Phi Beta Kappa in 1919 with majors in philosophy and economics. During his undergraduate years, he also became interested in psychology, and a meeting with Sigmund Freud in Vienna in 1920 — during which the founder of psychoanalysis failed to impress him — had a profound influence on him. After studying and teaching abroad, Allport returned to Harvard to teach social ethics and to pursue his Ph.D., which he received in 1922. He went on to become a full professor at Harvard in 1942, served as chairman of the psychology department, and received the Gold Medal Award of the American Psychological Foundation in 1963. He died in 1967.

Allport became known for his outspoken stances regarding racial prejudice, and he was hopeful about efforts being made to eradicate it. His book *The Nature of Prejudice* (1954) is still regarded as one of the most important and influential texts on the subject. The following excerpt from that book analyzes the connections between language and prejudice and explains some of the specific ways in which language can induce and shape prejudice.

WRITING TO DISCOVER: *While in high school and college, many students are associated with groups that bring together people of disparate racial and religious backgrounds but whose labels still carry with them positive or negative associations. You may have made such associations yourself without thinking twice about it, as in "He's just a jock," or "She's with the popular crowd — she'll never go out with me." To what group, if any, did you belong in high school? Briefly write about the effects on you and your classmates of cliques in your school. How did the labels associated with the different groups influence how you thought about the individual members of each group?*

Without words we should scarcely be able to form categories at all. A dog perhaps forms rudimentary generalizations, such as small-boys-are-to-be-avoided — but this concept runs its course on the conditioned reflex level, and does not become the object of thought as such. In order to hold a generalization in mind for reflection and recall, for identification and for action, we need to fix it in words. Without words our world would be, as William James said, an "empirical sand-heap."

NOUNS THAT CUT SLICES

In the empirical world of human beings there are some two and a half billion grains of sand corresponding to our category "the human race." We cannot possibly deal with so many separate entities in our thought, nor can we individualize even among the hundreds whom we encounter in our daily round. We must group them, form clusters. We welcome, therefore, the names that help us to perform the clustering.

The most important property of a noun is that it brings many grains of sand into a single pail, disregarding the fact that the same grains might have fitted just as appropriately into another pail. To state the matter technically, a noun *abstracts* from a concrete reality some one feature and assembles different concrete realities only with respect to this one feature. The very act of classifying forces us to overlook all other features, many of which might offer a sounder basis than the rubric we select. Irving Lee gives the following example:

> I knew a man who had lost the use of both eyes. He was called a "blind man." He could also be called an expert typist, a conscientious worker, a good student, a careful listener, a man who wanted a job. But he couldn't get a job in the department store order room where employees sat and typed orders which came over the telephone. The personnel man was impatient to get the interview over. "But you're a blind man," he kept saying, and one could almost feel his silent assumption that somehow the incapacity in one aspect made the man incapable in every other. So blinded by the label was the interviewer that he could not be persuaded to look beyond it.

Some labels, such as "blind man," are exceedingly salient and powerful. They tend to prevent alternative classification, or even cross-classification. Ethnic labels are often of this type, particularly if they refer to some highly visible feature, e.g., Negro, Oriental. They resemble the labels that point to some outstanding incapacity—*feeble-minded, cripple, blind man.* Let us call such symbols "labels of primary potency." These symbols act like shrieking sirens, deafening us to all finer discriminations that we might otherwise perceive. Even though the blindness of one man and the darkness of pigmentation of another may be defining attributes for some purposes, they are irrelevant and "noisy" for others.

Most people are unaware of this basic law of language—that every   5 label applied to a given person refers properly only to one aspect of his nature. You may correctly say that a certain man is *human, a philanthropist, a Chinese, a physician, an athlete.* A given person may be all of these; but the chances are that Chinese stands out in your mind as the symbol of primary potency. Yet neither this nor any other classificatory label can refer to the whole of a man's nature. (Only his proper name can do so.)

Thus each label we use, especially those of primary potency, distracts our attention from concrete reality. The living, breathing, complex individual—the ultimate unit of human nature—is lost to sight. As in the figure, the label magnifies one attribute out of all proportion to its true significance, and masks other important attributes of the individual.... .

A category, once formed with the aid of a symbol of primary potency, tends to attract more attributes than it should. The category labeled *Chinese* comes to signify not only ethnic membership but also reticence, impassivity, poverty, treachery. To be sure, . . . there may be genuine ethnic-linked traits, making for a certain *probability* that the member of an ethnic stock may have these attributes. But our cognitive process is not cautious. The labeled category, as we have seen, includes indiscriminately the defining attribute, probable attributes, and wholly fanciful, nonexistent attributes.

Even proper names—which ought to invite us to look at the individual person—may act like symbols of primary potency, especially if they arouse ethnic associations. Mr. Greenberg is a person, but since his name is Jewish, it activates in the hearer his entire category of Jews-as-a-whole. An ingenious experiment performed by Razran shows this point

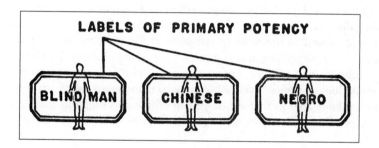

clearly, and at the same time demonstrates how a proper name, acting like an ethnic symbol, may bring with it an avalanche of stereotypes.

Thirty photographs of college girls were shown on a screen to 150 students. The subjects rated the girls on a scale from one to five for *beauty, intelligence, character, ambition, general likability*. Two months later the same subjects were asked to rate the same photographs (and fifteen additional ones introduced to complicate the memory factory). This time five of the original photographs were given Jewish surnames (Cohen, Kantor, etc.), five Italian (Valenti, etc.), and five Irish (O'Brien, etc.); and the remaining girls were given names chosen from the signers of the Declaration of Independence and from the Social Register (Davis, Adams, Clark, etc.).

When Jewish names were attached to photographs there occurred the following changes in ratings:

> decrease in liking
> decrease in character
> decrease in beauty
> increase in intelligence
> increase in ambition

For those photographs given Italian names there occurred:

> decrease in liking
> decrease in character
> decrease in beauty
> decrease in intelligence

Thus a mere proper name leads to prejudgments of personal attributes. The individual is fitted to the prejudiced ethnic category, and not judged in his own right.

While the Irish names also brought about depreciated judgment, the depreciation was not as great as in the case of the Jews and Italians. The falling of likability of the "Jewish girls" was twice as great as for "Italians" and five times as great as for "Irish." We note, however, that the "Jewish" photographs caused higher ratings in *intelligence* and in *ambition*. Not all stereotypes of out-groups are unfavorable.

The anthropologist, Margaret Mead, has suggested that labels of primary potency lose some of their force when they are changed from nouns into adjectives. To speak of a Negro soldier, a Catholic teacher, or a Jewish artist calls attention to the fact that some other group classifications are just as legitimate as the racial or religious. If George Johnson is spoken of not only as a Negro but also as a *soldier,* we have at least two attributes to know him by, and two are more accurate than one. To depict him truly as an individual, of course, we should have to name many more attributes. It is a useful suggestion that we designate ethnic and religious membership where possible with *adjectives* rather than *nouns.*

EMOTIONALLY TONED LABELS

Many categories have two kinds of labels—one less emotional and one more emotional. Ask yourself how you feel, and what thoughts you have, when you read the words *school teacher,* and then *school marm.* Certainly the second phrase calls up something more strict, more ridiculous, more disagreeable than the former. Here are four innocent letters: m-a-r-m. But they make us shudder a bit, laugh a bit, and scorn a bit. They call up an image of a spare, humorless, irritable old maid. They do not tell us that she is an individual human being with sorrows and troubles of her own. They force her instantly into a rejective category.

In the ethnic sphere even plain labels such as Negro, Italian, Jew, Catholic, Irish-American, French-Canadian may have emotional tone for a reason that we shall soon explain. But they all have their higher key equivalents: nigger, wop, kike, papist, harp, canuck. When these labels are employed we can be almost certain that the speaker *intends* not only to characterize the person's membership, but also to disparage and reject him.

Quite apart from the insulting intent that lies behind the use of certain labels, there is also an inherent ("physiognomic") handicap in many terms designating ethnic membership. For example, the proper names characteristic of certain ethnic memberships strike us as absurd. (We compare them, of course, with what is familiar and therefore "right.") Chinese names are short and silly; Polish names intrinsically difficult and outlandish.

Unfamiliar dialects strike us as ludicrous. Foreign dress (which, of course, is a visual ethnic symbol) seems unnecessarily queer.

But of all of these "physiognomic" handicaps the reference to color, clearly implied in certain symbols, is the greatest. The word Negro comes from the Latin *niger* meaning black. In point of fact, no Negro has a black complexion, but by comparison with other blonder stocks, he has come to be known as a "black man." Unfortunately *black* in the English language is a word having a preponderance of sinister connotations: the outlook is black, blackball, blackguard, black-hearted, black death, blacklist, blackmail, Black Hand. In his novel *Moby Dick,* Herman Melville considers at length the remarkably morbid connotations of black and the remarkably virtuous connotations of white.

Nor is the ominous flavor of black confined to the English language. A cross-cultural study reveals that the semantic significance of black is more or less universally the same. Among certain Siberian tribes, members of a privileged clan call themselves "white bones," and refer to all others as "black bones." Even among Uganda Negroes there is some evidence for a white god at the apex of the theocratic hierarchy; certain it is that a white cloth, signifying purity, is used to ward off evil spirits and disease.

There is thus an implied value-judgment in the very concept of *white race* and *black race.* One might also study the numerous unpleasant connotations of *yellow,* and their possible bearing on our conception of the people of the Orient. 　　15

Such reasoning should not be carried too far, since there are undoubtedly, in various contexts, pleasant associations with both black and yellow. Black velvet is agreeable, so too are chocolate and coffee. Yellow tulips are well liked; the sun and moon are radiantly yellow. Yet it is true that "color" words are used with chauvinistic overtones more than most people realize. There is certainly condescension indicated in many familiar phrases: dark as a nigger's pocket, darktown strutters, white hope (a term originated when a white contender was sought against the Negro heavyweight champion, Jack Johnson), the white man's burden, the yellow peril, black boy. Scores of everyday phrases are stamped with the flavor of prejudice, whether the user knows it or not.

We spoke of the fact that even the most proper and sedate labels for minority groups sometimes seem to exude a negative flavor. In many contexts and situations the very terms *French-Canadian, Mexican,* or *Jew,* correct and nonmalicious though they are, sound a bit opprobrious. The reason is that they are labels of social deviants. Especially in a culture where uniformity is prized, the name of *any* deviant carries with it *ipso facto* a negative value-judgment. Words like *insane, alcoholic, pervert* are presumably neutral designations of a human condition, but they are more: they are finger-pointing at a deviance. Minority groups are deviants, and for this reason, from the very outset, the most innocent labels in many situations imply a shading of disrepute. When we wish to highlight the deviance and denigrate it still further we use words of a higher emotional key: crackpot, soak, pansy, greaser, Okie, nigger, harp, kike.

Members of minority groups are often understandably sensitive to names given them. Not only do they object to deliberately insulting epithets, but sometimes see evil intent where none exists. Often the word Negro is spelled with a small *n*, occasionally as a studied insult, more often from ignorance. (The term is not cognate with white, which is not capitalized, but rather with Caucasian, which is.) Terms like "mulatto" or "octoroon" cause hard feeling because of the condescension with which they have often been used in the past. Sex differentiations are objectionable, since they seem doubly to emphasize ethnic difference: why speak of Jewess and not of Protestantess, or of Negress and not of whitess? Similar overemphasis is implied in the terms like Chinaman or Scotchman; why not American man? Grounds for misunderstanding lie in the fact that minority group members are sensitive to such shadings, while majority members may employ them unthinkingly.

THE COMMUNIST LABEL

Until we label an out-group it does not clearly exist in our minds. Take the curiously vague situation that we often meet when a person wishes to locate responsibility on the shoulders of some out-group whose nature he cannot specify. In such a case he usually employs the pronoun "they" without an antecedent. "Why don't they make these sidewalks wider?" "I hear they are going to build a factory in this town and hire a lot of foreigners." "I won't pay this tax bill; they can just whistle for their money." If asked "who?" the speaker is likely to grow confused and embarrassed. The common use of the orphaned pronoun *they* teaches us that people often want and need to designate out-groups (usually for the purpose of venting hostility) even when they have no clear conception of the out-group in question. And so long as the target of wrath remains vague and ill-defined specific prejudice cannot crystallize around it. To have enemies we need labels.

Until relatively recently [late 1940s]—strange as it may seem—there [20] was no agreed-upon symbol for *communist*. The word, of course, existed but it had no special emotional connotation, and did not designate a public enemy. Even when, after World War I, there was a growing feeling of economic and social menace in this country, there was no agreement as to the actual source of the menace.

A content analysis of the Boston *Herald* for the year 1920 turned up the following list of labels. Each was used in a context implying some threat. Hysteria had overspread the country, as it did after World War II. Someone must be responsible for the postwar malaise, rising prices, uncertainty. There must a villain. But in 1920 the villain was impartially designated by reporters and editorial writers with the following symbols:

> alien, agitator, anarchist, apostle of bomb and torch, Bolshevik, communist, communist laborite, conspirator, emissary of false promise, extremist, foreigner, hyphenated-American, incendiary, IWW, parlor anarchist, parlor pink, parlor socialist, plotter, radical, red, revolutionary, Russian agitator, socialist, Soviet, syndicalist, traitor, undesirable.

From this excited array we note that the *need* for an enemy (someone to serve as a focus for discontent and jitters) was considerably more apparent than the precise *identity* of the enemy. At any rate, there was no clearly agreed upon label. Perhaps partly for this reason the hysteria abated. Since no clear category of "communism" existed there was no true focus for the hostility.

But following World War II this collection of vaguely interchangeable labels became fewer in number and more commonly agreed upon. The out-group menace came to be designated almost always as *communist* or *red*. In 1920 the threat, lacking a clear label, was vague; after 1945 both symbol and thing became more definite. Not that people knew precisely what they meant when they said "communist," but with the aid of the term they were at least able to point consistently to *something* that inspired fear. The term developed the power of signifying menace and led to various repressive measures against anyone to whom the label was rightly or wrongly attached.

Logically, the label should apply to specifiable defining attributes, such as members of the Communist Party, or people whose allegiance is with the Russian system, or followers, historically, of Karl Marx. But the label came in for far more extensive use.

What seems to have happened is approximately as follows. Having suffered through a period of war and being acutely aware of devastating revolutions abroad, it is natural that most people should be upset, dreading to lose their possessions, annoyed by high taxes, seeing customary moral and religious values threatened, and dreading worse disasters to come. Seeking an explanation for this unrest, a single identifiable enemy is wanted. It is not enough to designate "Russia" or some other distant land. Nor is it satisfactory to fix blame on "changing social conditions." What is needed is a human agent near at hand: someone in Washington, someone in our schools, in our factories, in our neighborhood. If we *feel* an immediate threat, we reason, there must be a near-lying danger. It is, we conclude, communism, not only in Russia but also in America, at our doorstep, in our government, in our churches, in our colleges, in our neighborhood.

Are we saying that hostility toward communism is prejudice? Not necessarily. There are certainly phases of the dispute wherein realistic social conflict is involved. American values (e.g., respect for the person) and totalitarian values as represented in Soviet practice are intrinsically at odds. A realistic opposition in some form will occur. Prejudice enters only when

25

the defining attributes of *communist* grow imprecise, when anyone who favors any form of social change is called a communist. People who fear social change are the ones most likely to affix the label to any persons or practices that seem to them threatening.

For them the category is undifferentiated. It includes books, movies, preachers, teachers who utter what for them are uncongenial thoughts. If evil befalls—perhaps forest fires or a factory explosion—it is due to communist saboteurs. The category becomes monopolistic, covering almost anything that is uncongenial. On the floor of the House of Representatives in 1946, Representative Rankin called James Roosevelt a communist. Congressman Outland replied with psychological acumen, "Apparently everyone who disagrees with Mr. Rankin is a communist."

When differentiated thinking is at a low ebb—as it is in times of social crises—there is a magnification of two-valued logic. Things are perceived as either inside or outside a moral order. What is outside is likely to be called communist. Correspondingly—and here is where damage is done—whatever is called communist (however erroneously) is immediately cast outside the moral order.

This associative mechanism places enormous power in the hands of a demagogue. For several years Senator McCarthy managed to discredit many citizens who thought differently from himself by the simple device of calling them communist. Few people were able to see through this trick and many reputations were ruined. But the famous senator has no monopoly on the device. As reported in the Boston *Herald:* on November 1, 1946, Representative Joseph Martin, Republican leader in the House, ended his election campaign against his Democratic opponent by saying, "The people will vote tomorrow between chaos, confusion, bankruptcy, state socialism or communism, and the preservation of our American life, with all its freedom and its opportunities." Such an array of emotional labels placed his opponent outside the accepted moral order. Martin was re-elected....

Not everyone, of course, is taken in. Demagogy, when it goes too far, meets with ridicule. Elizabeth Dilling's book, *The Red Network,* was so exaggerated in its two-valued logic that it was shrugged off by many people with a smile. One reader remarked, "Apparently if you step off the sidewalk with your left foot you're a communist." But it is not easy in times of social strain and hysteria to keep one's balance, and to resist the tendency of a verbal symbol to manufacture large and fanciful categories of prejudiced thinking.

VERBAL REALISM AND SYMBOL PHOBIA

Most individuals rebel at being labeled, especially if the label is uncomplimentary. Very few are willing to be called *fascistic, socialistic,* or *anti-Semitic.* Unsavory labels may apply to others; but not to us.

An illustration of the craving that people have to attach favorable symbols to themselves is seen in the community where white people banded together to force out a Negro family that had moved in. They called themselves "Neighborly Endeavor" and chose as their motto the Golden Rule. One of the first acts of this symbol-sanctified band was to sue the man who sold property to Negroes. They then flooded the house which another Negro couple planned to occupy. Such were the acts performed under the banner of the Golden Rule.

Studies made by Stagner and Hartmann show that a person's political attitudes may in fact entitle him to be called a fascist or a socialist, and yet he will emphatically repudiate the unsavory label, and fail to endorse any movement or candidate that overtly accepts them. In short, there is a *symbol phobia* that corresponds to *symbol realism*. We are more inclined to the former when we ourselves are concerned, though we are much less critical when epithets of "fascist," "communist," "blind man," "school marm" are applied to others.

When symbols provoke strong emotions they are sometimes regarded no longer as symbols, but as actual things. The expressions "son of a bitch" and "liar" are in our culture frequently regarded as "fighting words." Softer and more subtle expressions of contempt may be accepted. But in these particular cases, the epithet itself must be "taken back." We certainly do not change our opponent's attitude by making him take back a word, but it seems somehow important that the word itself be eradicated.

Such verbal realism may reach extreme length.   35

> The City Council of Cambridge, Massachusetts, unanimously passed a resolution (December, 1939) making it illegal "to possess, harbor, sequester, introduce or transport, within the city limits, any book, map, magazine, newspaper, pamphlet, handbill, or circular containing the words Lenin or Leningrad."

Such naiveté in confusing language with reality is hard to comprehend unless we recall that word-magic plays an appreciable part in human thinking. The following examples, like the one preceding, are taken from Hayakawa.

> The Malagasy soldier must eschew kidneys, because in the Malagasy language the word for kidney is the same as that for "shot"; so shot he would certainly be if he ate a kidney.

> In May, 1937, a state senator of New York bitterly opposed a bill for the control of syphilis because "the innocence of children might be corrupted by a widespread use of the term. . . . This particular word creates a shudder in every decent woman and decent man."

This tendency to reify words underscores the close cohesion that exists between category and symbol. Just the mention of "communist," "Negro," "Jew," "England," "Democrats," will send some people into a panic of fear or a frenzy of anger. Who can say whether it is the word or the thing that annoys them? The label is an intrinsic part of any monopolistic category. Hence to liberate a person from ethnic or political prejudice it is necessary at the same time to liberate him from *word fetishism*. This fact is well known to students of general semantics who tell us that prejudice is due in large part to verbal realism and to symbol phobia. Therefore any program for the reduction of prejudice must include a large measure of semantic therapy.

THINKING CRITICALLY ABOUT THE READING

1. What is Allport's thesis, and where is it stated? (Glossary: *Thesis*)

2. In paragraph 2, why do you think Allport uses a metaphorical image—grains of sand—to represent people? (Glossary: *Figurative Language*) How does this metaphor help him present his point?

3. In paragraph 3, Allport uses Irving Lee's story of a blind man who was unable to get a job as an example of how powerful certain labels can be. (Glossary: *Examples*) What other quotations does he use as examples? What is the purpose of each one? Do you think they are effective? Why or why not?

4. Nouns, or names, provide an essential service in making categorization possible. Yet according to Allport, nouns are also words that "cut slices." What does he mean by that term? What is inherently unfair about nouns?

5. What are "labels of primary potency" (4)? Why does Allport equate them with "shrieking sirens"? Why are such labels important to his essay?

6. What does the experiment with the nonlabeled and labeled photos demonstrate? How do labels affect the way the mind perceives reality?

7. What does Allport mean by the "orphaned pronoun *they*" (19)? Why is it used so often in conversation?

8. What does Allport mean by *symbol phobia* (33)? How does this concept illustrate the unfairness of labeling others?

9. Allport wrote "The Language of Prejudice" in the early 1950s. Does this help explain why he devotes many paragraphs to the evolution of the label *communist*? What are the connotations of the word *communist* today? (Glossary: *Connotation/Denotation*)

LANGUAGE IN ACTION

Read the following brief article, which appeared in the *New York Times* on December 13, 1968. Then make a list of the arguments for and against the UN action. Do you think it's possible to legislate tolerance and tone down prejudice through the use—or nonuse—of language?

UN GROUP URGES DROPPING OF WORDS
WITH RACIST TINGE

In an effort to combat racial prejudice, a group of United Nations experts is urging sweeping revision of the terminology used by teachers, mass media, and others dealing with race.

Words such as *Negro, primitive, savage, backward, colored, bushman,* and *uncivilized* would be banned as either "contemptuous, unjust, or inadequate." They were described as aftereffects of colonialism.

The report said that the terms were "so charged with emotive potential that their use, with or without conscious pejorative intent, to describe or characterize certain ethnic, social, or religious groups, generally provoked an adverse reaction on the part of these groups."

The report said further that even the term *race* should be used with particular care since its scientific validity was debatable and that it "often served to perpetuate prejudice." The experts suggested that the word *tribe* should be used as sparingly as possible, since most of the "population groups" referred to by this term have long since ceased to be tribes or are losing their tribal character. A *native* should be called *inhabitant,* the group advised, and instead of *paganism* the words *animists, Moslems, Brahmans,* and other precise words should be used. The word *savanna* is preferable to *jungle,* and the new countries should be described as *developing* rather than *underdeveloped,* the experts said.

WRITING SUGGESTIONS

1. Make an extensive list of the labels that have been or could be applied to you at this time. Write an essay in which you discuss the labels that you find "truly offensive," those you can "live with," and those that you "like to be associated with." Explain your reasons for putting particular labels in each of these categories.

2. Allport states, "Especially in a culture where uniformity is prized, the name of *any* deviant carries with it *ipso facto* a negative value-judgment" (17). This was written in the 1950s. Since then, the turbulent 1960s, the political correctness movement of the 1980s and 1990s and the years since the millennium, and the mainstreaming of "alternative" cultures have all attempted to persuade people to accept differences and be more tolerant. Write an essay in which you consider Allport's statement today. Which labels that identify someone as different still carry a negative association? Have the social movements of the past decades changed in a fundamental way how we think about others? Do you think there is more acceptance of nonconformity today, or is a nonconformist or member of a minority still subjected to negative, though perhaps more subtle, labeling? Support your conclusions with examples from your own experience and from the depiction of current events in the popular media.

3. Allport wrote *The Nature of Prejudice* before the civil rights movement began in earnest, though he did live to see it grow and reach its climax at the famous 1963 march on Washington. (See Martin Luther King Jr.'s celebrated "I

Have a Dream" speech on pp. 200–203) Obviously, part of the civil rights movement was in the arena of language, and its leaders often used impressive rhetoric to confront the language of prejudice. Write an essay in which you analyze how the kinds of labels and symbols identified by Allport were used in speeches and documents both to justify the continuation of segregation and prejudice and to decry it. How did the leaders of the civil rights movement use language to their advantage? To what emotions or ideas did the language of the opposition appeal? The Internet and your library have vast information about the movement's genesis and history, so it may be difficult at first to decide on a specific area of research. Start by looking at how language was used by both sides in the battle over civil rights.

Signs of Infection

Bob Herbert

Bob Herbert was born in 1945 in Brooklyn, New York, but spent his early years in Montclair, New Jersey. He received a B.S. degree in journalism from the State University of New York (Empire State College) in 1988. Shortly after college, looking for work in journalism, he called the *Star-Ledger* in Newark, New Jersey, and to his great surprise was offered a job as a reporter. In 1973 he became the paper's night city editor. From 1976 to 1985 Herbert was a reporter and editor and eventually a columnist and member of the editorial board of the *New York Daily News.* Herbert later became a founding panelist of *Sunday Edition,* a weekly discussion program on WCBS-TV, and the host of *Hotline,* a weekly issues program on New York public television. After making a number of appearances from 1991 to 1993 on both *The Today Show* and *NBC Nightly News,* Herbert joined the *New York Times* as its first African American op-ed columnist, writing a twice-weekly column on politics, urban affairs, and social trends titled "In America." Asked by *The Progressive* magazine in 1995 what inspired him to write when he was growing up, Herbert replied: "I was reading newspapers from the time I was five years old. I would read anything. I especially liked Dickens, and I read *Oliver Twist* when I was about nine. I remember being awed. It never occurred to me that there was this kind of power in literature. So my little mind was won over."

In the following column, first published in the *New York Times* on April 16, 2007, Herbert reflects on the attack on the Rutgers women's basketball team by radio personality Don Imus. As he puts it, "The attention surrounding Mr. Imus's very public self-immolation is an opportunity for Americans to acknowledge that we have a problem."

WRITING TO DISCOVER: *When you heard of Don Imus's comments about the Rutgers University women's basketball team, what was your reaction? Were his comments simply another example of Imus's rather crude attempts at "humorously" echoing rap and gangsta talk, or do you think his comments signified something more seriously wrong with his character and with the audience to which he appeals?*

People in positions of great power are the ones who define those who are relatively lacking in power. So when Don Imus, a very powerful radio personality, dropped his disgusting verbal bomb on the members of the Rutgers women's basketball team, he sent a powerful message across the airwaves: that the young women on the team (the black ones, at least) were crude, ugly, and genetically inferior, and that all of the women were whores.

That message, which Mr. Imus insisted was meant to be funny, reinforced views already widely held in our society, which is why I could get
the following e-mail from a reader:

> "Who woulda thunk that the Imus idiocy and the Duke Debacle would
> hit home on the same day. Both stories bring to mind what my father
> told me 60 years ago: Stay away from colored women."

The attention surrounding Mr. Imus's very public self-immolation
is an opportunity for Americans to acknowledge that we have a problem. Not only is the society still permeated by racism and sexism and
the stereotypes they spawn, but we have allowed a debased and profoundly immature culture to emerge in which the coarsest, most socially
destructive images and language are an integral part of the everyday
discourse.

Gangsta rappers trapped in the throes of the Stockholm syndrome
have spent years encouraging black people to see themselves as niggers
and all women as whores. Michael Savage, one of the most prominent figures in talk radio, with an audience substantially larger than Don Imus's,
has called Diane Sawyer a "lying whore" and Barbara Walters a "double-
talking slut," according to Media Matters for America, a group that moni-
tors some of the excesses of talk radio.

The culture that has given us such wonders as jazz, blues, baseball,   5
Hollywood, the Broadway musical theater, rock 'n' roll, and on and on, is
now specializing in too many instances in language and entertainment fit
only for the gutter or a sewer.

Something has gone completely haywire when young American boys
and girls are listening to songs like "Can You Control Yo Hoe" and "Break
a Bitch Til I Die," by Snoop Dogg, formerly Snoop Doggy Dogg, formerly Cordozar Calvin Broadus.

"It's gotten pretty savage out there," said Tom Brokaw of NBC News
during an on-air discussion of the Imus situation.

Mr. Brokaw, who believes that firing Mr. Imus was the right thing to
do, said: "There's been an absence of civility in public discourse for some
time now. The use of language across the racial spectrum, and across the
political spectrum, and across the cultural spectrum, has been, in any way
you want to describe it, debased to a certain degree.

"The words that you hear used commonly on the street, or on the air,
or on radio, or in rap lyrics, are words that in the worst days of segregation
in this country, in the worst segregated parts of this country, you would
not have heard on radio. Now you hear them commonly."

The language, of course, is just a symptom. Mr. Brokaw went on to men-   10
tion, in a tone that sounded a bit sad and somewhat resigned, that Americans
had steadfastly refused to face the race issue honestly and head-on. "I had

hoped," he said, "I guess somewhat naively 20 years ago, that we would be in a far different place than we are now."

We should also be in a better place in the way that women are viewed and portrayed in the culture. And one of the first steps in a conversation about how to honestly address these issues should be a discussion of how to get more more blacks, other ethnic minorities, and women into positions of real authority in the major news and entertainment outlets.

Another part of the conversation should deal with why the bullying and degradation of other human beings is such a staple of popular entertainment in this country. One of the Rutgers players expressed astonishment Thursday night when Mr. Imus told her that making fun of people was how he'd made his living for many years.

The people who fought back against the racism and misogyny of the "Imus in the Morning" program need to keep the momentum going. Keep the pressure on the companies that sponsor this garbage. Keep the matter before the media.

Imus, Snoop Dogg, Michael Savage—it doesn't matter where the bigotry is coming from. What's important is to find the integrity and the strength to see it for what it is—a loathsome, soul-destroying disease—and then to respond accordingly.

THINKING CRITICALLY ABOUT THE READING

1. Discuss Herbert's opening sentence: "People in positions of power are the ones who define those who are relatively lacking in power." Do you think that Herbert is correct? Why or why not?

2. What is Herbert's thesis is this essay? (Glossary: *Thesis*) What evidence does he use to support it? (Glossary: *Evidence*)

3. How does the word *debased* relate to two other expressions that Herbert uses in his essay: "bullying" and "the degradation of other human beings"?

4. What does Herbert mean when he writes: "The language, of course, is just a symptom" (10)? If the language is a symptom, what is the disease?

5. How do you respond to Herbert's suggestion that the answer to the social ill he points to "should be a discussion of how to get more blacks, other minorities, and women into positions of real authority in the major news and entertainment outlets" (11)?

6. What is Herbert's tone in this essay? (Glossary: *Tone*) Angry? Aggressive? Reasoned? Thoughtful? Does his tone add to or detract from his argument, in your opinion?

LANGUAGE IN ACTION

Explain the message of this political cartoon. What is being criticized? How do you know? How do you think Herbert might respond to its message?

WRITING SUGGESTIONS

1. Using Andrew Sullivan's essay "What's So Bad About Hate?" (pp. 247–261) together with Herbert's essay, write an essay on bigotry. What is bigotry? How does it arise in a culture? How does a culture rid itself of the impulse to debase others?

2. Herbert believes that one way to counter "language and entertainment fit only for the gutter or sewer" is "to get more blacks, other ethnic minorities, and women into positions of real authority in the major news and entertainment outlets." Write an essay arguing either for or against this proposition, but take into account these potential counterarguments:
   - There is an audience for the content that Herbert objects to, and ratings and revenue seem to be driving the decline in values.
   - Blacks, other minorities, and women in some cases take an active role in promoting the degradation of language and cultural values in the entertainment industry.

From the Dixie Chicks to the St. Louis Rams: What Animal-Based Metaphors Reveal about Sexism[1]

ALLEEN PACE NILSEN

Alleen Pace Nilsen is a teacher and writer who specializes in children's literature and the study of sexist language. Born in 1936 in Phoenix, Arizona, she is a graduate of Brigham Young University and the University of Iowa. Between 1967 and 1969, Nilsen lived with her three young children and her husband in Kabul, Afghanistan. According to Nilsen, living for two years in one of the most isolated countries in Southwest Asia and observing the differences in the ways that men and women were treated made her think differently about what it means to be either male or female. When the family returned to the United States, she began looking at the English language and how it reflected some of the same kinds of sexism she had seen in Afghanistan, where a proverb advised, "If you see an old man, sit down and take a lesson. If you see an old woman, throw a stone."

Currently Nilsen is professor of English and director of English Education at Arizona State University. Her books on language study include *Pronunciation Contrasts in English* (1971); *Language Play: An Introduction to Linguistics* (1978); *The Language of Humor/The Humor of Language* (1983); and most recently, *Literature for Today's Young Adults* [with Ken Donelson] (2005) and *Names and Naming in Young Adult Literature* [coauthored with Don L. F. Nilsen] (2007). In the following essay, which was written for *Language Awareness*, Nilsen analyzes the ways that sexist language reveals the antifemale bias in our culture. According to Nilsen the "chicken metaphor" tells the whole story: a young girl is a *chick*, then she marries and begins feeling *cooped up*, so she goes to *hen parties* where she *cackles* with her friends. Then she has her *brood*. And when they *leave the nest*, she begins to *henpeck* her husband, and finally turns into an *old biddy*.

WRITING TO DISCOVER: *Think about the language you use every day. Think about how you use language with your classmates, your family, your friends, your neighbors, and your fellow workers. In what ways does language reflect you and your culture?*

---

1 Some of the observations in this piece come from Nilsen's earlier work, including *Sexism and Language* by Alleen Pace Nilsen, Haig Bosmajian, H. Lee Gershuny, and Julia P. Stanley (National Council of Teachers of English, 1977), and "Of Ladybugs and Billy Goats: What Animal Species Names Tell about Human Perceptions of Gender," published in *Metaphor and Symbolic Activity*, 11, no. 4 (1996): 257–271.

Over the last 150 years, American anthropologists have traveled to the corners of the earth to study other cultures, often focusing on those cultures termed "primitive." They either became linguists themselves or they took linguists with them to help in learning and analyzing languages. Even if the culture was one that no longer existed, they were interested in learning its language, because besides being tools of communication, the vocabulary and structure of a language tell much about the values held by its speakers.

However, in order to make useful observations about a culture, the culture need not be "primitive," nor do the people making observations need to be anthropologists and linguists. Anyone living in the United States who listens with a keen ear or reads with a perceptive eye can come up with startling new insights about the way American English reflects our values.

For example, American English is especially rich in metaphors based on farm and domestic animals because in 1910, something like one-third of all Americans lived on farms, with many more of us living in rural areas and others of us regularly visiting our "country cousins." Today less than 2 percent of Americans live on farms, which means that many fewer of us have the kinds of direct relationships with domesticated animals that speakers had at the turn of the last century. But because changes in language lag far behind changes in society, we continue using the barnyard metaphors that were common to our grandparents. For example, many Americans now grow up without ever coming in close contact with a real, live *goose*, but because of such terms as *Mother Goose rhymes, silly goose, goose bumps, goose pimples,* and *goose flesh,* most speakers know what a goose is. If they don't, they will miss out on the meanings of such metaphors as:

- *Your goose is cooked!* = You are in trouble, i.e. there's no way to get your stolen goose back.
- *Being goosed* = Being playfully prodded in the backside, something geese often did as they chased children.
- *Goose-stepping* = Nazi soldiers were described as *goose-stepping* because they marched without bending their knees.
- *Goose-egg* = Your score is zero. The *goose-egg* metaphor gains its power from the fact that geese are bigger than chickens or ducks and so the metaphor is saying something like "You have a big, fat zero."

In short, animal-based metaphors provide us with a glimpse of common beliefs and attitudes that reveal the attitudes of our cultural and linguistic ancestors and therefore the attitudes that we as a culture are likely to have inherited. In this essay, I will discuss some of the animal-based metaphors that are common in contemporary United States culture, and, more specifically, what these metaphors reveal about our culture's sexist attitudes and values.

CONTEMPORARY METAPHORS

I wrote the title of this article on the chalkboard in an Introduction to   5
Language class and asked students if they thought the political troubles of
the Dixie Chicks singing group were exacerbated by their name. I conjec-
tured that their name predisposed people to think of them as "chickens"
or cowards, which is why there was such an outcry when in 2003 Natalie
Maines apologized at a London concert for the Iraq war and said that she
was "ashamed that the president of the United States is from Texas." I
envisioned people saying to themselves, "Just who do these *chicks* think
they are—criticizing brave men going to war?"

My students said, "No!" My interpretation was wrong. A girl who grew
up in the South said the word *Dixie* was more responsible for the outrage than
was *Chicks* because *Dixie* stands for the South, and Southerners are taught to
be genteel and respectful of authority. Another student said that the success
of the name—the reason it caught people's attention in the first place—is
that its connotations are so far removed from those of the typical "southern
belle." When I said that my generation of feminists considered *chick* to be an
insulting term, some students were surprised because to them it simply means
a young female. Others said that by taking the name, the group was parading
its own strength by showing that they could turn the negative connotations
around, just as people have done with such terms as *black* and *queer*.

We then went on to talk about the connotations of *ram* in the name
of the *St. Louis Rams*. When I asked what this word made them think of,
they mentioned such things as the *Dodge Ram* truck, a *ramrod* muzzle, a
battering ram, to ram something down someone's throat, and to be *ram-
bunctious*. To stand *ramrod* straight is to be stiff or rigid. At this, someone
said the word had sexual connotations, and someone else said that *ram* is
to sheep and goats what *cock* is to chickens.

When I asked whether the Los Angeles Rams and the Dixie Chicks
could trade names, everyone laughed because they knew I wasn't being
serious. And while the Dixie Chicks are women and the St. Louis Rams
are men, the students also knew that I was talking about something bigger than the physical differences between males and females. I was talking
about the broader concept of gender which includes the physical differences plus all the expectations that people have for behavioral, social, and
psychological differences and the attitudes and expectations commonly
thought to belong more to one sex than the other.

ARCHETYPAL METAPHORS

Animal-based metaphors may be a language universal because since
prehistory humans have been observing animals and watching their
actions in an attempt to make sense of the world. For example, ancient

Egyptians chose the scarab or dung beetle as a sacred symbol of their Sun God because they saw similarities between the way the sun is rolled across the sky each day and then dropped behind the horizon and the way dung beetles roll a ball of manure and drop it into their nests.

Some animal terms are simply labels of convenience created to fill lexi-   10
cal gaps. These might be based on a similarity in appearance between the item needing a name and the shape of some part of an animal, as when pastries are described as *snails* or as *bear claws*. Other labels of convenience might be based on actions, as when we give children *bear hugs* or tell them to *run like a bunny*, while still others are based on size, as when smallness is implied by describing someone as a *shrimp* or as having *bird legs*. But if a speaker calls someone a *birdbrain*, their intended meaning is probably a reflection on the person's intellectual abilities rather than size. In this case, the usage has moved away from being a label of convenience toward being a judgmental metaphor. It is not always possible to know exactly when a usage crosses the line between simple communication and the expression of an attitude, because many terms do both. Also, terms which seem purely communicative to some speakers may seem judgmental to others. For example, the first speakers who used *kids* as a term for children or teenagers were comparing the actions and attitudes of young people to those of young goats—animals that are particularly frisky and annoying. Some editors of education journals disapprove of their authors referring to students as *kids* because they feel it is disparaging—comparable to describing someone as *monkeying around* or as being *stubborn as a mule*. My own feeling is that children who have grown up going to places like *Kids' World* or *Kids Zone* are not at all insulted to be referred to as *kids*, and if they happen to learn that young goats are also called *kids*, they probably think that goats borrowed the name from them, instead of the other way around.

The number of names and metaphors that speakers create for a particular species is a direct reflection of the closeness of the relationship between the species and humans. For example, we know that deer were important to our linguistic ancestors because English has not only the word *deer*, but also *buck* and *stag* for the male, *doe* for the female, *fawn* and *yearling* for the young, and *venison* for the meat. Such a full system is common for domestic animals, but not for wild animals where speakers seldom need to make gender and age distinctions for insects, fish, birds, small mammals, or for the kinds of animals usually seen in zoos, including giraffes, camels, elephants, monkeys, and baboons. With these kinds of animals, speakers simply use such generic descriptions as *an old fox, a mother rat, a female shark*, or *a male coyote*.

Because of their symbolic meanings and the way they communicate about ideas that people already have inklings of, many animal-based metaphors become part of the archetypal images that people hold about important and permanent aspects of their lives, including death, fear, love, the biological family, and the unknown. Carl Jung called such archetypal images "the collective unconscious" because people accept them without questioning their validity. Archetypal images come to people through myth, religion, drama, fantasy, literature, and as I am illustrating here, through linguistic metaphors and symbols.

The most interesting of these metaphors tell stories, "teaching" ideas and patterns that we are prone to accept without intellectual processing because people who write fables about animals have more poetic license than do the authors of realistic fictions. These authors are free to exaggerate and to make *fabulous,* i.e. "incredible and astonishing" claims that readers would be more likely to question if their characters were human. Aesop, a Greek storyteller who is thought to have been a slave, personified animals in such a delightful way that Aesop's fables are still told today with the purpose of teaching moral values to children. One theory is that Aesop used animals for his characters because it would have been dangerous for a slave to offend the high and mighty of the land whose selfishness and bad behavior he was illustrating. He wanted people to identify with his stories, but not so closely that they would think he was making fun of them. Today, many authors and artists who create books for young children follow Aesop's lead in making their stories about "people" in fur or feathers. The common belief is that it will be easier for children to identify with characters if they are not distracted by realistic characters portrayed as belonging to a race or gender different from their own.

Such fables communicate more than just the individual ideas represented by the metaphors that underly them. To illustrate this point, I am focusing here on four "fables" that I think are displayed—and also promoted—through the way that we as English speakers rely on animal-related metaphors for our modern communication.

Fable One: Male or Female? — The Most Basic of Questions

Because I have a reputation for working against sexist attitudes, a colleague came to ask me for a recommendation for a good children's book to give to a friend who had just had a baby. I responded with, "Oh, did she have a boy or a girl?" Of course my friend burst out laughing because if I were going to be truly nonsexist, it shouldn't have mattered. What I was thinking of recommending was not a nonsexist book, but a book that would counterbalance some of the sexist ideas and icons that surround infants the minute they are born.

English speakers have chosen various methods for communicating the all-important distinction between males and females. One method with animals is to develop new terms for both the male and the female, as with sheep, which are divided into *ewes* and *rams;* horses, which are divided into *mares* and *stallions* (or *studs*); and pigs, which are divided into *sows* and *boars.* Sometimes, human names common to one sex or the other are used for distinguishers, as when donkeys are divided into *jennies* and *jackasses,*

15

and goats are divided into *billygoats* and *nannygoats* (from *Nancy*). With turkeys, the male is identified as a *tom turkey* while the female has the more general name of a *hen turkey*.

The importance of cattle to people is shown by the wealth of terms we have, including *cattle* for a group, *calf* and *yearling* for the young, *heifer* for a young female who has not yet borne a calf, *cow* for a female who has given birth, *steer* for a male who has been castrated, *veal* as the meat from a young animal (most likely a male since the females are saved for breeding), and *beef* from an adult animal. The fact that cows are more valued than bulls (because the female provides milk for human consumption and is also the one who gives birth) is reflected in our everyday language, which uses *cow* as the "catch-all" term, as seen in such words as *cowboy, cow pasture, cow path, cowbell, cowcatcher,* and a *cow college* (slang for an agricultural school).

An illustration of how words move from being simple descriptors to being allegories that tell gender-related stories is the word *cat*. Male cats are called *tomcats,* while female cats are called *pussy cats. Pussy* is thought to come from a Late German or Scandinavian term for the female vulva, and is cognate with *pocket* or *pouch*. When used to refer to the female partner in sexual intercourse, *pussy* is generally considered vulgar or as edgy humor, as in the name of the "Pussy Galore" character in the old James Bond movies. As long as the term is used in relation to cats, or in a second-generation metaphor, to the plant commonly called a pussy willow because of its soft, small, gray buds, it has fairly neutral connotations. But when it is used as a judgmental metaphor intended to make listeners think of females, the connotations are negative. The Tenth Edition of Merriam-Webster's *Collegiate Dictionary* (1999) defines *pussycat* as "one that is weak, compliant, or amiable; SOFTY," and *pussyfoot* as "to tread or move warily or stealthily," and "to refrain from committing oneself."

Fable Two: With Different Species, Different Genders Are Valued

Many years ago, I had a vivid lesson in the preference of one gender over the other. I was teaching first grade in Fairfax County, Virginia, and in keeping with the magical feelings of a Northern Virginia spring, I arranged to take my first graders on a field trip to a chicken hatchery. All went well as we walked past dozens of incubators and watched the baby chicks pecking their way out of their shells and into the world. But then we came to a slow-moving conveyor belt carrying the baby chicks off to another part of the hatchery. About midway down the line, we had to walk around a man who was sitting on a stool and picking up each chick and giving it a cursory examination. He placed about half of the chicks back on the belt to move forward, but the others he dropped into a big barrel that was about three-fourths full of fluffy little bodies, still peeping and squawking—at least on the top layer, which was what I—along with the tallest first graders—could see. As soon as I understood what was happening, I hurried the children on out the door and back to the school bus.

I still remember the plaintive tone with which the smartest little girl in the class asked, "Why is he putting the baby chickens in the barrel?" I pretended not to hear her question because even now I'm not sure how I could explain to a six-year-old the man's profession of "sexing chickens," which means saving the females and discarding most of the males. This practice is common because the male's sole role is to fertilize the eggs for hatching; because most eggs are going to be eaten rather than hatched, the need for males is limited. This is why in our traditional vision of barnyards, there are many hens but only one rooster, jocularly referred to as the *cock of the walk*. The word "cock" is still very much alive in contemporary U.S. culture,* but the word "chicken" (like "cow") is most commonly used to refer to the species, which indicates the relative importance of one sex (female) over the other.

The opposite process has happened with peafowls. In appearance, *peacocks* (the male of the species) are dramatic, because of the bobbing crest of feathers on their heads and their blue/green tail feathers that can be fanned into large iridescent displays decorated with dark spots resembling eyes. *Peahens* are drab in comparison, and while *peahen* and *peacock* are the respective female and male designations, unlike with most barnyard animals, virtually everyone uses the male name *peacock* as the cover term. While dictionaries define both *peacock* and *peahen,* editors also acknowledge that "broadly speaking" *peacock* refers to the entire species.

An interesting aspect of the word *peacock* is that even when words contain a marker of sex (in this case, *cock*), speakers will sometimes overlook the matter of *sex* in favor of the broader term of *gender,* which includes emotional and psychological expectations. In today's world, it is women rather than men who dress in colorful clothing and give extra care to hair, fingernails, and jewelry. Because of this, speakers are more likely to think of women as fitting in with the second definition given in dictionaries for *peacock,* which includes such terms as "strutting," "a show-off," and "making a proud display."

A few years ago I conducted a study in which I asked speakers to write sentences showing me how they might use various animal terms when talking about people. Each respondent was asked to work with only six terms, and none of them had such matching terms as *peacock/peahen* or

20

---

* Until a couple of hundred years ago when puritanical speakers felt a need to clean up the language, roosters were known as *roost cocks,* an allusion to their enthusiasm for copulating with the hens. That most American speakers now refer to these animals as *roosters* shows that it is fairly easy for people to bring new words into a language, but that speakers continue to use such terms as *cocky, cocksure, to cock a gun, to cock an eye, a haycock,* and a *cocked hat* shows that deleting well-established words is not nearly as easy.

stallion/mare. I collected ten sentences for each of twenty different words. I analyzed the sentences to see what pronouns or other markers the writers used that would reveal whether they were thinking about males or females. Six of the ten sentences about peacocks were about females, compared with only two about males and two in which sex was not marked. The female-marked sentences were variations on "Tina is as colorful as a peacock," and "After donning her outfit, Mary paraded around like a peacock."

Fable Three: Males Are Expected To Be Bigger and More Powerful Than Females

Besides applying animal terms to humans, speakers also apply human names to animals. For example, size and power have traditionally been associated with males, and so when two species are similar, the larger or more powerful species might be given such a name as *king crab* while the smaller species will be called a *queen crab*. We see this in the names of a *king turtle* compared with a *queen turtle* and a *king snake* compared with a *queen snake*. There are many more species named after *kings* than after *queens* because the namers wanted to communicate both a large size and a royal quality. The *kingbird* has the alternate name of *American tyrant flycatcher; king cobras* are extremely venomous: and *king crabs, king penguins,* and *king salmon* are unusually large. On farms, *king snakes* are valued because they are voracious eaters of rodents, while the *king vulture* is extra large and powerful and is sometimes called the *king of vultures.*

Fable Four: For Females, Young and Small Is Good; Old and Large Is Bad

Authors of introductory books for children about the animal kingdom   25
find it necessary to explain that there are both male and female *lady bugs* and *seacows.* With children's books, the explanation stops at this point, but what is interesting to adults about these species and their feminine sounding names is that they represent female archetypes. The *lady bug,* which was originally called *Our Lady's Bug* as an allusion to the Virgin Mary, apparently reminded early speakers of a young and innocent female. *Seacows,* also called *dugongs,* get their feminine sounding name from the similarity of their bodies to those of milk cows.

The female archetype represented by the seacow is that of the older, unattractive, and overweight woman, the one who might also be called a *sow* or a *bitch.* The word *bitch* has taken on such negative connotations that speakers now hesitate to use it with female dogs. Over and over with animal metaphors, we see that the terms are positive when both the animal and the female being alluded to are young, but negative if both are middle-aged or older. *Playboy Bunnies* sounds way more appealing than would the phrase *Playboy Rabbits*. Similarly, referring to a girl as a *bird* is more appealing than referring to her as *an old crow* or *an old bat*. Referring to a young girl as *kittenish* or as a *sex kitten* is a kind of teasing with positive overtones, while identifying a woman as *catty* has negative overtones.

Young women are sometimes referred to as *fillies* or *birds*, while their mothers or grandmothers might be called *old nags, old crows,* or *old bats.* A "sweet young thing" might also be addressed as a *lamb,* while someone much older will be called a *crone,* a term for "a withered old woman," which is thought to come from the Dutch name for an old ewe. In the same class where the students told me I was wrong about the Dixie Chicks, a student brought up the phrase *old cronies,* which men use to describe their buddies. While it is less-than-complimentary, it is not nearly as negative as the female term *old crone.**

Contrary to popular opinion, *chick lit* did not start with Danielle Steele or Nora Roberts; it started hundreds of years ago with such old folktales as the one about *Chicken Little*. She was the foolish young thing — the archetypal Innocent — who experienced panic when a falling acorn hit her on the head and she caused general mayhem by running from animal to animal calling out "The sky is falling! The sky is falling!" A more positive archetypal image is that of *The Little Red Hen* — the archetypal Caregiver — who couldn't get anyone to help her plant the wheat, or water and harvest it, much less grind it and make it into bread. Only after she baked it into crusty loaves of bread did the other barnyard animals show an interest, but by then it was too late because she and her chicks ate it all up.

The Little Red Hen was a feminist before her time in that she demanded respect for her work and was assertive enough to keep the benefits of her labor for herself and her chicks. It is a fairly unusual story, because most of the world's folklore implies that as soon as a female is past the age of being a *chick,* she will begin going to *hen parties* and *cackling* with her friends. When she marries she will work hard to *feather her nest,* but after she has her *brood,* she will begin feeling *cooped up* and sorry that she has *put all of her eggs in one basket.* Finally she *henpecks* her husband and turns into *an old biddy.*

---

* We were only partially successful in checking out the source of *crony* in our classroom dictionary because the editors wrote that "perhaps" the term comes from *chronos,* referring to "time." If this is true, the feature being highlighted is that *old cronies* are men whose friendships have lasted a long time. However, this does not ring true to me because such words as *chronology, chronicles, synchronize,* and *chronometer,* all words descended from *chronos* and connected to the idea of time, have kept the *ch-* spelling. Written language changes much more slowly than does spoken language, and how words are spelled, especially when silent letters are kept, is a fairly reliable clue to the relationship of new words to old words. I suspect that calling a group of old men *cronies* is a kind of double insult because speakers are not only comparing the men to a bunch of animals, but to a bunch of "useless" female animals. This is similar to the way that speakers insult fussy old men by referring to them as *old maids.*

IN SUMMARY

Fables are defined as fictitious narratives that often include supernatu-   30
ral happenings and animal characters who speak and act like people for
the purpose of teaching "useful truths." There is a tendency for people to
think that the older a story is and the longer it has been part of society, the
closer it comes to being a universal truth. In this essay, I am asking speakers to question both the usefulness and the truthfulness of the mini-fables
that exist in many of the animal-based metaphors that we have inherited. I
think we can get insights from looking at them with fresh eyes.

For example, one of the linguistic customs illustrated in this essay is
how speakers have chosen to use the name of the most valued gender as
the cover term for such barnyard animals as chickens, geese, ducks, and
cows. Understanding this practice lends insight into why women are irritated when they are told that they are included as a subset of such terms
as *mankind, man on the street, chairman, man-made, the best man for the
job,* and *the common man.* If we use *man* as the cover term for our own
species, then we are following the unusual pattern of *peacock,* in which the
male is obviously so much more stunning than the female that his name
has taken over. This same concept also helps us to understand why there is
a general movement away from teaching students in grammar classes that
the singular masculine pronouns *he, him,* and *his* are appropriate whenever
the gender of the referent is unknown or is a mixed group, as often happens with such pronouns as *anyone, everybody,* and *someone,* which, even
though they appear to be singular, often refer to groups of people.

And while we might *cluck* at the practice of "sexing chickens" and
discarding most of the males, there is considerable evidence that since
the mid-1980s, when technology made it possible to determine the sex
of a fetus, the citizens of countries that are overpopulated and so no longer value females for their role in reproduction are beginning to practice
something similar to what I saw in the chicken hatchery, except that it is
the female fetuses that are being aborted. A March 10, 2008, BBC news
story, "Chinese Facing Shortage of Wives," told how a report from the
State Population and Family Planning Commission warned that by 2020,
China is expected to have 30 million more men than women, a gender
imbalance which will lead to social instability because men will not be able
to find wives. In 2000, 110 Chinese males were born for every 100 Chinese females, but in 2005 the number of males had risen to 118 for every
100 females, with the difference in southern areas of China being as great
as 130 boys to 100 girls. Similar statistics can be found for India and other
Asian countries.

Moving from the international scene to much closer at home, I will
close by illustrating the kinds of social and technological changes that have
occurred during my lifetime and that demonstrate why it no longer makes
sense to unthinkingly rely on "lessons" that grew out of a world that was

very different from the world of today, at least in industrialized countries where technology has brought tremendous changes.

I was born in 1936, and the difference between my life and my mother's and my grandmothers' lives illustrate some of these changes. My maternal grandmother gave birth to twelve children; my paternal grandmother gave birth to ten children; my mother gave birth to seven children; and I gave birth to three children. My paternal grandfather was a schoolteacher, a job that his wife could have physically done, but neither my maternal grandmother nor my mother would have been strong enough to do the physical labor that their husbands did. One ran a sawmill, while the other was a rancher and a cattleman. These were physically demanding jobs, and women's bodies are simply not made with the size or the strength of men's bodies. I do not know about my grandmothers' friends, but I know that none of my mother's friends could have done the jobs that their husbands did because they were ranchers, farmers, construction workers, and miners. Today, I and all of my friends have the physical strength to do the jobs that our husbands do—not because we are physically stronger, but because machines have taken over much of the physical lifting, digging, and pounding that used to be part of men's work. I, and many of my women friends, work alongside our husbands as teachers, attorneys, accountants, salespeople, store managers, computer programmers, and office workers. Because in many parts of the world workers are becoming valued for their training and their intellect more than for their physical strength, women's roles are changing.

Another reason that my grandmothers could not have done their husbands' jobs is that all their energy was taken up by giving birth to and raising their large families, which meant doing everything from home doctoring, to growing gardens and canning the food, sewing their children's clothes, feeding and milking the family cow, tending the chickens, and also managing to educate and encourage their children in civic and religious duties. Both of my grandmothers lost children to early deaths, and my mother's first pregnancy ended in a stillbirth. When my father came to my forty-eighth birthday party, he rejoiced for me but lamented that his mother died when she was forty-eight, and in his words "was an old woman." She never lived in a house with running water, and after her mid-thirties never smiled in a photo because she was missing a tooth and had no money for a dentist. 35

My own opinion is that she had very little to smile about.

THINKING CRITICALLY ABOUT THE READING

1. What is Nilsen's thesis in this essay? Where does she state her thesis? (Glossary: *Thesis*)

2. Why does Nilsen think metaphors are so important in determining our linguistic heritage? (Glossary: *Figures of Speech*)

3. What was Nilsen's conjecture about the Dixie Chicks' political problems? Why did her students find it incorrect?

4. How does Nilsen get her students to see the connection between the metaphors we use every day and "the broader concept of gender"(8)?

5. What are archetypal metaphors? Why are they important in the context of Nilsen's argument?

6. What relationship does Nilsen establish between mini-fables and the animal-based metaphors she discusses?

7. What connection does Nilsen make between her experience with the "sexing of chickens" and the 2008 BBC story "Chinese Facing Shortage of Wives"(32)?

8. In her summary Nilsen writes, "one of the linguistic customs illustrated in this essay is how speakers have chosen to use the name of the most valued gender as the cover term for such barnyard animals as chickens, geese, ducks, and cows. Understanding this practice lends insights into why women are irritated when they are told they are included as a subset of such terms as *mankind, man on the street, chairman, man-made, the best man for the job,* and *the common man.*" What does she mean?

LANGUAGE IN ACTION

Select five animal names from the following list: Beast, Bird, Bitch, Bull, Cat, Chicken, Cow, Dog, Fox, Jackass, Peacock, Pig, Rat, Shark, Shrew, Tiger, Tigress, Vulture, and Wolf. Before the next class session, ask friends or acquaintances to provide you with sentences in which these animal names are used metaphorically to refer to a person (e.g., "That guy was a real pool shark"). In class, discuss your sentences. How many of them were about males or females? Which ones were gender neutral? Reflecting both on your sample and Nilsen's essay, discuss the ways in which you think animal names reflect our culture and its values.

WRITING SUGGESTIONS

1. Nilsen cites an Afghan proverb, "If you see an old man, sit down and take a lesson. If you see an old woman, throw a stone." Write an essay in which you examine the values encapsulated within the proverbs of your culture or another culture in which you are interested. Do they reveal gender bias? Other kinds of bias? There are many sites on the Internet that provide lists of international proverbs. Here is one to help you get started: http://www.tentmaker.org/Quotes/international_proverbs.htm

2. If, as Nilsen argues, language reflects and solidifies deeply ingrained cultural attitudes, is there any hope that prejudice can be reduced by altering language? Write an essay in which you argue for or against the proposition that changing sexist language will help eliminate gender bias. Think about the kinds of evidence you will need to support your thesis and make a convincing argument.

The Meanings of a Word

GLORIA NAYLOR

Novelist and essayist Gloria Naylor was born in New York City in 1950.
She worked as a missionary for the Jehovah's Witnesses from 1967 to 1975
and then as a telephone operator until 1981, the year she graduated from
Brooklyn College. Naylor later started a graduate program in African American studies at Yale University. In her fiction, she explores the lives of African
American women, drawing freely from her own experiences and those of her
extended family. As Naylor has stated, "I wanted to become a writer because
I felt that my presence as a black woman and my perspective as a woman in
general had been underrepresented in American literature." She received
the American Book Award for First Fiction for *The Women of Brewster Place*
(1982), a novel that was later adapted for television. This success was followed by *Linden Hills* (1985), *Mama Day* (1988), *Bailey's Cafe* (1993), and
The Men of Brewster Place (1998). Her most recent novel is *1996* (2005), a
book that has been described as a "fictionalized memoir." Naylor's short fiction and essays have appeared widely, and she has also edited *Children of the
Night: Best Short Stories by Black Writers, 1967 to the Present* (1995).

  More than any other form of prejudiced language, racial slurs
are intended to wound and shame. In the following essay, which first
appeared in the *New York Times* in 1986, Naylor remembers a time when
a third-grade classmate called her a nigger. By examining the ways in
which words can take on meaning depending on who uses them and to
what purpose, Naylor concludes that "words themselves are innocuous; it
is the consensus that gives them true power."

WRITING TO DISCOVER: *Have you or someone you know ever been called
a derogatory name? Write about how this made you feel.*

Language is the subject. It is the written form with which I've managed to keep the wolf away from the door and, in diaries, to keep my
sanity. In spite of this, I consider the written word inferior to the spoken,
and much of the frustration experienced by novelists is the awareness that
whatever we manage to capture in even the most transcendent passages
falls far short of the richness of life. Dialogue achieves its power in the
dynamics of a fleeting moment of sight, sound, smell, and touch.

  I'm not going to enter the debate here about whether it is language that
shapes reality or vice versa. That battle is doomed to be waged whenever we
seek intermittent reprieve from the chicken and egg dispute. I will simply

take the position that the spoken word, like the written word, amounts to a nonsensical arrangement of sounds or letters without a consensus that assigns "meaning." And building from the meanings of what we hear, we order reality. Words themselves are innocuous; it is the consensus that gives them true power.

I remember the first time I heard the word *nigger*. In my third-grade class, our math tests were being passed down the rows, and as I handed the papers to a little boy in back of me, I remarked that once again he had received a much lower mark than I did. He snatched his test from me and spit out that word. Had he called me a nymphomaniac or a necrophiliac, I couldn't have been more puzzled. I didn't know what a nigger was, but I know that whatever it meant, it was something he shouldn't have called me. This was verified when I raised my hand, and in a loud voice repeated what he had said and watched the teacher scold him for using a "bad" word. I was later to go home and ask the inevitable question that every black parent must face—"Mommy, what does *nigger* mean?"

And what exactly did it mean? Thinking back, I realize that this could not have been the first time the word was used in my presence. I was part of a large extended family that had migrated from the rural South after World War II and formed a close-knit network that gravitated around my maternal grandparents. Their ground-floor apartment in one of the buildings they owned in Harlem was a weekend mecca for my immediate family, along with countless aunts, uncles, and cousins who brought along assorted friends. It was a bustling and open house with assorted neighbors and tenants popping in and out to exchange bits of gossip, pick up an old quarrel, or referee the ongoing checkers game in which my grandmother cheated shamelessly. They were all there to let down their hair and put up their feet after a week of labor in the factories, laundries, and shipyards of New York.

Amid the clamor, which could reach deafening proportions—two or   5
three conversations going on simultaneously, punctuated by the sound of a baby's crying somewhere in the back rooms or out on the street—there was still a rigid set of rules about what was said and how. Older children were sent out of the living room when it was time to get into the juicy details about "you-know-who" up on the third floor who had gone and gotten herself "p-r-e-g-n-a-n-t!" But my parents, knowing that I could spell well beyond my years, always demanded that I follow the others out to play. Beyond sexual misconduct and death, everything else was considered harmless for our young ears. And so among the anecdotes of the triumphs and disappointments in the various workings of their lives, the word *nigger* was used in my presence, but it was set within contexts and inflections that caused it to register in my mind as something else.

In the singular, the word was always applied to a man who had distinguished himself in some situation that brought their approval for his strength, intelligence, or drive:

"Did Johnny *really* do that?"

"I'm telling you, that nigger pulled in $6,000 of overtime last year. Said he got enough for a down payment on a house."

When used with a possessive adjective by a woman—"my nigger"—it became a term of endearment for her husband or boyfriend. But it could be more than just a term applied to a man. In their mouths it became the pure essence of manhood—a disembodied force that channeled their past history of struggle and present survival against the odds into a victorious statement of being: "Yeah, that old foreman found out quick enough—you don't mess with a nigger."

In the plural, it became a description of some group within the community that had overstepped the bounds of decency as my family defined it. Parents who neglected their children, a drunken couple who fought in public, people who simply refused to look for work, those with excessively dirty mouths or unkempt households were all "trifling niggers." This particular circle could forgive hard times, unemployment, the occasional bout of depression—they had gone through all of that themselves—but the unforgivable sin was a lack of self-respect.

A woman could never be a "nigger" in the singular, with its connotation of confirming worth. The noun *girl* was its closest equivalent in that sense, but only when used in direct address and regardless of the gender doing the addressing. *Girl* was a token of respect for a woman. The one-syllable word was drawn out to sound like three in recognition of the extra ounce of wit, nerve, or daring that the woman had shown in the situation under discussion.

"G-i-r-l, stop. You mean you said that to his face?"

But if the word was used in a third-person reference or shortened so that it almost snapped out of the mouth, it always involved some element of communal disapproval. And age became an important factor in these exchanges. It was only between individuals of the same generation, or from any older person to a younger (but never the other way around), that *girl* would be considered a compliment.

I don't agree with the argument that use of the word *nigger* at this social stratum of the black community was an internalization of racism. The dynamics were the exact opposite: the people in my grandmother's living room took a word that whites used to signify worthlessness or degradation and rendered it impotent. Gathering there together, they transformed *nigger* to signify the varied and complex human beings they knew themselves to be. If the word was to disappear totally from the mouths of even the most liberal of white society, no one in that room was naive enough to believe it would disappear from white minds. Meeting the word head-on, they proved it had absolutely nothing to do with the way they were determined to live their lives.

So there must have been dozens of times that *nigger* was spoken in front of me before I reached the third grade. But I didn't "hear" it until it was said by a small pair of lips that had already learned it could be a way to humiliate me. That was the word I went home and asked my mother about. And since she knew that I had to grow up in America, she took me in her lap and explained.

THINKING CRITICALLY ABOUT THE READING

1. How, according to Naylor, do words get meanings?

2. Why does the boy sitting behind Naylor call her a nigger (3)? Why is she confused by this name-calling?

3. When Naylor was growing up, what two meanings did the word *girl* convey? How were those meanings defined by the speaker? In what way was age an important factor in the correct uses of *girl*?

4. Why does Naylor disagree with the notion that the use of the word *nigger* within her community was an internalization of racism?

5. Naylor begins her essay with an abstract discussion about how words derive their meaning and power. How does this introduction tie in with her anecdote and discussion of the word *nigger*? (Glossary: *Abstract/Concrete*) Why is the introduction vital to the overall message of her essay?

6. Naylor says she must have heard the word *nigger* many times while she was growing up; yet she "heard" it for the first time when she was in the third grade (15). How does she explain this seeming contradiction? (Glossary: *Paradox*)

7. Define what *nigger* means to Naylor in the context of her family. (Glossary: *Definition*) Why do you suppose she offers so little in the way of definition of her classmate's use of the word?

8. How would you characterize Naylor's tone in her essay? (Glossary: *Tone*) Is she angry, objective, cynical, or something else? Cite examples of her diction to support your answer. (Glossary: *Diction*)

LANGUAGE IN ACTION

Naylor's essay discusses how those in her community used the word *nigger* for their own purposes and "rendered it impotent" (14). Nevertheless, the word still has a lot of negative power, as revealed in the following 1995 essay by Keith Woods, which was published by the Poynter Institute for Media Studies.

The consensus to which Naylor refers—here represented by Mark Fuhrman—gives the word that power, making news organizations report it in euphemisms or as a deleted expletive. You may remember that Mark Fuhrman was a Los Angeles homocide detective whose racial profiling and negative attitude toward African Americans made him one of the most controversial figures in the O. J. Simpson trial. In preparation for class discussion, think about your position on the following questions: What should be done about the word *nigger*? Should African Americans use it and try to "render it impotent" by creating their own prevailing context for it? Should the word be suppressed, forced into the fringes of racist thought, and represented in euphemisms? Or is there another way to address the word's negative power?

AN ESSAY ON A WICKEDLY POWERFUL WORD

When I heard Mark Fuhrman's voice saying the word "nigger," I heard a lynch mob. I saw the grim and gleeful faces of murderous white men. I felt the coarse, hairy rope. I smelled the sap of the hangin' tree and saw Billie Holiday's "strange fruit" dangling from its strongest limb.

What a wickedly powerful word, nigger. So many other slurs could have slithered from Fuhrman's tongue and revealed his racism without provoking those images.

Jiggaboo.

Spade.

Coon.

I hear the hatred in those words, but I don't feel the fire's heat the way I do when this white former policeman says nigger. Somewhere in that visceral reflex is the reason news organizations had to use that word this time around.

Somewhere in the sting of seeing it, hearing it, feeling it is the reason they should think hard before using it the next time.

In context, there is no other way to report what Mark Furhman said. "Racial epithet" doesn't quite get it, does it? "Spearchucker" is a racial epithet, but it doesn't make you see burnt crosses and white sheets. Just rednecks.

The "n-word" sounds silly, childish, something you'd say when you don't want your 3-year-old to know what you're talking about. And "n----?" What does that accomplish other than to allow newspapers the dubious out of saying, "Well, it's actually the reader who's saying nigger, not us."

When Mark Fuhrman or any person armed with a club or a gun or a bat or a judicial robe or a teaching certificate or any measure of power says "nigger," it's more than an insult. It summons all the historic and modern-day violence that is packed into those six letters.

Nigger is "Know your place."

Nigger is, "I am better than you."

Nigger is, "I can frame you or flunk you or beat you or kill you because ...".

Nigger is, "I own you."

You just can't convey that definition with n-dash-dash-dash-dash-dash. You can't communicate it with bleeps or blurbs or euphemisms. The problem is that sometimes the only way to do your job as a journalist is to say or write the word that furthers the mission of racists.

I'd like to believe that there's some lessening of harm every time the word sees the light of day. I once fantasized about a day when a group of black rappers or comedians would appropriate the white sheets and hoods of the KKK and

(continued)

go gallivanting across MTV or HBO and forever render that image so utterly ridiculous that no self-respecting racist would ever wear it again.

But then, Richard Pryor tried to appropriate nigger, didn't he? Took it right from the white folks and turned it into a career before he thought better of it. So did the rappers NWA ("Niggas With Attitudes"). So did my friends on the streets of New Orleans. So has a generation of young black people today.

Still, the definition didn't change.

Dick Gregory tried it. In the dedication of his autobiography, "Nigger," the comedian-turned-activist wrote: "Dear Momma—Wherever you are, if ever you hear the word "nigger" again, remember they are advertising my book."

He wrote that 31 years ago, but if Lucille Gregory were here to hear Mark Fuhrman, she'd surely know he wasn't talking about her son's book. The definition doesn't change. It doesn't hurt any less after three decades. No less after three centuries.

It's the same word, spiked with the same poison, delivering the same message of inferiority, degradation, hatred, and shame. The same word whether it's Fuhrman saying it or Huck Finn or Def Comedy Jam or Snoop Doggy Dogg or my old friends from Touro Street (because, they do call themselves nigger, you know).

It hurts every time it's in the paper or on the air or in the street. Every time. Sometimes there's no way around using it in the media, but only sometimes.

Could there come a day when you see it or read it or hear it from the homeboys so much that you hardly notice? When your eyebrow doesn't arch as often or your jaw suddenly drop when the six o'clock anchor plops the word onto your living room coffee table?

Maybe. And you might even say, that day, "Oh, they're just talking about niggers again."

Are we better off then?

WRITING SUGGESTIONS

1. Write an essay in which you describe the process through which you became aware of prejudice, either toward yourself or toward another person or group of people. Did a specific event spark your awareness, such as that detailed in your Writing to Discover entry? Or did you become aware of prejudice in a more gradual way? Did you learn about prejudice primarily from your peers, your parents, or someone else? How did your new awareness affect you? How have your experiences shaped the way you think and feel about prejudice today?

2. In addition to discussing the word *nigger*, Naylor talks about the use of *girl*, a word with far less negative baggage but one that can still be offensive when used in an inappropriate context. Write an essay in which you discuss your use of a contextually sensitive word. What is its strict definition? How do you use it? In what context(s) might its use be inappropriate? Why is the word used in different ways?

The B-Word? You Betcha

ANDI ZEISLER

Andi Zeisler is a cofounder and the editorial/creative director of *Bitch: Feminist Response to Pop Culture,* a nonprofit independent quarterly magazine published in Portland, Oregon. Founded by Zeisler and Lisa Jervis in Oakland, California, in 1996, *Bitch* publishes articles on politics, style, television shows, books, music, and art. According to its Web site, its mission is, in part, to be "a fresh, revitalizing voice for feminism, one that welcomes complex arguments, showcases witty and whip-smart critiques of popular culture, and refuses to ignore the contradictory and sometimes uncomfortable details that constitute the realities of life in an unequivocally gendered world".

Zeisler, who claims to have been a feminist as early as nine or ten, grew up in the suburbs of New York City and graduated from Colorado College in 1994 with a B.A. in fine art. A former pop-music columnist for the *SF Weekly* and the *East Bay Express,* Zeisler has contributed articles and illustrations to numerous publications, including *Ms., Mother Jones, Utne, BUST,* the *San Francisco Chronicle,* the *Women's Review of Books,* and *Hues.* Together with Jervis, Zeisler published the anthology *BITCHfest: Ten Years of Cultural Criticism from the Pages of Bitch Magazine* in 2006 and recently finished a book about feminism and popular culture for Seal Press. "The B-Word? You Betcha" was published on November 18, 2007, in the *Washington Post.*

WRITING TO DISCOVER: *"Bitch," or "the B-word," as it is often termed in polite conversation, has appeared with increasing frequency in the press in the last decade or so. What is the meaning of the word for you? Are you shocked by hearing the word spoken? Are you offended by its use, or do you take it for granted as a part of everyday conversation? Have you ever used the word in reference to a man? Write a paragraph or so exploring what the word means for you.*

When you work for a magazine called *Bitch,* the phone tends to ring a lot when the word pops up in the news.

When the New York City Council announced a symbolic ban on the word several months back, the phone rang. When New York Knicks coach Isiah Thomas defended his use of the term toward Anucha Browne Sanders, a former Knicks marketing executive who won a sexual harassment suit last month, it rang some more. And since one of Senator John McCain's supporters used the B-word to refer to Senator Hillary Rodham Clinton in a question last week, it has been ringing like crazy.

People want to know whether it is still a bad word. They want to know whether I support its use in public discourse. Or they already think it's a bad word and want to discuss whether its use has implications for free speech or sexual harassment or political campaigns.

The other thing about working for a magazine called *Bitch* is that you really can't cop to being totally sick of having this conversation. But I am. Still, I'll continue to say the same things I always say, partly because talking about the word is an occupational responsibility/hazard and partly because, despite the fatigue, I believe them.

So here goes: Bitch is a word we use culturally to describe any woman   5 who is strong, angry, uncompromising and, often, uninterested in pleasing men. We use the term for a woman on the street who doesn't respond to men's catcalls or smile when they say, "Cheer up, baby, it can't be that bad." We use it for the woman who has a better job than a man and doesn't apologize for it. We use it for the woman who doesn't back down from a confrontation.

So let's not be disingenuous. Is it a bad word? Of course it is. As a culture, we've done everything possible to make sure of that, starting with a constantly perpetuated mindset that deems powerful women to be scary, angry and, of course, unfeminine—and sees uncompromising speech by women as anathema to a tidy, well-run world.

It's for just these reasons that when Lisa Jervis and I started the magazine in 1996, no other title was even up for consideration. As young women who had been bombarded with the word for, say, daring to walk down the street in tank tops, we knew what kinds of insults would be hurled when we started publishing articles on sexism in consumer and popular culture.

When Lisa and I were on tour with a tenth-year anniversary anthology, men wandered up to us after several readings to ask, nervously, whether we hated men—or whether men were "allowed" to read the magazine. We always told them the same thing: If you actually read the magazine —which includes everything from essays on racism in the modeling industry to columns on the marketing of the HPV drug Gardasil—you'll find that it's not about hating men but about elevating women. But too many people don't see the difference. And, at least in part, that's why the B-word is still such a problematic term.

In fact, we hoped that we could reclaim it for mouthy, smart women in much the way that "queer" had been repurposed by gay radicals. As Lisa wrote in the magazine's mission statement, "If being an outspoken woman means being a bitch, we'll take that as a compliment, thanks."

I'm guessing that Hillary Clinton, though probably not a reader of   10 our magazine, has a somewhat similar stance on the word. After all, people who don't like Clinton have been throwing the slur at her since at least 1991. So everybody else in the room laughed knowingly when a woman at a campaign event in South Carolina last Monday asked McCain, "How do we beat the bitch?"

In fact, the most surprising thing about the whole dust-up (available on YouTube for the world to see) is that something like it didn't happen sooner. Sure, it was disrespectful of McCain to laugh off the insult. (Rather than admonishing the questioner, he called it an "excellent question," then added, "I respect Senator Clinton.") And sure, the woman who asked the question was transparently courting sound-bite fame. (Congratulations, faceless woman! Stay classy!) But for Clinton, this episode has to be pretty much a case of another day, another insult.

These days, the people hurling the term at Clinton are her direct opponents: Republicans, social conservatives, assorted Schlafly-ites and Coulter-ites, and that sludgy, amorphous pool of across-the-board woman-haters.

Their hatred for Clinton has nothing to do with whether she fits the Merriam-Webster Dictionary definition: "a malicious, spiteful, or domineering woman—sometimes used as a generalized term of abuse." It certainly has nothing to do with her stance on particular issues. When these people call Clinton (or House Speaker Nancy Pelosi, or Senator Dianne Feinstein or former vice-presidential candidate Geraldine Ferraro) a bitch, or even the cutesier "rhymes-with-witch," it's an expression of pure sexism—a hope that they can shut up not only one woman but every woman who dares to be assertive. Simply put: If you don't like Clinton's stance on, say, health care or Iraq, there are plenty of ways to say so without invoking her gender.

Plenty of people are lukewarm on Clinton, for a variety of reasons: her support for the anti-gay Defense of Marriage Act, her ham-fisted attempts to put forth a clear position on Iraq, the fear that she would be just as beholden to corporate interests as her predecessor. Then there are the women who chafe at the idea that they're expected to vote their sex rather than their specific politics. But very few of these people seem to worry that Clinton isn't warm enough, or that she's too dowdy or mannish or whatever can't-win descriptor is lobbed her way daily.

So the word remains as incendiary as ever. (Sorry, Senator McCain.)   15 Back in 1996, a time when the word was just barely squeaking past the censors on network TV, I would never have thought it could get any more loaded. (Same for the word "feminism," but that's a whole other story.) But the rise of the first serious female front-runner for the presidency has proved me wrong.

On the street, in music and in the boardroom, it's the word that won't go away. Isiah Thomas's somewhat bumbling claim during his sexual harassment trial that casual, off-the-cuff usage makes the term less problematic when done within the black community didn't fly with the judge, and it doesn't fly with plenty of other folks.

A few years ago, the *New York Times* reported on the phenomenon of men using the term to describe other men, a use that has roots in the social dynamics of prison populations but has since spread to the realms of sports, rap music, and junior high schools everywhere. The article reasoned that the term was becoming, if not respectable, then increasingly no big deal. I disagree—it's simply another way to denigrate women.

I'm all for a lively discussion of how the word is used in daily life: by men, by women, in jest, in earnest. But I don't foresee that dialogue taking place in a political arena that considers mere femaleness a deficiency. Talking about the use of the word —against Clinton, Browne Sanders, or everyday women everywhere—just isn't helpful if we don't also address the many unsaid words that follow in its wake.

My own definition of the term being what it is, I can confidently say that I want my next president to be a bitch, and that goes for men and women. Outspoken? Check. Commanding? Indeed. Unworried about pleasing everybody? Sure. Won't bow to pressure to be "nice"? You bet.

And guess what? I'm not even sure that person is Hillary Clinton.   20

THINKING CRITICALLY ABOUT THE READING

1. How does Zeisler define the word *bitch*? (Glossary: *Definition*) How does her definition differ from Merriam-Webster's definition of the word? Explain.

2. Why did Zeisler and Jervis name their magazine *Bitch*?

3. Why does Zeisler label "the B-word" a "problematic term" (8)?

4. What annoys Zeisler about the way Senator McCain responded to a supporter's use of the term with reference to Senator Clinton (10–11)?

5. What is Zeisler's advice to men who ask if they are "allowed" to read the magazine (8)?

6. Zeisler notes that the writer of an article in the *New York Times* concluded that the use of the word *bitch* was "no big deal," that through wide use it has been rendered less offensive than it once was (17). Why does Zeisler disagree with that assessment?

LANGUAGE IN ACTION

In a February 27, 2008, posting entitled "Snoop Dogg Briefly Erases the Word 'Bitch' from His Vocabulary," *New York* magazine's Daily Intel blogger Jada Yuan reported the following:

Has chronic curser Snoop Dogg reformed his dirty language? At Monday's Hip-Hop Summit Action Network awards gala at Capitale, honoree Snoop Dogg repented for some of the harsh language he's used against women in his songs. "I'm not trying to do anything to offend nobody, but y'all've got to understand, I'm from the East Side," he said. "I worked hard to become a man on my own. My mother showed me how, but she couldn't really teach me how to become a man. My father wasn't there. I never knocked him for that. But the playas that I learnt from, they taught me the wrong way. They taught me to call a woman a whore, a bitch. So that was what I was taught. It wasn't until once I got older and got married and had a daughter and had kids and started to realize that now my music is starting to swing in a different direction, because I understand that I was wrongfully taught." Inspiring words!

In a small group, discuss the common use of the word *bitch* in the context of rap and hip-hop, and how it differs from the use embraced by Zeisler. Respond to Snoop Dogg's explanation of his use of the term, and to the tone with which the Daily Intel blogger reports on his apparent decision to forgo it.

WRITING SUGGESTIONS

1. In paragraph 9, Zeisler writes that she and Jervis "hoped that we could reclaim [*bitch*] for mouthy, smart women in much the way that 'queer' had been repurposed by gay radicals." Read (or reread) Gloria Naylor's article "The Meanings of a Word" (pp. 291–294), in which Naylor discusses the way the community in which she was raised "transformed" the word *nigger* "to signify the varied and complex human beings they knew themselves to be." What are the similarities and differences in her analysis of that word's use and Zeisler's explanation of feminists' use of *bitch*?

2. Consider the following statement made by Zeisler in an interview with the *Boston Globe*'s Kate Bolick in 2006: "The mainstream media feels the need to define stuff against the word *feminism:* Is it feminist, is it not feminist, is it antifeminist? A lot of people are still scared of the word. But if we can convey that calling yourself a feminist doesn't mean that you have to stop wearing lipstick or shopping or whatever, that's good. I would rather have fashion magazines acknowledge that there is no perfect idealism and there's always going to be a compromise, but you should still go and call yourself a feminist anyhow." Should women who support feminist ideals embrace the words *feminism* and *feminist,* or should they shy away from them for fear of being pigeonholed as disagreeable and angry? Write an essay in which you express your perspective on this topic.

In Defense of the "Chick Flick"

GLORIA STEINEM

Gloria Steinem is a political activist, editor, lecturer, writer, and one of the country's leading advocates for women's rights. She was born in Toledo, Ohio, in 1934 and graduated from Smith College in 1956. After college she traveled to India to study and then returned to New York, where she helped to found two important magazines, *Ms.* and *New York* Steinem has published numerous articles and eight books: *The Thousand Indias* (1957), *The Beach Book* (1963), *Outrageous Acts and Everyday Rebellions* (1983), *Marilyn: Norma Jean* (1987), *Revolution from Within: A Book of Self-Esteem* (1992), *Moving Beyond Words* (1993), and *Doing Sixty and Seventy* (2006). Steinem was inducted into the National Women's Hall of Fame in Seneca Falls, New York, in 1993.

Steinem posted "In Defense of the 'Chick Flick'" on July 7, 2007, on the Web site of the Women's Media Center, a "non-partisan, non-profit progressive women's media organization" cofounded by Steinem in 2004. In the piece, Steinem speculates on what's behind the term "chick flick" and what happens if one inverts the term.

WRITING TO DISCOVER: *Do you and your friends use the term "chick flick"? Just what do you mean by that term? Write a brief definition of the term as you understand it, and provide some examples of films that support your definition.*

Here's a modest proposal to the young man on the plane from Los Angeles to Seattle who said of the movie that most passengers —male and female—voted to watch: "I don't watch chick flicks!"

So what exactly is a "chick flick"? I think you and I could probably agree that it has more dialogue than special effects, more relationships than violence, and relies for its suspense on how people live instead of how they die.

I'm not challenging your choice; I'm just questioning the term that encourages it. After all, if you think back to your school days, much of what you were assigned as great literature could have been dismissed as "chick lit." Indeed, the books you read probably only survived because they were written by famous guys.

Think about it: If *Anna Karenina* had been written by Leah Tolstoy, or *The Scarlet Letter* by Nancy Hawthorne, or *Madame Bovary* by Greta Flaubert, or *A Doll's House* by Henrietta Ibsen, or *The Glass Menagerie* by (a female) Tennessee Williams, would they have been hailed as universal? Suppose Shakespeare had really been The Dark Lady some people supposed. I bet most of her plays and all of her sonnets would have been dismissed as some Elizabethan version of ye olde "chick lit," only to be resurrected centuries later by stubborn feminist scholars.

Indeed, as long as men are taken seriously when they write about the female half of the world—and women aren't taken seriously when writing about themselves much less about men or male affairs—the list of Great Authors will be more about power than about talent.

Still, I know this is not your problem. Instead, let me appeal to your self-interest as well as your sense of fairness: If the "chick flick" label helps you to avoid the movies you don't like, why is there no label to guide you to the ones you do like?

Just as there are "novelists" and then "women novelists," there are "movies" and then "chick flicks." Whoever is in power takes over the noun—and the norm—while the less powerful get an adjective. Thus, we read about "African American doctors" but not "European American doctors," "Hispanic leaders" but not "Anglo leaders," "gay soldiers" but not "heterosexual soldiers," and so on.

That's also why you're left with only half a guide. As usual, bias punishes everyone. Therefore I propose, as the opposite of "chick flick" and an adjective of your very own, "prick flick." Not only will it serve film critics well, but its variants will add to the literary lexicon. For example, "prick lit" could characterize a lot of fiction, from Philip Roth to Bret Easton Ellis and beyond. "True prick" could guide readers to their preferred nonfiction, from the classics of Freud to the populist works of sociobiologists and even Rush Limbaugh.

Most of all, the simple label "prick flick" could lead you easily and quickly through the thicket of televised, downloaded, and theatrical releases to such attractions as:

- All the movies that glorify World War II. From classics with John Wayne and Ronald Reagan, those master actors who conveyed heroism without ever leaving the back lot, to Spielberg's *Band of Brothers*, in which the hero would rather die than be rescued, Hollywood has probably spent more on making movies about the war than this country spent on fighting it. After all, World War II was the last war in which this country was clearly right. Without frequent exposure to it, how are we to believe we still are?
- All the movies that glorify Vietnam, bloody regional wars, and the war on terrorism. These may not be as much fun to watch—you probably are aware that we aren't the winners here—but they allow you to enjoy mass mayhem in, say, South Asia or Africa or the Middle East that justifies whatever this country might do.
- All the movies that portray violence against women, preferably beautiful, sexy, half-naked women. These feature chainsaws and house parties for teenage guys, serial killers and sadistic rapists for ordinary male adults, plus cleverly plotted humiliations and deaths of powerful women for the well-educated misogynist.

- All the movies that insist female human beings are the only animals on earth that seek out and even enjoy their own pain. From glamorized versions of prostitution to such complex plots as *Boxing Helena,* a man's dream of amputating all a rebellious woman's limbs—and then she falls in love with him—these provide self-justification and how-to manuals for sadists.

As you can see, one simple label could guide you through diversity, and help other viewers to practice avoidance. 10

But if you really think about it, I'm hope-a-holic enough to think you might like to watch a chick flick after all.

THINKING CRITICALLY ABOUT THE READING

1. Steinem's essay is her half of an imaginary dialogue with "the young man on the plane." What argumentative advantage does she gain by using this technique?

2. In paragraph 4, Steinem speculates briefly about what the fate of some great literature would have been had it been written by women instead of by men. What point does she make by such speculation?

3. Starting in paragraph 6, Steinem puts forth a second, related argument that she hopes will "appeal to [the young man's] self-interest [and] sense of fairness": "bias punishes everyone" (8). How does this insight relate to what Steinem argues about the term "chick flick"?

4. What purposes would be served by the creation of the label "prick flick," as far as Steinem is concerned? Do you think she's serious about the need for such a term, or do you think she's being ironic? (Glossary: *Irony*)

5. Explain Steinem's last two sentences. Are they a fitting conclusion for her essay? (Glossary: *Beginnings and Endings*). Explain why or why not.

LANGUAGE IN ACTION

Using Steinem's argument about dominant language, analyze the father's statement in the cartoon below. What is the underlying assumption behind his statement? What would you say the cartoon's message is? How does the artist's way of drawing each character contribute to this message?

"Go bother your mother. She's only reading chick lit."

WRITING SUGGESTIONS

1. In calling her essay "a modest proposal" in her first paragraph, Steinem is making a tongue-in-cheek reference to Jonathan Swift's "A Modest Proposal" (pp. 227–233), in which he puts forth his plan for solving the problem of the Irish famine. Read, or reread, Swift's essay and write an essay of your own in which you explain the relationship between Steinem's essay and Swift's.

2. Categorization, like stereotyping, can be said to impose limitations on reality that are potentially unfair. For example, is it fair to say that there are two types of writing, "creative" and "nonfiction"? So-called creative writing is, after all, very often based on reality, and nonfiction writing very often uses fictional techniques and can be quite creative. Write an essay in which you explore the shortcomings of categorization, with special reference to categories commonly applied to film, literature, music, or something else of interest to you. To what extent is categorization useful, and to what degree does it deny something its uniqueness or special qualities?

"FOBs" vs. "Twinkies": The New Discrimination Is Intraracial

GRACE HSIANG

Grace Hsiang was born in San Jose, California, in 1986. In 2008 she graduated with a double major in international studies and literary journalism from the University of California, Irvine. Already building a career in writing, Hsiang has been published in the following magazines and news services: *Alternet, Pacific News Service/New America Media, WWS Magazine, Jaded Magazine, ISM Magazine,* and *13 Minutes.*

The following selection, written when Hsiang was working as an intern for Pacific News Service, first appeared on April 15, 2005. When asked what inspired her to write about her community and its struggles, she wrote the following: "I think the Asian American community has made significant strides in the last century and has really carved a presence. We are in films, fashion, and politics, and I'm proud of all the strides we've made. However, there is still a long way to go in the name of equality, and before we blame the outside or the other, we must look internally for change. I think if we face the problems within our community first it will allow us to face those outside."

WRITING TO DISCOVER: *If you are a member of a minority group, what subgroups within your community do you recognize? What tensions between members of that group are you aware of, and how do those tensions make themselves felt? Write several paragraphs describing the tensions as you understand them as well as explaining why you think they exist.*

Today in my sociology class, the teacher asked the students to volunteer our own experiences with racism or ethnic harassment. I imagined the responses would once again feature the ongoing battle between white vs. minority. Instead, to my surprise, most of the students told of being discriminated against and marginalized by members of their own ethnic group.

In the Asian community, the slurs heard most often are not terms such as "Chink" or "Jap," but rather "FOB" ("Fresh Off the Boat") or "whitewashed" (too assimilated). When Asian Americans hit puberty, they seem to divide into two camps, each highly critical of the other.

Members of the first cling to their ethnic heritage. They tend to be exclusive in their friendships, often accepting only "true Asians." They believe relationships should remain within the community, and may even opt to speak their parents' native language over English in public.

Members of the second group reject as many aspects of Asian culture as possible and concentrate on being seen as American. They go out of their way to refuse to date within the community, embrace friends outside their ethnic circle, and even boast to others about how un-Asian they are.

"My coworker is Vietnamese," 19-year-old Carol Lieu remarked, 5
"but she will yell at you if you speak it to her and pretend that she doesn't
understand."

Second-generation Asian Americans often face pressure from their
parents, who believe that the privileges we are allowed in this country
make us spoiled and ungrateful. Many of us very much want to belong to
our parents' community, but we cannot completely embody one culture
when we are living in another.

The pressures we face force many of us to feel we must choose one
culture over another. We can either cling to our parent's ideology or rebel
against it and try to be "American."

The problems start when those who have made one choice discrimi-
nate against those who have made the other. I've heard ethnocentric Asians
speak with disgust about Asians who wear Abercrombie and Fitch (which
is viewed as the ultimate "white" brand), or make fun of those who don't
know their parents' language.

This perspective even made it into the recent hit movie *Harold and
Kumar Go to White Castle*. John Cho's character complains about a girl
who is pursuing him despite his lack of interest: She "rambles on about
her East Asian Students Club or whatever. Then I have to actually pretend
that I give a s--t or she calls me a Twinkie . . . yellow on the outside, white
on the inside."

"People act disappointed that I can't speak Japanese fluently," a stu- 10
dent of Mexican and Japanese ancestry in my sociology class complained
this morning. "I don't see anyone giving me credit for speaking fluent
Gaelic."

On the other side, second-generation kids who refuse to assimilate are
called FOBs. The cars they drive are derided as "Rice Rockets," and their
pastimes and ways of dressing are stereotyped as exclusively Asian. "We
live in America," one freshman political science major recalls more assimilated friends telling her. "Don't bring your culture here."

Not all young Asian Americans buy into the dichotomy between
"FOBs" and "Twinkies." Many, like me, understand the term "Asian
American" in all its complexity, and embrace all sides of our identity.
Rather than identifying with one culture or another, my friends and I
accept both.

You should identify with your heritage "because that's who you are,"
Ricky Kim, founder of the online journal *Evil Monito,* has said. "But don't
be ignorant of the culture you grew up in—that's being ungrateful."

Asian Americans grow up experiencing enough difficulties living in a
predominantly white country with the face of a foreigner. The gap between
races is wide enough without drawing lines within ethnicities and communities. We can avoid this internal discrimination simply by recognizing that
we are of two cultures—and that in itself creates a new culture that should
be fully celebrated.

THINKING CRITICALLY ABOUT THE READING

1. What surprised Hsiang when students in her class were asked to discuss their "own experiences with racism and ethnic harassment" (1)? Why did it surprise her?

2. Hsiang writes that the split in the Asian community arises when children "hit puberty" (2). Why do you suppose the split occurs at this stage of development?

3. What pressures from their parents do Asian students often face, according to Hsiang? How does this relate to her topic?

4. In "What's So Bad about Hate?" (pp. 247–261), writer Andrew Sullivan discusses other varieties of "intragroup" prejudice and concludes: "[I]ts intensity comes in part, one senses, from the pain of being excluded for so long, of anger long restrained bubbling up and directing itself more aggressively toward an alleged traitor than an alleged enemy. It is the hate of the hated." Do you think Hsiang would agree? If not, in what way(s) might she take issue with Sullivan's conclusion?

5. Does Hsiang offer any solutions to the problem she identifies? Explain.

LANGUAGE IN ACTION

Hsiang refers in her essay to the cult comedy *Harold and Kumar Go to White Castle* (2004), which was recently reprised in *Harold and Kumar Escape from Guantanamo Bay* (2008). Both films provocatively address stereotypes of minority cultures in the United States, including but not limited to stereotypes of Korean Americans and Indian Americans. Search online for reviews of both films, paying particular attention to any discussion of the ways in which the films deal with racial stereotypes. What criticisms are raised? Do you agree or disagree with critics who think the comedies are, in fact, racist?

WRITING SUGGESTIONS

1. Hsiang's essay is important because it sheds light on a topic that is not often discussed: intraracial discrimination. Write an essay in which you express your own perspective on intraracial discrimination. Depending on your interests and experiences, you might focus on Arab American, African American, Hispanic American, or other communities within the United States. In writing your essay, consider the following questions: What role does skin color play in the discrimination exercised within a minority community? What role do different geographical origins, different levels/kinds of education, or other factors play?

2. Hsiang's essay has generated a great deal of discussion on the Web and elsewhere, especially among those who were not aware of intraracial discrimination. Write an essay based on Hsiang's in which you explore the ramifications of any intraracial discrimination you have experienced personally or have been aware of in your community. How does prejudice affect the self-esteem of the individuals involved? How does it affect the cohesion of the minority group? Does such prejudice reflect on the way the minority group as a whole is seen by the dominant culture?

Black Men and Public Space

Brent Staples

Brent Staples is an important voice in American culture. He was born in 1951 in Chester, Pennsylvania, an industrial city southwest of Philadelphia. He studied at Widener University in Chester and the University of Chicago, where he earned his Ph.D. in psychology. Formerly a teacher, Staples began his newspaper career as a reporter for the *Chicago Sun-Times.* He later became an editor for the *New York Times Book Review* and is now editor for the *New York Times* a member of the editorial board. His memoir *Parallel Time: Growing Up in Black and White* (1994) won the 1995 Anisfield-Wolff Award, also given to such notable African American writers as James Baldwin, Ralph Ellison, and Zora Neale Hurston.

"Black Men and Public Space" first appeared in 1986 in *Ms.* magazine as "Just Walk on By: A Black Man Ponders His Power to Alter Public Space." The revised version that we print here was published later the same year in *Harper's.* In the essay, Staples recounts his experiences moving through public spaces at night. After innocently scaring a woman one night, Staples writes, "It was in the echo of that terrified woman's footfalls that I first began to know the unwieldy inheritance I'd come into—the ability to alter public space in ugly ways."

WRITING TO DISCOVER: *Reflect on what you know about body language. Are you aware, for example, of the messages that might be conveyed by a person's physical features, gestures, and use of space? Try observing some people around you, in your dormitory, in the school cafeteria, or at work in order to gain some appreciation of the messages that they may be sending that either support or contradict their verbal messages.*

My first victim was a woman—white, well dressed, probably in her late twenties. I came upon her late one evening on a deserted street in Hyde Park, a relatively affluent neighborhood in an otherwise mean, impoverished section of Chicago. As I swung onto the avenue behind her, there seemed to be a discreet, uninflammatory distance between us. Not so. She cast back a worried glance. To her, the youngish black man—a broad six feet two inches with a beard and billowing hair, both hands shoved into the pockets of a bulky military jacket—seemed menacingly close. After a few more quick glimpses, she picked up her pace and was soon running in earnest. Within seconds, she disappeared into a cross street.

That was more than a decade ago. I was twenty-two years old, a graduate student newly arrived at the University of Chicago. It was in the echo of that terrified woman's footfalls that I first began to know the unwieldy inheritance I'd come into—the ability to alter public space in ugly ways. It was clear that she thought herself the quarry of a mugger, a rapist, or worse.

Suffering a bout of insomnia, however, I was stalking sleep, not defenseless wayfarers. As a softy who is scarcely able to take a knife to a raw chicken — let alone hold one to a person's throat — I was surprised, embarrassed, and dismayed all at once. Her flight made me feel like an accomplice in tyranny. It also made it clear that I was indistinguishable from the muggers who occasionally seeped into the area from the surrounding ghetto. The first encounter, and those that followed, signified that a vast, unnerving gulf lay between nighttime pedestrians — particularly women — and me. And I soon gathered that being perceived as dangerous is a hazard in itself. I only needed to turn a corner into a dicey situation, or crowd some frightened, armed person in a foyer somewhere, or make an errant move after being pulled over by a policeman. Where fear and weapons meet — and they often do in urban America — there is always the possibility of death.

In that first year, my first away from my hometown, I was to become thoroughly familiar with the language of fear. At dark, shadowy intersections, I could cross in front of a car stopped at a traffic light and elicit the *thunk, thunk, thunk, thunk* of the driver — black, white, male, or female — hammering down the door locks. On less traveled streets after dark, I grew accustomed to but never comfortable with people crossing to the other side of the street rather than pass me. Then there were the standard unpleasantries with policemen, doormen, bouncers, cabdrivers, and others whose business it is to screen out troublesome individuals *before* there is any nastiness.

I moved to New York nearly two years ago and I have remained an avid night walker. In central Manhattan, the near-constant crowd cover minimizes tense one-on-one street encounters. Elsewhere — in SoHo, for example, where sidewalks are narrow and tightly spaced buildings shut out the sky — things can get very taut indeed.

After dark, on the warrenlike streets of Brooklyn where I live, I often see women who fear the worst from me. They seem to have set their faces on neutral, and with their purse straps strung across their chests bandolier-style, they forge ahead as though bracing themselves against being tackled. I understand, of course, that the danger they perceive is not a hallucination. Women are particularly vulnerable to street violence, and young black males are drastically overrepresented among the perpetrators of that violence. Yet these truths are no solace against the kind of alienation that comes of being ever the suspect, a fearsome entity with whom pedestrians avoid making eye contact.

It is not altogether clear to me how I reached the ripe old age of twenty-two without being conscious of the lethality nighttime pedestrians attributed to me. Perhaps it was because in Chester, Pennsylvania, the small, angry industrial town where I came of age in the 1960s, I was scarcely noticeable against a backdrop of gang warfare, street knifings, and murders. I grew up one of the good boys, had perhaps a half-dozen fistfights. In retrospect, my shyness of combat has clear sources.

As a boy, I saw countless tough guys locked away; I have since buried several, too. They were babies, really—a teenage cousin, a brother of twenty-two, a childhood friend in his mid-twenties—all gone down in episodes of bravado played out in the streets. I came to doubt the virtues of intimidation early on. I chose, perhaps unconsciously, to remain a shadow—timid, but a survivor.

The fearsomeness mistakenly attributed to me in public places often has a perilous flavor. The most frightening of these confusions occurred in the late 1970s and early 1980s, when I worked as a journalist in Chicago. One day, rushing into the office of a magazine I was writing for with a deadline story in hand, I was mistaken for a burglar. The office manager called security and, with an ad hoc posse, pursued me through the labyrinthine halls, nearly to my editor's door. I had no way of proving who I was. I could only move briskly toward the company of someone who knew me.

Another time I was on assignment for a local paper and killing time before an interview. I entered a jewelry store on the city's affluent Near North Side. The proprietor excused himself and returned with an enormous red Doberman pinscher straining at the end of a leash. She stood, the dog extended toward me, silent to my questions, her eyes bulging nearly out of her head. I took a cursory look around, nodded, and bade her good night.

Relatively speaking, however, I never fared as badly as another black 10 male journalist. He went to nearby Waukegan, Illinois, a couple of summers ago to work on a story about a murderer who was born there. Mistaking the reporter for the killer, police officers hauled him from his car at gunpoint and but for his press credentials would probably have tried to book him. Such episodes are not uncommon. Black men trade tales like this all the time.

Over the years, I learned to smother the rage I felt at so often being taken for a criminal. Not to do so would surely have led to madness. I now take precautions to make myself less threatening. I move about with care, particularly late in the evening. I give a wide berth to nervous people on subway platforms during the wee hours, particularly when I have exchanged business clothes for jeans. If I happen to be entering a building behind some people who appear skittish, I may walk by, letting them clear the lobby before I return, so as not to seem to be following them. I have been calm and extremely congenial on those rare occasions when I've been pulled over by the police.

And on late-evening constitutionals I employ what has proved to be an excellent tension-reducing measure: I whistle melodies from Beethoven and Vivaldi and the more popular classical composers. Even steely New Yorkers hunching toward nighttime destinations seem to relax, and occasionally they even join in the tune. Virtually everybody seems to sense that a mugger wouldn't be warbling bright, sunny selections from Vivaldi's *Four Seasons.*

THINKING CRITICALLY ABOUT THE READING

1. What is Staples's purpose in this essay? (Glossary: *Purpose*)

2. Staples's essay was first published in *Ms.* magazine, a publication that was very influential for young women, particularly in the beginning of the women's movement. Why is Staples's essay appropriate for that magazine? (Glossary: *Audience*)

3. Why is Staples's realization that he might cause fear in someone in a public space so surprising to him? What does he say about himself that explains the surprise he experienced?

4. Staples provides several examples to support his thesis that people have been conditioned to respond negatively to him in public spaces. (Glossary: *Evidence*) Recount several of those experiences. How effective were these examples in helping him make his case?

5. Staples never discusses his situation as an example of the racial prejudice that exists all around him. Would his essay be more or less effective if he made such statements? Explain.

6. Staples begins his essay with the words: "My first victim was a woman—white, well dressed, probably in her late twenties." What effect did this beginning have on you? (Glossary: *Beginnings and Endings*)

7. What is one of the solutions that Staples has come up with to help him deal with strangers in public spaces? Are his solutions a concession to the fact that he sees no hope of changing attitudes around him, or are they an effort to change peoples' attitudes?

LANGUAGE IN ACTION

Brent Staples's essay is in part about the concept of "territoriality" and the nonverbal messages it sends. Most of our feelings of territoriality remain unconscious until "our territory" is violated. How would you react to each of the following situations?

a. after a class has been meeting for at least three weeks, someone deliberately sat in a seat that you have been regularly occupying

b. in your library or snack bar, if someone moved his or her books or food and sat down while you were temporarily away

c. in an uncrowded library or classroom, someone deliberately sat right next to you

d. in your dorm room or at home, someone deliberately sat (in a chair, at a desk, etc.) that "belongs" to you or another family member

You may wish to share your reactions with those of other members of your class. What conclusions can you draw about the way people regard invasions of their personal space?

WRITING SUGGESTIONS

1. Each of us makes an impression on those around us, either in public spaces or in more intimate surroundings. Each of us also has a more or less sensitive appreciation of the impressions we create on those around us. Describe the impression that you think you create in presenting yourself. Draw on examples of situations over time and in different settings that support the major ideas you are trying to present in your writing.

2. Write an essay that describes the various stereotypes that are created about students. What do you think of your fellow students? How do you think they regard you? How do students see themselves as a group? How does their body language reflect the way they see themselves? Do you think that most students see themselves as others do? Are the stereotypes that are applied to students fair in your judgment?

The Fourth of July

AUDRE LORDE

Audre Lorde (1934–1992) was a professor of English at Hunter College in New York City. Born in New York, she studied at Hunter and at Columbia University. Her published works include several volumes of poetry, such as *Undersong: Chosen Poems Old and New* (1982), which was revised in 1992; essay collections like *Sister Outsider* (1984) and *Burst of Light* (1988); and an autobiography, *Zami: A New Spelling of My Name* (1982). Her book of poems *The Arithmetics of Distance* appeared posthumously in 1993. The following selection from *Zami* eloquently communicates the tragedy of racism. Take special note of Lorde's tone as you read, particularly the way it intensifies as the essay continues and how it culminates in the anger of the final paragraph.

WRITING TO DISCOVER: *Reflect on an experience you had while traveling in which you came to realize that you were an outsider in a place around the corner or around the world. What effect did your new awareness have on you?*

The first time I went to Washington, D.C., was on the edge of the summer when I was supposed to stop being a child. At least that's what they said to us all at graduation from the eighth grade. My sister Phyllis graduated at the same time from high school. I don't know what she was supposed to stop being. But as graduation presents for us both, the whole family took a Fourth of July trip to Washington, D.C., the fabled and famous capital of our country.

It was the first time I'd ever been on a railroad train during the day. When I was little, and we used to go to the Connecticut shore, we always went at night on the milk train, because it was cheaper.

Preparations were in the air around our house before school was even over. We packed for a week. There were two very large suitcases that my father carried, and a box filled with food. In fact, my first trip to Washington was a mobile feast; I started eating as soon as we were comfortably ensconced in our seats, and did not stop until somewhere after Philadelphia. I remember it was Philadelphia because I was disappointed not to have passed by the Liberty Bell.

My mother had roasted two chickens and cut them up into dainty bite-size pieces. She packed slices of brown bread and butter and green pepper and carrot sticks. There were little violently yellow iced cakes with scalloped edges called "marigolds," that came from Cushman's Bakery. There was a spice bun and rock-cakes from Newton's, the West Indian bakery across Lenox Avenue from St. Mark's School, and iced tea in a wrapped mayonnaise jar. There were sweet pickles for us and dill pickles for my father, and peaches with the fuzz still on them, individually wrapped to keep them from bruising. And, for neatness, there were piles of napkins and a little tin box with a washcloth dampened with rosewater and glycerine for wiping sticky mouths.

I wanted to eat in the dining car because I had read all about them, but my mother reminded me for the umpteenth time that dining car food always cost too much money and besides, you never could tell whose hands had been playing all over that food, nor where those same hands had been just before. My mother never mentioned that black people were not allowed into railroad dining cars headed south in 1947. As usual, whatever my mother did not like and could not change, she ignored. Perhaps it would go away, deprived of her attention.

I learned later that Phyllis's high school senior class trip had been to Washington, but the nuns had given her back her deposit in private, explaining to her that the class, all of whom were white, except Phyllis, would be staying in a hotel where Phyllis "would not be happy," meaning, Daddy explained to her, also in private, that they did not rent rooms to Negroes. "We will take you to Washington, ourselves," my father had avowed, "and not just for an overnight in some measly fleabag hotel."

American racism was a new and crushing reality that my parents had to deal with every day of their lives once they came to this country. They handled it as a private woe. My mother and father believed that they could best protect their children from the realities of race in America and the fact of American racism by never giving them name, much less discussing their nature. We were told we must never trust white people, but *why* was never explained, nor the nature of their ill will. Like so many other vital pieces of information in my childhood, I was supposed to know without being told. It always seemed like a very strange injunction coming from my mother, who looked so much like one of those people we were never supposed to trust. But something always warned me not to ask my mother why she wasn't white, and why Auntie Lillah and Auntie Etta weren't, even though they were all that same problematic color so different from my father and me, even from my sisters, who were somewhere in-between.

In Washington, D.C., we had one large room with two double beds and an extra cot for me. It was a back-street hotel that belonged to a friend of my father's who was in real estate, and I spent the whole next day after Mass squinting up at the Lincoln Memorial where Marian Anderson had sung after the D.A.R. refused to allow her to sing in their auditorium because she was black. Or because she was "Colored," my father said as he told us the story. Except that what he probably said was "Negro," because for his times, my father was quite progressive.

I was squinting because I was in that silent agony that characterized all of my childhood summers, from the time school let out in June to the end of July, brought about by my dilated and vulnerable eyes exposed to the summer brightness.

I viewed Julys through an agonizing corolla of dazzling whiteness and   10
I always hated the Fourth of July, even before I came to realize the travesty such a celebration was for black people in this country.

My parents did not approve of sunglasses, nor of their expense.

I spent the afternoon squinting up at monuments to freedom and past presidencies and democracy, and wondering why the light and heat were both so much stronger in Washington, D.C., than back home in New York City. Even the pavement on the streets was a shade lighter in color than back home.

Late that Washington afternoon my family and I walked back down Pennsylvania Avenue. We were a proper caravan, mother bright and father brown, the three of us girls step-standards in-between. Moved by our historical surroundings and the heat of early evening, my father decreed yet another treat. He had a great sense of history, a flair for the quietly dramatic and the sense of specialness of an occasion and a trip.

"Shall we stop and have a little something to cool off, Lin?"

Two blocks away from our hotel, the family stopped for a dish of   15
vanilla ice cream at a Breyer's ice cream and soda fountain. Indoors, the soda fountain was dim and fan-cooled, deliciously relieving to my scorched eyes.

Corded and crisp and pinafored, the five of us seated ourselves one by one at the counter. There was I between my mother and father, and my two sisters on the other side of my mother. We settled ourselves along the white mottled marble counter, and when the waitress spoke at first no one understood what she was saying, and so the five of us just sat there.

The waitress moved along the line of us closer to my father and spoke again. "I said I kin give you to take out, but you can't eat here. Sorry." Then she dropped her eyes looking very embarrassed, and suddenly we heard what it was she was saying all at the same time, loud and clear.

Straight-backed and indignant, one by one, my family and I got down from the counter stools and turned around and marched out of the store, quiet and outraged, as if we had never been black before. No one would answer my emphatic questions with anything other than a guilty silence. "But we hadn't done anything!" This wasn't right or fair! Hadn't I written poems about Bataan and freedom and democracy for all?

My parents wouldn't speak of this injustice, not because they had contributed to it, but because they felt they should have anticipated it and avoided it. This made me even angrier. My fury was not going to be acknowledged by a like fury. Even my two sisters copied my parents' pretense that nothing unusual and anti-American had occurred. I was left to write my angry letter to the president of the United States all by myself, although my father did promise I could type it out on the office typewriter next week, after I showed it to him in my copybook diary.

The waitress was white, and the counter was white, and the ice cream   20
I never ate in Washington, D.C., that summer I left childhood was white,
and the white heat and the white pavement and the white stone monuments of my first Washington summer made me sick to my stomach for
the whole rest of that trip and it wasn't much of a graduation present
after all.

THINKING CRITICALLY ABOUT THE READING

1. Why do you think Lorde's family dealt with racism by ignoring it? How is
   Lorde different?

2. Why did Lorde dislike the Fourth of July as a child? Why does she dislike it
   as an adult? Lorde takes great care in describing the food her family took on
   the train with them to Washington. What is Lorde's purpose in describing the
   food? (Glossary: *Purpose*)

3. What is the role of silence in Lorde's family? How does it enable or impede
   the racism they experience?

4. Lorde's essay is not long or exaggerated, but it is a very effective indictment of
   a country that in 1947 held up the ideal of equality but reinforced institutions
   that argued against it. Identify some of the words Lorde uses to communicate
   her outrage when she writes of the racism that she and her family faced. How
   does her choice of words contribute to her message?

5. What is the tone of Lorde's essay? (Glossary: *Tone*) Identify passages to support your answer.

6. Do you see any irony in Lorde's title? (Glossary: *Irony*) In what way? Do you
   think it is an appropriate title for her essay?

LANGUAGE IN ACTION

Read the following poem by Maria Mazziotti Gillan, which depicts how
non-English speakers were treated in previous generations. Discuss the reasons for Gillan's anger. Is her anger Audre Lorde's? If so, in what ways?
How have they both dealt with their memories of incidents that have caused
them emotional pain?

PUBLIC SCHOOL NO. 18: PATERSON, NEW JERSEY

Miss Wilson's eyes, opaque
as blue glass, fix on me:
"We must speak English.
We're in America now."
I want to say, "I am American,"
but the evidence is stacked against me.

(continued)

My mother scrubs my scalp raw, wraps
my shining hair in white rags
to make it curl; Miss Wilson
drags me to the window, checks my hair
for lice. My face wants to hide.

At home, my words smooth in my mouth,
I chatter and am proud. In school,
I am silent; I grope for the right English
words, fear the Italian word will sprout
from my mouth like a rose.

I fear the progression of teachers
in their sprigged dresses,
their Anglo-Saxon faces.

Without words, they tell me
to be ashamed.
I am.
I deny that booted country
even from myself,
want to be still
and untouchable
as these women
who teach me to hate myself.

Years later, in a white
Kansas City house,
the psychology professor tells me
I remind him of the Mafia leader
on the cover of *Time* magazine.
My anger spits
venomous from my mouth:

I am proud of my mother,
dressed all in black,
proud of my father
with his broken tongue,
proud of the laughter
and noise of our house.

Remember me, ladies,
the silent one?
I have found my voice
and my rage will blow
your house down.

WRITING SUGGESTIONS

1. When read with the ideals of the American Revolution and the Constitution in mind, Lorde's essay is strongly ironic. Write an essay in which you capture what the Fourth of July means to you. How do your feelings relate to the stated ideals of our forebears? Choose your words carefully, and use specific personal experiences to support your general statements.

2. Imagine that you are Lorde in 1947. Write a letter to President Harry Truman in which you protest the reception you received in the nation's capital on the Fourth of July. Do not overstate your case. Show the president in what ways you and your family were treated unfairly rather than merely stating that you were discriminated against, and carefully choose words that will help President Truman see the irony of your experience.

5

EVERYDAY CONVERSATIONS

We reveal ourselves—where we come from, who we are, and who we'd like to be—in the language we use every day. At the same time, our use of language shapes us: In writing, speaking, or text messaging, we evolve as individuals in communication with other language users, exchanging signs and meanings and exploring new ways of defining ourselves and our place in the world. In this chapter, we offer a collection of readings that discuss two important variables that position us in relation to language: the "speech communities" to which we belong and the gender(s) with which we identify.

In the chapter's first section, "Exploring Our Speech Communities," six authors express different perspectives on the communities that shape how we use language. In the first reading in this section, Paul Roberts writes about how speech communities form based on such factors as age, geography, and social class, and how the language patterns we learn in our speech communities affect how the world perceives (and receives) us. In "Whither the Southern Accent?," Jeffrey Collins and Kristen Wyatt focus on the speech communities in a particular region: Specifically, they investigate the current state of southern dialects, which many believe to be under pressure from the homogenizing effects of mass media. In "Mute in an English-Only World," Chang-Rae Lee explores conflict among competing speech communities, using local legislation restricting foreign-language signage as a springboard for reflection on his mother's experience as a nonnative speaker in the urban northeastern United States. Daniel Seidel's "The Lost Art of the Rant" celebrates the rant, a particular kind of speech that some say has undergone a revival in recent years, with the Internet serving as a virtual soapbox. Finally, in a set of paired essays, journalists Jennifer 8. Lee and Charles McGrath discuss the educational and social changes issuing from the widespread use of specialized shorthand in instant messaging and text messaging. In "I Think, Therefore IM," Lee reports on teachers' responses to the infiltration of "IM-speak" into elementary school classrooms. In "The Pleasures of the Text," McGrath expresses grave reservations about the impact of text messaging not only on the way young people write, but also on the way they think and feel.

The second section of this chapter, "Gender and the Words We Use," addresses the ways in which language and gender intersect. In "You're Wearing *That*?: Understanding Mothers and Daughters in Conversation," Deborah Tannen reflects on her relationship with her mother toward the end of her mother's life and broadens these reflections into an arresting essay on the ways in which mothers and daughter communicate. In the selection that follows, "He and She: What's the Real Difference?" Clive Thompson reports on a computer program that can allegedly determine by analysis of the words used in a text whether the author is male or female. The development of the program naturally gives rise to a whole new set of fascinating questions regarding what constitutes gender and language usage. Next, Martha Irvine traces the history of the word *queer* from being synonymous with "odd" or "unusual" to its use as an anti-gay insult, to its being reclaimed, redefined, and embraced by the gay community. Finally, in a set of paired essays, John McWhorter and Audrey Bilger take on different aspects of sexism in language and suggest different means of countering it. McWhorter, in "Missing the Nose on Our Face," suggests that the "correct" English that language purists insist on is expendable, when the alternative reflects and fosters a more equitable society, while Bilger, in "On Language: You Guys," focuses on a particular instance of sexist language—the use of "you guys" to mean "you" (plural)—and recommends that it be rejected.

Speech Communities

PAUL ROBERTS

In "A Brief History of English" (pp. 84–93), linguist, teacher, and writer Paul Roberts uses the long view of history to discuss the relationship of major events in English history to the development of the English language. In the following selection, taken from the same book, *Understanding English* (1958), Roberts writes about the development of speech variations within the United States that are based on what he identifies as "speech communities." These communities—which sometimes have their own dialects, their own jargon, their own codes, meanings, and pronunciations—are formed by a variety of factors, according to Roberts, including "age, geography, education, occupation, social position."

WRITING TO DISCOVER: *Think about your own way of speaking. What factors do you believe are the most powerful influences on your own use of English—for example, your family; the region you grew up in; your peers? Do you have more than one way of speaking, depending on whom you are with or where you are?*

Imagine a village of a thousand people all speaking the same language and never hearing any language other than their own. As the decades pass and generation succeeds generation, it will not be very apparent to the speakers of the language that any considerable language change is going on. Oldsters may occasionally be conscious of and annoyed by the speech forms of youngsters. They will notice new words, new expressions, "bad" pronunciations, but will ordinarily put these down to the irresponsibility of youth, and decide piously that the language of the younger generation will revert to decency when the generation grows up.

It doesn't revert, though. The new expressions and the new pronunciations persist, and presently there is another younger generation with its own new expressions and its own pronunciations. And thus the language changes. If members of the village could speak to one another across five hundred years, they would probably find themselves unable to communicate.

Now suppose that the village divides itself and half the people move away. They move across the river or over a mountain and form a new village. Suppose the separation is so complete that the people of New Village have no contact with the people of Old Village. The language of both villages will change, drifting away from the language of their common

323

ancestors. But the drift will not be in the same direction. In both villages there will be new expressions and new pronunciations, but not the same ones. In the course of time the languages of Old Village and New Village will be mutually unintelligible with the language they both started with. They will also be mutually unintelligible with one another.

An interesting thing—and one for which there is no perfectly clear explanation—is that the rate of change will not ordinarily be the same for both villages. The language of Old Village changes faster than the language of New Village. One might expect that the opposite would be true—that the emigrants, placed in new surroundings and new conditions, would undergo more rapid language changes. But history reports otherwise. American English, for example, despite the violence and agony and confusion to which the demands of a new continent have subjected it, is probably essentially closer to the language of Shakespeare than London English is.

Suppose one thing more. Suppose Old Village is divided sharply into   5 an upper class and a lower class. The sons and daughters of the upper class go to preparatory school and then to the university; the children of the lower class go to work. The upper-class people learn to read and write and develop a flowering literature; the lower-class people remain illiterate. Dialects develop, and the speech of the two classes steadily diverges. One might suppose that most of the change would go on among the illiterate, that the upper-class people, conscious of their heritage, would tend to preserve the forms and pronunciations of their ancestors. Not so. The opposite is true. In speech, the educated tend to be radical and the uneducated conservative. In England one finds Elizabethan forms and sounds not among Oxford and Cambridge graduates but among the people of backward villages.

A village is a fairly simple kind of speech community—a group of people steadily in communication with one another, steadily hearing one another's speech. But the village is by no means the basic unit. Within the simplest village there are many smaller units—groupings based on age, class, occupation. All these groups play intricately on one another and against one another, and a language that seems at first a coherent whole will turn out on inspection to be composed of many differing parts. Some forces tend to make these parts diverge, other forces hold them together. Thus the language continues in tension.

THE SPEECH COMMUNITIES OF THE CHILD

The child's first speech community is ordinarily his family. The child learns whatever kind of language the family speaks—or, more precisely, whatever kind of language it speaks to him. The child's language learning, now and later, is governed by two obvious motives: the desire to communicate and the desire to be admired. He imitates what he hears. More or less successful imitations usually bring action and reward and tend to be repeated. Unsuccessful ones usually don't bring action and reward and tend to be discarded.

But since language is a complicated business it is sometimes the unsuccessful imitations that bring the reward. The child, making a stab at the word *mother,* comes out with *muzzer.* The family decides that this is just too cute for anything and beams and repeats *muzzer,* and the child, feeling that he's scored a bull's eye, goes on saying *muzzer* long after he has mastered *other* and *brother.* Baby talk is not so much invented by the child as sponsored by the parent.

Eventually the child moves out of the family and into another speech community—other children of his neighborhood. He goes to kindergarten and immediately encounters speech habits that conflict with those he has learned. If he goes to school and talks about his *muzzer,* it will be borne in on him by his colleagues that the word is not well chosen. Even *mother* may not pass muster, and he may discover that he gets better results and is altogether happier if he refers to his female parent as his ma or even his old lady.

Children coming together in a kindergarten class bring with them language that is different because it is learned in different homes. It is all to some degree unsuccessfully learned, consisting of not quite perfect imitations of the original. In school all this speech coalesces, differences tend to be ironed out, and the result differs from the original parental speech and differs in pretty much the same way.

The pressures on the child to conform to the speech of his age group, his speech community, are enormous. He may admire his teacher and love his mother, he may even—and even consciously—wish to speak as they do. But he *has* to speak like the rest of the class. If he does not, life becomes intolerable.

The speech changes that go on when the child goes to school are often most distressing to parents. Your little Bertram, at home, has never heard anything but the most elegant English. You send him to school, and what happens? He comes home saying things like "I done real good in school today, Mom." But Bertram really has no choice in the matter. If Clarence and Elbert and the rest of the fellows customarily say "I done real good," then Bertram might as well go around with three noses as say things like "I did very nicely."

Individuals differ of course, and not all children react to the speech community in the same way. Some tend to imitate and others tend to force imitation. But all to some degree have their speech modified by forces over which neither they nor their parents nor their teachers have any real control.

Individuals differ too in their sensitivity to language. For some, language is always a rather embarrassing problem. They steadily make boners, saying the right thing in the wrong place or the wrong way. They have a hard time fitting in. Others tend to change their language slowly, sticking stoutly to their way of saying things, even though their way differs from that of the majority. Still others adopt new language habits almost automatically, responding quickly to whatever speech environment they encounter.

Indeed some children of five or six have been observed to speak two   15 or more different dialects without much awareness that they are doing so. Most commonly, they will speak in one way at home and in another on the playground. At home they say, "I did very nicely" and "I haven't any"; these become at school, "I done real good" and "I ain't got none."

THE CLASS AS A SPEECH COMMUNITY

Throughout the school years, or at least through the American secondary school, the individual's most important speech community is his age group, his class. Here is where the real power lies. The rule is conformity above all things, and the group uses its power ruthlessly on those who do not conform. Language is one of the chief means by which the school group seeks to establish its entity, and in the high school this is done more or less consciously. The obvious feature is high school slang, picked up from the radio, from other schools, sometimes invented, changing with bewildering speed. Nothing is more satisfactory than to speak today's slang; nothing more futile than to use yesterday's.

There can be few tasks more frustrating than that of the secondary school teacher charged with the responsibility of brushing off and polishing up the speech habits of the younger generation. Efforts to make *real* into *really, ain't* into *am not, I seen him* into *I saw him, he don't* into *he doesn't* meet at best with polite indifference, at worst with mischievous counterattack.

The writer can remember from his own high school days when the class, a crashingly witty bunch, took to pronouncing the word *sure* as *sewer*. "Have you prepared your lesson, Arnold?" Miss Driscoll would ask. "Sewer, Miss Driscoll," Arnold would reply. "I think," said Miss Driscoll, who was pretty quick on her feet too, "that you must mean 'sewerly,' since the construction calls for the adverb not the adjective." We were delighted with the suggestion and went about saying "sewerly" until the very blackboards were nauseated. Miss Driscoll must have wished often that she had left it lay.

CONFRONTING THE ADULT WORLD

When the high school class graduates, the speech community disintegrates as the students fit themselves into new ones. For the first time in the experience of most of the students the speech ways of adult communities begin to exercise real force. For some people the adjustment is a relatively simple one. A boy going to work in a garage may have a good deal of new lingo to pick up, and he may find that the speech that seemed so racy and won such approval in the corridors of Springfield High leaves his more adult associates merely bored. But a normal person will adapt himself without trouble.

For others in other situations settling into new speech communities may be more difficult. The person going into college, into the business world, into scrubbed society may find that he has to think about and work on his speech habits in order not to make a fool of himself too often.   20

College is a particularly complicated problem. Not only does the freshman confront upperclassmen not particularly disposed to find the speech of Springfield High particularly cute, but the adult world, as represented chiefly by the faculty, becomes increasingly more immediate. The problems of success, of earning a living, of marriage, of attaining a satisfactory adult life loom larger, and they all bring language problems with them. Adaptation is necessary, and the student adapts.

The student adapts, but the adult world adapts too. The thousands of boys and girls coming out of the high schools each spring are affected by the speech of the adult communities into which they move, but they also affect that speech. The new pronunciation habits, developing grammatical features, different vocabulary do by no means all give way before the disapproval of elders. Some of them stay. Elders, sometimes to their dismay, find themselves changing their speech habits under the bombardment of those of their juniors. And then of course the juniors eventually become the elders, and there is no one left to disapprove.

THE SPACE DIMENSION

Speech communities are formed by many features besides that of age. Most obvious is geography. Our country was originally settled by people coming from different parts of England. They spoke different dialects to begin with and as a result regional speech differences existed from the start in the different parts of the country. As speakers of other languages came to America and learned English, they left their mark on the speech of the sections in which they settled. With the westward movement, new pioneers streamed out through the mountain passes and down river valleys, taking the different dialects west and modifying them by new mixtures in new environments.

Today we are all more or less conscious of certain dialect differences in our country. We speak of the "southern accent," the "Brooklyn accent," the "New England accent." Until a few years ago it was often said that American English was divided into three dialects: Southern American (south of the Mason-Dixon line); Eastern American (east of the Connecticut River); and Western American. This description suggests certain gross differences all right, but recent research shows that it is a gross oversimplification.

The starting point of American dialects is the original group of colonies. We had a New England settlement, centering in Massachusetts; a Middle Atlantic settlement, centering in Pennsylvania; a southern settlement, centering in Virginia and the Carolinas. These colonies were different in speech to begin with, since the settlers came from different parts of England. Their differences were increased as the colonies lived for a century and a half or so with only thin communication with either Mother England or each other. By the time of the Revolution the dialects were well established. Within each group there were of course subgroups. Richmond speech differed markedly from that of Savannah. But Savannah and Richmond were more like each other than they were like Philadelphia or Boston.

The Western movement began shortly after the Revolution, and dialects followed geography. The New Englanders moved mostly into upper New York State and the Great Lakes region. The Middle Atlantic colonists went down the Shenandoah Valley and eventually into the heart of the Midwest. The southerners opened up Kentucky and Tennessee, later the lower Mississippi Valley, later still Texas and much of the Southwest. Thus new speech communities were formed, related to the old ones of the seaboard, but each developing new characteristics as lines of settlement crossed.

New complications were added before and after the Revolution by the great waves of immigration of people from countries other than England: Swedes in Delaware, Dutch in New York, Germans and Scots-Irish in Pennsylvania, Irish in New England, Poles and Greeks and Italians and Portuguese. The bringing in of black slaves had an important effect on the speech of the South and later on the whole country. The Spanish in California and the Southwest added their mark. In [the twentieth and twenty-first centuries], movement of peoples goes on: the trek of southern blacks to northern and western cities, the migration of people from Arkansas, Oklahoma, and Texas to California. All these have shaped and are shaping American speech.

We speak of America as the melting pot, but the speech communities of this continent are very far from having melted into one. Linguists today can trace very clearly the movements of the early settlers in the still-living speech of their descendants. They can follow an eighteenth century speech community west, showing how it crossed this pass and followed that river, threw out an offshoot here, left a pocket there, merged with another group, halted, split, moved on once more. If all other historical evidence were destroyed, the history of the country could still be reconstructed from the speech of modern America.

SOCIAL DIFFERENCES

The third great shaper of speech communities is social class. This has been, and is, more important in England than in America. In England, class differences have often been more prominent than those of age or place. If you were the blacksmith's boy, you might know the son of the local baronet, but you didn't speak his language. You spoke the language of your social group, and he that of his, and over the centuries these social dialects remained widely separated.

England in the twentieth century has been much democratized, but the language differences are far from having disappeared. One can still tell much about a person's family, his school background, his general position in life by the way he speaks. Social lines are hard to cross, and language is perhaps the greatest barrier. You may make a million pounds and own several cars and a place in the country, but your vowels and consonants and nouns and verbs and sentence patterns will still proclaim to the world that you're not a part of the upper crust.

In America, of course, social distinctions have never been so sharp as they are in England. We find it somewhat easier to rise in the world, to move into social environments unknown to our parents. This is possible, partly, because speech differences are slighter; conversely, speech differences are slighter because this is possible. But speech differences do exist. If you've spent all your life driving a cab in Philly and, having inherited a fortune, move to San Francisco's Nob Hill, you will find that your language is different, perhaps embarrassingly so, from that of your new acquaintances.

Language differences on the social plane in America are likely to correlate with education or occupation rather than with birth — simply because education and occupation in America do not depend so much on birth as they do in other countries. A child without family connection can get himself educated at Harvard, Yale, or Princeton. In doing so, he acquires the speech habits of the Ivy League and gives up those of his parents.

Exceptions abound. But in general there is a clear difference between the speech habits of the college graduate and those of the high-school graduate. The cab driver does not talk like the Standard Oil executive, the college professor like the carnival pitch man, or an Illinois merchant like a sailor shipping out of New Orleans. New York's Madison Avenue and Third Avenue are only a few blocks apart, but they are widely separated in language. And both are different from Broadway.

It should be added that the whole trend of modern life is to reduce rather than to accentuate these differences. In a country where college education becomes increasingly everybody's chance, where executives and refrigerator salesmen and farmers play golf together, where a college professor may drive a cab in the summertime to keep his family alive, it becomes harder and harder to guess a person's education, income, and social status by the way he talks. But it would be absurd to say that language gives no clue at all.

GOOD AND BAD

Speech communities, then, are formed by many features: age, geography, education, occupation, social position. Young people speak differently from old people, Kansans differently from Virginians, Yale graduates differently from Dannemora graduates. Now let us pose a delicate question: aren't some of these speech communities better than others? That is, isn't better language heard in some than in others?

Well, yes, of course. One speech community is always better than all the rest. This is the group in which one happens to find oneself. The writer would answer unhesitatingly that the noblest, loveliest, purest English is that heard in the Men's Faculty Club of San Jose State College, San Jose, California. He would admit, of course, that the speech of some of the younger members leaves something to be desired; that certain recent immigrants from Harvard, Michigan, and other foreign parts need to work on the laughable oddities lingering in their speech; and that members of certain departments tend to introduce a lot of queer terms that can only be described as jargon. But in general the English of the Faculty Club is ennobling and sweet.

As a practical matter, good English is whatever English is spoken by the group in which one moves contentedly and at ease. To the bum on Main Street in Los Angeles, good English is the language of other L.A. bums. Should he wander onto the campus of UCLA, he would find the talk there unpleasant, confusing, and comical. He might agree, if pressed, that the college man speaks "correctly" and he doesn't. But in his heart he knows better. He wouldn't talk like them college jerks if you paid him.

If you admire the language of other speech communities more than you do your own, the reasonable hypothesis is that you are dissatisfied with the community itself. It is not precisely other speech that attracts you but the people who use this speech. Conversely, if some language strikes you as unpleasant or foolish or rough, it is presumably because the speakers themselves seem so.

To many people, the sentence "Where is he at?" sounds bad. It is bad, they would say, in and of itself. The sounds are bad. But this is very hard to prove, If "Where is he at?" is bad because it has bad sound combinations, then presumably "Where is the cat?" or "Where is my hat?" are just as bad, yet no one thinks them so. Well, then, "Where is he at?" is bad because it uses too many words. One gets the same meaning from "Where is he?" so why add the *at?* True. Then "He going with us?" is a better sentence than "Is he going with us?" You don't really need the *is,* so why put it in?

Certainly there are some features of language to which we can apply   40
the terms *good* and *bad, better* and *worse.* Clarity is usually better than
obscurity; precision is better than vagueness. But these are not often
what we have in mind when we speak of good and bad English. If we like
the speech of upper-class Englishmen, the presumption is that we admire
upper-class Englishmen—their characters, culture, habits of mind. Their
sounds and words simply come to connote the people themselves and
become admirable therefore. If we heard the same sounds and words from
people who were distasteful to us, we would find the speech ugly.

This is not to say that correctness and incorrectness do not exist in
speech. They obviously do, but they are relative to the speech community—
or communities—in which one operates. As a practical matter, correct
speech is that which sounds normal or natural to one's comrades.
Incorrect speech is that which evokes in them discomfort or hostility or
disdain.

THINKING CRITICALLY ABOUT THE READING

1. Why does Roberts begin with a discussion of "the village"? Is he referring
   literally to villages, or does "the village" stand in for something else? What
   does his extended example of "Old Village" and "New Village" (3–5) illustrate? (Glossary: *Beginnings and Endings; Examples*)

2. Roberts writes: "Baby talk is not so much invented by the child as sponsored
   by the parent" (8). Explain what he means by this. What are the most basic,
   and motivational, factors in a child's language learning?

3. When children go to school, they move into an entirely new speech community, where, according to Roberts, their speech is modified "by forces over
   which neither they nor their parents nor their teachers have any real control"
   (13). What are these forces? What are some of the ways in which the new
   speech community asserts itself and establishes its own identity?

4. "We speak of America as the melting pot, but the speech communities of this
   continent are very far from having melted into one" (28), writes Roberts.
   What factors have contributed to, and continue to foster, the multiplicity of
   speech communities across the United States?

5. According to Roberts, the impact in England of social class on shaping speech
   communities differs considerably from the impact of class on speech communities in the United States. What factors contribute to this difference? Do
   you think these differences are as relevant today as Roberts assumed they were
   when he wrote *Understanding English?*

6. Roberts asks the provocative question: "Aren't some of these speech communities better than others?" (35). What do you think he means by this? Is
   he referring to the language of the community, or the community members
   themselves? What kind of value judgments do you think we make about others based on their particular way of speaking?

LANGUAGE IN ACTION

In his 1995 memoir, *Dreams from My Father: A Story of Race and Inheritance*, Senator Barack Obama writes:

I learned to slip back and forth between my black and white worlds, understanding that each possessed its own language and customs and structures of meaning, convinced that with a bit of translation on my part the two worlds would eventually cohere. Still, the feeling that something wasn't quite right stayed with me, a warning that sounded whenever a white girl mentioned in the middle of conversation how much she liked Stevie Wonder or when a woman in the supermarket asked me if I played basketball; or when the school principal told me I was cool. I did like Stevie Wonder, I did love basketball, and I tried my best to be cool at all times. So why did such comments set me on edge?

Why do you think Obama was "set on edge" by the kinds of comments he mentions toward the end of the passage? Can you sympathize with his position? Do you believe that it's possible to make different language communities to which one belongs "eventually cohere"? Why or why not?

WRITING SUGGESTIONS

1. We are often simultaneous members of more than one speech community, especially as we move into young adulthood and are introduced to groups outside of our family. Each of these groups can have its own demands, rules of membership, culture, and identity, to which we must adapt with chameleon-like skill. Write about your own experience moving between or among groups, identifying the most influential groups on your life and what demands were made on you in order to belong. What did you have to do to adapt to each group? How did the groups differ? Were they mutually exclusive, or did they overlap on occasion? Do you consider any one of the groups to be superior to the other, or were they simply equal, but different? If it helps you organize your thinking, make a sketch or a map of your communities. Write an essay in which you discuss what you discover.

2. Roberts writes:

   If you admire the language of other speech communities more than you do your own, the reasonable hypothesis is that you are dissatisfied with the community itself. It is not precisely the other speech that attracts you but the people who use this speech. Conversely, if some language strikes you as unpleasant or foolish or rough, it is presumably because the speakers themselves seem so (38).

   Write an essay that supports or refutes his argument, providing examples from your own experience as evidence.

Whither the Southern Accent?

JEFFREY COLLINS AND KRISTEN WYATT

Jeffrey Collins and Kristen Wyatt are reporters for the Associated Press (AP). Collins, at the Columbia, South Carolina, AP bureau since 2000, teamed up in 2005 with Wyatt, who was at that time reporting from Roswell, Georgia, to write this article about the southern accent. According to Collins, the story was part of a broader series the AP did at that time about myths and realities of the American South. The article asks if the southern accent is, in fact, disappearing. Their answer: "That depends what accent you mean."

WRITING TO DISCOVER: *What associations do you have with southern accents? In your opinion, what does the accent say about the people who have one?*

"Y'all" isn't welcome in Erica Tobolski's class in voice and diction at the University of South Carolina. And forget about "fixin'," as in getting ready to do something, or "pin" when talking about the writing instrument.

Tobolski's class is all about getting rid of accents, mostly southern ones in the heart of the former Confederacy, and replacing them with Standard American Dialect, the uninflected tone of TV news anchors that oozes authority and refinement.

"We sort of avoid talking about class in this country, but clearly class is indicated by how we speak," she said.

"Many come to see me because they want to sound less country," she said. "They say, 'I don't want to lose my accent completely, but I want to be able to minimize it or modify it.'"

That was the case for sophomore Ali Huffstetler, who said she "luuuvs" the slow-paced softness of her upstate South Carolina magnolia mouth but wants to be able to turn it on and off depending on her audience.

"I went to New Hampshire to visit one of my best friends and all they kept saying was, 'Will you please talk, can you just talk for me?'" Huffstetler said. "I felt like a little puppet show."

Across the fast-growing South, accents are under assault, and not just from the modern-day Henry Higginses of academia. There's the flood of transplants from other regions, notions of southern upward mobility that require dropping the drawl, and stereotypes that "y'alls" and "suhs" signal low status or lack of intelligence.

But is the southern accent really disappearing?

That depends what accent you mean. The South, because of its rural, isolated past, boasts a diversity of dialects, from Appalachian twangs in several states to Elizabethan lilts in Virginia to Cajun accents in Louisiana to African-influenced Gullah accents on the coasts of Georgia and South Carolina.

One accent that has been all but wiped out is the slow juleps-in-the- 10 moonlight drawl favored by Hollywood portrayals of the South. To find that so-called plantation accent in most parts of the region nowadays requires a trip to the video store.

"The Rhett-and-Scarlett accent, that is disappearing, no doubt about it," said Bill Kretzschmar, a linguist at the University of Georgia and editor of the American Linguistic Atlas, which tracks speech patterns.

"Blame it on the boll weevil," he said, referring to the cotton pest. "That accent from plantation areas, which was never the whole South, has been in decline for a long time. The economic basis of that culture started going away at the turn of the last century," when the bugs nearly wiped out the South's cotton economy.

Even as the stereotypical southern accent gets rarer, other speech patterns take its place, and they're not any less southern. The Upland South accent, a faster-paced dialect native to the Appalachian mountains, is said to be spreading just as fast as the plantation drawl disappears.

"The one constant about language is, it's always changing," Kretzschmar said. "The southern accent is not going anywhere. But you have all kinds of mixtures and changes."

For a long-term study on whether the southern accent is disappear- 15 ing, University of Georgia linguists went to Roswell, Georgia, an Atlanta suburb that is just the kind of transient place that leads to the death of indigenous dialects. It's packed with strip malls and subdivisions with no cotton patches or peach trees in sight.

"I don't hear it," 21-year-old Roswell native Amanda Locher said of the accent. She's never lived outside the South, but even northern newcomers question her southernness. "People tell me I sound like I'm from up North. To hear a true southern accent, you'd have to go deeper south than here."

Adam Mach, a 25-year-old tire shop worker who moved to the Atlanta suburbs from Lafayette, La., has got a noticeable Louisiana lilt. But he said his accent seldom makes conversation because the area is such a melting pot of newcomers.

"Everybody I meet's not from here," he shrugged.

North Carolina State University linguist Walt Wolfram said it's a misconception among southerners that Yankee newcomers are stamping out traditional speech. More likely, he said, is that newcomers pick up local speech patterns.

"When people move here and don't think they've changed at all, they 20 go home and people say, 'Wow. You've turned southern.' They pick up enough to be identified as southern. So it's still there, still strongly identified with the South," Wolfram said.

But that doesn't mean that population change in the South isn't chipping away at old-timey dialects, especially in cities. Wolfram said the "dearest feature" of the southern accent—the vowel shift where one-syllable words like "air" come out in two syllables, "ay-ah"—is certainly vanishing. Other aspects—such as double-modal constructions like "might could"—are still pervasive.

Kretzschmar, who has recorded Roswell speakers for three years, said his suburban Atlanta studies have backed up his suspicion that the southern accent is morphing along with the urbanizing South.

"It's not really disappearing, but the circumstances of living make it different," he said. "People don't have connections with their neighbors to maintain their way of speech.

"The circumstances of how people get together and talk in the cities have changed; they're not constantly talking to people who talk just like them. But in the South outside the cities, you have a lot of similarities."

Georgia-bred humorist Roy Blount Jr. understands that people with strong southern accents are often perceived as "slow and dimwitted." But he thinks it's "sort of a shame" that people should feel the need to soften or even lose their accents.   25

"My father, who was a surely intelligent man, would say 'cain't.' He wouldn't say 'can't.' And, 'There ain't no way, just there ain't no way.' You don't want to say, 'There isn't any way.' That just spoils the whole thing," Blount said.

"I just think that there's a certain eloquence in southern vernacular that I wouldn't want to lose touch with . . . you ought to sound like where you come from."

But never fear. There are still plenty of professions that thrive on a good southern twang—from preachers to football coaches to a certain breed of courtroom litigators.

And South Carolina's Tobolski, an Indiana native who came south eight years ago, can help there, too. As a private coach she has even taught a politician she wouldn't name how to ratchet up his southern accent to make him appear more folksy before certain crowds—a technique she calls "code switching."

"He didn't want to lose his dialect entirely. He just wanted to be able to adapt."   30

"I don't think that any regional accent is going to be eliminated," she said. "There's still people who want to hang on to how they sound. That's who they are. That's their identity. And that goes from New Jersey to Minnesota to Wyoming to Georgia."

THINKING CRITICALLY ABOUT THE READING

1. Students at the University of South Carolina take a class in voice and diction for a number of reasons. List these reasons. Can you imagine such a class in, say, Boston, Massachusetts, or Brooklyn, New York?

2. Define Standard American Dialect. Where is it spoken and by whom?

3. According to the article, the movie-inspired "Rhett-and-Scarlett accent," referred to by linguists as the "plantation accent" (10), seems to be the rare accent that is, indeed, disappearing. How does the article explain this phenomenon?

4. University of Georgia linguists went to an Atlanta suburb for a long-term study on the southern accent. Why do you think they chose this location? What do their findings tell us about the effect of the "urbanizing South" on the southern accent?

5. What does humorist Roy Blount mean when he says, "You ought to sound like where you come from" (27)? Why do you think he might say this?

6. How would you describe "code switching"? Why would some people—politicians, for example—find the ability to move from accent to accent an advantage?

LANGUAGE IN ACTION

The Cambridge Online Survey of World Englishes (http://www.ling.cam. ac.uk/survey/) is one of several surveys that attempts to document the variety of "Englishes" spoken in different areas of the world. Take the survey, and then look at the results to date. How does your English compare with that of other English speakers? Do you seem to agree with the majority of speakers on most questions, or is your use of English relatively uncommon? What can you conclude from this?

WRITING SUGGESTIONS

1. Do you "sound like where you come from"? If so, is your accent something you are proud of or something you would rather not have? If not, do you wish you had an accent, or do you consider the lack of one an advantage? Write an essay in which you explain your position.

2. What would be lost in a country without accents? What would be gained? If you could wave a wand and make every person in the United States a speaker of Standard American Dialect, would you? Think for a moment about which position seems intuitively "right" to you—and then see how compelling an argument you can make for its opposite.

Mute in an English-Only World

CHANG-RAE LEE

Chang-Rae Lee was born in Korea in 1965 and immigrated to the United States with his family when he was three. A graduate of Yale University, Lee received his MFA degree from the University of Oregon and, by age twenty-nine, had published his first novel, *Native Speaker,* which garnered critical acclaim and numerous awards, including the Hemingway Foundation/PEN Award. *Native Speaker* addresses Lee's fascination with the cultural outsider, as do his subsequent novels, *GestureLife* (2000) and *Aloft* (2004). His fourth novel, *The Surrendered,* will be published by Penguin Group (USA) in 2009. Lee is currently a professor of creative writing and director of the Creative Writing Program at Princeton University. In his faculty profile for the Creative Writing Program's Web site, Lee writes of his novels, "The characters may not always be Asian Americans, but they will always be people who are thinking about the culture and how they fit or don't fit into it."

In a 2004 profile in the *New York Times Book Review,* Lee reveals that a character in *Native Speaker* was based on his mother, whose character fascinated him "because of the way she was so outside of things—you know, the great divide between her private human personality and the expression of it in public. I was always impressed by how interesting and smart, and sometimes even aggressive, she could be, but it was always in Korean. She was never that person in English." In "Mute in an English-Only World," a 1996 *New York Times* op-ed piece prompted by the passing of local signage laws regulating the use of foreign language, Lee portrays his mother directly, writing of her experience as an outsider in an English-only world.

WRITING TO DISCOVER: *Have you ever had the sense of being a stranger, an outsider, unable to express who you really are? What occasioned this "great divide" in your own experience?*

When I read of the troubles in Palisades Park, New Jersey, over the proliferation of Korean-language signs along its main commercial strip, I unexpectedly sympathized with the frustrations, resentments and fears of the longtime residents. They clearly felt alienated and even unwelcome in a vital part of their community. The town, like seven others in New Jersey, has passed laws requiring that half of any commercial sign in a foreign language be in English.

Now I certainly would never tolerate any exclusionary ideas about who could rightfully settle and belong in the town. But having been raised in a Korean immigrant family, I saw every day the exacting price and power of language, especially with my mother, who was an outsider in an English-only world.

In the first years we lived in America, my mother could speak only the most basic English, and she often encountered great difficulty whenever she went out.

We lived in New Rochelle, New York, in the early 70's, and most of the local businesses were run by the descendants of immigrants who, generations ago, had come to the suburbs from New York City. Proudly dotting Main Street and North Avenue were Italian pastry and cheese shops, Jewish tailors and cleaners and Polish and German butchers and bakers. If my mother's marketing couldn't wait until the weekend, when my father had free time, she would often hold off until I came home from school to buy the groceries.

Though I was only 6 or 7 years old, she insisted that I go out shop- 5 ping with her and my younger sister. I mostly loathed the task, partly because it meant I couldn't spend the afternoon playing catch with my friends but also because I knew our errands would inevitably lead to an awkward scene, and that I would have to speak up to help my mother.

I was just learning the language myself, but I was a quick study, as children are with new tongues. I had spent kindergarten in almost complete silence, hearing only the high nasality of my teacher and comprehending little but the cranky wails and cries of my classmates. But soon, seemingly mere months later, I had already become a terrible ham and mimic, and I would crack up my father with impressions of teachers, his friends and even himself. My mother scolded me for aping his speech, and the one time I attempted to make light of hers I rated a roundhouse smack on my bottom.

For her, the English language was not very funny. It usually meant trouble and a good dose of shame, and sometimes real hurt. Although she had a good reading knowledge of the language from university classes in South Korea, she had never practiced actual conversation. So in America, she used English flashcards and phrase books and watched television with us kids. And she faithfully carried a pocket workbook illustrated with stick-figure people and compound sentences to be filled in.

But none of it seemed to do her much good. Staying mostly at home to care for us, she didn't have many chances to try out sundry words and phrases. When she did, say, at the window of the post office, her readied speech would stall, freeze, sometimes altogether collapse.

One day was unusually harrowing. We ventured downtown in the new Ford Country Squire my father had bought her, an enormous station wagon that seemed as long—and deft—as an ocean liner. We were shopping for a special meal for guests visiting that weekend, and my mother had heard that a particular butcher carried fresh oxtails—which she needed for a traditional soup.

We'd never been inside the shop, but my mother would pause before   10
its window, which was always lined with whole hams, crown roasts and ropes of plump handmade sausages. She greatly esteemed the bounty with her eyes, and my sister and I did also, but despite our desirous cries she'd turn us away and instead buy the packaged links at the Finast supermarket, where she felt comfortable looking them over and could easily spot the price. And, of course, not have to talk.

But that day she was resolved. The butcher store was crowded, and as we stepped inside the door jingled a welcome. No one seemed to notice. We waited for some time, and people who entered after us were now being served. Finally, an old woman nudged my mother and waved a little ticket, which we hadn't taken. We patiently waited again, until one of the beefy men behind the glass display hollered our number.

My mother pulled us forward and began searching the cases, but the oxtails were nowhere to be found. The man, his big arms crossed, sharply said, "Come on, lady, whaddya want?" This unnerved her, and she somehow blurted the Korean word for oxtail, *soggori*.

The butcher looked as if my mother had put something sour in his mouth, and he glanced back at the lighted board and called the next number.

Before I knew it, she had rushed us outside and back in the wagon, which she had double-parked because of the crowd. She was furious, almost vibrating with fear and grief, and I could see she was about to cry.

She wanted to go back inside, but now the driver of the car we were   15
blocking wanted to pull out. She was shooing us away. My mother, who had just earned her driver's license, started furiously working the pedals. But in her haste she must have flooded the engine, for it wouldn't turn over. The driver started honking and then another car began honking as well, and soon it seemed the entire street was shrieking at us.

In the following years, my mother grew steadily more comfortable with English. In Korean, she could be fiery, stern, deeply funny and ironic; in English, just slightly less so. If she was never quite fluent, she gained enough confidence to make herself clearly known to anyone, and particularly to me.

Five years ago, she died of cancer, and some months after we buried her I found myself in the driveway of my father's house, washing her sedan. I liked taking care of her things; it made me feel close to her. While I was cleaning out the glove compartment, I found her pocket English workbook, the one with the silly illustrations. I hadn't seen it in nearly 20 years. The yellowed pages were brittle and dogeared. She had fashioned a plain-paper wrapping for it, and I wondered whether she meant to protect the book or hide it.

I don't doubt that she would have appreciated doing the family shopping on the new Broad Avenue of Palisades Park. But I like to think, too, that she would have understood those who now complain about the Korean-only signs.

I wonder what these same people would have done if they had seen my mother studying her English workbook—or lost in a store. Would they have nodded gently at her? Would they have lent a kind word?

THINKING CRITICALLY ABOUT THE READING

1. Why do you think New Jersey towns passed laws requiring all signs to be at least half in English? What explanation does Lee offer?

2. What strategies did Lee's mother develop to avoid having to speak English? How successful were they?

3. Why was Lee hesitant to go shopping with his mother? What fears did he have? Were they the same as his mother's?

4. Lee describes one particularly disastrous shopping encounter between his mother and a butcher. Describe the dynamic between them and the source of each person's irritation and anger.

5. What were Lee's thoughts when he found his mother's pocket English workbook in its plain-paper wrapping? In your opinion, was the book cover meant to protect the book or hide it? Explain.

6. Lee raises the possibility that we all, at one time or another, can be the alienated outsider looking in as well as the insider looking out. What question—and message—does Lee leave us with at the end of his essay? Why? (Glossary: *Beginnings and Endings*)

LANGUAGE IN ACTION

In an April 9, 1996, article in the *New York Times* called "Debating the Language of Signs," Robert Hanley writes about the Palisades Park, New Jersey, signage laws that Lee refers to in "Mute in an English-Only World":

Hong Gol Kim, owner of Nadri Tour and Travel, says 95 percent of his agency's business comes from Korean customers. So why, he asks, should he have to comply with a local law that requires him to put up a promotional sign with equal-sized letters in both Korean and English?

"The American people in the neighborhood don't come to my office," he said. "If my customers are 50-50—English and Korean—then I'll do a 50-50 sign."

For all his misgivings, he said he will follow the law, but only after he goes to court on May 22 to answer a summons. He said he wants the judge to explain the logic of the law to him.

Palisades Park is one of seven towns clustered near the George Washington Bridge that have responded to a growing Asian presence in their downtowns by imposing regulations on the Asian merchants. Since 1992, all seven towns have enacted laws requiring that half of any foreign-language commercial sign be in English. But the impact has been most noticeable here, where Asian-American merchants now own most of the 144 stores on the milelong commercial strip, Broad Avenue.

Longtime residents grumble that the younger Korean merchants cater only to the growing number of Asian residents despite admonitions from their elders to accept the new sign law and to try to serve everyone in town. Older residents seem wary, resentful and suspicious. Often, they flood the town's building inspector, John Candelmo, with calls complaining about perceived violations of the sign law.

"We have a lot of people in town who police the signs," he said.

The Mayor, Susan Spohn, said there was a need for more tolerance and cultural understanding. "The whole issue for many is—this is America, and signs should be in English," she said. "For a portion of the people—if they had their druthers—they'd have completely English signs. But we don't have a national language."

What is the logic of the law? Do you agree with it? Whose perspective do you find most convincing, as it is expressed in this article—that of the Korean merchants? the longtime non-Korean residents? the mayor?

WRITING SUGGESTIONS

1. In an interview in Brown University's *Daily Herald*, Lee was asked how his background as a Korean American informed his writing. He answered that his experience growing up in the United States in an immigrant family is "essential to my life and to my writing." Think about what informs your own writing. In an essay, list the experiences, people, and events that you consider essential to your own writing, and explain why they are essential.

2. In the same interview with the *Daily Herald*, the word *outsider* came up frequently as Lee talked about his novels. "The books are about the problems of being an outsider, the problems of assimilating. It's all about the kind of complicated engagement that we had as a family, being in a place that didn't really recognize us and didn't really see us and didn't really understand us, but that we wanted to be in." Do you think this "outsider" status could in part explain the interest we have in reading an essay like "Mute in an English-Only World"? Write an essay in which you explain the way(s) that such a vantage point might make writing more complex and/or more compelling.

The Lost Art of the Rant: How the Web Revived a Storied Tradition of Expletive-Laced Tirades

Daniel Seidel

Writer, editor, and translator Daniel Seidel was born in Princeton, New Jersey, in 1979. Since his graduation from Yale with a degree in English literature, his articles have appeared in *New York Runner, Running Times Magazine,* and on *Slate,* where his essay "The Lost Art of the Rant" was first posted on October 30, 2007. Among his translations from Italian is *Obsolete Objects in the Literary Imagination* (2006), by noted literary critic and historian Francesco Orlando.

Asked why he chose "the rant" as the subject of his essay for *Slate,* Seidel answered: "What inspired me to write 'The Lost Art of the Rant' was the idea of approaching a subject that I hadn't really seen written about, or that was often dismissed contemptuously as a sign of how the Internet is destroying modern civilization. I'm sure everyone, whether they like to admit it or not, has been entertained at some point by a well-executed rant, so I wanted to ask some basic questions: What is a rant, and What makes a good one?"

Writing to Discover: *Have you ever ranted verbally or in writing? If so, what was it about? For you, what makes a "good" rant?*

When Joe Torre recently decided not to accept the New York Yankees' offer of a one-year contract, Buster Olney, a baseball writer for ESPN, argued that only one person—Yankees reliever Mariano Rivera—had been more valuable than the former manager during the team's string of World Series wins. The next day, a response to Olney's piece appeared on fire-joemorgan.com, a site "where bad sports journalism comes to die." It read:

> Seriously, when Derek Jeter retires, are you really going to write that, hey, Jetes was a pretty sweet shortstop, but he was no Joe Torre when it comes to winning baseball games? If you had a crazy combo draft of players and managers in 2001, are you really taking Torre over Derek F____ing Fitzgerald Jeter, God of Baseball and Winner of life?

It went on from there. Throughout, the response was humorous, knowledgeable, a little angry, a little tongue-in-cheek, and sprinkled with expletives. It was, in short, a rant.

It was a particular kind of rant, however; a relatively new breed of an old beast. While there are many examples of literary rants—think of Dostoyesvky's *Notes From the Underground,* Beckett's crazed, starkly beautiful monologues, or Roth's eloquent diatribes—ranting used to be primarily an oral tradition, perfected in taverns and street corners and smoke-filled comedy clubs. The *Oxford English Dictionary* defines a rant as a "high-flown, extravagant, or bombastic speech or utterance; a piece of turgid declamation; a tirade." Merriam-Webster offers a drier and tamer definition—"to talk in a noisy, excited, or declamatory manner"—but also emphasizes the medium of speech.

Some of the first rants of the modern era—at least some of the first to be referred to as such—were associated with a short-lived, 17th-century English sect known (to their enemies) as the "Ranters." Its members' penchant for tobacco, alcohol, women, and swearing sprung from a belief in the divinity of all things and a rejection of the idea of sin altogether. They were frequently accused of blasphemy and of profaning religious rituals. A Ranter preacher, Abiezer Coppe, once swore for an entire hour while standing at the pulpit. Richard Baxter, a Puritan divine, recounted with horror the power that such "hideous words of Blasphemy" could have: "[A] Matron of great Note for Godliness and Sobriety, being perverted by them, turned so shameless a Whore, that she was Carted in the streets of London."

Oral tirades are still with us, of course, even if they're no longer as likely   5
to turn our matrons into whores. Yet the last decade or so has also seen more and more written rants, a form that has blossomed on the Web. The Web is often rightly criticized by the guardians of high culture for encouraging bilious discourse and sloppy writing, with cruel message-board postings and bloggers attacking one another at the slightest provocation. But in this new golden age of the rant, when the Web allows anyone to lash out about anything at all, it would be foolish to dismiss the more artful and entertaining instances of the genre with the artless ones.

Consider the following example from the "best-of-craigslist," which gathers some of the more outrageous postings from the site (not all of which advertise used furniture or extra concert tickets). In "NYC Subway Rant: Jesus Christ!," an anonymous author lists the "mental rolodex of the people I share the subway with on a daily basis . . . the monsters I can't get used to and won't accept." The list includes guys who wear sunglasses, the jerk who leans into you to look at the subway map, the "ghostfarter," and the lady that hugs the pole on a crowded train. All of these monsters have committed various sins against the cardinal law of riding the subway: Don't make it any more miserable than it already is.

A good rant, like this one, expresses a real passion, and it is often a passion that has been enflamed by a feeling of powerlessness. If the subway ranter had been able to "take a free shot [at the] gut" of the nail-clipping businessman (whose "nail shrapnel is flying every which way"), there would have been no need for the rant in the first place.

Such powerlessness can explode into violent language, but the rant also tends to possess a playful element as well. Take another Craigslist posting set on the subway, "to the girl on the metro with the cleavage." In this case, the author is trying to explain to a woman why he was looking at her cleavage. He points out that she shouldn't have worn that revealing top if she didn't want him staring at her chest. It eventually concludes: "So anyway, I just thought you should know my point of view on what happened. I am not a pervert. I was just a man on a metro, a man who saw something that pulled his mind out of the daily routine, and I held onto it dearly."

This protest of innocence—"I am not a pervert"—challenges one of the stereotypes of the cyber-addict whose perversions have finally found free rein on the anarchic Web. Indeed, it's not so much specialized perversions but rather quirky and unlikely subjects that people tend to rant about online. At rant.com, you can search the archives of *Rant* magazine and read some high-octane thoughts on dental hygienists and skunks. In a slightly more rarefied and ironic vein, the McSweeney's Web site publishes "Open Letters" to, among other things: "American Express"; "the intestinal parasites I managed to pick up in West Africa this summer"; "my sister's psychotic dogs"; "my lost bikini bra"; "the Amazon parrot I have been supporting for over 15 years who still tries to bite me for no apparent reason"; and "the birds nesting in my air conditioner."

Despite their evident passion, most of these letters have not   10
simply been dashed off in the heat of the moment but have been crafted to harmonize outrage with decorum, anger with artfulness: "I think you may have noticed my affection for other animals—including my own dog—and wrongly assumed that it extended to your snarling demented selves." Or: "While I am pleased that you have decided the air conditioner in my bedroom is the perfect place for you to reside, I feel obligated to voice a few concerns on behalf of the other inhabitants of our apartment. Please do not take this letter as a sign of ill will." These softer-edged letters may not seem to be rants at all, but they are merely embracing a frequently overlooked sense of the word—"a boisterous, riotous frolic or merry-making."

But wherever a rant may fall on this wide spectrum, there is neither the expectation of nor the desire for a response. The rant is an end in itself, an adrenaline-fueled literary catharsis. That's the paradox at the heart of ranting—its theatricality usually overwhelms all else, including the desire to change whatever outrage has elicited the rant in the first place.

It would be simplistic to think of blogging as a kind of sublimated ranting, since many blogs are earnestly committed to their subjects, and still more could not be accused of sublimating anything. But blogs do form a part of our cacophonous culture, one in which high-flown and bombastic speech flourishes. Far from deploring these noisy tirades indiscriminately, we should embrace their more skillful and playful practitioners, who are developing an entertaining variation on an old form and helping to put dental hygienists, skunks, and American Express in their places.

THINKING CRITICALLY ABOUT THE READING

1. Why do you think Seidel begins his essay with an example drawn from the world of sports? Are discussions of sports particularly prone to becoming rants? (Glossary: *Beginnings and Endings*)

2. The subhead *Slate* used to describe Seidel's essay is "How the Web Revived a Storied Tradition of Expletive-Laced Tirades." Describe some of the traditions Seidel mentions that were precursors of today's cyber-rants. What role has the Internet played in turning this oral form into a written one?

3. Seidel writes, "The Web is often rightly criticized by the guardians of high culture for encouraging bilious discourse and sloppy writing" (5). Do you agree with the "guardians of high culture" (and with Seidel, in this instance)? Would there likely be less "bilious discourse and sloppy writing" if the Web didn't exist?

4. According to Seidel, what makes a written rant "artful" or "good"?

5. Seidel writes that wherever a rant may fall on the broad spectrum he describes, "there is neither the expectation of nor the desire for a response" (11). If the written rant isn't meant to invite a response, what it is it for?

6. Discuss the ways in which Seidel's essay is, in a sense, itself a rant—a rant against "deploring . . . noisy tirades indiscriminately" (12). What is Seidel asking readers to embrace?

LANGUAGE IN ACTION

Look online for Craigslist's "Best of" page (http://www.craigslist.org/about/best/all) and search on "rant." Read one of the rants that looks interesting from its subject line (e.g., "Person with a wooden leg that lives above me"). Does the rant you chose conform to the definitions Seidel supplies for "rant" from the *Oxford English Dictionary* and Merriam-Webster? Does it meet the criteria Seidel supplies for a "good rant"? Why or why not?

WRITING SUGGESTIONS

1. If you've never written a rant, now is your chance. Write your own "open letter" about something or someone who has annoyed, insulted, or in some way irritated you in the past week. Once you have written your rant, sit back and describe how you feel about it.

2. Seidel writes that a good rant expresses real passion, yet it is a passion "that has been enflamed by a feeling of powerlessness" (7). What do you think he means by this? Explain in a short essay what you think the connection might be between powerlessness and rants. Also consider: What is the distinction between a rant and other passionate speech—even hate speech? In your essay about powerlessness/passion, consider integrating discussion of the more virulent "expressions of passion" described by Andrew Sullivan in "What's So Bad about Hate?" (pp. 247–261).

I Think, Therefore IM

JENNIFER 8. LEE

Jennifer 8. Lee was born in New York City in 1976 to Chinese immigrant parents. As a teenager, Lee gave herself her unusual middle name to bring her good fortune—something that has accompanied her throughout her career. Having grown up in New York City, Lee attended Harvard University, where she studied applied mathematics and economics. Before graduating in 1999, Lee honed her journalism skills with internships at the *Washington Post,* the *Wall Street Journal,* the *Boston Globe,* and *Newsday,* among other publications. A fluent Mandarin speaker, Lee also studied international relations at Beijing University for a year on a Harvard-Yenching fellowship.

Lee began writing for the *New York Times* as a summer intern in 1999. By 2001, she was on staff as a reporter, most recently for the *Times*'s local news blog, City Room. Her first book, *The Fortune Cookie Chronicles: Adventures in the World of Chinese Food,* was published in 2008. Lee's article about the impact of instant messaging on young people, "I Think, Therefore IM," first appeared in the *Times*'s Technology section on September 19, 2002. In it, Lee explores the different responses teachers have to the slow seepage into the classroom of language habits learned in the world of instant messaging.

WRITING TO DISCOVER: *Think about how instant messaging (IM) and its later permutation, text messaging, have affected the way you communicate. Do you find yourself using "IM-speak," consciously or unconsciously, when you write for school? Are there circumstances in which shortcuts have been helpful in your writing process? Explain.*

Each September Jacqueline Harding prepares a classroom presentation on the common writing mistakes she sees in her students' work.

Ms. Harding, an eighth-grade English teacher at Viking Middle School in Guernee, Ill., scribbles the words that have plagued generations of schoolchildren across her whiteboard:

There. Their. They're.

Your. You're.

To. Too. Two.

Its. It's.

This September, she has added a new list: u, r, ur, b4, wuz, cuz, 2.

When she asked her students how many of them used shortcuts like these in their writing, Ms. Harding said she was not surprised when most of them raised their hands. This, after all, is their online lingua franca: English adapted for the spitfire conversational style of Internet instant messaging.

Ms. Harding, who had seen such shortcuts creep into student papers over the last two years, said she gave her students a warning: "If I see this in your assignments, I will take points off."

"Kids should know the difference," said Ms. Harding, who decided to address this issue head-on this year. "They should know where to draw the line between formal writing."

As more and more teenagers socialize online, middle school and high school teachers like Ms. Harding are increasingly seeing a breezy form of Internet English jump from e-mail into schoolwork. To their dismay, teachers say that papers are being written with shortened words, improper capitalization and punctuation, and characters like &, $ and @.

Teachers have deducted points, drawn red circles and tsk-tsked at their classes. Yet the errant forms continue. "It stops being funny after you repeat yourself a couple of times," Ms. Harding said.

But teenagers, whose social life can rely as much these days on text communication as the spoken word, say that they use instant-messaging shorthand without thinking about it. They write to one another as much as they write in school, or more.

"You are so used to abbreviating things, you just start doing it unconsciously on schoolwork and reports and other things," said Eve Brecker, 15, a student at Montclair High School in New Jersey.

Ms. Brecker once handed in a midterm exam riddled with instant-messaging shorthand. "I had an hour to write an essay on *Romeo and Juliet*," she said. "I just wanted to finish before my time was up. I was writing fast and carelessly. I spelled 'you' 'u.'" She got a C.

Even terms that cannot be expressed verbally are making their way into papers. Melanie Weaver was stunned by some of the term papers she received from a 10th-grade class she recently taught as part of an internship. "They would be trying to make a point in a paper, they would put a smiley face in the end," said Ms. Weaver, who leaches at Alvernia College in Reading, PA. "If they were presenting an argument and they needed to present an opposite view, they would put a frown."

As Trisha Fogarty, a sixth-grade teacher at Houlton Southside School in Houlton, Maine, puts it, today's students are "Generation Text."

Almost 60 percent of the online population under age 17 uses instant messaging, according to Nielsen/NetRatings. In addition to cellphone text messaging, Weblogs and e-mail, it has become a popular means of flirting, setting up dates, asking for help with homework and keeping in contact with distant friends. The abbreviations are a natural outgrowth of this rapid-fire style of communication.

"They have a social life that centers around typed communication," said Judith S. Donath, a professor at the Massachusetts Institute of Technology's Media Lab who has studied electronic communication. "They have a writing style that has been nurtured in a teenage social milieu."

Some teachers see the creeping abbreviations as part of a continu- 15
ing assault of technology on formal written English. Others take it more
lightly, saying that it is just part of the larger arc of language evolution.

"To them it's not wrong," said Ms. Harding, who is 28. "It's acceptable because it's in their culture. It's hard enough to teach them the art of
formal writing. Now we've got to overcome this new instant-messaging
language."

Ms. Harding noted that in some cases the shorthand isn't even shorter.
"I understand 'cuz,' but what's with the 'wuz'? It's the same amount of
letters as 'was,' so what's the point?" she said.

Deborah Bova, who teaches eighth-grade English at Raymond Park
Middle School in Indianapolis, thought her eyesight was failing several
years ago when she saw the sentence "B4 we perform, ppl have 2 practice"
on a student assignment.

"I thought, 'My God, what is this?'" Ms. Bova said. "Have they lost
their minds?"

The student was summoned to the board to translate the sentence 20
into standard English: "Before we perform, people have to practice." She
realized that the students thought she was out of touch. "It was like 'Get
with it, Bova,'" she said. Ms. Bova had a student type up a reference list
of translations for common instant-messaging expressions. She posted a
copy on the bulletin board by her desk and took another one home to use
while grading.

Students are sometimes unrepentant.

"They were astonished when I began to point these things out to
them," said Henry Assetto, a social studies teacher at Twin Valley High
School in Elverson, Pa. "Because I am a history teacher, they did not think
a history teacher would be checking up on their grammar or their spelling," said Mr. Assetto, who has been teaching for 34 years.

But Montana Hodgen, 16, another Montclair student, said she was so
accustomed to instant-messaging abbreviations that she often read right
past them. She proofread a paper last year only to get it returned with the
messaging abbreviations circled in red.

"I was so used to reading what my friends wrote to me on Instant
Messenger that I didn't even realize that there was something wrong," she
said. She said her ability to separate formal and informal English declined
the more she instant messages. "Three years ago, if I had seen that, I
would have been used What is that?'"

The spelling checker doesn't always help either, students say. For one, 25
Microsoft Word's squiggly red spell-check lines don't appear beneath
single letters and numbers such as u, r, c, 2 and 4. Nor do they catch words
which have numbers in them such as "18r" and "b4" by default.

Teenagers have essentially developed an unconscious "accent" in their
typing, Professor Donath said. "They have gotten facile at typing and they
are not paying attention."

Teenagers have long pushed the boundaries of spoken language, introducing words that then become passé with adult adoption. Now teenagers are taking charge and pushing the boundaries of written language. For them, expressions like "oic" (oh I see), "nm" (not much), "jk" (just kidding) "lol" (laughing out loud), "brb" (be right back), and "ttyl" (talk to you later) are as standard as conventional English.

"There is no official English language," said Jesse Sheidlower, the North American editor of the *Oxford English Dictionary*. "Language is spread not because anyone dictates any one thing to happen. The decisions are made by the language and the people who use the language."

Some teachers find the new writing style alarming. "First of all, it's very rude, and it's very careless," said Lois Moran, a middle school English teacher at St. Nicholas school in Jersey City.

"They should be careful to write properly and not to put these little 30 codes in that they are in such a habit of writing to each other," said Ms. Moran, who has lectured her eighth-grade class on such mistakes.

Others say that the instant-messaging style might simply be a fad, something that students will grow out of. Or they see it as an opportunity to teach students about the evolution of language.

"I turn it into a very positive teachable moment for kids in the class," said Erika V. Karrcs, an assistant professor at the University of North Carolina at Chapel Hill who trains student teachers. She shows students how English has evolved since Shakespeare's time. Imagine Langston Hughes's writing in quick texting instead of 'Langston writing,' " she said. "It makes teaching and learning so exciting."

Other teachers encourage students to use messaging shorthand to spark their thinking processes. "When my children are writing first drafts, I don't care how they spell anything, as long as they are writing," said Ms. Fogarty, the sixth-grade teacher from Houlton, Maine. "If this lingo gets their thoughts and ideas onto paper quicker, the more power to them." But during editing and revising, she expects her students to switch to standard English.

Ms. Bova shares the view that instant-messaging language can help free up their creativity. With the help of students, she does not even need the cheat sheet to read the shorthand anymore.

"I think it's a plus," she said. "And I would say that with a + sign." 35

THINKING CRITICALLY ABOUT THE READING

1. The title of this piece is a punning allusion to a famous philosophical declaration made by the seventeenth-century French philosopher René Descartes: "I think, therefore I am." Why might Lee have made such an allusion in her title? (Glossary: *Allusion*)

2. What criticisms do teachers quoted in the article have about the use of instant-messaging shorthand? Do you agree with these criticisms? Explain.

3. Consider the example Melanie Weaver gave of students who used smiley faces and frowns in their papers to signal points they agreed or disagreed with (11). Do you think such usages should be forbidden? Why does Weaver seem to think they should?

4. One teacher seems particularly alarmed at how students "put these little codes in that they are in such a habit of writing to each other" (30). Do you think this teacher might be alarmed about something more than instant-messaging style? In what ways might generational differences between teachers and students, particularly teenagers, play a role in conflicts over language use?

5. Lee presents two sides of the argument about the use of messaging shorthand. What positive outcomes do teachers cite who welcome the use of IM in classroom writing?

6. What does the North American editor of the *Oxford English Dictionary* mean when he says, "There is no official English language" (28). How does this statement relate to what Lee writes about in this article?

LANGUAGE IN ACTION

Below are a few of the emoticons given as examples on Webopedia's "Text Messaging Abbreviations" page (http://www.webopedia.com/quick_ref/textmessageabbreviations.asp):

Icon	Meaning	Icon	Meaning	Icon	Meaning
:)	Standard smile	:-X	Kiss on the lips	:-!	"Foot in mouth"
:-)	With nose	`:-)	One eyebrow raised	:-D	Laughter
>-)	Evil grin	:-&	tongue tied	:*)	Drunk smile
:(	Sad or frown smile	:'-)	Happy Crying	:@	Exclamation "What???"
:-(	Sad with nose	;)	Winking smile	:-0	Yell
:-<	Super sad	I-O	Yawn	%-(	Confused
:P	Sticking tongue out (raspberry)	(:-D	Gossip, blabbermouth	:-----)	Long nose (Liar!)
(((H)))	Hugs	@-}---	Rose	<(-_-)>	Robot

In a small group, discuss whether these symbols are still in current use and accurately described. Whether they are or not, consider: How does it feel to have what's predominantly "youthspeak" explained and described on sites such as this? What's the purpose of doing so? To whom are the explanations offered, and why?

WRITING SUGGESTIONS

1. Many people use symbols in text messaging to express feelings (e.g., : l means, "I am bored"). In your opinion, is there a value in searching for the right words, as opposed to using a conventional symbol such as an emoticon, to express an emotion? Write an essay in which you take a position on the following: Does the use of emoticons enhance expression or does it "dumb it down"?

2. Place yourself in the shoes of a high school science teacher whose students argue that, because it's a science class, writing skillfully and using correct grammar and spelling are not necessary as long as the meaning is conveyed. Write an argument in which you try to explain and inspire the students about the value of good writing skills.

The Pleasures of the Text

CHARLES MCGRATH

Born in 1947 in Boston, Massachusetts, editor and journalist Charles McGrath graduated from Yale University. McGrath served from 1974 until 1997 as deputy editor of *The New Yorker* and subsequently became editor of the *New York Times Book Review,* where he remained for almost a decade. Currently a writer-at-large for the *New York Times,* McGrath wrote "The Pleasures of the Text" for the *New York Times Magazine,* where it was published on January 22, 2006. In it, McGrath reflects on the broader changes he sees—and in part fears—as a result of the proliferation of language habits learned from text messaging.

WRITING TO DISCOVER: *How often do you text message? Under what circumstances do you call and speak to someone instead? Do you think the medium (messaging via cell phone) changes what you say, or just how you say it?*

There used to be an ad on subway cars, next to the ones for bail bondsmen and hemorrhoid creams, that said: "if u cn rd ths u cn gt a gd job & mo pa." The ad was promoting a kind of stenography training that is now extinct, presumably. Who uses stenographers anymore? But the notion that there might be value in easily understood shorthand has proved to be prescient. If u cn rd these days, and, just as important, if your thumbs are nimble enough so that u cn als snd, you can conduct your entire emotional life just by transmitting and receiving messages on the screen of your cellphone. You can flirt there, arrange a date, break up, and—in Malaysia at least—even get a divorce.

Shorthand contractions, along with letter-number homophones ("gr8" and "2moro," for example), emoticons (like the tiresome colon-and-parenthesis smiley face) and acronyms (like the ubiquitous "lol," for "laughing out loud"), constitute the language of text-messaging—or txt msg, to use the term that txt msgrs prefer. Text-messaging is a refinement of computer instant-messaging, which came into vogue five or six years ago. But because the typical cellphone screen can accommodate no more than 160 characters, and because the phone touchpad is far less versatile than the computer keyboard, text-messaging puts an even greater premium on concision. Here, for example, is a text-message version of *Paradise Lost* disseminated by some scholars in England: "Devl kikd outa hevn coz jelus of jesus&strts war. pd'off wiv god so corupts man (md by god) wiv apel. devl stays serpnt 4hole life&man ruind. Woe un2mnkind."

As such messages go, that one is fairly straightforward and unadorned. There is also an entire code book of acronyms and abbreviations, ranging from CWOT (complete waste of time) to DLTBBB (don't let the bedbugs bite). And emoticonography has progressed way beyond the smiley-face stage, and now includes hieroglyphics to indicate drooling, for example (:-) . . .), as well as secrecy (:X), Hitler (/.#( ) and the rose (@{rcub};--). Keep these in mind; we'll need them later.

As with any language, efficiency isn't everything. There's also the issue of style. Among inventive users, and younger ones especially, text-messaging has taken on many of the characteristics of hip-hop, with so much of which it conveniently overlaps—in the substitution of "z" for "s," for example, "a," for "er" and "d" for "th." Like hip-hop, text-messaging is what the scholars call "performative"; it's writing that aspires to the condition of speech. And sometimes when it makes abundant use of emoticons, it strives not for clarity so much as a kind of rebus-like cleverness, in which showing off is part of the point. A text-message version of *Paradise Lost*—or of the prologue, anyway—that tries for a little more shnizzle might go like this: "Sing hvnly mewz dat on d :X mtntp inspyrd dat shephrd hu 1st tot d chozn seed in d begnin hw d hvn n erth @{rcub};— outa chaos."

Not that there is much call for Miltonic messaging these days. To use   5
the scholarly jargon again, text-messaging is "lateral" rather than "pen-etrative," and the medium encourages blandness and even mindlessness. On the Internet there are several Web sites that function as virtual Hallmark stores and offer ready-made text messages of breathtaking banality. There are even ready-made Dear John letters, enabling you to dump someone without actually speaking to him or her. Far from being considered rude, in Britain this has proved to be a particularly popular way of ending a relationship—a little more thoughtful than leaving an e-mail message but not nearly as messy as breaking up in person—and it's also catching on over here.

Compared with the rest of the world, Americans are actually laggards when it comes to text-messaging. This is partly for technical reasons. Because we don't have a single, national phone company, there are several competing and incompatible wireless technologies in use, and at the same time actual voice calls are far cheaper here than in most places, so there is less incentive for texting. But in many developing countries, mobile-phone technology has so far outstripped land-line availability that cellphones are the preferred, and sometimes the only, means of communication, and text messages are cheaper than voice ones. The most avid text-messagers are clustered in Southeast Asia, particularly in Singapore and the Philippines.

There are also cultural reasons for the spread of text-messaging else-where. The Chinese language is particularly well-suited to the telephone keypad, because in Mandarin the names of the numbers are also close to the sounds of certain words; to say "I love you," for example, all you have to do is press 520. (For "drop dead," it's 748.) In China, moreover, many people believe that to leave voice mail is rude, and it's a loss of face to make a call to someone important and have it answered by an underling. Text messages preserve everyone's dignity by eliminating the human voice.

This may be the universal attraction of text-messaging, in fact: it's a kind of avoidance mechanism that preserves the feeling of communication—the immediacy—without, for the most part, the burden of actual intimacy or substance. The great majority of text messages are of the "Hey, how are you, whassup?" variety, and they're sent sometimes when messenger and recipient are within speaking distance of each other—across classrooms, say, or from one row of a stadium to another. They're little electronic waves and nods that, just like real waves and nods, aren't meant to do much more than establish a connection—or disconnection, as the case may be—without getting into specifics.

"We're all wired together" is the collective message, and we'll signal again in a couple of minutes, not to say anything, probably, but just to make sure the lines are still working. The most depressing thing about the communications revolution is that when at last we have succeeded in making it possible for anyone to reach anyone else anywhere and at any time, it turns out that we really don't have much we want to say.

THINKING CRITICALLY ABOUT THE READING

1. McGrath writes of text messaging, "You can flirt there, arrange a date, break up and—in Malaysia at least—even get a divorce" (1). Traditionally, in Malaysia, a husband could divorce his wife by saying "I divorce you" to her three times. In recent years, text messages have been used for the same purpose (though the legitimacy of the practice has been challenged in court). What's the difference between divorcing one's wife via text message and divorcing her by an oral declaration?

2. In what ways does McGrath claim text messaging is similar to hip-hop?

3. What does it mean to say that text messaging is "lateral" rather than "penetrative" (5)? (If you can't tell from the context, look these terms up.) Do you agree with this judgment?

4. Why, according to McGrath, do Americans lag behind the rest of the world when it comes to text messaging? Is this distance significant?

5. What does McGrath mean when he says that for many people one of the most attractive aspects of text messaging is its use as an "avoidance mechanism" (8)? Do you find this aspect of text messaging attractive?

6. What does McGrath consider "the most depressing thing about the communications revolution" (9)? Why does he consider it depressing? Do you agree with this perspective?

LANGUAGE IN ACTION

The "if u cn rd ths" ads that McGrath refers to in his article were for a system of secretarial shorthand called Speedwriting, which is still taught in some places. Take a look at the Speedwriting company's promotional materials at http://www.speedwriting.co.uk/, paying special attention to the free sample lesson on the site. How does Speedwriting compare to the language of text messaging? How are they different?

WRITING SUGGESTIONS

1. McGrath repeats the tongue-in-cheek text-message version of *Paradise Lost* circulated, he says, by English scholars: "'Devl kikd outa hevn coz jelus of jesus&strts war. pd'off wiv god so corupts man (md by god) wiv apel. devl stays serpnt 4hole life&man ruind. Woe un2mnkind.'" This extreme "Cliff Notes" version of the text is meant as a joke, but it suggests a serious problem: What happens when one updates/translates a classic text for a modern audience? What is lost, and what might be gained, in modernizing works such as *The Great Gatsby* (in the movie *G*), *Othello* (in *O*), or Jane Austen's *Emma* (in *Clueless*)? Discuss this question in an essay, using one of these movies or another modern "retelling" of a classic story as your primary example.

2. Though McGrath and Jennifer 8. Lee are a generation apart by birth, and their articles were published less than four years apart (eons in the tech world), they both focus on the impact on language of today's technology-driven shorthand. How do their perspectives on messaging differ? Write an essay in which you compare and contrast their different concerns, and the ways in which their writing reflects those concerns.

You're Wearing *That?*: Understanding Mothers and Daughters in Conversation

DEBORAH TANNEN

Deborah Tannen, professor of linguistics at Georgetown University, was born in 1945 in Brooklyn, New York. Tannen received her B.A. in English from the State University of New York at Binghamton in 1966 and taught English in Greece until 1968. She then earned an M.A. in English litera-ture from Wayne State University in 1970. While pursuing her Ph.D in linguistics at the University of California, Berkeley, she received several prizes for her poetry and short fiction. Her work has appeared in *New York*, *Vogue*, and the *New York Times Magazine.*

As a noted linguist, Tannen has broadened the scope of the discipline by encouraging linguists to move beyond syntax and the history of lan-guage to everyday conversation. In the process, she has brought her ideas out of academia to a wider audience, publishing twenty-one books and over a hundred articles, including five best-selling books on how people's conversations affect relationships: *That's Not What I Meant!* (1986), *You Just Don't Understand* (1990), *Talking from 9 to 5* (1994), *The Argument Culture: Stopping America's War of Words* (1998), and *I Only Say This Because I Love You* (2001).

This essay, first published in the *Washington Post* on January 22, 2006, as "Oh, Mom. Oh, Honey: Why Do You Have to Say *That?*," is based on Tannen's book *You're Wearing* That?: *Understanding Mothers and Daughters in Conversation* (2006). The period in which Tannen was researching and writing this book coincided with the end of her mother's life. According to Tannen, the time she spent with her mother during this period not only intensified their relationship, it also "transformed [her] thinking about mother-daughter relationships."

WRITING TO DISCOVER: *Think about the title of the essay. Did your mother ever manage to stop you in your tracks with the all-too-familiar: "You're wearing that?" If so, what was your response? Think of some other stop-in-your-tracks comments by your parents. How did they make you feel?*

The five years I recently spent researching and writing a book about mothers and daughters also turned out to be the last years of my mother's life. In her late eighties and early nineties, she gradually weakened, and I spent more time with her, caring for her more intimately than I ever had before. This experience—together with her death before I finished writing—transformed my thinking about mother-daughter relationships and the book that ultimately emerged.

All along I had in mind the questions a journalist had asked during an interview about my research. "What is it about mothers and daughters?" she blurted out. "Why are our conversations so complicated, our relationships so fraught?" These questions became more urgent and more personal, as I asked myself: What had made my relationship with my mother so volatile? Why had I often ricocheted between extremes of love and anger? And what had made it possible for my love to swell and my anger to dissipate in the last years of her life?

Though much of what I discovered about mothers and daughters is also true of mothers and sons, fathers and daughters, and fathers and sons, there is a special intensity to the mother-daughter relationship because talk—particularly talk about personal topics—plays a larger and more complex role in girls' and women's social lives than in boys' and men's. For girls and women, talk is the glue that holds a relationship together—and the explosive that can blow it apart. That's why you can think you're having a perfectly amiable chat, then suddenly find yourself wounded by the shrapnel from an exploded conversation.

Daughters often object to remarks that would seem harmless to outsiders, like this one described by a student of mine, Kathryn Ann Harrison:

"Are you going to quarter those tomatoes?" her mother asked as   5
Kathryn was preparing a salad. Stiffening, Kathryn replied, "Well, I was. Is that wrong?"

"No, no," her mother replied. "It's just that personally, I would slice them." Kathryn said tersely, "Fine." But as she sliced the tomatoes, she thought, can't I do *anything* without my mother letting me know she thinks I should do it some other way?

I'm willing to wager that Kathryn's mother thought she had merely asked a question about a tomato. But Kathryn bristled because she heard the implication, "You don't know what you're doing. I know better."

I'm a linguist. I study how people talk to each other, and how the ways we talk affect our relationships. My books are filled with examples of conversations that I record or recall or that others record for me or report to me. For each example, I begin by explaining the perspective that I understand immediately because I share it: in mother-daughter talk, the daughter's, because I'm a daughter but not a mother. Then I figure out the logic of the other's perspective. Writing this book forced me to look at conversations from my mother's point of view.

I interviewed dozens of women of varied geographic, racial, and cultural backgrounds, and I had informal conversations or e-mail exchanges with countless others. The complaint I heard most often from daughters was, "My mother is always criticizing me." The corresponding complaint from mothers was, "I can't open my mouth. She takes everything as criticism." Both are right, but each sees only her perspective.

One daughter said, for example, "My mother's eyesight is failing,   10
but she can still spot a pimple from across the room." Her mother
doesn't realize that her comments—and her scrutiny—make the pimple
bigger.

Mothers subject their daughters to a level of scrutiny people usually
reserve for themselves. A mother's gaze is like a magnifying glass held
between the sun's rays and kindling. It concentrates the rays of imperfection on her daughter's yearning for approval. The result can be a
conflagration—*whoosh*.

This I knew: Because a mother's opinion matters so much, she has
enormous power. Her smallest comment—or no comment at all, just a
look—can fill a daughter with hurt and consequently anger. But this I
learned: Mothers, who have spent decades watching out for their children,
often persist in commenting because they can't get their adult children to
do what is (they believe) obviously right. Where the daughter sees power,
the mother feels powerless. Daughters and mothers, I found, both overestimate the other's power—and underestimate their own.

The power that mothers and daughters hold over each other derives,
in part, from their closeness. Every relationship requires a search for the
right balance of closeness and distance, but the struggle is especially intense
between mothers and daughters. Just about every woman I spoke to used
the word "close," as in "We're very close" or "We're not as close as I'd
like (or she'd like) to be."

In addition to the closeness/distance yardstick—and inextricable
from it—is a yardstick that measures sameness and difference. Mothers
and daughters search for themselves in the other as if hunting for treasure,
as if finding sameness affirms who they are. This can be pleasant: After her
mother's death, one woman noticed that she wipes down the sink, cuts
an onion and holds a knife just as her mother used to do. She found this
comforting because it meant her mother was still with her.

Sameness, however, can also make us cringe. One mother thought she   15
was being particularly supportive when she assured her daughter, "I know
what you mean," and described a matching experience of her own. But
one day her daughter cut her off: "Stop saying you know because you've
had the same experience. You don't know. This is my experience. The
world is different now." She felt her mother was denying the uniqueness
of her experience—offering *too* much sameness.

"I sound just like my mother" is usually said with distaste—as is the
wry observation, "Mirror mirror on the wall, I am my mother after all."

When visiting my parents a few years ago, I was sitting across from my
mother when she asked, "Do you like your hair long?"

I laughed, and she asked what was funny. I explained that in my
research, I had come across many examples of mothers who criticize their

daughters' hair. "I wasn't criticizing," she said, looking hurt. I let the matter drop. A little later, I asked, "Mom, what do you think of my hair?" Without hesitation, she said, "I think it's a little too long."

Hair is one of what I call the Big Three that mothers and daughters critique (the other two are clothing and weight). Many women I talked to, on hearing the topic of my book, immediately retrieved offending remarks that they had archived, such as, "I'm so glad you're not wearing your hair in that frumpy way anymore"; another had asked, "You did that to your hair on purpose?" Yet another told her daughter, after seeing her on television at an important presidential event, "You needed a haircut."

I would never walk up to a stranger and say, "I think you'd look better if you got your hair out of your eyes," but her mother might feel entitled, if not obligated, to say it, knowing that women are judged by appearance—and that mothers are judged by their daughters' appearance, because daughters represent their mothers to the world. Women must choose hairstyles, like styles of dress, from such a wide range of options, it's inevitable that others—mothers included—will think their choices could be improved. Ironically, mothers are more likely to notice and mention flaws, and their comments are more likely to wound.

But it works both ways. As one mother put it, "My daughters can turn my day black in a millisecond." For one thing, daughters often treat their mothers more callously than they would anyone else. For example, a daughter invited her mother to join a dinner party because a guest had bowed out. But when the guest's plans changed again at the last minute, her daughter simply uninvited her mother. To the daughter, her mother was both readily available and expendable.

There's another way that a mother can be a lightning rod in the storm of family emotions. Many mothers told me that they can sense and absorb their daughters' emotions instantly ("If she feels down, I feel down") and that their daughters can sense theirs. Most told me this to illustrate the closeness they cherish. But daughters sometimes resent the expectation that they have this sixth sense—and act on it.

For example, a woman was driving her mother to the airport following a visit, when her mother said petulantly, "I had to carry my own suitcase to the car." The daughter asked, "Why didn't you tell me your luggage was ready?" Her mother replied, "You knew I was getting ready." If closeness requires you to hear—and obey—something that wasn't even said, it's not surprising that a daughter might crave more distance.

Daughters want their mothers to see and value what they value in themselves; that's why a question that would be harmless in one context can be hurtful in another. For example, a woman said that she told her mother of a successful presentation she had made, and her mother asked, "What did you wear?" The woman exclaimed, in exasperation, "Who cares what I wore?!" In fact, the woman cared. She had given a lot of thought to selecting the right outfit. But her mother's focus on

20

clothing—rather than the content of her talk—seemed to undercut her professional achievement.

Some mothers are ambivalent about their daughters' success because it creates distance: A daughter may take a path her mother can't follow. And mothers can envy daughters who have taken paths their mothers would have liked to take, if given the chance. On the other hand, a mother may seem to devalue her daughter's choices simply because she doesn't understand the life her daughter chose. I think that was the case with my mother and me.

My mother visited me shortly after I had taken a teaching position at Georgetown University, and I was eager to show her my new home and new life. She had disapproved of me during my rebellious youth, and had been distraught when my first marriage ended six years before. Now I was a professor; clearly I had turned out all right. I was sure she'd be proud of me—and she was. When I showed her my office with my name on the door and my publications on the shelf, she seemed pleased and approving.

Then she asked, "Do you think you would have accomplished all this if you had stayed married?" "Absolutely not," I said. "If I'd stayed married, I wouldn't have gone to grad school to get my Ph.D."

"Well," she replied, "if you'd stayed married you wouldn't have had to." Ouch. With her casual remark, my mother had reduced all I had accomplished to the consolation prize.

I have told this story many times, knowing I could count on listeners to gasp at this proof that my mother belittled my achievements. But now I think she was simply reflecting the world she had grown up in, where there was one and only one measure by which women were judged successful or pitiable: marriage. She probably didn't know what to make of my life, which was so different from any she could have imagined for herself. I don't think she intended to denigrate what I had done and become, but the lens through which she viewed the world could not encompass the one I had chosen. Reframing how I look at it takes the sting out of this memory.

Reframing is often key to dissipating anger. One woman found that this technique could transform holiday visits from painful to pleasurable. For example, while visiting, she showed her mother a new purchase: two pairs of socks, one black and one navy. The next day she wore one pair, and her mother asked, "Are you sure you're not wearing one of each color?" In the past, her mother's question would have set her off, as she wondered, "What kind of incompetent do you think I am?" This time she focused on the caring: Who else would worry about the color of her socks? Looked at this way, the question was touching.

If a daughter can recognize that seeming criticism truly expresses concern, a mother can acknowledge that concern truly implies criticism—and bite her tongue. A woman who told me that this worked for her gave me an example: One day her daughter announced, "I joined Weight Watchers and already lost two pounds." In the past, the mother would have said, "That's great" and added, "You have to keep it up." This time she replied, "That's great"—and stopped there.

Years ago, I was surprised when my mother told me, after I began a letter to her "Dearest Mom," that she had waited her whole life to hear me say that. I thought this peculiar to her until a young woman named Rachael sent me copies of e-mails she had received from her mother. In one, her mother responded to Rachael's effusive Mother's Day card: "Oh, Rachael!!!!! That was so WONDERFUL!!! It almost made me cry. I've waited 25 years, 3 months and 7 days to hear something like that . . . ."

Helping to care for my mother toward the end of her life, and writing this book at the same time, I came to understand the emotion behind these parallel reactions. Caring about someone as much as you care about yourself, and the critical eye that comes with it, are two strands that cannot be separated. Both engender a passion that makes the mother-daughter relationship perilous—and precious.

THINKING CRITICALLY ABOUT THE READING

1. Much of what Tannen discovered in researching her book on mother-daughter relationships could be applied to mothers and sons, fathers and daughters, and fathers and sons—but there is a "special intensity to the mother-daughter relationship" (3), according to Tannen. What does Tannen think creates that special intensity? What is "the glue that holds a relationship together—and the explosive that can blow it apart" (3)?

2. Tannen records many examples of everyday conversations in her work as a linguist. Explain the process that she goes through to get to a better and broader understanding of each person's perspective in the conversation. Why does Tannen feel it is important to see things from both perspectives?

3. In her countless interviews and contacts with a diverse group of women, what complaint does Tannen report that she heard most often? Does this surprise you? Why or why not?

4. Tannen writes: "Where the daughter sees power, the mother feels powerless. Daughters and mothers, I found, both overestimate the other's power—and underestimate their own" (12). What does she mean by this? How does power affect the relationships between mothers and daughters?

5. Tannen refers to a technique she uses to change a memory, conflicting view, or incident between mother and daughter from painful to pleasurable. How does she do this? How did she come to terms with her own mother's apparent disappointment at her life choices?

6. Tannen concludes her essay by talking about "two strands that cannot be separated. Both engender a passion that makes the mother-daughter relationship perilous—and precious." What is she referring to here?

LANGUAGE IN ACTION

Do you feel the scenarios related by Tannen apply only to mothers and daughters? List instances of miscommunication or miscues within your own family that parallel Tannen's examples. Compare them with those of others in a small group. Does the mother-daughter relationship seem unique to you, as Tannen claims it is?

WRITING SUGGESTIONS

1. Tannen believes strongly that linguists can use their study and scientific analysis of language to help solve communications problems in the real world: "If a daughter can recognize that seeming criticism truly expresses concern, a mother can acknowledge that concern truly implies criticism—and bite her tongue" (31). Think about your own relationship with a parent of either sex. Do the solutions Tannen suggests seem applicable? Do you think they would work? In a short essay, explain why or why not.

2. Reread Paul Roberts's "Speech Communities" (pp. 323–331) and consider how Roberts's thinking in that essay might be applied to the specific mother-daughter relationship Tannen discusses. Also, consider what ways Tannen's piece might illuminate Roberts's piece. Write an essay in which you discuss the ways that each essay expands/complicates a view of how "language gaps" arise.

He and She: What's the Real Difference?

CLIVE THOMPSON

Clive Thompson was born in 1968 in Toronto, Canada, and received a B.A. in political science and English from the University of Toronto in 1987. He began his career writing about politics, but due to his lifelong interest in computers, switched to writing primarily about science technology. When asked to submit his biography for this book, Thompson wrote the following of this piece: "What interested me about this story was how the scientists used artificial intelligence to examine questions about male and female identity that are as old as the hills. Human philosophy and linguistics has for millennia been limited by the fact that human brains are only good at observing small collections of text at a time; when we try to think about the way language works, we rely on our knowledge of the thousands of books and articles we've read in our lifetime. But computers are able to scan millions and billions of pieces of human writing—allowing them to observe patterns that we ourselves would never be able to spot."

In 2002, Thompson began his year as a Knight Science Journalism Fellow at M.I.T. and started his blog, Collision Detection (www. collisioondetection.net). Since then, the blog has grown into a highly regarded and influential source of writing and research on technology and culture. Thompson is currently a contributing writer for the *New York Times Magazine* and a columnist for *Wired* magazine. He writes about gaming and technology for *Slate* and contributes regularly to *Discover, Fast Company,* and *New York* magazine, among others. This essay originally appeared in the *Boston Globe* on July 6, 2003.

WRITING TO DISCOVER: *Think about what we can learn about the author of a piece of writing aside from what the author tells us directly. Can you tell what a writer is like as a person, a writer's age, or if the writer is a male or female from the style of the writing? Explain how you came to your conclusions.*

Imagine, for a second, that no [author's name] is attached to this article. Judging by the words alone, can you figure out if I am a man or a woman?

Moshe Koppel can. This summer, a group of computer scientists—including Koppel, a professor at Israeli's Bar-Ilan University—are publishing two papers in which they describe the successful results of a gender-detection experiment. The scholars have developed a computer algorithm that can examine an anonymous text and determine, with accuracy rates of better than 80 percent, whether the author is male or female. For centuries, linguists and cultural pundits have argued heatedly about whether men and women communicate differently. But Koppel's group is the first to create an actual prediction machine.

A rather controversial one, too. When the group submitted its first paper to the prestigious journal *Proceedings of the National Academy of Sciences,* the referees rejected it "on ideological grounds," Koppel maintains. "They said, 'Hey, what do you mean? You're trying to make some claim about men and women being different, and we don't know if that's true. That's just the kind of thing that people are saying in order to oppress women!' And I said, 'Hey—I'm just reporting the numbers.'"

When they submitted their papers to other journals, the group made a significant tweak. One of the co-authors, Anat Shimoni, added her middle name "Rachel" to her byline, to make sure reviewers knew one member of the group was female. (The third scientist is a man, Shlomo Argamon.) The papers were accepted by the journals *Literary* and *Linguistic Computing and Text,* and are appearing over the next few months. Koppel says they haven't faced any further accusations of antifeminism.

The odd thing is that the language differences the researchers dis-   5
covered would seem, at first blush, to be rather benign. They pertain not to complex, "important" words, but to the seemingly quotidian parts of speech: the ifs, ands, and buts.

For example, Koppel's group found that the single biggest difference is that women are far more likely than men to use personal pronouns—"I," "you," "she," "myself," or "yourself" and the like. Men, in contrast, are more likely to use determiners—"a," "the," "that," and "these"—as well as cardinal numbers and quantifiers like "more" or "some." As one of the papers published by Koppel's group notes, men are also more likely to use "post-head noun modification with an *of* phrase"—phrases like "garden of roses."

It seems surreal, even spooky, that such seemingly throwaway words would be so revealing of our identity. But text-analysis experts have long relied on these little parts of speech. When you or I write a text, we pay close attention to how we use the main topic–specific words—such as, in this article, the words "computer" and "program" and "gender." But we don't pay much attention to how we employ basic parts of speech, which means we're far more likely to use them in unconscious but revealing patterns. Years ago, Donald Foster, a professor of English at Vassar College, unmasked Joe Klein as the author of the anonymous book *Primary Colors,* partly by paying attention to words like "the" and "and," and to quirks in the use of punctuation. "They're like fingerprints," says Foster.

To divine these subtle patterns, Koppel's team crunched 604 texts taken from the British National Corpus, a collection of 4,124 documents assembled by academics to help study modern language use. Half of the chosen texts were written by men and half by women; they ranged from novels such as Julian Barnes's *Talking It Over* to works of nonfiction (including even some pop ephemera, such as an instant-biography of the singer Kylie Minogue). The scientists removed all the topic-specific words, leaving the non-topic-specific ones behind.

Then they fed the remaining text into an artificial-intelligence sorting algorithm and programmed it to look for elements that were relatively unique to the women's set and the men's set. "The more frequently a word got used in one set, the more weight it got. If the word 'you' got used in the female set very often and not in the male set, you give it a stronger female weighting," Koppel explains.

When the dust settled, the researchers wound up zeroing in on barely   10
50 features that had the most "weight," either male or female. Not a big group, but one with ferocious predictive power: When the scientists ran their test on new documents culled from the British National Corpus, they could predict the gender of the author with over 80 percent accuracy.

It may be unnerving to think that your gender is so obvious, and so dominates your behavior, that others can discover it by doing a simple word-count. But Koppel says the results actually make a sort of intuitive sense. As he points out, if women use personal pronouns more than men, it may be because of the old sociological saw: Women talk about people, men talk about things. Many scholars of gender and language have argued this for years.

"It's not too surprising," agrees Deborah Tannen, a linguist and author of best-sellers such as *You Just Don't Understand: Women and Men in Conversation*. "Because what are [personal] pronouns? They're talking about people. And we know that women write more about people." Also, she notes, women typically write in an "involved" style, trying to forge a more intimate connection with the reader, which leads to even heavier pronoun use. Meanwhile, if men are writing more frequently about things, that would explain why they're prone to using quantity words like "some" or "many." These differences are significant enough that even when Koppel's team analyzed scientific papers—which would seem to be as content-neutral as you can get—they could still spot male and female authors. "It blew my mind," he says.

But this gender-spotting eventually runs into a $64,000 conceptual question: What the heck is gender, anyway? At a basic level, Koppel's group assumes that there are only two different states—you're either male or female. ("Computer scientists love a binary problem," as Koppel jokes.) But some theorists of gender, such as Berkeley's Judith Butler, have argued that this is a false duality. Gender isn't simply innate or biological, the argument goes; it's as much about how you act as what you are.

Tannen once had a group of students analyze articles from men's and women's magazines, trying to see if they could guess which articles had appeared in which class of publication. It wasn't hard. In men's magazines, the sentences were always shorter, and the sentences in women's magazines had more "feeling verbs," which would seem to bolster Koppel's findings. But here's the catch: The actual identity of the author didn't matter. When women wrote for men's magazines, they wrote in the "male" style. "It clearly was performance," Tannen notes. "It didn't matter whether the author was male or female. What mattered was whether the intended audience was male or female."

Critics charge that experiments in gender-prediction don't discover   15
inalienable male/female differences; rather, they help to create and exaggerate such differences. "You find what you're looking for. And that leads to this sneaking suspicion that it's all hardwired, instead of cultural," argues Janet Bing, a linguist at Old Dominion University in Norfolk, Virginia. She adds: "This whole rush to categorization usually works against women." Bing further notes that gays, lesbians, or transgendered people don't fit neatly into simple social definitions of male or female gender. Would Koppel's algorithm work as well if it analyzed a collection of books written mainly by them?

Koppel enthusiastically agrees it's an interesting question—but "we haven't run that experiment, so we don't know." In the end, he's hoping his group's data will keep critics at bay. "I'm just reporting the numbers," he adds, "but you can't be careful enough."

THINKING CRITICALLY ABOUT THE READING

1. Describe the gender-detection experiment performed by computer scientists at Israel's Bar-Ilan University. How was the experiment set up and carried out? What were the results?

2. What were the original concerns of the editors of *Proceedings of the National Academy of Sciences* when the researchers submitted the results of their experiment? How did the researchers respond to the concerns other editors had?

3. What words are women far more likely to use? What words are men more likely to use? Why are the words in both cases rather surprising?

4. Review paragraph 14 and explain how the research that Tannen did with her students extends the findings of the research that Koppel and his associates did. What role does audience play in the kinds of language that writers use? (Glossary: *Audience*)

5. What question(s) are not answered by Koppel's research, according to linguist Janet Bing?

6. Why do you suppose Thompson ends his article with a reiteration of the "I'm just reporting the numbers" quotation that he used earlier in his article? To what does Koppel refer when he's quoted at the end of the article by saying, "but you can't be careful enough"? (Glossary: *Beginnings and Endings*)

LANGUAGE IN ACTION

Using the tips that Thompson says are at the heart of the program developed to detect whether an author is more likely male or female, examine the following passages to see if you can make a calculated guess as to the sex of their authors. Make sure you are able to explain to your instructor or the members of your class why you could or could not make a judgment in each case. (The authors' names are found on p. 368.)

WRITER 1

I was saved from sin when I was going on thirteen. But not really saved. It happened like this. There was a big revival at my Auntie Reed's church. Every night for weeks there had been much preaching, singing, praying, and shouting, and some very hardened sinners had been brought to Christ, and the membership of the church had grown by leaps and bounds. Then just before the revival ended, they held a special meeting for children, "to bring the young lambs to the fold." My aunt spoke of it for days ahead. That night I was escorted to the front row and placed on the mourners' bench with all the other young sinners, who had not yet been brought to Jesus.

My aunt told me that when you were saved you saw a light, and something happened to you inside! And Jesus came into your life! And God was with you from then on! She said you could see and hear and feel Jesus in your soul. I believed her.

WRITER 2

The stealth of autumn catches one unaware. Was that a goldfinch perching in the early September woods, or just the first turning leaf? A red-winged blackbird or a sugar maple closing up shop for the winter? Keen-eyed as leopards, we stand still and squint hard, looking for signs of movement. Early-morning frost sits heavily on the grass, and turns barbed wire into a string of stars. On a distant hill, a small square of yellow appears to be a lighted stage. At last the truth dawns on us: Fall is staggering in, right on schedule, with its baggage of chilly nights, macabre holidays, and spectacular, heart-stoppingly beautiful leaves. Soon the leaves will start cringing on the trees, and roll up in clenched fists before they actually fall off. Dry seedpods will rattle like tiny gourds. But first there will be weeks of gushing color so bright, so pastel, so confettilike, that people will travel up and down the East Coast just to stare at it—a whole season of leaves.

WRITING SUGGESTIONS

1. In paragraph 13, Thompson writes of the research that Koppel's group has done: "But this gender-spotting eventually runs into a $64,000 conceptual question: What the heck is gender, anyway? At a basic level, Koppel's group assumes that there are only two different states—you're either male or female.

('Computer scientists love a binary problem,' as Koppel jokes.) But some theorists of gender, such as Berkeley's Judith Butler, have argued that this is a false duality. Gender isn't simply innate or biological, the argument goes; it's as much how you act as what you are." Write an essay in which you attempt to define the term *gender* using Thompson's essay as well as other sources that you find in your library or on the Internet.

2. If Deborah Tannen is correct, that the most important issue in word choice is the writer's intended audience, then it would seem that audience as a writer's concern is perhaps even more important than we have assumed. We are never sure who will read what we write, but we need to have an audience in mind as we write. Or do we? Is it possible to write for ourselves or for an audience so general that we don't have it clearly in mind? Write an essay in which you examine the concept of audience as it pertains to the writer's craft. Is it as important as writing teachers and theorists think? If so, why? What have writing experts said about audience that is important for us to know? You may find it helpful to read Linda Flower, "Writing for an Audience" (pp. 107–109)

Authors on page 367:

Writer 1: Langston Hughes, "Salvation"

Writer 2: Diane Ackerman, "Why Leaves Turn Color in the Fall"

"Queer" Evolution: Word Goes Mainstream

MARTHA IRVINE

Martha Irvine is a graduate of the University of Michigan and the Columbia Graduate School of Journalism and began her journalism career in 1986. She has worked for publications in Australia, New Zealand, Michigan, Minnesota, and New York. She is now a national writer for the Associated Press and writes stories about issues and trends in popular culture for juveniles and young adults.

"Queer Evolution," an Associated Press article, was first published in a number of newspapers across the country on November 27, 2003. Irvine said the following about how she got the idea for the article: "The 'Queer Evolution' idea came to me after hearing more friends using the word in casual conversation—some of it tied to the television shows *Queer as Folk* and *Queer Eye for the Straight Guy*, though not exclusively so. I was aware that the word is—especially to older generations—difficult to hear, and often considered offensive. But this didn't seem to be the case with younger people, gay or straight. I wanted to see if there was a story there—and indeed, there was."

WRITING TO DISCOVER: *What role does language play when discussing sexual and gender orientations different from your own? Why might it be important for you to be informed about such matters?*

Something queer is happening to the word "queer."

Originally a synonym for "odd" or "unusual," the word evolved into an anti-gay insult in the last century, only to be reclaimed by defiant gay and lesbian activists who chanted: "We're here, we're queer, get used to it."

Now "queer" is sneaking into the mainstream—and taking on a hipster edge as a way to describe any sexual orientation beyond straight.

Jay Edwards, a 28-year-old gay man from Houston, has noticed it.

"Hey Jay," a straight co-worker recently said. "Have you met the new guy? He's really cute and queer, too. Just your type!" 5

It's the kind of exchange that still makes many—gay or straight—wince. That's because, in the 1920s and '30s the word "queer" became synonymous with "pansy," "sissy," and even "pervert," says Gregory Ward, a Northwestern University linguist who teaches a course on language and sexuality.

Now, Ward says, the increasing use of "queer"—as in the prime-time TV show titles *Queer Eye for the Straight Guy* and *Queer as Folk*—is changing the word's image.

"It's really losing the hurtful and quasi-violent nature it had," Ward says.

Trish McDermott, vice president of "romance" at the Match.com online dating service, says she's seeing the word appear more often in personal ads.

The title of one current ad: "Nice Guy for the Queer Guy."   10

Meanwhile, a recent review in the *Chicago Tribune*'s Metromix entertainment guide defined the crowd in a new upscale bar as "model-types and young clubbers amid dressy Trixies, middle-aged Gold Coast cigar-chompers, and queer-eyed straight guys" (the latter term referring to straight men who've spiffed themselves up).

And while some in the gay community began using the word in the last decade or two as an umbrella term for "gay, lesbian, bisexual, and transgendered," today's young people say that "queer" encompasses even more.

"I love it because, in one word, you can refer to the alphabet soup of gay, lesbian, bisexual, questioning, 'heteroflexible,' 'omnisexual,' 'pansexual,' and all of the other shades of difference in that fluid, changing arena of human sexuality," says 27-year-old Stacy Harbaugh. She's the program coordinator for the Indiana Youth Group, a drop-in center in Indianapolis for youth who may place themselves into any of those categories.

"I find myself attracted to boy-like girls and girl-like boys," Harbaugh adds. "If 'lesbian' or 'bi' doesn't seem to fit, 'queer' certainly does."

Heteroflexible? Pansexual? The growing list of terms can be down-   15
right boggling.

James Cross, a 26-year-old Chicagoan, personally likes the term "metrosexual," meant to describe straight men like him who are into designer clothes, love art and fashion, and even enjoy shopping (much like "queer-eyed straight guys").

He's also noticed the word "queer" being bandied about more often, especially at the public relations firm where he works. But he says women are "definitely more comfortable" with it.

"I hate to admit it, but I certainly wear masks with the term. When I'm at work and talking with women, I'm down with it," he says. "But when I'm out on the rugby pitch or drinking beer with my 'bros,' I'm just one of the guys."

Indeed, use of a word that carries so much baggage can cause confusion.

Andy Rohr, a 26-year-old gay man living in Boston, noted that when   20
a straight co-worker told him she liked the show *Queer Eye for the Straight Guy,* she whispered the word 'queer,' he says.

Dan Cordella says he, too, is perplexed about what he "can and can't say."

"An entire generation of suburban youth was taught to practically walk on eggshells with their wording around those that, one, chose an alternative lifestyle and, two, were of a different ethnic background," says Cordella, a 26-year-old straight man who lives in New York and grew up outside Boston.

Ward, the Northwestern linguist, says that people are wise to use "queer" carefully because it is still "very context-sensitive."

"It really matters who says it and why they're saying it," he says.

Edwards, from Houston, says he likes when straight people are com-   25
fortable using it.

"If they can say the word with as much casualness and confidence as my gay friends, it lets me know that they are comfortable with who I am," he says.

Rohr, from Boston, is less sure about its use in everyday conversation but says it works with the *Queer Eye* title because its use is "archaic and unexpected."

"The bottom line is, I think the term has lost its political potency, if it ever had any, and has just become campy," he says.

Others, especially those with strong memories of the word as an insult, still find its use hurtful. "I believe this word continues to marginalize us," says Robin Tyler, a California-based activist and lesbian who's in her sixties.

THINKING CRITICALLY ABOUT THE READING

1. What does the evolution of the word *queer* suggest about the flexibility of the English language? Do other words go through similar evolutions in meaning? Can you think of some examples of such words?

2. Why might the word *queer* show a greater speed of evolution than other words in our vocabulary? Is the word of greater service today than it used to be? If so, why?

3. How are people who live alternative lifestyles reclaiming the word *queer*? What have they done to its earlier meanings?

4. Why does Gregory Ward, the Northwestern University linguist, think that people should still be careful how they use the word *queer*?

5. What does Irvine mean by claiming that *queer* has taken on a "hipster edge" today (3)?

6. Irvine uses a number of sources in reporting on the evolution of *queer*. Why doesn't she just report on what she *thinks* the word means and how she *thinks* it has changed over the years?

LANGUAGE IN ACTION

"Something queer is happening to the word 'queer,'" writes Irvine in opening her essay. What, if anything, has happened to the word since 2003, when Irvine wrote her essay? Go to Google and enter the word *queer*, then do a quick scan of the ways the word is used in context in the first ten hits that are returned. How many of them use the word primarily or exclusively in the sense Irvine describes as "new"? How many incorporate older uses of the word *queer*? What, if anything, can you conclude about the way the use of the word has continued to evolve?

WRITING SUGGESTIONS

1. One of the linguists quoted in the essay urges caution in using the word *queer* because it is "very context-sensitive" (23). What does he mean by this? Are there other words that you feel comfortable using in some situations and not in others? Write an essay describing your own experience with the use of the word *queer*.

2. Do words really have as much power as described in Irvine's article? Write an essay defending or criticizing the use of certain words that have sharply divergent meanings and that in one context might be considered inflammatory, in others complimentary. Explain the difference between the use of a word to defeat its negativity, and the "abuse" of a word as a means of insult. Where does one draw the line? You may find it helpful to read Gloria Naylor's "The Meanings of a Word" (pp. 291–294) before starting to write.

Missing the Nose on Our Face: Pronouns and the Feminist Revolution

JOHN H. MCWHORTER

Linguist, scholar, and cultural critic, John McWhorter was born in Philadelphia in 1965. McWhorter received a masters degree in American studies at New York University, followed by a Ph.D. in linguistics at Stanford University. He taught in the Department of Language and Linguistics at Cornell University before becoming associate professor of linguistics at the University of California, Berkeley. He is currently a Senior Fellow at the Manhattan Institute, where he writes for the Institute's Center for Race and Ethnicity. McWhorter is also a regular columnist for the *New York Sun* and makes frequent guest appearances on television news and discussion programs such as *20/20, All Things Considered,* and *Meet the Press.* His articles on race and cultural issues have appeared in such publications as the *Wall Street Journal,* the *New York Times,* the *Washington Post,* and the *Chronicle of Higher Education.* McWhorter is also the author of numerous books on language, linguistics, and race, including the best-seller *Losing the Race: Self-Sabotage in Black America* (2001); *The Power of Babel: A Natural History of Language* (2002); *Authentically Black: Essays on the Black Silent Majority* (2003); *Winning the Race: Beyond the Crisis in Black America* (2005); and his latest, *All About the Beat: Why Hip-Hop Can't Save Black America* (2008).

In an October 19, 2003, review in the *Washington Post* of McWhorter's *Doing Our Own Thing: The Degradation of Language and Music in America and Why We Should, Like, Care* (2003), Jonathan Yardley describes McWhorter as a "linguist of the modern school" who "believes that language is ever-evolving and that change is neither good nor bad but simply change." According to Yardley, McWhorter's own prose "too often takes a decidedly ungrammatical turn." Clearly, McWhorter practices what he preaches, even in the title of his essay, "Missing the Nose on Our Face," which is a chapter from *Word on the Street: Debunking the Myth of a "Pure" Standard English* (2001). In this essay, McWhorter discusses possible solutions to the sexism inherent in English, a language that "has no pronoun that was originally gender-neutral."

WRITING TO DISCOVER: *How conscious are you of the issue of sexism and gender-neutrality in language? Does it bother you when you hear a sentence like "Somebody left his book here," when the speaker is not sure whether the "somebody" was male or female?*

Here are three sentences of ordinary English:

Ask one of the musicians whether they lost a page of this score.

Somebody left their book here.

If a student asks for an extension, tell them no.

Thoroughly everyday pieces of English, no? And yet as unobjectionable as those mundane little utterances may seem, according to the rules of classroom grammar, they are considered wrong. *To wit,* what we are often told is that the use of *they, them,* or *their* to refer to single persons is a mistake because *they, them* and *their* are plural words.

Yet the question is what singular pronoun we are supposed to use here. Instead of the offending plural pronouns, we have often been told by many official sources that it is better to use *he, him,* or *his*:

Ask one of the musicians whether he lost a page of this score.

Somebody left his book here.

If a student asks for an extension, tell him no.

This, however, does not sit quite right with many of us, especially in light of the profound change in the roles of women in Western societies over the past several decades. Using *he, him* and *his* seems to imply that musicians, students, and, well, somebodies of the world are all men, or at least so often men that the occasional females are just so much static.

In older grammars, pundits often actually came right out and said that men were higher than women in the cosmic order of things, as in an admonition from 1500s to "let us keep a natural order, and set the man before the woman for maners sake," since after all, "the worthier is preferred and set before." Even by the 1700s, however, this was beginning to seem a rather bald thing to put down in black and white (if not to think), and the party line became that *he* was intended as gender-neutral, since English has no pronoun that was originally gender-neutral.

This is nonsense. To decree a pronoun gender-neutral in a book has no effect on how we link language to basic meanings, and for all of us, a sentence like *Somebody left his book here* calls up the image of a boy or man leaving the book. As a matter of fact, applying the sentence to the image of a girl or woman leaving the book seems downright inappropriate because of the obvious male connotation of *he*.

In any case, a bad odor has grown around this gender-neutral feint of late, as the feminist revolution has led a call to eliminate words and expressions from the language that promote the conception that the levers of power in society are the province of men. The commitment that has substituted *police officer* for *policeman* and *chairperson* for *chairman* has led in the pronoun department to a long overdue rethinking of the gender-neural pronoun issue. One of the most popular suggestions has been to use *he or she,* both in speech and in writing. This construction becomes more prevalent with every year:

> Ask one of the musicians whether he or she lost a page of this score.
>
> Somebody left his or her book here.
>
> If a student asks for an extension, tell him or her no.

He or she is founded upon good intentions, but ultimately it will not do. For one thing, the man is still first. Why not *she or he?* But then, two wrongs don't make a right—why should women be first either? If one argues that this would redress millennia of oppression, one might ask how we would decide exactly when the oppression had been redressed, and besides, *then* what would we do?

Moreover, as a look at the above sentences shows, *he or she* is a construction of inherently limited domain. Conscious and forced, it could never go beyond writing and formal speech. There is not a single language out of the over 5,000 on earth in which people spontaneously refer to unisex subjects as "he or she" in conversation, including English. It's one thing to use this in a paper (albeit with that nagging Why-should-men-come-first? problem), lecture, speech, or announcement. However, imagine anyone using *he or she* chewing on a mouthful of pizza while watching a football game on the tube. When we are rattling along in real time in the real world, our concern, while we juggle shopping bags and avoid offending and fix our hair, is the subject we are addressing. A cooked construction like *he or she* is not a piece of spontaneous language, but a statement of allegiance to gender-neutral speech. As laudable as this is, to genuflect to an allegiance to a broad sociopolitical position in the middle of a casual discussion of anything else is no more natural than to genuflect to any number of other noble issues outside of our topic, such as concern with injustice or love of our children. In other words, *he or she* is strictly conscious, whereas spoken language is inherently unconscious, like breathing, or walking without falling. What this means is that if our response to the *they* issue is to decree that *he or she* is the proper form, then while we have applied a Band-Aid to formal speech, we are meanwhile leaving casual speech with the same old *they* that grammarians make us feel guilty about.

One variation on this theme, particularly hip lately, is to switch between *he/him/his* and *she/her/her* in alternate sentences. This one, however, is as hopelessly conscious as *he or she.* Doing this takes a kind of close attention to one's text flow that is virtually impossible outside of writing or careful, planned speech, such as lectures. Once again, there is no language on earth in which people spontaneously alternate their pronouns like this, and there's a reason. This switching also has this disadvantage: Whether spoken or written, each particular use of the male or female pronoun calls up an image of that particular gender, which is both awkward and ends up calling attention to itself instead of to the content of the utterance. To say *he*, especially to audiences familiar with the problems with the gender-neutral fallacy, gives the little jolt of seeming sociologically unsavory; when the speaker or writer corrects this by saying *she* a while later, this usage is distracting as well because after all, women aren't the only ones referred to either. To say *she* first still creates this problem, and even when *he* is used second, it still creates the jolt, especially if the reference to *she* occurred a while ago. In any case, because of the heavy self-monitoring required, this kind of self-conscious alternation is unlikely to ever go beyond a tiny segment of society with a particularly strong interest in demonstrating their commitment to gender-neutral speech.

Of course, some might say that I lack imagination in declaring that *he or she* and the switching are alien to spontaneous speech, and that our goal ought to be to change the very nature of spontaneous speech for the future. I am the last one to dismiss idealism, but there are times when it is best described as quixotic. In that vein, we must ask how realistic it is to imagine, say, children using *he or she* or switching pronouns between sentences. Like *Billy and I went to the store* and *whom*, these devices are the kind of thing only learnable as artificial second layers. They will always flake away with two drinks, laughter, or even simple social comfort.

Then there is *s/he*, which is a complete disaster. This one makes no   10
pretense of being intended for spoken language; it is as unpronounceable as the glyph that the artist formerly known as Prince adopted. Even in writing, however, just look at it—it's too darned ugly to be used as frequently as a pronoun has to be. Imagine great literature splattered with *s/he*'s!

Why are we stuck with all of these awkward little concoctions for written English while condemned to "misusing" *they* in spoken English? The source of the problem here is that there happens to have been no originally singular gender-neutral pronoun in English. Many, many languages do not distinguish between males and females with their third person pronouns. For example, the Finnish pronoun *hän* can refer to either a man or a woman, which is why Finns new to English often mistakenly refer to a woman as *he*. This lack has even led some people to try to work up their own gender-neutral pronoun to bestow on English, but to date, proposals like *hesh, hirm, co, et, E, ho, mon, ne, po*, and *thon* have had distinctly marginal impact on English (yes, people actually have suggested that these be used!). It's not that it's impossible to introduce new words into a language, of course: words like *humongous* and *zillion* do not descend nobly from ancient roots, but were instead made up and somehow hung on. However, around the world, languages are much more resistant to accepting new words, made up or foreign, which are as central to their grammar as pronouns are. It can happen: none other than *they, them*, and *their* were actually taken from Scandinavian after Danes invaded Britain—the originals were the now impossible-looking *hi, heo*, and *hira*. Yet it is still a sometime thing, and even these pronouns entered the language gradually, without any individual commanding that it be so. It is all but impossible for such things to catch on when the introducer is a sole person brandishing a pamphlet.

"The entire question is unlikely to be resolved in the near future" intones the latest edition of the *American Heritage Dictionary*, after a fine capsule summary of the *they/he/she* or *she/s/he* conundrum. The fact is, however, that the issue has been brilliantly resolved for several centuries, if only our grammarians would wake up and realize that language is a lava lamp and not a clockworks. English has long offered a very simple solution that could neatly apply to both casual and formal speech, sail over the problems of whether men or women are to go first, and spare us the drain on the mental battery of parlor tricks like switching between sentences. Notice that in the last paragraph, I said that English has no *originally* singular gender-neutral pronoun. It does, however, have a *presently* singular gender-neutral pronoun, and that is none other than the *they*, which all of us use in this function all of the time despite the frowns of prescriptivists.

We are told that because it is a plural pronoun, *they* must not be used to refer to single persons because it "doesn't make sense." However, the fact is that today, *they* is indeed both a singular and a plural pronoun, as indicated by the fact that all English speakers use it so. *They* is singular as well as plural for the simple reason that the language has changed and made it so. The idea that *they* is only a plural pronoun is an illusion based on the fallacy of treating the English of one thousand years ago as if it was somehow hallowed, rather than just one arbitrary stage of an endless evolution over time.

I say that we know *they* can be singular because people use it that way so regularly, but it is tempting to suppose that English speakers may have just gotten lazy and infected each other with a bad habit. But once again, we gain perspective on this by looking at languages elsewhere. The French pronoun *vous* began as the plural *you*, originally used with people of the highest rank with the implication that they were such awesome personages that they were more like two people, rather like a person today might facetiously refer to themselves as "we" to connote a certain aristocracy. (Note the use of *themselves* in that last sentence—does it really look like a mistake?) Over time, *vous* came to be used to refer to single people as a mark of respect, and gradually percolated down to indicating respect for ordinary people of authority or even just one's elders. Thus today, within the first month of French instruction we learn that single persons are referred to as *vous* when we are conveying respect (*Comment allez-vous?*), and no one in France or elsewhere considers this to "not make sense"—it happened, and it just is.

In the same month we are also taught that "we" is *nous*, as in *Nous prenons du café chaque matin*, "We drink coffee every morning." However, once we get to France, one of the first things we learn about French as it is actually spoken casually is that "we" is usually rendered with the

15

singular gender-neutral pronoun on. *On prend du café chaque matin* has not exclusively meant "one drinks coffee every morning" for centuries, and is so commonly used to mean "we," and not just "in the streets" but even among educated folk, that mastering spoken French usually entails unlearning the *nous* that textbooks emphasize. Again, the claim that this "doesn't make sense" would be meaningless—it wouldn't have eons ago when *on* still only meant "one," but it has long since acquired this new meaning, to no one's objection.

Things are even more far out in Italian, where the polite form of "you" is *lei,* which also means "she"! Thus *lei parla* means both "she speaks" and "you speak." The reason for this is that centuries ago, noble women were addressed as "she," and this percolated down first to women in ordinary society, and then spread even to men! Things are similar even in the plural—to address two people respectfully one uses *loro,* the word which is also used for "they." One would search in vain for any Italian newspaper editorial where someone complained that these usages don't make sense. They wouldn't have made sense 1,500 years ago when these changes had yet to occur, but this is today, when these changes have taken place. These usages create no confusion and thus make perfect sense.

And then we return to English and recall once again that our own *you* began as plural, with *thou* being the original second-person singular form. As we saw, there were once indignant grammarians who decried the use of *you* in the singular as illogical. Today, however, *thou* is now relegated to the Bible and jocular imitations of archaic speech, while *you* is both plural and singular. None of us [has] any sense of singular *you* as in any way wrong or sloppy; and the fact that it used to be a plural word only is something we only learn about in books like this one. In other words, the use of *you* changed over time, and now, whatever its original use happened to be, it has had a new one longer than anyone can now remember.

Language change is ever thus. In the beginning a word has one meaning or use. Then as the meaning or use begins to change, prescriptivist grammarians call the new form sloppy and wrong. This sort of thing cannot stop the language from changing because nothing can. Instead it just creates a situation where people use the new form casually when Aunt Lucy isn't looking but avoid it in formal speech. Eventually, the new form becomes so prevalent that it starts popping up even in formal language (*whole nother*); the grammarians give up and jump on the latest new forms (*Hopefully, she'll come*); and before long no one, grammarian or civilian, even remembers that the now accepted form was even ever considered a problem (singular *you*). The old criticisms, the trees felled to provide the paper on which they were written, and the insecurity they sowed in millions of people—all of it served no more purpose than throwing salt over our shoulder to ward off bad luck.

In this light, our modern grammarians' discomfort with singular *they* is nothing but this comical intermediate stage in an inevitable change, as misguided and futile as the old grumbles about singular *you.* As much as we might like pronouns to stick to their little corners and hone to a perfect model where there is one form for each person/number combination with no overlaps, the fact is that very few languages ever maintain things this way, and if they do, it's by accident. We have to be told by Aunt Lucy that *they* "cannot" refer to one person, and the reason this never occurs to us until we are told is because in Modern English, *they* indeed *can* refer to one person. That's why we use it that way and are understood when we do. We are no more wrong in allowing *they, them,* and *their* to change in this way than the French speakers were who started saying *on prend du café* or the Italians who started calling their monsignors *lei;* or the Middle English speakers who started saying *Charles, you have to do it* instead of *Charles, thou hast to do it;* or the horselike mammals who started developing longer necks on their way to evolving into giraffes. Like life forms, languages are always changing. We would no more expect one to be the way it used to be than we would expect whales to still be bearlike critters bumbling around the seashore. (Yes, this is what whales began as!) Most importantly, language change goes the whole nine yards—nothing in it is exempt, not sounds, not word order, not word meanings, and certainly not good old pronouns.

Thus English has already taken care of the unisex pronoun issue—we   20
don't need *he or she, s/he,* "Look-Ma-I'm-politically-correct" switching, *co, hesh,* or *thon;* because we have *they.* The *they* case is particularly exasperating in that singular *they* has been available to English speakers for several centuries. The only thing keeping us from taking advantage of it has been the power of the prescriptivist hoax, starting with Lowth and Murray's inevitable whacks at it back in the 1700s. The next time someone tells you that *they* must be used only to refer to plural things, ask *them* to explain why it is okay to use *you* in the singular or what's wrong with the sentence *Comment allez-vous, Guillaume?,* and see what *they* come up with.

THINKING CRITICALLY ABOUT THE READING

1. What are some of the problems with the supposedly gender-neutral use of the phrase "he or she"? Why does McWhorter call it a "cooked" construction?

2. How did the masculine *he* become the "gender-neutral" pronoun in the eighteenth century? Why does McWhorter decry this usage?

3. What are the reasons for the feminist attempt to eliminate sexist pronouns from our language?

4. McWhorter talks about the difference between "conscious" language and "unconscious" language, formal speech and casual speech, spoken language and written language. What are the differences? When is one or the other used? Why is one deemed "proper" and the other not?

5. What does McWhorter find so objectionable about the solutions that use the construction *s/he,* or *he/him/his* and *she/her/her* in alternate sentences?

6. McWhorter says that the insistence on limiting the use of the word *they* to its plural meaning is "an illusion based on the fallacy of treating the English of one thousand years ago as if it was somehow hallowed" (13). What does he mean? What does this reveal about his perspective on the evolution of language?

LANGUAGE IN ACTION

How would you remedy the pronoun problems in McWhorter's opening examples of "ordinary English":

Ask one of the musicians whether they lost a page of this score.
Somebody left their book here.
If a student asks for an extension, tell them no.

Try some of the "awkward little constructions" McWhorter refers to. Do they work for you? In your view, do they succeed in purging the sentence of sexism, or do they simply scream: Look how politically correct I am!

WRITING SUGGESTIONS

1. Go to the library or local bookstore and examine some of the many reference books dedicated to English grammar and language usage. Look up "pronouns" in several of the books and compare their rules. Do any of the books address the issues of gender-neutrality and sexism? What reasoning seems to be behind any solutions they might recommend? Write an essay in which you discuss what you find, especially as it relates to the recommendations made by McWhorter in his essay.

2. Think about McWhorter's approach to grammar in general and his willingness, if not delight, in breaking the rules set down by traditional grammarians. Do you think that grammatical rules and regulations can have a positive impact on the language, or do you agree with McWhorter that nothing *can* stop a language from changing, and further, that nothing *should* stop its natural evolution? From your own point of view, defend or criticize McWhorter's approach.

On Language: You Guys

AUDREY BILGER

Born in 1960 in Fairmont, West Virginia, Audrey Bilger earned a Ph.D. in English from the University of Virginia and currently teaches courses in literature and gender studies at Claremont McKenna College. She is the author of *Laughing Feminism: Subversive Comedy in Frances Burney, Maria Edgeworth, and Jane Austen* (1998), and editor of Jane Collier's eighteenth-century satire *An Essay on the Art of Ingeniously Tormenting* (2003). In addition to her work on early women writers, Bilger is a noted feminist whose articles have appeared in the *Paris Review*, the *Los Angeles Times, Women's Review of Books,* and *ROCKRGRL,* a magazine and organization advocating for female artists in the music business. She is a frequent contributor to *Bitch: Feminist Response to Popular Culture,* a magazine devoted to feminist analysis and media criticism, where her essay "On Language: You Guys" first appeared. The essay was later reprinted in *Bitchfest: Ten Years of Cultural Criticism from the Pages of* Bitch *Magazine,* edited by Lisa Jervis and Andi Zeisler.

When Bilger first posted her request on a university listserv in 2002 for stories or comments about the use of the phrase "you guys," she set off a flood of responses from the women's study community, ranging from "What's your problem?" to suggestions for replacing "guys" with "y'all." These comments formed the basis for her essay, which critiques the ubiquitous use of the term.

WRITING TO DISCOVER: *Think about how you use gender-specific language in your own informal conversation. How do you typically greet a group of female friends? Do you use the word* guys *to refer to women? What is your reaction to someone else's use of "guys" when talking to a group of women?*

Oprah says it. My yoga instructor says it. College students around the country say it. The cast of *Friends* says it, as do my own friends, over and over again. At least ten to twenty times a day, I hear someone say "you guys" to refer to groups or pairs that include and in some cases consist entirely of women. I get e-mail all the time asking after my (female) partner and me: "How's everything with you guys?" or "What are you guys doing for the holidays?" In informal speech and writing, the phrase has become so common in American English that it's completely invisible to many who use it. In response to my post on the topic, participants on WMST-L, a listserv for women's studies teachers and scholars hosted by the University of Maryland, report that it's not confined to young people, nor is it an altogether recent development (some of the participants' older relatives used it in the '50s and '60s). Furthermore, the usage is beginning to spread to Canada, England, and Australia, largely through the influence of American television.

What's the problem? people ask when I question this usage. The language has evolved, and now "guys" is gender neutral, they say. Even those who consider themselves feminists—who conscientiously choose "he or she" over "he"; use "flight attendant," "chairperson," and "restaurant server"; and avoid gender-specific language as much as possible—seem quite willing to accept "you guys" as if it were generic. But let's do the math: One guy is clearly male; two or more guys are males. How does a word become gender neutral just by being plural? And then how do you explain something like Heyyouguys.com, "The Man's Search Engine"? Can the same culture that says "it's a guy thing" to refer to anything that women just don't get about male behavior view a woman as one of the guys?

Current dictionaries, such as *Merriam-Webster's Collegiate Dictionary*, eleventh edition, tell us that "guys" may be "used in plural to refer to the members of a group regardless of sex"; but then, we need to keep in mind that dictionaries are not apolitical. They record the state of language and reflect particular ways of seeing the world. (This same tome offers the word "wicked" as one synonym for "black.") My 1979 ninth edition of *Webster's* includes no reference to gender-free guys, an indication that "you guys" had not yet become a standard form of address.

In "The Ascent of Guy," a 1999 article in *American Speech*, Steven J. Clancy writes, "Contrary to everything we might expect because of the pressures of 'politically correct' putative language reforms, a new generic noun is developing right before our eyes." Although Clancy doesn't take issue with the development (as you could probably guess from his disparaging tone on the whole idea of feminist language reform), his report ought to make us stop and think. During the same decades in which feminist critiques of generic uses of "man" and "he" led to widespread changes in usage—no mean feat—"you guys" became even more widely accepted as an informal and allegedly gender-free phrase. What Clancy concludes is that English contains a "cognitive framework in which strongly masculine words regularly show a development including specifically male meanings (man, he, guy) along with gender nonspecific forms . . . whereas in English, feminine words do not undergo such changes." In practice, that is, terms signifying maleness have been more readily perceived as universal than those signifying femaleness. Or, to put it another way, if you call a group of men "you gals," they're not going to think you're just celebrating our common humanity.

And this should trouble us. After all, haven't we been largely pleased   5
by the way the media has worked to adopt at least a semblance of non-sexist language? Newscasters and other public figures make an effort to avoid obviously gender-biased words, and major publications such as the

New York Times and the *Wall Street Journal* do the same. In spite of vocal criticism from those who view such shifts as preposterous, genuine feminist language reform has gained some ground. But as is the case with all advances brought about by feminism and other progressive movements, we need to stay on top of things—or else we may wake up one day to find them gone. This seemingly innocent phrase may be operating like a computer virus, worming its way into our memory files and erasing our sense of why we worry about sexism in language to begin with.

Up until a couple of years ago, I used the phrase as much as anyone, and I never gave it a thought. "You guys" sounds casual, friendly, harmless. When two female friends told me one day that it bothered them to be called "you guys," my wounded ego began an internal rant: *I'm* a literature and gender studies professor, *I* know about language, *I* spend much of my time teaching and writing against sexism, and here were people whose opinions I valued telling me that *I* was being patriarchal, impossible! And then I started listening. I listened first to my own defensive indignation. Clearly, my friends had touched a nerve. Deep down I knew that they were right: Calling women "guys" makes femaleness invisible. It says that man—as in a male person—is still the measure of all things.

Once I copped to being in the wrong, I started hearing the phrase with new ears. Suddenly it seemed bizarre to me when a speaker at an academic conference addressed a room full of women as "you guys"; when a man taking tickets from me and some friends told us all to enjoy the show, "you guys"; and on and on. It was as if these speakers were not really seeing what was before their eyes.

Alice Walker, a vocal opponent of this usage, recounts how she and filmmaker Pratibha Parmar toured the U.S. supporting the film *Warrior Marks* and were discouraged to find that in question-and-answer sessions audience members continually referred to them as "you guys." "Each night, over and over, we told the women greeting us: We are not 'guys.' We are women. Many failed to get it. Others were amused. One woman amused us, she had so much difficulty not saying 'you guys' every two minutes, even after we'd complained" (from "Becoming What We're Called," in 1997's *Anything We Love Can Be Saved*). Because it took me the better part of a year to eradicate this usage from my own speech, and after hearing friends—whom I've encouraged to follow suit—apologize when they slip back into it, I feel like I understand the problem from the inside out. Most of us are familiar with the idea of internalized oppression, the subtle process by which members of disenfranchised groups come to accept their own lesser status. We need to recognize that accepting "guys" as a label for girls and women is a particularly insidious example of that process.

Many people on WMST-L have offered alternatives, ranging from the Southern "y'all" or less regionally marked "you all," to the Midwestern "yoonz" or "you-uns," to the apparently unhip "people," which is associated, it seems, with nerdy high-school teachers and coaches. "Folks" received the most support as a truly gender-free option. Some suggested "gyns" as a playful feminist variant. A more radical solution might be to use a word like "gals" as generic and get men used to hearing themselves included in a female-specific term. Although the majority of those who posted and wrote to me privately viewed the spread of "guys" as something to resist (with many noting how they sometimes regressed), others expressed hope that the phrase would indeed free itself from masculine connotations over time. One professor writes, almost wistfully, "I, for one, have always liked the formulation 'you guys' and wholeheartedly wish it were gender neutral. English could use a gender-neutral term to refer to a group of people (or even to individuals for that matter) . . . I've had students (female) be offended when I've used 'you guys' to them, but I still like it for some reason." I think many feminists who find "you guys" acceptable would similarly like to believe that it is indeed nonsexist. It's a powerful phrase precisely because it seems so warm and cozy. But we ought to ask what we are protecting when we claim that "you guys" is no big deal.

Sherryl Kleinman, professor of sociology at the University of North   10 Carolina in Chapel Hill, has dedicated herself to eliminating the usage. She argues, in "Why Sexist Language Matters" (published in *Center Line,* the newsletter of the Orange County Rape Crisis Center), that male-based generics function as "reinforcers" of a "system in which 'man' in the abstract and men in the flesh are privileged over women." With the help of two former students, Kleinman developed a small card to leave at establishments where "you guys" is spoken (it's available to download at www.youall2.freeservers.com). The card succinctly explains what's at stake in this usage and suggests alternatives. She reports that distributing the card has aroused some anger. After dining with a group of female friends and being called "you guys" several times by the server, Kleinman left the card along with a generous tip. The server followed the women out of the restaurant and berated them for what he perceived to be an insult. Christian Helms, who designed the card's artwork, comments, "It's interesting how something that is supposedly 'no big deal' seems to get people so worked up."

Most of us have probably had the experience of pointing out some type of sexist expression or behavior to acquaintances and being accused of being "too sensitive" or "too PC" and told to "lighten up." It's certainly easier just to go along with things, to avoid making people uncomfortable, to accept what we think will do no harm. If you feel this way about "you guys," you might want to consider Alice Walker's view of the expression: "I see in its use some women's obsequious need to be accepted, at any cost, even at the cost of erasing their own femaleness, and that of other women. Isn't it at least ironic that after so many years of struggle for women's liberation, women should end up calling themselves this?"

So open your ears and your mouth. Tell people that women and girls aren't "guys." Stop saying it yourself. Feminist language reform is an ongoing process that requires a supportive community of speakers. The more we raise our voices, the less likely it is that women and girls will be erased from speech.

THINKING CRITICALLY ABOUT THE READING

1. Bilger cites *Merriam-Webster's Collegiate Dictionary,* eleventh edition, which states that "guys" may be "used in plural to refer to the members of a group regardless of sex" (3). What are her objections to this usage? Why does she consider it important to identify the edition that contains that definition?

2. What is the significance of the findings by Steven L. Clancy in his 1999 article "The Ascent of Guy" (4)? What differences are there in the way "strongly masculine words" and "feminine words" change and develop into more universal meanings?

3. What caused Bilger to go through the process of purging the use of "guys" from her conversation? Why was it so difficult to do? What advice does she offer on what we all can do to eliminate male-oriented language?

4. What does Bilger mean by the phrase "internalized oppression" (8)? How is it expressed in language?

5. What is the central argument presented by sociologist Sherryl Kleinman, who wrote the article "Why Sexist Language Matters" (10)? What do Kleinman and Bilger believe is at stake in pursuing feminist language reform?

6. What is Alice Walker's view of the subject? What is the irony of feminists' using the word *guys* in their own conversation?

LANGUAGE IN ACTION

Bilger talks about a business card that sociologist Sherryl Kleinman leaves at places such as restaurants, where "you guys" is all-too-commonly used in addressing a group of women:

"Hey, You Guys!"

Imagine someone walking up to a group of guys and saying, "Hey, girls, how're ya doing?" We doubt they'd be amused! So isn't it weird that women are supposed to accept — even like — being called "one of the guys"? We're also supposed to like "freshman," "chairman," and "mankind."

(continued)

Get over it, some people say. Those words are generic. They apply to everyone. But then how come so-called generics are always male? What if generics ended in "white"? Freshwhite, chairwhite, whitekind, and "Hey, you whiteys!" Would people of color like being called "one of the whites"? The term "guys" makes women invisible by lumping them in with men. Let's quit doing that. When you're talking to a group of customers, gender really doesn't matter, so why not replace "you guys" with "you all," "folks," or "y'all." Or simply say, "What can I get you?" That would take care of us all.

Thanks for your help.

What is your response to this card? Do you think it represents an effective strategy for making changes in people's attitudes? Would you still think so if you were a restaurant server who received it? Explain.

WRITING SUGGESTIONS

1. Think about the instances in which you have used the word *guys* to describe more than one woman, or, if you don't use that term, then list the circumstances under which you've heard it used. Do you agree with Bilger that it's critical that women confront the usage and say, in no uncertain terms, that women and girls *aren't* guys? Write an essay stating your opinion about the use of "you guys." Include examples from your personal experience. You may find it helpful to read Nancy Stevens's letter to the edition of the *New York Times* entitled "Women Aren't Guys" on pages 208–209 before you start writing.

2. Like Bilger in "You Guys," John McWhorter in "Missing the Nose on Our Face" responds to the problem of sexism embedded in language. Write an essay in which you describe each author's approach to the problem and compare their solutions.

6

MEDIA AND ADVERTISING

Media, and the advertising they convey, are like the air we breathe: ubiquitous, life-supporting, yet sometimes also toxic. Both are so pervasive that we rarely stop to question the motives driving them or what it is they persuade us to do and think. If you are like most Americans, much of what you know about the world is dictated by what you see, hear, read (and download) from the media. Every day, in ever-increasing amounts, we learn, communicate, and entertain ourselves not face-to-face but through Internet blogs, social networks, YouTube, Wikipedia, iPods, cell phones, television, radio, newspapers, magazines, and movies—to name only some of the most popular conduits. To understand the tremendous power that the media industry wields in our lives, we need to look closely at today's mass media and how they have evolved in recent times.

In the first section of this chapter, "Fake News . . . Real News," the writers offer five distinct views of what to look for in measuring the truth (or, as "fake news" pundit Stephen Colbert might put it, the "truthiness") of what the media presents, what we should value, and whom and what we should believe. The core question is not how much information we receive but how much of that information translates into knowledge.

The title of Greg Beato's essay, "Amusing Ourselves to Depth," is the first clue to his unusual suggestion that the satirical fake news of *The Onion* is more trustworthy and honest than that of most mainstream newspapers. In "Selection, Slanting, and Charged Language," Newman and Genevieve Birk give us a crash course on how the language people use subtly shapes perceptions. They introduce us to three simple but powerful concepts—selecting, slanting, and charging—that when understood, will change forever the way we read, watch, or listen to the media. Neil Postman and Steve Powers take on network television news of the precable and pre-Internet era. Their essay, "Television News: The Language of Pictures," lobs harsh criticism at the network television news that delivered entertainment at the expense of journalism—a critique one could readily translate to the practices of today's more "advanced" media. In "The Cult of the Amateur," Andrew Keen critiques one exponent of today's media, the blogosphere, with its "endless digital forest of mediocrity" that threatens to replace the expertise and intelligent analysis of professional journalists with superficial opinion. His essay is paired with blogger Annalee Newitz's "What Happens When Blogs Go Mainstream?" No amateur herself, Newitz subscribes to an unusually high standard of quality research, sourcing, and editing and sees blogging as a way to "shake up the way news is made and culture is analyzed."

The second section of this chapter, "Advertising and the Art of Persuasion," covers a range of views on the power of advertising in our lives. In the opening selection, "The Hard Sell: Advertising in America," Bill Bryson provides a historical perspective and context for the world of advertising, whose roots he locates in the late nineteenth and early twentieth centuries. William Lutz challenges advertisers and their manipulative language in "Weasel Words" and exposes some of the secrets of successful advertising language. In his essay "Lead Us into Temptation," advertising historian James Twitchell takes us on a journey to the heart of modern material consumer culture: the Mall, a.k.a. "Mallcondoville," "a vast continuum of interconnected structures and modes of organizing work, shopping, and living, all based on principles of enclosure, control, and consumption." Jean Kilbourne, whose essay "Jesus Is a Brand of Jeans" is paired with Twitchell's, digs under the surface of some gleaming ads to reveal a massive propaganda effort to make people believe that "products are more important than people" and that the path to love, freedom, and happiness lies in the "consumption of material objects." Finally, in "Barricading the Branded Village," Naomi Klein turns to yet another aspect of advertising: the relationship between merchandising and corporate censorship, which, according to Klein, is changing the cultural landscape.

Amusing Ourselves to Depth

GREG BEATO

Greg Beato's articles, book and music reviews, interviews, and columns have appeared in more than seventy publications worldwide, including *SPIN, Blender, Business 2.0, Wired, Mother Jones,* the *Washington Post,* and the *International Herald Tribune.* A graduate of the University of California, Berkeley (B.A. English, 1986) and Emerson College (M.F.A. Writing, 1990), Beato lives and works in San Francisco. As a contributing editor at *Reason* magazine, he writes a monthly column about pop culture, where this selection appeared in November 2007.

Beato, a long-time fan of *The Onion,* decided that the paper's twentieth anniversary was a good time to look at the reasons for its phenomenal success. What particularly struck him was the fact that *The Onion* had such a huge print circulation—placing it in the top ten most-read newspapers in the country—when other print newspapers were rapidly losing readership. "*The Onion* has proved that people still will read a print-based product," says Beato, "so it seemed like a good thing to point out."

WRITING TO DISCOVER: *Do you read a newspaper to get the news? Do you watch any of the "fake news" shows such as* The Daily Show *or* The Colbert Report? *In your opinion, is there ever a time when fake news is better than "real" news?*

In August 1988, college junior Tim Keck borrowed $7,000 from his mom, rented a Mac Plus, and published a 12-page newspaper. His ambition was hardly the stuff of future journalism symposiums: He wanted to create a compelling way to deliver advertising to his fellow students. Part of the first issue's front page was devoted to a story about a monster running amok at a local lake; the rest was reserved for beer and pizza coupons.

Almost 20 years later, *The Onion* stands as one of the newspaper industry's few great success stories in the post-newspaper era. Currently, it prints 710,000 copies of each weekly edition, roughly 6,000 more than the *Denver Post,* the nation's ninth-largest daily. Its syndicated radio dispatches reach a weekly audience of 1 million, and it recently started producing video clips too. Roughly 3,000 local advertisers keep *The Onion* afloat, and the paper plans to add 170 employees to its staff of 130 this year.

Online it attracts more than 2 million readers a week. Type *onion* into Google, and *The Onion* pops up first. Type *the* into Google, and *The Onion* pops up first.

But type "best practices for newspapers" into Google, and *The Onion* is nowhere to be found. Maybe it should be. At a time when traditional newspapers are frantic to divest themselves of their newsy, papery legacies, *The Onion* takes a surprisingly conservative approach to innovation. As much as it has used and benefited from the Web, it owes much of its success to low-tech attributes readily available to any paper but nonetheless in short supply: candor, irreverence, and a willingness to offend.

While other newspapers desperately add gardening sections, ask read-   5
ers to share their favorite bratwurst recipes, or throw their staffers to ravenous packs of bloggers for online question-and-answer sessions, *The Onion* has focused on reporting the news. The fake news, sure, but still the news. It doesn't ask readers to post their comments at the end of stories, allow them to rate stories on a scale of one to five, or encourage citizen-satire. It makes no effort to convince readers that it really does understand their needs and exists only to serve them. *The Onion*'s journalists concentrate on writing stories and then getting them out there in a variety of formats, and this relatively old-fashioned approach to newspapering has been tremendously successful.

Are there any other newspapers that can boast a 60 percent increase in their print circulation during the last three years? Yet as traditional newspapers fail to draw readers, only industry mavericks like *The New York Times*' Jayson Blair and *USA Today*'s Jack Kelley have looked to *The Onion* for inspiration.

One reason *The Onion* isn't taken more seriously is that it's actually fun to read. In 1985 the cultural critic Neil Postman published the influential *Amusing Ourselves to Death*, which warned of the fate that would befall us if public discourse were allowed to become substantially more entertaining than, say, a Neil Postman book. Today newspapers are eager to entertain—in their Travel, Food, and Style sections, that is. But even as scope creep has made the average big-city tree killer less portable than a 10-year-old laptop, hard news invariably comes in a single flavor: Double Objectivity Sludge.

Too many high priests of journalism still see humor as the enemy of seriousness: If the news goes down too easily, it can't be very good for you. But do *The Onion* and its more fact-based acolytes, *The Daily Show* and *The Colbert Report*, monitor current events and the way the news media report on them any less rigorously than, say, the *Columbia Journalism Review* or *USA Today*?

During the last few years, multiple surveys by the Pew Research Center and the Annenberg Public Policy Center have found that viewers of *The Daily Show* and *The Colbert Report* are among America's most informed citizens. Now, it may be that Jon Stewart isn't making anyone smarter; perhaps America's most informed citizens simply prefer comedy over the stentorian drivel the network anchormannequins dispense. But at the very least, such surveys suggest that news sharpened with satire doesn't cause the intellectual coronaries Postman predicted. Instead, it seems to correlate with engagement.

It's easy to see why readers connect with *The Onion*, and it's not just   10
the jokes: Despite its "fake news" purview, it's an extremely honest publication. Most dailies, especially those in monopoly or near-monopoly markets, operate as if they're focused more on not offending readers (or advertisers) than on expressing a worldview of any kind.

The Onion takes the opposite approach. It delights in crapping on pieties and regularly publishes stories guaranteed to upset someone: "Christ Kills Two, Injures Seven In Abortion-Clinic Attack." "Heroic PETA Commandos Kill 49, Save Rabbit." "Gay Pride Parade Sets Mainstream Acceptance of Gays Back 50 Years." There's no predictable ideology running through those headlines, just a desire to express some rude, blunt truth about the world.

One common complaint about newspapers is that they're too negative, too focused on bad news, too obsessed with the most unpleasant aspects of life. *The Onion* shows how wrong this characterization is, how gingerly most newspapers dance around the unrelenting awfulness of life and refuse to acknowledge the limits of our tolerance and compassion. The perfunctory coverage that traditional newspapers give disasters in countries cursed with relatability issues is reduced to its bare, dismal essence: "15,000 Brown People Dead Somewhere." Beggars aren't grist for Pulitzers, just punch lines: "Man Can't Decide Whether to Give Sandwich to Homeless or Ducks." Triumphs of the human spirit are as rare as vegans at an NRA barbecue: "Loved Ones Recall Local Man's Cowardly Battle With Cancer."

Such headlines come with a cost, of course. Outraged readers have convinced advertisers to pull ads. Ginger Rogers and Denzel Washington, among other celebrities, have objected to stories featuring their names, and former *Onion* editor Robert Siegel once told a lecture audience that the paper was "very nearly sued out of existence" after it ran a story with the headline "Dying Boy Gets Wish: To Pork Janet Jackson."

But if this irreverence is sometimes economically inconvenient, it's also a major reason for the publication's popularity. It's a refreshing antidote to the he-said/she-said balancing acts that leave so many dailies sounding mealy-mouthed. And while *The Onion* may not adhere to the facts too strictly, it would no doubt place high if the Pew Research Center ever included it in a survey ranking America's most trusted news sources.

During the last few years, big-city dailies have begun to introduce   15
"commuter" papers that function as lite versions of their original fare. These publications share some of *The Onion*'s attributes: They're free, they're tabloids, and most of their stories are bite-sized. But while they may be less filling, they still taste bland. You have to wonder: Why stop at price and paper size? Why not adopt the brutal frankness, the willingness to pierce orthodoxies of all political and cultural stripes, and apply these attributes to a genuinely reported daily newspaper?

Today's publishers give comic strips less and less space. Editorial cartoonists and folksy syndicated humorists have been nearly eradicated. Such changes have helped make newspapers more entertaining—or at least less dull—but they're just a start. Until today's front pages can amuse our staunchest defenders of journalistic integrity to severe dyspepsia, if not death, they're not trying hard enough.

THINKING CRITICALLY ABOUT THE READING

1. What was the motivation for *The Onion*'s creator, Tim Keck, to start a newspaper while he was still in college? In what way did the first story forecast the direction of the "news" reported by *The Onion*?

2. In Beato's opinion, what makes *The Onion* "one of the newspaper industry's few great success stories in the post-newspaper era" (2)?

3. Why did Beato choose the title "Amusing Ourselves to Depth"? What does the title suggest about Beato's view of entertainment in the news media?

4. Research has shown that viewers of *The Daily Show* and *The Colbert Report* "are among America's most informed citizens" (9). How does Beato use this fact to argue against Neil Postman's notion that too much entertainment in news is dangerous?

5. How, according to Beato, does *The Onion* handle "the unrelenting awfulness of life" (12) that traditional papers refuse to confront?

6. Is Beato suggesting that fake news is better than "real" news, or is he saying something else?

LANGUAGE IN ACTION

Go to *The Onion*'s Web site (www.theonion.com) and read the latest installment of "American Voices." Now look up the "straight news" version of the featured story on the Web site of the *New York Times, USA Today*, or another mainstream newspaper. How do the treatments of the story differ? What does one source offer that the other does not?

WRITING SUGGESTIONS

1. Headlines in *The Onion* are often all one needs to understand the story being satirized. In paragraphs 11 and 12, Beato lists a number of *Onion* headlines, and in doing so, berates the traditional media for their perfunctory coverage of certain countries and situations. Visit *The Onion* online (www.theonion. com), select some of your favorite headlines, and discuss how *The Onion* uses

satire to expose a real problem. Do you agree or disagree with Beato's argument that "news sharpened with satire" (9) can be more effective than the news presented "straight"?

2. Do you agree with Beato when he writes, in reference to *The Daily Show*: "[P]erhaps America's most informed citizens simply prefer comedy over the stentorian drivel the network anchormannequins dispense" (9)? Write an essay in which you defend or challenge Beato's suggestion that fake news might just be more "real" than real news.

Selection, Slanting, and Charged Language

Newman P. Birk and Genevieve B. Birk

The more we learn about language and how it works, the more abundantly clear it becomes that our language shapes our perceptions of the world. Because most people have eyes to see, ears to hear, noses to smell, tongues to taste, and skins to feel, it seems as though our perceptions of reality should be pretty similar. We know, however, that this is not the case, and language, it seems, makes a big difference in how we perceive our world. In effect, language acts as a filter, heightening certain perceptions, dimming others, and totally voiding still others.

In the following selection from their book *Understanding and Using Language* (1972), Newman and Genevieve Birk discuss how we use words, especially the tremendous powers that slanted and charged language wields. As a writer, you will be particularly interested to learn just how important your choice of words is. After reading what the Birks have to say, you'll never read another editorial, watch another commercial, or listen to another politician in quite the same way.

Writing to Discover: *Choose three different people and write a description of a person, an object, or an event from each of their perspectives. Consider how each would relate to the subject you chose, what details each would focus on, and the attitude each would have toward that subject.*

A. THE PRINCIPLE OF SELECTION

Before it is expressed in words, our knowledge, both inside and outside, is influenced by the principle of selection. What we know or observe depends on what we notice; that is, what we select, consciously or unconsciously, as worthy of notice or attention. As we observe, the principle of selection determines which facts we take in.

Suppose, for example, that three people, a lumberjack, an artist, and a tree surgeon, are examining a large tree in the forest. Since the tree itself is a complicated object, the number of particulars or facts about it that one could observe would be very great indeed. Which of these facts a particular observer will notice will be a matter of selection, a selection that is determined by his interests and purposes. A lumberjack might be interested in the best way to cut the tree down, cut it up and transport it to the lumber mill. His interest would then determine his principle of selection in observing and thinking about the tree. The artist might consider painting a picture of the tree, and his purpose would furnish his principle of selection. The tree surgeon's professional interest in the physical health of the tree might establish a principle of selection for him. If each man were now required to write an exhaustive, detailed report on everything he observed about the tree, the facts supplied by each would differ, for each would report those facts that his particular principle of selection led him to notice.[1]

The principle of selection holds not only for the specific facts that people observe but also for the facts they remember. A student suddenly embarrassed may remember nothing of the next ten minutes of class discussion but may have a vivid recollection of the sensation of the blood mounting, as he blushed, up his face and into his ears. In both noticing and remembering, the principle of selection applies, and it is influenced not only by our special interest and point of view but by our whole mental state of the moment.

The principle of selection then serves as a kind of sieve or screen through which our knowledge passes before it becomes our knowledge. Since we can't notice everything about a complicated object or situation or action or state of our own consciousness, what we do notice is determined by whatever principle of selection is operating for us at the time we gain the knowledge.

It is important to remember that what is true of the way the principle of selection works for us is true also for the way it works for others. Even before we or other people put knowledge into words to express meaning, that knowledge has been screened or selected. Before an historian or an economist writes a book, or before a reporter writes a news article, the facts that each is to present have been sifted through the screen of a principle of selection. Before one person passes on knowledge to another, that knowledge has already been selected and shaped, intentionally or unintentionally, by the mind of the communicator.

B. THE PRINCIPLE OF SLANTING

When we put our knowledge into words, a second process of selection, the process of slanting, takes place. Just as there is something, a rather mysterious principle of selection, which chooses for us what we will notice, and what will then become our knowledge, there is also a principle which operates, with or without our awareness, to select certain facts and feelings from our store of knowledge, and to choose the words and emphasis that we shall use to communicate our meaning.[2] Slanting may be defined as the process of selecting (1) knowledge—factual and attitudinal; (2) words; and (3) emphasis, to achieve the intention of the communicator. Slanting is present in some degree in all communication:

---

1. Of course, all three observers would probably report a good many facts in common—the height of the tree, for example, and the size of the trunk. The point we wish to make is that each observer would give us a different impression of the tree because of the different principle of selection that guided his observation.

2. Notice that the "principle of selection" is at work as *we take in* knowledge, and that slanting occurs *as we express* our knowledge in words.

one may *slant for* (favorable slanting), *slant against* (unfavorable slanting), or *slant both ways* (balanced slanting). . . .

C. SLANTING BY USE OF EMPHASIS

Slanting by use of the devices of emphasis is unavoidable,[3] for emphasis is simply the giving of stress to subject matter, and so indicating what is important and what is less important. In speech, for example, if we say that Socrates was *a wise old man,* we can give several slightly different meanings, one by stressing *wise,* another by stressing *old,* another by giving equal stress to *wise* and *old,* and still another by giving chief stress to *man.* Each different stress gives a different slant (favorable or unfavorable or balanced) to the statement because it conveys a different attitude toward Socrates or a different judgment of him. Connectives and word order also slant by the emphasis they give: consider the difference in slanting or emphasis produced by *old but wise, old and wise, wise but old.* In writing, we cannot indicate subtle stresses on words as clearly as in speech, but we can achieve our emphasis and so can slant by the use of more complex patterns of word order, by choice of connectives, by underlining heavily stressed words, and by marks of punctuation that indicate short or long pauses and so give light or heavy emphasis. Question marks, quotation marks, and exclamation points can also contribute to slanting.[4] It is impossible either in speech or in writing to put two facts together without giving some slight emphasis or slant. For example, if we have in mind only two facts about a man, his awkwardness and his strength, we subtly slant those facts favorably or unfavorably in whatever way we may choose to join them.

More Favorable Slanting	*Less Favorable Slanting*
He is awkward and strong.	He is strong and awkward.
He is awkward but strong.	He is strong but awkward.
Although he is somewhat awkward, he is very strong.	He may be strong, but he's very awkward.

With more facts and in longer passages it is possible to maintain a delicate balance by alternating favorable emphasis and so producing a balanced effect.

All communication, then, is in some degree slanted by the *emphasis* of the communicator.

---

3. When emphasis is present—and we can think of no instance in the use of language in which it is not—it necessarily influences the meaning by playing a part in the favorable, unfavorable, or balanced slant of the communicator. We are likely to emphasize by voice stress, even when we answer *yes* or *no* to simple questions.

4. Consider the slanting achieved by punctuation in the following sentences: He called the Senator an honest man? *He* called the Senator an honest man? He called the Senator an honest man! He said one more such "honest" senator would corrupt the state.

D. SLANTING BY SELECTION OF FACTS

To illustrate the technique of slanting by selection of facts, we shall examine three passages of informative writing which achieve different effects simply by the selection and emphasis of material. Each passage is made up of true statements or facts about a dog, yet the reader is given three different impressions. The first passage is an example of objective writing or balanced slanting, the second is slanted unfavorably, and the third is slanted favorably.

1. Balanced Presentation

Our dog, Toddy, sold to us as a cocker, produces various reactions in various people. Those who come to the back door she usually growls and barks at (a milkman has said that he is afraid of her); those who come to the front door, she whines at and paws; also she tries to lick people's faces unless we have forestalled her by putting a newspaper in her mouth. (Some of our friends encourage these actions; others discourage them. Mrs. Firmly, one friend, slaps the dog with a newspaper and says, "I know how hard dogs are to train.") Toddy knows and responds to a number of words and phrases, and guests sometimes remark that she is a "very intelligent dog." She has fleas in the summer, and she sheds, at times copiously, the year round. Her blonde hairs are conspicuous when they are on people's clothing or on rugs or furniture. Her color and her large brown eyes frequently produce favorable comment. An expert on cockers would say that her ears are too short and set too high and that she is at least six pounds too heavy.

The passage above is made up of facts, verifiable facts,[5] deliberately selected and emphasized to produce a *balanced* impression. Of course not all the facts about the dog have been given—to supply *all* the facts on any subject, even such a comparatively simple one, would be an almost impossible task. Both favorable and unfavorable facts are used, however, and an effort has been made to alternate favorable and unfavorable details so that neither will receive greater emphasis by position, proportion, or grammatical structure.   10

2. Facts Slanted Against

That dog put her paws on my white dress as soon as I came in the door, and she made so much noise that it was two minutes before she had quieted down enough for us to talk and hear each other. Then the gas man came and she did a great deal of barking. And her hairs are on the

---

5. *Verifiable facts* are facts that can be checked and agreed upon and proved to be true by people who wish to verify them. That a particular theme received a failing grade is a verifiable fact; one needs merely to see the theme with the grade on it. That the instructor should have failed the theme is not, strictly speaking, a verifiable fact, but a matter of opinion. That women on the average live longer than men is a verifiable fact; that they live better is a matter of opinion, *a value judgment.*

rug and on the furniture. If you wear a dark dress they stick to it like lint. When Mrs. Firmly came in, she actually hit the dog with a newspaper to make it stay down, and she made some remark about training dogs. I wish the Birks would take the hint or get rid of that noisy, short-eared, overweight "cocker" of theirs.

This unfavorably slanted version is based on the same facts, but now these facts have been selected and given a new emphasis. The speaker, using her selected facts to give her impression of the dog, is quite possibly unaware of her negative slanting.

Now for a favorably slanted version:

3. Facts Slanted For

What a lively and responsible dog! When I walked in the door, there she was with a newspaper in her mouth, whining and standing on her hind legs and wagging her tail all at the same time. And what an intelligent dog. If you suggest going for a walk, she will get her collar from the kitchen and hand it to you, and she brings Mrs. Birk's slippers whenever Mrs. Birk says she is "tired" or mentions slippers. At a command she catches balls, rolls over, "speaks," or stands on her hind feet and twirls around. She sits up and balances a piece of bread on her nose until she is told to take it; then she tosses it up and catches it. If you are eating something, she sits up in front of you and "begs" with those big dark brown eyes set in that light, buff-colored face of hers. When I got up to go and told her I was leaving, she rolled her eyes at me and sat up like a squirrel. She certainly is a lively and intelligent dog.

Speaker 3, like Speaker 2, is selecting from the "facts" summarized in balanced version 1, and is emphasizing his facts to communicate his impression.

All three passages are examples of *reporting* (i.e., consist only of verifiable facts), yet they give three very different impressions of the same dog because of the different ways the speakers slanted the facts. Some people say that figures don't lie, and many people believe that if they have the "facts," they have the "truth." Yet if we carefully examine the ways of thought and language, we see that any knowledge that comes to us through words has been subjected to the double screening of the principle of selection and the slanting of language. . . .

Wise listeners and readers realize that the double screening that is   15
produced by the principle of selection and by slanting takes place even when people honestly try to report the facts as they know them. (Speakers 2 and 3, for instance, probably thought of themselves as simply giving information about a dog and were not deliberately trying to mislead.) Wise listeners and readers know too that deliberate manipulators of language, by mere selection and emphasis, can make their slanted facts appear to support almost any cause.

In arriving at opinions and values we cannot always be sure that the facts that sift into our minds through language are representative and relevant and true. We need to remember that much of our information about politics, governmental activities, business conditions, and foreign affairs comes to us selected and slanted. More than we realize, our opinions on these matters may depend on what newspaper we read or what news commentator we listen to. Worthwhile opinions call for knowledge of reliable facts and reasonable arguments for and against—and such opinions include beliefs about morality and truth and religion as well as about public affairs. Because complex subjects involve knowing and dealing with many facts on both sides, reliable judgments are at best difficult to arrive at. If we want to be fairminded, we must be willing to subject our opinions to continual testing by new knowledge, and must realize that after all they *are* opinions, more or less trustworthy. Their trustworthiness will depend on the representativeness of our facts, on the quality of our reasoning, and on the standard of values that we choose to apply.

We shall not give here a passage illustrating the unscrupulous slanting of facts. Such a passage would also include irrelevant facts and false statements presented as facts, along with various subtle distortions of fact. Yet to the uninformed reader the passage would be indistinguishable from a passage intended to give a fair account. If two passages (2 and 3) of casual and unintentional slanting of facts about a dog can give such contradictory impressions of a simple subject, the reader can imagine what a skilled and designing manipulation of facts and statistics could do to mislead an uninformed reader about a really complex subject. An example of such manipulation might be the account of the United States that Soviet propaganda has supplied to the average Russian. Such propaganda, however, would go beyond the mere slanting of the facts: it would clothe the selected facts in charged words and would make use of the many other devices of slanting that appear in charged language.

E. SLANTING BY USE OF CHARGED WORDS

In the passages describing the dog Toddy, we were illustrating the technique of slanting by the selection and emphasis of facts. Though the facts selected had to be expressed in words, the words chosen were as factual as possible, and it was the selection and emphasis of facts and not of words that was mainly responsible for the two distinctly different impressions of the dog. In the passages below we are demonstrating another way of slanting—by the use of charged words. This time the accounts are very similar in the facts they contain; the different impressions of the subject, Corlyn, are produced not by different facts but by the subtle selection of charged words.

The passages were written by a clever student who was told to choose as his subject a person in action, and to write two descriptions, each using the "same facts." The instructions required that one description be slanted positively and the other negatively, so that the first would make the reader favorably inclined toward the person and the action, and the second would make him unfavorably inclined.

Here is the favorably charged description. Read it carefully and form your   20
opinion of the person before you go on to read the second description.

Corlyn

Corlyn paused at the entrance to the room and glanced about. A well-cut black dress draped subtly about her slender form. Her long blonde hair gave her chiseled features the simple frame they required. She smiled an engaging smile as she accepted a cigarette from her escort. As he lit it for her she looked over the flame and into his eyes. Corlyn had that rare talent of making every male feel that he was the only man in the world.

She took his arm and they descended the steps into the room. She walked with an effortless grace and spoke with equal ease. They each took a cup of coffee and joined a group of friends near the fire. The flickering light danced across her face and lent an ethereal quality to her beauty. The good conversation, the crackling logs, and the stimulating coffee gave her a feeling of internal warmth. Her eyes danced with each leap of the flames.

Taken by itself this passage might seem just a description of an attractive girl. The favorable slanting by use of charged words has been done so skillfully that it is inconspicuous. Now we turn to the unfavorable slanted description of the "same" girl in the "same" actions:

Corlyn

Corlyn halted at the entrance to the room and looked around. A plain black dress hung on her thin frame. Her stringy bleached hair accentuated her harsh features. She smiled an inane smile as she took a cigarette from her escort. As he lit it for her she stared over the lighter and into his eyes. Corlyn had a habit of making every male feel that he was the last man on earth.

She grasped his arm and they walked down the steps and into the room. Her pace was fast and ungainly, as was her speed. They each reached for some coffee and broke into a group of acquaintances near the fire. The flickering light played across her face and revealed every flaw. The loud talk, the fire, and the coffee she had gulped down made her feel hot. Her eyes grew more red with each leap of the flames.

When the reader compares these two descriptions, he can see how charged words influence the reader's attitude. One needs to read the two descriptions several times to appreciate all the subtle differences between them. Words, some rather heavily charged, others innocent-looking but lightly charged, work together to carry to the reader a judgment of a person and a situation. If the reader had seen only the first description of Corlyn, he might well have thought that he had formed his "own judgment on the basis of the facts." And the examples just given only begin to suggest the techniques that may be used in heavily charged language. For one thing, the two descriptions of Corlyn contain no really good example of the use of charged abstractions; for another, the writer was obliged by the assignment to use the same set of facts and so could not slant by selecting his material.

F. SLANTING AND CHARGED LANGUAGE

...When slanting of facts, or words, or emphasis, or any combination of the three *significantly influences* feelings toward, or judgments about, a subject, the language used is charged language. . . .

Of course communications vary in the amount of charge they carry and in their effect on different people; what is very favorably charged for one person may have little or no charge, or may even be adversely charged, for others. It is sometimes hard to distinguish between charged and uncharged expression. But it is safe to say that whenever we wish to convey any kind of inner knowledge—feelings, attitudes, judgments, values—we are obliged to convey that attitudinal meaning through the medium of charged language; and when we wish to understand the inside knowledge of others, we have to interpret the charged language that they choose, or are obliged to use. Charged language, then, is the natural and necessary medium for the communication of charged or attitudinal meaning. At times we have difficulty in living with it, but we should have even greater difficulty in living without it.

Some of the difficulties in living with charged language are caused 25
by its use in dishonest propaganda, in some editorials, in many political speeches, in most advertising, in certain kinds of effusive salesmanship, and in blatantly insincere, or exaggerated, or sentimental expressions of emotion. Other difficulties are caused by the misunderstandings and misinterpretations that charged language produces. A charged phrase misinterpreted in a love letter; a charged word spoken in haste or in anger; an acrimonious argument about religion or politics or athletics or fraternities; the frustrating uncertainty produced by the effort to understand the complex attitudinal meaning in a poem or play or a short story—these troubles, all growing out of the use of charged language, may give us the feeling that Robert Louis Stevenson expressed when he said, "The battle goes sore against us to the going down of the sun."

But however charged language is abused and whatever misunderstandings it may cause, we still have to live with it—and even by it. It shapes our attitudes and values even without our conscious knowledge; it gives purpose to, and guides, our actions; through it we establish and maintain relations with other people and by means of it we exert our greatest influence on them. Without charged language, life would be but half life. The relatively uncharged language of bare factual statement, though it serves its informative purpose well and is much less open to abuse and to misunderstanding, can describe only the bare land of factual knowledge; to communicate knowledge of the turbulencies and the calms and the deep currents of the sea of inner experience we must use charged language.

THINKING CRITICALLY ABOUT THE READING

1. What is the Birks's purpose in this essay? (Glossary: *Purpose*) Do they seem more intent on explaining or on arguing their position? Point to specific language they use that led you to your conclusion. (Glossary: *Diction*)

2. How do the Birks organize their essay? (Glossary: *Organization*) Do you think the organizational pattern is appropriate given their subject matter and purpose? Explain.

3. According to the Birks, how is slanting different from the principle of selection? What devices can a speaker or writer use to slant knowledge? When is it appropriate, if at all, to slant language?

4. Do you find the examples about Toddy the dog and Corlyn particularly helpful? (Glossary: *Examples*) Why or why not? What would have been lost, if anything, had the examples not been included?

5. Why is it important for writers and others to be aware of charged words? What can happen if you use charged language unknowingly? What are some of the difficulties in living in a world with charged language?

6. The Birks wrote this essay in 1972, when people were not as sensitive to sexist language as they are today. (Glossary: *Sexist Language*) Reread several pages of their essay, paying particular attention to the Birks's use of pronouns and to the gender of the people in their examples. Suggest ways in which the Birks's diction could be changed so as to eliminate any sexist language.

LANGUAGE IN ACTION

According to the editors of *Newsweek,* the March 8, 1999, "Voices of the Century: Americans at War" issue "generated more than two hundred passionate responses from civilians and veterans." The following five letters are representative of those the editors received and published in the issue of March 29, 1999. Carefully read each letter, looking for slanting and charged language. Point out the verifiable facts you find. How do you know these facts are verifiable?

Kudos for your March 8 issue, "Voices of the Century: Americans at War." This issue surely ranks among the best magazines ever published. As a military historian, I gained a better perspective of this turbulent century from this single issue than from many other sources combined. The first-person accounts are the genius of the issue. And your selection of storytellers was truly inspired. The "Voices of the Century" is so powerful that I will urge all of my friends to read it, buying copies for those who are not subscribers. Many persons today, especially those born after WWII, do not comprehend or appreciate the defining events of this century. How can we be more confident that they will be aware of our vital past when making important social and political decisions during the next century? I have great confidence in the American spirit and will, but this missing perspective is my principal concern as I leave this nation to the ministry of my daughters, my grandchildren, and their generation. Why not publish "Voices of the Century" as a booklet and make it readily available to all young people? Why not urge every school system to make it required reading prior to graduation from high school?

–Alan R. McKie, Springfield, VA

Your March 8 war issue was a powerfully illustrated essay of the men and women who have served our country and the people of other lands in so many capacities. But it was the photos that touched my soul and made me cry all over again for the human loss, *my* loss. As I stared at the pictures of the injured, dead, dying, and crying, I felt as though I were intruding on their private hell. God bless all of them, and my sincere thanks for a free America.

–Deborah Ames, Sparks, NV

I arrived in this country at 15 as a Jewish refugee from Nazism. I became an American soldier at 19 and a U.S. Foreign Service officer at 29. As a witness to much of the history covered in your special issue, I wanted to congratulate *Newsweek* on a superb job. In your excellent introduction, I found only one word with which I take issue: that "after the war Rosie and her cohort *happily* went back to the joys of motherhood and built the baby boom." Rosie and her cohort were forced back into their traditional gender roles, and it took the women's movement another generation or two to win back the gains achieved during the war.

–Lucian Heichler, Frederick, MD

Editor's note: The word "happily" was carefully chosen. Contemporary surveys indicated that most of the American women who joined the work force because of World War II were glad to get back to family life when it was over.

On the cover of your "Americans at War" issue, you have the accompanying text "From WWI to Vietnam: The Grunts and the Great Men—In Their Own Words." In each of these wars, the grunts *were* the great men.

–Paula S. McGuire, Charlotte, NC

Your March 8 issue was painful for me and other members of my family as a result of the photograph you included on page 62 showing a wounded soldier being dragged from the line of fire during the Tet Offensive.

(**continued**)

My family had previously confirmed with the photographer that the soldier was my youngest brother, Marine Cpl. Robert Mack Harrelson. His bullet-riddled body fought hard to survive and, with the assistance of many excellent, caring members of our U.S. Military Medical Staff, he was able to regain some degree of normalcy after his return. But the injuries he received were too great to overcome, resulting in the military funeral he had requested. The rekindled grief brought on by your photo is keenly felt throughout our large family, and especially so by our dear 85-year-old mother, who still speaks of Bob as though he might reappear at any time. In spite of the photo, I sincerely congratulate your fine publication for reminding the world of the tragedy of war.

—LOWELL L. HARRELSON, Bay Minette, AL

WRITING SUGGESTIONS

1. Describe a day at your school or university. Begin with details that help you create a single dominant impression. Be careful to select only details that support the attitude and meaning you wish to convey. Once you've finished, compare your essay with those of your peers. In what ways do the essays differ? How are they the same? How does this writing exercise reinforce the Birks's discussion of the principle of selection?

2. When used only positively or only negatively, charged words can alienate the reader and bring the author's reliability into question. Consider the Birks's two examples of Corlyn. In the first example Corlyn can do no wrong, and in the second she can do nothing right. Using these two examples as a guide, write your own multiparagraph description of a person you know well. Decide on the overall impression you want to convey to your readers, and use charged words—both positive and negative—to create that impression.

3. Find a newspaper or magazine editorial on a subject that you have strong opinions about. Analyze the writer's selection of facts and use of charged language. How well does the writer present different viewpoints? Is the editorial convincing? Why or why not? After researching the topic further in your library or on the Internet, write a letter to the editor in response to the editorial. In your letter, use information from your research to make a point about the subject. Also comment on any charged or slanted language the editor used. Mail your letter to the editor.

Television News: The Language of Pictures

NEIL POSTMAN AND STEVE POWERS

Neil Postman (1931–2003)—media theory pioneer, cultural commentator, educator, and prolific and provocative writer—authored twenty books, starting in 1961 with *Television and the Teaching of English*. Among his other books on language, education, the media, and communications theory are *Teaching as a Subversive Activity* (1971), *Amusing Ourselves to Death: Public Discourse in the Age of Show Business* (1985), *Conscientious Objections: Stirring Up Trouble about Language, Technology and Education* (1988), *Technopoly: The Surrender of Culture to Technology* (1992), and *Building a Bridge to the 18th Century: How the Past Can Improve Our Future* (1999). Postman was a contributing editor to the *Nation,* and his more than 200 articles and essays appeared in the *New York Times Magazine,* the *Atlantic Monthly,* and the *Harvard Education Review,* among other publications. He also edited *Et Cetera,* a journal of semantics. A native of Brooklyn, New York, Postman was a graduate of the State University of New York at Fredonia and Columbia University. In 1971, he founded the program in media ecology at New York University's Steinhardt School of Education. In 1993, he was appointed university professor in the School of Education and was chairman of the Department of Culture and Communication until 2002.

Steve Powers, born in New York City in 1934, has had a long and varied career as a professional musician, news correspondent, and educator. Starting his professional radio career in Connecticut, he later became a fixture in the New York news scene as an anchor/reporter at WNYW-TV, where he won an Emmy Award; as host of "Steve Powers News-Talk" on WMCA; as a correspondent at the ABC Radio Network; and as newsperson for Fox Five television. He recently retired after forty-five years as a newscaster on WQXR-FM in New York City.

In the 1980s, Powers returned to New York University, where he earned a Ph.D. in media studies, and he began teaching at St. John's University in 1993. His interest in media literacy led him to team up with Neil Postman to write *How to Watch TV News* (1992), an influential book that analyzes television as a news source. The book has remained in wide circulation since its publication in 1992 and was revised in 2008.

In the following selection, taken from that book, Postman and Powers look closely at what we as viewers are getting when we watch the news on television. They conclude that unless we come to television news with a "prepared mind ... a news program is only a kind of rousing light show."

WRITING TO DISCOVER: *Where and how do you get news of what is happening in the world? Do you read a print newspaper or go to a news source online? What other sources do you go to on a regular basis?*

When a television news show distorts the truth by altering or manufacturing facts (through re-creations), a television viewer is defenseless even
if a re-creation is properly labeled. Viewers are still vulnerable to misinformation since they will not know (at least in the case of docudramas)
what parts are fiction and what parts are not. But the problems of verisi-
militude posed by re-creations pale to insignificance when compared to the
problems viewers face when encountering a straight (no-monkey-business)
show. All news shows, in a sense, are re-creations in that what we hear and
see on them are attempts to represent actual events, and are not the events
themselves. Perhaps, to avoid ambiguity, we might call all news shows "re-
presentations" instead of "re-creations." These re-presentations come to us
in two forms: language and pictures.

    . . . It is often said that a picture is worth a thousand words. Maybe
so. But it is probably equally true that one word is worth a thousand pictures, at least sometimes—for example, when it comes to understanding
the world we live in. Indeed, the whole problem with news on television
comes down to this: all the words uttered in an hour of news coverage
could be printed on one page of a newspaper. And the world cannot be
understood in one page. Of course, there is a compensation: television
offers pictures, and the pictures move. Moving pictures are a kind of language in themselves, but the language of pictures differs radically from
oral and written language, and the differences are crucial for understanding television news.

    To begin with, pictures, especially single pictures, speak only in par-
ticularities. Their vocabulary is limited to concrete representation. Unlike
words and sentences, a picture does not present to us an idea or concept
about the world, except as we use language itself to convert the image
to idea. By itself, a picture cannot deal with the unseen, the remote, the
internal, the abstract. It does not speak of "man," only of *a* man; not of
"tree," only of *a* tree. You cannot produce an image of "nature," any more
than an image of "the sea." You can only show a particular fragment of the
here-and-now—a cliff of a certain terrain, in a certain condition of light;
a wave at a moment in time, from a particular point of view. And just as
"nature" and "the sea" cannot be photographed, such larger abstractions
as truth, honor, love, and falsehood cannot be talked about in the lexicon
of individual pictures. For "showing of" and "talking about" are two very
different kinds of processes: individual pictures give us the world as object;
language, the world as idea. There is no such thing in nature as "man" or
"tree." The universe offers no such categories or simplifications; only flux
and infinite variety. The picture documents and celebrates the particularities
of the universe's infinite variety. Language makes them comprehensible.

    Of course, moving pictures, video with sound, may bridge the gap
by juxtaposing images, symbols, sound, and music. Such images can present emotions and rudimentary ideas. They can suggest the panorama of
nature and the joys and miseries of humankind.

Picture—smoke pouring from the window, cut to people coughing, an ambulance racing to a hospital, a tombstone in a cemetery. 5

Picture—jet planes firing rockets, explosions, lines of foreign soldiers surrendering, the American flag waving in the wind.

Nonetheless, keep in mind that when terrorists want to prove to the world that their kidnap victims are still alive, they photograph them holding a copy of a recent newspaper. The dateline on the newspaper provides the proof that the photograph was taken on or after that date. Without the help of the written word, film and videotape cannot portray temporal dimensions with any precision. Consider a film clip showing an aircraft carrier at sea. One might be able to identify the ship as Soviet or American, but there would be no way of telling where in the world the carrier was, where it was headed, or when the pictures were taken. It is only through language—words spoken over the pictures or reproduced in them—that the image of the aircraft carrier takes on specific meaning.

Still, it is possible to enjoy the image of the carrier for its own sake. One might find the hugeness of the vessel interesting; it signifies military power on the move. There is a certain drama in watching the planes come in at high speeds and skid to a stop on the deck. Suppose the ship were burning: that would be even more interesting. This leads to an important point about the language of pictures. Moving pictures favor images that change. That is why violence and dynamic destruction find their way onto television so often. When something is destroyed violently it is altered in a highly visible way; hence the entrancing power of fire. Fire gives visual form to the ideas of consumption, disappearance, death—the thing that burned is actually taken away by fire. It is at this very basic level that fires make a good subject for television news. Something was here, now it's gone, and the change is recorded on film.

Earthquakes and typhoons have the same power. Before the viewer's eyes the world is taken apart. If a television viewer has relatives in Mexico City and an earthquake occurs there, then he or she may take a special interest in the images of destruction as a report from a specific place and time; that is, one may look at television pictures for information about an important event. But film of an earthquake can be interesting even if the viewer cares nothing about the event itself. Which is only to say, as we noted earlier, that there is another way of participating in the news—as a spectator who desires to be entertained. Actually to see buildings topple is exciting, no matter where the buildings are. The world turns to dust before our eyes.

Those who produce television news in America know that their medium favors images that move. That is why they are wary of "talking heads," people who simply appear in front of a camera and speak. When talking heads appear on television, there is nothing to record or document, no change in process. In the cinema the situation is somewhat different. On a movie screen, close-ups of a good actor speaking dramatically can 10 sometimes be interesting to watch. When Clint Eastwood narrows his eyes and challenges his rival to shoot first, the spectator sees the cool rage of the Eastwood character take visual form, and the narrowing of the eyes is dramatic. But much of the effect of this small movement depends on the size of the movie screen and the darkness of the theater, which make Eastwood and his every action "larger than life."

The television screen is smaller than life. It occupies about 15 percent of the viewer's visual field (compared to about 70 percent for the movie screen). It is not set in a darkened theater closed off from the world but in the viewer's ordinary living space. This means that visual changes must be more extreme and more dramatic to be interesting on television. A narrowing of the eyes will not do. A car crash, an earthquake, a burning factory are much better.

With these principles in mind, let us examine more closely the structure of a typical newscast, and here we will include in the discussion not only the pictures but all the nonlinguistic symbols that make up a television news show. For example, in America, almost all news shows begin with music, the tone of which suggests important events about to unfold. The music is very important, for it equates the news with various forms of drama and ritual—the opera, for example, or a wedding procession—in which musical themes underscore the meaning of the event. Music takes us immediately into the realm of the symbolic, a world that is not to be taken literally. After all, when events unfold in the real world, they do so without musical accompaniment. More symbolism follows. The sound of teletype machines can be heard in the studio, not because it is impossible to screen this noise out, but because the sound is a kind of music in itself. It tells us that data are pouring in from all corners of the globe, a sensation reinforced by the world map in the background (or clocks noting the time on different continents). The fact is that teletype machines are rarely used in TV news rooms, having been replaced by silent computer terminals. When seen, they have only a symbolic function.

Already, then, before a single news item is introduced, a great deal has been communicated. We know that we are in the presence of a symbolic event, a form of theater in which the day's events are to be dramatized. This theater takes the entire globe as its subject, although it may look at the world from the perspective of a single nation. A certain tension is present, like the atmosphere in a theater just before the curtain goes up. The tension is represented by the music, the staccato beat of the teletype machines, and often the sight of news workers scurrying around typing reports and answering phones. As a technical matter, it would be no problem to build a set in which the newsroom staff remained off camera, invisible to the viewer, but an important theatrical effect would be lost. By being busy on camera, the workers help communicate urgency about the events at hand, which suggests that situations are changing so rapidly that constant revision of the news is necessary.

The staff in the background also helps signal the importance of the person in the center, the anchor, "in command" of both the staff and the news. The anchor plays the role of host. He or she welcomes us to the newscast and welcomes us back from the different locations we visit during the filmed reports.

Many features of the newscast help the anchor to establish the impression of control. These are usually equated with production values in broadcasting. They include such things as graphics that tell the viewer what is being shown, or maps and charts that suddenly appear on the screen and disappear on cue, or the orderly progression from story to story. They also include the absence of gaps, or "dead time," during the broadcast, even the simple fact that the news starts and ends at a certain hour. These common features are thought of as purely technical matters, which a professional crew handles as a matter of course. But they are also symbols of a dominant theme of television news: the imposition of an orderly world—called "the news"—upon the disorderly flow of events.

While the form of a news broadcast emphasizes tidiness and control, its content can best be described as fragmented. Because time is so precious on television, because the nature of the medium favors dynamic visual images, and because the pressures of a commercial structure require the news to hold its audience above all else, there is rarely any attempt to explain issues in depth or place events in their proper context. The news moves nervously from a warehouse fire to a court decision, from a guerrilla war to a World Cup match, the quality of the film most often determining the length of the story. Certain stories show up only because they offer dramatic pictures. Bleachers collapse in South America: hundreds of people are crushed—a perfect television news story, for the cameras can record the face of disaster in all its anguish. Back in Washington, a new budget is approved by Congress. Here there is nothing to photograph because a budget is not a physical event; it is a document full of language and numbers. So the producers of the news will show a photo of the document itself, focusing on the cover where it says "Budget of the United States of America." Or sometimes they will send a camera crew to the government printing plant where copies of the budget are produced. That evening, while the contents of the budget are summarized by a voice-over, the viewer sees stacks of documents being loaded into boxes at the government printing plant. Then a few of the budget's more important provisions will be flashed on the screen in written form, but this is such a time-consuming process—using television as a printed page—that the producers keep it to a minimum. In short, the budget is not televisable, and for that reason its time on the news must be brief. The bleacher collapse will get more time that evening.

While appearing somewhat chaotic, these disparate stories are not just dropped in the news program helter-skelter. The appearance of a scattershot story order is really orchestrated to draw the audience from one story to the next—from one section to the next—through the commercial breaks to the end of the show. The story order is constructed to hold and build the viewership rather than place events in context or explain issues in depth.

Of course, it is a tendency of journalism in general to concentrate on the surface of events rather than underlying conditions; this is as true for the newspaper as it is for the newscast. But several features of television undermine whatever efforts journalists may make to give sense to the world. One is that a television broadcast is a series of events that occur in sequence, and the sequence is the same for all viewers. This is not true for a newspaper page, which displays many items simultaneously, allowing readers to choose the order in which they read them. If newspaper readers want only a summary of the latest tax bill, they can read the headline and the first paragraph of an article, and if they want more, they can keep reading. In a sense, then, everyone reads a different newspaper, for no two readers will read (or ignore) the same items.

But all television viewers see the same broadcast. They have no choices. A report is either in the broadcast or out, which means that anything which is of narrow interest is unlikely to be included. As NBC News executive Reuven Frank once explained:

> A newspaper, for example, can easily afford to print an item of conceivable interest to only a fraction of its readers. A television news program must be put together with the assumption that each item will be of some interest to everyone that watches. Every time a newspaper includes a feature which will attract a specialized group it can assume it is adding at least a little bit to its circulation. To the degree a television news program includes an item of this sort . . . it must assume that its audience will diminish.

The need to "include everyone," an identifying feature of commercial television in all its forms, prevents journalists from offering lengthy or complex explanations, or from tracing the sequence of events leading up to today's headlines. One of the ironies of political life in modern democracies is that many problems which concern the "general welfare" are of interest only to specialized groups. Arms control, for example, is an issue that literally concerns everyone in the world, and yet the language of arms control and the complexity of the subject are so daunting that only a minority of people can actually follow the issue from week to week and month to month. If it wants to act responsibly, a newspaper can at least make available more information about arms control than most people want. Commercial television cannot afford to do so.

But even if commercial television could afford to do so, it wouldn't. The fact that television news is principally made up of moving pictures prevents it from offering lengthy, coherent explanations of events. A television news show reveals the world as a series of unrelated, fragmentary moments. It does not—and cannot be expected to—offer a sense of

20

coherence or meaning. What does this suggest to a TV viewer? That the viewer must come with a prepared mind—information, opinions, a sense of proportion, an articulate value system. To the TV viewer lacking such mental equipment, a news program is only a kind of rousing light show. Here a falling building, there a five-alarm fire, everywhere the world as an object, much without meaning, connections, or continuity.

THINKING CRITICALLY ABOUT THE READING

1. Examine the writers' diction in the opening paragraph. (Glossary: *Diction*) What is their attitude toward television news? (Glossary: *Attitude*) What about their language led you to this conclusion? Does their diction throughout the essay support the impression created in the opening paragraph?

2. What is Postman and Powers's main point about television news? (Glossary: *Thesis*) Where do they state their position? What changes, if any, do they want to see readers and viewers make as a result of reading this article?

3. What kinds of evidence do Postman and Powers provide to support their position? (Glossary: *Evidence*) Which evidence do you find most persuasive? Least persuasive? Explain.

4. In what ways does the language of pictures differ from spoken and written language? Why, according to Postman and Powers, are these differences important for understanding television news?

5. Why do scenes of violence and dynamic destruction have such appeal to viewers? Why do television producers avoid "talking heads"? In comparison to the movies, why must visual changes "be more extreme and more dramatic . . . on television" (11)?

6. In what ways can television news be considered a form of theater? According to Postman and Powers, how are news telecasts staged? What is the one dominant theme of television news, and how is this theme orchestrated?

LANGUAGE IN ACTION

Postman and Powers suggest that pictures of destruction are entertaining because they show rapid and large-scale change. This, in turn, implies that pictures are chosen for the emotional effect they may have. Discuss your response to the following news photograph in terms of its emotional effect. Keep in mind both the feeling the scene itself creates and that created by the destruction that is the implied aftermath of the soldier's action. Postman and Powers also say that images can be converted to ideas. What ideas does this photograph convey about war? Explain how language could translate this image into different ideas about war or the military. How do such "translations" illustrate Postman and Powers's main point about language and pictures?

(**continued**)

WRITING SUGGESTIONS

1. Select several pictures from a photo album—of a wedding, or graduation, or a recent trip you took with friends. Do the pictures capture or tell the story of the event, or did you really have to be there to get the whole story? If a video of the event is available, watch it for the sake of comparison. Write an essay in which you discuss the limitations of still photographs in capturing an event.

2. Watch (and videotape, if possible) at least two networks' versions of the same day's evening news. How are the news shows the same? Different? To what extent do the news telecasts support the analysis of news programs presented by Postman and Powers? Report your findings in an essay.

3. What was the impact of television news reporting on such memorable events as the Gulf War, the O. J. Simpson trial, the death and funeral of Princess Diana, President Clinton's impeachment trial, the death of John F. Kennedy Jr., September 11th, the war in Iraq, or another newsworthy event? Research the event you choose in your library or on the Internet. Be sure to read accounts of your event in newspapers and magazines at the time it was happening. As you write an essay about the event, consider the following questions: To what extent can it be said that television news actually creates rather than reports the news? What impact do you think live coverage of events has on our perceptions of them? In what ways is live coverage different from an anchor's retelling of the news?

The Cult of the Amateur

ANDREW KEEN

Andrew Keen—writer, media personality, and Silicon Valley entrepreneur—is noted for his provocative analysis and commentary on technology, media, and culture. Born in London in 1960, Keen graduated from the University of London with a degree in modern history, after which he did graduate work at the University of California, Berkeley. He entered the Internet boom (and bust) in the mid-1990s with his own Internet start-up, AudioCafe.com, which lasted until 2000. He is the founder and host of AfterTV, a podcast chat show, whose guests "excavate the social, cultural and political consequences of the digital media revolution." Keen's commentaries can be read on such blog sites as *ZDNet, Britannica,* and *iHollywood Forum,* and he is a frequent guest on television and radio news programs (both fake and real) such as *The Colbert Report, The NewsHour with Jim Lehrer, The Today Show, Fox News, CNN International,* and National Public Radio's *Weekend Edition.* His articles have appeared in numerous publications, including the *Los Angeles Times,* the *San Francisco Chronicle,* the *Wall Street Journal, Forbes, Entertainment Weekly, Fast Company,* and the *Weekly Standard.*

   An article Keen wrote for the *Weekly Standard,* "Web 2.0: The second generation of the Internet has arrived. It's worse than you think," compared Web 2.0 to Marxism and brought Keen considerable notoriety. The article became the basis for his 2007 book, *The Cult of the Amateur: How the Internet Is Killing Our Culture,* which is described by *New York Times* book critic Michiko Kakutani as "a shrewdly argued jeremiad against the digerati effort to dethrone cultural and political gatekeepers and replace experts with the 'wisdom of the crowd.'" The following essay is the introduction to *The Cult of the Amateur.*

WRITING TO DISCOVER: *The Internet has become, for many, the primary source for information, news, and entertainment. How do you use the Web? Do you feel that Internet sources are completely reliable and credible, or are you sometimes skeptical about the "truth" of the information you receive?*

If I didn't know better, I'd think it was 1999 all over again. The boom has returned to Silicon Valley, and the mad utopians are once again running wild. I bumped into one such evangelist at a recent San Francisco mixer.

   Over glasses of fruity local Chardonnay, we swapped notes about our newest new things. He told me his current gig involved a new software for publishing music, text, and video on the Internet.

   "It's MySpace meets YouTube meets Wikipedia meets Google," he said. "On steroids."

In reply, I explained I was working on a polemic about the destructive impact of the digital revolution on our culture, economy, and values.

"It's ignorance meets egoism meets bad taste meets mob rule," I said, 5 unable to resist a smile. "On steroids."

He smiled uneasily in return. "So it's Huxley meets the digital age," he said. "You're rewriting Huxley for the twenty-first century." He raised his wine glass in my honor. "To *Brave New World 2.0!*"

We clinked wine glasses. But I knew we were toasting the wrong Huxley. Rather than Aldous, the inspiration behind this book comes from his grandfather, T. H. Huxley, the nineteenth-century evolutionary biologist and author of the "infinite monkey theorem." Huxley's theory says that if you provide infinite monkeys with infinite typewriters, some monkey somewhere will eventually create a masterpiece—a play by Shakespeare, a Platonic dialogue, or an economic treatise by Adam Smith.[1]

In the pre-Internet age, T. H. Huxley's scenario of infinite monkeys empowered with infinite technology seemed more like a mathematical jest than a dystopian vision. But what had once appeared as a joke now seems to foretell the consequences of a flattening of culture that is blurring the lines between traditional audience and author, creator and consumer, expert and amateur. This is no laughing matter.

Today's technology hooks all those monkeys up with all those typewriters. Except in our Web 2.0 world, the typewriters aren't quite typewriters, but rather networked personal computers, and the monkeys aren't quite monkeys, but rather Internet users. And instead of creating masterpieces, these millions and millions of exuberant monkeys—many with no more talent in the creative arts than our primate cousins—are creating an endless digital forest of mediocrity. For today's amateur monkeys can use their networked computers to publish everything from uninformed political commentary, to unseemly home videos, to embarrassingly amateurish music, to unreadable poems, reviews, essays, and novels.

At the heart of this infinite monkey experiment in self-publishing 10 is the Internet diary, the ubiquitous blog. Blogging has become such a mania that a new blog is being created every second of every minute of every hour of every day. We are blogging with monkeylike shamelessness about our private lives, our sex lives, our dream lives, our lack of lives, our Second Lives. At the time of writing there are fifty-three million blogs on the Internet, and this number is doubling every six months. In the time it took you to read this paragraph, ten new blogs were launched.

If we keep up this pace, there will be over five hundred million blogs by 2010, collectively corrupting and confusing popular opinion about

---

1. For more about Huxley's theory, see Jorge Luis Borges's 1939 essay "The Total Library."

everything from politics, to commerce, to arts and culture. Blogs have become so dizzyingly infinite that they've undermined our sense of what is true and what is false, what is real and what is imaginary. These days, kids can't tell the difference between credible news by objective professional journalists and what they read on joeshmoe.blogspot.com. For these Generation Y utopians, every posting is just another person's version of the truth; every fiction is just another person's version of the facts.

Then there is Wikipedia, an online encyclopedia where anyone with opposable thumbs and a fifth-grade education can publish anything on any topic from AC/DC to Zoroastrianism. Since Wikipedia's birth, more than fifteen thousand contributors have created nearly three million entries in over a hundred different languages—none of them edited or vetted for accuracy. With hundreds of thousands of visitors a day, Wikipedia has become the third most visited site for information and current events; a more trusted source for news than the CNN or BBC Web sites, even though Wikipedia has no reporters, no editorial staff, and no experience in newsgathering. It's the blind leading the blind—infinite monkeys providing infinite information for infinite readers, perpetuating the cycle of misinformation and ignorance.

On Wikipedia, everyone with an agenda can rewrite an entry to their liking—and contributors frequently do. *Forbes* recently reported, for example, a story of anonymous McDonald's and Wal-Mart employees furtively using Wikipedia entries as a medium for deceptively spreading corporate propaganda. On the McDonald's entry, a link to Eric Schlosser's *Fast Food Nation* conveniently disappeared; on Wal-Mart's somebody eliminated a line about underpaid employees making less than 20 percent of the competition.[2]

But the Internet's infinite monkey experiment is not limited to the written word. T. H. Huxley's nineteenth-century typewriter has evolved into not only the computer, but also the camcorder, turning the Internet into a vast library for user-generated video content. One site, YouTube, is a portal of amateur videos that, at the time of writing, was the world's fastest-growing site,[3] attracting sixty-five thousand new videos daily and boasting sixty million clips being watched each day; that adds up to over twenty-five million new videos a year,[4] and some twenty-five billion hits. In the fall of 2006, this overnight sensation was bought by Google for over a billion and a half dollars.

YouTube eclipses even the blogs in the inanity and absurdity of its content. Nothing seems too prosaic or narcissistic for these videographer monkeys. The site is an infinite gallery of amateur movies showing poor fools dancing, singing, eating, washing, shopping, driving, cleaning, 15

---

2. Evan Hessel, "Shillipedia," *Forbes,* June 19, 2006.
3. http://mashable.com/2006/07/22/youtube-is-worlds-fastest-growing-website/
4. Scott Wooley, "Video Fixation," *Forbes,* October 16, 2006.

sleeping, or just staring into their computers. In August 2006, one hugely popular video called "The Easter Bunny Hates You" showed a man in a bunny suit harassing and attacking people on the streets; according to *Forbes* magazine, this video was viewed more than three million times in two weeks. A few other favorite subjects include a young woman watching another YouTube user who is watching yet another user—a virtual hall of mirrors that eventually leads to a woman making a peanut butter and jelly sandwich in front of the television; a Malaysian dancer in absurdly short skirts grooving to Ricky Martin and Britney Spears; a dog chasing its tail; an Englishwoman instructing her viewers how to eat a chocolate and marmalade cookie; and, in a highly appropriate addition to the YouTube library, a video of dancing stuffed monkeys.

What's more disturbing than the fact that millions of us willingly tune in to such nonsense each day is that some Web sites are making monkeys out of us without our even knowing it. By entering words into Google's search engine, we are actually creating something called "collective intelligence," the sum wisdom of all Google users. The logic of Google's search engine, what technologists call its algorithm, reflects the "wisdom" of the crowd. In other words, the more people click on a link that results from a search, the more likely that link will come up in subsequent searches. The search engine is an aggregation of the ninety million questions we collectively ask Google each day; in other words, it just tells us what we already know.

This same "wisdom" of the crowd is manifested on editor-free news-aggregation sites such as Digg and Reddit. The ordering of the headlines on these sites reflects what other users have been reading rather than the expert judgment of news editors. As I write, there is a brutal war going on in Lebanon between Israel and Hezbollah. But the Reddit user wouldn't know this because there is nothing about Israel, Lebanon, or Hezbollah on the site's top twenty "hot" stories. Instead, subscribers can read about a flat-chested English actress, the walking habits of elephants, a spoof of the latest Mac commercial, and underground tunnels in Japan. Reddit is a mirror of our most banal interests. It makes a mockery of traditional news media and turns current events into a childish game of Trivial Pursuit.

The *New York Times* reports that 50 percent of all bloggers blog for the sole purpose of reporting and sharing experiences about their personal lives. The tagline for YouTube is "Broadcast Yourself." And broadcast ourselves we do, with all the shameless self-admiration of the mythical Narcissus. As traditional mainstream media is replaced by a personalized one, the Internet has become a mirror to ourselves. Rather than using it to seek news, information, or culture, we use it to actually BE the news, the information, the culture.

This infinite desire for personal attention is driving the hottest part of the new Internet economy—social-networking sites like MySpace,

Facebook, and Bebo. As shrines for the cult of self-broadcasting, these sites have become tabula rasas of our individual desires and identities. They claim to be all about "social networking" with others, but in reality they exist so that we can advertise ourselves: everything from our favorite books and movies, to photos from our summer vacations, to "testimonials" praising our more winsome qualities or recapping our latest drunken exploits. It's hardly surprising that the increasingly tasteless nature of such self-advertisements has led to an infestation of anonymous sexual predators and pedophiles.

But our cultural standards and moral values are not all that are at 20 stake. Gravest of all, the very traditional institutions that have helped to foster and create our news, our music, our literature, our television shows, and our movies are under assault as well. Newspapers and newsmagazines, one of the most reliable sources of information about the world we live in, are flailing, thanks to the proliferation of free blogs and sites like Craigslist that offer free classifieds, undermining paid ad placements. In the first quarter of 2006, profits plummeted dramatically at all the major newspaper companies—down 69 percent at the New York Times Company, 28 percent at the Tribune Company, and 11 percent at Gannett, the nation's largest newspaper company. Circulation is down, too. At the *San Francisco Chronicle,* ironically one of the newspapers of record for Silicon Valley, readership was down a dizzying 16 percent in the middle two quarters of 2005 alone.[5] And in 2007, Time, Inc., laid off almost 300 people, primarily from editorial, from such magazines as *Time, People,* and *Sports Illustrated.*

Those of us who still read the newspaper and magazines know that people are buying less music, too. Thanks to the rampant digital piracy spawned by file-sharing technology, sales of recorded music dropped over 20 percent between 2000 and 2006.[6]

In parallel with the rise of YouTube, Hollywood is experiencing its own financial troubles. Domestic box office sales now represent less than 20 percent of Hollywood's revenue and, with the levelling off of DVD sales and the rampant global piracy, the industry is desperately searching for a new business model that will enable it to profitably distribute movies on the Internet. According to *The New Yorker* film critic David Denby, many studio executives in Hollywood are now in a "panic" over declining revenue. One bleak consequence is cuts. Disney, for example, announced 650 job cuts in 2006, and an almost 50 percent drop in the number of animated movies produced annually.[7]

---

5. Audit Bureau of Circulations, September 2005, reports. BBC News, January 23, 2006. (http://news.bbc.co.uk/2/hi/entertainment/4639066.stm.)

6. Jeff Howe, "No Suit Required," *Wired,* September 2006.

7. Frank Ahrens, "Disney to Reorganize Its Lagging Movie Studios," *Washington Post,* July 20, 2006.

Old media is facing extinction. But if so, what will take its place? Apparently, it will be Silicon Valley's hot new search engines, social media sites, and video portals. Every new page on MySpace, every new blog post, every new YouTube video adds up to another potential source of advertising revenue lost to mainstream media. Thus, Rupert Murdoch's canny—or desperate—decision in July 2005 to buy MySpace for five hundred and eighty million dollars. Thus, the $1.65 billion sale of YouTube and the explosion of venture capital funding YouTube copycat sites. And, thus, the seemingly unstoppable growth at Google where, in the second quarter of 2006, revenue surged to almost two and a half billion dollars.

What happens, you might ask, when ignorance meets egoism meets bad taste meets mob rule?

The monkeys take over. Say good-bye to today's experts and cultural   25
gatekeepers—our reporters, news anchors, editors, music companies, and Hollywood movie studios. In today's cult of the amateur,[8] the monkeys are running the show. With their infinite typewriters, they are authoring the future. And we may not like how it reads.

THINKING CRITICALLY ABOUT THE READING

1. What is evolutionary biologist T. H. Huxley's "infinite monkey" theorem? How does Keen relate it to today's "Web 2.0 world"?

2. What does Keen mean when he writes: "Blogs have become so dizzyingly infinite that they've undermined our sense of what is true and what is false, what is real and what is imaginary" (11)? Do you agree with him that this is a cause for concern?

3. According to Keen, Wikipedia has become a more trusted news source for some people than the CNN or BBC news Web sites. Why does this disturb him? What are Keen's key criticisms of Wikipedia?

4. What is Keen's central criticism of "user-generated video content" such as YouTube?

5. Explain what Keen means when he writes that search engines "are making monkeys out of us without our even knowing it" (16)?

6. Consider what social-networking sites such as MySpace and Facebook are intended to do. What does Keen mean when he calls these sites "shrines for the cult of self-broadcasting" and "tabula rasas of our individual desires and identities" (19)?

7. Keen gravely states that "[o]ld media is facing extinction" (23). What are the examples he offers? (Glossary: *Examples*) What about this most concerns him?

---

8. The term "cult of the amateur" was first coined by Nicholas Carr in his essay "The Amorality of Web 2.0," roughtype.com, October 3, 2005.

LANGUAGE IN ACTION

How do you use the Internet? List your most frequently visited sites and the reason you go to each. Think about how your use of the Internet has changed over time. List what sites you go to less frequently, or stopped going to altogether, and why you stopped or switched to something else. Discuss your list, and your reflections, with a small group in your class. How do your lists compare?

WRITING SUGGESTIONS

1. Keen writes that the "wisdom" of the crowd (which he considers "mob rule") manifests itself in an extreme form on news-aggregation sites such as Digg and Reddit, where the headlines are presented in an order determined, not by a trained news editor, but by "votes" of readers themselves. On the Reddit site, for example, the promotional copy reads: "Reddit is a source for what's new and popular online. Vote on links that you like or dislike and help decide what's popular, or submit your own!" Write an essay in which you take a position on user participation in news content and placement. How much control do you think readers should have over what content is presented? Which do you trust more: the editor-free news-aggregation sites, or the editorial judgment of more traditional journalism? Or is there room for both? Explain.

2. In a 2007 interview with Jeffrey Brown on the PBS *NewsHour with Jim Lehrer*, Keen talked about what many call the "democratization" of the Internet, which he calls "the cult of the amateur." In his opinion, user-generated Internet content is undermining reliable, professional, and quality content and replacing it with content that is "unreliable, inane, and often rather corrupt." Do you agree with Keen's analysis? Write an essay in defense of his position, or present a contrasting view, citing your own use of the Internet as an example.

What Happens When Blogs Go Mainstream?

ANNALEE NEWITZ

Writer, author, blogger Annalee Newitz was born in Irvine, California, "just after the New Left died and shortly before abortion was legalized," as she describes it on her blog, *Techsploitation.com*. Newitz received her Ph.D. in English and American studies at University of California, Berkeley, in 1998 and taught there until 1999, when she became a full-time writer and editor.

Newitz has written extensively about pop culture and media, technology, and science for a wide array of outlets, including *New York Magazine, Popular Science, New Scientist, Salon.com,* the *Silicon Valley Metro,* and numerous alternative weeklies, academic journals, and anthologies. She has founded a progressive political webzine, *Bad Subjects,* and published several books, including *White Trash: Race and Class in America* (1997); *The Bad Subjects Anthology* (1998); *Pretend We're Dead: Capitalist Monsters in American Pop Culture* (2006); and *She's Such a Geek: Women Write about Science, Technology, and Other Nerdy Stuff* (2007), which she coedited with Charlie Anders.

Newitz's blog *Techsploitation* is a nationally syndicated column that runs weekly in the *San Francisco Bay Guardian* and on *AlterNet* and appears regularly in papers in the United States and abroad. Newitz has recently moved from *Wired* magazine, where she was a contributing editor and writer, to Gawker Media network, where she will run the blog *io9,* a "place where science and futurism overlap with politics."

Like Andrew Keen, Newitz is greatly concerned about what blogs actually *should* be doing. "Now that I am editing and writing [*Techsploitation*]," she wrote, "I worry a lot about what will happen to this once-upstart medium as it merges with more traditional media." By going mainstream, Newitz fears blogs will lose their edge—allowing self-censorship and "narrowing the range of what it's permissible to talk about in a public forum."

WRITING TO DISCOVER: *Do you write a blog? If so, why do you keep it? Do you have favorite blogs? If so, what makes them your favorite? If you neither write nor read blogs, do you feel you're missing out on something?*

Six years ago I wrote a column titled "Blog Anxiety," which was all about how bloggers make me nervous and jealous with their lightning-fast news cycles. I bemoaned my inability to commit words to public record without waiting for editorial oversight and without waiting for publication day (inevitably several days if not weeks after I had written those words).

I talked about how bloggers can cite sources they've talked to informally and how they seem blissfully unburdened by concerns about injecting a personal perspective into their writing. That was before It All Changed. And by "It All Changed," I don't just mean that I became a blogger, which I did. More profoundly, I mean that blogs themselves have changed.

They are not the subterranean upstart media without rules anymore. I'm certainly not the first person to observe that blogs are fast becoming indistinguishable from mainstream media, and indeed places like the *New York Times* and the *Washington Post* have blogs that are often more newsy than the papers themselves. This blurring between formerly mainstream media and formerly alternative media means that the upstarts are having to follow old-school rules.

While I can't speak for all bloggers, I prefer not to publish anything on my blog that hasn't been edited. I don't want readers to see my spelling errors and craptastic leaps in logic, thank you very much (of course you'll still see many, but not as many as you would if there were no edits). I also spend a fair amount of time on the phone or on e-mail interviewing sources for my posts, as well as doing research. And I won't publish anything that I think will get me sued, is libelous, or is just plain wrong, even if it's funny. What I'm saying is that my blog is not exactly the unedited, stream-of-consciousness outpourings of a person in pajamas. Well, OK, I am often in pajamas.

Recently I was reading a conversation thread on Metafilter, one of my 5 favorite still-subterranean Web sites for smart talk and slagging. Somebody mentioned my science fiction blog io9.com, then snarked at me for starting a blog when I was on record saying that blogs freak me out. An unedited discussion full of spiky banter and maniacal analysis followed — exactly the kind of conversation I once associated with all blogs. People were nastier than they would have been if writing for a mainstream publication, but the cool ideas-to-noise ratio was nevertheless far higher than you'd ever get in *USA Today* or CNN.

And this brings me to what scares me about blogs now. I worry that instead of taking the Metafilter ethos mainstream, many blogs are leaving it behind. That's not because we have editors or talk to sources — I'm happy to see bloggers doing that.

It's because our audiences are starting to be as big as those of the mainstream media, and the mainstream media have taught us to be afraid of saying what we really think to those audiences. They've taught us that we should tiptoe around hot-button issues like climate change and sex and delay publishing stories that might upset the government until such a time as the government is comfortable with those stories.

This is the source of my blog anxiety in 2008. Will blogs take on all the bad habits of the mainstream media, self-censoring when we should be publishing? Or will bloggers help the media progress just a little bit further toward independence of thought and bravery in publication?

It's still too early to tell. Even the most mainstream blogs don't suffer the same pressures that mainstream publications like the *New York*

Times do. Blogs don't have the 100-year histories of many newspapers and magazines—they don't have the huge staffs and long, elaborate relationships with corporations and governments and famous, influential people. And I am glad we don't have that history. I hope we can make our own, new history and shake up the way news is made and culture is analyzed. And then, in 30 years, I hope a new medium will come along and kick our asses too.

THINKING CRITICALLY ABOUT THE READING

1. What caused Newitz anxiety in 2002 when she wrote a column titled "Blog Anxiety"? Six years later, what is the source of her anxiety about "formerly alternative media" (3)?

2. What distinguishes Newitz's blogging from the "stream-of-consciousness outpourings of a person in pajamas" (4) usually associated with bloggers? What standards does she apply to her blog that others might not?

3. Newitz uses the community blog *Metafilter* as an example of a "still-subterranean" Web site that maintains a "cool ideas-to-noise ratio" far higher than that of *USA Today* or CNN (5). What basic concerns about blogs going mainstream does Newitz address in discussing this example?

4. What does Newitz mean by "self-censoring"? How does self-censoring work in the media? What are the results of such self-censoring?

5. What are some of the pressures that mainstream publications such as the *New York Times* are under that most blogs are not? How do these pressures affect the news that is reported?

6. What is Newitz's conclusion? (Glossary: *Beginnings and Endings*) What is her hope for the future?

LANGUAGE IN ACTION

Take a look at today's Metafilter (http://www.metafilter.com/). Then go to the front page of a mainstream online news source such as CNN.com (www.cnn.com), the *San Francisco Chronicle* (http://www.sfgate.com), or *USA Today* (http://www.usatoday.com/). How much overlap is there among the top stories covered? Why do you think this is? Do you prefer one site's coverage over the other's?

WRITING SUGGESTIONS

1. In a 2007 *AlterNet* column entitled "Wikipedia Activism," Newitz wrote:

> When I edit Wikipedia, I am fighting for the future. There are certain things and people whose memories I want preserved for generations to come so that curious searchers a century from now will

know the full story. Via Wikipedia, they will get more than stories of great politicians and giant corporations from glossy histories. I want this user-edited, online encyclopedia to tell tales of the brave and the marginal as well as the notorious and the powerful. That's why I've become a Wikipedia activist.

Andrew Keen, on the other hand, appears to have quite a different take on Wikipedia when he writes in "Cult of the Amateur" (p. 415):

> Then there is Wikipedia, an online encyclopedia where anyone with opposable thumbs and a fifth-grade education can publish anything on any topic from AC/DC to Zoroastrianism. . . . On Wikipedia, everyone with an agenda can rewrite an entry to their liking—and contributors frequently do.

Write an essay on these opposing perspectives of Wikipedia. Whose position do you find more persuasive? Why?

2. Write an essay about your use of new media as a source of news and entertainment. How have your attitudes and habits changed over time? Do you see the "digital revolution" as largely beneficial, or do you see it as having a negative effect on standards and credible content?

The Hard Sell: Advertising in America

BILL BRYSON

Journalist and author Bill Bryson was born in Des Moines, Iowa, in 1951, but spent most of his adult life in Great Britain, beginning with a backpacking trip to Europe in the early 1970s. He settled in England with his wife in 1977, where he worked as a journalist, eventually becoming chief copy editor of the business section of the *Times,* and then national news editor for the *Independent.* Bryson's interest in language is reflected in his *A Dictionary of Troublesome Words* (1987), *The Mother Tongue: English and How It Got That Way* (1990), *Shakespeare: The World as Stage* (2007), and most recently, *Bryson's Dictionary for Writers and Editors* (2008). Among his many books on travel are *The Lost Continent: Travels in Small-Town America* (1989), *Neither Here Nor There: Travels in Europe* (1992), *A Walk in the Woods: Rediscovering America on the Appalachian Trail* (1998), and *Bill Bryson's African Diary* (2002). Bryson's 2003 book on science, *A Short History of Nearly Everything,* won the prestigious Royal Society Aventis Prize for science writing. His memoir, *The Life and Times of the Thunderbolt Kid,* was published in 2006.

The following essay is a chapter in Bryson's *Made in America: An Informal History of the English Language in the United States* (1994). In it, he provides a historical perspective on advertising and explores some of the trends that have appeared over the years. It may surprise many people to learn that advertising as we know it is a modern invention, spanning only about a century. During that time, however, the influence of advertisements has grown so much that they now shape the way we see the world.

WRITING TO DISCOVER: *Reactions to advertising vary, but most people would say that ads are a necessary evil and that they ignore them whenever possible. Yet advertising is a multibillion-dollar industry, which is financed by what we buy and sell. Think about some recent TV shows you've watched or newspapers you've read. Jot down the names of the products you saw advertised. Do you buy any of these products? Write about the influences, if any, advertising seems to have on the way you spend your money.*

In 1885, a young man named George Eastman formed the Eastman Dry Plate and Film Company in Rochester, New York. It was rather a bold thing to do. Aged just thirty-one, Eastman was a junior clerk in a bank on a comfortable but modest salary of $15 a week. He had no background in business. But he was passionately devoted to photography and had become increasingly gripped with the conviction that anyone who could develop a simple, untechnical camera, as opposed to the cumbersome, outsized, fussily complex contrivances then on the market, stood to make a fortune.

Eastman worked tirelessly for three years to perfect his invention, supporting himself in the meantime by making dry plates for commercial photographers, and in June 1888 produced a camera that was positively dazzling in its simplicity: a plain black box just six and a half inches long by three and a quarter inches wide, with a button on the side and a key for advancing the film. Eastman called his device the *Detective Camera*. Detectives were all the thing—Sherlock Holmes was just taking off with American readers—and the name implied that it was so small and simple that it could be used unnoticed, as a detective might.

The camera had no viewfinder and no way of focusing. The *photographer* or *photographist* (it took a while for the first word to become the established one) simply held the camera in front of him, pressed a button on the side, and hoped for the best. Each roll took a hundred pictures. When the roll was fully exposed, the anxious owner sent the entire camera to Rochester for developing. Eventually he received the camera back, freshly loaded with film, and—assuming all had gone well—one hundred small circular pictures, two and a half inches in diameter.

Often all didn't go well. The film Eastman used at first was made of paper, which tore easily and had to be carefully stripped of its emulsion before the exposures could be developed. It wasn't until the invention of celluloid roll film by a sixty-five-year-old Episcopal minister named Hannibal Goodwin in Newark, New Jersey—this truly was the age of the amateur inventor—that amateur photography became a reliable undertaking. Goodwin didn't call his invention *film* but *photographic pellicule,* and, as was usual, spent years fighting costly legal battles with Eastman without ever securing the recognition or financial payoff he deserved—though eventually, years after Goodwin's death, Eastman was ordered to pay $5 million to the company that inherited the patent.

In September 1888, Eastman changed the name of the camera to   5
Kodak—an odd choice, since it was meaningless, and in 1888 no one gave meaningless names to products, especially successful products. Since British patent applications at the time demanded a full explanation of trade and brand names, we know how Eastman arrived at his inspired name. He crisply summarized his reasoning in his patent application: "First. It is short. Second. It is not capable of mispronunciation. Third. It does not resemble anything in the art and cannot be associated with anything in the art except the Kodak." Four years later the whole enterprise was renamed the Eastman Kodak Company.

Despite the considerable expense involved—a Kodak camera sold for $25, and each roll of film cost $10, including developing—by 1895, over 100,000 Kodaks had been sold and Eastman was a seriously wealthy man. A lifelong bachelor, he lived with his mother in a thirty-seven-room mansion with twelve bathrooms. Soon people everywhere were talking about snapshots, originally a British shooting term for a hastily executed shot. Its photographic sense was coined by the English astronomer Sir John Herschel, who also gave the world the terms *positive* and *negative* in their photographic senses.

From the outset, Eastman developed three crucial strategies that have been the hallmarks of virtually every successful consumer goods company since. First, he went for the mass market, reasoning that it was better to make a little money each from a lot of people rather than a lot of money from a few. He also showed a tireless, obsessive dedication to making his products better and cheaper. In the 1890s, such an approach was widely perceived as insane. If you had a successful product you milked it for all it was worth. If competitors came along with something better, you bought them out or tried to squash them with lengthy patent fights or other bullying tactics. What you certainly did not do was create new products that made your existing lines obsolescent. Eastman did. Throughout the late 1890s, Kodak introduced a series of increasingly cheaper, niftier cameras—the Bull's Eye model of 1896, which cost just $12, and the famous slim-line Folding Pocket Kodak of 1898, before finally in 1900 producing his eureka model: the little box Brownie, priced at just $1 and with film at 15 cents a reel (though with only six exposures per reel).

Above all, what set Eastman apart was the breathtaking lavishness of his advertising. In 1899 alone, he spent $750,000, an unheard-of sum, on advertising. Moreover, it was *good* advertising: crisp, catchy, reassuringly trustworthy. "You press the button—we do the rest" ran the company's first slogan, thus making a virtue of its shortcomings. Never mind that you couldn't load or unload the film yourself. Kodak would do it for you. In 1905, it followed with another classic slogan: "If It Isn't an Eastman, It Isn't a Kodak."

Kodak's success did not escape other businessmen, who also began to see virtue in the idea of steady product refinement and improvement. AT&T and Westinghouse, among others, set up research laboratories with the idea of creating a stream of new products, even at the risk of displacing old ones. Above all, everyone everywhere began to advertise.

Advertising was already a well-established phenomenon by the turn   10
of the twentieth century. Newspapers had begun carrying ads as far back as the early 1700s, and magazines soon followed. (Benjamin Franklin has the distinction of having run the first magazine ad, seeking the whereabouts of a runaway slave, in 1741.) By 1850, the country had its first *advertising agency,* the American Newspaper Advertising Agency, though its function was to buy advertising space rather than come up with creative campaigns. The first advertising agency in the modern sense was N. W. Ayer & Sons of Philadelphia, established in 1869. *To advertise* originally carried the sense of to broadcast or disseminate news. Thus a nineteenth-century newspaper that called itself the *Advertiser* meant

that it had lots of news, not lots of ads. By the early 1800s the term had been stretched to accommodate the idea of spreading the news of the availability of certain goods or services. A newspaper notice that read "Jos. Parker, Hatter" was essentially announcing that if anyone was in the market for hats, Jos. Parker had them. In the sense of persuading members of the public to acquire items they might not otherwise think of buying—items they didn't know they needed—advertising is a phenomenon of the modern age.

By the 1890s, advertising was appearing everywhere—in newspapers and magazines, on *billboards* (an Americanism dating from 1850), on the sides of buildings, on passing streetcars, on paper bags, even on matchbooks, which were invented in 1892 and were being extensively used as an advertising medium within three years.

Very early on, advertisers discovered the importance of a good slogan. Many of our more venerable slogans are older than you might think. Ivory Soap's "99 44/100 percent pure" dates from 1879. Schlitz has been calling itself "the beer that made Milwaukee famous" since 1895, and Heinz's "57 varieties" followed a year later. Morton Salt's "When it rains, it pours" dates from 1911, the American Florist Association's "Say it with flowers" was first used in 1912, and the "good to the last drop" of Maxwell House coffee, named for the Maxwell House Hotel in Nashville, where it was first served, has been with us since 1907. (The slogan is said to have originated with Teddy Roosevelt, who pronounced the coffee "good to the last drop," prompting one wit to ask, "So what's wrong with the last drop?")

Sometimes slogans took a little working on. Coca-Cola described itself as "the drink that makes a pause refreshing" before realizing, in 1929, that "the pause that refreshes" was rather more succinct and memorable. A slogan could make all the difference to a product's success. After advertising its soap as an efficacious way of dealing with "conspicuous nose pores," Woodbury's Facial Soap came up with the slogan "The skin you love to touch" and won the hearts of millions. The great thing about a slogan was that it didn't have to be accurate to be effective. Heinz never actually had exactly "57 varieties" of anything. The catchphrase arose simply because H. J. Heinz, the company's founder, decided he liked the sound of the number. Undeterred by considerations of verity, he had the slogan slapped on every one of the products he produced, already in 1896 far more than fifty-seven. For a time the company tried to arrange its products into fifty-seven arbitrary clusters, but in 1969 it gave up the ruse altogether and abandoned the slogan.

Early in the 1900s, advertisers discovered another perennial feature of marketing—the *giveaway*, as it was called almost from the start. Consumers soon became acquainted with the irresistibly tempting notion that if they bought a particular product they could expect a reward—the chance to receive a prize, a free book (almost always ostensibly dedicated to the general improvement of one's well-being but invariably a thinly disguised plug for the manufacturer's range of products), a free sample, or a rebate in the form of a shiny dime, or be otherwise endowed with some gratifying bagatelle. Typical of the genre was a turn-of-the-century tome called *The Vital Question Cook Book,* which was promoted as an aid to livelier meals, but which proved upon receipt to contain 112 pages of recipes all involving the use of Shredded Wheat. Many of these had a certain air of desperation about them, notably the "Shredded Wheat Biscuit Jellied Apple Sandwich" and the "Creamed Spinach on Shredded Wheat Biscuit Toast." Almost all involved nothing more than spooning some everyday food on a piece of shredded wheat and giving it an inflated name. Nonetheless the company distributed no fewer than four million copies of *The Vital Question Cook Book* to eager consumers.

The great breakthrough in twentieth-century advertising, however, 15
came with the identification and exploitation of the American consumer's Achilles' heel: anxiety. One of the first to master the form was King Gillette, inventor of the first safety razor and one of the most relentless advertisers of the early 1900s. Most of the early ads featured Gillette himself, who with his fussy toothbrush mustache and well-oiled hair looked more like a caricature of a Parisian waiter than a captain of industry. After starting with a few jaunty words about the ease and convenience of the safety razor—"Compact? Rather!"—he plunged the reader into the heart of the matter: "When you use my razor you are exempt from the dangers that men often encounter who allow their faces to come in contact with brush, soap, and barbershop accessories used on other people."

Here was an entirely new approach to selling goods. Gillette's ads were in effect telling you that not only did there exist a product that you never previously suspected you needed, but if you *didn't* use it you would very possibly attract a crop of facial diseases you never knew existed. The combination proved irresistible. Though the Gillette razor retailed for a hefty $5—half the average workingman's weekly pay—it sold by the millions, and King Gillette became a very wealthy man. (Though only for a time, alas. Like many others of his era, he grew obsessed with the idea of the perfectibility of mankind and expended so much of his energies writing books of convoluted philosophy with titles like *The Human Drift* that he eventually lost control of his company and most of his fortune.)

By the 1920s, advertisers had so refined the art that a consumer could scarcely pick up a magazine without being bombarded with unsettling questions: "Do You Make These Mistakes in English?"; "Will Your Hair Stand Close Inspection?"; "When Your Guests Are Gone—Are You Sorry You Ever Invited Them?" (because, that is, you lack social polish); "Did Nature fail to put roses in your cheeks?"; "Will There be a Victrola in Your Home This Christmas?"[1] The 1920s truly were the Age of Anxiety. One

---

1. The most famous 1920s ad of them all didn't pose a question, but it did play on the reader's anxiety: "They Laughed When I Sat Down, but When I Started to Play . . ." It was originated by the U.S. School of Music in 1925.

ad pictured a former golf champion, "now only a wistful onlooker," whose career had gone sour because he had neglected his teeth. Scott Tissues mounted a campaign showing a forlorn-looking businessman sitting on a park bench beneath the bold caption "A Serious Business Handicap—These Troubles That Come from Harsh Toilet Tissue." Below the picture the text explained "65 percent of all men and women over 40 are suffering from some form of rectal trouble, estimates a prominent specialist connected with one of New York's largest hospitals. 'And one of the contributing causes,' he states, 'is inferior toilet tissue.'" There was almost nothing that one couldn't become uneasy about. One ad even asked: "Can You Buy a Radio Safely?" Distressed bowels were the most frequent target. The makers of Sal Hepatica warned: "We rush to meetings, we dash to parties. We are on the go all day long. We exercise too little, and we eat too much. And, in consequence, we impair our bodily functions—often we retain food within us too long. And when that occurs, poisons are set up—*Auto-Intoxication begins.*"

In addition to the dread of auto-intoxication, the American consumer faced a gauntlet of other newly minted maladies—*pyorrhea, halitosis* (coined as a medical term in 1874, but popularized by Listerine beginning in 1922 with the slogan "Even your best friend won't tell you"), *athlete's foot* (a term invented by the makers of Absorbine Jr. in 1928), *dead cuticles, scabby toes, iron-poor blood, vitamin deficiency* (*vitamins* had been coined in 1912, but the word didn't enter the general vocabulary until the 1920s, when advertisers realized it sounded worryingly scientific), *fallen stomach, tobacco breath,* and *psoriasis,* though Americans would have to wait until the next decade for the scientific identification of the gravest of personal disorders—*body odor,* a term invented in 1933 by the makers of Lifebuoy soap and so terrifying in its social consequences that it was soon abbreviated to a whispered *B.O.*

The white-coated technicians of American laboratories had not only identified these new conditions, but—miraculously, it seemed—simultaneously come up with cures for them. Among the products that were invented or rose to greatness in this busy, neurotic decade were *Cutex* (for those deceased cuticles), *Vick's VapoRub, Geritol, Serutan* ("Natures spelled backwards," as the voiceover always said with somewhat bewildering reassurance, as if spelling a product's name backward conferred some medicinal benefit), *Noxema* (for which read: "knocks eczema"), *Preparation H, Murine* eyedrops, and *Dr. Scholl's Foot Aids.*[2] It truly was an age of miracles—one in which you could even cure a smoker's cough by smoking, so long as it was Old Golds you smoked, because, as the slogan proudly if somewhat untruthfully boasted, they contained "Not a cough

---

2. And yes, there really was a Dr. Scholl. His name was William Scholl; he was a real doctor, genuinely dedicated to the well-being of feet, and they are still very proud of him in his hometown of La Porte, Indiana.

in a carload." (As late as 1953, L&M cigarettes were advertised as "just what the doctor ordered!")

By 1927, advertising was a $1.5-billion-a-year industry in the United   20
States, and advertising people were held in such awe that they were asked not only to mastermind campaigns but even to name the products. An ad man named Henry N. McKinney, for instance, named *Keds* shoes, *Karo* syrup, *Meadow Gold* butter, and *Uneeda Biscuits.*

Product names tended to cluster around certain sounds. Breakfast cereals often ended in *-ies (Wheaties, Rice Krispies, Frosties);* washing powders and detergents tended to be gravely monosyllabic (*Lux, Fab, Tide, Duz*). It is often possible to tell the era of a product's development by its termination. Thus products dating from the 1920s and early 1930s often ended in *-ex (Pyrex, Cutex, Kleenex, Windex)*, while those ending in *master (Mixmaster, Toastmaster)* generally betray a late 1930s or early-1940s genesis. The development of *Glo-Coat* floor wax in 1932 also heralded the beginning of American business's strange and long-standing infatuation with illiterate spellings, a trend that continued with *ReaLemon* juice in 1935, *Reddi-Wip* whipped cream in 1947, and many hundreds of others since, from *Tastee-Freez* drive-ins to *Toys 'Я' Us*, along with count-less others with a *Kwik, E-Z,* or *U* (as in *While-U-Wait*) embedded in their titles. The late 1940s saw the birth of a brief vogue for endings in *matic,* so that car manufacturers offered vehicles with *Seat-O-Matic* levers and *Cruise-O-Matic* transmissions, and even fitted sheets came with *Ezy-Matic* corners. Some companies became associated with certain types of names. Du Pont, for instance, had a special fondness for words ending in *-on.* The practice began with *nylon*—a name that was concocted out of thin air and owes nothing to its chemical properties—and was followed with *Rayon, Dacron, Orlon,* and *Teflon,* among many others. In recent years the com-pany has moved on to what might be called its *Star Trek* phase with such compounds as *Tyvek, Kevlar, Sontara, Condura, Nomex,* and *Zemorain.*

Such names have more than passing importance to their owners. If American business has given us a large dose of anxiety in its ceaseless quest for a healthier *bottom line* (a term dating from the 1930s, though not part of mainstream English until the 1970s), we may draw some comfort from the thought that business has suffered a great deal of collective anxiety over protecting the names of its products.

A certain cruel paradox prevails in the matter of preserving brand names. Every business naturally wants to create a product that will dom-inate its market. But if that product so dominates the market that the brand name becomes indistinguishable in the public mind from the prod-uct itself—when people begin to ask for a *thermos* rather than a "Thermos brand vacuum flask"—then the term has become generic and the owner faces the loss of its trademark protection. That is why advertisements and labels so often carry faintly paranoid-sounding lines like "Tabasco is the registered trademark for the brand of pepper sauce made by McIlhenny

Co." and why companies like Coca-Cola suffer palpitations when they see a passage like this (from John Steinbeck's *The Wayward Bus*):

> "Got any coke?" another character asked.
> "No," said the proprietor. "Few bottles of Pepsi-Cola. Haven't had any coke for a month.... It's the same stuff. You can't tell them apart."

An understandable measure of confusion exists concerning the distinction between patents and trademarks and between trademarks and trade names. A *patent* protects the name of the product and its method of manufacture for seventeen years. Thus from 1895 to 1912, no one but the Shredded Wheat Company could make shredded wheat. But because patents require manufacturers to divulge the secrets of their products—and thus make them available to rivals to copy when the patent runs out— companies sometimes choose not to seek their protection. *Coca-Cola*, for one, has never been patented. A *trademark* is effectively the name of a product, its *brand name*. A *trade name* is the name of the manufacturer. So *Ford* is a trade name, *Taurus* a trademark. Trademarks apply not just to names, but also to logos, drawings, and other symbols and depictions. The MGM lion, for instance, is a trademark. Unlike patents, trademark protection goes on forever, or at least as long as the manufacturer can protect it.

For a long time, it was felt that this permanence gave the holder an   25
unfair advantage. In consequence, America did not enact its first trademark law until 1870, almost a century after Britain, and then it was declared unconstitutional by the Supreme Court. Lasting trademark protection did not begin for American companies until 1881. Today, more than a million trademarks have been issued in the United States and the number is rising by about thirty thousand a year.

A good trademark is almost incalculably valuable. Invincible-seeming brand names do occasionally falter and fade. *Pepsodent, Rinso, Chase & Sanborn, Sal Hepatica, Vitalis, Brylcreem,* and *Burma-Shave* all once stood on the commanding heights of consumer recognition but are now defunct or have sunk to the status of what the trade calls "ghost brands"—products that are still produced but little promoted and largely forgotten. For the most part, however, once a product establishes a dominant position in a market, it is exceedingly difficult to depose it. In nineteen of twenty-two categories, the company that owned the leading American brand in 1925 still has it today— *Nabisco* in cookies, *Kellogg's* in breakfast cereals, *Kodak* in film, *Sherwin Williams* in paint, *Del Monte* in canned fruit, *Wrigleys* in chewing gum, *Singer* in sewing machines, *Ivory* in soap, *Campbell's* in soup, *Gillette* in razors. Few really successful brand names of today were not just as familiar to your grandparents or even great-grandparents, and a well-established brand name has a sort of self-perpetuating power. As *The Economist* has noted: "In the category of food blenders, consumers were still ranking General Electric second twenty years after the company had stopped making them."

An established brand name is so valuable that only about 5 percent of the sixteen thousand or so new products introduced in America each year bear all-new brand names. The others are variants on an existing product — *Tide with Bleach, Tropicana Twister Light Fruit Juices,* and so on. Among some types of product a certain glut is evident. At last count there were 220 types of branded breakfast cereal in America. In 1993, according to an international business survey, the world's most valuable brand was *Marlboro,* with a value estimated at $40 billion, slightly ahead of *Coca-Cola.* Among the other ten brands were *Intel, Kellogg*'s*, Budweiser, Pepsi, Gillette,* and *Pampers. Nescafé* and *Bacardi* were the only foreign brands to make the top ten, underlining American dominance.

Huge amounts of effort go into choosing brand names. General Foods reviewed 2,800 names before deciding on *Dreamwhip.* (To put this in proportion, try to think of just ten names for an artificial whipped cream.) Ford considered more than twenty thousand possible car names before finally settling on *Edsel* (which proves that such care doesn't always pay), and Standard Oil a similar number of names before it opted for *Exxon.* Sometimes, however, the most successful names are the result of a moment's whimsy. *Betty Crocker* came in a flash to an executive of the Washburn Crosby Company (later absorbed by General Mills), who chose *Betty* because he thought it sounded wholesome and sincere and *Crocker* in memory of a beloved fellow executive who had recently died. At first the name was used only to sign letters responding to customers' requests for advice or information, but by the 1950s, Betty Crocker's smiling, confident face was appearing on more than fifty types of food product, and her loyal followers could buy her recipe books and even visit her "kitchen" at the General Foods headquarters.

Great efforts also go into finding out why people buy the brands they do. Advertisers and market researchers bandy about terms like *conjoint analysis technique, personal drive patterns, Gaussian distributions, fractals,* and other such arcana in their quest to winnow out every subliminal quirk in our buying habits. They know, for instance, that 40 percent of all people who move to a new address will also change their brand of toothpaste, that the average supermarket shopper makes fourteen impulse decisions in each visit, that 62 percent of shoppers will pay a premium for mayonnaise even when they think a cheaper brand is just as good, but that only 24 percent will show the same largely irrational loyalty to frozen vegetables.

To preserve a brand name involves a certain fussy attention to linguistic and orthographic details. To begin with, the name is normally expected to be treated not as a noun but as a proper adjective — that is, the name should be followed by an explanation of what it does: *Kleenex facial tissues, Q-Tip cotton swabs, Jell-O brand gelatin dessert, Sanka brand decaffeinated coffee.* Some types of products — notably cars — are granted an exemption, which explains why General Motors does not have to advertise *Cadillac self-propelled automobiles* or the like. In all cases, the name may not explicitly describe the product's function, though it may hint at what it does. Thus *Coppertone* is acceptable; *Coppertan* would not be.

The situation is more than a little bizarre. Having done all they can to make their products household words, manufacturers must then in their advertisements do all in their power to imply that they aren't. Before trademark law was clarified, advertisers positively encouraged the public to treat their products as generics. Kodak invited consumers to "Kodak as you go," turning the brand name into a dangerously ambiguous verb. It would never do that now. The American Thermos Product Company went so far as to boast, "Thermos is a household word," to its considerable cost. Donald F. Duncan, Inc., the original manufacturer of the *Yo-Yo*, lost its trademark protection partly because it was amazingly casual about capitalization in its own promotional literature. "In case you don't know what a yo-yo is ..." one of its advertisements went, suggesting that in commercial terms Duncan didn't. Duncan also made the elemental error of declaring, "If It Isn't a Duncan, It Isn't a Yo-Yo," which on the face of it would seem a reasonable claim, but was in fact held by the courts to be inviting the reader to consider the product generic. Kodak had long since stopped saying "If it isn't an Eastman, it isn't a Kodak."

Because of the confusion, and occasional lack of fastidiousness on the part of their owners, many dozens of products have lost their trademark protection, among them *aspirin, linoleum, yo-yo, thermos, cellophane, milk of magnesia, mimeograph, lanolin, celluloid, dry ice, escalator, shredded wheat, kerosene,* and *zipper.* All were once proudly capitalized and worth a fortune.

On July 1, 1941, the New York television station WNBT-TV interrupted its normal viewing to show, without comment, a Bulova watch ticking. For sixty seconds the watch ticked away mysteriously, then the picture faded and normal programming resumed. It wasn't much, but it was the first television *commercial.*

Both the word and the idea were already well established. The first commercial—the term was used from the very beginning—had been broadcast by radio station WEAF in New York on August 28, 1922. It lasted for either ten or fifteen minutes, depending on which source you credit. Commercial radio was not an immediate hit. In its first two months, WEAF sold only $550 worth of airtime. But by the mid-1920s, sponsors were not only flocking to buy airtime but naming their programs after their products— *The Lucky Strike Hour, The A&P Gypsies, The Lux Radio Theater,* and so on. Such was the obsequiousness of the radio networks that by the early 1930s, many were allowing the sponsors to take complete artistic and production control of the programs. Many of the most popular shows were actually written by the advertising agencies, and the agencies naturally seldom missed an opportunity to work a favorable mention of the sponsor's products into the scripts.

With the rise of television in the 1950s, the practices of the radio   35
era were effortlessly transferred to the new medium. Advertisers inserted
their names into the program title — *Texaco Star Theater, Gillette Cav-
alcade of Sports, Chesterfield Sound-Off Time, The U.S. Steel Hour, Kraft
Television Theater, The Chevy Show, The Alcoa Hour, The Ford Star Revue,
Dick Clark's Beechnut Show,* and the arresting hybrid *The Lux-Schlitz Playhouse,* which seemed to suggest a cozy symbiosis between soapflakes and
beer. The commercial dominance of program titles reached a kind of hysterical peak with a program officially called *Your Kaiser Dealer Presents
Kaiser-Frazer "Adventures in Mystery" Starring Betty Furness in "Byline."*
Sponsors didn't write the programs any longer, but they did impose a
firm control on the contents, most notoriously during a 1959 *Playhouse
90* broadcast of *Judgment at Nuremberg,* when the sponsor, the American
Gas Association, managed to have all references to gas ovens and the gas-
sing of Jews removed from the script.

Where commercial products of the late 1940s had scientific-sounding
names, those of the 1950s relied increasingly on secret ingredients. Gleem
toothpaste contained a mysterious piece of alchemy called *GL-70.*[3] There
was never the slightest hint of what GL-70 was, but it would, according
to the advertising, not only rout odor-causing bacteria but "wipe out their
enzymes!"

A kind of creeping illiteracy invaded advertising, too, to the dismay
of many. When Winston began advertising its cigarettes with the slogan
"Winston tastes good like a cigarette should," nationally syndicated
columnists like Sydney J. Harris wrote anguished essays on what the
world was coming to — every educated person knew it should be "as a
cigarette should" — but the die was cast. By 1958, Ford was advertising that you could "travel smooth" in a Thunderbird Sunliner and the
maker of Ace Combs was urging buyers to "comb it handsome" — a
trend that continues today with "pantihose that fits you real comfortable" and other grammatical manglings too numerous and dispiriting
to dwell on.

We may smile at the advertising ruses of the 1920s — frightening people with the threat of "fallen stomach" and "scabby toes" — but in fact
such creative manipulation still goes on, albeit at a slightly more sophisticated level. The *New York Times Magazine* reported in 1990 how an
advertising copywriter had been told to come up with some impressive
labels for a putative hand cream. She invented the arresting and healthful-
sounding term *oxygenating moisturizers* and wrote accompanying copy with

---

3. For purposes of research, I wrote to Procter & Gamble, Gleem's manufacturer,
asking what GL-70 was, but the public relations department evidently thought it eccentric
of me to wonder what I had been putting in my mouth all through childhood and declined
to reply.

references to "tiny bubbles of oxygen that release moisture into your skin." This done, the advertising was turned over to the company's research and development department, which was instructed to come up with a product that matched the copy.

If we fall for such commercial manipulation, we have no one to blame but ourselves. When Kentucky Fried Chicken introduced "Extra Crispy" chicken to sell alongside its "Original" chicken, and sold it at the same price, sales were disappointing. But when its advertising agency persuaded it to promote "Extra Crispy" as a premium brand and to put the price up, sales soared. Much the same sort of verbal hypnosis was put to work for the benefit of the fur industry. Dyed muskrat makes a perfectly good fur, for those who enjoy cladding themselves in dead animals, but the name clearly lacks stylishness. The solution was to change the name to *Hudson seal*. Never mind that the material contained not a strand of seal fur. It sounded good, and sales skyrocketed.

Truth has seldom been a particularly visible feature of American adver- 40
tising. In the early 1970s, Chevrolet ran a series of ads for the Chevelle boasting that the car had "109 advantages to keep it from becoming old before its time." When looked into, it turned out that these 109 vaunted features included such items as rearview mirrors, backup lights, balanced wheels, and many other components that were considered pretty well basic to any car. Never mind; sales soared. At about the same time, Ford, not to be outdone, introduced a "limited edition" Mercury Monarch at $250 below the normal list price. It achieved this, it turned out, by taking $250 worth of equipment off the standard Monarch.

And has all this deviousness led to a tightening of the rules concerning what is allowable in advertising? Hardly. In 1986, as William Lutz relates in *Doublespeak,* the insurance company John Hancock launched an ad campaign in which "real people in real situations" discussed their financial predicaments with remarkable candor. When a journalist asked to speak to these real people, a company spokesman conceded that they were actors and "in that sense they are not real people."

During the presidential campaign [in 1982], the Republican National Committee ran a television advertisement praising President Reagan for providing cost-of-living pay increases to federal workers "in spite of those sticks-in-the-mud who tried to keep him from doing what we elected him to do." When it was pointed out that the increases had in fact been mandated by law since 1975 and that Reagan had in any case three times tried to block them, a Republican official responded: "Since when is a commercial supposed to be accurate?" Quite.

In linguistic terms, perhaps the most interesting challenge facing advertisers today is that of selling products in an increasingly multicultural society. Spanish is a particular problem, not just because it is spoken over such a widely scattered area but also because it is spoken in so many different forms. Brown sugar is *azucar negra* in New York, *azucar prieta* in

Miami, *azucar morena* in much of Texas, and *azucar pardo* pretty much everywhere else—and that's just one word. Much the same bewildering multiplicity applies to many others. In consequence, embarrassments are all but inevitable.

In mainstream Spanish, *bichos* means *insects*, but in Puerto Rico it means *testicles*, so when a pesticide maker promised to bring death to the *bichos*, Puerto Rican consumers were at least bemused, if not alarmed. Much the same happened when a maker of bread referred to its product as *un bollo de pan* and discovered that to Spanish-speaking Miamians of Cuban extraction that means a woman's private parts. And when Perdue Chickens translated its slogan "It takes a tough man to make a tender chicken" into Spanish, it came out as the slightly less macho "It takes a sexually excited man to make a chick sensual."

Never mind. Sales soared.   45

THINKING CRITICALLY ABOUT THE READING

1. Why do you think Bryson begins his essay with an extensive passage on George Eastman before even mentioning advertising, the focus of his essay? Why is this background information important to the rest of the essay? (Glossary: *Beginnings and Endings*) What do you need to consider when writing an introduction to an essay?

2. What is Bryson's purpose in this essay—to express personal thoughts and feelings, to inform his audience, or to argue a particular position? (Glossary: *Purpose*) What in his essay leads you to this conclusion?

3. Bryson peppers his essay with examples from the world of business and advertising. (Glossary: *Examples*) These examples serve not only to illustrate the points he makes but also to help establish his authority on the subject. Which examples do you find most effective? Least effective? Explain why.

4. It is important for companies to prevent their trademarks from becoming household words because they could lose their trademark protection. For example, advertisements for Kleenex and Xerox urge people to ask for a *tissue* or say they're going to *copy* a paper. Identify two or three current trademarks that you think could lose their trademark protection in the future, and explain your reasoning for choosing each trademark.

5. Bryson discusses what he calls a "creeping illiteracy" (37) that has invaded advertising. What form does this illiteracy take? In what ways might using poor English benefit advertisers?

6. In talking about the powers of advertising to persuade, Bryson discusses *commercial manipulation* and *verbal hypnosis* (39). What exactly does he mean by each term? How have advertisers used these techniques to sell their products? How do you think you as a consumer can guard against such advertising practices?

7. According to Bryson, what is one of the more interesting linguistic challenges facing today's advertisers?

LANGUAGE IN ACTION

In 1976, the Committee on Public Doublespeak (a committee of the National Council of Teachers of English) gave Professor Hugh Rank of Governors State University its Orwell Award for the Intensify/Downplay schema he developed to help people analyze public persuasion. As Rank explains, "All people *intensify* (commonly by *repetition, association, composition*) and *downplay* (commonly by *omission, diversion, confusion*) as they communicate in words, gestures, numbers, etc. But, 'professional persuaders' have more training, technology, money, and media access than the average citizen. Individuals can better cope with organized persuasion by recognizing the common ways that communication is intensified or downplayed, and by considering who is saying what to whom, with what intent and what result." Look closely at Rank's schema on pages 438–39, listing the questions you can ask yourself about any type of advertisement.

Use Rank's schema to analyze the World War I Navy recruitment posters on pages 440–41. Find examples of intensifying and downplaying in each. Then check out today's Navy recruitment efforts at www.navy .com. Have the government's persuasive techniques changed?

WRITING SUGGESTIONS

1. Think of a product that you have used and been disappointed by, one that has failed to live up to its advertising claims. Write a letter to the manufacturer in which you describe your experience with the product and explain why you believe the company's advertisements have been misleading. Send your letter to the president of the company or to the director of marketing.

2. Many product names are chosen because of their connotative or suggestive values. (Glossary: *Connotation/Denotation*) For example, the name *Tide* for a detergent suggests the power of the ocean tides and the rhythmic surge of cleansing waters; the name *Pride* for the wax suggests how the user will feel after using the product; the name *100% Natural* for the cereal suggests that the consumer is getting nothing less than nature's best; and the name *Taurus* for the Ford car suggests the strength and durability of a bull. Test what Bryson has said about brand names by exploring the connotations of the brand names in one of the following categories: cosmetics, deodorants, candy, paint, car batteries, fast-food sandwiches, pain relievers, disposable diapers, or cat food. Report your findings in an essay.

3. In paragraph 12, Bryson reminds us that successful advertisers have always known the importance of good slogans. Some early slogans, such as the American Florist Association's "Say it with flowers," are still in use today even though they were coined years ago. Research five or six current product slogans that Bryson doesn't mention—like Microsoft's "Where do you want to go?" or Just for Men's "So natural no one can tell"—and write an essay in which you discuss the importance of slogans to advertising campaigns. How, for example, do slogans serve to focus, direct, and galvanize advertising campaigns? What do you think makes some slogans work and others fail? What

makes a slogan memorable? As you start this project, you may find it helpful to search out materials in your library or on the Internet relating to slogans in general and how they engage people.

INTENSIFY

Repetition

How often have you seen the ad? On TV? In print? Do you recognize the **brand name? trademark? logo? company? package?** What key words or images repeated within ad? Any repetition patterns (*alliteration, anaphora, rhyme*) used? Any **slogan?** Can you hum or sing the **musical theme** or **jingle?** How long has this ad been running? How old were you when you first heard it? (For information on frequency, duration, and costs of ad campaigns, see *Advertising Age.*)

Association

What **"good things"** - already loved or desired by the intended audience - are associated with the product? Any links with basic needs (*food, activity, sex, security*)? With an appeal to save or gain money? With desire for certitude or outside approval (from *religion, science,* or the *"best," "most,"* or *"average" people*)? With desire for a sense of space (*neighborhood, nation, nature*)? With desire for love and belonging (*intimacy, family, groups*)? With other human desires (*esteem, play, generosity, curiosity, creativity, completion*)? Are **"bad things"** - things already hated or feared - stressed, as in a **"scare-and-sell"** ad? Are *problems* presented, with products as *solutions?* Are the speakers (models, endorsers) **authority figures:** people you respect, admire? Or **friend figures:** people you'd like as friends, identify with, or would like to be?

Composition

Look for the basic strategy of *"the pitch": Hi . . . TRUST ME . . . YOU NEED . . . HURRY . . . BUY.* What are the **attention-getting (HI)** words, images, devices? What are the **confidence-building (TRUST ME)** techniques: words, images, smiles, endorsers, brand names? Is the main **desire-stimulation (YOU NEED)** appeal focused on our benefit-seeking *to get* or *to keep* a *"good,"* or *to avoid* or *to get rid of* a *"bad"*? Are you the **"target audience"**? If not, who is? Are you part of an unintended audience ? When and where did the ads appear? Are **product claims** made for: *superiority, quantity, beauty, efficiency, scarcity, novelty, stability, reliability, simplicity, utility, rapidity,* or *safety?* Are any **"added values"** suggested or implied by using any of the association techniques (see above)? Is there any **urgency-stressing (HURRY)** by words, movement, pace? Or is a "soft sell" conditioning for *later* purchase? Are there specific **response-triggering** words **(BUY):** to buy, to do, to call? Or is it conditioning (image building or public relations) to make us *"feel good"* about the company, to get favorable public opinion on *its* side (against government regulations. laws, taxes)? **Persuaders seek some kind of response!**

Omission

What "bad" aspects, disadvantages, drawbacks, hazards, have been **omitted** from the ad? Are there some unspoken assumptions? An unsaid story? Are some things implied or suggested, but not explicitly stated? Are there concealed problems concerning the **maker**, the **materials**, the **design**, the **use**, or the **purpose of the product? Are there any unwanted or harmful side effects:** *unsafe, unhealthy, uneconomical, inefficient, unneeded?* Does any **"disclosure law"** exist (or is needed) requiring public warning about a concealed hazard? In the ad, what gets less time, less attention, smaller print? *(Most ads are true, but incomplete.)*

Diversion

What benefits (low cost, high speed, etc.) get high priority in the ad's claim and promises? Are these **your** priorities? Significant, important to you? Is there any **"bait-and-switch"**? *(Ad stresses low cost, but the actual seller switches buyer's priority to high quality.)* Does ad divert focus from **key issues,** important things *(e.g., nutrition, health, safety)*? Does ad focus on **side-issues,** unmeaningful trivia *(common in parity products)*? Does ad divert attention from your other choices, other options: buy something else, use less, use less often, rent, borrow, share, do without? *(Ads need not show other choices, but you should know them.)*

Confusion

Are the words clear or ambiguous? Specific or vague? Are claims and promises absolute, or are there qualifying words *("may help," "some")*? Is the claim measurable? Or is it **"puffery"**? *(Laws permit most "sellers's talk" of such general praise and subjective opinions.)* Are the words common, understandable, familiar? Uncommon? Jargon? Any parts difficult to "translate" or explain to others? Are analogies clear? Are comparisons within the same kind? Are examples related? Typical? Adequate? Enough examples? Any contradictions? Inconsistencies? Errors? Are there frequent changes, variations, revisions *(in size, price, options, extras, contents, packaging)*? Is it too complex: too much, too many? Disorganized? Incoherent? Unsorted? Any confusing statistics? Numbers? Do you know exact costs? Benefits? Risks? Are **your own goals,** priorities, and desires clear or vague? Fixed or shifting? Simple or complex? *(Confusion can also exist within us as well as within an ad. If any confusion exists: slow down, take care.)*

DOWNPLAY

Weasel Words: The Art of Saying Nothing at All

WILLIAM LUTZ

William Lutz was born in 1940 in Racine, Wisconsin. A professor of English at Rutgers University at Camden, Lutz holds a Ph.D. in Victorian literature, linguistics and rhetoric, and a law degree from the Rutgers School of Law. Lutz is the author or coauthor of numerous books having to do with language, including *Webster's New World Thesaurus* (1985) and *The Cambridge Thesaurus of American English* (1994). Considered an expert on language, Lutz has worked with many corporations and government agencies to promote clear, "plain" English. A member of the Pennsylvania bar, he was awarded the Pennsylvania Bar Association Clarity Award for the Promotion of Plain English in Legal Writing in 2001.

Lutz is best known for his series of books on "doublespeak": *Doublespeak: From Revenue Enhancement to Terminal Living* (1989), *The New Doublespeak: Why No One Knows What Anyone's Saying Anymore* (1996), and *Doublespeak Defined: Cut Through the Bull**** and Get to the Point* (1999). Lutz edited the *Quarterly Review of Doublespeak* from 1980 to 1994.

The term *doublespeak* comes from the Newspeak vocabulary of George Orwell's novel *Nineteen Eighty-Four*. It refers to speech or writing that presents two or more contradictory ideas in such a way that an unsuspecting audience is not consciously aware of the contradiction and is likely to be deceived. As chair of the National Council of Teachers of English's Committee on Public Doublespeak, Lutz has been a watchdog of public officials and business leaders who use language to "mislead, distort, deceive, inflate, circumvent, and obfuscate." Each year the committee presents the Orwell Awards, recognizing the most outrageous uses of public doublespeak in government and business.

In the following excerpt from his book *Doublespeak,* Lutz reveals some of the ways that advertisers use language to imply great things about products and services without promising anything at all. With considerable skill, advertisers can produce ads that make us believe a certain product is better than it is without actually lying about it. Lutz's word-by-word analysis of advertising claims reveals how misleading—and ridiculous—these slogans and claims can be.

WRITING TO DISCOVER: *Imagine what it would be like if you were suddenly transported to a world in which there were no advertisements and no one trying to sell you a product. Write about how you would decide what to buy. How would you learn about new products? Would you prefer to live in such a world? Why or why not?*

WEASEL WORDS

One problem advertisers have when they try to convince you that the product they are pushing is really different from other, similar products is that their claims are subject to some laws. Not a lot of laws, but there are some designed to prevent fraudulent or untruthful claims in advertising. Even during the happy years of nonregulation under President Ronald Reagan, the FTC did crack down on the more blatant abuses in advertising claims. Generally speaking, advertisers have to be careful in what they say in their ads, in the claims they make for the products they advertise. Parity claims are safe because they are legal and supported by a number of court decisions. But beyond parity claims there are weasel words.

Advertisers use weasel words to appear to be making a claim for a product when in fact they are making no claim at all. Weasel words get their name from the way weasels eat the eggs they find in the nests of other animals. A weasel will make a small hole in the egg, suck out the insides, then place the egg back in the nest. Only when the egg is examined closely is it found to be hollow. That's the way it is with weasel words in advertising: Examine weasel words closely and you'll find that they're as hollow as any egg sucked by a weasel. Weasel words appear to say one thing when in fact they say the opposite, or nothing at all.

"Help" — The Number One Weasel Word

The biggest weasel word used in advertising doublespeak is "help." Now "help" only means to aid or assist, nothing more. It does not mean to conquer, stop, eliminate, end, solve, heal, cure, or anything else. But once the ad says "help," it can say just about anything after that because "help" qualifies everything coming after it. The trick is that the claim that comes after the weasel word is usually so strong and so dramatic that you forget the word "help" and concentrate only on the dramatic claim. You read into the ad a message that the ad does not contain. More importantly, the advertiser is not responsible for the claim that you read into the ad, even though the advertiser wrote the ad so you would read that claim into it.

The next time you see an ad for a cold medicine that promises that it "helps relieve cold symptoms fast," don't rush out to buy it. Ask yourself what this claim is really saying. Remember, "help" means only that the medicine will aid or assist. What will it aid or assist in doing? Why, "relieve" your cold "symptoms." "Relieve" only means to ease, alleviate, or mitigate, not to stop, end, or cure. Nor does the claim say how much relieving this medicine will do. Nowhere does this ad claim it will cure anything. In fact, the ad doesn't even claim it will *do* anything at all. The ad only claims that it will aid in relieving (not curing) your cold symptoms, which are probably a runny nose, watery eyes, and a headache. In other words, this medicine probably contains a standard decongestant and some aspirin. By the way, what does "fast" mean? Ten minutes, one hour, one day? What is fast to one person can be very slow to another. Fast is another weasel word.

Ad claims using "help" are among the most popular ads. One says, 5 "Helps keep you young looking," but then a lot of things will help keep you young looking, including exercise, rest, good nutrition, and a facelift. More importantly, this ad doesn't say the product will keep you young, only "young *looking.*" Someone may look young to one person and old to another.

A toothpaste ad says, "Helps prevent cavities," but it doesn't say it will actually prevent cavities. Brushing your teeth regularly, avoiding sugars in food, and flossing daily will also help prevent cavities. A liquid cleaner ad says, "Helps keep your home germ free," but it doesn't say it actually kills germs, nor does it even specify which germs it might kill.

"Help" is such a useful weasel word that it is often combined with other action-verb weasel words such as "fight" and "control." Consider the claim, "Helps control dandruff symptoms with regular use." What does it really say? It will assist in controlling (not eliminating, stopping, ending, or curing) the *symptoms* of dandruff, not the cause of dandruff nor the dandruff itself. What are the symptoms of dandruff? The ad deliberately leaves that undefined, but assume that the symptoms referred to in the ad are the flaking and itching commonly associated with dandruff. But just shampooing with *any* shampoo will temporarily eliminate these symptoms, so this shampoo isn't any different from any other. Finally, in order to benefit from this product, you must use it regularly. What is "regular use"—daily, weekly, hourly? Using another shampoo "regularly" will have the same effect. Nowhere does this advertising claim say this particular shampoo stops, eliminates, or cures dandruff. In fact, this claim says nothing at all, thanks to all the weasel words.

Look at ads in magazines and newspapers, listen to ads on radio and television, and you'll find the word "help" in ads for all kinds of products. How often do you read or hear such phrases as "helps stop ... ," "helps overcome ... ," "helps eliminate ... ," "helps you feel ... ," or "helps you look ..."? If you start looking for this weasel word in advertising, you'll be amazed at how often it occurs. Analyze the claims in the ads using "help," and you will discover that these ads are really saying nothing.

There are plenty of other weasel words used in advertising. In fact, there are so many that to list them all would fill the rest of this book. But, in order to identify the doublespeak of advertising and understand the real meaning of an ad, you have to be aware of the most popular weasel words in advertising today.

Virtually Spotless

One of the most powerful weasel words is "virtually," a word so 10 innocent that most people don't pay any attention to it when it is used in an advertising claim. But watch out. "Virtually" is used in advertising claims that appear to make specific, definite promises when there is no promise. After all, what does "virtually" mean? It means "in essence or effect, although not in fact." Look at that definition again. "Virtually" means *not in fact*. It does *not* mean "almost" or "just about the same as," or anything else. And before you dismiss all this concern over such a small word, remember that small words can have big consequences.

In 1971 a federal court rendered its decision on a case brought by a woman who became pregnant while taking birth control pills. She sued the manufacturer, Eli Lilly and Company, for breach of warranty. The woman lost her case. Basing its ruling on a statement in the pamphlet accompanying the pills, which stated that, "When taken as directed, the tablets offer virtually 100 percent protection," the court ruled that there was no warranty, expressed or implied, that the pills were absolutely effective. In its ruling, the court pointed out that, according to *Webster's Third New International Dictionary*, "virtually" means "almost entirely" and clearly does not mean "absolute" (*Whittington* v. *Eli Lilly and Company*, 333 F. Supp. 98). In other words, the Eli Lilly company was really saying that its birth control pill, even when taken as directed, *did not in fact* provide 100 percent protection against pregnancy. But Eli Lilly didn't want to put it that way because then many women might not have bought Lilly's birth control pills.

The next time you see the ad that says that this dishwasher detergent "leaves dishes virtually spotless," just remember how advertisers twist the meaning of the weasel word "virtually." You can have lots of spots on your dishes after using this detergent and the ad claim will still be true, because what this claim really means is that this detergent does not *in fact* leave your dishes spotless. Whenever you see or hear an ad claim that uses the word "virtually," just translate that claim into its real meaning. So the television set that is "virtually trouble free" becomes the television set that is not in fact trouble free, the "virtually foolproof operation" of any appliance becomes an operation that is in fact not foolproof, and the product that "virtually never needs service" becomes the product that is not in fact service free.

New and Improved

If "new" is the most frequently used word on a product package, "improved" is the second most frequent. In fact, the two words are almost always used together. It seems just about everything sold these days is "new and improved." The next time you're in the supermarket, try counting the number of times you see these words on products. But you'd better do it while you're walking down just one aisle, otherwise you'll need a calculator to keep track of your counting.

Just what do these words mean? The use of the word "new" is restricted by regulations, so an advertiser can't just use the word on a product or in an ad without meeting certain requirements. For example, a product is considered new for about six months during a national advertising campaign. If the product is being advertised only in a limited test market area, the word can be used longer, and in some instances has been used for as long as two years.

What makes a product "new"? Some products have been around for a   15
long time, yet every once in a while you discover that they are being advertised as "new." Well, an advertiser can call a product new if there has been "a material functional change" in the product. What is "a material functional change," you ask? Good question. In fact it's such a good question it's being asked all the time. It's up to the manufacturer to prove that the product has undergone such a change. And if the manufacturer isn't challenged on the claim, then there's no one to stop it. Moreover, the change does not have to be an improvement in the product. One manufacturer added an artificial lemon scent to a cleaning product and called it "new and improved," even though the product did not clean any better than without the lemon scent. The manufacturer defended the use of the word "new" on the grounds that the artificial scent changed the chemical formula of the product and therefore constituted "a material functional change."

Which brings up the word "improved." When used in advertising, "improved" does not mean "made better." It only means "changed" or "different from before." So, if the detergent maker puts a plastic pour spout on the box of detergent, the product has been "improved," and away we go with a whole new advertising campaign. Or, if the cereal maker adds more fruit or a different kind of fruit to the cereal, there's an improved product. Now you know why manufacturers are constantly making little changes in their products. Whole new advertising campaigns, designed to convince you that the product has been changed for the better, are based on small changes in superficial aspects of a product. The next time you see an ad for an "improved" product, ask yourself what was wrong with the old one. Ask yourself just how "improved" the product is. Finally, you might check to see whether the "improved" version costs more than the unimproved one. After all, someone has to pay for the millions of dollars spent advertising the improved product.

Of course, advertisers really like to run ads that claim a product is "new and improved." While what constitutes a "new" product may be subject to some regulation, "improved" is a subjective judgment. A manufacturer changes the shape of its stick deodorant, but the shape doesn't improve the function of the deodorant. That is, changing the shape doesn't affect the deodorizing ability of the deodorant, so the manufacturer calls it "improved." Another manufacturer adds ammonia to its liquid cleaner and calls it "new and improved." Since adding ammonia does affect the cleaning ability of the product, there has been a "material functional change" in the product, and the manufacturer can now call its cleaner "new," and "improved" as well. Now the weasel words "new and improved" are plastered all over the package and are the basis for a multimillion-dollar ad campaign. But after six months the word "new" will have to go, until someone can dream up another change in the product. Perhaps it will be adding color to the liquid, or changing the shape of the package, or maybe adding a new dripless pour spout, or perhaps a ___. The "improvements" are endless, and so are the new advertising claims and campaigns.

"New" is just too useful and powerful a word in advertising for advertisers to pass it up easily. So they use weasel words that say "new" without really saying it. One of their favorites is "introducing," as in, "Introducing improved Tide," or "Introducing the stain remover." The first is simply saying, here's our improved soap; the second, here's our new advertising campaign for our detergent. Another favorite is "now," as in, "Now there's Sinex," which simply means that Sinex is available. Then there are phrases like "Today's Chevrolet," "Presenting Dristan," and "A fresh way to start the day." The list is really endless because advertisers are always finding new ways to say "new" without really saying it. If there is a second edition of [my] book, I'll just call it the "new and improved" edition. Wouldn't you really rather have a "new and improved" edition of [my] book rather than a "second" edition?

Acts Fast

"Acts" and "works" are two popular weasel words in advertising because they bring action to the product and to the advertising claim. When you see the ad for the cough syrup that "Acts on the cough control center," ask yourself what this cough syrup is claiming to do. Well, it's just claiming to "act," to do something, to perform an action. What is it that the cough syrup does? The ad doesn't say. It only claims to perform an action or do something on your "cough control center." By the way, what and where is your "cough control center"? I don't remember learning about that part of the body in human biology class.

Ads that use such phrases as "acts fast," "acts against," "acts to pre- 20 vent," and the like are saying essentially nothing, because "act" is a word empty of any specific meaning. The ads are always careful not to specify exactly what "act" the product performs. Just because a brand of aspirin claims to "act fast" for headache relief doesn't mean this aspirin is any better than any other aspirin. What is the "act" that this aspirin performs? You're never told. Maybe it just dissolves quickly. Since aspirin is a parity product, all aspirin is the same and therefore functions the same.

Works Like Anything Else

If you don't find the word "acts" in an ad, you will probably find the weasel word "works." In fact, the two words are almost interchangeable in advertising. Watch out for ads that say a product "works against," "works like," "works for," or "works longer." As with "acts," "works" is the same meaningless verb used to make you think that this product really does something, and maybe even something special or unique. But "works," like "acts," is basically a word empty of any specific meaning.

Like Magic

Whenever advertisers want you to stop thinking about the product and to start thinking about something bigger, better, or more attractive than the product, they use that very popular weasel word "like." The word "like" is the advertiser's equivalent of a magician's use of misdirection. "Like" gets you to ignore the product and concentrate on the claim the advertiser is making about it. "For skin like peaches and cream" claims the ad for a skin cream. What is this ad really claiming? It doesn't say this cream will give you peaches-and-cream skin. There is no verb in this claim, so it doesn't even mention using the product. How is skin ever like "peaches and cream"? Remember, ads must be read literally and exactly, according to the dictionary definition of words. (Remember "virtually" in the Eli Lilly case.) The ad is making absolutely no promise or claim whatsoever for this skin cream. If you think this cream will give you soft, smooth, youthful-looking skin, you are the one who has read that meaning into the ad.

The wine that claims "It's like taking a trip to France" wants you to think about a romantic evening in Paris as you walk along the boulevard after a wonderful meal in an intimate little bistro. Of course, you don't really believe that a wine can take you to France, but the goal of the ad is to get you to think pleasant, romantic thoughts about France and not about how the wine tastes or how expensive it may be. That little word "like" has taken you away from crushed grapes into a world of your own imaginative making. Who knows, maybe the next time you buy wine, you'll think those pleasant thoughts when you see this brand of wine, and you'll buy it. Or, maybe you weren't even thinking about buying wine at all, but now you just might pick up a bottle the next time you're shopping. Ah, the power of "like" in advertising.

How about the most famous "like" claim of all, "Winston tastes good like a cigarette should"? Ignoring the grammatical error here, you might want to know what this claim is saying. Whether a cigarette tastes good or bad is a subjective judgment because what tastes good to one person may well taste horrible to another. Not everyone likes fried snails, even if they are called escargot. (*De gustibus non est disputandum,* which was probably the Roman rule for advertising as well as for defending the games in the Colosseum.) There are many people who say all cigarettes taste terrible, other people who say only some cigarettes taste all right, and still others who say all cigarettes taste good. Who's right? Everyone, because taste is a matter of personal judgment.

Moreover, note the use of the conditional, "should." The complete claim is, "Winston tastes good like a cigarette should taste." But should cigarettes taste good? Again, this is a matter of personal judgment and probably depends most on one's experiences with smoking. So, the Winston ad is simply saying that Winston cigarettes are just like any other cigarette: Some people like them and some people don't. On that statement R. J. Reynolds conducted a very successful multimillion-dollar advertising campaign that helped keep Winston the number-two-selling cigarette in the United States, close behind number one, Marlboro.

CAN IT BE UP TO THE CLAIM?

Analyzing ads for doublespeak requires that you pay attention to every word in the ad and determine what each word really means. Advertisers try to wrap their claims in language that sounds concrete, specific, and objective, when in fact the language of advertising is anything but. Your job is to read carefully and listen critically so that when the announcer says that "Crest can be of significant value ..." you know immediately that this claim says absolutely nothing. Where is the doublespeak in this ad? Start with the second word.

Once again, you have to look at what words really mean, not what you think they mean or what the advertiser wants you to think they mean. The ad for Crest only says that using Crest "can be" of "significant value." What really throws you off in this ad is the brilliant use of "significant." It draws your attention to the word "value" and makes you forget that the ad only claims that Crest "can be." The ad doesn't say that Crest *is* of value, only that it is "able" or "possible" to be of value, because that's all that "can" means.

It's so easy to miss the importance of those little words, "can be." Almost as easy as missing the importance of the words "up to" in an ad. These words are very popular in sale ads. You know, the ones that say, "Up to 50% Off!" Now, what does that claim mean? Not much, because the store or manufacturer has to reduce the price of only a few items by 50 percent. Everything else can be reduced a lot less, or not even reduced. Moreover, don't you want to know 50 pecent off of what? Is it 50 percent off the "manufacturer's suggested list price," which is the highest possible price? Was the price artificially inflated and then reduced? In other ads, "up to" expresses an ideal situation. The medicine that works "up to ten times faster," the battery that lasts "up to twice as long," and the soap that gets you "up to twice as clean" all are based on ideal situations for using those products, situations in which you can be sure you will never find yourself.

UNFINISHED WORDS

Unfinished words are a kind of "up to" claim in advertising. The claim that a battery lasts "up to twice as long" usually doesn't finish the comparison — twice as long as what? A birthday candle? A tank of gas? A cheap battery made in a country not noted for its technological achievements? The implication is that the battery lasts twice as long as batteries made by other battery makers, or twice as long as earlier model batteries made by the advertiser, but the ad doesn't really make these claims. You read these claims into the ad, aided by the visual images the advertiser so carefully provides.

Unfinished words depend on you to finish them, to provide the words the advertisers so thoughtfully left out of the ad. Pall Mall cigarettes were once advertised as "A longer finer and milder smoke." The question is, longer, finer, and milder than what? The aspirin that claims it contains "Twice as

30

much of the pain reliever doctors recommend most" doesn't tell you what pain reliever it contains twice as much of. (By the way, it's aspirin. That's right; it just contains twice the amount of aspirin. And how much is twice the amount? Twice of what amount?) Panadol boasts that "nobody reduces fever faster," but, since Panadol is a parity product, this claim simply means that Panadol isn't any better than any other product in its parity class. "You can be sure if it's Westinghouse," you're told, but just exactly what it is you can be sure of is never mentioned. "Magnavox gives you more" doesn't tell you what you get more of. More value? More television? More than they gave you before? It sounds nice, but it means nothing, until you fill in the claim with your own words, the words the advertiser didn't use. Since each of us fills in the claim differently, thead and the product can become all things to all people, and not promise a single thing.

Unfinished words abound in advertising because they appear to promise so much. More importantly, they can be joined with powerful visual images on television to appear to be making significant promises about a product's effectiveness without really making any promises. In a television ad, the aspirin product that claims fast relief can show a person with a headache taking the product and then, in what appears to be a matter of minutes, claiming complete relief. This visual image is far more powerful than any claim made in unfinished words. Indeed, the visual image completes the unfinished words for you, filling in with pictures what the words leave out. And you thought that ads didn't affect you. What brand of aspirin do you use?

Some years ago, Ford's advertisements proclaimed "Ford LTD— 700 percent quieter." Now, what do you think Ford was claiming with these unfinished words? What was the Ford LTD quieter than? A Cadillac? A Mercedes Benz? A BMW? Well, when the FTC asked Ford to substantiate this unfinished claim, Ford replied that it meant that the inside of the LTD was 700 percent quieter than the outside. How did you finish those unfinished words when you first read them? Did you even come close to Ford's meaning?

COMBINING WEASEL WORDS

A lot of ads don't fall neatly into one category or another because they use a variety of different devices and words. Different weasel words are often combined to make an ad claim. The claim, "Coffee-Mate gives coffee more body, more flavor," uses unfinished words ("more" than what?) and also uses words that have no specific meaning ("body" and "flavor"). Along with "taste" (remember the Winston ad and its claim to taste good), "body" and "flavor" mean nothing because their meaning is entirely subjective. To you, "body" in coffee might mean thick, black, almost bitter coffee, while I might take it to mean a light brown, delicate coffee. Now, if you think you understood that last sentence, read it again, because it said nothing of objective value; it was filled with weasel words of no specific meaning: "thick," "black," "bitter," "light brown," and "delicate." Each of those words has no specific, objective meaning, because each of us can interpret them differently.

Try this slogan: "Looks, smells, tastes like ground-roast coffee." So, are you now going to buy Taster's Choice instant coffee because of this ad? "Looks," "smells," and "tastes" are all words with no specific meaning and depend on your interpretation of them for any meaning. Then there's that great weasel word "like," which simply suggests a comparison but does not make the actual connection between the product and the quality. Besides, do you know what "ground-roast" coffee is? I don't, but it sure sounds good. So, out of seven words in this ad, four are definite weasel words, two are quite meaningless, and only one has clear meaning.

Remember the Anacin ad—"Twice as much of the pain reliever doc- 35 tors recommend most"? There's a whole lot of weaseling going on in this ad. First, what's the pain reliever they're talking about in this ad? Aspirin, of course. In fact, any time you see or hear an ad using those words "pain reliever," you can automatically substitute the word "aspirin" for them. (Makers of acetaminophen and ibuprofen pain relievers are careful in their advertising to identify their products as nonaspirin products.) So, now we know that Anacin has aspirin in it. Moreover, we know that Anacin has twice as much aspirin in it, but we don't know twice as much as what. Does it have twice as much aspirin as an ordinary aspirin tablet? If so, what is a ordinary aspirin tablet, and how much aspirin does it contain? Twice as much as Excedrin or Bufferin? Twice as much as a chocolate chip cookie? Remember those unfinished words and how they lead you on without saying anything.

Finally, what about those doctors who are doing all that recommending? Who are they? How many of them are there? What kind of doctors are they? What are their qualifications? Who asked them about recommending pain relievers? What other pain relievers did they recommend? And there are a whole lot more questions about this "poll" of doctors to which I'd like to know the answers, but you get the point. Sometimes, when I call my doctor, she tells me to take two aspirin and call her office in the morning. Is that where Anacin got this ad?

THINKING CRITICALLY ABOUT THE READING

1. What are weasel words? How, according to Lutz, did they get their name?

2. Lutz is careful to illustrate each of the various kinds of weasel words with examples of actual usage. (Glossary: *Examples*) What do these examples add to his essay? Which ones do you find most effective? Explain.

3. According to Lutz, why is *help* the biggest weasel word used by advertisers (3–8)? In what ways does it help them present their products without having to make promises about actual performance?

4. Why is *virtually* a particularly effective weasel word (10–12)? Why can advertisers get away with using words that literally mean the opposite of what they want to convey?

5. When advertisers use the word *like*, they often create a simile — "Ajax cleans *like* a white tornado." (Glossary: *Figures of Speech*) What, according to Lutz, is the power of similes in advertising (22–24)? Explain by citing several examples of your own.

6. What kinds of claims fit into Lutz's "unfinished words" category (29–32)? Why are they weasels? What makes them so difficult to detect?

7. Lutz uses the strategy of division and classification to develop this essay. (Glossary: *Division and Classification*) Explain how he uses this strategy. Why do you suppose Lutz felt the need to create the "Combining Weasel Words" category? Did the headings in the essay help you follow his discussion? What would be lost had he not included them?

LANGUAGE IN ACTION

Select one eye-catching advertisement from a magazine. Jot down any words that Lutz would describe as weasels. How does recognizing such language affect your impression of the product being advertised? What would happen to the text of the ad if the weasels were eliminated? Share your analysis with others in your class.

WRITING SUGGESTIONS

1. Choose something that you own and like — a mountain bike, a CD or DVD collection, luggage, a comfortable sofa, a stereo, or anything else that you are glad you bought. Imagine that you need to sell it to raise some money for a special weekend, and to do so you need to advertise on radio. Write copy for a 30-second advertising spot in which you try to sell your item. Include a slogan or make up a product name and use it in the ad. Then write a short essay about your ad in which you discuss the features of your item you chose to highlight, the language you used to make it sound as appealing as possible, and how your slogan or name makes the advertisement more memorable.

2. Pay attention to the ads for companies that offer rival products or services (for example, Apple and IBM, Coca-Cola and Pepsi-Cola, Burger King and McDonald's, Charles Schwab and Smith Barney, and AT&T and MCI). Focusing on a single pair of ads, analyze the different appeals that companies make when comparing their products or services to those of the competition. To what audience does each ad appeal? How many weasel words can you detect? How does each ad use Intensify/Downplay (pp. 438–39) techniques to its product's advantage? Based on your analysis, write an essay about the advertising strategies companies use when in head-to-head competition with the products of other companies.

3. Look at several issues of one popular women's or men's magazine (such as *Cosmopolitan, Vogue, Elle, Glamour, Sports Illustrated, GQ, Playboy, Car and Driver, Field and Stream*), and analyze the advertisements they contain. What types of products or services are advertised? Which ads caught your eye? Why? Are the ads made up primarily of pictures, or do some have a lot of text? Do you detect any relationship beween the ads and the editorial content of the magazine? Write an essay in which you present the findings of your analysis.

Lead Us into Temptation

JAMES B. TWITCHELL

Cultural critic and advertising historian James B. Twitchell was born in Burlington, Vermont, in 1943. After graduating from the University of Vermont in 1962, he attended the University of North Carolina at Chapel Hill, where he earned his Ph.D. in 1969. Later he embarked on a career in education, teaching first at Duke University and then at the California State College at Bakersfield. Currently, he is professor of English and advertising at the University of Florida, Gainesville, where he has taught since 1972. Among the courses he teaches is Advertising and Culture, in which he interprets American culture in terms of commercialism. His many books include *Adcult USA: The Triumph of Advertising in American Culture* (1996), *For Shame: The Loss of Common Decency in American Culture* (1997), *Twenty Ads That Shook the World: The Century's Most Groundbreaking Advertising and How It Changed Us All* (2000), *Branded Nation: The Marketing of Megachurch, College Inc., and Museumworld* (2004), and his most recent book, *Shopping for God: How Christianity Went from In Your Heart to In Your Face* (2007).

The selection that follows is taken from the opening chapter of his 1999 book *Lead Us into Temptation: The Triumph of American Materialism*, which Twitchell described as "A Brief Consumer Guide to Consumption, Commercialism, and the Meaning of Stuff."

WRITING TO DISCOVER: *Think about your personal shopping habits. When you buy clothing, for example, are you attracted to certain brands? What are those brands, and what makes them more enticing than others?*

Of all "-isms" of the twentieth century none has been more misunderstood, more criticized, and more important than materialism. Who but fools, toadies, hacks, and occasional loopy Libertarians have ever risen to its defense? Yet the fact remains that while materialism may be the most shallow of the twentieth century's various -isms, it has been the one to ultimately triumph. The world of commodities seems so antithetical to the world of ideas that it seems almost heresy to point out the obvious: most of the world most of the time spends most of its energy producing and consuming more and more stuff.

The really interesting question may be not why are we so materialistic? but why are we so unwilling to acknowledge and explore what seems to be the central characteristic of modern life?

When the French wished to disparage the English in the nineteenth century, they called them a nation of shopkeepers. When the rest of the world now wishes to disparage Americans, they call us a nation of consumers. And they are right. Almost all mature American cities have a Market

Street and almost all of us have been there. No longer. We are developing and rapidly exporting a new material culture, a "mallcondo" culture.

The bus lines today terminate not at Market Street but at the Mall, the heart of our new modern urbia. All around mallcondoville is a vast continuum of interconnected structures and modes of organizing work, shopping, and living, all based on principles of enclosure, control, and consumption.

Most of us have not entered the mallcondo cocoon . . . yet. But we are on our way. We have the industrial "park," the "gated" community, the corporate "campus," the "domed" stadium, all of which play on the same conception of Xanadu's pleasure dome. Get inside. In the modern world the Kubla Khan down at the bank or over at the insurance company is not building a mallcondo dome around the natural world, but around a commercial one. Few are willing or able to live outside except, of course, the poor. "If you lived here, you'd be home by now" is no idle billboard; it is the goal of middle-class life.

To the rest of the world we do indeed seem not just born to shop, but alive to shop. We spend more time tooling around the mallcondo—three to four times as many hours as our European counterparts—and we have more stuff to show for it. According to some estimates we have about four times as many things as Middle Europeans, and who knows how much more than the less developed parts of the world. The quantity and disparity is increasing daily, even though, as we see in Russia and China, the "emerging nations" are playing a frantic game of catch up.

THE IMPACT OF THE BABY BOOM

This burst of mallcondo commercialism has happened recently—in my lifetime—and it is moving outward around the world at the speed of television. The average American consumes twice as many goods and services as in 1950; in fact, the poorest fifth of the current population buys more than the average fifth did in 1955. Little wonder that the average new home of today is twice as large as the average house constructed after World War II. We have to put that stuff somewhere—quick!—before it turns to junk.

Manufacturing both things and their meanings is what mallcondo culture is all about, especially for the baby boomers. If Greece gave the world philosophy, Britain gave drama, Austria gave music, Germany gave politics, and Italy gave art, then America has recently contributed mass-produced and mass-consumed objects. "We bring good things to life" is no offhand claim but the contribution of the last century. Think about it: did anyone before the 1950s—except the rich—ever shop just for fun? Now the whole world wants to do it.

Sooner or later we are going to have to acknowledge the uncomfortable fact that this amoral commercial culture has proved potent because human beings love things. In fact, to a considerable degree, we live for things. Humans like to exchange things. In all cultures we buy things, steal things, and hoard things. From time to time, some of us collect vast amounts of things such as tulip bulbs, paint drippings on canvases, bits of minerals. Others collect such stuff as thimbles, shoes, even libraries of videocassettes. Often these objects have no observable use.

We live through things. We create ourselves through things. And we change ourselves by changing our things. We often depend on such material for meaning. In the West, we have even developed the elaborate algebra of commercial law to decide how things are exchanged, divested, and recaptured. Remember, we call these things goods as in "goods and services." Academics aside, we do not call them bads. This sounds simplistic, but it is crucial to understanding the powerful allure of materialism, consumption, mallcondo culture, and all that it carries with it. 10

Things are in the saddle, no doubt about it. We put them there. If some of us want to think that things are riding us, that's fine. The rest of us know better.

THE COMPLEXITY OF CONSUMING COMMERCIALISM

That consumption gives meaning to life seems to be rearranging the terms, getting things backwards. But think about it: do we work in order to have the leisure to buy things, or is the leisure to buy things how we make work necessary? We forever talk about how work gives meaning—labore est orare—but it may be consumption that we are referring to. Give a banana to a monkey and he eats it right away. Give him a bundle and he gets confused. He has no idea what to do with surplus. Should he hoard, should he gorge himself, should he share? This used to be a problem only for the rich; now the rest of us can share the perplexity.

I never want to imply that, in creating order in our lives, consumption is doing something to us that we are not covertly responsible for. We are not victims of consumption. Just as we make our media, our media make us. Again, commercialism is not making us behave against our "better judgment." Commercialism is our better judgment. Not only are we willing to consume, and not only does consuming make us happy, "getting and spending" is what gives our lives order and purpose. We have a deluding tendency to consider advertising, packaging, fashion, branding, and the rest of the movement of goods in the way we consider many other cultural sequences, like politics and religion, as somehow "out there" beyond our control. Not so.

Our desire to individualize experience causes us to forget that there is a continual interaction between forces—between people and their leaders, between males and females, between readers and writers, between young and old, even between producers and consumers—in which there is a struggle not for dominance, but for expansion. In the language of William Blake, the endeavor is not to separate the Prolific and the Devourers, not to blame one for the condition of the other, but to realize that in the shifting of forces is the excitement and the danger of change. In this sense, commercialism is just another site in which the sometimes opposing forces of a culture are brought to bear on each other. The resulting friction is often quite hot.

I make this point now because commercial speech—how we talk   15 about manufactured things—has become one of the primary hotspots of modern culture. It has been blamed for the rise of eating disorders, the spreading of affluenza, the epidemic of depression, the despoiling of cultural icons, the corruption of politics, the carnivalization of holy times like Christmas, and the gnat-life attention span of our youth. All of this is true. Commercialism contributes. But it is by no means the whole truth. Commercialism is more a mirror than a lamp. That we demonize it, that we see ourselves as helpless and innocent victims of its overpowering force, that it has become scapegoat du jour, tells far more about our eagerness to be passive in the face of complexity than about our understanding of how it does its work.

Anthropologists tell us that consumption habits are gender specific. Men seem to want stuff in early adolescence and post-midlife. That's when the male collecting impulse seems to be felt. Boys gather playing marbles first, Elgin marbles later. Women seem to gain potency as consumers after childbirth, almost as if getting and spending is a nesting impulse. There are no women stamp collectors of note. They do save letters, however, far more often then men do.

Historians, however, tell us to be careful about such stereotyping. While it is clear that women are the primary consumers of commercial objects today, this has only been the case since the Industrial Revolution. Certainly in the pre-industrial world, men were the chief hunter-gatherers. If we can trust works of art to accurately portray how booty was split (and art historians like John Berger and Simon Schama think we can), then males were the prime consumers of fine clothes, heavily decorated furniture, gold and silver articles and, of course, paintings in which they could be shown displaying their stuff.

Once a surplus was created, as happened in the nineteenth century, women joined the fray in earnest. They were not duped. The hegemonic, phallocentric patriarchy did not brainwash them into thinking goods mattered. The Industrial Revolution produced more and more things not because production is what machines do, and not because nasty producers twisted their handlebar mustaches and whispered, "We can talk women into buying anything," but because both sexes are powerfully attracted to the world of things. Stuff is not nonsense. The material world magnetizes us and we focus much energy on our relationship with it.

Marx himself knew this better than anyone else. In the Communist Manifesto he writes:

> The bourgeoisie, by the rapid improvement of all instruments of production, by the immensely facilitated means of communication, draws all, even the most barbarian nations into civilization. The cheap prices of its commodities are the heavy artillery with which it batters down all Chinese walls…It compels all nations, on pain of extinction, to adopt the bourgeois mode of production; it compels them to introduce what it calls civilization into their midst, i.e., to become bourgeois themselves. In one word, it creates a world after its own image.

Marx uses this insight to motivate the heroic struggle against capitalism. But as we have seen, especially in the last few decades, it proved feckless. The struggle should not be to deter capitalism and its mad consumptive ways, but to appreciate how it works so its furious energy may be understood and exploited.   20

MY ARGUMENT IN A NUTSHELL

I am going to put forward a seemingly naive thesis to understand the triumph of our commodity culture: (1) Humans are consumers by nature. We are tool users because we like to use what tool using can produce. In other words, tools are not the ends but the means. Further, materialism does not crowd out spiritualism; spiritualism is more likely a substitute when objects are scarce. When we have few things, we make the next world holy. When we have plenty, we enchant the objects around us. The hereafter becomes the here and now. You deserve a break today, not in the next life. (2) Consumers are rational. They are often fully aware that they are more interested in consuming aura than objects, sizzle than steak, meaning than material, packaging than product. In fact, if you ask them—as academic critics are usually loath to do—they are quite candid in explaining that the Nike swoosh, the Polo pony, the Guess? label, the DKNY logo are what they are after. They are not duped by advertising, packaging, branding, fashion, or merchandising. They actively seek and enjoy what surrounds the object, especially when they are young. (3) We need to question the criticism that consumption almost always leads to "buyer's remorse." Admittedly the circular route from desire to purchase to disappointment to renewed desire is never-ending, but it may be followed because the other route from melancholy to angst is worse. In other words, in a world emptied of external values, consuming what looks to be overpriced kitsch may be preferable to consuming nothing. And

(4) we need to rethink the separation between production and consumption, for they are more alike than separate, and occur not at different times and places but simultaneously.

Ironically the middle-aged critic, driving about in his well-designed Volvo (unattractive and built to stay that way), is unable to provide much insight into his own consumption practices, although he can certainly criticize the bourgeois afflictions of others. Ask him to explain the difference between "Hilfiger" inscribed on the oversize shirts worn outside pants slopped down to the thighs, and his rear window university decal (My child goes to Yale, sorry about yours), and you will be met with a blank stare. If you were to then suggest that what that decal and automotive nameplate represent is as overpriced as Calvin Klein's initials on a plain white T-shirt, he would pout that you can't compare apples and whatevers. If you were to say next that aspiration and affiliation is at the heart of both displays, he would say that you just don't get it, just don't get it at all.

But don't talk to critics if you want to understand the potency of American consumer culture. Ask any group of teenagers what democracy means to them and you will hear an extraordinary response. Democracy is the right to buy anything you want. Freedom's just another word for lots of things to buy. Appalling perhaps, but there is something to their answer. Being able to buy what you want when and where you want it was, after all, the right that made 1989 a watershed year in Eastern Europe.

Recall as well that freedom to shop was another way to describe the right to be served in a restaurant that provided a focus for the early civil rights movement. Go back farther. It was the right to consume freely that sparked the fires of separation of this country from England. The freedom to buy what you want (even if you can't pay for it) is what most foreigners immediately spot as what they like about our culture, even though in the next breath they will understandably criticize it.

Paradoxically, buying stuff is not just our current popular culture, it 25 is how we understand the world. High culture has pretty much disappeared, desperately needing such infusions of life-preserving monies from taxpayer-supported endowments and tax free foundations to keep it from gasping away. One might well wonder if there is anything more to American life than shopping. After all, we are all consumers now, consumers of everything—consumers of health services, consumers of things and ideas, consumers of political representation, even consumers of what high culture there is left.

The new model citizen wearing his Calvins and eating his Paul Newman popcorn while applying his Michael Jordan cologne, described by both Left and Right, is the citizen consumer, the one who makes rational choices based on assimilating all the available information. Thinking ends in action and that action is buying. W. H. Auden may have lampooned this creature as the drone of the modern state ("The Unknown

Citizen"), but it seems it is not the state that makes the drone, but the drone that makes the state.

THE CASE OF SEVEN-YEAR-OLD MOLLIE

We learn early that shopping around is the way to organize experience. Enid Nemy reports in my favorite part of the *New York Times,* "Metropolitan Diary," this passing tidbit: "Seven-year-old Mollie Kurshan of Ridgewood, N.J., recently attended The Nutcracker with her grandmother at the New York State Theater at Lincoln Center. There was a Sugar Plum Fairy and beautiful costumes, Mollie told her mother, and, best of all 'They stopped in the middle so you could go shopping.' The Kurshans now have a cute little wooden nutcracker, bought at the gift shop during intermission."

By the time she gets to school, Mollie may see her education as something to purchase. Many of my students think of themselves as buyers of a degree. They can even tell you how much a credit hour costs. In addition, when we talk about how much a credit hour is worth, we mean in dollars and cents. A diploma is valued for how much it improves your starting wage.

Just look at the admission process, complete with competition for financial assistance. Schools live and die by what *US News & World Report* or *Money* magazine says about them. You make a deal with one school. You show the deal to other schools. They make counteroffers. It's just like car shopping.

Why go to a prestigious school? Not for good teaching—you are   30 almost assured of being treated poorly in the full professor/teaching assistant configuration. No, you go because the school name improves the relative worth of the line on the vita, the certificate. The assumption is that you pay your money, you get your degree.

Mollie will also learn that what she experienced in Lincoln Center is the norm for what was once called High Culture. Art today is almost always commodified. Juliet B. Schor, a Harvard economist who wrote *The Overworked American* and then *The Overspent American,* quotes a museum curator sheepishly explaining why his museum had to be combined with a shopping mall: "The fact is that shopping is the chief cultural activity in the United States." He is right, as the endless catalogs from the Metropolitan or the Museum of Modern Art attest. Not only are all major museum shows sponsored by corporate interests, but they all end in the same spot: the gift shop.

Mollie may discover that shopping for stuff is so powerful that it sets not just mallcondo culture but our biological clocks. The weekend developed so that shopping day—Saturday—would be set aside and formalized for consuming. Blue laws were passed because clearly Saturday was not enough, and the desire was spilling over to the Sabbath. The year is punctuated by shopping extravaganzas from Christmas to Valentine's Day to Mother's Day to Halloween. By the age of ten, we all know what Mollie Kurshan is learning: what to buy and when. We even know when prices fall: Washington's birthday, Labor Day, after Christmas.

Mollie even knows that objects themselves have seasons. Take candy, for instance. She knows exactly what kind of candy to expect as these days pass by: candy canes, sugar hearts, chocolate, candy corn. As she grows up she will even know what to buy during the day. Take fluids; we have coffee breaks, teatime, cocktail hour, and nightcap. The night belongs to Michelob. One of the biggest marketing problems Coca-Cola had was being thought of only as a hot weather drink. It created the image of Santa Claus, the one recognized by Mollie—a construction of adman Haddon Sundbloom—in order to show Santa drinking a summertime beverage in the dead of winter.

Shopping is so powerful that it even generates our urban architecture. Since the 1950s, towns and cities have grown in grids around not office buildings or schools but malls. Look at Atlanta or Los Angeles. The city of the future is spoked outward from a shopping hub. What of transportation? Every fifth time Mollie's mom gets in the car it is to go buy something. Why do people go to New York City? The third most important reason is to go shopping. Shopping—as Mollie will learn—is not just how we organize our life at various times. It is our life, especially when we are young.

Is this hyperbole? Is it possible for any of us to take a trip and not buy   35
a souvenir? Getting there may be half the fun, but when you return home the experience may be forgotten without the aide memoire. The anxiety of returning empty-handed means we may lose the event. Kodak used this as a way to sell cameras. Show pictures of faraway places and people will travel to faraway places and take pictures of exactly what the ad showed. They were not duped or tricked by this process. We were there, we saw the picture, we "took" a picture just like it. We brought it home. Of course perception is reality, as the ad says. Is there any other kind?

THE CARNIVALIZATION OF SHOPPING

"Fill 'er up," we say as we motor through life from one defining purchase to another. On our journeying juggernauts we tape tributes onto our bumpers so all can see that we have been there, done that. Sometimes what we memorialize is not the trip but the purchase, not the thing but the image of it. On the bumpers of self we slap stickers: "Shop 'til you drop," "He who dies with the most toys wins," "People who say money can't buy happiness, don't know where to shop," "When the going gets tough, the tough go shopping," "But I can't be overdrawn! I still have some checks left!," "I'm spending my grandchildren's inheritance," "Nouveau riche is better than no riche at all," "A woman's place is in the mall." For those who want a thought larger than what fits on a car bumper, here is a greeting card. It says, "Work to Live, Live to Love, Love to Shop, so you see...if I buy enough things I'll never have to work at love again." Wink wink, we say, but under the irony is truth.

Let me reiterate what is central to my thesis and so overlooked in much academic cultural criticism. We were not suddenly transformed from customers to consumers by wily manufacturers eager to unload a surplus of crapular products. We are many things, but what we are not are victims of capitalism. With few exceptions (food, shelter, sex), our needs are cultural, not natural. We have created a surfeit of things because we enjoy the process of getting and spending. The consumption ethic may have started in the early 1900s and hit full tilt after the midcentury, but the desire is ancient. Whereas kings and princes once thought they could solve problems by possessing and amassing things, we now say, "Count us in." Whereas the Duchess of Windsor once said, "All my friends know that I'd rather shop than eat," we now say, "Hey, wait for me."

Generations ago, consumption played out its Saturnalian excesses alongside the church, literally, at the carnival. Mardi Gras and Lent were connected. Consumption, then denial. It was the world turned upside down, then right side up. We used to go into the dark cathedral looking for life's meaning and then do a little shopping on the side. Now we just go straight to the mall. If you travel about the globe, you will find that millions are quietly queuing up waiting their turn to start shopping. Woe to that government or church that tries to turn them back.

By standards of stuff, the last half century of our national life has been wildly successful. We have achieved unprecedented prosperity and personal freedom. We are healthier, we work at less exhausting jobs, and we live longer than ever. Most of this has been made possible by consuming things, ironically spending more and more time at the carnival, less and less in church.

THE MIXED BLESSING

"Wanting," "desiring," "needing" are the gerunds that lubricated   40
this strain of capitalism and made our culture so compelling for have-nots around the world. In the last generation we have almost completely reversed the poles of shame so that where we were once ashamed of consuming too much (religious shame), we are now often ashamed of consuming the wrong brands (shoppers' shame).

Was it worth it? Are we happier for it? Was it fair? Did some of us suffer inordinately for the excesses of others? What are we going to do when all this stuff we have shopped for becomes junk? How close is the connection between the accumulation of goods and the fact that America also leads the industrialized world in rates of murder, violent crime, juvenile violent crime, imprisonment, divorce, abortion, single-parent households, obesity, teen suicide, cocaine consumption, per capita consumption of all drugs, pornography production, and pornography consumption?

These are important questions and we need to continually talk about them. I'm not going to. However, there is a mixed aspect of the material world that I will have to confront. The cornucopia of stuff—which I will address under the rubrics of advertising, fashion, branding, and marketing— is to a considerable number of people an experience that is not just boring but banal, almost obscene. The fact is that the carnival is a world of brazen excess, full of sound and excitement but signifying little in the way of philosophical depth. Most critics of mallcondo culture usually feel this antipathy toward commercialism in midlife, after they have chased the meaning of objects and have settled into a routine of low and simplified consumption. In advertising lingo, they no longer change brands because they have made their affiliations. For them the carnival is over and the church is beckoning.

WHERE THE GENERATION GAP BEGINS

Yeats forecast this split between wanting and no longer interested via a sexual metaphor. In "Sailing to Byzantium" he wrote of the world of youthful urges from which the speaker is now alien:

> That is no country for old men. The young
> In one another's arms, birds in trees—
> Those dying generations—at their song,
> The salmon-falls, the mackerel-crowded seas,
> Fish, flesh, or fowl, commend all summer long
> Whatever is begotten, born, and dies.
> Caught in that sensual music all neglect
> Monuments of unaging intellect.

To translate this "sensual music" into a consumerist apology: once you have passed through "prime-branding time" you are almost impossible to sell to. The mall carnival is not for you. You become in our culture, "a paltry thing, / A tattered coat upon a stick" . . . forgotten. Very little entertainment, let alone information, flows your way because no one is willing to pay the freight to send it. You better find your own Byzantium in far off High Aesthetica because you are not going to find it here in Lower Vulgaria. No one really makes movies for you (blockbusters are for the kids), programs television for you (check who watches primetime), publishes books and magazines for you (look at the bestseller lists or the flood of magazines like *Details, Rolling Stone, Wired*) because, although you have the money, your kids spend it. No wonder you become a critic of a culture that has made you a pariah.

There was no generation gap two generations ago. Fashions, like moral and ethical values, flowed down from above, from old to young,   45 rich to poor. But the money in materialism is to be made from tapping those with excess disposable time and money—the young. Ironically, the only way to return to a culture that served the mature would be if everyone over forty made it a habit to change brands of everything every week or so just like the kids.

This generation gap and the hostility it has engendered is part of the reason we have recently been so passionate about condemning commercialism, and yet so unwilling to examine its workings. These are our kids. We have raised them. They have (gasp!) our values. Clearly we are perplexed about how they act, and just as clearly we have selectively forgotten how important consumption was for us. Their excitement in consumption has been little studied, perhaps because while it is so unfocused, so common, so usual, it is also so youthful. . . .

THINKING CRITICALLY ABOUT THE READING

1. Consider Twitchell's title, "Lead Us into Temptation." What does he seem to be saying about us as consumers?

2. Explain Twitchell's "mallcondo" culture. What are the features of "mallcondoville" and on what principles are they based? Why does he compare the "mallcondo cocoon" (5) to Xanadu's pleasure dome?

3. Twitchell states that what mallcondo culture is really about, especially for those born after World War II, is "manufacturing both things and their meanings" (8). What does he mean by this?

4. Twitchell agrees that commercialism contributes to those things people criticize it for, from corruption in politics to eating disorders. "But it is by no means the whole truth," he writes. "Commercialism is more a mirror than a lamp" (15). Explain this metaphor. (Glossary: *Figures of Speech*)

5. Explain Twitchell's statement that "[a]rt today is almost always commodified" (31). What are some examples that he offers? (Glossary: *Examples*)

6. How does Twitchell use the "case of seven-year-old Mollie" to illustrate his thesis that "shopping around is the way to organize experience" (27)?

7. Explain what Twitchell means by the "carnivalization of shopping." How does this concept illustrate his central thesis?

LANGUAGE IN ACTION

What statement is the following cartoon "Sign Language" making about the influence of advertising and commercialism on our beliefs and behavior? Does the cartoon exaggerate the power of advertising in our lives?

(**continued**)

WRITING SUGGESTIONS

1. Twitchell refers to a number of famous poems in his essay:

   - William Wordsworth, "The World Is Too Much with Us" (1806)
   - Samuel Taylor Coleridge, "Kubla Khan: Or a Vision in a Dream. A Fragment" (c. 1798)
   - William Blake, "The Marriage of Heaven and Hell" (c. 1793)
   - W. H. Auden, "The Unknown Citizen" (1939)

   Select one of these references, read and analyze the poem, and describe how effectively (or ineffectively) Twitchell has used it to illustrate his points and underscore his themes. Is there a literary reference, music lyric, film, or television show that you might use for the same purpose? Use your own reference to help illustrate and support the central thesis of your essay.

2. Twitchell is at odds with much of academic cultural criticism that creates victims out of consumers. In "Jesus Is a Brand of Jeans" (pp. 466–71), Jean Kilbourne sees the power of advertising differently, telling in 2001, "The truth is that there's no way not to be influenced by advertising." Read Kilbourne's essay, then write an essay comparing their central themes, starting with Twitchell's view that "We are many things, but what we are not are victims of capitalism" (37).

Jesus Is a Brand of Jeans

JEAN KILBOURNE

Author, lecturer, filmmaker, and educator Jean Kilbourne is internation-
ally recognized for her work on the impact of advertising on women and
the culture at large. Born in Junction City, Kansas, in 1943, Kilbourne
received her B.A. from Wellesley College, followed by a doctorate in education from Boston University. Kilbourne's seminal study of the adverse
affects of advertising on women, *Deadly Persuasion: Why Women and
Girls Must Fight the Addictive Power of Advertising* (1999), won the Distinguished Publication Award from the Association for Women in Psychology. It was re-released in paperback in 2000 with the title *Can't Buy
My Love: How Advertising Changes the Way We Think and Feel.* Her latest
book, coauthored with Diane E. Levin, is *So Sexy So Soon: The New Sexu-
alized Childhood and What Parents Can Do to Protect Their Kids* (2008).
Kilbourne's award-winning educational films include *Killing Us Softly:
Advertising's Image of Women,* followed by *Still Killing Us Softly* and *Killing Us Softly 3;* and a series of videos on alcohol and smoking: *Deadly
Persuasion: The Advertising of Alcohol & Tobacco; Spin the Bottle: Sex, Lies
& Alcohol; Slim Hopes; Pack of Lies;* and *Calling the Shots.* A recognized
expert on gender issues, addictions, and the media, Kilbourne has advised
two surgeons general and served on both the National Advisory Council on Alcohol Abuse and Alcoholism and the Massachusetts Governor's
Commission on Sexual and Domestic Violence. Her many articles have
appeared in the *International Journal of Advertising, Journal of Media
Literacy, Media and Values, USA Today,* and the *New York Times,* among
other publications.

Her essay "Jesus Is a Brand of Jeans" was first published in the *New
Internationalist* in September 2006. In it, she dissects what she refers to
as advertising's "giant propaganda effort" that includes thousands of messages that "link our deepest emotions to products, that objectify people
and trivialize our most heartfelt moments and relationships—just to sell
us something."

WRITING TO DISCOVER: *Think about what kind of advertising attracts
you most. What are your favorite ads? What makes those ads stand out from
all of the others? Do they usually result in your making a purchase?*

A recent ad for Thule car-rack systems features a child in the backseat
of a car, seatbelt on. Next to the child, assorted sporting gear is carefully
strapped into a child's carseat. The headline says: "We Know What Matters to You." In case one misses the point, further copy adds: "Your gear
is a priority."

Another ad features an attractive young couple in bed. The man is on top of the woman, presumably making love to her. However, her face is completely covered by a magazine, open to a double-page photo of a car. The man is gazing passionately at the car. The copy reads, "The ultimate attraction."

These ads are meant to be funny. Taken individually, I suppose they might seem amusing or, at worst, tasteless. As someone who has studied ads for a long time, however, I see them as part of a pattern: just two of many ads that state or imply that products are more important than people. Ads have long promised us a better relationship via a product: *buy this and you will be loved.* But more recently they have gone beyond that proposition to promise us a relationship with the product itself: *buy this and it will love you.* The product is not so much the means to an end, as the end itself.

After all, it is easier to love a product than a person. Relationships with human beings are messy, unpredictable, sometimes dangerous. "When was the last time you felt this comfortable in a relationship?" asks an ad for shoes. Our shoes never ask us to wash the dishes or tell us we're getting fat. Even more important, products don't betray us. "You can love it without getting your heart broken," proclaims a car ad. One certainly can't say that about loving a human being, as love without vulnerability is impossible.

We are surrounded by hundreds, thousands of messages every day   5
that link our deepest emotions to products, that objectify people and trivialize our most heartfelt moments and relationships. Every emotion is used to sell us something. Our wish to protect our children is leveraged to make us buy an expensive car. A long marriage simply provides the occasion for a diamond necklace. A painful reunion between a father and his estranged daughter is dramatized to sell us a phone system. Everything in the world—nature, animals, people—is just so much stuff to be consumed or to be used to sell us something.

The problem with advertising isn't that it creates artificial needs, but that it exploits our very real and human desires. Advertising promotes a bankrupt concept of *relationship.* Most of us yearn for committed relationships that will last. We are not stupid: we know that buying a certain brand of cereal won't bring us one inch closer to that goal. But we are surrounded by advertising that yokes our needs with products and promises us that *things* will deliver what in fact they never can. In the world of advertising, lovers are things and things are lovers.

It may be that there is no other way to depict relationships when the ultimate goal is to sell products. But this apparently bottomless consumerism not only depletes the world's resources, it also depletes our inner resources. It leads inevitably to narcissism and solipsism. It becomes difficult to imagine a way of relating that isn't objectifying and exploitative.

TUNED IN

Most people feel that advertising is not something to take seriously. Other aspects of the media are serious—the violent films, the trashy talk shows, the bowdlerization of the news. But not advertising! Although much more attention has been paid to the cultural impact of advertising in recent years than ever before, just about everyone still feels personally exempt from its influence. What I hear more than anything else at my lectures is; "I don't pay attention to ads . . . I just tune them out . . . they have no effect on me." I hear this most from people wearing clothes emblazoned with logos. In truth, we are all influenced. There is no way to tune out this much information, especially when it is designed to break through the "tuning out" process. As advertising critic Sut Jhally put it: "To not be influenced by advertising would be to live outside of culture. No human being lives outside of culture."

Much of advertising's power comes from this belief that it does not affect us. As Joseph Goebbels said: "This is the secret of propaganda: those who are to be persuaded by it should be completely immersed in the ideas of the propaganda, without ever noticing that they are being immersed in it." Because we think advertising is trivial, we are less on guard, less critical, than we might otherwise be. While we're laughing, sometimes sneering, the commercial does its work.

Taken individually, ads are silly, sometimes funny, certainly nothing   10
to worry about. But cumulatively they create a climate of cynicism that is poisonous to relationships. Ad after ad portrays our real lives as dull and ordinary, commitment to human beings as something to be avoided. Because of the pervasiveness of this kind of message, we learn from childhood that it is far safer to make a commitment to a product than to a person, far easier to be loyal to a brand. Many end up feeling romantic about material objects yet deeply cynical about other human beings.

UNNATURAL PASSIONS

We know by now that advertising often turns people into objects. Women's bodies—and men's bodies too these days—are dismembered, packaged and used to sell everything from chainsaws to chewing gum, champagne to shampoo. Self-image is deeply affected. The self-esteem of girls plummets as they reach adolescence partly because they cannot possibly escape the message that their bodies are objects, and imperfect objects at that. Boys learn that masculinity requires a kind of ruthlessness, even brutality.

Advertising encourages us not only to objectify each other but to feel passion for products rather than our partners. This is especially dangerous when the products are potentially addictive, because addicts do feel they are in a relationship with their substances. I once heard an alcoholic joke that Jack Daniels was her most constant lover. When I was a smoker, I felt that my cigarettes were my friends. Advertising reinforces these beliefs, so we are twice seduced—by the ads and by the substances themselves.

The addict is the ideal consumer. Ten percent of drinkers consume over sixty percent of all the alcohol sold. Most of them are alcoholics or people in desperate trouble—but they are also the alcohol industry's very best customers. Advertisers spend enormous amounts of money on psychological research and understand addiction well. They use this knowledge to target children (because if you hook them early they are yours for life), to encourage all people to consume more, in spite of often dangerous consequences for all of us, and to create a climate of denial in which all kinds of addictions flourish. This they do with full intent, as we see so clearly in the "secret documents" of the tobacco industry that have been made public in recent years.

The consumer culture encourages us not only to buy more but to seek our identity and fulfillment through what we buy, to express our individuality through our "choices" of products. Advertising corrupts relationships and then offers us products, both as solace and as substitutes for the intimate human connection we all long for and need.

In the world of advertising, lovers grow cold, spouses grow old, children grow up and away—but possessions stay with us and never change. Seeking the outcomes of a healthy relationship through products cannot work. Sometimes it leads us into addiction. But at best the possessions can never deliver the promised goods. They can't make us happy or loved or less alone or safe. If we believe they can, we are doomed to disappointment. No matter how much we love them, they will never love us back. 15

Some argue that advertising simply reflects societal values rather than affecting them. Far from being a passive mirror of society, however, advertising is a pervasive medium of influence and persuasion. Its influence is cumulative, often subtle and primarily unconscious. A former editor-in-chief of *Advertising Age*, the leading advertising publication in North America, once claimed: "Only eight percent of an ad's message is received by the conscious mind. The rest is worked and re-worked deep within, in the recesses of the brain."

Advertising performs much the same function in industrial society as myth did in ancient societies. It is both a creator and perpetuator of the dominant values of the culture, the social norms by which most people govern their behavior. At the very least, advertising helps to create a climate in which certain values flourish and others are not reflected at all.

Advertising is not only our physical environment, it is increasingly our spiritual environment as well. By definition, however, it is only interested in materialistic values. When spiritual values show up in ads, it is only in order to sell us something. Eternity is a perfume by Calvin Klein,

Infiniti is an automobile, Hydra Zen a moisturizer, and Jesus is a brand of jeans.

Sometimes the allusion is more subtle, as in the countless alcohol ads featuring the bottle surrounded by a halo of light. Indeed products such as jewelry shining in a store window are often displayed as if they were sacred objects. Advertising co-opts our sacred symbols in order to evoke an immediate emotional response. Media critic Neil Postman referred to this as "cultural rape."

It is commonplace to observe that consumerism has become the reli-   20
gion of our time (with advertising its holy text), but the criticism usually stops short of what is at the heart of the comparison. Both advertising and religion share a belief in transformation, but most religions believe that this requires sacrifice. In the world of advertising, enlightenment is achieved instantly by purchasing material goods. An ad for a watch says, "It's not your handbag. It's not your neighborhood. Its not your boy-friend. It's your watch that tells most about who you are." Of course, this cheapens authentic spirituality and transcendence. This junk food for the soul leaves us hungry, empty, malnourished.

SUBSTITUTE STORIES

Human beings used to be influenced primarily by the stories of our particular tribe or community, not by stories that are mass-produced and market-driven. As George Gerbner, one of the world's most respected researchers on the influence of the media, said: "For the first time in human history, most of the stories about people, life and values are told not by parents, schools, churches, or others in the community who have some-thing to tell, but by a group of distant conglomerates that have something to sell."

Although it is virtually impossible to measure the influence of adver-tising on a culture, we can learn something by looking at cultures only recently exposed to it. In 1980 the Gwich' in tribe of Alaska got television, and therefore massive advertising, for the first time. Satellite dishes, video games and VCRs were not far behind. Before this, the Gwich'in lived much the way their ancestors had for generations. Within 10 years, the young members of the tribe were so drawn by television they no longer had time to learn ancient hunting methods, their parents' language or their oral history. Legends told around campfires could not compete with Beverly Hills 90210. Beaded moccasins gave way to Nike sneakers, and "tundra tea" to Folger's instant coffee.

As multinational chains replace local character, we end up in a world in which everyone is Gapped and Starbucked. Shopping malls kill vibrant downtown centers locally and create a universe of uniformity internation-ally. We end up in a world ruled by, in John Maynard Keynes's phrase, the values of the casino. On this deeper level, rampant commercialism undermines our physical and psychological health, our environment and our civic life, and creates a toxic society.

Advertising creates a world view that is based upon cynicism, dissatisfaction and craving. Advertisers aren't evil. They are just doing their job, which is to sell a product; but the consequences, usually unintended, are often destructive. In the history of the world, there has never been a propaganda effort to match that of advertising in the past 50 years. More thought, more effort, more money goes into advertising than has gone into any other campaign to change social consciousness. The story that advertising tells is that the way to be happy, to find satisfaction —and the path to political freedom, as well—is through the consumption of material objects. And the major motivating force for social change throughout the world today is this belief that happiness comes from the market.

THINKING CRITICALLY ABOUT THE READING

1. Kilbourne points out two ads in the beginning of her essay that she sees as part of a pattern of how we relate to advertising and the products that are being pitched. What is that pattern? Discuss the difference between "buy this and you will be loved" and "buy this and it will love you."

2. The problem with advertising, according to Kilbourne, "isn't that it creates artificial needs, but that it exploits our very real and human desires" (6). How does she think ads accomplish this kind of exploitation? What examples does she use? (Glossary: *Examples*)

3. In her view, how does advertising promote a "climate of cynicism that is poisonous to relationships" (10)?

4. In what context does Kilbourne introduce the ideas of Nazi propagandist Joseph Goebbels? Why does she do so?

5. Advertising is often accused of turning people into objects. What is the danger in this objectification? How does Kilbourne link such objectification to addiction?

6. Explain what Kilbourne means when she states that advertising and religion share a belief in transformation. What kind of transformation is she referring to?

7. How did the introduction of advertising, via television, change the Alaskan Gwich'in tribe? What can we learn from the tribe's experience?

LANGUAGE IN ACTION

Take a look at the following image, along with its caption, from the *New York Times*:

(**continued**)

NEW YORK—March 10, 2008—A news headline referring to Gov. Eliot Spitzer scrolls above a billboard advertising "America's Next Top Model" in New York's Times Square on Monday, March 10, 2008. Spitzer has been caught on a federal wiretap arranging to meet with a high-priced prostitute at a Washington hotel last month, according to a person briefed on the federal investigation. (Robert Caplin/The New York Times)

What do you make of the juxtaposition of the scrolling headline and the billboard for the popular television show? What do you think Kilbourne might make of it?

WRITING SUGGESTIONS

1. Kilbourne used the Alaskan Gwich'in tribe as an example of how media and advertising can produce great changes in a culture, almost overnight. China might provide an equally powerful example. China's economy has grown by leaps and bounds, because its products feed consumer demand in the United States and elsewhere, and, as a result, China is developing its own burgeoning consumer society. Do some research on China's economy and the growth of consumerism there. Keeping in mind Kilbourne's account of the Alaskan tribe and what she views as their loss of traditional cultural attributes, write an article reporting some of the changes that have occurred in China recently due to their growing "consumer ethic."

2. In his essay "Lead Us into Temptation," James Twitchell says that "commercialism is more a mirror than a lamp." Kilbourne uses the same metaphor, but to make a point: "Some argue that advertising simply reflects societal values rather than affecting them. Far from being a passive mirror of society, however, advertising is a pervasive medium of influence and persuasion" (16). Think about Twitchell's and Kilbourne's differing approaches to the links between consumerism and advertising, and write an essay comparing their views.

Barricading the Branded Village

NAOMI KLEIN

Journalist, author, and political and social activist Naomi Klein was born in Montreal, Canada, in 1970, and lives in Toronto. A graduate of the University of Toronto, Klein was a Miliband Fellow at the London School of Economics and holds an honorary Doctor of Civil Laws from the University of King's College, Nova Scotia. Her first book, *No Logo: Taking Aim at the Brand Bullies,* was published in 2000 and became an international best-seller. It was shortly followed by *Fences and Windows: Dispatches from the Front Lines of the Globalization Debate* (2002), a collection of columns, speeches, essays, and articles about the rise of the anti-globalization movement. Her latest book is *Shock Doctrine: The Rise of Disaster Capitalism* (2007). Her regular columns for the *Nation,* the *Guardian* (U.K.), and the *Globe and Mail* (Canada) are syndicated around the world, and her articles appear in numerous publications, including *Newsweek International,* the *New York Times,* the *Village Voice,* and *Ms.* Her reports from Iraq for *Harper*'s in 2004 won the James Aronson Award for Social Justice Journalism. In that same year, Klein released *The Take,* a feature-length documentary about Argentina's factory workers, which she coproduced with her husband, Avi Lewis. The film was an official selection of the Venice Biennale and won the Best Documentary Jury Prize at the American Film Institute's Film Festival in Los Angeles.

The reading selection we reproduce here is taken from a chapter in *No Logo* entitled "Corporate Censorship." In it, Klein warns that the decisions made by corporations about what goes on the shelves in a store, or what kinds of books and music are stocked, can have enormous consequences, because "those who make these choices have the power to reengineer the cultural landscape."

WRITING TO DISCOVER: *Klein is concerned that mega-retailers such as Wal-Mart are determining what books we read and what music we listen to. Where do you buy your books and music? Do you detect any difference in what is available for purchase between, say, your local music store and Kmart? If so, to what do you ascribe these differences?*

Every other week I pull something off the shelf that I don't think is of Wal-Mart quality.

> —Teresa Stanton, manager of Wal-Mart's store in Cheraw, South Carolina,
> on the chain's practice of censoring magazines with provocative covers, in
> the *Wall Street Journal,* October 22, 1997

In some instances, the assault on choice has moved beyond predatory retail and monopolistic synergy schemes and become what can only

be described as straightforward censorship: the active elimination and suppression of material. Most of us would define censorship as a restriction of
content imposed by governments or other state institutions, or instigated—
particularly in North American societies—by pressure groups for political or
religious reasons. It is rapidly becoming evident, however, that this definition is drastically outdated. Although there will always be a Jesse Helms and
a Church Lady to ban a Marilyn Manson concert, these little dramas are fast
becoming sideshows in the context of larger threats to free expression.

Corporate censorship has everything to do with the themes of the last
two chapters: media and retail companies have inflated to such bloated
proportions that simple decisions about what items to stock in a store or
what kind of cultural product to commission—decisions quite properly
left to the discretion of business owners and culture makers—now have
enormous consequences: those who make these choices have the power
to reengineer the cultural landscape. When magazines are pulled from
Wal-Mart's shelves by store managers, when cover art is changed on CDs
to make them Kmart-friendly, or when movies are refused by Blockbuster
Video because they don't conform to the chain's "family entertainment"
image, these private decisions send waves through the culture industries,
affecting not just what is readily available at the local big box but what gets
produced in the first place.

Both Wal-Mart and Blockbuster Video have their roots in the southern
U.S. Christian heartland—Blockbuster in Texas, Wal-Mart in Arkansas.
Both retailers believe that being "family" stores is at the core of their finan-
cial success, the very key to their mass appeal. The model (also adopted by
Kmart), is to create a one-size-fits-all family-entertainment center, where
Mom and Dad can rent the latest box-office hit and the new Garth Brooks
release a few steps away from where Johnny can get *Tomb Raider 2* and
Melissa can co-angst with Alanis.

To protect this formula, Blockbuster, Wal-Mart, Kmart and all the
large supermarket chains have a policy of refusing to carry any material that could threaten their image as a retail destination for the whole
family. The one-stop-shopping recipe is simply too lucrative to risk. So
magazines are rejected by Wal-Marts and supermarket chains—which
together account for 55 percent of U.S. newsstand sales—for offenses
ranging from too much skin on the cover girls, to articles on "His &
Her Orgasms" or "Coming Out: Why I Had to Leave My Husband for
Another Woman."[1] Wal-Mart's and Kmart's policy is not to stock CDs
with cover art or lyrics deemed overly sexual or touching too explicitly on
topics that reliably scandalize the heartland: abortion, homosexuality and
satanism. Meanwhile, Blockbuster Video, which controls 25 percent of
the home-video market in the U.S., carries plenty of violent and sexually
explicit movies but it draws the line at films that receive an NC-17 rating,

---

1. *Wall Street Journal,* 22 October 1997, A1.

a U.S. designation meaning that nobody under seventeen can see the film, even accompanied by an adult.

To hear the chains tell it, censoring art is simply one of several services   5 they provide to their family-oriented customers, like smiling faces and low prices. "Our customers understand our music and video merchandising decisions are a common-sense attempt to provide the type of material they might want to purchase," says Dale Ingram, Wal-Mart director of corporate relations. Blockbuster's line is: "We respect the needs of families as well as individuals."[2]

Wal-Mart can afford to be particularly zealous since entertainment products represent only a fraction of its business anyway. No one hit record or movie has the power to make a dent in Wal-Mart's bottom line, a fact that makes the retailer unafraid to stand up to the entertainment industry's best-selling artists and defend its vision of a shopping environment where power tools and hip-hop albums are sold in adjoining aisles. The most well known of these cases involved the chain's refusal to carry Nirvana's second hit album, *In Utero*, even though the band's previous album had gone quadruple platinum, because it objected to the back-cover artwork portraying fetuses. "Country artists like Vince Gill and Garth Brooks are going to sell much better for Wal-Mart than Nirvana," Wal-Mart spokesperson Trey Baker blithely said at the time.[3] Facing a projected loss of 10 percent (Wal-Mart's then share of U.S. music sales), Warner and Nirvana backed down and changed the artwork. They also changed the title of the song "Rape Me" to "Waif Me." Kmart Canada took a similar attitude to the Prodigy's 1997 release *Fat of the Land,* on the basis that the cover art and the lyrics in the songs "Smack My Bitch Up" and "Funky Shit" just wouldn't fit in at the Mart. "Our typical customer is a married working mother and we felt it was inappropriate for a family store," said manager Allen Letch.[4] Like Nirvana, the British bad boys complied with their label's subsequent request and issued a cleaned-up version.

Such censorship, in fact, has become so embedded in the production process that it is often treated as simply another stage of editing. Because of Blockbuster's policy, some major film studios have altogether stopped making films that will be rated NC-17. If a rare exception is made, the studios will cut two versions—one for the theaters, one sliced and diced for Blockbuster. What producer, after all, would be willing to forgo 25 percent of video earnings before their project is even out of the gate? As film director David Cronenberg told *The New Yorker,* "The assumption now seems to be that every movie should be watchable by a kid. . . . So the pressure on anyone who wants to make a grownup movie is enormous."[5]

---

2. *New York Times,* 12 November 1996.
3. *Billboard,* 2 October 1993.
4. *Globe and Mail,* 7 January 1998, C2.
5. "Guardian Angels," *New Yorker,* 25 November 1996, 47.

Many magazines, including *Cosmopolitan* and *Vibe,* have taken to showing advance copies of new issues to big boxes and supermarkets before they ship them out. Why risk having to deal with the returns if the issue is deemed too risqué? "If you don't let them know in advance, they will delist the title and never carry it again," explains Dana Sacher, circulation director of *Vibe.* "This way, they don't carry one issue, but they might carry the next one."[6]

Since bands put out a record every couple of years—not one a month—they don't have the luxury of warning Wal-Mart about a potentially contentious cover and hoping for better luck on the next release. Like film producers, record labels are instead acting preemptively, issuing two versions of the same album—one for the big boxes, bleeped, airbrushed, even missing entire songs. But while that has been the strategy for multi-platinum-selling artists like the Prodigy and Nirvana, bands with less clout often lose the opportunity to record their songs the way they intended, preempting the objections of family-values retailers by issuing only pre-sanitized versions of their work.

In large part, the complacency surrounding the Wal-Mart and Block- 10
buster strain of censorship occurs because most people are apt to think of corporate decisions as non-ideological. Businesses make business decisions, we tell ourselves—even when the effects of those decisions are clearly political. And when retailers dominate the market to the extent that these chains do today, their actions can't help raising questions about the effect on civil liberties and public life. As Bob Merlis, a spokesperson for Warner Brothers Records explains, these private decisions can indeed have very public effects. "If you can't buy the record then we can't sell it," he says. "And there are some places where these mass merchandisers are the only game in town."[7] So in much the same way that Wal-Mart has used its size to get cheaper prices out of suppliers, the chain is also using its heft to change the kind of art that its "suppliers" (i.e., record companies, publishers, magazine editors) provide.

CENSORSHIP IN SYNERGY

While the instances of corporate censorship discussed so far have been a direct by-product of retail concentration, they represent only the most ham-fisted form of corporate censorship. More subtly—and perhaps more interestingly—the culture industry's wave of mergers is breeding its own blockages to free expression, a kind of censorship in synergy.

---

6. *Wall Street Journal,* 22 October 1997, A1.
7. *Sacramento Bee,* 10 December 1997, E1.

One of the reasons that producers are not standing up to puritanical retailers is that those retailers, distributors and producers are often owned, in whole or in part, by the same companies. Nowhere is this conflict of interest more in play than in the relationship between Paramount Films and Blockbuster Video. Paramount is hardly positioned to lead the charge against Blockbuster's conservative stocking policy, because if indeed such a policy is the most cost-effective way to draw the whole family into the video store, then who is Paramount to take money directly out of mutual owner Viacom's pockets? Similar conflicts arise in the aftermath of Disney's 1993 purchase of Miramax, the formerly independent film company. On the one hand, Miramax now has deep resources to throw behind commercially risky foreign films like Roberto Benigni's *Life Is Beautiful;* on the other, when the company decides whether or not to carry a politically controversial and sexually explicit work like Larry Clarke's *Kids,* it cannot avoid weighing how that decision will reflect on Disney and ABC's reputations as family programmers, with all the bowing to pressure groups that that entails.

Such potential conflicts become even more disturbing when the media holdings involved are not only producing entertainment but also news or current affairs. When newspapers, magazines, books and television stations are but one arm of a conglomerate bent on "absolute open communication" (as Sumner Redstone puts it), there is obvious potential for the conglomerate's myriad financial interests to influence the kind of journalism that is produced. Of course, newspaper publishers meddling in editorial content to further their own financial interests is as old a story as the small-town paper owner who uses the local *Herald* or *Gazette* to get his buddy elected mayor. But when the publisher is a conglomerate, its fingers are in many more pots at once. As multinational conglomerates build up their self-enclosed, self-promoting worlds, they create new and varied possibilities for conflict of interest and censorship. Such pressures range from pushing the magazine arm of the conglomerate to give a favorable review to a movie or sitcom produced by another arm of the conglomerate, to pushing an editor not to run a critical story that could hurt a merger in the works, to newspapers being asked to tiptoe around judicial or regulatory bodies that award television licenses and review anti-trust complaints. And what is emerging is that even tough-minded editors and producers who unquestioningly stand up to external calls for censorship—whether from vocal political lobbies, Wal-Mart managers or their own advertisers—are finding these intracorporate pressures much more difficult to resist.

The most publicized of the synergy-censorship cases occurred in September 1998 when ABC News killed a Disney-related story prepared by its award-winning investigative team of correspondent Brian Ross and producer Rhonda Schwartz. The story began as a broad investigation of allegations of lax security at theme parks and resorts, leading to the inadvertent hiring of sex offenders, including pedophiles, as park employees.

Because Disney was to be only one of several park owners under the   15
microscope, Ross and Schwartz got the go-ahead on the story. After all,
it wasn't the first time the team had faced the prospect of reporting on
their parent company. In March 1998, ABC newsmagazine *20/20* had
aired their story about widespread sweatshop labor in the U.S. territory of
Saipan. Though it focused its criticism on Ralph Lauren and the Gap, the
story did mention in passing that Disney was among the other American
companies contracting to the offending factories.

But reporting has a life of its own and as Ross and Schwartz progressed on the theme-park investigation, they found that Disney wasn't on
the periphery, but was at the center of this story. When they handed in two
drafts of what had turned into a sex-and-scandal exposé of Disney World,
David Westin, president of ABC News, rejected the drafts. "They didn't
work," said network spokeswoman Eileen Murphy.[8] Even though Disney
denies the allegations of lax security, first made in the book *Disney: The
Mouse Betrayed,* and even though CEO Michael Eisner is on record saying
"I would prefer ABC not cover Disney,"[9] ABC denies the story was killed
because of pressure from its parent company. Murphy did say, however,
that "we would generally not embark on an investigation that focused
solely on Disney, for a whole variety of reasons, one of which is that whatever you come up with, positive or negative, will seem suspect."[10]

The most vocal criticism of the affair came from *Brill's Content,* the
media-watch magazine founded in 1998 by Steven Brill. The publication
lambasted ABC executives and journalists for their silence in the face of
censorship, accusing them of caving in to their own internalized "Mouse-
Ke-Fear." In his previous incarnation as founder of the Court TV cable
network and *American Lawyer* magazine, Steven Brill had some firsthand
experience with censorship in synergy. After selling his miniature media
empire to Time Warner in 1997, Brill claims that he faced pressure on
several different stories that brushed up against the octopus-like tentacles
of the Time Warner/Turner media empire. In a memo excerpted in *Vanity
Fair,* Brill writes that company lawyers tried to suppress a report in *American Lawyer* about a Church of Scientology lawsuit against *Time* magazine
(owned by Time Warner) and asked Court TV to refrain from covering
a trial involving Warner Music. He also claims to have received a request
from Time Warner's chief financial officer, Richard Bressler, to "kill a
story" about William Baer, the director of the Federal Trade Commission's
Bureau of Competition—ironically, the very body charged with reviewing
the Time Warner-Turner merger for any violation of anti-trust law.[11]

---

8. Gail Shister, Knight Ridder Newspapers, 20 October 1998.
9. "Fresh Air," National Public Radio, 29 September 1998.
10. Lawrie Mifflin, "ABC News Reporter Discovers the Limits of Investigating
Disney," *New York Times,* 19 October 1998.
11. Jennet Conant, "Don't Mess with Steve Brill," *Vanity Fair,* August 1997, 62–74.

Despite the alleged meddling, all the stories in question made it to print or to air, but Brill's experience still casts a shadow over the future of press freedom inside the merged giants. Individual crusading editors and producers have always carried the flag for journalists' right to do their job, but in the present climate, for every crusader there will be many more walking on eggs for fear of losing their job. And it's not surprising that some have begun to see trouble everywhere, second-guessing the wishes of top executives in ways more creative and paranoid than the executives may even dare to imagine themselves. This is the truly insidious nature of self-censorship: it does the gag work more efficiently than an army of bullying and meddling media moguls could ever hope to accomplish.

THINKING CRITICALLY ABOUT THE READING

1. Klein writes that censorship is typically defined as the active elimination and restriction of content imposed by governments and/or political and religious pressure groups, but that corporate censorship makes that definition outdated. What is "corporate censorship"? How does it work in a retail environment?

2. What is the prime motivation behind the attempt by "big box" stores to control the products they sell?

3. What is Klein's greatest concern about corporate censorship?

4. We are apt to think that the decisions businesses make are nonideological, Klein warns, and that helps make us complacent about this type of censorship. Explain how, in Klein's view, these everyday merchandising decisions can be both ideological and political in their effect.

5. Klein writes that "the culture industry's wave of mergers is breeding its own blockages to free expression, a kind of censorship in synergy" (11). Define *synergy* in this context. How does media concentration affect artists and the distribution of the art that's produced? Give examples.

6. Discuss the possible conflicts of interest that can result when the holdings of media conglomerates produce both entertainment and news. What are some of the pressures on journalists that result from concentrated media ownership?

7. Klein writes about the "insidious nature of self-censorship" (18). How does this work in the context of corporate censorship?

LANGUAGE IN ACTION

How do you define censorship? List instances in which you have experienced censorship in your own life, including restrictions imposed by government, religious, and political organizations, as well as from the corporate sector. Compare your list with others in your class.

WRITING SUGGESTIONS

1. CDs that carry an adult-content warning sticker are not sold at Wal-Mart. Wal-Mart's policy on this issue states the following:

    > *Wal-Mart will not stock music with parental guidance stickers. While Wal-Mart sets high standards, it would not be possible to eliminate every image, word or topic that an individual might find objectionable. And the goal is not to eliminate the need for parents to review the merchandise their children buy. The policy simply helps eliminate the most objectionable material from Wal-Mart's shelves.*

    Klein calls this refusal to stock potentially objectionable materials censorship; Wal-Mart would call it successful target marketing and good customer service. Who is right, in your opinion? Write an essay comparing the two differing views; give your own opinion and defend it with examples.

2. The nonpartisan, nonprofit organization Free Press (www.freepress.net) is dedicated to increasing informed public participation in crucial media policy debates. In a feature on its Web site called "Who Owns the Media: The Big Six" (http://www.freepress.net/ownership/chart/main), it echoes concerns expressed by Naomi Klein about the potential for censorship brought about by media concentration:

    > *The U.S. media landscape is dominated by massive corporations that, through a history of mergers and acquisitions, have concentrated their control over what we see, hear and read. In many cases these giant companies are vertically integrated, controlling everything from initial production to final distribution.*

    Among the companies it profiles is the Walt Disney Company, which in 2006 had revenues of $34.3 billion:

    > *The Walt Disney Company owns the ABC Television Network, cable networks including ESPN, the Disney Channel, SOAPnet, A&E and Lifetime, 227 radio stations, music and book publishing companies, production companies Touchstone, Miramax and Walt Disney Pictures, Pixar Animation Studios, the cellular service Disney Mobile, and theme parks around the world.*

    With these facts in mind, write an essay in which you argue for or against the proposition that this media concentration presents risks to our basic freedoms.

7

LANGUAGE DEBATE: SHOULD LEARNING BE CENSORED?

This chapter opens with a provocative question: Should learning be censored? If you're anything like our students, you will probably immediately respond—Of course not! Before moving on to the next topic, though, you should take a minute to look at your own experience as a student and citizen of a learning community, and ask yourself: *Is* learning censored at my school and in my community? If so, how, and by whom? To what extent does such censorship impede my learning? To what extent does it affect the world outside the classroom? Finally, what should we do about it?

Vigorous campus debates on the issues of speech codes, First Amendment rights, political correctness, and the virtues and sins of various kinds of free expression give students ample opportunity to examine these issues firsthand. It is imperative that as members of a learning community, we neither uncritically embrace nor thoughtlessly dismiss movements that seek to increase sensitivity to the larger problems of prejudice and discrimination in our society or that attempt to propagate moral codes and value lessons. As members of our college communities, we need to know as much as we can about these movements and to articulate in both speech and writing what we think. What you learn about censorship now, while you're in school, and how you act as a result of what you learn, will significantly affect both how you conduct yourself in the wider world and the way that world works.

This chapter assembles the work of six well-known writers, each arguing from a different perspective, in a debate about censorship and core values in our society. In the opening essay, "We Are Free to Be You, Me, Stupid, and Dead," Roger Rosenblatt goes to the fundamentals of language itself—"our sauntering, freewheeling, raucous, stumbling, unbridled, unregulated, unorthodox words"—to champion unbridled freedom of speech. In his essay "Pornography, Obscenity, and the Case for Censorship," conservative pundit Irving Kristol counters the liberal view by arguing for censorship of pornography and obscenity, which, in his opinion, threaten our civilization, our humanity, and our democracy. Next is Stanley Fish with his "Free-Speech Follies." Fish lambastes those, on college campuses in particular, who "cry the First Amendment" at the least provocation, invoking First Amendment rights "when there are no First Amendment issues in sight." Stuart Taylor Jr., in "How Campus Censors Squelch Freedom of Speech," argues that First Amendment rights are violated routinely on college campuses in the name of the fight against racial or sexual "harassment." As a result, Taylor argues, "censorship is thriving" on college campuses. The debate closes with a pair of essays on the specific topic of the censorship of educational materials. In her essay "The Language Police," educator Diane Ravitch explores the pressures brought by "partisans of both left and right" to push books and stories "through a sieve of political correctness," leaving students with only a highly censored "thin gruel" to read. Anna Quindlen gets the last word in the debate with her essay "With a No. 2 Pencil, Delete: The Destruction of Literature in the Name of Children," in which she reveals the not-so-subtle efforts of the educational establishment to homogenize and sanitize literature and reading material aimed at children. Using a metaphor that recalls Ravitch's "thin gruel," Quindlen describes the result of such misguided efforts as "pabulum for students who deserve something tastier."

We Are Free to Be You, Me, Stupid, and Dead

ROGER ROSENBLATT

Journalist, author, and essayist Roger Rosenblatt was born in 1940 in New York City. He received his Ph.D. in English and American literature in 1968 from Harvard University, where he also taught and directed the freshman English program. He began his career as a journalist in 1975 as literary editor for the *New Republic* before joining the *Washington Post* as a columnist. From 1980 to 1988, Rosenblatt was senior editor and essayist at *Time* magazine, where his essays won two George Polk Awards, among other major recognition. Rosenblatt currently appears regularly on the *PBS NewsHour with Jim Lehrer*, where his commentaries have won both a Peabody Award and an Emmy.

Rosenblatt's nonfiction books, which cover a wide range of social and cultural themes, include *Children at War*, which was a finalist for the National Book Critics Circle Award and won the Robert F. Kennedy Book Prize; *Witness: The World Since Hiroshima* (1985); *Life Itself: Abortion in the American Mind* (1992); *Rules for Aging* (2000); and *Anything Can Happen: Notes on My Inadequate Life and Yours* (2003). His first novel, *Lapham Rising*, was published in 2006, followed by *Beet* in 2008. He is also the author of five plays, including the 1991 play *Free Speech in America*.

"We Are Free to Be You, Me, Stupid, and Dead" comes from Rosenblatt's essay collection *Where We Stand: Thirty Reasons for Loving Our Country* (2002). In defending the right to freedom of speech given by the Constitution, Rosenblatt cites a number of colorful examples of protected speech that many of us would find objectionable, while reminding us "that the Founding Fathers . . . actually meant it when they allowed someone to do something that would outrage the rest of us."

WRITING TO DISCOVER: *Think about your personal definition of "free speech." Does it mean the freedom to say anything you want—to anyone, about anyone, using any words you please? Do you think freedom of speech can go too far? Do you set limits for yourself and others, and if so, what are they?*

Everyone loves free expression as long as it isn't exercised. Several years ago, Mahmoud Abdul-Rauf, a basketball player for the Denver Nuggets, refused to stand up for the playing of the national anthem because of personal religious convictions. The National Basketball Association greeted his decision by suspending him from the league until someone suggested that the Founding Fathers had actually meant it when they allowed someone to do something that would outrage the rest of us.

Similarly, major league baseball suspended John Rocker, the famous nut-case relief pitcher for the Atlanta Braves, when Rocker said that he did not want to ride New York City's Number 7 subway with all those single moms, queers, and illegal aliens. The court did not interfere, perhaps because the Constitution only states that government has no right to prevent free expression; it grants no affirmative licenses. I don't really get the difference between the two cases, but I know that Rocker had a perfect, or rather imperfect, right to sound like a jackass.

The rights of jackasses are more than a national staple. The strange beauty of American freedom is that it is ungovernable, that it always runs slightly ahead of human temperament. You think you know what you will tolerate. A man on a soapbox speaks out for China. Fine. An editorial calls for sympathy with the Taliban. (Gulp) okay. But then a bunch of Nazis want to march around Skokie, Illinois, or Harlem, and, hold on a minute! And what the hell is this? An art exhibit called "African-American Flag" in New Jersey. Or this? An exhibit in the Phoenix Art Museum called "What Is the Proper Way to Display the US Flag?"

Now that one was a doozie. The exhibit required observers to walk across an American flag on the floor to get to what was displayed on a wall. "That's my flag, and I'm going to defend it," said a visitor to the museum as he tried to take the flag from the floor. "No son of a bitch is going to do that."

The thing that I like best about sons of bitches doing that and worse,   5 as long as they do not cry "fire" in a crowded room, is (a) it enhances my appreciation of the wild courage of the Founders, and (b) it expands my mind, which could use some expanding. Freedom is like a legal drug. *How far will we go?* is not a rhetorical question here. Another exhibit in Chicago showed a flag with the word "think" where the stars should have been. Think. I hate it when that happens.

You think you know how far freedom will go in America, and then you meet another jackass. In the 1990s, I wrote a story for the *New York Times Magazine* about the Philip Morris company called "How Do They Live with Themselves?" The answer to that question, which came from the company executives I interviewed, turned out to be "Quite comfortably, thanks." The reason that their consciences did not seem to bother them about manufacturing an addictive lethal product was that their customers were engaging in the blessed American activity of freedom of choice. They were right—at least until new laws or lawsuits would prove them wrong. People technically had the choice of becoming addicted to cigarettes or not. I doubt that any of the Philip Morris people would ever step on the flag.

Since free is the way people's minds were made to be, it has been instructive for me to spend time in places where freedom was limited. In the Soviet Union, it was fascinating to see how many ways the workers of the world managed to squeeze free thought through the cracks of their utopian cells: the secret publication of books, the pirated music, the tricky subversive lines of poetry read at vast gatherings of tens of thousands. And the below-the-surface comedy. I was checking out of a hotel in Tbilisi. Checking out of Russian hotels was always a feat—they didn't have dollars, they didn't have rubles, no one had ever checked out before. The clerk at the desk spoke little English, and she wanted to tell me that another, more fluent, clerk would be along shortly. "Mr. Rosenblatt," she said. "Would you mind coming back in fifteen years?" We both exploded in laughter because we knew it was remotely possible.

The mind expands, the mind settles, then is shaken up, resists, and expands again. One of the great ongoing stupidities of the country are school boards and library committees that ban certain books they deem dangerous. On the positive side, though, the folks who do the banning offer some delightful defenses for their decisions. The three literary works most frequently banned in our country are *Macbeth, King Lear,* and *The Great Gatsby.* The reason school boards offer for banning *Macbeth* is that the play promotes witchcraft. Perhaps it does. One doesn't think of *Macbeth* as promoting things, but if it did, witchcraft would be it. They don't say why they want to ban *King Lear.* Promotes ingratitude, I suppose. I assume that *The Great Gatsby* promotes Long Island.

Sometimes the reasons offered for censoring certain works are obscure, thus intriguing. In Georgia, the Harry Potter books were recently burned because they were said to encourage kids to want to be sorcerers. In Spokane, Washington, they wanted to remove the children's picture book *Where's Waldo?* from the elementary school library. People objected to *Where's Waldo?,* they said, because it contains "explicit subject matter." A plea for surrealism, I imagine. In Springfield, Virginia, they banned a book called *Hitler's Hang-Ups* because it offered "explicit sexual details about Hitler's life." Given the *other* tendencies of Hitler's life, I should think the sexual details would be relatively acceptable. And, in the town of Astoria, Oregon, a book called *Wait Till Helen Comes* was challenged in an elementary school for giving "a morbid portrayal of death." Now they've gone too far.

THINKING CRITICALLY ABOUT THE READING

1. Rosenblatt opens his essay with the statement: "Everyone loves free expression as long as it isn't exercised." What does he mean by this statement? How does it apply to the two sports figures he cites as examples?

2. What is Rosenblatt getting at when he says that we "think" we know what we will tolerate? What do his examples of the Nazis in Skokie and the flag exhibit in the art museum tell us about the limits of our tolerance?

3. Rosenblatt refers to the "wild courage of the Founders" (5). Explain why he chose the phrase "wild courage."

4. Why were the Philip Morris executives comfortable with their position as purveyors of "an addictive lethal product" like cigarettes? How does this fit in with free expression as described by Rosenblatt?

5. Describe Rosenblatt's experience in the then–Soviet Union, and why it was instructive. How, according to Rosenblatt, did Soviet citizens express free thought in a repressive society? What did the desk clerk at the hotel mean when she asked, "Would you mind coming back in fifteen years"?

6. What is the central argument of Rosenblatt's essay? Does he believe that free speech should never be curtailed? Cite evidence from the essay to support your answer. (Glossary: *Argument; Evidence*)

Pornography, Obscenity, and the Case for Censorship

IRVING KRISTOL

Writer, editor, and political and social critic Irving Kristol was born in New York City in 1920 and educated at City College of New York, a hotbed of radical left-wing intellectualism in the 1930s and 1940s, where Kristol became involved early on in progressive movements. Upon graduating in 1940, however, Kristol gradually developed a philosophy at the opposite end of the political spectrum. Often referred to as the "godfather of neoconservatism," he was managing editor of *Commentary* (1947–1952), a magazine later called the "neocon Bible," and has written numerous books on issues of concern to conservatives, including *On the Democratic Idea in America* (1972), *Two Cheers for Capitalism* (1978), and *Reflections of a Neoconservative: Looking Back, Looking Ahead* (1983). *Neoconservatism: Autobiography of an Idea* (1995) is a collection of essays Kristol wrote over fifty years that follows the establishment of the neocon approach. Kristol's articles have appeared in the *New York Times, Harper*'s, the *Atlantic, Fortune, Foreign Affairs,* and *Yale Review,* among other places, and he is a member of the board of contributors of the *Wall Street Journal.* He is a distinguished fellow at the American Enterprise Institute and father of the noted neoconservative *New York Times* columnist William Kristol.

"Pornography, Obscenity, and the Case for Censorship" was first published on May 28, 1971, in the *New York Times Magazine.* It has since been reprinted in numerous anthologies. In it, Kristol makes a well-reasoned, highly controversial case for media censorship, saying, "For almost a century now, a great many intelligent, well-meaning and articulate people have argued eloquently against any kind of censorship of art and entertainment. . . . Somehow, things have not worked out as they were supposed to. . . ."

WRITING TO DISCOVER: *Has any song, movie, book, or work of art ever offended you so much that you felt it should be censored? Do you think censoring art is ever justified? Why or why not?*

Being frustrated is disagreeable, but the real disasters in life begin when you get what you want. For almost a century now, a great many intelligent, well-meaning and articulate people — of a kind generally called liberal or intellectual, or both — have argued eloquently against any kind of censorship of art and/or entertainment. And within the past 10 years, the courts and the legislatures of most Western nations have found these arguments persuasive—so persuasive that hardly a man is now alive who clearly remembers what the answers to these arguments were. Today, in the United States and other democracies, censorship has to all intents and purposes ceased to exist.

Is there a sense of triumphant exhilaration in the land? Hardly. There is, on the contrary, a rapidly growing unease and disquiet. Somehow, things have not worked out as they were supposed to, and many notable civil libertarians have gone on record as saying this was not what they meant at all. They wanted a world in which *Desire Under the Elms* could be produced, or *Ulysses* published, without interference by philistine busybodies holding public office. They have got that, of course; but they have also got a world in which homosexual rape takes place on the stage, in which the public flocks during lunch hours to witness varieties of professional fornication, in which Times Square has become little more than a hideous market for the sale and distribution of printed filth that panders to all known (and some fanciful) sexual perversions.

But disagreeable as this may be, does it really matter? Might not our unease and disquiet be merely a cultural hangover—a "hangup," as they say? What reason is there to think that anyone was ever corrupted by a book?

This last question, oddly enough, is asked by the very same people who seem convinced that advertisements in magazines or displays of violence on television do indeed have the power to corrupt. It is also asked, incredibly enough and in all sincerity, by people—e.g., university professors and school teachers—whose very lives provide all the answers one could want. After all, if you believe that no one was ever corrupted by a book, you have also to believe that no one was ever improved by a book (or a play or a movie). You have to believe, in other words, that all art is morally trivial and that, consequently, all education is morally irrelevant. No one, not even a university professor, really believes that.

To be sure, it is extremely difficult, as social scientists tell us, to trace   5 the effects of any single book (or play or movie) on an individual reader or any class of readers. But we all know, and social scientists know it too, that the ways in which we use our minds and imaginations do shape our characters and help define us as persons. That those who certainly know this are nevertheless moved to deny it merely indicates how a dogmatic resistance to the idea of censorship can—like most dogmatism—result in a mindless insistence on the absurd.

I have used these harsh terms—"dogmatism" and "mindless"—advisedly. I might also have added "hypocritical." For the plain fact is that none of us is a complete civil libertarian. We all believe that there is some point at which the public authorities ought to step in to limit the "self expression" of an individual or a group, even where this might be seriously intended as a form of artistic expression, and even where the artistic transaction is between consenting adults. A playwright or theatrical director might, in this crazy world of ours, find someone willing to commit suicide on the stage, as called for by the script. We would not allow that—any more than we would permit scenes of real physical torture on the stage, even if the victim were a willing masochist. And I know of no one, no matter how free in spirit, who argues that we ought to permit gladiatorial contests in Yankee Stadium, similar to those once performed in the Colosseum at Rome—even if only consenting adults were involved.

The basic point that emerges is one that Prof. Walter Berns has powerfully argued: no society can be utterly indifferent to the ways its citizens publicly entertain themselves.* Bearbaiting and cockfighting are prohibited only in part out of compassion for the suffering animals; the main reason they were abolished was because it was felt that they debased and brutalized the citizenry who flocked to witness such spectacles. And the question we face with regard to pornography and obscenity is whether, now that they have such strong legal protection from the Supreme Court, they can or will brutalize and debase our citizenry. We are, after all, not dealing with one passing incident—one book, or one play, or one movie. We are dealing with a general tendency that is suffusing our entire culture.

I say pornography *and* obscenity because, though they have different dictionary definitions and are frequently distinguishable as "artistic" genres, they are nevertheless in the end identical in effect. Pornography is not objectionable simply because it arouses sexual desire or lust or prurience in the mind of the reader or spectator; this is a silly Victorian notion. A great many non-pornographic works—including some parts of the Bible—excite sexual desire very successfully. What is distinctive about pornography is that, in the words of D. H. Lawrence, it attempts "to do dirt on [sex] . . . [It is an] insult to a vital human relationship."

In other words, pornography differs from erotic art in that its whole purpose is to treat human beings obscenely, to deprive human beings of their specifically human dimension. That is what obscenity is all about. It is light years removed from, any kind of carefree sensuality—there is no continuum between Fielding's "Tom Jones" and the Marquis de Sade's "Justine." These works have quite opposite intentions. To quote Susan Sontag: "What pornographic literature does is precisely to drive a wedge between one's existence as a full human being and one's existence as a sexual being—while in ordinary life a healthy person is one who prevents such a gap from opening up." This definition occurs in an essay *defending* pornography—Miss Sontag is a candid as well as gifted critic—so the definition, which I accept, is neither tendentious nor censorious.

Along these same lines, one can point out—as C. S. Lewis pointed out some years back—that it is no accident that in the history of all   10

---

* This is as good a place as any to express my profound indebtedness to Walter Berns's superb essay, "Pornography vs. Democracy," in the winter, 1971, issue of *The Public Interest*.

literatures obscene words—the so-called "four-letter words"—have always been the vocabulary of farce or vituperation. The reason is clear: they reduce men and women to some of their mere bodily functions—they reduce man to his animal component, and such a reduction is an essential purpose of farce or vituperation.

Similarly, Lewis also suggested that it is not an accident that we have no offhand, colloquial, neutral terms—not in any Western European language at any rate—for our most private parts. The words we do use are either (a) nursery terms, (b) archaisms, (c) scientific terms or (d) a term from the gutter (i.e., a demeaning term). Here I think the genius of language is telling us something important about man. It is telling us that man is an animal with a difference: he has a unique sense of privacy, and a unique capacity for shame when this privacy is violated. Our "private parts" are indeed private, and not merely because convention prescribes it. This particular convention is indigenous to the human race. In practically all primitive tribes, men and women cover their private parts; and in practically all primitive tribes, men and women do not copulate in public.

It may well be that Western society, in the latter half of the twentieth century, is experiencing a drastic change in sexual mores and sexual relationships. We have had many such "sexual revolutions" in the past—and the bourgeois family and bourgeois ideas of sexual propriety were themselves established in the course of a revolution against eighteenth-century "licentiousness"—and we shall doubtless have others in the future. It is, however, highly improbable (to put it mildly) that what we are witnessing is the Final Revolution which will make sexual relations utterly unproblematic, permit us to dispense with any kind of ordered relationships between the sexes, and allow us freely to redefine the human condition. And so long as humanity has not reached that utopia, obscenity will remain a problem.

One of the reasons it will remain a problem is that obscenity is not merely about sex, any more than science fiction is about science. Science fiction, as every student of the genre knows, is a peculiar vision of power: what it is really about is politics. And obscenity is a peculiar vision of humanity: what it is really about is ethics and metaphysics.

Imagine a man—a well-known man, much in the public eye—in a hospital ward, dying an agonizing death. He is not in control of his bodily functions, so that his bladder and his bowels empty themselves of their own accord. His consciousness is overwhelmed and extinguished by pain, so that he cannot communicate with us, nor we with him. Now, it would be, technically, the easiest thing in the world to put a television camera in his hospital room and let the whole world witness this spectacle. We don't do it—at least we don't do it as yet—because we regard this as an *obscene* invasion of privacy. And what would make the spectacle obscene is that we would be witnessing the extinguishing of humanity in a human animal.

Incidentally, in the past our humanitarian crusaders against capital   15
punishment understood this point very well. The abolitionist literature
goes into great physical detail about what happens to a man when he is
hanged or electrocuted or gassed. And their argument was—and is—that
what happens is shockingly obscene, and that no civilized society should
be responsible for perpetrating such obscenities, particularly since in the
nature of the case there must be spectators to ascertain that this horror was
indeed being perpetrated in fulfillment of the law.

Sex—like death—is an activity that is both animal and human. There
are human sentiments and human ideals involved in this animal activity.
But when sex is public, the viewer does not see—cannot see—the sentiments and the ideals. He can only see the animal coupling. And that
is why, when men and women make love, as we say, they prefer to be
alone—because it is only when you are alone that you can make love, as
distinct from merely copulating in an animal and casual way. And that,
too, is why those who are voyeurs, if they are not irredeemably sick, also
feel ashamed at what they are witnessing. When sex is a public spectacle, a
human relationship has been debased into a mere animal connection.

It is also worth noting that this making of sex into an obscenity is
not a mutual and equal transaction, but is rather an act of exploitation
by one of the partners—the male partner. I do not wish to get into the
complicated question as to what, if any, are the essential differences—as
distinct from conventional and cultural differences—between male and
female. I do not claim to know the answer to that. But I do know—and
I take it as a sign which has meaning—that pornography is, and always
has been, a man's work; that women rarely write pornography; and that
women tend to be indifferent consumers of pornography.* My own guess,
by way of explanation, is that a woman's sexual experience is ordinarily
more suffused with human emotion than is a man's, that men are more
easily satisfied with autoerotic activities, and that men can therefore more
easily take a more "technocratic" view of sex and its pleasures. Perhaps this
is not correct. But whatever the explanation, there can be no question that
pornography is a form of "sexism," as the Women's Liberation Movement
calls it, and that the instinct of Women's Lib has been unerring in perceiving that, when pornography is perpetrated, it is perpetrated against them,
as part of a conspiracy to deprive them of their full humanity.

But even if all this is granted, it might be said—and doubtless will be
said—that I really ought not to be unduly concerned. Free competition

---

* There are, of course, a few exceptions—but of a kind that prove the rule. *L'Histoire
d'O,* for instance, written by a woman, is unquestionably the most *melancholy* work of pornography ever written. And its theme is precisely the dehumanization accomplished by
obscenity.

in the cultural marketplace—it is argued by people who have never otherwise had a kind word to say for laissez faire—will automatically dispose
of the problem. The present fad for pornography and obscenity, it will be
asserted, is just that, a fad. It will spend itself in the course of time; people
will get bored with it, will be able to take it or leave it alone in a casual
way, in a "mature way," and, in sum, I am being unnecessarily distressed
about the whole business. The *New York Times*, in an editorial, concludes
hopefully in this vein.

"In the end . . . the insensate pursuit of the urge to shock, carried
from one excess to a more abysmal one, is bound to achieve its own antidote in total boredom. When there is no lower depth to descend to, ennui
will erase the problem."

I would like to be able to go along with this line of reasoning, but I   20
cannot. I think it is false, and for two reasons, the first psychological, the
second political.

The basic psychological fact about pornography and obscenity is that
it appeals to and provokes a kind of sexual regression. The sexual pleasure
one gets from pornography and obscenity is autoerotic and infantile; put
bluntly, it is a masturbatory exercise of the imagination, when it is not
masturbation pure and simple. Now, people who masturbate do not get
bored with masturbation, just as sadists don't get bored with sadism, and
voyeurs don't get bored with voyeurism.

In other words, infantile sexuality is not only a permanent temptation
for the adolescent or even the adult—it can quite easily become a permanent, self-reinforcing neurosis. It is because of an awareness of this possibility of regression toward the infantile condition, a regression which
is always open to us, that all the codes of sexual conduct ever devised by
the human race take such a dim view of autoerotic activities and try to
discourage autoerotic fantasies. Masturbation is indeed a perfectly natural
autoerotic activity, as so many sexologists blandly assure us today. And
it is precisely because it is so perfectly natural that it can be so dangerous
to the mature or maturing person, if it is not controlled or sublimated in
some way. That is the true meaning of Portnoy's complaint. Portnoy, you
will recall, grows up to be a man who is incapable of having an adult sexual relationship with a woman; his sexuality remains fixed in an infantile
mode, the prison of his autoerotic fantasies. Inevitably, Portnoy comes to
think, in a perfectly *infantile* way, that it was all his mother's fault.

It is true that, in our time, some quite brilliant minds have come to
the conclusion that a reversion to infantile sexuality is the ultimate mission and secret destiny of the human race. I am thinking in particular of
Norman O. Brown, for whose writings I have the deepest respect. One of
the reasons I respect them so deeply is that Mr. Brown is a serious thinker
who is unafraid to face up to the radical consequences of his radical theories. Thus, Mr. Brown knows and says that for his kind of salvation to be
achieved, humanity must annul the civilization it has created—not merely

the civilization we have today, but all civilization—so as to be able to make the long descent backwards into animal innocence.

What is at stake is civilization and humanity, nothing less. The idea that "everything is permitted," as Nietzsche put it, rests on the premise of nihilism and has nihilistic implications. I will not pretend that the case against nihilism and for civilization is an easy one to make. We are here confronting the most fundamental of philosophical questions, on the deepest levels. But that is precisely my point—that the matter of pornography and obscenity is not a trivial one, and that only superficial minds can take a bland and untroubled view of it.

In this connection, I might also point out those who are primarily   25
against censorship on liberal grounds tell us not to take pornography or obscenity seriously, while those who are for pornography and obscenity, on radical grounds, take it very seriously indeed. I believe the radicals—writers like Susan Sontag, Herbert Marcuse, Norman O. Brown, and even Jerry Rubin—are right, and the liberals are wrong. I also believe that those young radicals at Berkeley, some five years ago, who provoked a major confrontation over the public use of obscene words, showed a brilliant political instinct. Once the faculty and administration had capitulated on this issue—saying: "Oh, for God's sake, let's be adult: what difference does it make anyway?"—once they said that, they were bound to lose on every other issue. And once Mark Rudd could publicly ascribe to the president of Columbia a notoriously obscene relationship to his mother, without provoking any kind of reaction, the S.D.S. had already won the day. The occupation of Columbia's buildings merely ratified their victory. Men who show themselves unwilling to defend civilization against nihilism are not going to be either resolute or effective in defending the university against anything.

I am already touching upon a political aspect of pornography when I suggest that it is inherently and purposefully subversive of civilization and its institutions. But there is another and more specifically political aspect, which has to do with the relationship of pornography and/or obscenity to democracy, and especially to the quality of public life on which democratic government ultimately rests.

Though the phrase, "the quality of life," trips easily from so many lips these days, it tends to be one of those clichés with many trivial meanings and no large, serious one. Sometimes it merely refers to such externals as the enjoyment of cleaner air, cleaner water, cleaner streets. At other times it refers to the merely private enjoyment of music, painting or literature. Rarely does it have anything to do with the way the citizen in a democracy views himself—his obligations, his intentions, his ultimate self-definition.

Instead, what I would call the "managerial" conception of democracy is the predominant opinion among political scientists, sociologists and economists, and has, through the untiring efforts of these scholars, become the conventional journalistic opinion as well. The root idea behind this "managerial" conception is that democracy is a "political system" (as they say) which can be adequately defined in terms of—can be fully reduced to—its mechanical arrangements. Democracy is then seen as a set of rules and procedures, and *nothing but* a set of rules and procedures, whereby majority rule and minority rights are reconciled into a state of equilibrium. If everyone follows these rules and procedures, then a democracy is in working order. I think this is a fair description of the democratic idea that currently prevails in academia. One can also fairly say that it is now the liberal idea of democracy par excellence.

I cannot help but feel that there is something ridiculous about being this kind of a democrat, and I must further confess to having a sneaking sympathy for those of our young radicals who also find it ridiculous. The absurdity is the absurdity of idolatry—of taking the symbolic for the real, the means for the end. The purpose of democracy cannot possibly be the endless functioning of its own political machinery. The purpose of any political regime is to achieve some version of the good life and the good society. It is not at all difficult to imagine a perfectly functioning democracy which answers all questions except one—namely, why should anyone of intelligence and spirit care a fig for it?

There is, however, an older idea of democracy—one which was fairly   30
common until about the beginning of this century—for which the conception of the quality of public life is absolutely crucial. This idea starts from the proposition that democracy is a form of self-government, and that if you want it to be a meritorious polity, you have to care about what kind of people govern it. Indeed, it puts the matter more strongly and declares that, if you want self-government, you are only entitled to it if that "self" is worthy of governing. There is no inherent right to self-government if it means that such government is vicious, mean, squalid and debased. Only a dogmatist and a fanatic, an idolater of democratic machinery, could approve of self-government under such conditions.

And because the desirability of self-government depends on the character of the people who govern, the older idea of democracy was very solicitous of the condition of this character. It was solicitous of the individual self, and felt an obligation to educate it into what used to be called "republican virtue." And it was solicitous of that collective self which we call public opinion and which, in a democracy, governs us collectively. Perhaps in some respects it was nervously over-solicitous—that would not be surprising. But the main thing is that it cared, cared not merely about the machinery of democracy but about the quality of life that this machinery might generate.

And because it cared, this older idea of democracy had no problem in principle with pornography and/or obscenity. It censored them—and it did so with a perfect clarity of mind and a perfectly clear conscience. It was not about to permit people capriciously to corrupt themselves. Or, to put it more precisely: in this version of democracy, the people took some care not to let themselves be governed by the more infantile and irrational parts of themselves.

I have, it may be noticed, uttered that dreadful word, "censorship." And I am not about to back away from it. If you think pornography and/or obscenity is a serious problem, you have to be for censorship. I'll go even further and say that if you want to prevent pornography and/or obscenity from becoming a problem, you have to be for censorship. And lest there be any misunderstanding as to what I am saying, I'll put it as bluntly as possible: if you care for the quality of life in our American democracy, then you have to be for censorship.

THINKING CRITICALLY ABOUT THE READING

1. What is the downside, in Kristol's opinion, of unfettered, uncensored expression in arts and entertainment? What is the outcome, as he sees it, of "dogmatic resistance to the idea of censorship" (5)?

2. Explain Kristol's central argument about the power of art to improve or to corrupt lives. (Glossary: *Argument*) Do you believe that anyone has ever been corrupted by a book?

3. Kristol utilizes extreme examples, mostly hypothetical, to bolster his argument for censorship. What are some of his examples? Can you cite any examples of instances where entertainment crosses the line? (Glossary: *Examples*)

4. In Kristol's opinion, what is the purpose of pornography? Why does he find sex as "a public spectacle" (16) problematic if not abhorrent?

5. What is Kristol's theory about the "political aspect of pornography" (26)?

6. What are the issues of "quality of life" (27) that Kristol refers to? How does this notion of "quality of life" relate to American democracy?

The Free-Speech Follies

STANLEY FISH

Stanley Fish, noted scholar, author, and professor of literature and law, was born in 1938 in New York City. Fish earned his Ph.D. in English literature at Yale University and taught at the University of California at Berkeley, Johns Hopkins University, and Duke University, where he was both professor of English and professor of law. In 1999, Fish became dean of the College of Liberal Arts and Sciences at the University of Illinois at Chicago, and after his retirement in 2005, he joined the law faculty at Florida International University in Miami. A noted Milton scholar and expert on literary theory, Fish has written numerous books on a wide range of subjects, including *Surprised by Sin: The Reader in Paradise Lost* (1997), *Doing What Comes Naturally: Change, Rhetoric, and the Practice of Theory in Literary and Legal Studies* (1989), and *How Milton Works* (2001). His latest book, *Save the World on Your Own Time* (2008), is a sharp critique of academia for forgetting that its mission is "[n]ot to practice politics, but to study it; not to proselytize for or against religious doctrines, but to describe them; not to affirm or condemn Intelligent Design, but to explain what it is and analyze its appeal."

Fish is a regular contributor to the *New York Times* op-ed page and the *Chronicle of Higher Education,* where his essay "The Free-Speech Follies" appeared in 2003. In this essay, Fish firmly sets forth his argument that the cry of "First Amendment rights" is too often used, especially on college campuses, to defend speech that the Constitution was not designed to protect.

WRITING TO DISCOVER: *Some feel that speech that attacks a certain racial or ethnic groups is protected under the First Amendment, no matter how repellent the speech itself is or how much one might disagree with it. Do you agree? Why or why not?*

The modern American version of crying wolf is crying First Amendment. If you want to burn a cross on a black family's lawn or buy an election by contributing millions to a candidate or vilify Jerry Falwell and his mother in a scurrilous "parody," and someone or some government agency tries to stop you, just yell "First Amendment rights" and you will stand a good chance of getting to do what you want to do.

In the academy, the case is even worse: Not only is the First Amendment pressed into service at the drop of a hat (especially whenever anyone is disciplined for anything), it is invoked ritually when there are no First Amendment issues in sight.

Take the case of the editors of college newspapers who will always cry First Amendment when something they've published turns out to be the cause of outrage and controversy. These days the offending piece or editorial or advertisement usually involves (what is at least perceived to be) an attack on Jews. In January of this year, the *Daily Illini*, a student newspaper at the University of Illinois at Urbana–Champaign, printed a letter from a resident of Seattle with no university affiliation. The letter ran under the headline "Jews Manipulate America" and argued that because their true allegiance is to the state of Israel, the president should "separate Jews from all government advisory positions"; otherwise, the writer warned, "the Jews might face another Holocaust."

When the predictable firestorm of outrage erupted, the newspaper's editor responded by declaring, first, that "we are committed to giving all people a voice"; second, that, given this commitment, "we print the opinions of others with whom we do not agree"; third, that to do otherwise would involve the newspaper in the dangerous acts of "silencing" and "self-censorship"; and, fourth, that "what is hate speech to one member of a society is free speech to another."

Wrong four times.   5

I'll bet the *Daily Illini* is not committed to giving all people a voice—the KKK? man-boy love? advocates of slavery? would-be Unabombers? Nor do I believe that the editors sift through submissions looking for the ones they disagree with and then print those. No doubt they apply some principles of selection, asking questions like, Is it relevant, or Is it timely, or Does it get the facts right, or Does it present a coherent argument?

That is, they exercise judgment, which is quite a different thing from silencing or self-censorship. No one is silenced because a single outlet declines to publish him; silencing occurs when that outlet (or any other) is forbidden by the state to publish him on pain of legal action; and that is also what censorship is.

As for self-censoring, if it is anything, it is what we all do whenever we decide it would be better not to say something or cut a sentence that went just a little bit too far or leave a manuscript in the bottom drawer because it is not yet ready. Self-censorship, in short, is not a crime or a moral failing; it is a responsibility.

And, finally, whatever the merits of the argument by which all assertions are relativised—your hate speech is my free speech—this incident has nothing to do with either hate speech or free speech and everything to do with whether the editors are discharging or defaulting on their obligations when they foist them off on an inapplicable doctrine, saying in effect, "The First Amendment made us do it."

More recently, the same scenario played itself out at Santa Rosa Junior   10
College. This time it was a student who wrote the offending article. Titled "Is Anti-Semitism Ever the Result of Jewish Behavior?" it answered the

question in the affirmative, creating an uproar that included death threats, an avalanche of hate mail, and demands for just about everyone's resignation. The faculty adviser who had approved the piece said, "The First Amendment isn't there to protect agreeable stories."

He was alluding to the old saw that the First Amendment protects unpopular as well as popular speech. But what it protects unpopular speech *from* is abridgment by the government of its free expression; it does not protect unpopular speech from being rejected by a newspaper, and it confers no positive obligation to give your pages over to unpopular speech, or popular speech, or any speech.

Once again, there is no First Amendment issue here, just an issue of editorial judgment and the consequences of exercising it. (You can print anything you like; but if the heat comes, it's yours, not the Constitution's.)

In these controversies, student editors are sometimes portrayed, or portray themselves, as First Amendment heroes who bravely risk criticism and censure in order to uphold a cherished American value. But they are not heroes; they are merely confused and, in terms of their understanding of the doctrine they invoke, rather hapless.

Not as hapless, however, as the Harvard English department, which made a collective fool of itself three times when it invited, disinvited and then reinvited poet Tom Paulin to be the Morris Gray lecturer. Again the flash point was anti-Semitism. In his poetry and in public comments, Paulin had said that Israel had no right to exist, that settlers on the West Bank "should be shot dead," and that Israeli police and military forces were the equivalent of the Nazi SS. When these and other statements came to light shortly before Paulin was to give his lecture, the department voted to rescind the invitation. When the inevitable cry of "censorship, censorship" was heard in the land, the department flip-flopped again, and a professor-spokesman declared, "This was a clear affirmation that the department stood strongly by the First Amendment."

It was of course nothing of the kind; it was a transparent effort of a   15
bunch that had already put its foot in its mouth twice to wriggle out of trouble and regain the moral high ground by striking the pose of First Amendment defender. But, in fact, the department and its members were not First Amendment defenders (a religion they converted to a little late), but serial bunglers.

What should they have done? Well, it depends on what they wanted to do. If they wanted to invite this particular poet because they admired his poetry, they had a perfect right to do so. If they were aware ahead of time of Paulin's public pronouncements, they could have chosen either to say something by way of explanation or to remain silent and let the event speak for itself; either course of action would have been at once defensible and productive of risk. If they knew nothing of Paulin's anti-Israel sentiments (difficult to believe of a gang of world-class researchers) but found out about them after the fact, they might have said, "Oops, never mind" or toughed it out—again alternatives not without risk. But at each stage, whatever they did or didn't do would have had no relationship whatsoever to any First Amendment right—Paulin had no right to be invited—or obligation—there was no obligation either to invite or disinvite him, and certainly no obligation to reinvite him, unless you count the obligations imposed on yourself by a succession of ill-thought-through decisions. Whatever the successes or failures here, they were once again failures of judgment, not doctrine.

In another case, it looked for a moment that judgment of an appropriate kind was in fact being exercised. The University of California at Berkeley houses the Emma Goldman Papers Project, and each year the director sends out a fund-raising mailer that always features quotations from Goldman's work. But this January an associate vice chancellor edited the mailer and removed two quotations that in context read as a criticism of the Bush administration's plans for a war in Iraq. He explained that the quotations were not randomly chosen and were clearly intended to make a "political point, and that is inappropriate in an official university situation."

The project director (who acknowledged that the quotes were selected for their contemporary relevance) objected to what she saw as an act of censorship and a particularly egregious one given Goldman's strong advocacy of free expression.

But no one's expression was being censored. The Goldman quotations are readily available and had they appeared in the project's literature in a setting that did not mark them as political, no concerns would have been raised. It is just, said the associate vice chancellor, that they are inappropriate in this context, and, he added, "It is not a matter of the First Amendment."

Right, it's a matter of whether or not there is even the appearance   20 of the university's taking sides on a partisan issue; that is, it is an empirical matter that requires just the exercise of judgment that associate vice chancellors are paid to perform. Of course he was pilloried by members of the Berkeley faculty and others who saw First Amendment violations everywhere.

But there were none. Goldman still speaks freely through her words. The project director can still make her political opinions known by writing letters to the editor or to everyone in the country, even if she cannot use the vehicle of a university flier to do so. Everyone's integrity is preserved. The project goes on unimpeded, and the university goes about its proper academic business. Or so it would have been had the administration stayed firm. But it folded and countermanded the associate vice chancellor's decision.

At least the chancellor had sense enough to acknowledge that no one's speech had been abridged. It was just, he said, an "error in judgment." Aren't they all?

Are there then no free-speech issues on campuses? Sure there are; there just aren't very many. When Toni Smith, a basketball player at Manhattanville College, turned her back to the flag during the playing of the national anthem in protest against her government's policies, she was truly exercising her First Amendment rights, rights that ensure that she cannot be compelled to an affirmation she does not endorse (see *West Virginia* v. *Barnette*). And as she stood by her principles in the face of hostility, she truly was (and is) a First Amendment hero, as the college newspaper editors, the members of the Harvard English department, and the head of the Emma Goldman Project are not. The category is a real one, and it would be good if it were occupied only by those who belong in it.

THINKING CRITICALLY ABOUT THE READING

1. What is Fish's central thesis? How does he establish his argument? How does it relate to the title of the essay? (Glossary: *Thesis; Argument*)

2. Fish gives an example of a college newspaper editor who used the First Amendment as the defense for publishing an article that could be interpreted as hate speech. What arguments did the editor offer for printing the piece? How does Fish counter those arguments?

3. Fish writes that he finds value in "self-censorship." What does he mean by this?

4. How does Fish argue against the "old saw that the First Amendment protects unpopular as well as popular speech" (11)?

5. Fish states that the Harvard English department's decisions regarding the appearance of a controversial poet were "failures of judgment, not doctrine" (16). Explain.

6. Why does Fish agree with the official at UC Berkeley that removing certain Emma Goldman quotes from a campus mailer was "not a matter of the First Amendment" (19), despite the fact that they were political in nature?

7. How does Fish differentiate between a true "First Amendment hero" (13, 23) such as the Manhattanville College basketball player and those who, invoking the First Amendment, are simply "crying wolf" (1)?

How Campus Censors Squelch Freedom of Speech

Stuart Taylor Jr.

Journalist, legal scholar, and commentator Stuart Taylor is a senior writer and columnist for the *National Journal* and a contributing editor at *Newsweek.* After earning his law degree from Harvard Law School in 1977, Taylor began his career as a lawyer at a prominent Washington, D.C., law firm. Soon he changed course, becoming a reporter for the *Baltimore Sun* and *Evening Sun,* and later covering the Supreme Court for the Washington bureau of the *New York Times,* work for which he was nominated for a Pulitzer Prize in 1988. As a senior writer with American Lawyer Media, Taylor wrote a widely syndicated weekly opinion column focusing on legal-political issues. His analysis and commentary on politics, government, and the law have also made him a much-sought-after guest on television and radio news outlets including CNN, Fox News Channel, PBS, and National Public Radio. Taylor is a senior fellow at the Brookings Institute, where he specializes in constitutional law and the Supreme Court. He lives in Washington, D.C., with his wife and two daughters.

His essay "How Campus Censors Squelch Freedom of Speech" appeared on *Atlantic Online* on July 14, 2003, and was one of Taylor's weekly columns for the *National Journal.* Taylor continues writing about the double standard that many journalists and academics apply to free speech controversies. In a 2007 opinion piece, he wrote about the "thinly veiled speech codes, misleadingly called anti-'harassment' policies" and the "loopy radicals" who "despise intellectual diversity" and who dominate all things political on campus.

WRITING TO DISCOVER: *How do you define "politically correct"? In your experience on campus, do you feel that your own speech or opinions, or those of someone you know, have been curtailed or suppressed because they were not "politically correct"?*

Steve Hinkle, a student at California Polytechnic State University, was posting fliers around campus last November 12 that advertised a speech to be given the next evening. The fliers contained a photo of the speaker, black conservative Mason Weaver, and the words "It's OK to Leave the Plantation," the name of a book in which Weaver likens African-American dependence on government programs to slavery.

When Hinkle approached a public bulletin board in the lounge of the campus Multicultural Center, some African-American students who were

501

sharing pizzas nearby objected. They told Hinkle not to post the flier because they found it "offensive" and "disrespectful." By all accounts, his response was something like, "How do you know it's offensive? Why can't we talk about it?" The offended students then said that the flier violated the Multicultural Center's "posting policy," and threatened to call the campus police. Hinkle left, without posting the flier.

That was not the end of the matter, however. One black student did call campus police, with what was recorded as a report of "a suspicious white male passing out literature of an offensive racial nature." She and others also urged university authorities to discipline Hinkle, a member of the Cal Poly College Republicans, for what she called "hate speech" (i.e., the flier).

Incredibly, university authorities did just that, under the pretext of punishing Hinkle for "disruption" of what complaining students later claimed to have been a Bible study dinner and meeting. (Nobody had told Hinkle that this was a "meeting" at all, and he saw no Bibles.)

This episode provides a window into the politically correct censorship   5
that pollutes so many of our nation's campuses. For seeking peacefully and politely to exercise his First Amendment rights, Hinkle was subjected to a seven-hour disciplinary hearing, from which his lawyer was barred. He was found guilty of "disruption" of the "meeting." And he was ordered to apologize to the offended students, in writing, or face much stiffer penalties, possibly including expulsion. All of this is to go on Hinkle's permanent record, perhaps hurting his chances of getting into graduate school.

The bottom line is that like many other campuses, "Cal Poly gives some people the power to veto what others have to say," says Thor L. Halvorssen, the head of the Foundation for Individual Rights in Education (FIRE), a nonpartisan, Philadelphia-based free speech group that has come to Hinkle's defense.

Cal Poly's legal counsel, Carlos Cordova, responded to a complaint from FIRE by claiming in a May 9 letter that "many of your factual assertions . . . are incorrect" and by denying that the disciplining of Hinkle was motivated by the perceived offensiveness of the flier. But Cordova did not specifically dispute any of the facts recounted in the first four paragraphs above, which are based in part on notes prepared by Hinkle's faculty adviser at the hearing. Those facts amount to an egregious violation of the First Amendment.

Cal Poly is but one of hundreds of campuses that penalize student speech of which they disapprove. This censorship regime has attracted little attention since the mid-1990s, after successful legal challenges at the University of Michigan, the University of Wisconsin, and Stanford University seemed to foretell the demise of speech codes.

But in fact, campus censorship lives on, often justified under the guise of enforcing vague rules against racial or sexual "harassment." Administrators typically interpret these rules to encompass any speech that offends nonwhite students or insults the left-liberal-radical-feminist-postmodernist orthodoxies of the academic class. The rules are typically enforced by campus kangaroo courts with no semblance of fairness.

Here are some representative examples of rules that appear to be current as far as FIRE could tell from checking university Web sites: Georgetown warns against "expression" that is "inappropriate" and that severely offends others on matters of "race, ethnicity, religion, gender, or sexual preference." (Would that include quoting Justice Antonin Scalia's acerbic dissent from the June 26 Supreme Court decision upholding gay rights?) At the University of Massachusetts, students can be disciplined for speaking in ways that create a "sexually offensive" environment, or for displaying "offensive or sexually suggestive" pictures, cartoons, or posters. At Princeton, they can be disciplined for "unwanted sexual attention that makes a person feel uncomfortable." (Asking for a date after being once turned down?) At Brown, "unwelcome verbal expressions," "degrading language," "jokes or innuendoes," "sounds or whistles," and "gestures" can amount to sexual harassment. At Dartmouth, "sexual harassment [can be] subtle and indirect, possibly even unintentional." Many campuses define "leering" as a form of harassment. A training document once used at the University of Maryland even warned against "holding or eating food provocatively." (Handle bananas with care.)

It is unclear how often such provisions are enforced. In any event, they hang over campus speech like a Sword of Damocles. Their vagueness and overbreadth violate students' First Amendment rights in the case of public universities and may violate their contractual rights in the case of those private universities that advertise themselves as devoted to free and open debate. Such rules nonetheless persist because few students or professors have the stomach to challenge them.

The good news is that since 1999 those willing to fight back have a potent ally. FIRE has battled campus censors with great success since its founding by two men whose passion for the freedoms of speech, association, and religion transcends their politics: left-leaning lawyer Harvey A. Silverglate of Boston and right-leaning University of Pennsylvania professor Alan Charles Kors.

FIRE typically employs the threat of public exposure to persuade campus administrators to back off in individual censorship-through-discipline cases. It has also produced pamphlets informing students in detail of their legal rights. And in the past few months, FIRE has helped launch a litigation offensive against speech codes that is designed to make it "clear to universities across the country that they infringe on students' rights at their own peril," in Silverglate's words, by winning a succession of definitive judicial rulings. The defendants so far have been Shippensburg University, in central Pennsylvania (whose code prohibited conduct that "annoys, threatens, or alarms a person or group"); Citrus College, near Los Angeles (which has already surrendered); and 28,000-student Texas Tech University.

Texas Tech bans "communications [that] humiliate any person," such as "sexual innuendoes" or "referring to an adult as 'girl,' 'boy,' or 'honey.'" Like many other campuses, it also quarantines demonstrations, protests, and other free speech activities to a single "free speech zone"—at Tech, a 20-foot-wide gazebo that can hold about 40 people. On the rest of the campus, students must seek official approval at least six days in advance to hold protests or demonstrations, make speeches, distribute newspapers or literature, or engage in other free speech activities.

FIRE champions flag-burners as well as flag-wavers, anti-Bush and   15
anti-American dissidents as well as conservatives. In February, for example, it helped persuade Texas Tech not to confine a protest against President Bush's Iraq policies to the gazebo. But the vast majority of the students and professors complaining of campus censorship are to the right of center. *American Enterprise* magazine recently published some numbers that help explain this: At top universities—including Brown, Cornell, Stanford, and the University of California (Berkeley)—the ratio of professors registered in parties of the left (including Democrats) to those in parties of the right (including Republicans) in many departments ranges from almost 10-to-1 to more than 20-to-1. And many of them think of free speech as a right reserved to the politically correct.

Despite the cries of "McCarthyism" raised by the Left since September 11, there has been only a smattering of unwarranted attacks on leftist or anti-American speech. And on campus, you are a lot less likely to be disciplined for assailing President Bush than for assailing militant Islam. Take the Ethiopian student at San Diego State University who reproached some Saudi students in September 2001 for gleefully celebrating, in Arabic, the murders of 3,000 people at the World Trade Center and the Pentagon. A university committee warned the Ethiopian—not the Saudis—that offending fellow students in this way could get him suspended or expelled.

Political biases aside, campus censors commit a fundamental error in supposing that devotion to civil rights requires shielding traditionally subordinated groups from hurt feelings by suppressing the civil liberties of others. As Kors has put it, "No one who tells people that they are too weak to live with freedom, legal equality, the Bill of Rights, or academic freedom is their friend."

THINKING CRITICALLY ABOUT THE READING

1. What brought Steve Hinkle to the attention of the African American students in the lounge of the Multicultural Center? What was the nature of his offense, in their eyes?

2. Taylor writes that, despite actions on some campuses to end speech codes, campus censorship lives on. What examples does he provide? Describe some of the speech code rules that Taylor lists.

3. Taylor makes his case that speech rules, whether tacit or made explicit in student speech code manuals, violate the rights of students. Describe the specific rights to which he is referring.

4. Taylor mentions the Foundation for Individual Rights in Education (FIRE), a nonpartisan free-speech group. What are some of the tactics this group uses in defense of people such as Hinkle?

5. Taylor describes the ways in which Texas Tech handles demonstrations, protests, and other free-speech activities. What are these policies? Why does Taylor find them so problematic?

6. Taylor states that "the vast majority of the students and professors complaining of campus censorship are to the right of center" (15), and he backs this up with statistics from the American Enterprise Institute. How does he use this evidence to support his notion of bias in the way free speech is handled on campus?

The Language Police

DIANE RAVITCH

Diane Ravitch is a distinguished educator who has been influential in both the private and public sectors. She is currently Research Professor of Education at New York University and holds the Brown Chair of Education at the Brookings Institution in Washington, D.C. Ravitch received her B.A. from Wellesley College and her Ph.D. in history from Columbia University. A prolific author, she has published, among others, the following books: *The American Reader: Words That Moved a Nation* (1993); *New Schools for a New Century: The Redesign of Urban Education* (edited with Joseph Viteritti; 1997); *Left Back: A Century of Failed School Reforms* (2000); *Brookings Papers on Education Policy 2002* (2002); and *The Language Police: How Pressure Groups Restrict What Students Learn* (2003).

In the following article, taken from the Summer 2003 issue of the *American Educator* and drawn from her book *The Language Police*, Ravitch describes the kinds of censorship, from both the political left and political right, that have had such a powerful impact on the education of young people in America.

WRITING TO DISCOVER: *Consider the textbooks, including this one, that you use in your classes. Do you detect any attempts on the part of the publishers to make the content "politically correct"—that is, to alter the language or the content to decrease the risk of offending a particular group or political view? Do you think a textbook such as this one is "left-leaning," "right-leaning," or balanced? What factors do you take into account in your analysis?*

The word *censorship* refers to the deliberate removal of language, ideas, and books from the classroom or library because they are deemed offensive or controversial. The definition gets fuzzier, however, when making a distinction between censorship and selection. Selection is not censorship. Teachers have a responsibility to choose readings for their students based on their professional judgment of what students are likely to understand and what they need to learn. (It is also important to remember that people have a First Amendment right to complain about textbooks and library books they don't like.)

Censorship occurs when school officials or publishers (acting in anticipation of the legal requirements of certain states) delete words, ideas, and topics from textbooks and tests for no reason other than their fear of controversy. Censorship may take place before publication, as it does when publishers utilize guidelines that mandate the exclusion of certain language and topics, and it may happen after publication, as when parents and community members pressure school officials to remove certain books from school libraries or classrooms. Some people believe that censorship occurs only when government officials impose it, but publishers censor their products in order to secure government contracts. So the result is the same.

Censors on the political right aim to restore an idealized vision of the past, an Arcadia of happy family life, in which the family was intact, comprising a father, a mother, two or more children, and went to church every Sunday. Father was in charge, and Mother took care of the children. Father worked; Mother shopped and prepared the meals. Everyone sat around the dinner table at night. It was a happy, untroubled setting into which social problems seldom intruded. Pressure groups on the right believe that what children read in school should present this vision of the past to children and that showing it might make it so. They believe strongly in the power of the word, and they believe that children will model their behavior on whatever they read. If they read stories about disobedient children, they will be disobedient; if they read stories that conflict with their parents' religious values, they might abandon their religion. Critics on the right urge that whatever children read should model appropriate moral behavior.

Censors from the political left believe in an idealized vision of the future, a utopia in which egalitarianism prevails in all social relations. In this vision, there is no dominant group, no dominant father, no dominant race, and no dominant gender. In this world, youth is not an advantage, and disability is not a disadvantage. There is no hierarchy of better or worse; all nations and all cultures are of equal accomplishment and value. All individuals and groups share equally in the roles, rewards, and activities of society. In this world to be, everyone has high self-esteem, eats healthy foods, exercises, and enjoys being different. Pressure groups on the left feel as strongly about the power of the word as those on the right. They expect that children will be shaped by what they read and will model their behavior on what they read. They want children to read only descriptions of the world as they think it should be in order to help bring this new world into being.

For censors on both the right and the left, reading is a means of role 5 modeling and behavior modification. Neither wants children and adolescents to encounter books, textbooks, or videos that challenge their vision of what was or what might be, or that depict a reality contrary to that vision.

I. CENSORSHIP FROM THE RIGHT

In the 1980s, after a century of attacks on textbooks—animated by a search for anti-confederate or pro-communist sentiment, or any acknowledgement of evolution—right-wing censors launched an impassioned crusade against immoral books and textbooks and shifted their focus to religious and moral issues. Groups such as the Reverend Jerry Falwell's Moral Majority, Phyllis Schlafly's Eagle Forum, the Reverend Donald Wildmon's American Family Association, Dr. James Dobson's Focus on the Family, the Reverend Pat Robertson's National Legal Foundation, and Beverly La-Haye's Concerned Women for America, along with Mel and Norma Gabler's Educational Research Analysts in Texas, pressured local school districts and state boards of education to remove books that they considered objectionable.

The New Right attacked textbooks for teaching secular humanism, which they defined as a New Age religion that ignored biblical teachings and shunned moral absolutes. If it was right to exclude the Christian religion from the public schools, they argued, then secular humanism should be excluded too. If it was acceptable to teach secular humanism, they said, then Christian teaching should have equal time. The textbooks, said the critics, failed to distinguish between right and wrong, and thus taught the "situation ethics" of "secular humanism." They disapproved of portrayals of abortion, out-of-wedlock pregnancy, homosexuality, suicide, drug use, foul language, or other behavior that conflicted with their religious values. The right-wing critics also opposed stories that showed dissension within the family; such stories, they believed, would teach children to be disobedient and would damage families. They also insisted that textbooks must be patriotic and teach a positive view of the nation and its history.

The teaching of evolution was extensively litigated in the 1980s. The scientific community weighed in strongly on the side of evolution as the only scientifically grounded theory for teaching about biological origins. Fundamentalist Christians, however, insisted that public schools should give equal time to teaching the biblical version of creation. Several southern legislatures passed laws requiring "balanced treatment" of evolution and creationism, but such laws were consistently found to be unconstitutional by federal courts that held that evolution is science, and creationism is religion. In 1987, the United States Supreme Court ruled 7-2 against Louisiana's "balanced treatment" law. Yet fundamentalist insistence on "creation science" or "intelligent design" continued unabated. When states debated the adoption of science textbooks or science standards, critics demanded that competing theories should get equal time. In 2000, Republican primary voters in Kansas defeated two state school board members who had voted to remove evolution from the state's science standards.

The religious right mounted numerous challenges to textbooks in the 1980s. The most important was the case of *Mozert* v. *Hawkins County Board of Education* in Tennessee. In 1983, fundamentalist Christian parents in Hawkins County objected to the elementary school textbooks that were required reading in their schools. The readers were published by Holt, Rinehart, and Winston (now owned by Harcourt). The parents complained that the textbooks promoted secular humanism, satanism, witchcraft, fantasy, magic, the occult, disobedience, dishonesty, feminism, evolution, telepathy, one-world government, and New Age religion. They also asserted that some of the stories in the readers belittled the government, the military, free enterprise, and Christianity. At first, the parents wanted the textbooks removed from the local public schools. Eventually, however, they sought only that their own children be allowed to read alternate books that did not demean their religious views.

The parents received legal support from the Concerned Women for   10 America. The school board was backed by the liberal People for the American Way. The battle turned into an epic left-right political showdown: One side claimed that the case was about censorship, and the other side argued that it was about freedom of religion.

For five years the case garnered national headlines as it wound its way up and down the federal court system. In 1987, the parents lost in federal appeals court, and in 1988, the U.S. Supreme Court decided not to review the appellate court decision. The judges decided that "mere exposure" to ideas different from those of the parents' religious faith did not violate the First Amendment's guarantee of free exercise of religion.

Defenders of the Holt Basic Readers celebrated their legal victory, but it was a hollow one. In *Battleground*, a comprehensive account of the case, author Stephen Bates noted that the Holt readers were "once the most popular reading series in the nation," but were brought to "the verge of extinction" by the controversy associated with the court case. If publishers learned a lesson from the saga of the Holt reading series, it was the importance of avoiding controversy by censoring themselves in advance and including nothing that might attract bad publicity or litigation. The 1986 revision of the series, designed to replace the 1983 edition that was on trial in Tennessee, omitted some of the passages that fundamentalist parents objected to. The Holt readers won the legal battle but were commercially ruined. This was not a price that any textbook publisher would willingly pay.

A third major area for litigation in the 1980s involved efforts to ban books, both those that were assigned in class and those that were available in the school library. The first major test came not in the South, but in the Island Trees Union Free School District in New York. There, the local board directed school officials to remove ten books from their libraries because of their profanity and explicit sexual content, including Bernard Malamud's *The Fixer,* Richard Wright's *Black Boy,* Kurt Vonnegut's *Slaughterhouse-Five,* and Eldridge Cleaver's *Soul on Ice.* The courts traditionally deferred to school officials when it came to curriculum and other policy-making, but in this instance the students who objected to the school officials' decision won by a narrow one-vote margin. In 1982, the U.S. Supreme Court ruled that the students had a "right to receive information." The decision was far from conclusive, however, as the justices wrote seven opinions, none of which had majority support.

Many book-banning incidents were never challenged in the courts. In the 1970s and 1980s, school officials in different sections of the country removed certain books from school libraries or from classroom use, including J. D. Salinger's *The Catcher in the Rye,* John Steinbeck's *Grapes of Wrath,* Aldous Huxley's *Brave New World,* George Orwell's *1984,* MacKinley Kantor's *Andersonville,* and Gordon Parks's *Learning Tree.* In most cases, parents criticized the books' treatment of profanity, sex, religion, race, or violence.

The battle of the books shifted to Florida in the late 1980s. In Columbia   15 County, a parent (who was a fundamentalist minister) complained to the local school board about a state-approved textbook used in an elective course for high school students. The parent objected to the book because it included Chaucer's "The Miller's Tale" and Aristophanes's *Lysistrata.* The school board banned the book and its decision was upheld in federal district court and in an appellate court. In Bay County, a parent complained about Robert Cormier's *I Am the Cheese,* a work of adolescent fiction that contains some mild profanity and not especially explicit sexual scenes. The school superintendent suppressed not only that book, but required teachers to write a rationale for every book they intended to assign unless it was on the state-approved list. The superintendent then proscribed a long list of literary classics that he deemed controversial, including several of Shakespeare's plays, Charles Dickens's *Great Expectations,* F. Scott Fitzgerald's *Great Gatsby,* and Ernest Hemingway's *A Farewell to Arms.* Parents, teachers, and students sued the local school board and the superintendent to prevent the book-banning, and a federal district judge ruled that it was acceptable to remove books because of vulgar language but not because of disagreement with the ideas in them. The litigation soon became moot, however, when the superintendent retired, and all of the books were restored in that particular district.

During the 1980s and 1990s, and after, there were numerous challenges to books by parents and organized groups. Many were directed against adolescent fiction, as authors of this genre became increasingly explicit about sexuality and more likely to utilize language and imagery that some adults considered inappropriate for children. The thirty "most frequently attacked" books from 1965 to the early 1980s included some that offended adults from different ends of the political spectrum. Some were assigned in class; others were in the school library. The list included such books as *The Adventures of Huckleberry Finn* by Mark Twain, *The Diary of a Young Girl* by Anne Frank, *Black Like Me* by John Howard Griffin, *The Scarlet Letter* by Nathaniel Hawthorne, *The Catcher in the Rye* by J. D. Salinger, and *Go Ask Alice* by anonymous.

By 2000, the American Library Association's list of the "most attacked" books had changed considerably. Most of the classics had fallen away. At the beginning of the new millennium, the most challenged books were of the Harry Potter series, assailed because of their references to the occult, satanism, violence, and religion, as well as Potter's dysfunctional family. Most of the other works that drew fire were written specifically for adolescents. Some of these books were taught in classes; others were available in libraries.

The most heated controversy over textbooks in the early 1990s involved a K–6 reading series called Impressions, which was published by Holt, Rinehart, and Winston. The Impressions series consisted of grade-by-grade anthologies with a cumulative total of more than 800 reading selections from authors such as C. S. Lewis, Lewis Carroll, the Brothers Grimm, Rudyard Kipling, Martin Luther King Jr., and Laura Ingalls Wilder. Its purpose was to replace the old-fashioned "Dick and Jane"-style reader with literary anthologies of high interest for children.

The texts may have been altogether too interesting because they captured the avid attention of conservative family groups across the country. Before they became infamous among right-wing groups, the books were purchased by more than 1,500 elementary schools in 34 states. A small proportion of the series' literary selections, some of them drawn from classic fairy tales, described magic, fantasy, goblins, monsters, and witches.

Right-wing Christian groups, including Focus on the Family, Citizens for Excellence in Education, and the Traditional Values Coalition, organized against the Impressions series. The controversy became especially fierce in the early 1990s in California. The state-approved textbooks came under fire in half of California's school districts. Large numbers of parents turned out for school board meetings to demand the removal of the readers they claimed were terrifying their children. One district glued together some pages in the books to satisfy critics. Some districts dropped the series. Critics objected to stories about death, violence, and the supernatural. They charged that the series was promoting a New Age religion of paganism, the occult, and witchcraft. In one district, angry parents initiated a recall campaign against two local school board members who supported the books (the board members narrowly survived the recall vote). In another district, an evangelical Christian family filed a lawsuit charging that the district—by using the Impressions textbooks—violated the Constitution by promoting a religion of "neo-paganism" that relied on magic, trances, a veneration for nature and animal life, and a belief in the supernatural. In 1994, a federal appeals court ruled that the textbook series did not violate the Constitution.

Public ridicule helped to squelch some of the ardor of those who wanted to censor books. Editorial writers across California uniformly opposed efforts to remove the Impressions series from the public schools, providing important encouragement for public officials who were defending the books. The editorial writers read the books and saw that they contained good literature. Most reckoned that children do not live in a hermetically sealed environment. Children, they recognized, see plenty of conflict and violence on television and in real life as well. They confront, sooner or later, the reality of death and loss. Most know the experience of losing a family member, a pet, a friend. Over the generations, fairy tales have served as a vehicle for children to deal with difficult situations and emotions. Even the Bible, the most revered of sacred documents in Western culture, is replete with stories of violence, betrayal, family dissension, and despicable behavior.

One cannot blame parents for wanting to protect their children's innocence from the excesses of popular culture. However, book censorship far exceeds reasonableness; usually, censors seek not just freedom from someone else's views, but the power to impose their views on others. Parents whose religious beliefs cause them to shun fantasy, magic, fairy tales, and ghost stories will have obvious difficulties adjusting to parts of the literature curriculum in public schools today. They would have had equal difficulty adjusting to the literary anthologies in American public schools 100 years ago, which customarily included myths and legends, stories about disobedient children, even tales of magical transformation. It may be impossible for a fundamentalist Christian (or Orthodox Jew or fundamentalist Muslim) to feel comfortable in a public institution that is committed to tolerance and respect among all creeds and promotion of none. This conflict cannot be avoided. Much of what is most imaginative in our culture draws upon themes that will prove objectionable to fundamentalist parents of every religion. Schools may offer alternative readings to children of fundamentalist parents, but they cannot provide readings of a sectarian nature, nor should the schools censor or ban books at the insistence of any religious or political group.

Even though the religious right has consistently lost court battles, its criticisms have not been wasted on educational publishers. The Impressions series, for all its literary excellence, was not republished and quietly vanished.

Fear of the pressures that sank the Impressions series has made publishers gun-shy about any stories that might anger fundamentalists. Textbook publishers are understandably wary about doing anything that would unleash hostile charges and countercharges and cause a public blow-up over their product.

Publishers of educational materials do not want controversy (general   25 publishers, of course, love controversy because it sells books in a competitive marketplace). Even if a publisher wins in court, its books are stigmatized as "controversial." Even if a textbook is adopted by a district or state over protests, it will lose in other districts that want to avoid similar battles. It is a far, far better thing to have no protests at all. Publishers know that a full-fledged attack, like the one waged against Impressions, means death to their product. And the best recipe for survival in a marketplace dominated by the political decisions of a handful of state boards is to delete whatever might offend anyone.

II. CENSORSHIP FROM THE LEFT

The left-wing groups that have been most active in campaigns to change textbooks are militantly feminist and militantly liberal. These groups hope to bring about an equitable society by purging certain language and images from textbooks.

Lee Burress, a leader of anticensorship activities for many years in the National Council of Teachers of English, describes in *The Battle of the Books* how feminists and liberals became censors as they sought to "raise consciousness" and to eliminate "offensive" stories and books. Joan DelFattore, in *What Johnny Shouldn't Read*, writes that political correctness, taken to its extreme, "denotes a form of intellectual terrorism in which people who express ideas that are offensive to any group other than white males of European heritage may be punished, *regardless of the accuracy or relevance of what they say*" (italics in the original). The censors from the left and right, she says, compel writers, editors, and public officials to suppress honest questions and to alter facts "solely to shape opinion." Once a society begins limiting freedom of expression to some points of view, then "all that remains is a trial of strength" to see whose sensibilities will prevail.

While the censors on the right have concentrated most of their ire on general books, the censors on the left have been most successful in criticizing textbooks. Although left-wing censors have occasionally targeted books too, they have achieved their greatest influence by shaping the bias guidelines of the educational publishing industry. Educational publishers have willingly acquiesced even to the most farfetched demands for language censorship, so long as the campaign's stated goal is "fairness." Only a George Orwell could fully appreciate how honorable words like *fairness* and *diversity* have been deployed to impose censorship and uniformity on everyday language.

The organization that led the left-wing censorship campaign was the Council on Interracial Books for Children (CIBC). Founded in 1966 in New York City, CIBC was active over the next quarter-century as the best-known critic of racism and sexism in children's books and textbooks. Directing its critiques not as much to the general public as to the publishing industry and educators, CIBC issued publications and conducted seminars for librarians and teachers to raise their consciousness about racism and sexism.

CIBC ceased its organizational life in 1990; its most enduring legacy proved to be its guidelines, which explained how to identify racism, sexism, and ageism, as well as a variety of other isms. They were the original template for the detailed bias guidelines that are now pervasive in the education publishing industry and that ban specific words, phrases, roles, activities, and images in textbooks and on tests. The CIBC guidelines are still cited; they circulate on many Web sites, and they continue to serve as training materials for bias and sensitivity reviewers. 30

CIBC's initial goal was to encourage publishers to include more realistic stories and more accurate historical treatments about blacks, Hispanics, Native Americans, and women. It awarded annual prizes for the best new children's books by minority writers. However, soon after it was founded in the mid-1960s, the nation's political and cultural climate changed dramatically. In the wake of riots and civil disorders in major American cities, including New York, the racial integration movement was swept away by movements for racial separatism and black power. CIBC was caught up in the radicalism of the times. Its goals shifted from inclusion to racial assertiveness, from the pursuit of racial harmony to angry rhetoric about colonialism and the "educational slaughter" of minority children. As its militancy grew, CIBC insisted that only those who were themselves members of a minority group were qualified to write about their own group's experience. It demanded that publishers subsidize minority-owned bookstores, printers, and publishers. It urged teachers and librarians to watch for and exclude those books that violated its bias guidelines.

CIBC's critiques of racial and gender stereotyping undoubtedly raised the consciousness of textbook publishers about the white-only world of their products and prompted necessary revisions. However, in the early 1970s, CIBC demanded elimination of books that it deemed "anti-human," racist, and sexist.

CIBC attacked numerous literary classics as racist, including Hugh Lofting's Dr. Dolittle books, Pamela Travers's *Mary Poppins,* Harriet Beecher Stowe's *Uncle Tom's Cabin,* Theodore Taylor's *The Cay,* Ezra Jack Keats's books (*Snowy Day* and *Whistle for Willie*), Roald Dahl's *Charlie and the Chocolate Factory,* and William H. Armstrong's *Sounder.* The American publisher of Dr. Dolittle, agreeing that the series contained stereotypical images of Africans, expurgated the books to remove offensive illustrations and text. The original version of the books has now disappeared from library shelves and bookstores.

CIBC attacked fairy tales as sexist, asserting that they promote "stereotypes, distortions, and anti-humanism." It charged that such traditional tales as "Little Red Riding Hood," "Cinderella," "Jack and the Beanstalk," "Snow-White," "Beauty and the Beast," "The Princess and the Pea," "Rumpelstiltskin," and "Hansel and Gretel" were irredeemably sexist because they portrayed females as "princesses or poor girls on their way to becoming princesses, fairy godmothers or good fairies, wicked and evil witches, jealous and spiteful sisters, proud, vain, and hateful stepmothers, or shrewish wives." The "good" females were depicted as beautiful, the "bad" ones as evil witches. The males were powerful and courageous, while the females were assigned to "traditional" roles as helpers. Typically, the characters in fairy tales rose from poverty to great wealth, CIBC complained, but no one ever asked about the "socioeconomic causes of their condition"; no one ever talked about the need for "collective action" to overcome injustice. In the eyes of CIBC, fairy tales were not only rife with sexist stereotypes, but with materialism, elitism, ethnocentrism, and racism too.

CIBC's *Human (and Anti-Human) Values in Children's Books* listed 35 235 children's books published in 1975. Each was evaluated against a checklist that measured whether it was racist, sexist, elitist, materialist, age-ist, conformist, escapist, or individualist; or whether it was opposed to those values or indifferent to them; whether it "builds a positive image of females/minorities" or "builds a negative image of females/minorities"; whether it "inspires action versus oppression"; and whether it is "cultur-ally authentic." Only members of a specific group reviewed books about their own group: Blacks reviewed books about blacks, Chicanos reviewed books about Chicanos, and so on. Few of the books reviewed had any lasting significance, and few of them are still in print a quarter-century later. One that is still read is John D. Fitzgerald's *The Great Brain Does It Again,* which CIBC rated as racist, sexist, materialist, individualist, con-formist, and escapist.

The author Nat Hentoff reacted angrily to what he called CIBC's "righteous vigilanteism." Although he agreed with the council's egali-tarian goals, he warned that its bias checklists and its demands for political correctness would stifle free expression. He interviewed other writers who complained about the CIBC checklist but were fearful of being identified. CIBC's efforts to eliminate offensive books and to rate books for their political content, he argued, were creating a climate in which "creative imagination, the writer's and the child's, must hide to survive." Its drive against "individualism," he said, was antithetical to literature and the literary imagination: "Collectivism is for politics," he said, not for writers.

In retrospect, CIBC appears to have had minimal impact on general books. Despite having been denounced as racist, *The Cay* and *Sounder* remain commercially successful. Fairy tales continue to enchant children (although they are seldom found in textbooks and are usually bowdler-ized). The public was only dimly aware, if at all, of CIBC's lists of ste-reotypes, its reviews, and its ratings. Publishers kept printing and selling children's books that defied CIBC's strictures.

Where CIBC did make a difference, however, was with publishers of K–12 textbooks. Textbook houses could not risk ignoring CIBC or its labeling system. No publisher could afford to enter a statewide adoption process with a textbook whose contents had been branded racist or sexist or ageist or handicapist or biased against any other group. The publish-ers' fear of stigma gave CIBC enormous leverage. When publishers began writing their own bias guidelines in the late 1960s and early 1970s, they consulted with CIBC or hired members of its editorial advisory board to counsel them about identifying bias. James Banks, a member of the CIBC advisory board, wrote the bias guidelines for McGraw-Hill; his wife, Cherry A. McGee Banks, was one of the main writers of the Scott Foresman–Addison Wesley guidelines.

CIBC multiplied its effectiveness when it worked in tandem with the National Organization for Women (NOW), which was also founded in 1966. Unlike CIBC, which operated from New York City, NOW had chapters in every state. CIBC and NOW frequently collaborated to fight sexism and to promote language censorship in the publishing industry and in textbooks. Feminist groups, some associated with NOW, others operating independently, testified at state hearings against unacceptable textbooks, pressured state and local school boards to exclude such books, and lobbied publishers to expunge sexist language from their books. Feminists demanded a 50-50 ratio of girls and boys, women and men, in every book. They counted illustrations to see how many female characters were represented. They noted whether girls and women were in passive or active roles as compared to boys and men. They made lists of the occupations represented, insisted that women have equal representation in professional roles, and objected if illustrations showed women as housewives, baking cookies, or sewing. They hectored publishers, textbook committees, and school boards with their complaints. And they made a difference.

In 1972, a group called Women on Words and Images published 40 a pamphlet titled *Dick and Jane as Victims: Sex Stereotyping in Children's Readers* that documented the imbalanced representation of boys and girls in reading textbooks. In the most widely used readers of the mid-1960s, boys were more likely to be lead characters and to play an active role as compared to girls, who were portrayed as dependent, passive, and interested only in shopping and dressing up. At textbook hearings around the country, feminist groups brandished the book and demanded changes. Within a year of the pamphlet's appearance, the authors reported that they had drawn national attention to the problem. Publishers consulted with them for advice about how to revise their materials. By the mid-1970s, every major publishing company had adopted guidelines that banned sexist language and stereotypes from their textbooks.

By adopting bias guidelines, the publishers agreed to police their products and perform the censorship demanded by the politically correct left and the religious right. Publishers found it easier to exclude anything that offended anybody, be they feminists, religious groups, racial and ethnic groups, the disabled, or the elderly, rather than to get into a public controversy and see their product stigmatized. It was not all that difficult to delete a story or a paragraph or a test item, and most of the time no one noticed anyway.

The publishers reacted differently to pressure groups from the left and right. Companies did not share the Christian fundamentalist values of right-wing groups; they sometimes fought them in court, as Holt did in the *Mozert* v. *Hawkins* case described earlier. By contrast, editors at the big publishing companies often agreed quietly with the feminists and civil rights groups that attacked their textbooks; by and large, the editors and the left-wing critics came from the same cosmopolitan worlds and held similar political views. The publishers and editors did not mind if anyone thought them unsympathetic to the religious right, but they did not want to be considered racist by their friends, family, and professional peers. Nor did they oppose feminist demands for textbook changes, which had the tacit or open support of their own female editors. In retrospect, this dynamic helps to explain why the major publishing companies swiftly accepted the sweeping linguistic claims of feminist critics and willingly yielded to a code of censorship.

By the end of the 1980s, every publisher had complied with the demands of the critics, both from left and right. Publishers had established bias guidelines with which they could impose self-censorship and head off the outside censors, as well as satisfy state adoption reviews. Achieving demographic balance and excluding sensitive topics had become more important to their success than teaching children to read or to appreciate good literature. Stories written before 1970 had to be carefully screened for compliance with the bias guidelines; those written after 1970 were unlikely to be in compliance unless written for a textbook publisher. So long as books and stories continue to be strained through a sieve of political correctness, fashioned by partisans of both left and right, all that is left for students to read will be thin gruel.

THINKING CRITICALLY ABOUT THE READING

1. Controversies over political correctness often take the form of isolated incidents or situations, many of them based on college campuses and in college classrooms: for example, an instructor or student says something that offends administrators, other instructors, or students. The participants in such cases are often strident about their concerns, and authorities rush in to put pressure on the parties to resolve their differences. What, according to Ravitch, makes the question of political correctness in the world of textbook publishing different from political correctness on college campuses?

2. Ravitch describes how in the 1980s, the religious right mounted numerous challenges to textbook content. Describe the "New Right's" attack on "secular humanism." What is "secular humanism"? Why is it a favorite target of the religious right?

3. In what segment of the publishing business have left-leaning groups had the most influence? Who are the most powerful interest groups on the left? How do these groups use "fairness" to promote their type of censorship, in Ravitch's view?

4. Describe the "checklist" that the Council on Interracial Books for Children (CIBC) uses to evaluate educational materials. What are some of the key elements on the list? Why do some liberals, such as Nat Hentoff, object to this practice?

5. How do the attempts from the political Left to censor seem to differ, in Ravitch's account of them, from those that emanate from the Right? In what ways might they be the same? Are the differences significant to Ravitch? Do you think she's more sympathetic to one end of the spectrum than to the other?

6. Do you know for certain whether or not your texts have undergone censorship? Does the fact that it is difficult to know if censorship has taken place make the issue more or less important for you? Why?

7. To what extent is the publishing industry's "bottom line" the real problem with respect to the work of the language police? Is the public concerned about censorship in textbooks, or is this an "invisible issue" for most people? Does the public want unbiased textbooks? Who, or what group, could be put in charge of guaranteeing bias-free textbooks?

With a No. 2 Pencil, Delete: The Destruction of Literature in the Name of Children

ANNA QUINDLEN

Born in 1953, author and Pulitzer Prize–winning journalist Anna Quindlen began her career in journalism immediately following her graduation from Barnard College. Starting out as a reporter for the *New York Post,* she later joined the *New York Times,* where in the years from 1977 to 1995 she went from city hall reporter to metropolitan deputy editor to the syndicated columnist of "Life in the 30's" and "Public and Private." Only the third woman in the paper's history to write a regular op-ed column, she was awarded the Pulitzer Prize for Commentary in 1992. In 1999, Quindlen joined *Newsweek,* where she writes the column "Last Word." Quindlen is the first author to appear simultaneously on the *New York Times* best-seller lists for fiction, nonfiction, and self-help. Her columns are collected in the books *Living Out Loud* (1988), *Thinking Out Loud* (1994), and *Loud and Clear* (2004). Her novels include *Object Lessons* (1991), *One True Thing* (1995), *Black and Blue* (1998), *Blessings* (2002), and *Rise and Shine* (2006); among her nonfiction works are *A Short Guide to a Happy Life* (2000) and *Being Perfect* (2005).

In an interview with Barnes & Noble's *Book* magazine, Quindlen talked about her book *How Reading Changed My Life* (1998) and about her admiration for a librarian at her children's school who designed a whole lesson around the issue of banning books, rather than taking books deemed objectionable off the shelves. Young people should read books like *Catcher in the Rye,* and then "discuss why it upsets adults so much," Quindlen said. "I just think that's much more useful than withholding reading material." That same issue is at the center of her essay "With a No. 2 Pencil, Delete: The Destruction of Literature in the Name of Children," which appeared in her *Newsweek* column in October 2007. In it, Quindlen writes about how the homogenization-through-censorship of educational material and literature is a betrayal, not of the authors but of the students themselves.

WRITING TO DISCOVER: *As a student, you have taken many standardized tests, some of which include excerpts from literary works and other professionally published materials. Does it matter to you that these excerpts and essays might have been "sanitized" or otherwise edited? Do you think that, in the interest of not offending any person or group, such editing might be justified?*

You can imagine how honored I was to learn that my work was going to be mangled for the sake of standardized testing. I got the word just after a vigilant parent had discovered that statewide English tests in New York had included excerpts from literary writers edited so nonsensically that the work had essentially lost all meaning. Isaac Bashevis Singer, Annie Dillard, even Chekhov—the pool of those singled out for red-penciling by bureaucrats was a distinguished one, and I found myself a little disappointed that I had not been turned into reading-comp pabulum.

But the state of Georgia was more accommodating. The folks at the Educational Testing Service, one of America's most powerful monopolies, were preparing something called the Georgia End-of-Course Tests and wanted to use an excerpt from a book I'd written called *How Reading Changed My Life.*

In the sentence that read "The Sumerians first used the written word to make laundry lists, to keep track of cows and slaves and household goods," the words "and slaves" had been deleted.

And in the sentence "And soon publishers had the means, and the will, to publish anything—cookbooks, broadsides, newspapers, novels, poetry, pornography, picture books for children," someone had drawn a black line through the word "pornography" and written edit!

I got off easy. In the Singer excerpt on New York's Regents exam, which was about growing up a Jew in prewar Poland, all references to Jews and Poles were excised. Dillard's essay about being the only white child in a library in the black section of town became almost unintelligible after all references to race were obliterated. The New York State Education Department's overheated guidelines are written so broadly that only the words "the" and "but" seem safe. "Does the material require the parent, teacher or examinee to support a position that is contrary to their religious beliefs or teaching?" the guidelines ask. "Does the material assume that the examinee has experience with a certain type of family structure?" As Jeanne Heifetz, an opponent of the required Regents exams who uncovered the editing, wrote, "Almost no piece of writing emerges from this process unscathed." Nor could any except the most homogenized piece of pap about Cape Cod tide pools.

"The words 'slave' and 'pornography' deal with controversial issues that could cause an emotional reaction in some students that could distract them from the test and affect their performance," wrote the ETS supernumerary snipping at my sentences.

This was in a week when students likely heard of another suicide bomber in Israel, the gunpoint abduction of a teen-ager in Utah and the arrest of an R&B star for appearing on videotape having sex with an underage girl. And they're going to be distracted by the words "slaves" and "pornography"?

That's the saddest thing here: not the betrayal of writers by bureaucrats, but the betrayal of kids by educators. Everyone complains that teenagers don't read enough good stuff; the lists of banned books in school libraries are thick with quality, with Steinbeck and Margaret Atwood.

Everyone complains that students are not intellectually engaged; controversial issues are excised from those staggeringly boring textbooks. Everyone complains that kids are not excited about school; the point of school increasingly seems to be incessant testing that doesn't even have the grace to be mildly interesting. By the standards of the Regents tests, *The Catcher in the Rye* is unacceptable. ("Does the material require a student to take a position that challenges parental authority?") So are *To Kill a Mockingbird* and *The Merchant of Venice*.

Here is the most shocking question among the New York state guidelines: "Does the material assume values not shared by all test takers?" There is no book worth reading, no poem worth writing, no essay worth analyzing, that assumes the same values for all. That sentence is the death of intellectual engagement.

The education officials in New York have now backed down from   10
their cut-and-paste-without-permission position, faced with an angry mob of distinguished writers. But what do the kids learn from this? That the written word doesn't really matter much, that it can be weakened at will. That no one trusts a student to understand that variations in opinion and background are both objectively interesting and intellectually challenging. That some of the most powerful people involved in their education have reduced them to the lowest common denominator.

I like kids, have a brace of them around here, and I'm damned (edit!) if I'm going to abet some skewed adult vision of their febrile emotional state. Unlike those in New York, the people preparing tests for the state of Georgia at least had the common courtesy to ask permission to mess with my stuff. I declined. It's not that one or two words are particularly precious; I have hacked away at my own sentences to get them to fit tidily in this space. But not to make pabulum for students who deserve something tastier.

THINKING CRITICALLY ABOUT THE READING

1. What is the tone of Quindlen's opening paragraph? (Glossary: *Beginnings and Endings; Tone*) In what sense is she "honored" to have been included in the Georgia End-of-Course Tests and "disappointed" at having been left out of the New York State tests?

2. Quindlen cites several examples of the way her *How Reading Changed My Life* was edited for the Georgia tests. What was the rationale behind the editing? Do you find the rationale convincing?

3. What examples of editing does Quindlen cite from the New York Regents exam? What was the rationale behind these edits? What, in Quindlen's view, was their actual effect?

4. What examples does Quindlen give of "the betrayal of kids by educators" (8)? Do you agree with her charges?

5. What does Quindlen mean by the "death of intellectual engagement" (9)?

6. What does Quindlen say that kids learn from the "cut-and-paste-without-permission" (10) practices of the New York State educational system, and others like it? Do you think her position is defensible?

7. What argument strategy is Quindlen using when she writes, "It's not that one or two words are particularly precious; I have hacked away at my own sentences to get them to fit tidily into this space" (11)? (Glossary: *Argument*) Is it effective?

WRITING SUGGESTIONS: DEBATING THE ISSUE

1. In the essays included in this chapter, Roger Rosenblatt and Stuart Taylor both argue for the rights of people to speak openly, or as Rosenblatt states, the "rights of jackasses" to be outrageous and not be silenced or punished. Write an essay describing each author's basic argument, comparing and contrasting their evidence and conclusions. What would you say are the underlying political/philosophical differences between them? Be sure to supply evidence from the essays to support your conclusion.

2. In "Pornography, Obscenity, and the Case for Censorship," Irving Kristol poses a question to which his essay was intended to provide an answer: "What reason is there to think that anyone was ever corrupted by a book?" The question is at the heart of a debate that has been with us as long as art and entertainment—plays, books, television, movies, video games, and Internet Web sites, to name just a few kinds—have been with us. Do some research on a historical or contemporary debate on the corrupting influence of a particular work of art or entertainment. Some possiblities—drawn from a seemingly endless supply—are below:
   - *Doom* or *Mortal Kombat* (video games)
   - *Teletubbies* (television show)
   - Batman and Robin (comic book heroes)
   - *The Catcher in the Rye* (novel)
   - pinball machines

   Do you believe that books—or video games, or television shows, etc.—can and do corrupt? Consider drawing on the arguments and evidence cited by Kristol, Ravitch, and any of the other authors whose work is included in this chapter, and cite evidence from your research to support your position.

3. The First Amendment states: "Congress shall make no law respecting an establishment of religion, or prohibiting the free exercise thereof; or abridging the freedom of speech, or of the press; or the right of the people peaceably to assemble, and to petition the Government for a redress of grievances." In this chapter, all of the authors deal with different aspects of freedom of expression, but Stanley Fish and Stuart Taylor explicitly make arguments about what rights are actually guaranteed by the First Amendment. Compare and contrast the approaches, conclusions, and remedies in evidence in the two essays. Where do the two authors agree? Where do they disagree? Finally, take a position on whose understanding of the First Amendment is, in your view, ultimately most convincing.

4. In "How Campus Censors Squelch Freedom of Speech," Stuart Taylor cites a number of examples of how, in his view, "political correctness" is championed on campus at the expense of freedom of expression. In the eleventh edition of *Merriam-Webster's Collegiate Dictionary*, the phrase "politically correct" (first used in 1936) is defined as "conforming to a belief that language and practices which could offend political sensibilities (as in matters of sex or race) should be eliminated." The *Concise Oxford English Dictionary* (11th ed.) defines "political correctness" as "the careful avoidance of forms of expression or action that are perceived to exclude or insult groups of people who are socially disadvantaged or discriminated against." Research the history of "political correctness," and write an essay describing that history and discussing the factors that brought a "politically correct" standard to college campuses. Using examples from at least two of the essays in this chapter, as well as any examples you might have from your own experience, describe the relationship between "political correctness" and censorship.

5. The American Library Association (ALA) compiles lists of the authors and books that individuals, parents, or groups seek most often to remove from library shelves or keep out of the classroom. Included in their list of the top ten "most challenged" books in 2007 are Mark Twain's *The Adventures of Huckleberry Finn*, Alice Walker's *The Color Purple*, and Maya Angelou's *I Know Why the Caged Bird Sings*. The ALA takes the position that even when these objections are made with good intentions, that is, to protect children, they are still censorship: "Censorship can be subtle, almost imperceptible, as well as blatant and overt, but, nonetheless, harmful." Take a look at the ALA's data on challenges to books at http://www.ala.org/ala/oif/bannedbooksweek/challengedbanned/challengedbanned.cfm#mfcb, and read or reread Diane Ravitch's take on the subject in "The Language Police." Then, write an essay expressing your own perspective on the subject of book banning. What do you think about a community's rights when it comes to what books libraries can put on their shelves? What do you think of the ALA's warning about censorship? Are there limits to what you would consider appropriate in a school library?

6. The Web site for Parents Against Bad Books in Schools (http://www.pabbis .com/), located in the state of Virginia, is loaded with information about how to ban objectionable books from schools, including a "List of Lists" noting books that have been found objectionable by some (and on what grounds), a "Sample Book Review Documentation Form," and links to like-minded groups and organizations. Spend some time on the site, and use the information you find there to evaluate a book read while you were in school (K–12). Would it likely pass muster? Should it? (Is it on the PABBIS "List of Lists" already?) Write an essay in which you discuss what's at stake, for groups like PABBIS and for students. Do you find the PABBIS mission sympathetic, or do you object to it? On what grounds? Use one or more of the essays in this chapter to support your position.

7. Put yourself in a hypothetical situation: you are a writer whose work revolves around documenting gang life on the streets in a big city. The language people use under these conditions is tough, often profane, abusive, and violent. In attempting to get your work published, you run into an editor who deletes and replaces words, and, as in Quindlen's essay "With a No. 2 Pencil, Delete," edits your work to the point that it loses not only its meaning but also its

purpose. Write a defense of your work, explaining why the language as recorded is essential to the work. Use the arguments and evidence in one or more of the essays in this chapter to bolster your position.

8. Much of the discussion in this chapter has been about the censorship of language, but the censorship of images can be equally powerful. In recent years, a heated controversy has arisen over the U.S. government's policy, in place since 1991, banning the media release of photographs showing returning casualties (i.e., coffins) from war. In 2004, a military contractor fired a Kuwait-based cargo worker whose photograph of flag-draped coffins appeared on the front page of the *Seattle Times;* the case made a media star of the cargo worker and evoked an outcry over the government's policy. In 2005, in response to a series of Freedom of Information Act requests and a lawsuit, the government finally released more than 700 images of the return of American casualties to Dover Air Force Base and other U.S. military facilities. However, many of the images released were heavily censored—or "redacted," as the government puts it. Here are three of them:

These images are housed at the Web site of the National Security Archives (NSA), an independent research institute that operates from The George Washington University and archives these and other declassified government documents at http://www.gwu.edu/%7Ensarchiv/index.html. The NSA offers the following commentary:

> "I cannot imagine that the members of these honor guards want their own faces blacked out from the public homage that is due," [Director of the NSA Thomas] Blanton said. "Honor guard is the most solemn duty for anybody in the military, not something for the censors to hide."

> The photos released by the Pentagon were taken by U.S. government photographers, not by journalists. "There is nothing macabre or ghoulish about these images," said [University of Delaware professor Ralph] Begleiter. "These are among the most respectful images created of American casualties of war—far less wrenching than images we regularly see from the battlefield. They're taken under carefully controlled circumstances by military photographers covering honor ceremonies." (http://www.gwu .edu/%7Ensarchiv/NSAEBB/NSAEBB152/index.htm)

What is your reaction to the controversy over the images? Why do you think the government imposed a ban on media release of the images in the first place? What is your reaction to the "redaction" of the images the Pentagon ultimately released? Do some research on the controversy, starting with the NSA's Web site. Then write an essay in which you offer your reasoned explanation of the government's actions and argue for or against the appropriateness of the measures they have taken. Use the arguments and examples from one or more of the reading selections in this chapter to support your position.

8

LANGUAGE DEBATE: SHOULD ENGLISH BE THE LAW?

Since Great Britain gained control over what is now the United States, English has been the dominant language in our country. Despite the multitude of cultures and ethnicities that comprise the United States, English has until now been a common thread linking them. It may be somewhat surprising, then, that there is no official U.S. language. Now, even as English literacy becomes a necessity for people in many parts of the world, some people in the United States believe its primacy is being threatened at home. Much of the current controversy focuses on Hispanic communities with large Spanish-speaking populations, who may feel little or no pressure to learn English. Most would agree that in order for everyone to participate in our society, some way must be found to bridge the linguistic and cultural divide.

Recent government efforts in this regard have included bilingual programs in schools, on ballots, for providing emergency notices, and so on. The goal of the programs is to maintain a respect for the heritage and language of the non-English speakers while they learn the English language. The programs have come under fire, however, from those who believe that the U.S. government should conduct itself only in English. If people come here, the argument goes, they should assume the responsibility of learning the native language as quickly as possible. And, English-only proponents reason, if immigrants do not or are not willing to learn English, the government should not accommodate them in another language. Some believe that there should be a mandate that the official language of the United States is English and that the government will conduct business in no other language. Many state governments have, in fact, already made such a declaration.

The other side of the argument has two components. One is the belief that it is discriminatory to mandate English because those who do not speak it are then denied basic rights until they learn the language. The second part of this argument is that the current situation is nothing new: There have always been groups of immigrants that were slow to assimilate into American culture, but they all eventually integrated, and the controversy will resolve itself. Furthermore, English is not threatened, and its use does not need to be legislated. Indeed, according to English-only critics, declaring English the official U.S. language could create far more problems than it solves.

The first two selections address the issue head on. Robert King asks "Should English Be the Law?" in the context of our history and that of countries around the world. He notes that compared to similar situations in other countries, including the French Canadian separatist crisis just to our north, the problems here seem almost trivial. If being American still means anything unique, he concludes, we should be able to enjoy our linguistic diversity rather than be threatened by it. Charles Krauthammer's "In Plain English: Let's Make It Official" obviously comes to the opposite conclusion. Krauthammer claims, "History has blessed us, because of the accident of our origins, with a linguistic unity that brings a critically needed cohesion to a nation as diverse, multiracial and multiethnic as America."

The last four selections provide a rich context for the English-only debate. In "Why and When We Speak Spanish in Public," Myriam Marquez explains why she and her parents continue to speak Spanish when they are together, why they "haven't adopted English as our official family language." She knew that in order to get ahead in this country she had to learn English, but she contends that "[b]eing an American has very little to do with what language we use during our free time in a free country." In "Saying 'Adios' to Spanglish," Leticia Salais recounts an interesting change of attitude from being ashamed of her Spanish language and heritage while growing up to embracing it as an adult in the workplace and at home raising her two young boys. In the essay "From Outside, In," Barbara Mellix shares her literacy journey. She tells of growing up in Greeleyville, South Carolina, a world that was predominantly black, and learning to speak both Black English and Standard or "proper" English. She remembers feeling more comfortable using the "ordinary everyday speech of 'country' coloreds." As an African American and a speaker of the Black English vernacular, Mellix struggled for years with feelings of inferiority when confronted with the "proper" language of those she called the "others." She always thought of herself as person "who stood outside Standard English, hugging to herself a disabling mistrust of a language she thought could not represent a person with her history and experience"—until she took a college writing course and discovered the liberating and "generative power of language." Finally, in Caroline Hwang's "The Good Daughter," a young Korean American writer shares with us the anguish of her confounding search for identity in America. As she sadly laments, "My parents didn't want their daughter to be Korean, but they didn't want her to be American, either." How to deal with the "halfwayness" of a life in the middle is a question that, for Hwang, does not admit of a quick or easy answer.

Should English Be the Law?

ROBERT D. KING

Scholar and teacher Robert D. King was born in Mississippi in 1936. He graduated from the Georgia Institute of Technology in 1959 with a degree in mathematics, beginning a distinguished and diverse career in academe. After a brief stint at IBM, King went to the University of Wisconsin, receiving a Ph.D. in German linguistics in 1965. He was hired by the University of Texas at Austin to teach German that same year and has spent more than three decades there teaching linguistics and Asian studies in addition to German. He also served as the dean of the College of Liberal Arts from 1979 until 1989 and currently holds the Audre and Bernard Rapoport Regents Chair of Liberal Arts. Indian studies have captured his attention lately, and his most recent book is *Nehru and the Language Politics of India,* published in 1996.

The language politics of the United States has become a hot topic in recent years as well. In the following selection, first published in the April 1997 issue of the *Atlantic,* King provides historical background and perspective on the English-only debate.

WRITING TO DISCOVER: *What reasons can you give in favor of not making English the official language of the United States?*

We have known race riots, draft riots, labor violence, secession, antiwar protests, and a whiskey rebellion, but one kind of trouble we've never had: a language riot. Language riot? It sounds like a joke. The very idea of language as a political force—as something that might threaten to split a country wide apart—is alien to our way of thinking and to our cultural traditions.

This may be changing. On August 1 of last year [1996] the U.S. House of Representatives approved a bill that would make English the official language of the United States. The vote was 259 to 169, with 223 Republicans and thirty-six Democrats voting in favor and eight Republicans, 160 Democrats, and one independent voting against. The debate was intense, acrid, and partisan. On March 25 of last year [1996] the Supreme Court agreed to review a case involving an Arizona law that would require public employees to conduct government business only in English. Arizona is one of several states that have passed "Official English" or "English Only" laws. The appeal to the Supreme Court followed a 6-to-5 ruling, in October of 1995, by a federal appeals court striking down the Arizona law. These events suggest how divisive a public issue language could become in America—even if it has until now scarcely been taken seriously.

Traditionally, the American way has been to make English the national language—but to do so quietly, locally, without fuss. The Constitution is silent on language: the Founding Fathers had no need to legislate that English be the official language of the country. It has always been taken for granted that English *is* the national language, and that one must learn English in order to make it in America.

To say that language has never been a major force in American history or politics, however, is not to say that politicians have always resisted linguistic jingoism. In 1753 Benjamin Franklin voiced his concern that German immigrants were not learning English: "Those [Germans] who come hither are generally the most ignorant Stupid Sort of their own Nation. . . . they will soon so out number us, that all the advantages we have will not, in My Opinion, be able to preserve our language, and even our government will become precarious." Theodore Roosevelt articulated the unspoken American linguistic-melting-pot theory when he boomed, "We have room for but one language here, and that is the English language, for we intended to see that the crucible turns our people out as Americans, of American nationality, and not as dwellers in a polyglot boarding house." And: "We must have but one flag. We must also have but one language. That must be the language of the Declaration of Independence, of Washington's Farewell address, of Lincoln's Gettysburg speech and Second Inaugural."

OFFICIAL ENGLISH

TR's linguistic tub-thumping long typified the tradition of American politics. That tradition began to change in the wake of the anything-goes attitudes and the celebration of cultural differences arising in the 1960s. A 1975 amendment to the Voting Rights Act of 1965 mandated the "bilingual ballot" under certain circumstances, notably when the voters of selected language groups reached five percent or more in a voting district. Bilingual education became a byword of educational thinking during the 1960s. By the 1970s linguists had demonstrated convincingly—at least to other academics—that black English (today called African-American vernacular English or Ebonics) was not "bad" English but a different kind of authentic English with its own rules. Predictably, there have been scattered demands that black English be included in bilingual-education programs.

It was against this background that the movement to make English the official language of the country arose. In 1981 Senator S. I. Hayakawa, long a leading critic of bilingual education and bilingual ballots, introduced in the U.S. Senate a constitutional amendment that not only would have made English the official language but would have prohibited federal and state laws and regulations requiring the use of other languages. His English Language Amendment died in the Ninety-seventh Congress.

In 1983 the organization called U.S. English was founded by Hayakawa and John Tanton, a Michigan ophthalmologist. The primary purpose of the organization was to promote English as the official language of the United States. (The best background readings on America's "neolinguisticism" are the books *Hold Your Tongue,* by James Crawford, and *Language Loyalties,* edited by Crawford, both published in 1992.) Official English initiatives were passed by California in 1986, by Arkansas, Mississippi, North Carolina, North Dakota, and South Carolina in 1987, by Colorado, Florida, and Arizona in 1988, and by Alabama in 1990. The majorities voting for these initiatives were generally not insubstantial: California's, for example, passed by 73 percent.

It was probably inevitable that the Official English (or English-only— the two names are used almost interchangeably) movement would acquire a conservative, almost reactionary undertone in the 1990s. Official English is politically very incorrect. But its cofounder John Tanton brought with him strong liberal credentials. He had been active in the Sierra Club and Planned Parenthood, and in the 1970s served as the national president of Zero Population Growth. Early advisers of U.S. English resist ideological pigeonholing: they included Walter Annenberg, Jacques Barzun, Bruno Bettelheim, Alistair Cooke, Denton Cooley, Walter Cronkite, Angier Biddle Duke, George Gilder, Sidney Hook, Norman Podhoretz, Arnold Schwarzenegger, and Karl Shapiro. In 1987 U.S. English installed as its president Linda Chávez, a Hispanic who had been prominent in the Reagan Administration. A year later she resigned her position, citing "repugnant" and "anti-Hispanic" overtones in an internal memorandum written by Tanton. Tanton, too, resigned, and Walter Cronkite, describing the affair as "embarrassing," left the advisory board. One board member, Norman Cousins, defected in 1986, alluding to the "negative symbolic significance" of California's Official English initiative, Proposition 63. The current chairman of the board and CEO of U.S. English is Mauro E. Mujica, who claims that the organization has 650,000 members.

The popular wisdom is that conservatives are pro and liberals con. True, conservatives such as George Will and William F. Buckley Jr. have written columns supporting Official English. But would anyone characterize as conservatives the present and past U.S. English board members Alistair Cooke, Walter Cronkite, and Norman Cousins? One of the strongest opponents of bilingual education is the Mexican American writer Richard Rodriguez, best known for his eloquent autobiography, *Hunger of Memory* (1982). There is a strain of American liberalism that defines itself in nostalgic devotion to the melting pot.

For several years relevant bills awaited consideration in the U.S. House 10 of Representatives. The Emerson Bill (H.R. 123), passed by the House last August, specifies English as the official language of government, and requires that the government "preserve and enhance" the official status of English. Exceptions are made for the teaching of foreign languages; for actions necessary for public health, international relations, foreign trade, and the protection of the rights of criminal defendants; and for the use of "terms of art" from languages other than English. It would, for example, stop the Internal Revenue Service from sending out income-tax forms and instructions in languages other than English, but it would not ban the use of foreign languages in census materials or documents dealing with national security. "*E Pluribus Unum*" can still appear on American money. U.S. English supports the bill.

What are the chances that some version of Official English will become federal law? Any language bill will face tough odds in the Senate, because some western senators have opposed English-only measures in the past for various reasons, among them a desire by Republicans not to alienate the growing number of Hispanic Republicans, most of whom are uncomfortable with mandated monolingualism. Texas Governor George W. Bush, too, has forthrightly said that he would oppose any English Only proposals in his state. Several of the Republican candidates for President in 1996 (an interesting exception is Phil Gramm) endorsed versions of Official English, as has Newt Gingrich. While governor of Arkansas, Bill Clinton signed into law an English-only bill. As President, he has described his earlier action as a mistake.

Many issues intersect in the controversy over Official English: immigration (above all), the rights of minorities (Spanish-speaking minorities in particular), the pros and cons of bilingual education, tolerance, how best to educate the children of immigrants, and the place of cultural diversity in school curricula and in American society in general. The question that lies at the root of most of the uneasiness is this: Is America threatened by the preservation of languages other than English? Will America, if it continues on its traditional path of benign linguistic neglect, go the way of Belgium, Canada, and Sri Lanka — three countries among many whose unity is gravely imperiled by language and ethnic conflicts?

LANGUAGE AND NATIONALITY

Language and nationalism were not always so intimately intertwined. Never in the heyday of rule by sovereign was it a condition of employment that the King be able to speak the language of his subjects. George I spoke no English and spent much of his time away from England, attempting to use the power of his kingship to shore up his German possessions. In the Middle Ages nationalism was not even part of the picture: one owed loyalty to a lord, a prince, a ruler, a family, a tribe, a church, a piece of land, but not to a nation and least of all to a nation as a language unit. The capital city of the Austrian Hapsburg empire was Vienna, its ruler a monarch with effective control of peoples of the most varied and incompatible ethnicities, and languages, throughout Central and Eastern Europe. The official language, and the lingua franca as well, was German. While it stood—and it stood for hundreds of years—the empire was an anachronistic relic of what for most of human history had been the normal relationship between country and language: none.

The marriage of language and nationalism goes back at least to Romanticism and specifically to Rousseau, who argued in his *Essay on the Origin of Languages* that language must develop before politics is possible and that language originally distinguished nations from one another. A little-remembered aim of the French Revolution—itself the legacy of Rousseau—was to impose a national language on France, where regional languages such as Provençal, Breton, and Basque were still strong competitors against standard French, the French of the Ile de France. As late as 1789, when the Revolution began, half the population of the south of France, which spoke Provençal, did not understand French. A century earlier the playwright Racine said that he had had to resort to Spanish and Italian to make himself understood in the southern French town of Uzès. After the Revolution nationhood itself became aligned with language.

In 1846 Jacob Grimm, one of the Brothers Grimm of fairy-tale fame but better known in the linguistic establishment as a forerunner of modern comparative and historical linguists, said that "a nation is the totality of people who speak the same language." After midcentury, language was invoked more than any other single criterion to define nationality. Language as a political force helped to bring about the unification of Italy and of Germany and the secession of Norway from its union with Sweden in 1905. Arnold Toynbee observed—unhappily—soon after the First World War that "the growing consciousness of Nationality had attached itself neither to traditional frontiers nor to new geographical associations but almost exclusively to mother tongues." 15

The crowning triumph of the new desideratum was the Treaty of Versailles, in 1919, when the allied victors of the First World War began redrawing the map of Central and Eastern Europe according to nationality as best they could. The magic word was "self-determination," and none of Woodrow Wilson's Fourteen Points mentioned the word "language" at all. Self-determination was thought of as being related to "nationality," which today we would be more likely to call "ethnicity"; but language was simpler to identify than nationality or ethnicity. When it came to drawing the boundary lines of various countries—Czechoslovakia, Yugoslavia, Romania, Hungary, Albania, Bulgaria, Poland—it was principally language that guided the draftsman's hand. (The main exceptions were Alsace-Lorraine, South Tyrol, and the German-speaking parts of Bohemia and Moravia.) Almost by default language became the defining characteristic of nationality.

And so it remains today. In much of the world, ethnic unity and cultural identification are routinely defined by language. To be Arab is to speak Arabic. Bengali identity is based on language in spite of the division of Bengali-speakers between Hindu India and Muslim Bangladesh. When eastern Pakistan seceded from greater Pakistan in 1971, it named itself Bangladesh: *desa* means "country"; *bangla* means not the Bengali people or the Bengali territory but the Bengali language.

Scratch most nationalist movements and you find a linguistic grievance. The demands for independence of the Baltic states (Latvia, Lithuania, and Estonia) were intimately bound up with fears for the loss of their respective languages and cultures in a sea of Russianness. In Belgium the war between French and Flemish threatens an already weakly fused country. The present atmosphere of Belgium is dark and anxious, costive; the metaphor of divorce is a staple of private and public discourse. The lines of terrorism in Sri Lanka are drawn between Tamil Hindus and Sinhalese Buddhists—and also between the Tamil and Sinhalese languages. Worship of the French language fortifies the movement for an independent Quebec. Whether a united Canada will survive into the twenty-first century is a question too close to call. Much of the anxiety about language in the United States is probably fueled by the "Quebec problem": unlike Belgium, which is a small European country, or Sri Lanka, which is halfway around the world, Canada is our close neighbor.

Language is a convenient surrogate for nonlinguistic claims that are often awkward to articulate, for they amount to a demand for more political and economic power. Militant Sikhs in India call for a state of their own: Khalistan ("Land of the Pure" in Punjabi). They frequently couch this as a demand for a linguistic state, which has a certain simplicity about it, a clarity of motive—justice, even, because states in India are normally linguistic states. But the Sikh demands blend religion, economics, language, and retribution for sins both punished and unpunished in a country where old sins cast long shadows.

Language is an explosive issue in the countries of the former Soviet   20
Union. The language conflict in Estonia has been especially bitter. Ethnic Russians make up almost a third of Estonia's population, and most of them do not speak or read Estonian, although Russians have lived in Estonia for more than a generation. Estonia has passed legislation requiring knowledge of the Estonian language as a condition of citizenship. Nationalist groups in independent Lithuania sought restrictions on the use of Polish—again, old sins, long shadows.

In 1995 protests erupted in Moldova, formerly the Moldavian Soviet Socialist Republic, over language and the teaching of Moldovan history. Was Moldovan history a part of Romanian history or of Soviet history? Was Moldova's language Romanian? Moldovan—earlier called Moldavian—*is* Romanian, just as American English and British English are both English. But in the days of the Moldavian SSR, Moscow insisted that the two languages were different, and in a piece of linguistic nonsense required Moldavian to be written in the Cyrillic alphabet to strengthen the case that it was not Romanian.

The official language of Yugoslavia was Serbo-Croatian, which was never so much a language as a political accommodation. The Serbian and Croatian languages are mutually intelligible. Serbian is written in the Cyrillic alphabet, is identified with the Eastern Orthodox branch of the Catholic Church, and borrows its high-culture words from the east—from Russian and Old Church Slavic. Croatian is written in the Roman alphabet, is identified with Roman Catholicism and borrows its high-culture words from the west—from German, for example, and Latin. One of the first things the newly autonomous Republic of Serbia did, in 1991, was to pass a law decreeing Serbian in the Cyrillic alphabet the official language of the country. With Croatia divorced from Serbia, the Croatian and Serbian languages are diverging more and more. Serbo-Croatian has now passed into history, a language-museum relic from the brief period when Serbs and Croats called themselves Yugoslavs and pretended to like each other.

Slovakia, relieved now of the need to accommodate to Czech cosmopolitan sensibilities, has passed a law making Slovak its official language. (Czech is to Slovak pretty much as Croatian is to Serbian.) Doctors in state hospitals must speak to patients in Slovak, even if another language would aid diagnosis and treatment. Some 600,000 Slovaks—more than 10 percent of the population—are ethnically Hungarian. Even staff meetings in Hungarian-language schools must be in Slovak. (The government dropped a stipulation that church weddings be conducted in Slovak after heavy opposition from the Roman Catholic Church.) Language inspectors are told to weed out "all sins perpetrated on the regular Slovak language." Tensions between Slovaks and Hungarians, who had been getting along, have begun to arise.

The twentieth century is ending as it began—with trouble in the Balkans and with nationalist tensions flaring up in other parts of the globe. (Toward the end of his life Bismarck predicted that "some damn fool thing in the Balkans" would ignite the next war.) Language isn't always part of the problem. But it usually is.

UNIQUE OTHERNESS

Is there no hope for language tolerance? Some countries manage to   25
maintain their unity in the face of multilingualism. Examples are Finland, with a Swedish minority, and a number of African and Southeast Asian countries. Two others could not be more unlike as countries go: Switzerland and India.

German, French, Italian, and Romansh are the languages of Switzerland. The first three can be and are used for official purposes; all four are designated "national" languages. Switzerland is politically almost hyperstable. It has language problems (Romansh is losing ground), but they are not major, and they are never allowed to threaten national unity.

Contrary to public perception, India gets along pretty well with a host of different languages. The Indian constitution officially recognizes nineteen languages, English among them. Hindi is specified in the constitution as the national language of India, but that is a pious postcolonial fiction: outside the Hindi-speaking northern heartland of India, people don't want to learn it. English functions more nearly than Hindi as India's lingua franca.

From 1947, when India obtained its independence from the British, until the 1960s blood ran in the streets and people died because of language. Hindi absolutists wanted to force Hindi on the entire country, which would have split India between north and south and opened up other fracture lines as well. For as long as possible Jawaharlal Nehru, independent India's first Prime Minister, resisted nationalist demands to redraw the capricious state boundaries of British India according to language. By the time he capitulated, the country had gained a precious decade to prove its viability as a union.

Why is it that India preserves its unity with not just two languages to contend with, as Belgium, Canada, and Sri Lanka have, but nineteen? The answer is that India, like Switzerland, has a strong national identity. The two countries share something big and almost mystical that holds each together in a union transcending language. That something I call "unique otherness."

The Swiss have what the political scientist Karl Deutsch called "learned   30 habits, preferences, symbols, memories, and patterns of landholding": customs, cultural traditions, and political institutions that bind them closer to one another than to people of France, Germany, or Italy living just across the border and speaking the same language. There is Switzerland's traditional neutrality, its system of universal military training (the "citizen army"), its consensual allegiance to a strong Swiss franc—and fondue, yodeling, skiing, and mountains. Set against all this, the fact that Switzerland has four languages doesn't even approach the threshold of becoming a threat.

As for India, what Vincent Smith, in the *Oxford History of India,* calls its "deep underlying fundamental unity" resides in institutions and beliefs such as caste, cow worship, sacred places, and much more. Consider *dharma, karma,* and *maya,* the three root convictions of Hinduism; India's historical epics; Gandhi; *ahimsa* (nonviolence); vegetarianism; a distinctive cuisine and way of eating; marriage customs; a shared past; and what the Indologist Ainslie Embree calls "Brahmanical ideology." In other words, "We are Indian; we are different."

Belgium and Canada have never managed to forge a stable national identity; Czechoslovakia and Yugoslavia never did either. Unique otherness immunizes countries against linguistic destabilization. Even Switzerland and especially India have problems; in any country with as many different languages as India has, language will never *not* be a problem. However, it is one thing to have a major illness with a bleak prognosis; it is another to have a condition that is irritating and occasionally painful but not life-threatening.

History teaches a plain lesson about language and governments: there is almost nothing the government of a free country can do to change language usage and practice significantly, to force its citizens to use certain languages in preference to others, and to discourage people from speaking a language they wish to continue to speak. (The rebirth of Hebrew in Palestine and Israel's successful mandate that Hebrew be spoken and written by Israelis is a unique event in the annals of language history.) Quebec has since the 1970s passed an array of laws giving French a virtual monopoly in the province. One consequence—unintended, one wishes to believe—of these laws is that last year kosher products imported for Passover were kept off the shelves, because the packages were not labeled in French. Wise governments keep their hands off language to the extent that it is politically possible to do so.

We like to believe that to pass a law is to change behavior; but passing laws about language, in a free society, almost never changes attitudes or behavior. Gaelic (Irish) is living out a slow, inexorable decline in Ireland despite enormous government support of every possible kind since Ireland gained its independence from Britain. The Welsh language, in contrast, is alive today in Wales in spite of heavy discrimination during its history. Three out of four people in the northern and western counties of Gwynedd and Dyfed speak Welsh.

I said earlier that language is a convenient surrogate for other national 35 problems. Official English obviously has a lot to do with concern about immigration, perhaps especially Hispanic immigration. America may be threatened by immigration; I don't know. But America is not threatened by language.

The usual arguments made by academics against Official English are commonsensical. Who needs a law when, according to the 1990 census, 94 percent of American residents speak English anyway? (Mauro E. Mujica, the chairman of U.S. English, cites a higher figure: 97 percent.) Not many of today's immigrants will see their first language survive into the second generation. This is in fact the common lament of first-generation immigrants: their children are not learning their language and are losing the culture of their parents. Spanish is hardly a threat to English, in spite of isolated (and easily visible) cases such as Miami, New York City, and pockets of the Southwest and southern California. The everyday language of south Texas is Spanish, and yet south Texas is not about to secede from America.

But empirical, calm arguments don't engage the real issue: language is a symbol, an icon. Nobody who favors a constitutional ban against flag burning will ever be persuaded by the argument that the flag is, after all, just a "piece of cloth." A draft card in the 1960s was never merely a piece of paper. Neither is a marriage license.

Language, as one linguist has said, is "not primarily a means of communication but a means of communion." Romanticism exalted language, made it mystical, sublime—a bond of national identity. At the same time, Romanticism created a monster: it made of language a means for destroying a country.

America has that unique otherness of which I spoke. In spite of all our racial divisions and economic unfairness, we have the frontier tradition, respect for the individual, and opportunity; we have our love affair with the automobile; we have in our history a civil war that freed the slaves and was fought with valor; and we have sports, hot dogs, hamburgers, and milk shakes—things big and small, noble and petty, important and trifling. "We are Americans; we are different."

If I'm wrong, then the great American experiment will fail—not because of language but because it no longer means anything to be an American; because we have forfeited that "willingness of the heart" that F. Scott Fitzgerald wrote was America; because we are not long joined by Lincoln's "mystic chords of memory." 40

We are not even close to the danger point. I suggest that we relax and luxuriate in our linguistic richness and our traditional tolerance of language differences. Language does not threaten American unity. Benign neglect is a good policy for any country when it comes to language, and it's a good policy for America.

THINKING CRITICALLY ABOUT THE READING

1. According to King, "It has always been taken for granted that English *is* the national language, and that one must learn English in order to make it in America" (3). What has changed in recent years to make learning English a political issue?

2. What does King mean when he says, "Official English is politically very incorrect" (8)?

3. What, according to King, makes the English-only issue so controversial? What other issues complicate the decision to make English the nation's language?

4. Why do you think King takes time to explain the evolution of the relationship between language and nationality in Europe and the rest of the world? What insights into the English-only issue does this brief history of language and culture give you? Explain.

5. What does King mean by the term "unique otherness"? What do you see as America's "unique otherness"? Do you agree with King's assessment that America's "unique otherness" will help us transcend our language differences? Why or why not?

6. King concludes that "[b]enign neglect is a good policy for any country when it comes to language, and it's a good policy for America" (41). Do you share King's optimistic view?

In Plain English: Let's Make It Official

CHARLES KRAUTHAMMER

Pulitzer Prize–winning columnist and commentator Charles Krauthammer was born in 1950 in New York City to parents of French citizenship. He grew up in Montreal and graduated from McGill University in 1970. The following year he continued his studies in political science as a Commonwealth Scholar at Balliol College, Oxford. In 1972 he moved to the United States and enrolled in Harvard Medical School, earning his M.D. in psychiatry in 1975. In 1978 he joined Jimmy Carter's administration to direct planning in psychiatric research, and later he served as speechwriter for Vice President Walter Mondale and senior editor at the *New Republic.* As a journalist, Krauthammer quickly gained a reputation for his clear prose and sound arguments. He is widely recognized and respected for his political and social columns, which appear regularly in the *Washington Post, Time,* the *New Republic,* and the *Weekly Standard.* In 1985 he published *Cutting Edges: Making Sense of the Eighties,* a collection of his essays. One critic commented that "Krauthammer is at his best when he writes not so much about 'hard' politics as about political culture . . . and beyond that about the contemporary social climate in general."

In the following essay, first published in *Time* on June 12, 2006, Krauthammer presents the case for making English the official language of the United States. He strongly believes that America's unprecedented success as a nation can be traced to the unifying force of the English language.

WRITING TO DISCOVER: *Our country's elected officials are struggling with the question of whether or not to make English our official language. Make a list of the reasons why you think it should or should not be the language of the land for all official transactions.*

Growing up (as I did) in the province of Québec, you learn not just the joys but also the perils of bilingualism. A separate national identity, revolving entirely around "Francophonie," became a raging issue that led to social unrest, terrorism, threats of separation and a referendum that came within a hair's breadth of breaking up Canada.

Canada, of course, had no choice about bilingualism. It is a country created of two nations at its birth, and has ever since been trying to cope with that inherently divisive fact. The U.S., by contrast blessed with a single common language for two centuries, seems blithely and gratuitously to be ready to import bilingualism with all its attendant divisiveness and antagonisms.

One of the major reasons for America's great success as the world's first "universal nation," for its astonishing and unmatched capacity for assimilating immigrants, has been that an automatic part of acculturation was the acquisition of English. And yet during the great immigration debate now raging in Congress, the people's representatives cannot make up their minds whether the current dominance of English should be declared a national asset, worthy of enshrinement in law.

The Senate could not bring itself to declare English the country's "official language." The best it could do was pass an amendment to the immigration bill tepidly declaring English the "national language." Yet even that was too much for Senate Democratic leader Harry Reid, who called that resolution "racist."

Less hyperbolic opponents point out that granting special official   5 status to English is simply unnecessary: America has been accepting foreign-language-speaking immigrants forever—Brooklyn is so polyglot it is a veritable Babel—and yet we've done just fine. What's the great worry about Spanish?

The worry is this. Polyglot is fine. When immigrants, like those in Brooklyn, are members of a myriad of linguistic communities, each tiny and discrete, there is no threat to the common culture. No immigrant presumes to make the demand that the state grant special status to his language. He may speak it in the street and proudly teach it to his children, but he knows that his future and certainly theirs lie inevitably in learning English as the gateway to American life.

But all of that changes when you have an enormous, linguistically monoclonal immigration as we do today from Latin America. Then you get not Brooklyn's successful Babel but Canada's restive Québec. Monoclonal immigration is new for the U.S., and it changes things radically. If at the turn of the twentieth century, Ellis Island had greeted teeming masses speaking not 50 languages but just, say, German, America might not have enjoyed the same success at assimilation and national unity that it has.

Today's monoclonal linguistic culture is far from hypothetical. Growing rapidly through immigration, it creates large communities—in some places already majorities—so overwhelmingly Spanish speaking that, in time, they may quite naturally demand the rights and official recognition for Spanish that French has in French-speaking Québec.

That would not be the end of the world—Canada is a decent place—but the beginning of a new one for the U.S., a world far more complicated and fraught with division. History has blessed us with all the freedom and advantages of multiculturalism. But it has also blessed us, because of the accident of our origins, with a linguistic unity that brings a critically needed cohesion to a nation as diverse, multiracial and multiethnic as America. Why gratuitously throw away that priceless asset? How mindless to call the desire to retain it "racist."

I speak three languages. My late father spoke nine. When he became a   10
naturalized American in midcentury, it never occurred to him to demand
of his new and beneficent land that whenever its government had business
with him—tax forms, court proceedings, ballot boxes—that it should
be required to communicate in French, his best language, rather than
English, his last and relatively weakest.

English is the U.S.'s national and common language. But that may
change over time unless we change our assimilation norms. Making
English the official language is the first step toward establishing those
norms. "Official" means the language of the government and its institutions. "Official" makes clear our expectations of acculturation. "Official"
means that every citizen, upon entering America's most sacred political
space, the voting booth, should minimally be able to identify the words
President and Vice President and county commissioner and judge. The
immigrant, of course, has the right to speak whatever he wants. But he
must understand that when he comes to the U.S., swears allegiance and
accepts its bounty, he undertakes to join its civic culture. In English.

THINKING CRITICALLY ABOUT THE READING

1. According to Krauthammer, what has been one of the most important reasons for America's success as a nation?

2. How does Krauthammer counter those people who believe that "granting special official status to English is simply unnecessary" (5)?

3. What is "monoclonal immigration" (7)? In what ways does monoclonal immigration affect assimilation and national unity? Explain.

4. How does Krauthammer answer the question, "What's the great worry about Spanish" (5)? What do you see as his greatest fear?

5. Why does Krauthammer believe that "linguistic unity" is so important for the United States at this point in its history? Do you agree with his assessment of the situation? Explain why or why not.

6. What, for Krauthammer, is the difference between declaring English "the 'national language'" and making English the "'official language'" (4)? What does he believe the label "official" will mean for future generations?

Why and When We Speak Spanish in Public

Myriam Marquez

An award-winning columnist for the *Orlando Sentinel,* Myriam Marquez was born in Cuba in 1954 and grew up in South Florida. After graduating from the University of Maryland in 1983 with a degree in journalism and a minor in political science, she worked for United Press International in Washington, D.C., and in Maryland, covering the Maryland legislature as statehouse bureau chief. Marquez joined the editorial board of the *Sentinel* in 1987 and, since 1990, has been writing three weekly columns. Her commentaries focus on state and national politics, the human condition, civil liberties, and issues important to women and Hispanics. She is a founding board member of the YMCA Achievers program, which aims to help Hispanic students succeed in high school. Since 2000, Marquez has tutored public school children in reading. The Florida Society of Newspaper Editors awarded her its highest award for commentary in 2003.

As a Hispanic, Marquez recognizes that English is the "common language" in America but knows that being American has little if anything to do with what language one speaks. In this article, which first appeared in the *Orlando Sentinel* on July 5, 1999, she explains why she and her parents, all bilingual, continue to speak Spanish when they are together, even though they have lived in the United States for forty years.

WRITING TO DISCOVER: *How would you feel if you met a friend and her parents in a public place and they spoke a language other than English in your presence?*

When I'm shopping with my mother or standing in line with my step-dad to order fast food or anywhere else we might be together, we're going to speak to one another in Spanish.

That may appear rude to those who don't understand Spanish and overhear us in public places.

Those around us may get the impression that we're talking about them. They may wonder why we would insist on speaking in a foreign tongue, especially if they knew that my family has lived in the United States for 40 years and that my parents do understand English and speak it, albeit with difficulty and a heavy accent.

Let me explain why we haven't adopted English as our official family language. For me and most of the bilingual people I know, it's a matter of respect for our parents and comfort in our cultural roots.

It's not meant to be rude to others. It's not meant to alienate anyone   5
or to Balkanize America.

It's certainly not meant to be an American—what constitutes an
"American" being defined by English speakers from North America.

Being an American has very little to do with what language we use
during our free time in a free country. From its inception, this country
was careful not to promote a government-mandated official language.

We understand that English is the common language of this country
and the one most often heard in international business circles from Peru to
Norway. We know that, to get ahead here, one must learn English.

But that ought not mean that somehow we must stop speaking in our
native tongue whenever we're in a public area, as if we were ashamed of
who we are, where we're from. As if talking in Spanish—or any other language, for that matter—is some sort of litmus test used to gauge American patriotism.

Throughout this nation's history, most immigrants—whether from   10
Poland or Finland or Italy or wherever else—kept their language through
the first generation and, often, the second. I suspect that they spoke among
themselves in their native tongue—in public. Pennsylvania even provided
voting ballots written in German during much of the 1800s for those who
weren't fluent in English.

In this century, Latin American immigrants and others have fought for
this country in U.S.-led wars. They have participated fully in this nation's
democracy by voting, holding political office, and paying taxes. And they
have watched their children and grandchildren become so "American"
that they resist speaking in Spanish.

You know what's rude?

When there are two or more people who are bilingual and another
person who speaks only English and the bilingual folks all of a sudden start
speaking Spanish, which effectively leaves out the English-only speaker. I
don't tolerate that.

One thing's for sure. If I'm ever in a public place with my mom or dad
and bump into an acquaintance who doesn't speak Spanish, I will switch
to English and introduce that person to my parents. They will respond in
English, and do so with respect.

THINKING CRITICALLY ABOUT THE READING

1. How does Marquez explain the fact that she and her parents "haven't adopted
   English as our official family language"(4)? If you were standing next to the
   three of them and they were speaking Spanish, would you consider their
   behavior rude? Why or why not?

2. Marquez claims that "from its inception, this country was careful not to promote a government-mandated official language"(7). Why do you suppose the

U.S. government has steered clear of legislating an official language? Is there a need for such legislation now?

3. For Marquez, "being an American has very little to do with what language we use during our free time in a free country"(7). Do you think that the English-only debate gets muddied when people see language as "some sort of litmus text used to gauge American patriotism"(9)? Explain.

4. Under what circumstances would Marquez stop speaking Spanish and use English? If you were or are bilingual, would you behave the same way in similar situations? Explain.

Saying "Adios" to Spanglish

LETICIA SALAIS

Leticia Salais grew up, as she tells us, "in the poorest neighborhood of El Paso, Texas," where she did everything she could to shake off her poor background, including not speaking Spanish. The result was that she did not speak Spanish very fluently and instead used a combination of English and Spanish known as Spanglish. Salais married and moved to Tucson, Arizona, and began work in a nursing home. With the birth of her first child she continued to distance herself and now her family from her Hispanic culture by deciding to teach her son English as his first and perhaps only language. Her work in a nursing home helping people who were struggling with language and her growing desire to learn Spanish more fluently and appreciate her background more fully, however, caused her to think differently about the value of bilingualism and to take a different approach in the rearing of her second son: His first language is Spanish, and he's now helping his older brother to become bilingual. Salais's experiences in the workforce and as a young mother have caused her to become a strong advocate for bilingualism as an empowering and enriching force in our culture.

Salais's essay first appeared in *Newsweek* on December 8, 2007.

WRITING TO DISCOVER: *If you grew up in a home where a language other than English was spoken, how did you feel about letting other people know about it? If you grew up speaking only English at home, would you have welcomed the opportunity to speak another language and be bilingual?*

Niños, vengan a comer. My 18-month-old son pops out from behind the couch and runs to his high chair. My 7-year-old has no idea what I just said. He yells out from the same hiding spot: "What did you say?" My older son does not suffer from hearing loss. He is simply not bilingual like his brother, and did not understand that I was telling him to come eat.

Growing up in the poorest neighborhoods of El Paso, Texas, I did everything I could to escape the poverty and the color of my skin. I ran around with kids from the west side of town who came from more-affluent families and usually didn't speak a word of Spanish. I spoke Spanish well enough, but I pretended not to understand it and would not speak a word of it. In school, I refused to speak Spanish even with my Hispanic friends. I wanted nothing to do with it. While they joined Chicano clubs, all I wanted to do was be in the English literacy club. Even at home, the only person to whom I spoke Spanish was my mom, and that's only because she wouldn't have understood me otherwise.

After I got married and moved to Tucson, Arizona, I thought I was in heaven. Though I was actually in the minority, I felt right at home with my Anglo neighbors. When I got pregnant with my first son, I decided that English would be his first language and, if I could help it, his only language. I never spoke a word of Spanish around him, and when his grandparents asked why he did not understand what they were saying, I made excuses. He understands but he's very shy. He understands the language but he refuses to speak it. In reality, I didn't want him to speak it at all.

In a land of opportunity, I soon realized I had made a big mistake. I was denying my son one of the greatest gifts I had to offer: the ability to be bilingual. I saw the need for interpreters on a daily basis in the health field where I worked. Even trips to the grocery store often turned into an opportunity to help someone who could not understand English or vice versa.

In the nursing home where I worked, I met a wonderful group of   5
Spanish-speaking individuals, whom I bonded with right away. I longed to speak like they did, enunciating the words correctly as they rolled off their tongues. It sounded like music to me. I started watching Spanish *telenovelas* and listening to Spanish morning shows on the radio just to improve my vocabulary. I heard words that had never been uttered around me growing up in a border town where people spoke a mixture of Spanish and English. A co-worker from Peru had the most eloquent way of speaking in a language that I recognized as Spanish yet could not fully comprehend. Did I also cheat myself of being bilingual?

Today I can take any English word and, like magic, easily find its Spanish equivalent. I now live a life that is fully bilingual. I hunger for foreign movies from Spain and the interior of Mexico just to challenge myself by trying to guess what all the words mean. I even surprise my mom when she doesn't understand what I'm saying. I know she is proud that I no longer speak Spanglish, and I am no longer embarrassed to speak Spanish in public. I see it as a secret language my husband and I share when we don't want those around us to understand what we are saying. I quickly offer the use of my gift when I see someone struggling to speak English or to understand Spanish, and I quietly say a prayer of thanks that I am not in his or her shoes. I feel empowered and blessed that I can understand a conversation in another language and quickly translate it in my head.

My second son has benefited from my bilingual tongue. I speak only Spanish to him while my husband speaks only English; I am proud to say that his first language was Spanish. My 7-year-old, on the other hand, still has a way to go. I'm embarrassed that I foolishly kept my beautiful native language from him. I hope I have not done irreversible damage. A couple of years ago, I began speaking to him only in Spanish, but I had not yet heard him utter a complete sentence back.

Then, as if my prayers were answered, from behind the couch, I heard a tiny voice exclaim, *Ven, mira esto.* It was my older son instructing his little brother to come look at what he was doing. Maybe I won't be his first bilingual teacher, but it looks like he's already learning from another expert—his bilingual brother. Maybe it's not too late after all.

THINKING CRITICALLY ABOUT THE READING

1. What is the lesson that Salais has learned, and why does she think it important enough to share with her readers?

2. How effective is the beginning of Salais's essay? How does it help her illustrate the bilingual issues she addresses? (Glossary: *Beginnings and Endings*)

3. Why did Salais reject her Hispanic culture and language while growing up?

4. What, in later life, convinced Salais that she had made a mistake in rejecting her Hispanic heritage and language?

5. What did Salais realize once she became a parent with regard to her Hispanic culture and language?

6. How do you react to the following statement that Salais makes about Spanish in paragraph 6: "I see it as a secret language my husband and I share when we don't want those around us to understand what we are saying"? In your opinion, does her statement support her argument or stand in contradiction to it? Explain. (Glossary: *Argumentation*)

From Outside, In

BARBARA MELLIX

A native of Greeleyville, South Carolina, Barbara Mellix graduated from the University of Pittsburgh in 1984. She received her M.F.A. in creative writing from the same institution two years later. After teaching for a year at Pittsburgh's Greensburg campus, she returned to her alma mater as assistant to the dean of the College of Arts and Sciences. She is currently executive assistant dean of the College of Arts and Sciences, director of the college's advising center, and a teacher of composition at the University of Pittsburgh.

In this article, which first appeared in the *Georgia Review* in 1988, Mellix explains how she grew up speaking what amounted to two languages: "the ordinary everyday speech of 'country' coloreds and 'proper' English." She understood when she could speak Black English and when she should speak Standard English, but she always felt uncomfortable with the standard version. It was in a college writing class as an adult that Mellix took on the language of the outside world and discovered its remarkable power.

WRITING TO DISCOVER: *Do you speak two versions of English, one at home among family members and friends and another in public among people you don't know? What differentiates these two versions? What makes the two versions necessary for you?*

Two years ago, when I started writing this paper, trying to bring order out of chaos, my ten-year-old daughter was suffering from an acute attack of boredom. She drifted in and out of the room complaining that she had nothing to do, no one to "be with" because none of her friends were at home. Patiently I explained that I was working on something special and needed peace and quiet, and I suggested that she paint, read, or work with her computer. None of these interested her. Finally, she pulled up a chair to my desk and watched me, now and then heaving long, loud sighs. After two or three minutes (nine or ten sighs), I lost my patience. "Looka here, Allie," I said, "you are too old for this kinda carryin' on. I done told you this is important. You wronger than dirt to be in here haggin' me like this and you know it. Now git on outta here and leave me off before I put my foot all the way down."

I was at home, alone with my family, and my daughter understood that this way of speaking was appropriate in that context. She knew, as a matter of fact, that it was almost inevitable; when I get angry at home, I speak some of my finest, most cherished Black English. Had I been speaking to my daughter in this manner in certain other environments, she would have been shocked and probably worried that I had taken leave of my sense of propriety.

Like my children, I grew up speaking what I considered two distinctly different languages—Black English and Standard English (or as I thought of them then, the ordinary everyday speech of "country" coloreds and "proper" English)—and in the process of acquiring these languages, I developed an understanding of when, where, and how to use them. But unlike my children, I grew up in a world that was primarily black. My friends, neighbors, minister, teachers—almost everybody I associated with every day—were black. And we spoke to one another in our own special language: *That sho is a pretty dress you got on. If she don' soon leave me off I'm gon tell her head a mess. I was so mad I could'a pissed a blue rod. He all the time trying to low-rate somebody. Ain't that just about the nastiest thing you ever set ears on?*

Then there were the "others," the "proper" blacks, transplanted relatives and one-time friends who came home from the city for weddings, funerals, and vacations. To these we spoke Standard English. "Ain't?" my mother would yell at me when I used the term in the presence of "others." "You *know* better than that." And I would hang my head in shame and say the "proper" word.

I remember one summer sitting in my grandmother's house in   5
Greeleyville, South Carolina, when it was full of the chatter of city relatives who were home on vacation. My parents sat quietly, only now and then volunteering a comment or answering a question. My mother's face took on a strained expression when she spoke. I could see that she was being careful to say just the right words in just the right way. Her voice sounded thick, muffled. And when she finished speaking, she would lapse into silence, her proper smile on her face. My father was more articulate, more aggressive. He spoke quickly, his words sharp and clear. But he held his proud head higher, a signal that he, too, was uncomfortable. My sisters and brothers and I stared at our aunts, uncles, and cousins, speaking only when prompted. Even then, we hesitated, formed our sentences in our minds, then spoke softly, shyly.

My parents looked small and anxious during those occasions, and I waited impatiently for our leave-taking when we would mock our relatives the moment we were out of their hearing. "Reeely," we would say to one another, flexing our wrists and rolling our eyes, "how dooo you stan' this heat? Chile, it just too hyooo-mid for words." Our relatives had made us feel "country," and this was our way of regaining pride in ourselves while getting a little revenge in the bargain. The words bubbled in our throats and rolled across our tongues, a balming.

As a child I felt this same doubleness in uptown Greeleyville where the whites lived. "Ain't that a pretty dress you're wearing!" Toby, the town policeman, said to me one day when I was fifteen. "Thank you very much," I replied, my voice barely audible in my own ears. The words felt wrong in my mouth, rigid, foreign. It was not that I had never spoken that phrase before—it was common in Black English, too—but I was extremely conscious that this was an occasion for proper English. I had taken out my English and put it on as I did my church clothes, and I felt as if I were wearing my Sunday best in the middle of the week. It did not matter that Toby had not spoken grammatically correct English. He was white and could speak as he wished. I had something to prove. Toby did not.

Speaking Standard English to whites was our way of demonstrating that we knew their language and could use it. Speaking it to Standard-English-speaking blacks was our way of showing them that we, as well as they, could "put on airs." But when we spoke Standard English, we acknowledged (to ourselves and to others—but primarily to ourselves) that our customary way of speaking was inferior. We felt foolish, embarrassed, somehow diminished because we were ashamed to be our real selves. We were reserved, shy in the presence of those who owned and/or spoke *the* language.

My parents never set aside time to drill us in Standard English. Their forms of instruction were less formal. When my father was feeling particularly expansive, he would regale us with tales of his exploits in the outside world. In almost fluent English, complete with dialogue and flavored with gestures and embellishment, he told us about his attempt to get a haircut at a white barbershop; his refusal to acknowledge one of the town merchants until the man addressed him as "Mister"; the time he refused to step off the sidewalk uptown to let some whites pass; his airplane trip to New York City (to visit a sick relative) during which the stewardess and porters—recognizing that he was a "gentleman"—addressed him as "Sir." I did not realize then—nor, I think, did my father—that he was teaching us, among other things, Standard English and the relationship between language and power.

My mother's approach was different. Often, when one of us said, "I'm gon wash off my feet," she would say, "And what will you walk on if you wash them off?" Everyone would laugh at the victim of my mother's "proper" mood. But it was different when one of us children was in a proper mood. "You think you are so superior," I said to my oldest sister one day when we were arguing and she was winning. "Superior!" my sister mocked. "You mean I am acting 'biggidy'?" My sisters and brothers sniggered, then joined in teasing me. Finally, my mother said, "Leave your sister alone. There's nothing wrong with using proper English." There was a half-smile on her face. I had gotten "uppity," had "put on airs" for no good reason. I was at home, alone with the family, and I hadn't been prompted by one of my mother's proper moods. But there was also a proud light in my mother's eyes; her children were learning English very well.

Not until years later, as a college student, did I begin to understand our ambivalence toward English, our scorn of it, our need to master it, to own and be owned by it—an ambivalence that extended to the public-school classroom. In our school, where there were no whites, my teachers taught Standard English but used Black English to do it. When my grammar-school teachers wanted us to write, for example, they usually said something like, "I want y'all to write five sentences that make a statement. Anybody get done before the rest can color." It was probably almost those exact words that led me to write these sentences in 1953 when I was in the second grade:

> The white clouds are pretty.
>
> There are only 15 people in our room.
>
> We will go to gym.
>
> We have a new poster.
>
> We may go out doors.

Second grade came after "Little First" and "Big First," so by then I knew the implied rules that accompanied all writing assignments. Writing was an occasion for proper English. I was not to write in the way we spoke to one another: The white clouds pretty; There ain't but 15 people in our room; We going to gym; We got a new poster; We can go out in the yard. Rather I was to use the language of "other": clouds *are*, there *are*, we *will*, we *may*.

My sentences were short, rigid, perfunctory, like the letters my mother wrote to relatives:

> Dear Papa,
>
> How are you? How is Mamie? Fine I hope. We are fine. We will come to see you Sunday. Cousin Ned will give us a ride.
>
> Love,
>
> Daughter

The language was not ours. It was something from outside us, something we used for special occasions.

But my coloring on the other side of that second-grade paper is different. I drew three hearts and a sun. The sun has a smiling face that radiates and envelops everything it touches. And although the sun and its world are enclosed in a circle, the colors I used—red, blue, green, purple, orange, yellow, black—indicates that I was less restricted with drawing and coloring than I was with writing Standard English. My valentines were not just red. My sun was not just a yellow ball in the sky.

By the time I reached the twelfth grade, speaking and writing Standard-English had taken on new importance. Each year, about half of the newly graduated seniors of our school moved to large cities—particularly in the North—to live with relatives and find work. Our English teacher constantly corrected our grammar: "Not 'ain't,' but 'isn't.'" We seldom wrote papers, and even those few were usually plot summaries of short stories. When our teacher returned the papers, she usually lectured on the importance of using Standard English: "I *am;* you *are;* he, she, or it *is,*" she would say, writing on the chalkboard as she spoke. "How you gon git a job talking about 'I is,' or 'I isn't' or 'I ain't'?"

In Pittsburgh, where I moved after graduation, I watched my   15 aunt and uncle—who had always spoken Standard English when in Greeleyville—switch from Black English to Standard English to a mixture of the two, according to where they were or who they were with. At home and with certain close relatives, friends, and neighbors, they spoke Black English. With those less close, they spoke a mixture. In public and with strangers, they generally spoke Standard English.

In time, I learned to speak Standard English with ease and to switch smoothly from Black to Standard or a mixture, and back again. But no matter where I was, no matter what the situation or occasion, I continued to write as I had in school:

> Dear Mommie,
>
> How are you? How is everybody else? Fine I hope. I am fine. So are Aunt and Uncle. Tell everyone I said hello. I will write again soon.
>
>   Love,
>
>   Barbara

At work, at a health insurance company, I learned to write letters to customers. I studied form letters and letters written by co-workers, memorizing the phrases and the ways in which they were used. I dictated:

> Thank you for your letter of January 5. We have made the changes in your coverage you requested. Your new premium will be $150 every three months. We are pleased to have been of service to you.

In a sense, I was proud of the letters I wrote for the company: they were proof of my ability to survive in the city, the outside world—an indication of my growing mastery of English. But they also indicate that writing was still mechanical for me, something that didn't require much thought.

Reading also became a more significant part of my life during those early years in Pittsburgh. I had always liked reading, but now I devoted more and more of my spare time to it. I read romances, mysteries, popular novels. Looking back, I realized that the books I liked best were simple, unambiguous: good versus bad and right versus wrong with right rewarded and wrong punished, mysteries unraveled and all set right in the end. It was how I remembered life in Greeleyville.

Of course I was romanticizing. Life in Greeleyville had not been so very uncomplicated. Back there I had been—first as a child, then as a young woman with limited experience in the outside world—living in a relatively closed-in society. But there were implicit and explicit principles that guided our way of life and shaped our relationships with one another and the people outside—principles that a newcomer would find elusive and baffling. In Pittsburgh, I had matured, become more experienced: I had worked at three different jobs, associated with a wider range of people, married, had children. This new environment with different prescripts for living required that I speak Standard English much of the time, and slowly, imperceptibly, I had ceased seeing a sharp distinction between myself and "others." Reading romances and mysteries, characterized by dichotomy, was a way of shying away from change, from the person I was becoming.

But that other part of me—that part which took great pride in my ability to hold a job writing business letters—was increasingly drawn to the new developments in my life and the attending possibilities, opportunities for even greater change. If I could write letters for a nationally known business, could I not also do something better, more challenging, more important? Could I not, perhaps, go to college and become a school teacher? For years, afraid and a little embarrassed, I did no more than imagine this different me, this possible me. But sixteen years after coming north, when my younger daughter entered kindergarten, I found myself unable—or unwilling—to resist the lure of possibility. I enrolled in my first college course: Basic Writing, at the University of Pittsburgh.

For the first time in my life, I was required to write extensively about   20
myself. Using the most formal English at my command, I wrote these sentences near the beginning of the term:

> One of my duties as a homemaker is simply picking up after others. A day seldom passes that I don't search for a mislaid toy, book, or gym shoe, etc. I change the Ty-D-Bol, fight "ring around the collar," and keep our laundry smelling "April fresh." Occasionally, I settle arguments between my children and suggest things to do when they're bored. Taking telephone messages for my oldest daughter is my newest (and sometimes most aggravating) chore. Hanging the toilet paper is my most insignificant.

My concern was to use "appropriate" language, to sound as if I belonged in a college classroom. But I felt separate from the language—as if it did not and could not belong to me. I couldn't think and feel genuinely in that language, couldn't make it express what I thought and felt about being a housewife. A part of me resented, among other things, being judged by such things as the appearance of my family's laundry and toilet bowl, but in that language I could only imagine and write about a conventional housewife.

For the most part, the remainder of the term was a period of adjustment, a time of trying to find my bearings as a student in a college composition class, to learn to shut out my Black English whenever I composed, and to prevent it from creeping into my formulations; a time for trying to grasp the language of the classroom and reproduce it in my prose; for trying to talk about myself in that language, reach others through it. Each experience of writing was like standing naked and revealing my imperfection, my "otherness." And each new assignment was another chance to make myself over in language, reshape myself, make myself "better" in my rapidly changing image of a student in a college composition class.

But writing became increasingly unmanageable as the term progressed, and by the end of the semester, my sentences sounded like this:

> My excitement was soon dampened, however, by what seemed like a small voice in the back of my head saying that I should be careful with my long awaited opportunity. I felt frustrated and this seemed to make it difficult to concentrate.

There is a poverty of language in these sentences. By this point, I knew that the clichéd language of my housewife essay was unacceptable, and I generally recognized trite expressions. At the same time, I hadn't yet mastered the language of the classroom, hadn't yet come to see it as belonging to me. Most notable is the lifelessness of the prose, the apparent absence of a person behind the words. I wanted those sentences—and the rest of the essay—to convey the anguish of yearning to, at once, become something more and yet remain the same. I had the sensation of being split in two, part of me going into a future the other part didn't believe possible. As that person, the student writer at that moment, I was essentially mute. I could not—in the process of composing—use the language of the old me, yet I couldn't imagine myself in the language of "others."

I found this particularly discouraging because at midsemester I had been writing in a much different way. Note the language of this introduction to an essay I had written then, near the middle of the term:

> Pain is a constant companion to the people in "Footwork." Their jobs are physically damaging. Employers are insensitive to their feelings and in many cases add to their problems. The general public wounds them further by treating them with disgrace because of what they do for a living. Although the workers are as diverse as they are similar, there is a definite link between them. They suffer a great deal of abuse.

The voice here is stronger, more confident, appropriating terms like "physically damaging," "wounds them further," "insensitive," "diverse"—terms I couldn't have imagined using when writing about my own experience—and shaping them into sentences like "Although the workers are as diverse as they are similar, there is a definite link between them." And there is the sense of a personality behind the prose, someone who sympathizes with the workers. "The general public wounds them further by treating them with disgrace because of what they do for a living."

What causes these differences? I was, I believed, explaining other people's thoughts and feelings, and I was free to move about in the language of "others" so long as I was speaking *of* others. I was unaware that I was transforming into my best classroom language my own thoughts and feelings about people whose experiences and ways of speaking were in many ways similar to mine.

The following year, unable to turn back or to let go of what had   25
become something of an obsession with language (and hoping to catch and hold the sense of control that had eluded me in Basic Writing), I enrolled in a research writing course. I spent most of the term learning how to prepare for and write a research paper. I chose sex education as my subject and spent hours in libraries, searching for information, reading, taking notes. Then (not without messiness and often demoralizing frustration) I organized my information into categories, wrote a thesis statement, and composed my paper—a series of paragraphs and quotations spaced between carefully constructed transitions. The process and results felt artificial, but as I would later come to realize I was passing through a necessary stage. My sentences sounded like this:

> This reserve becomes understandable with examination of who the abusers are. In an overwhelming number of cases, they are people the victims know and trust. Family members, relatives, neighbors, and close family friends commit seventy-five percent of all reported sex crimes against children, and parents, parent substitutes and relatives are the offenders in thirty to eighty percent of all reported cases. While assault by strangers does occur, it is less common, and is usually a single episode. But abuse by family members, relatives and acquaintances may continue for an extended period of time. In cases of incest, for example, children are abused repeatedly for an average of eight years. In such cases, "the use of physical force is rarely necessary because of the child's trusting, dependent relationship with the offender. The child's cooperation is often facilitated by the adult's position of dominance, an offer of material goods, a threat of physical violence, or a misrepresentation of moral standards."

The completed paper gave me a sense of profound satisfaction, and I read it often after my professor returned it. I know now that what I was pleased with was the language I used and the professional voice it helped me maintain. "Use better words," my teacher had snapped at me one day after reading the notes I'd begun accumulating from my research, and slowly I began taking on the language of my sources. In my next set of notes, I used the word "vacillating"; my professor applauded. And by the time I composed the final draft, I felt at ease with terms like "overwhelming number of cases," "single episode," and "reserve," and I shaped them into sentences similar to those of my "expert" sources.

If I were writing the paper today, I would of course do some things differently. Rather than open with an anecdote—as my teacher suggested—I would begin simply with a quotation that caught my interest as I was researching my paper (and which I scribbled, without its source, in the margin of my notebook): "Truth does not do so much good in the world as the semblance of truth does evil." The quotation felt right because it captured what was for me the central idea of my essay—an idea that emerged gradually during the making of my paper—and expressed it in a way I would like to have said it. The anecdote, a hypothetical situation I invented to conform to the information in the paper, felt forced and insincere because it represented—to a great degree—my teacher's understanding of the essay, *her* idea of what in it was most significant. Improving upon my previous experiences with writing, I was beginning to think and feel in the language I used, to find my own voices in it, to sense that how one speaks influences how one means. But I was not yet secure enough, comfortable enough with the language to trust my intuition.

Now that I know that to seek knowledge, freedom, and autonomy means always to be in the concentrated process of becoming—always to be venturing into new territory, feeling one's way at first, then getting one's balance, negotiating, accommodating, discovering one's self in ways that previously defined "others"—I sometimes get tired. And I ask myself why I keep on participating in this highbrow form of violence, this slamming against perplexity. But there is no real futility in the question, no hint of that part of the old me who stood outside Standard English, hugging to herself a disabling mistrust of a language she thought could not represent a person with her history and experience. Rather, the question represents a person who feels the consequences of her education, the weight of her possibilities as a teacher and writer and human being, a voice in society. And I would not change that person, would not give back the good burden that accompanies my growing expertise, my increasing power to shape myself in language and share that self with "others."

"To speak," says Frantz Fanon, "means to be in a position to use a certain syntax, to grasp the morphology of this or that language, but it means above all to assume a culture, to support the weight of civilization."[1] To write means to do the same, but in a more profound sense. However, Fanon also says that to achieve mastery means to "get" in a position of power, to "grasp," to "assume." This I have learned—both as a student and subsequently as a teacher—can involve tremendous emotional and psychological conflict for those attempting to master academic discourse. Although as a beginning student writer I had a fairly good grasp of ordinary spoken English and was proficient at what Labov calls "code-switching" (and what John Baugh in *Black Street Speech* terms "style shifting"), when I came face to face with the demands of academic writing, I grew increasingly self-conscious, constantly aware of my status as a black and a speaker of one of the many Black English vernaculars—a traditional outsider. For the first time, I experienced my sense of doubleness as something

---

1. *Black Skin, White Masks* (1952; rpt. New York: Grove Press, 1967), pp. 17–18.

menacing, a built-in enemy. Whenever I turned inward for salvation, the balm so available during my childhood, I found instead this new fragmentation which spoke to me in many voices. It was the voice of my desire to prosper, but at the same time it spoke of what I had relinquished and could not regain: a safe way of being, a state of powerlessness which exempted me from responsibility for who I was and might be. And it accused me of betrayal, of turning away from blackness. To recover balance, I had to take on the language of the academy, the language of "others." And to do that, I had to learn to imagine myself as a part of the culture of that language, and therefore someone free to manage that language, to take liberties with it. Writing and rewriting, practicing, experimenting, I came to comprehend more fully the generative power of language. I discovered—with the help of some especially sensitive teachers—that through writing one can continually bring new selves into being, each with new responsibilities and difficulties, but also with new possibilities. Remarkable power, indeed. I write and continually give birth to myself.

THINKING CRITICALLY ABOUT THE READING

1. Explain the meaning of Mellix's title. In what ways does it reflect the journey she describes in her personal narrative?

2. Mellix remembers growing up "speaking what I considered two distinctly different languages—Black English and Standard English" (3). Through experience she learned when, where, and how to use each language. In what kinds of situations did she use Black English? And in what situations, Standard English? How did she feel about this "doubleness"?

3. For Mellix as a young woman, what did it mean to speak Standard English to whites? To Standard-English-speaking blacks? What was the pain of having to use Standard English?

4. What strategies did Mellix's parents use to teach her Standard English and the relationship between language and power? What do you see as the "power" of language?

5. Describe the transformation that Mellix experienced in her college composition class. What exactly did she learn about herself and her use of language?

The Good Daughter

CAROLINE HWANG

Freelance writer and editor Caroline Hwang was born in Milwaukee, Wisconsin. After graduating from the University of Pennsylvania in 1991, she entered the world of popular magazines, holding editorial positions at *Glamour, Mademoiselle,* and *Redbook.* She later earned an M.F.A. from New York University. She recently published her first novel, *In Full Bloom* (2003), and was a featured reader during the Asian American Writers' Workshop series in New York City.

In the following essay, which first appeared in *Newsweek* in 1998, Hwang illuminates the difficulty of growing up as the daughter of Korean immigrant parents.

WRITING TO DISCOVER: *What is your cultural identity? Do you consider yourself an American, or do you identify with another culture? How comfortable do you feel with this identity? Explain why you feel as you do.*

The moment I walked into the dry-cleaning store, I knew the woman behind the counter was from Korea, like my parents. To show her that we shared a heritage, and possibly get a fellow countryman's discount, I tilted my head forward, in shy imitation of a traditional bow.

"Name?" she asked, not noticing my attempted obeisance.[1]

"Hwang," I answered.

"Hwang? Are you Chinese?"

Her question caught me off-guard. I was used to hearing such queries   5 from non-Asians who think Asians all look alike, but never from one of my own people. Of course, the only Koreans I knew were my parents and their friends, people who've never asked me where I came from, since they knew better than I.

I ransacked my mind for the Korean words that would tell her who I was. It's always struck me as funny (in a mirthless sort of way) that I can more readily say "I am Korean" in Spanish, German, and even Latin than I can in the language of my ancestry. In the end, I told her in English.

The dry-cleaning woman squinted as though trying to see past the glare of my strangeness, repeating my surname under her breath. "Oh, *Fxuang,*" she said, doubling over with laughter. "You don't know how to speak your name."

I flinched. Perhaps I was particularly sensitive at the time, having just dropped out of graduate school. I had torn up my map for the future, the one that said not only where I was going but who I was. My sense of identity was already disintegrating.

---

1. *obeisance:* a gesture or movement that expresses respect or deference.

When I got home, I called my parents to ask why they had never bothered to correct me. "Big deal," my mother said, sounding more flippant than I knew she intended. (Like many people who learn English in a classroom, she uses idioms that don't always fit the occasion.) "So what if you can't pronounce your name? You are American," she said.

Though I didn't challenge her explanation, it left me unsatisfied. The   10
fact is, my cultural identity is hardly that clear-cut.

My parents immigrated to this country 30 years ago, two years before I was born. They told me often, while I was growing up, that, if I wanted to, I could be president someday, that here my grasp would be as long as my reach.

To ensure that I reaped all the advantages of this country, my parents saw to it that I became fully assimilated. So, like any American of my generation, I whiled away my youth strolling malls and talking on the phone, rhapsodizing over Andrew McCarthy's blue eyes, or analyzing the meaning of a certain upperclassman's offer of a ride to the Homecoming football game.

To my parents, I am all American, and the sacrifices they made in leaving Korea—including my mispronounced name—pale in comparison to the opportunities those sacrifices gave me. They do not see that I straddle two cultures, nor that I feel displaced in the only country I know. I identify with Americans, but Americans do not identify with me. I've never known what it's like to belong to a community—neither one at large, nor of an extended family. I know more about Europe than the continent my ancestors unmistakably come from. I sometimes wonder, as I did that day in the dry cleaner's, if I would be a happier person had my parents stayed in Korea.

I first began to consider this thought around the time I decided to go to graduate school. It had been a compromise: my parents wanted me to go to law school; I wanted to skip the starched-collar track and be a writer—the hungrier the better. But after 20-some years of following their wishes and meeting all of their expectations, I couldn't bring myself to disobey or disappoint. A writing career is riskier than law, I remember thinking. If I'm a failure and my life is a washout, then what does that make my parents' lives?

I know that many of my friends had to choose between pleasing their   15
parents and being true to themselves. But for the children of immigrants, the choice seems more complicated, a happy outcome impossible. By making the biggest move of their lives for me, my parents indentured me to the largest debt imaginable—I owe them the fulfillment of their hopes for me.

It tore me up inside to suppress my dream, but I went to school for a Ph.D. in English literature, thinking I had found the perfect compromise. I would be able to write at least about books while pursuing a graduate degree. Predictably, it didn't work out. How could I labor for five years in a program I had no passion for? When I finally left school, my parents were disappointed, but since it wasn't what they wanted me to do, they weren't devastated. I, on the other hand, felt I was staring at the bottom of the abyss. I had seen the flaw in my life of halfwayness, in my planned life of compromises.

I hadn't thought about my love life, but I had a vague plan to make concessions there, too. Though they raised me as an American, my parents expect me to marry someone Korean and give them grandchildren who look like them. This didn't seem like such a huge request when I was 14, but now I don't know what I'm going to do. I've never been in love with someone I dated, or dated someone I loved. (Since I can't bring myself even to entertain the thought of marrying the non-Korean men I'm attracted to, I've been dating only those I know I can stay clear-headed about.) And as I near that age when the question of marriage stalks every relationship, I can't help but wonder if my parents' expectations are responsible for the lack of passion in my life.

My parents didn't want their daughter to be Korean, but they don't want her fully American, either. Children of immigrants are living paradoxes. We are the first generation and the last. We are in this country for its opportunities, yet filial duty binds us. When my parents boarded the plane, they knew they were embarking on a rough trip. I don't think they imagined the rocks in the path of their daughter who can't even pronounce her own name.

THINKING CRITICALLY ABOUT THE READING

1. Why is not being able to properly pronounce her name in Korean so important to Hwang? What does it signify for her about her life in America?

2. Why is being a success so important for Hwang? Why might it be more important for her than for the average American?

3. Hwang writes in paragraph 16: "I had seen the flaw in my life of halfwayness, in my planned life of compromises." What does she mean?

4. What does Hwang's plight reveal about whether or not English should be our national language?

5. Is Hwang's complaint about not knowing whether she is Korean or American somewhat diminished by the fact that she writes well in English? Explain.

6. If her language is not the only but perhaps one of the strongest indicators of who she is, hasn't Hwang already shown herself to be an American? Or is the issue more complicated? Explain.

WRITING SUGGESTIONS: DEBATING THE ISSUE

1. While it's no secret that English is the common language of the United States, few of us know, as Myriam Marquez is quick to remind us, that our country has been "careful not to promote a government-mandated official language"(7). Why do you suppose that our federal government has chosen to keep its hands off the language issue? If it has not been necessary to mandate English in the past, why do you think that people now feel a need to declare English the "official language" of the United States? Write an essay in which you give your own opinion on this issue.

2. Robert D. King explains that "[i]n much of the world, ethnic unity and cultural identification are routinely defined by language" (17). To what extent is this true in the United States? Why is it sometimes difficult for nonnative speakers of English who immigrate to the United States to take ownership of Standard English? Write an essay in which you explore what it means to take ownership of language. Does one need this ownership to succeed?

3. Barbara Mellix tells us what it was like growing up torn between the worlds of Black English and Standard English, and Myriam Marquez explains the bilingual world she shares with her parents. What insights, if any, do their personal reflections give us into the English-only debate? Where do you think each of these writers stands on the issue of English-only?

4. Write an essay in which you frame the English-only debate as a political issue, a social issue, an economic issue, or some combination of the three. In this context, what do you see as the relationship between language and power?

5. The selections from King and Krauthammer address immigrant assimilation from an academic viewpoint, but it is a highly personal subject for those who come here. After all, they must confront their English-language deficiencies right from the start. When American students study a foreign language at school, however, almost all of the speaking and instruction is in English until they progress far enough to understand instruction and detailed conversations in the other language. Think about your classroom experience in learning a foreign language. What are the most difficult challenges for you in language studies? Are you comfortable expressing yourself in the language? If you absolutely needed to communicate in that language, how well could you do it? How do you respond to people who are just learning English? Do you get impatient with them or assume that they are poorly educated? Write an essay about how well you think you would do if suddenly you had to function in another country with a different language. How would you deal with those who were impatient with your language skills or dismissive of you? How self-conscious do you think you would be?

6. Readers have strong feelings about and respond both positively and negatively to Leticia Salais's views on Spanglish, bilingualism, childrearing, and her level of appreciation for her own heritage. Write an essay in which you defend or take issue with the way she has thought about her situation at various points in her life and the way she has acted as a result. Would you have acted in the same way? If not, how might you have approached the situation differently?

7. Caroline Hwang was born in America and writes well enough in English to be an editor, a freelance writer, and the author of a novel. But, as she writes in paragraph 13, her parents "do not see that I straddle two cultures, nor that I feel displaced in the only country I know. I identify with Americans, but Americans do not identify with me." Write an essay in which you examine Hwang's case and the case of others who find themselves in the same position. Did her parents fail her in not giving her a foundation in their own language and culture that was the equal of her American cultural heritage? Did our educational system put an exclusive and, therefore, detrimental emphasis on English and Americanization? Does Hwang herself bear any responsibility for her predicament? What could have been done to eliminate or, at least, alleviate her feelings of "halfwayness"?

8. The Federal Maritime Commission has issued a clear explanation of the law with respect to the "Ability to Speak English" in its Basis for Discrimination Web site: www.fmc.gov/bureaus/equal_employment_nopportunity/ basisfordescrimination.asp. It reads as follows:

> Employers who require that their employees be able to speak English must show that fluency in English is a bona fide occupational qualification or a business necessity, for the position in question. Further, an employer's rule which requires employees to speak English at all times, including during their work break and lunch time, is one example of an employment practice which discriminates against persons whose primary language is not English.

> However, an employer may require employees to speak only English at certain times and this would not be discriminatory, if the employer shows that the rule is justified by business necessity. The employer must clearly inform its employees of the general circumstances under which they are required to speak only English and the consequences of violating the rule.

After considering both the cartoon above and the Maritime Commission guidelines, write an essay about the potential problems in the workplace that could arise when non–English speakers have certain jobs. Why do some employment opportunities require English while others do not? Is the double standard discriminatory or appropriate, in your opinion?

9

LANGUAGE DEBATE: WHAT'S ALL THE FUSS ABOUT NATURAL, ORGANIC, LOCAL FOODS?

Few topics elicit more interest and evoke more discussion than the food we eat. Bookstores abound with books about food; numerous cooking shows on television and at least one dedicated cable channel celebrate the seemingly infinite variety of ingredients and ways to prepare them; self-described "foodies" spend large sums of money, time, and energy to book a table at an exclusive restaurant and savor the perfect meal. Food has been an inspiration for writers and painters, a weapon in war-torn countries, and the mainstay of many a multinational industry. But how many of us stop to think—really think—about the foods we eat every day? Do we know where the food we ate this morning was actually grown? Do we know whether or not chemical fertilizers and pesticides were used to grow it? Do we know, finally, if the food we eat is really good for us?

Whether we actually know a lot about the food we eat or not, we all tend to have opinions about it. Some people swear by the benefits of natural, organic, locally grown whole foods and are willing to pay extra for them. Others embrace fashionable diets and food trends touting firmer bodies, longer life, or better health. Still others habitually buy and consume the skillfully marketed and imaginatively packaged processed foods that the food industry saturates the marketplace with each year—foods that taste good but are of questionable nutritional value.

You can see evidence of this array of attitudes toward food by watching television almost any evening. A significant proportion of the commercials that you'll see will be touting health regimens, snack foods, gourmet products, soft drinks, nutritional supplements, heat-and-eat meals, weight loss products, beer, supermarkets, and restaurant chains. These seemingly disparate goods share a common thread: Whether the target market is upscale or downscale, interested in healthy eating or only in what tastes good, convenience seems to be the name of the game. In fact, some would say that we have become a society of grazers, eating our meals on the run. As a nation we tend to cook less and eat out more than we did in generations past, and many of us flock to restaurants that serve super-size portions or advertise "all-you-can-eat" specials. In a closely related development, obesity has become one of the most pressing public health problems in America over the last twenty years. Is this the way we want to identify ourselves and our relationship with food? Probably not.

To start our discussion of this issue, we have selected six writers with different perspectives on the subject of food in America. In the first reading, "Putting It Back Together Again: Processed Foods," Michael Pollan explains how corn and soybeans have come to play such dominant roles in America's food industry and reveals how food manufacturers have managed to pack more calories into the average American's diet each day. In "Called Home," Barbara Kingsolver discusses how her family took a year off to explore the personal and environmental benefits of growing their own food and buying locally what they could not produce. She explains how each of us could benefit from a course in agricultural basics so that we could better understand what goes into the production of the foods we eat.

The connotations of *natural*—like *fresh, organic, local,* and *wholesome*—let consumers think they are buying something that will be good for them. Not necessarily so, says Sarah Federman in "What's Natural about Our Natural Products?" We know *natural* sounds good, but because the word is unregulated, it is never really clear what it means when attached to any given product. In "Claims Crazy: Which Can You Believe?" nutritionist Bonnie Liebman examines this and other, similar claims that food manufacturers put in their advertisements and on their labels. She exposes unreliable, unregulated "structure/function claims" that use euphemism to sell products, and she tells how to differentiate these specious claims from those that are based on scientific evidence.

In a similar vein, Field Maloney questions the organic-food movement in "Is Whole Foods Wholesome?" Using the Whole Foods supermarket chain as his case in point, he wonders whether "the organic-food movement is in danger of exacerbating the growing gap between rich and poor in this country by contributing to a two-tiered national food supply, with healthy food for the rich." Finally, community food systems expert Mark Winne offers his commentary on the food gap in America in "The Poor Get Diabetes, the Rich Get Local and Organic," where he discusses two promising programs for closing this gap and democratizing the nation's food supply.

Putting It Back Together Again: Processed Foods

MICHAEL POLLAN

Writer, journalist, and educator Michael Pollan was born in 1955 and grew up on Long Island. In 1977 he graduated from Bennington College. He attended Mansfield College, Oxford University, and received a master's degree in English from Columbia University in 1981. As a writer, Pollan is fascinated by food, agriculture, gardening, drugs, and architecture—those places where the human and natural worlds intersect. His award-winning nonfiction books include *Second Nature: A Gardener's Education* (1991), *A Place of My Own: The Education of an Amateur Builder* (1997), *The Botany of Desire: A Plant's-Eye View of the World* (2001), *The Omnivore's Dilemma: A Natural History of Four Meals* (2006), and *In Defense of Food: An Eater's Manifesto* (2008). Since 1987 Pollan has been a contributing writer to the *New York Times Magazine,* and his articles on various food-related topics have appeared in *Esquire, Harper's, Gourmet, Condé Nast Traveler, Mother Jones,* and *Vogue.* He has taught at the University of Pittsburgh and the University of Wisconsin and is currently the John S. and James L. Knight Professor of Journalism at the University of California, Berkeley, where he directs the Knight Program in Science and Environmental Journalism.

In the following selection, excerpted from *The Omnivore's Dilemma,* Pollan examines the world of processed foods and questions whatever happened to "good old food." As you read, note how Pollan highlights the food industry's use of jargon and doublespeak to manipulate the reality of what's happening to our food.

WRITING TO DISCOVER: *Take a moment to reflect on your experiences with food. How would you describe your daily diet and your eating habits? Do you try to eat a nutritionally balanced diet, or are you a junk food junkie? Where do you usually eat? Do you regularly take time out to have a sit-down meal with others, or do you tend to eat on the run?*

The dream of liberating food from nature is as old as eating. People began processing food to keep nature from taking it back: What is spoilage, after all, if not nature, operating through her proxy microorganisms, repossessing our hard-won lunch? So we learned to salt and dry and cure and pickle in the first age of food processing, and to can, freeze, and vacuum-pack in the second. These technologies were blessings, freeing people from nature's cycles of abundance and scarcity, as well as from the tyranny of the calendar or locale: Now a New Englander could eat sweet corn, or something reminiscent of it, in January, and taste a pineapple for the first time in his life. As Massimo Montanari, an Italian food historian, points out, the fresh, local, and seasonal food we prize today was for most of human history "a form of slavery," since it left us utterly at the mercy of the local vicissitudes of nature.

Even after people had learned the rudiments of preserving food, however, the dream of liberating food from nature continued to flourish—indeed, to expand in ambition and confidence. In the third age of food processing, which begins with the end of World War II, merely preserving the fruits of nature was deemed too modest: The goal now was to improve on nature. The twentieth-century prestige of technology and convenience combined with advances in marketing to push aside butter to make shelf space for margarine, replace fruit juice with juice drinks and then entirely juice-free drinks like Tang, cheese with Cheez Whiz, and whipped cream with Cool Whip.

Corn, a species that had been a modest beneficiary of the first two ages of food processing (having taken well to the can and the freezer), really came into its own during the third. You would never know it without reading the ingredient label (a literary genre unknown until the third age), but corn is the key constituent of all four of these processed foods. Along with the soybean, its rotational partner in the field, corn has done more than any other species to help the food industry realize the dream of freeing food from nature's limitations and seducing the omnivore into eating more of a single plant than anyone would ever have thought possible.

In fact, you would be hard-pressed to find a late-model processed food that isn't made from corn or soybeans. In the typical formulation, corn supplies the carbohydrates (sugars and starches) and soy the protein; the fat can come from either plant. (Remember what George Naylor said about the real produce of his farm: not corn and soybeans but "energy and protein.") The longer the ingredient label on a food, the more fractions of corn and soybeans you will find in it. They supply the essential building blocks, and from those two plants (plus a handful of synthetic additives) a food scientist can construct just about any processed food he or she can dream up.

A few years ago, in the days when "food security" meant something 5
very different than it does today, I had the chance to visit one of the small handful of places where this kind of work is done. The Bell Institute, a leafy corporate campus on the outskirts of Minneapolis, is the research-and-development laboratory for General Mills, the sixth-largest food company in the world. Here nine hundred food scientists spend their days designing the future of food—its flavor, texture, and packaging.

Much of their work is highly secretive, but nowhere more so than in the cereals area. Deep in the heart of the heart of the Bell Institute, down in the bowels of the laboratory, you come to a warren of windowless rooms called, rather grandly, the Institute of Cereal Technology.

I was permitted to pass through a high-security conference room furnished with a horseshoe-shaped table that had a pair of headphones at every seat. This was the institute's inner sanctum, the cereal situation room, where General Mills executives gather to hear briefings about new products.

The secrecy surrounding the successor to Cocoa Pebbles struck me as laughable, and I said so. But as an executive explained to me, "Recipes are not intellectual property; you can't patent a new cereal. All you can hope for is to have the market to yourself for a few months to establish your brand before a competitor knocks off the product. So we're very careful not to show our hand." For the same reason, the institute operates its own machine shop, where it designs and builds the machines that give breakfast cereals their shapes, making it that much harder for a competitor to knock off, say, a new marshmallow bit shaped to resemble a shooting star. In the interests of secrecy, the food scientists would not talk to me about current projects, only past failures, like the breakthrough cereal in the shapes of little bowling pins and balls. "In focus group the kids loved it," the product's rueful inventor told me, "but the mothers didn't like the idea of kids bowling their breakfast across the table." Which is why bowling pin cereal never showed up in your supermarket.

In many ways breakfast cereal is the prototypical processed food: four cents' worth of commodity corn (or some other equally cheap grain) transformed into four dollars' worth of processed food. What an alchemy! Yet it is performed straightforwardly enough: by taking several of the output streams issuing from a wet mill (corn meal, corn starch, corn sweetener, as well as a handful of tinier chemical fractions) and then assembling them into an attractively novel form. Further value is added in the form of color and taste, then branding and packaging. Oh yes, and vitamins and minerals, which are added to give the product a sheen of healthfulness and to replace the nutrients that are lost whenever whole foods are processed. On the strength of this alchemy the cereals group generates higher profits for General Mills than any other division. Since the raw materials in processed foods are so abundant and cheap (ADM and Cargill will gladly sell them to all comers) protecting whatever is special about the value you add to them is imperative.

I think it was at General Mills that I first heard the term "food system." Since then, I've seen in the pages of *Food Technology,* the monthly bible of the food-processing industry, that this term seems to be taking over from plain old "food." Food system is glossier and more high-tech than food, I guess; it also escapes some of the negative connotations that got attached to "processed food" during the sixties. It's probably as good a term as any when you're describing, as that magazine routinely does, new edible materials constructed from "textured vegetable protein," or a nutraceutical breakfast cereal so fortified with green tea, grape seed extract, and antioxidants that it's not even called a cereal but a "healthy heart system."

Exactly what corn is doing in such food systems has less to do with   10
nutrition or taste than with economics. For the dream of liberating food
from nature, which began as a dream of the eaters (to make it less perishable), is now primarily a dream of the feeders—of the corporations that
sell us our food. No one was clamoring for synthetic cheese, or a cereal
shaped like a bowling pin; processed food has become largely a supply-
driven business—the business of figuring out clever ways to package and
market the glut of commodities coming off the farm and out of the wet
mills. Today the great advantages of processing food redound to the processors themselves. For them, nature is foremost a problem—not so much
of perishable food (though that's always a concern when your market is
global) as of perishable profits.

Like every other food chain, the industrial food chain is rooted at
either end in a natural system: the farmer's field at one end, and the human
organism at the other. From the capitalist's point of view, both of these
systems are less than ideal.

The farm, being vulnerable to the vicissitudes of weather and pests,
is prone to crises of over- and underproduction, both of which can hurt
business. Rising raw material prices cut into profits, obviously enough. Yet
the potential boon of falling raw material prices—which should allow you
to sell a lot more of your product at a lower price—can't be realized in the
case of food because of the special nature of your consumer, who can eat
only so much food, no matter how cheap it gets. (Food industry executives used to call this the problem of the "fixed stomach"; economists
speak of "inelastic demand.") Nature has cursed the companies working
the middle of the food chain with a recipe for falling rates of profits.

The growth of the American food industry will always bump up against
this troublesome biological fact: Try as we might, each of us can eat only
about fifteen hundred pounds of food a year. Unlike many other products—
CDs, say, or shoes—there's a natural limit to how much food we can each
consume without exploding. What this means for the food industry is that
its natural rate of growth is somewhere around 1 percent per year—1 percent being the annual growth rate of the American population. The problem is that Wall Street won't tolerate such an anemic rate of growth.

This leaves companies like General Mills and McDonald's with two
options if they hope to grow faster than the population: figure out how
to get people to spend more money for the same three-quarters of a ton
of food, or entice them to actually eat more than that. The two strategies.
are not mutually exclusive, of course, and the food industry energetically
pursues them both at the same time. Which is good news indeed for the
hero of our story, for it happens that turning cheap corn into complex
food systems is an excellent way to achieve both goals.

Building processed food out of a commodity like corn doesn't com-   15
pletely cushion you from the vicissitudes of nature, but it comes close.

The more complex your food system, the more you can practice "substitutionism" without altering the taste or appearance of the product. So if the price of hydrogenated fat or lecithin derived from corn spikes one day, you simply switch to fat or lecithin from soy, and the consumer will never know the difference. (This is why ingredient labels says things like "Contains one or more of the following: corn, soybean, or sunflower oil.") As a management consultant once advised his food industry clients, "The further a product's identity moves from a specific raw material—that is, the more processing steps involved—the less vulnerable is its processor" to the variability of nature.

In fact, there are lots of good reasons to complicate your product—or, as the industry prefers to say, to "add value" to it. Processing food can add months, even years, to its shelf life, allowing you to market globally. Complicating your product also allows you to capture more of the money a consumer spends on food. Of a dollar spent on a whole food such as eggs, $0.40 finds its way back to the farmer. By comparison; George Naylor will see only $0.04 of every dollar spent on corn sweeteners; ADM and Coca-Cola and General Mills capture most of the rest. (Every farmer I've ever met eventually gets around to telling the story about the food industry executive who declared, "There's money to be made in food, unless you're trying to grow it.") When Tyson food scientists devised the chicken nugget in 1983, a cheap bulk commodity—chicken—overnight became a high-value-added product, and most of the money Americans spend on chicken moved from the farmer's pocket to the processor's.

As Tyson understood, you want to be selling something more than a commodity, something more like a service: novelty, convenience, status, fortification, lately even medicine. The problem is, a value-added product made from a cheap commodity can itself become a commodity, so cheap and abundant are the raw materials. That lesson runs straight through the history of a company like General Mills, which started out in 1926 as a mill selling whole wheat flour: ground wheat. When that product became a cheap commodity, the company kept ahead of the competition by processing the grain a bit more, creating bleached and then "enriched" flour. Now they were adding value, selling not just wheat but an idea of purity and health, too. In time, however, even enriched white flour became a commodity, so General Mills took another step away from nature—from the farm and the plants in question—by inventing cake mixes and sweetened breakfast cereals. Now they were selling convenience, with a side of grain and corn sweetener, and today they're beginning to sell cereals that sound an awful lot like medicines. And so it goes, the rushing stream of ever cheaper agricultural commodities driving food companies to figure out new and ever more elaborate ways to add value and so induce us to buy more.

When I was in Minneapolis I spoke to a General Mills vice president who was launching a new line of organic TV dinners, a product that at first blush sounded like an oxymoron. The ingredient list went on forever, brimming with additives and obscure fractions of corn: maltodextrin, corn starch, xanthan gum. It seems that even organic food has succumbed to the economic logic of processing. The executive patiently explained that selling unprocessed or minimally processed whole foods will always be a fool's game, since the price of agricultural commodities tends to fall over time, whether they're organic or not. More food coming off the farm leads to either falling profits—or more processing.

The other problem with selling whole foods, he explained, is that it will always be hard to distinguish one company's corn or chickens or apples from any other company's. It makes much more sense to turn the corn into a brand-name cereal, the chicken into a TV dinner, and the apples into a component in a nutraceutical food system.

This last is precisely what one company profiled in a recent issue of   20
Food Technology has done. TreeTop has developed a "low-moisture, naturally sweetened apple piece infused with a red-wine extract." Just eighteen grams of these apple pieces have the same amount of cancer-fighting "flavonoid phenols as five glasses of wine and the dietary fiber equivalent of one whole apple." Remember the sixties dream of an entire meal served in a pill, like the Jetsons? We've apparently moved from the meal-in-a-pill to the pill-in-a-meal, which is to say, not very far at all. Either way, the message is: We need food scientists to feed us. Of course, it was fortified breakfast cereal that first showed the way, by supplying more vitamins and minerals than any mere grain could hope to. Nature, these products implied, was no match for food science.

The news of TreeTop's breakthrough came in a recent *Food Technology* trend story titled "Getting More Fruits and Vegetables into Food." I had thought fruits and vegetables were *already* foods, and so didn't need to be gotten into them, but I guess that just shows I'm stuck in the food past. Evidently we're moving into the fourth age of food processing, in which the processed food will be infinitely better (i.e., contain more of whatever science has determined to be the good stuff) than the whole foods on which they're based. The food industry has gazed upon nature and found it wanting—and has gotten to work improving it.

Back in the seventies, a New York food additive manufacturer called International Flavors & Fragrances used its annual report to defend itself against the rising threat of "natural foods" and explain why we were better off eating synthetics. Natural ingredients, the company pointed out rather scarily, are a "wild mixture of substances created by plants and animals for completely non-food purposes—their survival and reproduction." These dubious substances "came to be consumed by humans at their own risk."

Now, thanks to the ingenuity of modern food science, we had a choice. We could eat things designed by humans for the express purpose of being eaten by people—or eat "substances" designed by natural selection for its own purposes: to, say, snooker a bee or lift a wing or (eek!) make a baby. The meal of the future would be fabricated "in the laboratory out of a wide variety of materials," as one food historian wrote in 1973, including not only algae and fungi but also petrochemicals. Protein would be extracted directly from petroleum and then "spun and woven into 'animal' muscle—long, wrist-thick tubes of 'filet steak.'" (Come to think of it, agribusiness has long since mastered this trick of turning petroleum into steak, though it still needs corn and cattle to do it.)

All that's really changed since the high-tech food future of the sixties is that the laboratory materials out of which these meals will be constructed are nominally natural—the relative prestige of nature and modern chemistry having traded places in the years since the rise of environmentalism. And besides, why go to the trouble and expense of manufacturing food from petroleum when there is such a flood of cheap carbon coming off the farm? So instead of creating foods whole cloth from completely synthetic materials, the industry is building them from fortified apple bits, red-wine extract, flavor fractions derived from oranges, isoflavones from soy, meat substitutes fashioned from mycoprotein, and resistant starches derived from corn. ("Natural raspberry flavor" doesn't mean the flavor came from a raspberry; it may well have been derived from corn, just not from something synthetic.) But the underlying reductionist premise—that a food is nothing more than the sum of its nutrients—remains undisturbed. So we break down the plants and animals into their component parts and then reassemble them into high-value-added food systems. The omnivore's predilection to eat a variety of species is tricked by this protean plant, and even the biological limit on his appetite is overcome.

Resistant starch, the last novelty on that list of ingredients, has the corn refiners particularly excited today. They've figured out how to tease a new starch from corn that is virtually indigestible. You would not think this is a particularly good thing for a food to be, unless of course your goal is to somehow get around the biological limit on how much each of us can eat in a year. Since the body can't break down resistant starch, it slips through the digestive track without ever turning into calories of glucose—a particular boon, we're told, for diabetics. When fake sugars and fake fats are joined by fake starches, the food industry will at long last have overcome the dilemma of the fixed stomach: whole meals you can eat as often or as much of as you like, since this food will leave no trace. Meet the ultimate—the utterly elastic!—industrial eater. 25

THINKING CRITICALLY ABOUT THE READING

1. According to Pollan, what are the "three ages" of food processing? What sets the third age apart from the first two?

2. In paragraphs 6–8, Pollan describes the Institute of Cereal Technology at General Mills. What were your impressions of this facility and its methods? Does this knowledge affect your attitude toward breakfast cereals? Explain.

3. What is a "food system"? How is it different from "food" or "processed food"? In general, how does the language of the food industry that Pollan discusses strike you? On a scale of 1 to 10, with 1 being very objective and 10 being very deceptive, how objective is the industry's language?

4. What major problem confronts the American food industry as it tries to grow? How have companies attempted to solve this problem? What problems for the American public have been created in the process?

5. Pollan quotes a management consultant to the food industry as saying, "The further a product's identity moves from a specific raw material—that is, the more processing steps involved—the less vulnerable is its processor" (15) to the variability of nature. What does this mean to you, an American consumer?

6. Pollan cites chicken nuggets as an example of a "high-value-added product." What other high-value-added products do you regularly consume? For whom is the value added—the consumer? The farmer? The processor?

Called Home

BARBARA KINGSOLVER

The popular and prolific author Barbara Kingsolver was born in 1955 in eastern Kentucky. Although she has kept a journal since she was a child, she never dreamed that she might one day become a published writer. After graduating from DePaul University with a major in biology, Kingsolver traveled in Greece and France, taking a variety of jobs to support herself. After returning to the United States she earned a master's degree in biology and ecology at the University of Arizona. It was here that she took a writing course from the celebrated novelist Francine Prose and decided to try to make a living as a writer. Kingsolver first worked as a science writer and later as a features writer for journals and newspapers. She has since published two collections of her essays, *High Tide in Tucson* (1995) and *Small Wonder* (2002). In addition to several volumes of nonfiction, poetry, and an oral history, she has also written five novels, *The Bean Trees* (1988), *Animal Dreams* (1990), *Pigs in Heaven* (1993), *The Poisonwood Bible* (1997), and *Prodigal Summer* (2002). Most of her work, both fiction and nonfiction, features social commentary on some level.

In "Called Home," taken from her most recent book, *Animal, Vegetable, Miracle: A Year of Food Life* (2007), Kingsolver weighs in on the debate about food that is currently center stage in America. She tells the story of how Americans in a generation or two have drifted away from their agricultural roots and no longer know how foods grow. She believes that Americans need to give up their addiction to processed foods and begin to cultivate a "genuine food culture."

WRITING TO DISCOVER: *What do you know about the foods that grow in your region and how to care for them? Have you ever had your own vegetable garden or helped someone with theirs? What did you learn from this experience? If you have not had firsthand experience with a garden, where do you get your fruits and vegetables?*

I live now in a county whose economic base is farming. A disastrous summer will mean some of our neighbors will lose their farms. Others will have to keep farming *and* go looking for a job at the end of a long commute. We'll feel the effects in school enrollments, local businesses, shifts in land use and tax structure. The health of our streams, soils, and forests is also at stake, as lost farms get sold to developers whose business is to rearrange (drastically) the topsoil and everything on it. When I recognize good agricultural sense, though, I'm not just thinking of my town but also my species. It's not a trivial difference: praying for or against rainfall during a drought. You can argue that wishes don't count, but humans are good at making our dreams manifest and we do, historically speaking, get what we wish for. What are the just deserts for a species too selfish or preoccupied to hope for rain when the land outside is dying? Should we be buried under the topsoil in our own clean cars, to make room for wiser creatures?

We'd surely do better, if only we *knew* any better. In two generations we've transformed ourselves from a rural to an urban nation. North American children begin their school year around Labor Day and finish at the beginning of June with no idea that this arrangement was devised to free up children's labor when it was needed on the farm. Most people of my grandparents' generation had an intuitive sense of agricultural basics: when various fruits and vegetables come into season, which ones keep through the winter, how to preserve the others. On what day autumn's first frost will likely fall on their county, and when to expect the last one in spring. Which crops can be planted before the last frost, and which must wait. Which grains are autumn-planted. What an asparagus patch looks like in August. Most importantly: what animals and vegetables thrive in one's immediate region and how to live well on those, with little else thrown into the mix beyond a bag of flour, a pinch of salt, and a handful of coffee. Few people of my generation, and approximately none of our children, could answer any of those questions, let alone all. This knowledge has vanished from our culture.

We also have largely convinced ourselves it wasn't too important. Consider how Americans might respond to a proposal that agriculture was to become a mandatory subject in all schools, alongside reading and mathematics. A fair number of parents would get hot under the collar to see their kids' attention being pulled away from the essentials of grammar, the all-important trigonometry, to make room for down-on-the-farm stuff. The baby boom psyche embraces a powerful presumption that education is a key to moving *away* from manual labor, and dirt—two undeniable ingredients of farming. It's good enough for us that somebody, somewhere, knows food production well enough to serve the rest of us with all we need to eat, each day of our lives.

If that is true, why isn't it good enough for someone else to know multiplication and the contents of the Bill of Rights? Is the story of bread, from tilled ground to our table, less relevant to our lives than the history of the thirteen colonies? Couldn't one make a case for the relevance of a subject that informs choices we make *daily*—as in, What's for dinner? Isn't ignorance of our food sources causing problems as diverse as overdependence on petroleum, and an epidemic of diet-related diseases?

If this [essay] is not exactly an argument for reinstating food-production classes in schools (and it might be), it does contain a lot of what you might learn there. From our family's gas-station beginnings we have traveled far enough to discover ways of taking charge of one's food, and even knowing where it has been. This is the story of a year in which we made every

5

attempt to feed ourselves animals and vegetables whose provenance we really knew. We tried to wring most of the petroleum out of our food chain, even if that meant giving up some things. Our highest shopping goal was to get our food from so close to home, we'd know the person who grew it. Often that turned out to be *us*, as we learned to produce more of what we needed, starting with dirt, seeds, and enough knowledge to muddle through. Or starting with baby animals and enough sense to refrain from naming them.

This is not a how-to [essay] aimed at getting you cranking out your own food. We ourselves live in a region where every other house has a garden out back, but to many urban people the idea of growing your food must seem as plausible as writing and conducting your own symphonies for your personal listening pleasure. If that is your case, think of the agricultural parts of the story as a music appreciation course for food—acquainting yourself with the composers and conductors can improve the quality of your experience. Knowing the secret natural history of potatoes, melons, or asparagus gives you a leg up on detecting whether those in your market are wholesome kids from a nearby farm, or vagrants who idled away their precious youth in a boxcar. Knowing how foods grow is to know how and when to look for them; such expertise is useful for certain kinds of people, namely, the ones who eat, no matter where they live or grocery shop.

Absence of that knowledge has rendered us a nation of wary label-readers, oddly uneasy in our obligate relationship with the things we eat. We call our food animals by different names after they're dead, presumably sparing ourselves any vision of the beefs and the porks running around on actual hooves. Our words for unhealthy contamination—"soilea" or "dirty"—suggest that if we really knew the number-one ingredient of a garden, we'd all head straight into therapy. I used to take my children's friends out to the garden to warm them up to the idea of eating vegetables, but this strategy sometimes backfired: they'd back away slowly saying, "Oh *man*, those things touched *dirt!*" Adults do the same by pretending it all comes from the clean, well-lighted grocery store. We're like petulant teenagers rejecting our mother. We *know* we came out of her, but *ee-ew*.

We don't know beans about beans. Asparagus, potatoes, turkey drumsticks—you name it, we don't have a clue how the world makes it. I usually think I'm exaggerating the scope of the problem, and then I'll encounter an editor (at a well-known nature magazine) who's nixing the part of my story that refers to pineapples growing from the ground. She insisted they grew on trees. Or, I'll have a conversation like this one:

"What's new on the farm?" asks my friend, a lifelong city dweller who likes for me to keep her posted by phone. She's a gourmet cook, she cares about the world, and has been around a lot longer than I have. This particular conversation was in early spring, so I told her what was up in the garden: peas, potatoes, spinach.

"Wait a minute," she said. "When you say, 'The potatoes are up,' what   10
do you mean?" She paused, formulating her question: "What part of a
potato comes *up?*"

"Um, the plant part," I said. "The stems and leaves."

"Wow," she said. "I never knew a potato *had* a plant part."

Many bright people are really in the dark about vegetable life. Biology
teachers face kids in classrooms who may not even believe in the meta-
morphosis of bud to flower to fruit and seed, but rather, some continuum
of pansies becoming petunias becoming chrysanthemums; that's the only
reality they witness as landscapers come to campuses and city parks and
surreptitiously yank out one flower before it fades from its prime, replacing it with another. (My biology-professor brother pointed this out to
me.) The same disconnection from natural processes may be at the heart
of our country's shift away from believing in evolution. In the past, principles of natural selection and change over time made sense to kids who'd
watched it all unfold. Whether or not they knew the terms, farm families
understood the processes well enough to imitate them: culling, selecting,
and improving their herds and crops. For modern kids who intuitively
believe in the spontaneous generation of fruits and vegetables in the produce section, trying to get their minds around the slow speciation of the
plant kingdom may be a stretch. . . .

When we walked as a nation away from the land, our knowledge of
food production fell away from us like dirt in a laundry-soap commercial.
Now, it's fair to say, the majority of us don't want to be farmers, see farmers,
pay farmers, or hear their complaints. Except as straw-chewing figures in
children's books, we don't quite believe in them anymore. When we give it
a thought, we mostly consider the food industry to be a *thing* rather than a
person. We obligingly give 85 cents of our every food dollar to that thing,
too—the processors, marketers, and transporters. And we complain about
the high price of organic meats and vegetables that might send back more
than three nickels per buck to the farmers: those actual humans putting
seeds in the ground, harvesting, attending livestock births, standing in the
fields at dawn casting their shadows upon our sustenance. There seems to be
some reason we don't want to compensate or think about these hardwork-
ing people. In the grocery store checkout corral, we're more likely to learn
which TV stars are secretly fornicating than to inquire as to the whereabouts
of the people who grew the cucumbers and melons in our carts.

This drift away from our agricultural roots is a natural consequence   15
of migration from the land to the factory, which is as old as the Industrial
Revolution. But we got ourselves uprooted entirely by a drastic reconfigu-
ration of U.S. farming, beginning just after World War II. Our munitions
plants, challenged to beat their swords into plowshares, retooled to make
ammonium nitrate surpluses into chemical fertilizers instead of explosives.
The next explosions were yields on midwestern corn and soybean fields.
It seemed like a good thing, but some officials saw these new surpluses as

reason to dismantle New Deal policies that had helped farmers weather the economic uncertainties notorious to their vocation. Over the next decades, nudged by industry, the government rewrote the rules on commodity subsidies so these funds did not safeguard farmers, but instead guaranteed a supply of cheap corn and soybeans.

These two crops, formerly food for people and animals, became something entirely new: a standardized raw material for a new extractive industry, not so different from logging or mining. Mills and factories were designed for a multibranched production line as complex as the one that turns iron and aluminum ores into the likes of automobiles, paper clips, and antiperspirants. But instead, this new industry made piles of corn and soybeans into high-fructose corn syrup, hydrogenated oils, and thousands of other starch- or oil-based chemicals. Cattle and chickens were brought in off the pasture into intensely crowded and mechanized CAFOs (concentrated animal feeding operations) where corn—which is no part of a cow's natural diet, by the way—could be turned cheaply and quickly into animal flesh. All these different products, in turn, rolled on down the new industrial food pipeline to be processed into the soft drinks, burgers, and other cheap foods on which our nation now largely runs—or sits on its bottom, as the case may be.

This is how 70 percent of all our midwestern agricultural land shifted gradually into single-crop corn or soybean farms, each one of them now, on average, the size of Manhattan. Owing to synthetic fertilizers and pesticides, genetic modification, and a conversion of farming from a naturally based to a highly mechanized production system, U.S. farmers now produce 3,900 calories per U.S. citizen, per day. That is twice what we need, and 700 calories a day more than they grew in 1980. Commodity farmers can only survive by producing their maximum yields, so they do. And here is the shocking plot twist: as the farmers produced those extra calories, the food industry figured out how to get them into the bodies of people who didn't really *want* to eat 700 more calories a day. That is the well-oiled machine we call Late Capitalism.

Most of those calories enter our mouths in forms hardly recognizable as corn and soybeans, or even vegetable in origin: high-fructose corn syrup (HFCS) owns up to its parentage, but lecithin, citric acid, maltodextrin, sorbitol, and xanthan gum, for example, are also manufactured from corn. So are beef, eggs, and poultry, in a different but no less artificial process. Soybeans also become animal flesh, or else a category of ingredient known as "added fats." If every product containing corn or soybeans were removed from your grocery store, it would look more like a hardware store. Alarmingly, the lightbulbs might be naked, since many packaging materials also now contain cornstarch.

With so many extra calories to deliver, the packages have gotten bigger. The shapely eight-ounce Coke bottle of yesteryear became twenty ounces of carbonated high-fructose corn syrup and water; the accompanying meal morphed similarly. So did the American waistline. U.S. consumption of "added fats" has increased by one-third since 1975, and our HFCS is up by 1000 percent. About a third of all our calories now come from what is known, by community consent, as junk food.

No cashier held a gun to our heads and made us supersize it, true enough. But humans have a built-in weakness for fats and sugar. We evolved in lean environments where it was a big plus for survival to gorge on calorie-dense foods whenever we found them. Whether or not they understand the biology, food marketers know the weakness and have exploited it without mercy. Obesity is generally viewed as a failure of personal resolve, with no acknowledgment of the genuine conspiracy in this historical scheme. People actually did sit in strategy meetings discussing ways to get all those surplus calories into people who neither needed nor wished to consume them. Children have been targeted especially; food companies spend over $10 billion a year selling food brands to kids, and it isn't broccoli they're pushing. Overweight children are a demographic in many ways similar to minors addicted to cigarettes, with one notable exception: their parents are usually their suppliers. We all subsidize the cheap calories with our tax dollars, the strategists make fortunes, and the overweight consumers get blamed for the violation. The perfect crime.

All industrialized countries have experienced some commodification of agriculture and increased consumption of processed foods. But nowhere else on earth has it become normal to layer on the love handles as we do. (Nude beaches are still popular in Europe.) Other well-fed populations have had better luck controlling caloric excess through culture and custom: Italians eat Italian food, the Japanese eat Japanese, and so on, honoring ancient synergies between what their land can give and what their bodies need. Strong food cultures are both aesthetic and functional, keeping the quality and quantity of foods consumed relatively consistent from one generation to the next. And so, while the economies of many Western countries expanded massively in the late twentieth century, their citizens did not.

Here in the U.S. we seem puzzled by these people who refrain from gluttony in the presence of a glut. We've even named a thing we call the French Paradox: How can people have such a grand time eating cheese and fattened goose livers and still stay slim? Having logged some years in France, I have some hunches: they don't suck down giant sodas; they consume many courses in a meal but the portions of the fatty ones tend to be tiny; they smoke like chimneys (though that's changing); and they draw out meals sociably, so it's not just about shoveling it in. The all-you-can-eat buffet is an alien concern to the French, to put it mildly. Owing to certain rules about taste and civility in their heads, their bodies seem to know when enough is enough. When asked, my French friends have confided with varying degrees of tact that the real paradox is how people manage to consume, so very much, the scary food of America.

Why do we? Where are *our* ingrained rules of taste and civility, our ancient treaties between our human cravings and the particular fat of our land? Did they perhaps fly out the window while we were eating in a speeding car?

Food culture in the United States has long been cast as the property of a privileged class. It is nothing of the kind. Culture is the property of a species. Humans don't do everything we crave to do—that is arguably what makes us human. We're genetically predisposed toward certain behaviors that we've collectively decided are unhelpful; adultery and racism are possible examples. With reasonable success, we mitigate those impulses through civil codes, religious rituals, maternal warnings—the whole bag of tricks we call culture. Food cultures concentrate a population's collective wisdom about the plants and animals that grow in a place, and the complex ways of rendering them tasty. These are mores of survival, good health, and control of excess. Living without such a culture would seem dangerous.

And here we are, sure enough in trouble. North America's native cuisine met the same unfortunate fate as its native people, save for a few relics like the Thanksgiving turkey. Certainly, we still have regional specialties, but the Carolina barbecue will almost certainly have California tomatoes in its sauce (maybe also Nebraska-fattened feedlot hogs), and the Louisiana gumbo is just as likely to contain Indonesian farmed shrimp. If either of these shows up on a fast-food menu with lots of added fats or HFCS, we seem unable either to discern or resist the corruption. We have yet to come up with a strong set of generalized norms, passed down through families, for savoring and sensibly consuming what our land and climate give us. We have, instead, a string of fad diets convulsing our bookstores and bellies, one after another, at the scale of the national best seller. Nine out of ten nutritionists (unofficial survey) view this as evidence that we have entirely lost our marbles. A more optimistic view might be this: these sets of mandates captivate us because we're looking hard for a food culture of our own. A profit-driven food industry has exploded and nutritionally bankrupted our caloric supply, and we long for a Food Leviticus to save us from the sinful roil of cheap fats and carbs.

What the fad diets don't offer, though, is any sense of national and biological integrity. A food culture is not something that gets *sold* to people. It arises out of a place, a soil, a climate, a history, a temperament, a collective sense of belonging. Every set of fad-diet rules is essentially framed in the negative, dictating what you must give up. Together they've helped us form powerfully negative associations with the very act of eating. Our most celebrated models of beauty are starved people. But we're still an animal that must eat to live. To paraphrase a famous campaign slogan: it's the biology, stupid. A food culture of anti-eating is worse than useless.

People hold to their food customs because of the *positives:* comfort, nourishment, heavenly aromas. A sturdy food tradition even calls to

25

outsiders; plenty of red-blooded Americans will happily eat Italian, French, Thai, Chinese, you name it. But try the reverse: hand the Atkins menu to a French person, and run for your life.

Will North Americans ever have a food culture to call our own? Can we find or make up a set of rituals, recipes, ethics, and buying habits that will let us love our food and eat it too? Some signs point to "yes." Better food—more local, more healthy, more sensible—is a powerful new topic of the American conversation. It reaches from the epicurean quarters of Slow Food convivia to the matter-of-fact Surgeon General's Office; from Farm Aid concerts to school lunch programs. From the rural routes to the inner cities, we are staring at our plates and wondering where that's *been*. For the first time since our nation's food was ubiquitously local, the point of origin now matters again to some consumers. We're increasingly wary of an industry that puts stuff in our dinner we can't identify as animal, vegetable, mineral, or what. The halcyon postwar promise of "better living through chemistry" has fallen from grace. "No additives" is now often considered a plus rather than the minus that, technically, it is.

We're a nation with an eating disorder, and we know it. The multiple maladies caused by bad eating are taking a dire toll on our health—most tragically for our kids, who are predicted to be this country's first generation to have a *shorter* life expectancy than their parents. That alone is a stunning enough fact to give us pause. So is a government policy that advises us to eat more fruits and vegetables, while doling out subsidies *not* to fruit and vegetable farmers, but to commodity crops destined to become soda pop and cheap burgers. The Farm Bill, as of this writing, could aptly be called the Farm Kill, both for its effects on small farmers and for what it does to us, the consumers who are financing it. The Green Revolution of the 1970s promised that industrial agriculture would make food cheaper and available to more people. Instead, it has helped more of us become less healthy.

A majority of North Americans do understand, at some level, that our food choices are politically charged, affecting arenas from rural culture to international oil cartels and global climate change. Plenty of consumers are trying to get off the petroleum-driven industrial food wagon: banning fast food from their homes and schools, avoiding the unpronounceable ingredient lists. However, *banning* is negative and therefore fails as a food culture per se.

Something positive is also happening under the surface of our nation's food preference paradigm. It could be called a movement. It includes gardeners who grow some of their own produce—one-quarter of all U.S. households, according to the U.S. Census Bureau. Just as importantly, it's the city dwellers who roll their kids out of bed on Saturday mornings and head down to the farmers' markets to pinch the tomatoes and inhale the spicy-sweet melons—New York, alone, has about a quarter million such shoppers. It involves the farmers' markets themselves, along with a new breed of restaurant owner (and customer) dedicated to buying locally produced food. It has been embraced by farmers who manage to keep family farms by thinking outside the box, learning to grow organic peppers or gourmet mushrooms. It engages schoolchildren and teachers who are bringing food-growing curricula into classrooms and lunchrooms from Berkeley, California, to my own county in southern Appalachia. It includes the kids who get dirty in those outdoor classrooms planting tomatoes and peppers at the end of third grade, then harvesting and cooking their own pizza when they start back into fourth. And it owes a debt to parents who can watch those kids getting dirty, and not make a fuss.

At its heart, a genuine food culture is an affinity between people and the land that feeds them. Step one, probably, is to *live* on the land that feeds them, or at least on the same continent, ideally the same region. Step two is to be able to countenance the ideas of "food" and "dirt" in the same sentence, and three is to start poking into one's supply chain to learn where things are coming from. . . . It's not at all necessary to live on a food-producing farm to participate in this culture. But it is necessary to know such farms exist, understand something about what they do, and consider oneself basically in their court. . . .

Will our single-family decision to step off the nonsustainable food grid give a big black eye to that petroleum-hungry behemoth? . . . We only knew, when we started, that similar choices made by many families at once were already making a difference: organic growers, farmers' markets, and small exurban food producers now comprise the fastest-growing sector of the U.S. food economy. A lot of people at once are waking up to a troublesome truth about cheap fossil fuels: we are going to run out of them. Our jet-age dependence on petroleum to feed our faces is a limited-time-only proposition. Every food calorie we presently eat has used dozens or even hundreds of fossil-fuel calories in its making: grain milling, for example, which turns corn into the ingredients of packaged foods, costs ten calories for every one food calorie produced. That's *before* it gets shipped anywhere. By the time my children are my age, that version of dinnertime will surely be an unthinkable extravagance.

I enjoy denial as much as the next person, but this isn't rocket science: our kids will eventually have to make food differently. They could be assisted by some familiarity with how vegetables grow from seeds, how animals grow on pasture, and how whole ingredients can be made into meals, gee whiz, right in the kitchen. My husband and I decided our children would not grow up without knowing a potato has a plant part. We would take a food sabbatical, getting our hands dirty in some of the actual dying arts of food production. We hoped to prove—at least to ourselves—that a family living on or near green land need not depend for its life on industrial food. We were writing our Dear John letter to a roomie that smells like exhaust fumes and the feedlot.

But sticking it to the Man (whoever he is) may not be the most   35
inspired principle around which to organize one's life. We were also after
tangible, healthy pleasures, in the same way that boycotting tobacco, for
example, brings other benefits besides the satisfaction of withholding your
money from Philip Morris. We hoped a year away from industrial foods
would taste so good, we might actually enjoy it. The positives, rather than
the negatives, ultimately nudged us to step away from the agribusiness
supply line and explore the local food landscape. Doing the right thing,
in this case, is not about abstinence-only, throwing out bread, tightening
your belt, wearing a fake leather belt, or dragging around feeling righteous
and gloomy. Food is the rare moral arena in which the ethical choice is
generally the one more likely to make you groan with pleasure. Why resist
that?

THINKING CRITICALLY ABOUT THE READING

1. Kingsolver claims that a knowledge of agricultural basics "has vanished from
   our culture" (2). What does she mean by agricultural basics, and what have
   we all lost by not having an "intuitive sense" (2) of these basics? According to
   Kingsolver, why is it important that each of us knows how foods grow?

2. Do you agree with Kingsolver that most of us "don't know beans about
   beans" (8)?

3. In what ways did corn and soybeans change the face of American agriculture
   in the years immediately after World War II? What impact have these two
   crops had on the American diet?

4. What does Kingsolver mean by "food culture" (21)? What is the food culture
   of the French or Italians, for example? How do these food cultures differ from
   that of the United States? Explain.

5. What does Kingsolver find wrong or lacking in America's current food culture? What promising signs does she note to show that our food culture might
   be changing?

6. What steps does Kingsolver suggest we take in order to establish a genuine
   American food culture?

What's Natural about Our Natural Products?

SARAH FEDERMAN

A freelance writer, Sarah Federman was born in New York City in 1976. She graduated from the University of Pennsylvania in 1998, where she majored in intellectual history. A strong interest in alternative medicine led her to work at the Institute for Health and Healing at California Pacific Medical Center in San Francisco. In 2003 she returned to New York to work in media advertising. Currently, she works with media software technology in Paris, France.

Federman wrote the following essay expressly for *Language Awareness*. She first became curious about the word *natural* as an undergraduate when she defended its use as a meaningful word on food labels in a debate with one of her professors. Since that time, however, Federman has had a change of heart. As she reports in her essay, the meaning of *natural* is elusive and extremely difficult to pin down.

WRITING TO DISCOVER: *What do you think you're buying when you purchase a product with the word* natural *on its label? Do you use any natural products on a regular basis? Do you think such products are better for you than their regular alternatives? Are you willing to pay more for a natural product? Why or why not?*

Whether you're picking up Nature's Energy Supplements, Natrol, Nature's Way, Naturade, Nature's Gate, or Nature's Herbs in the vitamin aisle, attending a lecture on "Natural Sleep Aids," or diving into a bowl of Quaker 100% Natural Granola, you cannot escape the hype. Variations of the words "nature" and "natural" are used for product naming: to distinguish alternative medicine practitioners from their western counterparts and as slogans or names for everything from toothpaste to blue jeans. In a recent issue of *Delicious* magazine, for example, these words were used 85 times in the first 40 pages, with advertisements using them 8 times! Now pet owners can even skim through a copy of *Natural Dog* or *Natural Cat* while waiting at the vet.

Nowhere is the buzzword "natural" more prevalent than at the local grocery store where Fantastic Soups, Enrico's Pizza Sauce, Health Valley Cereals, and Celestial Seasonings tea, among others, brag unabashedly about the "naturalness" of their products. I often find myself seduced by the lure of the "natural" label on goods and services. I throw Tom's Natural Toothpaste, Pop-Secret Natural Flavored Popcorn, and Grape-Nuts Natural Wheat and Barley Cereal into my shopping cart with the utmost confidence that these natural varieties prove far superior to their "unnatural" or "less natural" counterparts. Recently, I took a closer look at the labels of my revered products only to discover the widespread abuse of the word "natural." The word "natural" has become more a marketing ploy than a way to communicate meaningful information about a product.

But this is not news. More than a decade ago the Consumers Union first sounded the alarm about "natural." The report alerted consumers to the fact that their beloved Quaker 100% Natural Cereal contained 24 percent sugar, not to mention the nine grams of fat which, according to the March 1999 *Nutrition Action Healthletter*, is the same as a small McDonald's hamburger. But despite the best efforts of the Union, nothing has changed. In fact, things have gotten worse, *especially* in the cereal aisle where 22 varieties, including Froot Loops, proclaim their commitment to "natural" ingredients. Berry Berry Kix, a brightly colored kids' cereal, promises "natural Fruit Flavors." Sure there is some grape juice, right after the sugar, partially hydrogenated oils, and corn syrup, and some strawberry juice, right after the dicalcium and trisodium phosphates. That's it for the fruits, the rest is corn meal and starch.

The Consumer Union's report also pointed out products using "natural" as an "indeterminate modifier," rather than as an adjective to convey some meaningful information about the product. In other words, placing the word "natural" in a slogan or product description without having it refer to anything in particular. For example, most major U.S. supermarkets sell Kraft's Natural Shredded Non-Fat Cheese, Natural Reduced Fat Swiss, and Natural Cheese Cubes. But don't dare to ask the question, What does that mean? Kraft has done nothing special with the cheese itself; "natural" in this case presumably relates to the shredding, reducing, and cubing process. What is natural cubing?

To me, a "natural" product or service suggests any or all of the following: a healthy alternative, an environmentally friendly product, vegetarian, and or produced without synthetic chemicals. Friends and family have also taken natural to mean wholesome, pure, low-fat, healthy, organic, and, simply, better. The meanings given in one popular dictionary, however, prove less specific: 1) determined by nature, 2) of or relating to nature, 3) having normal or usual character, 4) grown without human care, 5) not artificial, 6) present in or produced by nature. Interestingly, these definitions make no value judgments. There is nothing in the dictionary meaning to suggest, for instance, that a natural banana (one grown in the wild) is healthier than one raised by banana farmers. This positive spin we add ourselves.

Unlike using "low-fat," "organic," and "vegetarian," food manufacturers can use "natural" any way they choose. The Nutritional Labeling and Education Act of 1990 (ULEA) restricted the use of the following terms on food labels: low fat, low sodium, low cholesterol, low calorie, lean,

5

extra lean, reduced, good source, less, fewer, light, and more. A calorie-free product, for example, must have fewer than 5 calories per serving, while a cholesterol-free product must have 2 milligrams or less of cholesterol per serving. *Mother Earth News* reports that products labeled "organic" must align themselves with one of the 40 sets of organic standards, most often the California Organic Foods Act of 1990. This leaves "natural" as one of the few unregulated words.

Health-food companies and mainstream producers use the word to create an aura around the product. Actually, they use the word and "we" create the aura, allowing them to get away with higher prices or simply to take up more shelf space at the supermarket. For example, every month thousands of bags of Lays "Naturally Baked" Potato Chips travel through desert and farmland to enable us to "Ohh, ahh" and purchase these natural wonders. When first seeing this name, I had visions of organic farms and rugged, healthy farmers cultivating a much-loved product. Unfortunately, a closer look at the label served to shatter rather than support my countryside fantasy. While the ingredients reveal less fat per serving than the standard chip (1.5 grams versus 9 grams), I found nothing that explained the meaning of "naturally baked." Do you think this means they leave the chips out in the sun to crispen up? Probably not, so why does this natural process cost more per ounce (5.5 ounces for $1.99 versus 7.5 ounces) when it uses less fat?

Motts and Delmonte use "natural" to promote a new line without knocking their standard product. Motts applesauce has three products on the shelf of my local San Francisco market—"Apple Sauce," "Natural Apple Sauce," and "Chunky Apple Sauce." A comparison of the labels reveals that the "natural" version has no corn syrup added. Now, if they just wrote "no corn syrup added" on the label, we consumers would immediately become aware that there is, indeed, sweetener added to their standard version. Delmonte Fruit Cocktail has a two-product line-up with "Fruit Naturals" right next to "Fruit Cocktail." The natural variety costs 6 cents more and actually has *fewer* ingredients, presumably requiring less manufacturing. The natural version has no sugar and preservatives; the standard version has added corn syrup and sugar.

Fantastic, maker of dried soups and instant mixes, uses "natural" to connote something about the food and the type of person who may buy it. Under the heading Instant Black Beans, Fantastic writes "All Natural. Vegetarian." A vegetarian product, we know, means without meat. But what does "all natural" mean? Adding this phrase right before Vegetarian suggested to me that this product should appeal to vegetarians and self-proclaimed naturals. Mildly health-conscious people surely would prefer to ally themselves with natural rather than unnatural foods. Whether or not this product serves as a healthy alternative to other brands is irrelevant because the point is that Fantastic could sell you artery-clogging lard and still use the word.

Next to vitamins, bottled beverages probably use the word more   10
than any other product. Every Snapple bottle promises an "all natural"
treat, although the most natural iced tea is quite simply brewed tea with
ice. In Snapple's case, you end up paying more for tasty sugar water,
but with Hansen's Natural Soda you are outright deceived. Hansen's
soda has exactly the same ingredients as Sprite and 7-Up minus the
sodium citrate. Blue Sky Natural Soda has fructose sweetener, caramel
color, and something called tartaric acid. Doesn't Blue Sky Natural
Soda sound refreshing? Too bad your intestines can't distinguish it from
Coca-Cola.

At least we have natural bottled water as an alternative. Or do we?
The Natural Resources Defense Council, a national environmental group,
found dangerous amounts of arsenic in Crystal Geyser's "Natural" Spring
water. A four-year study revealed that one-third of the 103 bottled waters
tested contained contaminants beyond safe federal limits. Odwalla "Natural" Spring Water, another popular beverage company, especially among
health-food lovers, had high bacteria counts in a number of bottles. Hey,
bacteria are natural so what's the problem? The problem is that natural or
not, some bacteria make us sick. So it seems you cannot win with beverages. "Natural" serves as a meaningless label, a deceptive marketing tool,
or means "contains natural critters and natural toxins that may make you
sick." Best to just purchase a "Pur" (pronounced "pure") water filter; just
don't ask what they mean by pure.

Some products come closer to meeting my expectations. The Hain
Food Group, a "natural-food producer" whose projected 1999 annual
sales are $300 million, manufactures soup called "Healthy Naturals."
Although the split peas are not certified organic, Hain uses no preservatives or MSG. The ingredients are listed as water, split green peas,
carrots, celery, onion powder, and spices. This product lives up to my
notion of natural. But even Hain veers from their presumed commitment
to health food. The 14 product "Hain Kidz" line, introduced early in
1999, includes marshmallow crispcereal and snack bars, gummybear-like
candy, and animal cookies. It appears that as major brands (Krafts, Motts,
Quaker) increasingly tout their new-found "naturalness," health-food
companies such as Hain have started going toward more "unnatural"
products.

So as the line between specialty health-food company and standard
food producer becomes more elusive, I begin to wonder why the extra
cost? Why do plain peas and carrots cost *more* than highly refined and processed soups? And how did we get to a point where we need a special label
to tell us that the product is what it says it is? Before I infuse one more
dollar into this industry, I will assuredly read the list of ingredients more
carefully and do some research at www.naturalinvesting.com and www
.naturalhomemagazine.com.

THINKING CRITICALLY ABOUT THE READING

1. According to Federman, what is the literal meaning of the word *natural*? What connotations do consumers bring to the word? (Glossary: *Connotation/Denotation*)

2. What restrictions does the Nutritional Labeling and Education Act of 1990 place on what manufacturers can say on food labels? How is the word *organic* regulated? What restrictions, if any, are imposed on the use of the term *natural*?

3. What does Federman point to as the two main reasons that companies use the word *natural*? What does she mean when she says companies "use the word and 'we' create the aura" (7)?

4. Why do you think Federman talks about Kraft's Natural Shredded Non-Fat Cheese and Lays "Naturally Baked" Potato Chips? Name some other products whose labels use the word *natural* or *naturally* in an unclear or ambiguous manner.

5. Why do you suppose manufacturers charge more for their "natural" products when, in fact, these products may cost less to produce?

Claims Crazy: Which Can You Believe?

BONNIE LIEBMAN

Bonnie Liebman was born in Brooklyn, New York, in 1952 and graduated from the University of Maryland in 1974. After receiving a master's degree in nutritional sciences from Cornell University in 1977, she became director of nutrition at the Center for Science in the Public Interest, a Washington, D.C.–based nonprofit consumer advocacy organization. CSPI advocates honest food labeling and advertising, safer and more nutritious foods, and pro-health alcohol policies. Liebman's work at CSPI has focused on the links between diet and heart disease, cancer, stroke, osteoporosis, and other health-related issues, such as vitamin supplements, food labeling, and advertising. She has testified at hearings held by congressional committees and federal agencies, and her articles regularly appear in *Ladies Circle, Essence,* and *Pharmaceutical Executive.* She is coauthor of *Salt: The Brand Name Guide to Sodium Content* (1983). In the following article, which first appeared in the June 2003 issue of *CSPI's Nutrition Action Healthletter,* Liebman examines the crazy world of food advertising and instructs her readers how to differentiate the three main types of product claims.

WRITING TO DISCOVER: *Do you have any favorite food commercials? What do you find appealing about these particular advertisements? What connections, if any, do you see between your own purchasing and eating patterns and the claims or appeals food advertisers make to you and your peers? Explain.*

It's a brave new world. Walk down the aisles of any supermarket these days and you'll see claims that were never there before. Cereals that will help you "lose more weight!" Fruit drinks with "energy-releasing B-vitamins!" Raisins with antioxidants that "can slow the effects of aging."

It's been more than a decade since Congress passed a law that overhauled food labels and required companies to get the Food and Drug Administration's approval before making claims that mention a disease. But food companies, emboldened by the success of the supplement industry, have discovered a back door into the claims business.

And that leaves consumers on their own, trying to separate the good from the bad.

Here's a quiz for the astute shopper: Which (one or more) of these claims can appear on a food or supplement label without approval from the Food and Drug Administration?

(a) improves memory
(b) relieves stress

> (c) suppresses appetite
> (d) helps reduce difficulty in falling asleep
> (e) supports the immune system

The answers: a, b, c, and e. They're called "structure/function claims,"   5
because they describe how a food or supplement affects the body's structure (say, the skeleton) or its function (for example, digestion). And manufacturers can slap one on virtually any food or supplement with or without
evidence to back it up.

"The law says that structure/function claims can't be misleading, but
the FDA has never said how much evidence a company needs to substantiate a claim," says Bruce Silverglade, director of legal affairs for the
Center for Science in the Public Interest, publisher of *Nutrition Action
Healthletter.*

Is one good study enough? What if that study is contradicted by a
dozen others? "With no rules ensuring uniformity in structure/function
claims, the resulting free-for-all could end up confusing consumers and
encouraging them to buy unhealthy foods," says Representative Henry
Waxman. The California Democrat is one of the strongest advocates of
honest food labeling in Congress.

The FDA has no rules, in part because, until recently, structure/func-
tion claims only showed up on supplements.

NO APPROVAL NEEDED

In 1994, under strong industry pressure, Congress passed the Dietary
Supplement Health and Education Act. The law gives supplement-makers
free rein to make structure/function claims, as long as the companies:

- notify the FDA within 30 days after using a new claim, and
- print the following disclaimer on the label:

> These statements have not been evaluated by the Food and Drug
> Administration. This product is not intended to diagnose, treat,
> cure, or prevent any disease.

"Not evaluated" is right. "The FDA doesn't even look at the evidence   10
behind structure/function claims," says Silverglade. "It just makes sure
that the supplement doesn't make a disease claim—one that's approved
only for drugs."

According to the law, a disease claim promises to "diagnose, cure, mitigate, treat, or prevent disease." If a supplement makes a disease claim, then legally it becomes a drug. "Drugs must be pre-approved for safety and effectiveness, so that would make the supplement illegal," explains Silverglade.

But the distinction between a structure/function claim and a disease claim can be subtle. For example, "helps restore sexual vigor, potency, and performance" is a disease claim, says the FDA. In contrast, "arouses sexual desire" is a structure/function claim. (see "A Fine Line").

A Fine Line

Which claims need FDA approval and which don't? When does a claim cross the line between offering to "affect the structure or function of the body" and promising to "prevent, treat, cure, mitigate, or diagnose" a disease? It's not easy to tell.

In January 2000, the FDA tried to answer that question, at least for claims on supplements. Here are some examples of claims that fall into each category.

No Prior Approval Needed (Structure/Function Claim)	Approval Needed (Disease Claim)
Helps maintain normal cholesterol levels	Lowers cholesterol
Maintains healthy lung function	Maintains healthy lung function in smokers
Provides relief of occasional constipation	Provides relief of chronic constipation
Suppresses appetite to aid weight loss	Suppresses appetite to treat obesity
Supports the immune system	Supports the body's antiviral capabilities
Relief of occasional heartburn or acid indigestion	Relief of persistent heartburn or acid indigestion
For relief of occasional sleeplessness	Helps reduce difficulty in falling asleep
Arouses sexual desire	Helps restore sexual vigor, potency, and performance

Other structure/function claims that need no prior approval

• Improves memory • Helps you relax • For hair loss associated with aging

- Improves strength
- Promotes digestion
- Boosts stamina
- For common symptoms of PMS

- Helps enhance muscle tone or size
- Relieves stress
- Helps promote urinary tract health
- Maintains intestinal flora

- Prevents wrinkles
- For relief of muscle pain after exercise
- To treat or prevent nocturnal leg muscle cramps
- For hot flashes

Got that?

"Studies show that consumers can't distinguish between disease claims and structure/function claims," says Silverglade.

And if shoppers can't, why should food companies bother with health 15 claims when they can say just about anything they want by using structure/function claims?

TEXTBOOK TALK

"For years, the law has allowed structure/function claims on foods," explains Silverglade. "But companies rarely made them, probably because they didn't have much appeal."

The classic example was a statement like "calcium builds strong bones." "Structure/function claims were supposed to be something you might read in a textbook," says Silverglade.

Instead, the industry was fired up about health claims — that a food could, "as part of an overall diet," help reduce the risk of heart disease, cancer, or osteoporosis. In 1990, Congress passed a law permitting health claims, but with clear limits.

"The FDA had to approve the claim, and the food couldn't be too high in harmful nutrients like saturated fat or sodium or too low in vitamins and minerals," says Silverglade. "And the FDA could only approve the claim if it was backed by 'significant scientific agreement.'" In other words, the claim had to be supported by strong and consistent evidence.

Since 1990, the FDA has approved 14 health claims (see 20 "The 'A' List"). Apparently, that hasn't been enough for the food industry.

The "A" List: Approved Health Claims

Here are the 14 (slightly edited) health claims that the FDA has approved. Some are more popular than others.

- Diets rich in **whole grain foods** and other plant foods and low in total fat, saturated fat, and cholesterol may help reduce the risk of **heart disease** and certain **cancers.**
- Diets containing foods that are good sources of **potassium** and low in sodium may reduce the risk of **high blood pressure** and **stroke.**
- A diet low in **total fat** may reduce the risk of some **cancers.**
- Three grams of soluble fiber from [**oatmeal**] daily in a diet low in saturated fat and cholesterol may reduce the risk of **heart disease.** This [cereal] has [two] grams per serving.
- While many factors affect **heart disease**, diets low in **saturated fat** and **cholesterol** may reduce the risk of this disease.
- Diets low in **sodium** may reduce the risk of **high blood pressure.**
- Low fat diets rich in **fiber**-containing **grains, fruits,** and **vegetables** may reduce the risk of some types of **cancer.**
- Diets low in saturated fat and cholesterol that include 25 grams of soy **protein** per day may reduce the risk of **heart disease.** One serving of this product provides at least [6.25 g] of soy protein.
- Healthful diets with adequate **folate** may reduce a woman's risk of having a child with a **brain or spinal cord defect.**
- Two or three servings per day with meals, providing 3.4 grams of **plant stanol esters** daily, added to a diet low in saturated fat and cholesterol may reduce the risk of **heart disease.** [Benecol Spread] contains [1.7 g] stanol esters per serving.
- Diets low in saturated fat and cholesterol and rich in **fruits, vegetables,** and **grains** that contain some types of fiber, particularly **soluble fiber,** may reduce the risk of **heart disease.**
- Does not promote **tooth decay.**
- Low fat diets rich in **fruits** and **vegetables** containing **vitamin A, vitamin C,** and **fiber** may reduce the risk of some types of **cancer.**
- Regular exercise and a healthy diet with enough **calcium** help teens and young adult white and Asian women maintain good

bone health and may reduce their high risk of **osteoporosis** later in life.

NOTE: Each food that makes a health claim must meet specific criteria. For example, foods with the soy claim must contain at least 6.25 grams of soy protein per serving and be low in saturated fat and cholesterol. "Does not promote tooth decay" can only appear on sugar-free foods that contain maltitol, xylitol, or other sugar alcohols. Foods that make health claims must also meet general criteria. They can't be high in fat, saturated fat, cholesterol, or sodium and must have some naturally occurring nutrients.

TOWER OF BABEL

The Grocery Manufacturers of America, like other industry groups, has been hot under the collar over health claims for years.

The FDA approves claims "only where there is overwhelming science to support a diet/disease relationship, thus preventing the public from learning about new scientific developments until they have matured into hard science," a GMA spokesperson told Congress in May 2001. "As a result, the FDA has approved only a handful of disease/health claims. . . ."

Not to worry, GMA. Last December [2002], the FDA created a new kind of health claim. The agency announced that it would allow health claims for foods based on preliminary evidence as long as the label qualified it with a disclaimer like "this evidence is not conclusive."

These preliminary health claims haven't shown up on many foods yet. But even when they do, most companies will no doubt stick with anything-goes structure/function claims.

Why shouldn't they? Even preliminary health claims require approval and are prohibited on unhealthy or empty-calorie foods. What's more, structure/function claims have gotten jazzier. Goodbye, textbook. Hello, Madison Avenue.

"The supplement industry made a mint with structure/function claims," observes Silverglade. "Why should the food industry bother with health claims when they've got a free ride with structure/function claims? Food companies don't even have to notify the FDA or print a disclaimer, like supplement companies do."

Structure/function claims are starting to hit the marketplace . . . and no one's watching. So far, many are showing up on decent foods, like fruit juice and fruit (see "The Bottom Line"). But it's only a matter of time before they start to pop up in the cookie, chip, and soft-drink aisles.

Says Waxman: "The growth of structure/function claims for foods threatens to return us to the days when the Secretary of Health and Human Services called the food marketplace a 'Tower of Babel' for the consumer."

The Bottom Line

Here's how to tell one claim from another:

- **Solid Health Claims.** These reliable claims—based on solid evidence—name a disease like cancer, stroke, or heart disease; usually refer to a "diet" that's low (or high) in some nutrient; and can't appear on unhealthy or empty-calorie foods.
- **Preliminary Health Claims.** These unreliable claims are based on incomplete, shaky evidence. They have a disclaimer that ranges from the cautious ("the FDA has determined that this evidence is limited and not conclusive") to the silly ("the FDA concludes that there is little scientific evidence supporting this claim"). They can't appear on unhealthy or empty-calorie foods.
- **Structure/Function Claims.** These unreliable claims require no approval—in practice, that may mean no evidence. Instead of diseases, look for words like "maintains," "supports," and "enhances" and euphemisms (like "optimizes bone health"). They can appear on any food.

THINKING CRITICALLY ABOUT THE READING

1. What is a "structure/function claim"? What does Liebman see as the problem of such claims for consumers? Why do many food companies favor using structure/function claims?

2. According to the Food and Drug Administration, when does a supplement become a drug?

3. Currently, the food industry can use two types of health claims—"solid health claims" and "preliminary health claims." What is the essential difference between the two? Why, according to Liebman, is the food industry likely to use structure/function claims on its products more than health claims?

4. Now that you understand the different types of claims that manufacturers can make, do you think that food companies are deliberately trying to deceive consumers, or simply trying to sell their products in a highly competitive marketplace? Do you think that some claims put customers at real risk? Explain.

Is Whole Foods Wholesome?

FIELD MALONEY

A 1997 graduate of Princeton University, Field Maloney grew up in western Massachusetts, where his parents own a cider farm. After college he worked in the fiction department at the *New Yorker*. In addition to the *New Yorker,* his articles regularly appear in *Slate, Gourmet Magazine,* and the *New York Times.* A wine and beer enthusiast, Maloney is currently writing *CRUSH: A Clerk's Tale,* a book that will combine memoir and reporting. Having immersed himself in all aspects of wine culture from the vineyard to the winery to the retail store aisle, he plans to tell the story of American wine from the colonial era to the modern day.

In the following article, first posted on *Slate* on March 17, 2006, Maloney takes a close look at the "haute-crunchy supermarket chain" Whole Foods and asks the all-important question: "Is it really as virtuous as it appears to be?" In answering this question, Maloney uses specific examples to expose what he believes are several dark secrets of the organic-food movement.

WRITING TO DISCOVER: *When you hear the words* organic *and* sustainability, *what comes to mind? Do these words have positive or negative connotations for you? Explain.*

It's hard to find fault with Whole Foods, the haute-crunchy supermarket chain that has made a fortune by transforming grocery shopping into a bright and shiny, progressive experience. Indeed, the road to wild profits and cultural cachet has been surprisingly smooth for the supermarket chain. It gets mostly sympathetic coverage in the local and national media and red-carpet treatment from the communities it enters. But does Whole Foods have an Achilles' heel? And more important, does the organic movement itself, whose coattails Whole Foods has ridden to such success, have dark secrets of its own?

Granted, there's plenty that's praiseworthy about Whole Foods. John Mackey, the company's chairman, likes to say, "There's no inherent reason why business cannot be ethical, socially responsible, and profitable." And under the umbrella creed of "sustainability," Whole Foods pays its workers a solid living wage—its lowest earners average $13.15 an hour—with excellent benefits and health care. No executive makes more than 14 times the employee average. (Mackey's salary last year was $342,000.) In January, Whole Foods announced that it had committed to buy a year's supply of power from a wind-power utility in Wyoming.

But even if Whole Foods has a happy staff and nice windmills, is it really as virtuous as it appears to be? Take the produce section, usually located in the geographic center of the shopping floor and the spiritual heart of a Whole Foods outlet. (Every media profile of the company invariably contains a paragraph of fawning produce porn, near-sonnets about "gleaming melons" and "glistening kumquats.") In the produce section of Whole Foods' flagship New York City store at the Time Warner Center, shoppers browse under a big banner that lists "Reasons To Buy Organic." On the banner, the first heading is "Save Energy." The accompanying text explains how organic farmers, who use natural fertilizers like manure and compost, avoid the energy waste involved in the manufacture of synthetic fertilizers. It's a technical point that probably barely registers with most shoppers but contributes to a vague sense of virtue.

Fair enough. But here's another technical point that Whole Foods fails to mention and that highlights what has gone wrong with the organic-food movement in the last couple of decades. Let's say you live in New York City and want to buy a pound of tomatoes in season. Say you can choose between conventionally grown New Jersey tomatoes or organic ones grown in Chile. Of course, the New Jersey tomatoes will be cheaper. They will also almost certainly be fresher, having traveled a fraction of the distance. But which is the more eco-conscious choice? In terms of energy savings, there's no contest: Just think of the fossil fuels expended getting those organic tomatoes from Chile. Which brings us to the question: Setting aside freshness, price, and energy conservation, should a New Yorker just instinctively choose organic, even if the produce comes from Chile? A tough decision, but you can make a self-interested case for the social and economic benefit of going Jersey, especially if you prefer passing fields of tomatoes to fields of condominiums when you tour the Garden State.

Another heading on the Whole Foods banner says "Help the   5
Small Farmer." "Buying organic," it states, "supports the small, family farmers that make up a large percentage of organic food producers." This is semantic sleight of hand. As one small family farmer in Connecticut told me recently, "Almost all the organic food in this country comes out of California. And five or six big California farms dominate the whole industry." There's a widespread misperception in this country—one that organic growers, no matter how giant, happily encourage—that "organic" means "small family farmer." That hasn't been the case for years, certainly not since 1990, when the Department of Agriculture drew up its official guidelines for organic food. Whole Foods knows this well, and so the line about the "small family farmers that make up a large percentage of organic food producers" is sneaky. There are a lot of small, family-run organic farmers, but their share of the organic crop in this country, and of the produce sold at Whole Foods, is minuscule.

A nearby banner at the Time Warner Center Whole Foods proclaims "Our Commitment to the Local Farmer," but this also doesn't hold up to scrutiny. More likely, the burgeoning local-food movement is making Whole Foods uneasy. After all, a multinational chain can't promote a "buy local" philosophy without being self-defeating. When I visited the Time Warner Whole Foods last fall—high season for native fruits and vegetables on the East Coast—only a token amount of local produce was on display. What Whole Foods does do for local farmers is hang glossy pinups throughout the store, what they call "grower profiles," which depict tousled, friendly looking organic farmers standing in front of their crops. This winter, when I dropped by the store, the only local produce for sale was a shelf of upstate apples, but the grower profiles were still up. There was a picture of a sandy-haired organic leek farmer named Dave, from Whately, Mass., above a shelf of conventionally grown yellow onions from Oregon. Another profile showed a guy named Ray Rex munching on an ear of sweet corn he grew on his generations-old, picturesque organic acres. The photograph was pinned above a display of conventionally grown white onions from Mexico.

These profiles may be heartwarming, but they also artfully mislead customers about what they're paying premium prices for. If Whole Foods marketing didn't revolve so much around explicit (as well as subtly suggestive) appeals to food ethics, it'd be easier to forgive some exaggerations and distortions.

Of course, above and beyond social and environmental ethics, and even taste, people buy organic food because they believe that it's better for them. All things being equal, food grown without pesticides is healthier for you. But American populism chafes against the notion of good health for those who can afford it. Charges of elitism—media wags, in otherwise flattering profiles, have called Whole Foods "Whole Paycheck" and "wholesome, healthy for the wholesome, wealthy"—are the only criticism of Whole Foods that seems to have stuck. Which brings us to the newest kid in the organic-food sandbox: Wal-Mart, the world's biggest grocery retailer, has just begun a major program to expand into organic foods. If buying food grown without chemical pesticides and synthetic fertilizers has been elevated to a status-conscious lifestyle choice, it could also be transformed into a bare-bones commodity purchase.

When the Department of Agriculture established the guidelines for organic food in 1990, it blew a huge opportunity. The USDA—under heavy agribusiness lobbying—adopted an abstract set of restrictions for organic agriculture and left "local" out of the formula. What passes for organic farming today has strayed far from what the shaggy utopians who got the movement going back in the '60s and '70s had in mind. But if these pioneers dreamed of revolutionizing the nation's food supply, they surely didn't intend for organic to become a luxury item, a high-end lifestyle choice.

It's likely that neither Wal-Mart nor Whole Foods will do much to   10
encourage local agriculture or small farming, but in an odd twist, Wal-Mart,
with its simple "More for Less" credo, might do far more to democratize
the nation's food supply than Whole Foods. The organic-food movement
is in danger of exacerbating the growing gap between rich and poor in this
country by contributing to a two-tiered national food supply, with healthy
food for the rich. Could Wal-Mart's populist strategy prove to be more
"sustainable" than Whole Foods'? Stranger things have happened.

THINKING CRITICALLY ABOUT THE READING

1. According to Maloney, what public image does the supermarket chain Whole Foods have?

2. What does Maloney find deceptive about the "Reasons to Buy Organic" banner in the produce section of Whole Foods' New York City store? In your opinion, is he being a nit-picker, or does he have a valid complaint? Explain.

3. In what ways should the "local-food movement" make a big supermarket chain like Whole Foods uneasy?

4. Given that foods grown without chemical fertilizers and pesticides are better for you, do you think it is fair that these organic products are priced in a way that makes it prohibitive for many Americans to buy them? Do you think stores like Whole Foods are elitist? Why or why not?

5. How do you think Maloney would answer his concluding question: "Could Wal-Mart's populist strategy prove to be more 'sustainable' than Whole Foods'"? How would you answer this question? Explain.

The Poor Get Diabetes, the Rich Get Local and Organic

MARK WINNE

Mark Winne was born in Englewood, New Jersey, in 1950. Shortly after graduating from Bates College in 1973, he became involved in community food systems in Maine and Massachusetts. In 1979 Winne joined the Hartford Food System, a nonprofit organization, as executive director, and while working there earned a master of science degree in community economic development from the University of Southern New Hampshire. During his almost twenty-five years as director of Hartford Food System, he developed and organized numerous community food projects, including food co-ops, community gardens, farmers' markets, and food banks throughout Connecticut. As founder and chairman of the Working Lands Alliance, Winne advocated for farmland preservation. Thousands of low-income families and hundreds of Connecticut farmers have benefited from the programs he developed, and these programs, in turn, have become models for the rest of the country. As a writer, consultant, and food activist, Winne currently speaks out on what he sees as the most pressing food issue of the day, namely how healthful and affordable food has become less and less accessible to low-income Americans since the 1960s. In his book *Closing the Food Gap: Resetting the Table in the Land of Plenty* (2008), Winne discusses the growing food-gap problem between rich and poor and offers some realistic solutions.

In the following excerpt from this book, Winne points out that hunger, obesity, and diabetes run high among low-income families and addresses the need to have better food options made available to these citizens. His vision for making healthful local and organic foods available to all Americans is both hopeful and realistic.

WRITING TO DISCOVER: *Are organic foods a part of your regular diet? If yes, what are your reasons for buying and eating these foods? If no, what, if anything, is holding you back from buying and eating organic?*

As a class, lower income people have been well represented in some of the best-covered food stories of our day, particularly hunger, obesity, and diabetes. As these issues have faded in and out of the public's eye over the last 25 years, another food trend was rapidly becoming a national obsession—namely, local and organic.

At about the same time that Berkeley diva Alice Waters was first showing us how to bestow style and grace on something as ordinary as a local tomato, the Reagan administration's anti-poor policies were driving an unprecedented number of people into soup kitchens and food banks. And as organic food advocates were putting the finishing touches on what was to become the first national standard for organic food, supermarket chains were nailing plywood across their city store windows bidding farewell to lower income America.

Organic food and agriculture had barely climbed out of the bassinet in 1989 when *60 Minutes* ran its now famous Alar story. The exposure it received before 40 million television viewers ignited a firestorm of consumer reaction that eventually made organic food the fastest growing segment of the U.S. food industry.

Yuppie families reacted first. Like every parent since time immemorial, these parents wanted what was best for their children, and the emerging evidence that our food supply was tainted accelerated their desire for the healthiest and safest food possible. Though the research surrounding the health and safety attributes of various foods remained foggy, competing claims opened up a never ending number of consumer options. One's food choices may be vegetarian, vegan, organic, grass-fed, free-range, humanely raised, or some combination of these. As to the source of this food, it could range from "generally local when it's easy to get" to "obsessively local and will eat nothing else."

In low-income circles, however, such food anxieties got little traction.   5 Between getting to a food store where the bananas weren't black and having enough money to buy *any* food at all, low-income shoppers had little inclination to parse the differences between grass-fed and grass-finished. But this didn't imply that their awareness of organic food was nonexistent, nor did it mean that low-income consumers were less likely to buy organic if they had the chance.

LOW-INCOME SHOPPERS SPEAK

To better understand a variety of issues, the Hartford Food System, a Connecticut-based nonprofit organization that I directed for 24 years, would often meet with low-income families to get their point of view. On one such occasion, we asked eight members of Hartford's Clay/Arsenal neighborhood to discuss local and organic food. Like other impoverished urban neighborhoods, Clay/Arsenal was entirely devoid of good quality food stores, and their residents experienced hunger, obesity, and diabetes at rates that were two to three times the national average. This group was comprised exclusively of Hispanic and African American residents.

First off, the group expressed an immediate consensus that fresh, inexpensive food—the food they generally preferred—was unavailable in their neighborhood. Everyone agreed that traveling to a full-line supermarket was a hassle because it required one or two long bus rides or an expensive taxi fare. As a result, they did their major shopping once or twice a month, and when they shopped, price was their most important consideration.

When asked what the word *organic* meant to them, the residents answered "real food," "natural," "healthy," and "you know what's in it." While they believed that organic food was preferable to food they described as "processed," "full of chemicals," or "toxic," they said that buying organic food wasn't even an option, because it was simply not available to them. One young woman made a point of saying that she didn't trust the environment where she lived or the food she ingested. "Everything gives you cancer these days," she said. Conversely, there was an underlying tone of confidence in the safety and healthfulness of food that they could identify as local and organic.

Their awareness of the benefits of local and organic food was very high. For the elderly, there was the nostalgic association with tastes, places, and times gone by. For those with young children, there was an apprehension that nearly everything associated with their external environment, including food, was a threat. Like parents of all races, education levels, and occupations, these moms wanted what was best for their children as well, even when they knew that what was best was not available to them.

LOCAL AND ORGANIC GO MAINSTREAM

"In a burst of new interest in food," spouted *Newsweek*'s 2006 food   10
issue, "Americans are demanding—and paying for—the freshest and least chemically treated products available." Whole Foods' John Mackey told the *Wall Street Journal,* "The organic-food lifestyle is not a fad . . . It's a value system, a belief system. It's penetrating into the mainstream."

As we cast our eye over the sheer effulgence of American food, there appears to be no limit to the type and number of food products for those who are motivated by taste, environmental concern, animal welfare, political correctness, or simple virtue. Niman Ranch produces a pork to die for, and costs significantly more than the factory-farmed alternative. Don't want to spend the "best four years of your life" eating swill from the college cafeteria trough? Select from any of hundreds of colleges and universities that are now featuring "sustainable dining" (some inspired by master chef Alice Waters). And when you just can't find anything that satisfies your organic lifestyle where you live, you can always pack up and leave. The *New York Times* style page featured a number of families who had the financial wherewithal to escape from New York City to the Hudson River valley. Once there, the families "began eating strictly organic foods." One couple said they had moved because the wife was pregnant with their second child and "we decided that the children needed to be in nature."

Sounds pretty good. In fact, it just may be the latest incarnation of the American dream. But what about those who can't escape or afford to eat "strictly organic" or for whom "buying local" means the past-code date, packaged baloney at the neighborhood bodega? How do we fulfill the desire for healthy and sustainably produced food that is increasingly shared by all?

There are two general directions that have shown promise in closing this food gap: one is through private, largely nonprofit projects and the other is through public policy. At the Hartford Food System we founded the Holcomb Farm Community Supported Agriculture (CSA) Farm that made an explicit commitment to distribute about 40 percent of its local and organic produce to the city's low-income community. Using a hybrid method of funding, CSAs like the Holcomb Farm (Just Food in New York City and the Western Massachusetts Food Bank in Hadley are other examples) have been organized around the country to ensure that CSAs are not solely the province of a white, bright elite. Other models like the People's Grocery in Oakland are using mobile markets to bring high quality, healthy food into communities that are underserved by supermarkets.

Public policy advocacy has leveraged federal and state funding to provide special farmers' market vouchers to low-income women, children, and elders (Farmers Market Nutrition Program). These small denomination coupons have opened an increasing share of the nation's 4,500 farmers' markets to a wider demographic of shoppers. Along the same lines, a small but steady stream of farmers' markets are installing swipe card machines to enable food stamp recipients to use their electronic benefit transfer (EBT) cards to buy local food. And in what might be the biggest breakthrough yet, the national Women, Infant, and Children Program (WIC) will be implementing a new fruit and vegetable program that is potentially worth hundreds of million dollars to lower income consumers and local farmers.

While it may be some time before we see a Whole Foods open in East Harlem, nonprofit organizations like the Philadelphia-based Food Trust have secured millions of dollars in state financing to develop food stores in underserved urban and rural Pennsylvania communities. As part of an overall economic development strategy, these stores are not only providing new sources of healthy and affordable food to low-income families, they are also expanding employment opportunities and the local property tax base.

These projects and policies have inched us closer to bridging the divide between the haves and have-nots, but unless every segment of society rejects the notion that there is one food system for the poor, and one for everyone else, these gains will remain marginal.

THINKING CRITICALLY ABOUT THE READING

1. What does Winne see as the link between lower-income people and hunger, obesity, and diabetes? In what ways is food a class issue?

2. Why do you suppose many supermarkets closed their city stores in the 1980s? What has been the impact of these closings on low-income urban residents? Do you agree with Winne that "it may be some time before we see a Whole Foods open in East Harlem" (15)? What do you think is holding such companies back from moving into our urban neighborhoods?

3. What myths about low-income consumers does Winne challenge? Were you guilty of believeing any of these myths? Explain.

4. What did the Hartford Food System discover when its members discussed local and organic food options with residents of an impoverished urban neighborhood?

5. According to Winne, how can America close the food gap and "fulfill the desire for healthy and sustainably produced food that is increasingly shared by all" (12)?

WRITING SUGGESTIONS: DEBATING THE ISSUE

1. Michael Pollan tells a story about a food industry executive who once declared, "There's money to be made in food, unless you're trying to grow it" (16). What, if anything, is wrong with this picture, in your opinion? Do you agree with the food industry's claim that "selling unprocessed or minimally processed whole foods will always be a fool's game" (18)? Using evidence from several of the articles in this chapter, write an essay in which you argue for more unprocessed foods in the American diet.

2. In the selection "Called Home," which has been excerpted from *Animal, Vegetable, Miracle*, Barbara Kingsolver wonders, "Will North Americans ever have a food culture to call our own? Can we find or make up a set of rituals, recipes, ethics, and buying habits that will let us love our food and eat it too?" (28). In your opinion, how do Americans behave around food? Do you think we have anything close to what Kingsolver would call an American food culture? Write an essay in which you explore the food culture that might evolve in the United States as people become more educated about food.

3. What for you are the connotations of the words *natural, fresh, organic, local,* and *sustainable*? Do you believe that these words are inherently deceptive? What do you think you are buying when you purchase a product with one or more of these words on its label? Should these words be regulated in advertisements for food products? Sarah Federman, for example, claims that " 'natural' has become more a marketing ploy than a way to communicate meaningful information about a product" (2). Write an essay either for or against regulating words like *natural, fresh, organic, local,* and *sustainable,* using examples from ads you find in print or on television.

4. According to Pollan, what is the problem with the ways the food industry is using corn and soybeans? What was your reaction to Pollan's claim that "from these two plants (plus a handful of synthetic additives) a food scientist can construct just about any processed food he or she can dream up" (4)? What does Kingsolver have to say about corn and soybeans? Test Pollan's claim by examining the labels on food products in your cabinets or at the local grocery store. How much of each product is from corn or soybeans? Write a report on your findings.

5. Kingsolver claims that most Americans know very little about "agricultural basics," that is, where their food comes from. On a scale of one to ten, ten being extremely knowledgeable, how would you rate your own knowledge of agriculture? Have you ever grown any of your own food or worked on a farm? Have you ever had a "food-production class" or known anyone who has? What does Kingsolver see as the value of these classes? Do you think that such classes would help Americans think differently about the foods they eat? Write an essay in which you argue for or against the requirement of at least one food-production class in high school or college.

6. To what extent is food a political, social, and economic issue in the United States? Do you believe, like Mark Winne, that a "food gap" exists? How difficult is it for low-income people to eat well in America? Is it simply a matter of money, or are other factors like education involved? Do you agree with John Mackey, chairman of Whole Foods, that the "organic-food lifestyle is not a fad . . . It's a value system, a belief system. It's penetrating into the mainstream" (10)? Using evidence from at least three of the selections in this chapter and your own experience and observations, write an essay in which you explore the "food gap" between the haves and have-nots today and steps that can be taken to lessen the gap.

7. What kinds of foods are being served in your school's dining rooms? Is your university or college among the hundreds nationwide featuring what Mark Winne calls "sustainable dining"? If so, find out what it took to implement such a program and ask fellow students what they think about it. If not, find out why not. Write an article for your school newspaper in which you either tout the campus "sustainable dining" program and suggest improvements that could be made, or argue for the implementation of such a program.

8. What kinds of claims do advertisements for food routinely make? What strategies do they use to persuade us to buy and consume? Skim a few magazines or surf the Web and collect at least four ads connected by the type of food product they sell. (If you're feeling energetic, you might use a digital camera to take photos of ads you find on the street, on billboards, or in store windows.) You might, for example, choose ads for breakfast cereals; snack foods; "heat-and-serve" meals; or minimally processed foods, like sugar, beef, or milk. Make a copy or print out each of the ads, and analyze each one, paying particular attention to the types of claims it makes and the strategies of persuasion it uses. Does your analysis support Liebman's conclusion that structure/function claims dominate because they are not regulated? Present your findings in a brief essay.

9. Take a look at adbusters.org/spoofads/food, a collection of "spoof" ads for food products created by AdBusters, a self-described "global network of artists, activists, writers, pranksters, students, educators and entrepreneurs who want to advance the new social activist movement of the information age." Then compare them to actual ads you have found treating the same products. What claims do the AdBusters ads make? How do they manipulate the strategies made by mainstream advertisers for different ends? Write an essay in which you discuss what the spoof ads can teach us about the real ones.

Appendix: Finding, Evaluating, and Documenting Sources

The research paper is an important part of a college education for good reason. In writing such a paper, you acquire a number of indispensable research skills that you can adapt to other college assignments and, after graduation, to important life tasks.

The real value of writing a research paper, however, goes beyond acquiring basic skills; it is a unique hands-on learning experience. The purpose of a research paper is not to present a collection of quotations that show you can report what others have said about your topic. Rather, your goal is to analyze, evaluate, and synthesize the materials you research—and thereby learn how to do so with any topic. You learn how to view the results of research from your own perspective and arrive at an informed opinion of a topic.

Writing a researched essay is not very different from the other writing you will be doing in your college writing course. You will find yourself drawing heavily on what you have learned in "Writing in College" (pp. 15–38). First you determine what you want to write about. Then you decide on a purpose, consider your audience, develop a thesis, collect your evidence, write a first draft, revise and edit, and prepare a final copy. What differentiates the researched paper from other kinds of papers is your use of outside sources and how you acknowledge them.

In this chapter you will learn how to locate print and Internet sources and how to evaluate and analyze these sources. You will also find guidelines for creating a list of Works Cited according to MLA (Modern Language Association) rules. For important advice on integrating source material into your paper and avoiding plagiarism, see "Writing in College," pages 15–38.

FINDING SOURCES

The distinction between print sources and electronic sources is fast disappearing. Many sources that used to appear only in print are now available in electronic format as well; some, in fact, are moving entirely to electronic format, as a more efficient and in many cases less expensive means of distribution.

There are, however, still important distinctions between print sources (or their electronic equivalent) and Internet sources. Many of the sources you will find through an Internet search will not be as reliable as those that traditionally appeared in print. For this reason, in most cases you should use print sources or their electronic versions (books, newspapers, journals, periodicals, encyclopedias, pamphlets, brochures, and government publications) as your primary tools for research. These sources, unlike many Internet sources, are often reviewed by experts in the field before they are published, are generally overseen by a reputable publishing company or organization, and are examined by editors and fact checkers for accuracy and reliability. Unless you are instructed otherwise, you should try to use these sources in your research.

The best place to start any search for sources is your college library's home page (see figure below). Here you will find links to the computerized catalog of book holdings, online reference works, periodical databases, electronic journals, and a list of full-text databases. You'll also find links for subject study guides and for help conducting your research.

Search through your library's reference works, electronic catalog, periodical indexes, and other databases to generate a preliminary listing of books, magazine and newspaper articles, public documents and reports, and other sources that may be helpful in exploring your topic. At this early stage, it is better to err on the side of listing too many sources. Then, later on, you will not have to backtrack to find sources you discarded too hastily.

Sources that you find through an Internet search can also be informative and valuable additions to your research. The Internet is especially useful in providing recent data, stories, and reports. For example, you might

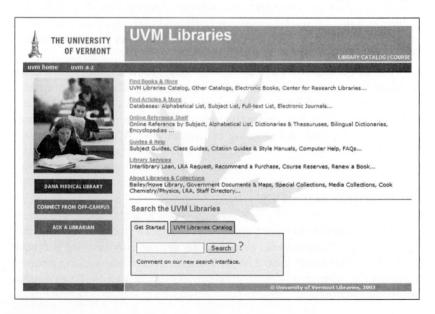

find a just-published article from a university laboratory, or a news story in your local newspaper's online archives. Generally, however, Internet sources should be used alongside sources you access through your college library and not as a replacement for them. Practically anyone with access to a computer and an Internet connection can put text and pictures on the Internet; there is often no governing body that checks for content or accuracy. Therefore, while the Internet offers a vast number of useful and carefully maintained resources, it also contains much unreliable information. It is your responsibility to determine whether a given Internet source should be trusted.

If you do not know how to access the Internet, or if you need more instruction on conducting Internet searches, go to your on-campus computer center for more information, or consult one of the many books written for Internet beginners. You can also access valuable information for searching the Internet at Diana Hacker's *Research and Documentation Online* <www.dianahacker.com.resdoc>.

Using Keyword Searches and Subject Directories to Locate Information

KEYWORD SEARCHES.   When searching for sources about your topic in an electronic database, in the library's computerized catalog, or on the Internet, you should start with a keyword search. To make the most efficient use of your time, you will want to know how to conduct a keyword search that is likely to yield solid sources and leads for your research project. As obvious or simple as it may sound, the key to a successful keyword search is the quality of the keywords you generate about your topic. You might find it helpful to start a list of potential keywords as you begin your research and add to it as your work proceeds. Often you will discover combinations of keywords that will lead you right to the sources you need.

Databases and library catalogs index sources by author, title, and year of publication, as well as by subject headings assigned by a cataloger who has previewed the source. The key here is to find a keyword that matches one of the subject headings. Once you begin to locate sources that are on your topic, be sure to note the subject headings listed for each source. You can use these subject headings as keywords to lead you to additional book sources or to articles in periodicals, using full-text databases like *Info Trac, LexisNexis, Expanded Academic ASAP*, or *JSTOR* to which your library subscribes. The figure on page 610 shows a typical book entry in a computer catalog. Notice the additional subject headings, which can be used as possible keywords.

The keyword search process is somewhat different—more wide open—when you are searching on the Web. It is always a good idea to look for search tips on the help screens or advanced search instructions for the search engine you are using before initiating a keyword search.

When you type in a keyword in the "Search" box on a search engine's home page, the search engine electronically scans Web sites looking to match your keyword to titles and texts. On the Web, the quality of the search terms—keywords—is determined by the relevance of the hits on the first page or two that comes up. While it is not uncommon for an Internet search to yield between 500,000 and 1,000,000 hits, the search engine's algorithm puts the best sources up front. If after scanning the first couple of pages of results you determine that these sites seem off topic, you will need to refine your search terms to either narrow or broaden your search.

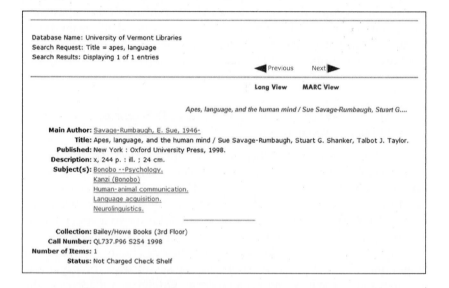

Database Name: University of Vermont Libraries
Search Request: Title = apes, language
Search Results: Displaying 1 of 1 entries

◀ Previous   Next ▶

Long View   MARC View

Apes, language, and the human mind / Sue Savage-Rumbaugh, Stuart G....

Main Author: Savage-Rumbaugh, E. Sue, 1946-
Title: Apes, language, and the human mind / Sue Savage-Rumbaugh, Stuart G. Shanker, Talbot J. Taylor.
Published: New York : Oxford University Press, 1998.
Description: x, 244 p. : ill. ; 24 cm.
Subject(s): Bonobo --Psychology.
Kanzi (Bonobo)
Human-animal communication.
Language acquisition.
Neurolinguistics.

Collection: Bailey/Howe Books (3rd Floor)
Call Number: QL737.P96 S254 1998
Number of Items: 1
Status: Not Charged Check Shelf

Refining Keyword Searches on the Web

While some variation in command terms and characters exists among electronic databases and popular search engines on the Internet, the following functions are almost universally accepted. If you have a particular question about refining your keyword search, seek assistance by clicking on "Help" or "Advanced Search."

- Use quotation marks or parentheses to indicate that you are searching for words in exact sequence—e.g., "whooping cough"; (Supreme Court).
- Use AND or a plus sign (+) between or before words to narrow your search by specifying that all words need to appear in a document—e.g., tobacco AND cancer; Shakespeare + sonnet.

- Use NOT or a minus sign (−) between or before words to narrow your search by eliminating unwanted words—e.g., monopoly NOT game, cowboys–Dallas.
- Use OR to broaden your search by requiring that only one of the words need appear—e.g., buffalo OR bison.
- Use an asterisk (*) to indicate that you will accept variations of a term—e.g., "food label*" for food labels, food labeling, and so forth.

During her initial search for her paper on censorship in schools (see pp. 32–38), student Tara E. Ketch typed in "school censorship." This produced an unmanageable 2,690,000 results.

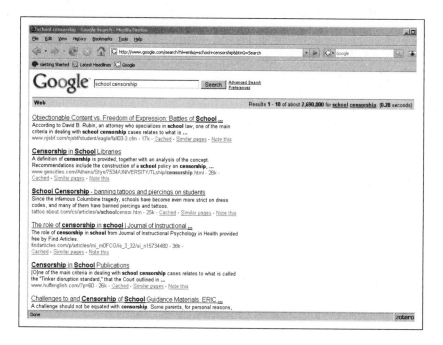

After thinking about how to narrow her search, she decided to type in "school censorship" + literature. This search yielded a more manageable 2,150 results (see screen shot on p. 612). As she refined her topic further, Ketch was able to narrow her searches even more effectively.

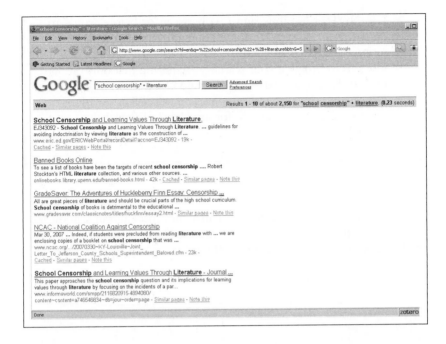

SUBJECT DIRECTORIES.   If you are undecided as to exactly what you want to write about, the subject directories on the home pages of search engines make it easy to browse the Web by various subjects and topics for ideas that interest you. Subject directories can also be a big help if you have a topic but are undecided about your exact research question or if you simply want to see if there is enough material to supplement your research work with print sources. Once you choose a subject area in the directory, you can select more specialized sub-directories, eventually arriving at a list of sites closely related to your topic.

The most common question students have at this stage of a Web search is, "How can I tell if I'm looking in the right place?" There is no straight answer; if more than one subject area sounds plausible, you will have to dig more deeply into each of their subdirectories, using logic and the process of elimination to determine which one is likely to produce the best leads for your topic. In most cases, it doesn't take long—usually just one or two clicks—to figure out whether you're searching in the right subject area. If you click on a subject area and none of the topics listed in its subdirectories seems to pertain even remotely to your research topic, try a different subject area. As you browse through various subject directories and subdirectories, keep a running list of keywords associated with your topic that you can use in subsequent keyword searches.

EVALUATING SOURCES

You will not have to spend much time in the library to realize that you do not have time to read every print and online source that appears relevant. Given the abundance of print and Internet sources, the key to successful research is identifying those books, articles, Web sites, and other online sources that will help you most. You must evaluate your potential sources to determine which materials you will read, which you will skim, and which you will simply eliminate. Here are some evaluation strategies and questions to assist you in identifying your most promising sources.

Strategies for evaluating print and online sources

EVALUATING A BOOK

- Read the dust jacket or cover copy for insights into the book's coverage and currency as well as the author's expertise.
- Scan the table of contents and identify any promising chapters.
- Read the author's preface, looking for his or her thesis and purpose.
- Check the index for key words or key phrases related to your research topic.
- Read the opening and concluding paragraphs of any promising chapter; if you are unsure about its usefulness, skim the whole chapter.
- Does the author have a discernable bias?

EVALUATING AN ARTICLE

- What do you know about the journal or magazine publishing the article? Scholarly journals (*American Economic Review, Journal of Marriage and the Family, The Wilson Quarterly*) publish articles about original research written by authorities in the field. Research essays always cite their sources in footnotes or bibliographies. Popular news and general interest magazines (*National Geographic, Smithsonian, Time, Ebony*), on the other hand, publish informative, entertaining, and easy-to-read articles written by editorial staff or freelance writers. Popular essays sometimes cite sources but often do not.
- What is the reputation of the journal or magazine? Determine the publisher or sponsor. Is it an academic institution or a commercial enterprise or individual? Does the publisher or publication have a reputation for accuracy and objectivity?
- Who are the readers of this journal or magazine?
- What are the author's credentials?
- Consider the title or headline of the article as well as the opening paragraph or two and the conclusion. Does the source appear to be too general or too technical for your needs and audience?

- For articles in journals, read the abstract (a summary of the main points) if there is one. Examine any photographs, charts, graphs, or other illustrations that accompany the article. Determine how useful they might be for your research purposes.

EVALUATING A WEB SITE

- Consider the type of Web site. Is this site a personal blog or a professional publication? Often the URL, especially the top-level domain name, can give you a clue about the kinds of information provided and the type of organization behind the site. Common suffixes include:

    .com—business/commercial/personal
    .edu—educational institution
    .gov—government sponsored
    .net—various types of networks
    .org—nonprofit organization, but also some commercial/personal

- Be advised that *.org* is not regulated like *.edu* and *.gov*, for example. Most nonprofits use *.org*, but many commercial and personal sites do as well.
- Examine the home page of the site. Does the content appear to be related to your research topic?
- Is there an *About* link on the home page that takes you to background information on the site's sponsor? Is there a mission statement, history, or statement of philosophy? Can you verify whether the site is official—actually sanctioned by the organization or company?
- Identify the author of the site. What are the author's qualifications for writing on this subject?
- Is a print equivalent available? Is the Web version more or less extensive than the print version?
- When was the site last updated? Is the content current enough for your purposes?

You can find sources on the Internet itself that offer useful guidelines for evaluating electronic sources. One excellent example was created by reference librarians at the Wolfgram Memorial Library of Widener University. Google *Wolfgram evaluate web pages* or visit www3.widener.edu/Academics/Libraries/Wolfgram_Memorial_Library/Evaluate_Web_Pages/659/.

On the basis of your evaluation, select the most promising books, articles, and Web sites to pursue in depth for your research project.

ANALYZING SOURCES

Before beginning to take notes, it is essential that you carefully analyze your sources for their thesis, overall argument, amount and credibility of evidence, bias, and reliability in helping you explore your research topic. Look for the writers' main ideas, key examples, strongest arguments, and conclusions. Read critically. While it is easy to become absorbed in sources that support your own beliefs, always seek out several sources with opposing viewpoints, if only to test your own position. Look for information about the authors themselves—information that will help you determine their authority and where they position themselves in the broader conversation on the issue. You should also know the reputation and special interests of book publishers and magazines, because you are likely to get different views—conservative, liberal, international, feminist—on the same topic depending on the publication you read. Use the following checklist to assist you in analyzing your print and online sources.

Checklist for analyzing print and online sources

- What is the writer's thesis or claim?
- How does the writer support this thesis? Does the evidence seem reasonable and ample, or is it mainly anecdotal?
- Does the writer consider opposing viewpoints?
- Does the writer have any obvious political or religious biases? Is the writer associated with any special-interest groups such as Planned Parenthood, Greenpeace, Amnesty International, or the National Rifle Association?
- Is the writer an expert on the subject? Do other writers mention this author in their work?
- Is important information documented through footnotes or links so that it can be verified or corroborated in other sources?
- What is the author's purpose—to inform or to argue for a particular position or action?
- Do the writer's thesis and purpose clearly relate to your research topic?
- Does the source reflect current thinking and research in the field?

DEVELOPING A WORKING BIBLIOGRAPHY

As you discover books, journal and magazine articles, newspaper stories, and Web sites that you think might be helpful, you need to start maintaining a record of important information about each source. This record, called a working bibliography, will enable you to know where sources are located as well as what they are when it comes time to consult them or acknowledge them in your list of works cited or final bibliography (see pp. 24–31 and 38). In all likelihood, your working bibliography will contain more sources than you actually consult and include in your list of works cited.

One method for creating a working bibliography is to make a separate bibliography card, using a 3- by 5-inch index card, for each work that you think might be helpful to your research. As your collection of cards grows, alphabetize them by the authors' last names. By using a separate card for each book, article, or Web site, you can continually edit your working bibliography, dropping sources that did not prove helpful for one reason or another and adding new ones.

With the computerization of most library resources, you now have the option to copy and paste bibliographic information from the library computer catalog and periodical indexes or from the Internet into a document on your computer that you can edit/add/delete/search throughout the research process. Or you can track your project online with the Bedford Bibliographer at www.bedfordstmartins.com/bibliographer. The advantage of the copy/paste option over the index card method is accuracy, especially in punctuation, spelling, and capitalization—details that are essential in accessing Internet sites.

Checklist for a working bibliography of print and online soures

FOR BOOKS
- Library call number
- Names of all authors, editors, and translators
- Title and subtitle
- Publication data:
    Place of publication (city and state)
    Publisher's name
    Date of publication
- Edition (if not first) and volume number (if applicable)

FOR PERIODICAL ARTICLES
- Names of all authors
- Name and subtitle of article
- Title of journal, magazine, or newspaper
- Publication data:
    Volume number and issue number
    Date of issue
    Page numbers

FOR INTERNET SOURCES
- Names of all authors and/or editors
- Title and subtitle of the document

- Title of the longer work to which the document belongs (if applicable)
- Title of the site or discussion list
- Name of company or organization that owns the Web site
- Date of release, online posting, or latest revision
- Format of online source (Web page, .pdf, podcast)
- Date you accessed the site
- Electronic address (URL)

FOR OTHER SOURCES

- Name of author, government agency, organization, company, recording artist, personality, etc.
- Title of the work
- Format (pamphlet, unpublished diary, interview, television broadcast, etc.)
- Publication or production data:

  Name of publisher or producer
  Date of publication, production, or release
  Identifying codes or numbers (if applicable)

DOCUMENTING SOURCES: SAMPLE WORKS CITED ENTRIES

In this section you will find general MLA guidelines for creating a works cited list, followed by sample entries that cover the citation situations you will encounter most often. Make sure that you follow the formats as they appear on the following pages.

GENERAL GUIDELINES

- Begin the list on a new page following the last page of text.
- Organize the list alphabetically by author's last name. If the entry has no author name, alphabetize by the first major word of the title.
- Double-space within and between entries.
- Begin each entry at the left margin. If the entry is longer than one line, indent the second and subsequent lines five spaces or one-half inch.
- Do not number entries.
- End your entry with the medium in which you accessed the source ("Print," for sources in this section).

Books

BOOKS BY ONE AUTHOR

List the author's last name first, followed by a comma and first name. Follow with the city of publication and a shortened version of publisher's name—for example, *Houghton* for *Houghton Mifflin,* or *Cambridge UP* for *Cambridge University Press.* End with the date of publication.

> Pinker, Steven. *The Language Instinct: How the Mind Creates Language.* New York: Morrow, 1994. Print.

BOOKS BY TWO OR THREE AUTHORS

List the first author (following order on title page) in the same way as for a single-author book; list subsequent authors first name first in the order they appear on the title page.

> Jones, Charisse, and Kumea Shorter–Gooden. *Shifting: The Double Lives of Black Women in America.* New York: HarperCollins, 2003. Print.

BOOKS BY FOUR OR MORE AUTHORS

List the first author in the same way as for a single-author book, followed by a comma and the abbreviation *et al.* ("and others").

> Chomsky, Noam, et al. *Acts of Aggression.* New York: Seven Stories, 1999. Print.

TWO OR MORE BOOKS BY THE SAME AUTHOR

List two or more books by the same author in alphabetical order by title. List the first book by the author's name. After the first book, in place of the author's name substitute three unspaced hyphens followed by a period.

> Lederer, Richard. *Anguished English.* Charleston: Wyrick, 1987. Print.
> ---. *Crazy English.* New York: Pocket Books, 1990. Print.

REVISED EDITION

> Aitchison, Jean. *Language Change: Process or Decay?* 2nd ed. Cambridge: Cambridge UP, 1991. Print.

EDITED BOOK

> Douglass, Frederick. *Narrative of the Life of Frederick Douglass, an American Slave, Written by Himself.* Ed. Benjamin Quarles. Cambridge: Belknap, 1960. Print.

TRANSLATION

> Dumas, Alexandre. *The Knight of Maison Rouge.* Trans. Julie Rose. New York: Modern Library, 2003. Print.

CORPORATE AUTHOR

> The Carnegie Foundation for the Advancement of Teaching. *Campus Life: In Search of Community.* Princeton: Princeton UP, 1990. Print.

MULTIVOLUME WORK

> Cassidy, Frederic G., and J. H. Hall, eds. *Dictionary of American Regional English.* 3 vols. Cambridge: Harvard UP, 1885. Print.

ANTHOLOGY

Rosa, Alfred, Paul Eschholz, and Beth Simon, eds. *Language: Introductory Readings.* 7th ed. Boston: Bedford/St. Martin's, 2008. Print.

WORK IN AN ANTHOLOGY

Giovanni, Nikki. "Campus Racism 101." *Subject and Strategy.* Ed. Paul Eschholz and Alfred Rosa. 11th ed. Boston: Bedford/St. Martin's, 2008. 249–257. Print.

SECTION OR CHAPTER IN A BOOK

Lamott, Anne. "Shitty First Drafts." *Bird by Bird: Some Instructions on Writing and Life.* New York: Pantheon, 1994. 21–27. Print.

Periodicals

ARTICLE IN A JOURNAL WITH CONTINUOUS PAGINATION
THROUGHOUT AN ANNUAL VOLUME

Some journals paginate issues continuously, by volume; that is, the page numbers in one issue pick up where the previous issue left off. For these journals, follow the volume number by the date of publication in parentheses.

Gazzaniga, Michael S. "Right Hemisphere Language Following Brain Bisection: A Twenty-Year Perspective." *American Psychologist* 38 (1983): 528–49. Print.

ARTICLE IN A JOURNAL WITH SEPARATE PAGINATION IN EACH ISSUE

Some journals paginate by issue; each issue begins with page 1. For these journals, follow the volume number with a period and the issue number. Then give the date of publication in parentheses.

Douglas, Ann. "The Failure of the New York Intellectuals." *Raritan* 17.4 (1998): 1–23. Print.

ARTICLE IN A WEEKLY OR BIWEEKLY MAGAZINE

Keizer, Garret. "Sound and Fury: The Politics of Noise in a Loud Society." *Harper's Magazine* Mar. 2001: 39–48. Print.

ARTICLE IN A NEWSPAPER

If an article in a newspaper or magazine appears discontinuously— that is, if it starts on one page and skips one or more pages before continuing—include only the first page followed by a plus sign.

Wade, Nicholas. "A Prolific Genghis Khan, It Seems, Helped People the World." *New York Times* 11 Feb. 2003, late ed.: D3+. Print.

EDITORIAL OR LETTER TO THE EDITOR

Rose, Lowell C. "Public Education's Trojan Horse?" Editorial. *Phi Delta Kappan* 85.1 (2003): 2. Print.

McEwan, Barbara. Letter. *Nature Conservancy* 52.4 (2002): 6. Print.

Electronic sources

The following guidelines and models for citing information retrieved from the Internet and other electronic sources have been adapted from the most recent advice of the MLA, as detailed in the *MLA Handbook for Writers of Research Papers*, 7th ed. (2009) and from the "MLA Style" section on the MLA's Web site at www.mla.org. When listing an electronic source in your list of works cited, include the following elements, if they are available and relevant, in the reference.

- **Author.** Write the name of the author, editor, compiler, or translator of the source with the last name first, followed by a comma and the first name. If appropriate, follow the name with an abbreviation such as *ed.* If no author is given, begin with the title.
- **Title.** Write the title of the poem, short story, article, essay, or similar short work within a scholarly project, database, or periodical in quotation marks. If you are citing an entire online book, the title should be italicized.
- **Electronic print information.** Give the title of the scholarly project, database, periodical, or professional or personal site (italicized), or, for a professional or personal site with no title, give a general description, such as *Home page*. If citing an online journal, provide journal and issue number, if available, and page numbers (or "n. pag." if no page numbers are given). For most online sources, follow the title with the sponsor or publisher of the site (or "n.p." if none is given), date of publication or last update (or "n.d." if no date is given), and medium ("Web"). Electronic sources that originally appeared in print should also provide print publication information, if available. (See, for example, the first entry below under "Online Book or Part of a Book.")
- **Access information.** The final elements to add are the date you accessed the source and the medium of the source. **Note:** Because most online sources are easily locatable using a search engine, the electronic address, or URL, of the source need not be supplied unless your instructor requires it. If this is the case, add the URL in angle brackets (e.g., <www.mla.org>) immediately following the date of access.

ONLINE BOOK OR PART OF BOOK

Hawthorne, Nathaniel. *Twice-Told Tales.* Ed. George Parsons Lathrop. Boston: Houghton, 1883. *Eldritchpress.org.* Web. 1 Mar. 2008.

Woolf, Virginia. "Kew Gardens." *Monday or Tuesday.* New York: Harcourt, 1921. N. pag. *Bartleby.com: Great Books Online.* Web. 28 Feb. 2008.

WORK IN A SCHOLARLY PROJECT OR DATABASE

Hodge, James T. "Bibliographic Description of *Agrippa.*" *The* Agrippa *Files.* The Transcriptions Project, UC Santa Barbara, n.d. Web. 11 Jul. 2008.

WORK FROM ONLINE SUBSCRIPTION SERVICE SUCH AS *INFOTRAC*

McEachern, William Ross. "Teaching and Learning in Bilingual Countries: The
    Examples of Belgium and Canada." *Education* 123 (2002): 103. *Expanded
    Academic ASAP Plus.* Web. 15 Aug. 2008.

Sanders, Joshunda. "Think Race Doesn't Matter? Listen to Eminem." *San Francisco
    Chronicle* 20 July 2003. *Lexis Nexis Academic.* 14 Nov. 2008.

ARTICLE IN AN ONLINE SCHOLARLY JOURNAL

Rist, Thomas. "Religion, Politics, Revenge: The Dead in Renaissance Drama." *Early
    Modern Literary Studies* 9.1 (May 2003): n. pag. Web. 28 Feb. 2008.

ARTICLE IN AN ONLINE MAGAZINE

Lamott, Anne. "Because I'm the Mother." *Salon.com.* Salon Media Group, 4 July 2003.
    Web. 10 Sept. 2008.

ARTICLE IN AN ONLINE NEWSPAPER

Morley, Jefferson. "In Schwarzenegger, Online Pundits See American Delusions,
    Opportunities." *Washington Post.* Washington Post, 9 Oct. 2003. Web. 2 Dec. 2008.

ARTICLE IN AN ONLINE REFERENCE WORK

"Vietnam War." *The Concise Columbia Electronic Encyclopedia.* 6th ed. *Encyclopedia.com.*
    HighBeam Research, 2008. Web. 29 Sept. 2008.

CD-ROM

Shakespeare, William. *Macbeth.* Ed. A. R. Branmuller. New York: Voyager, 1994.
    CD-ROM.

"Proactive." *The Oxford English Dictionary.* 2nd ed. Oxford: Oxford UP, 1992. CD-ROM.

E-MAIL

Walker, Alexis. "Re: Gender and Language Issues." Message to the author. 15 June
    2008. E-mail.

POSTING TO A DISCUSSION LIST

Baker, John. "Re: Actionable offense: Scrouge." *The Linguist List.* American Dialect
    Society, 8 Jul. 2008. Web. 11 Jul. 2008.

PROFESSIONAL ONLINE SITE

National Organization for Women. National Organization for Women, 2008. Web.
    10 May 2008.

Other Sources

TELEVISION OR RADIO PROGRAM

"Chicago 1968." *The American Experience.* Writ. Chana Gazit. Narr. W. S. Merwin. PBS.
    WNET, New York, 13 Nov. 1997. Television.

MOVIE, VIDEOTAPE, RECORD, OR SLIDE PROGRAM

The X Files. Dir. Rob Bowman. Perf. David Duchovny, Gillian Anderson, Martin Landau, Blythe Danner, and Armin Mueller-Stahl. Twentieth Century Fox, 1998. DVD.

An Oral Historian's Work. With Edward D. Ives. Northeast Archives of Folklore and Oral History, 1987. Videocassette.

PERSONAL INTERVIEW

Losambe, Lokangaka. Personal interview. 16 Jan. 2004.

PUBLIC PRESENTATION OR CLASS LECTURE

Hayford, Helen. "Robert Frost and the Language of New England." Johnson State Coll., Johnson, VT. 20 Feb. 2003. Lecture.

CARTOON

Smaller, Barbara. Cartoon. *The New Yorker* 31 Mar. 2003: 50. Print.

MAP OR CHART

"Map of Maine." Map. *Maine Map and Guide.* Yarmouth: Delorme, 2003. Print.

ADVERTISEMENT

Verizon Wireless. Advertisement. *Newsweek* 6 Oct. 2003: 40. Print.

Glossary of Rhetorical and Linguistic Terms

Abstract See *Concrete/Abstract*.

Accent Characteristics of pronunciation that reflect regional or social identity.

Acronym A word made from the initial letters (in some cases, the first few letters) of a phrase or organization; for example, NATO (North Atlantic Treaty Organization) and scuba (self-contained underwater breathing apparatus).

Allusion A passing reference to a familiar person, place, or thing drawn from history, the Bible, mythology, or literature. An allusion is an economical way for a writer to capture the essence of an idea, atmosphere, emotion, or historical era, as in "The scandal was his Watergate," "He saw himself as a modern Job," or "Everyone there held those truths to be self-evident."

American Sign Language (ASL, Ameslan) A system of communication used by deaf people in the United States, consisting of hand symbols that vary in the shape of the hands, the direction of their movement, and their position in relation to the body. It is different from finger spelling, in which words are signed in the order in which they are uttered, thus preserving English structure and syntax.

Analogy A special form of comparison in which the writer explains something complex or unfamiliar by comparing it to something familiar: "A transmission line is simply a pipeline for electricity. In the case of a water pipeline, more water will flow through the pipe as water pressure increases. The same is true of a transmission line for electricity." When a subject is unobservable or abstract, or when readers may have trouble understanding it, analogy is particularly useful.

Argument A strategy for developing an essay. To argue is to attempt to convince a reader to agree with a point of view, to make a given decision, or to pursue a particular course of action. Logical argument is based on reasonable explanations and appeals to the reader's intelligence. See also *Persuasion, Logical Fallacies, Deduction,* and *Induction*.

Attitude A writer's opinion of a subject, which may be very positive, very negative, or somewhere between these two extremes. See also *Tone*.

Audience The intended readership for a piece of writing. For example, the readers of a national weekly newsmagazine come from all walks of life and have diverse opinions, attitudes, and educational experiences. In contrast, the readership for an organic chemistry journal may be comprised of people with similar scientific interests and educational backgrounds. The essays in this book are intended for general readers, intelligent people who may lack specific information about the subjects being discussed.

Beginnings and Endings   A *beginning* is the sentence, group of sentences, or section that introduces an essay. Good beginnings usually identify the thesis or main idea, attempt to interest the reader, and establish a tone. Some effective ways to begin essays include (1) telling an anecdote that illustrates the thesis, (2) providing a controversial statement or opinion that engages the reader's interest, (3) presenting startling statistics or facts, (4) defining a term that is central to the discussion that follows, (5) asking thought-provoking questions, (6) providing a quotation that illustrates the thesis, (7) referring to a current event that helps to establish the thesis, or (8) showing the significance of the subject or stressing its importance to the reader.

An *ending* is the sentence or group of sentences that brings an essay to closure. Good endings are well planned; they are the natural outgrowths of the essays themselves and give readers a sense of finality or completion. Some of the techniques mentioned above for beginnings may be effective for endings as well.

Biased Language   Language that is used by a dominant group within a culture to maintain its supposed superior position and to disempower others. See also *Racist Language* and *Sexist Language*.

Bidialectalism   The use of two dialects of the same language.

Bilingual Education   Teaching in a child's primary language, which may or may not be the language of the dominant population.

Black English   A vernacular variety of English used by some black people; it may be divided into Standard Black English and Black English Vernacular (BEV). See also *Ebonics*.

Brainstorming   A discovery technique in which writers list everything they know about a topic, freely associating one idea with another. When writers brainstorm, they also make lists of questions about aspects of the topic for which they need information. See also *Clustering* and *Freewriting*.

Cause and Effect Analysis   A strategy for developing an essay. Cause and effect analysis answers the question *why*. It explains the reasons for an occurrence or the consequences of an action. Whenever a question asks *why*, answering it will require discovering a *cause* or series of causes for a particular *effect*; whenever a question asks *what if*, its answer will point out the effect or effects that can result from a particular cause.

Classification   See *Division and Classification*.

Cliché   An expression that has become ineffective through overuse, such as *quick as a flash, dry as dust, jump for joy*, and *slow as molasses*. Writers normally avoid such trite expressions and seek instead to express themselves in fresh and forceful language. See also *Figures of Speech*.

Clustering   A discovery technique in which a writer puts a topic or keyword in a circle at the center of a blank page and then generates main ideas about that topic, circling each idea and connecting it with a line to the topic in the center. Writers often repeat the process in order to add specific examples and details to each main idea. This technique allows writers to generate material and sort it into meaningful clusters at the same time. See also *Brainstorming* and *Freewriting*.

Coherence   A quality of good writing that results when all of the sentences, paragraphs, and longer divisions of an essay are naturally connected. Coherent writing is achieved through (1) a logical sequence of ideas (arranged in chronological order, spatial order, order of importance, or some other appropriate order), (2) the thoughtful repetition of keywords and ideas, (3) a pace suitable for your topic and your reader, and (4) the use of transitional words and expressions. Coherence should not be confused with unity. See also *Unity* and *Transitions.*

Colloquial Expressions   Informal expressions that are typical of a particular language. In English, phrases such as *come up with, be at loose ends,* or *get with the program* are colloquial expressions. Such expressions are acceptable in formal writing only if they are used for a specific purpose.

Comparison and Contrast   A strategy for developing an essay. In comparison and contrast, the writer points out the similarities and differences between two or more subjects in the same class or category. The function of any comparison and contrast is to clarify—to reach some conclusion about the items being compared and contrasted. An effective comparison and contrast does not dwell on obvious similarities or differences; instead, it tells readers something significant that they may not already know.

Conclusions   See *Beginnings and Endings.*

Concrete/Abstract   A *concrete word* names a specific object, person, place, or action that can be directly perceived by the senses: *car, bread, building, book, John F. Kennedy, Chicago,* or *hiking.* An *abstract word,* in contrast, refers to general qualities, conditions, ideas, actions, or relationships that cannot be directly perceived by the senses: *bravery, dedication, excellence, anxiety, friendship, thinking,* or *hatred.*

　　　　Although writers must use both concrete and abstract language, good writers avoid using too many abstract words. Instead, they rely on concrete words to define and illustrate abstractions. Because concrete words appeal to the senses, they are easily comprehended by a reader.

Connotation/Denotation   Both terms refer to the meanings of words. *Denotation* is the dictionary meaning of a word, its literal meaning. *Connotation,* on the other hand, is a word's implied or suggested meaning. For example, the denotation of *lamb* is a "a young sheep." The connotations of lamb are numerous: *gentle, docile, weak, peaceful, blessed, sacrificial, blood, spring, frisky, pure, innocent,* and so on. Good writers are sensitive to both the denotations and the connotations of words and use these meanings to advantage in their writing.

Deduction   The process of reasoning that moves from stated premises to a conclusion that follows necessarily. This form of reasoning moves from the general to the specific. See also *Induction* and *Syllogism.*

Definition   A strategy for developing an essay. A definition, which states the meaning of a word, may be either brief or extended; it may be part of an essay or an entire essay itself.

Denotation   See *Connotation/Denotation.*

Description   A strategy for developing an essay. Description tells how a person, place, or thing is perceived by the five senses. Objective description reports these sensory qualities factually, whereas subjective description gives the writer's interpretation of them.

Descriptivism   A school of linguistic analysis that seeks to describe linguistic facts as they are. See also *Prescriptivism.*

Dialect　A variety of language, usually regional or social, that is set off from other varieties of the same language by differences in pronunciation, vocabulary, and grammar.

Diction　A writer's choice and use of words. Good diction is precise and appropriate— the words mean exactly what the writer intends, and the words are well suited to the writer's subject, intended audience, and purpose. The word-conscious writer knows, for example, that there are differences among *aged, old,* and *elderly; blue, navy,* and *azure;* and *disturbed, angry,* and *irritated.* Furthermore, this writer knows when to use each word. See also *Connotation/ Denotation.*

Direct Quotation　A writer's use of the exact words of a source. Direct quotations, which are put in quotation marks, are normally reserved for important ideas stated memorably, for especially clear explanations by authorities, and for proponents' arguments conveyed in their own words. See also *Paraphrase, Summary,* and *Plagiarism.*

Division and Classification　A strategy for developing an essay. *Division* involves breaking down a single large unit into smaller subunits, or separating a group of items into discrete categories. *Classification,* on the other hand, involves arranging or sorting people, places, or things into categories according to their differing characteristics, thus making them more manageable for the writer and more understandable for the reader. Division, then, takes apart, while classification groups together. Although the two processes can operate separately, most often they work hand in hand.

Doublespeak　According to doublespeak expert William Lutz, "Doublespeak is a blanket term for language which pretends to communicate but doesn't, language which makes the bad seem good, the negative appear positive, the unpleasant attractive, or at least tolerable. It is language which avoids, shifts, or denies responsibility."

Ebonics　A term coined in 1973 for African American Vernacular English (AAVE). Public debate centers on whether it is a dialect of English or a separate language with its own grammatical rules and rhythms. See also *Black English.*

Endings　See *Beginnings and Endings.*

English-Only Movement　The ongoing attempts, which began in the Senate in 1986, to declare English the official language of the United States. Although these attempts have failed thus far at the federal level, a number of states have passed various forms of English-only legislation.

Essay　A relatively short piece of nonfiction in which the writer attempts to make one or more closely related points. A good essay is purposeful, informative, and well organized.

Ethnocentricity　The belief that one's culture (including language) is at the center of things and that other cultures (and languages) are inferior.

Euphemism　A pleasing, vague, or indirect word or phrase that is substituted for one that is considered harsh or offensive. For example, *pacify* is a euphemism for *bomb, pavement deficiency* for *pothole, downsize* or *release from employment* for *fire.*

Evidence　The data on which a judgment or argument is based or by which proof or probability is established. Evidence usually takes the form of statistics, facts, names, examples or illustrations, and opinions of authorities.

Examples Ways of illustrating, developing, or clarifying an idea. Examples enable writers to show and not simply to tell readers what they mean. The terms *example* and *illustration* are sometimes used interchangeably. An example may be anything from a statistic to a story; it may be stated in a few words or go on for several pages. An example should always be *relevant* to the idea or generalization it is meant to illustrate. An example should also be *representative*. In other words, it should be typical of what the writer is trying to show.

Exemplification A strategy for developing an essay. In exemplification, the writer uses examples—facts, opinions, anecdotes, or statistics—to make ideas more vivid and understandable. Exemplification is used in all types of essays. See also *Examples*.

Fallacy See *Logical Fallacies*.

Figures of Speech Brief, imaginative comparisons that highlight the similarities between things that are basically dissimilar. They make writing vivid and interesting and therefore more memorable. Following are the most common figures of speech:

Simile: An implicit comparison introduced by *like* or *as.* "The fighter's hands were like stone."

Metaphor: An implied comparison that uses one thing as the equivalent of another. "All the world's a stage."

Onomatopoeia: The use of words whose sound suggests the meaning, as in *buzz, hiss,* and *meow.*

Personification: A special kind of simile or metaphor in which human traits are assigned to an inanimate object. "The engine coughed and then stopped."

Freewriting A discovery technique that involves writing for a brief uninterrupted period of time—ten or fifteen minutes—on anything that comes to mind. Writers use freewriting to discover new topics, new strategies, and other new ideas. See also *Brainstorming* and *Clustering*.

Gobbledygook The use of technical or unfamiliar words that confuse rather than clarify an issue for an audience.

Grammar The system of a language including its parts and the methods for combining them.

Idiom A word or phrase that is used habitually with a particular meaning in a language. The meaning of an idiom is not always readily apparent to nonnative speakers of that language. For example, *catch cold, hold a job, make up your mind,* and *give them a hand* are all idioms in English.

Illustration See *Examples*.

Indo-European Languages A group of languages descended from a supposed common ancestor and now widely spoken in Europe, North and South America, Australia, New Zealand, and parts of India.

Induction A process of reasoning whereby a conclusion about all members of a class is reached by examining only a few members of the class. This form of reasoning moves from a set of specific examples to a general statement or principle. As long as the evidence is accurate, pertinent, complete, and sufficient to represent the assertion, the conclusion of the inductive argument can be regarded as valid; if, however, readers can spot inaccuracies in the evidence or point to contrary evidence, they have good reason to doubt the assertion as it stands. Inductive reasoning is the most common of argumentative structures. See also *Deduction*.

Introductions   See *Beginnings and Endings*.

Irony   The use of words to suggest something different from their literal meaning. A writer can use irony to establish a special relationship with the reader and to add an extra dimension or twist to the meaning.

Jargon   See *Technical Language*.

Language   Words, their pronunciation, and the conventional and systematic methods for combining them as used and understood by a community.

Lexicography   The art of dictionary-making.

Linguistic Relativity Hypothesis   The belief that the structure of a language shapes the way speakers of that language view reality. Also known as the Sapir-Whorf Hypothesis after Edward Sapir and Benjamin Lee Whorf.

Logical Fallacies   Errors in reasoning that render an argument invalid. Some of the more common logical fallacies are listed here:

> *Oversimplification:* The tendency to provide simple solutions to complex problems. "The reason we have inflation today is that OPEC has unreasonably raised the price of oil."
>
> *Non sequitur* ("It does not follow"): An inference or conclusion that does not follow from established premises or evidence. "It was the best movie I saw this year, and it should get an Academy Award."
>
> *Post hoc, ergo propter hoc* ("After this, therefore because of this"): Confusing chance or coincidence with causation. Because one event comes after another one, it does not necessarily mean that the first event caused the second. "I won't say I caught cold at the hockey game, but I certainly didn't have it before I went there."
>
> *Begging the question:* Assuming in a premise that which needs to be proven. "If American autoworkers built a better product, foreign auto sales would not be so high."
>
> *False analogy:* Making a misleading analogy between logically unconnected ideas. "He was a brilliant basketball player; therefore, there's no question in my mind that he will be a fine coach."
>
> *Either/or thinking:* The tendency to see an issue as having only two sides. "Used car salesmen are either honest or crooked."

Logical Reasoning   See *Deduction* and *Induction*.

Metaphor   See *Figures of Speech*.

Narration   A strategy for developing an essay. To narrate is to tell a story, to tell what happened. Although narration is most often used in fiction, it is also important in nonfiction, either by itself or in conjunction with other strategies. A good narrative essay has four essential features. The first is *context:* The writer makes clear when the action happened, where it happened, and to whom. The second is *point of view:* The writer establishes and maintains a consistent relationship to the action, either as a participant or as a reporter simply looking on. The third is *selection of detail:* The writer carefully chooses what to include, focusing on those actions and details that are most important to the story while merely mentioning or actually eliminating others. The fourth is *organization:* The writer organizes the events of the narrative into an appropriate sequence, often a strict chronology with a clear beginning, middle, and end.

Objective/Subjective *Objective writing* is factual and impersonal, whereas *subjective writing,* sometimes called impressionistic writing, relies heavily on personal interpretation.

Onomastics The study of the meaning and origins of proper names of persons and places.

Onomatopoeia See *Figures of Speech.*

Organization In writing, the thoughtful arrangement and presentation of one's points or ideas. Narration is often organized chronologically, whereas other kinds of essays may be organized point by point or from most familiar to least familiar. Argument may be organized from least important to most important. There is no single correct pattern of organization for a given piece of writing, but good writers are careful to discover an order of presentation suitable for their subject, audience, and purpose.

Paradox A seemingly contradictory statement that may nonetheless be true. For example, *we little know what we have until we lose it* is a paradoxical statement.

Paragraph A series of closely related sentences and the single most important unit of thought in an essay. The sentences in a paragraph adequately develop its central idea, which is usually stated in a topic sentence. A well-written paragraph has several distinguishing characteristics: a clearly stated or implied topic sentence, adequate development, unity, coherence, and an appropriate organizational pattern.

Paraphrase A restatement of the information a writer is borrowing. A paraphrase closely parallels the presentation of the ideas in the original, but it does not use the same words or sentence structure. See also *Direct Quotation, Summary,* and *Plagiarism.*

Personification See *Figures of Speech.*

Persuasion An attempt to convince readers to agree with a point of view, to make a given decision, or to pursue a particular course of action. See also *Argument, Induction,* and *Deduction.*

Phonetics The study of speech sounds.

Phonology The study of sounds systems in languages.

Plagiarism The use of someone else's ideas in their original form or in an altered form without proper documentation. Writers avoid plagiarism by (1) putting direct quotations within quotation marks and properly citing them and (2) documenting any idea, explanation, or argument that is borrowed and presented in a summary or paraphrase, making it clear where the borrowed material begins and ends. See also *Direct Quotation, Paraphrase,* and *Summary.*

Point of View The grammatical person of the speaker in an essay. For example, a first-person point of view uses the pronoun *I* and is commonly found in autobiography and the personal essay; a third-person point of view uses the pronouns *he, she,* or *it* and is commonly found in objective writing.

Prescriptivism A grammar that seeks to explain linguistic facts as they should be. See also *Descriptivism.*

Process Analysis A strategy for developing an essay. Process analysis answers the question *how* and explains how something works or gives step-by-step directions for doing something.

Propaganda Ideas, facts, or rumors purposely spread to further one's cause or to damage the cause of an opponent.

Purpose   What a writer wants to accomplish in a particular composition—his or her reason for writing. The three general purposes of writing are *to express* thoughts and feelings and lessons learned from life experiences, *to inform* readers about something about the world around them, or *to persuade* readers to accept some belief or take some action.

Racist Language   A form of biased language that makes distinctions on the basis of race and deliberately or subconsciously suggests that one race is superior to all others.

Rhetorical Questions   Questions that are asked but require no answer from the reader. "When will nuclear proliferation end?" is such a question. Writers use rhetorical questions to introduce topics they plan to discuss or to emphasize important points.

Sapir-Whorf Hypothesis   See *Linguistic Relativity Hypothesis.*

Semantics   The study of meanings in a language.

Sexist Language   A form of biased language that makes distinctions on the basis of sex and shows preference for one sex over the other.

Signal Phrase   A phrase alerting the reader that borrowed information is to follow. A signal phrase usually consists of the author's name and a verb (for example, "Keesbury argues") and helps to integrate direct quotations, paraphrases, and summaries into the flow of a paper.

Simile   See *Figures of Speech.*

Slang   The unconventional, very informal language of particular subgroups in a culture. Slang words such as *zonk, split, rap, cop,* and *stoned* are acceptable in formal writing only if they are used for a specific purpose. A writer might use slang, for example, to re-create authentic dialogue in a story.

Specific/General   *General words* name groups or classes of objects, qualities, or actions. *Specific words,* on the other hand, name individual objects, qualities, or actions within a class or group. To some extent the terms *general* and *specific* are relative. For example, *dessert* is a class of things. *Pie,* however, is more specific than *dessert* but more general than *pecan pie* or *chocolate cream pie.* Good writing judiciously balances the general with the specific. Writing with too many general words is likely to be dull and lifeless because general words do not create vivid responses in the reader's mind. On the other hand, writing that relies exclusively on specific words may lack focus and direction, which more general statements provide.

Standard English   A variety of English that is used by the government and the media and that is taught in the schools. It is often best expressed in written form.

Style   The individual manner in which a writer expresses his or her ideas. Style is created by the author's particular selection of words, construction of sentences, and arrangement of ideas.

Subjective   See *Objective/Subjective.*

Summary   A condensed form of the essential idea of a passage, article, or entire chapter. A summary is always shorter than the original. See also *Paraphrase, Direct Quotation,* and *Plagiarism.*

Syllogism   An argument that utilizes deductive reasoning and consists of a major premise, a minor premise, and a conclusion. For example,
All trees that lose leaves are deciduous. (major premise)
Maple trees lose their leaves. (minor premise)

Therefore, maple trees are deciduous. (conclusion)

See also *Deduction*.

Symbol   A person, place, or thing that represents something beyond itself. For example, the eagle is a symbol of America, and the bear is a symbol of Russia.

Syntax   The way words are arranged to form phrases, clauses, and sentences. Syntax also refers to the grammatical relationships among the words themselves.

Taboo Language   Language that is avoided in a given society. Almost all societies have language taboos.

Technical Language   The special vocabulary of a trade or profession. Writers who use technical language do so with an awareness of their audiences. If the audience is a group of peers, technical language may be used freely. If the audience is a more general one, technical language should be used sparingly and carefully so as not to sacrifice clarity. Technical language that is used only to impress, hide the truth, or cover insecurities is termed *jargon* and is not condoned. See also *Diction*.

Thesis   A statement of the main idea of an essay, the point the essay is trying to make. A thesis may sometimes be implied rather than stated directly.

Tone   The manner in which a writer relates to an audience, the "tone of voice" used to address readers. Tone may be described as friendly, serious, distant, angry, cheerful, bitter, cynical, enthusiastic, morbid, resentful, warm, playful, and so forth. A particular tone results from a writer's diction, sentence structure, purpose, and attitude toward the subject. See also *Attitude*.

Topic Sentence   The sentence that states the central idea of a paragraph and thus limits and controls the subject of the paragraph. Although the topic sentence normally appears at the beginning of the paragraph, it may appear at any other point, particularly if the writer is trying to create a special effect. See also *Paragraph*.

Transitions   Words or phrases that link the sentences, paragraphs, and larger units of an essay in order to achieve coherence. Transitional devices include parallelism, pronoun references, conjunctions, and the repetition of key ideas, as well as the many transitional expressions such as *moreover, on the other hand, in addition, in contrast,* and *therefore*. See also *Coherence*.

Unity   A quality that is achieved in an essay when all the words, sentences, and paragraphs contribute to its thesis. The elements of a unified essay do not distract the reader. Instead, they all harmoniously support a single idea or purpose.

Usage   The way in which words and phrases are actually used in a language community. See also *Descriptivism* and *Prescriptivism*.

Rhetorical Contents

CAUSE AND EFFECT ANALYSIS

COMPARISON AND CONTRAST

NARRATION

PROCESS ANALYSIS

(*continued from page ii*)

Gordon Allport. "The Language of Prejudice." From *The Nature of Prejudice* by Gordon Allport. Copyright © 1979, 1985, 1954 by Addison-Wesley Publishing Company, Inc. Reprinted by permission of Perseus Books Publishers, a member of Perseus Books, LLC.

Greg Beato. "Amusing Ourselves To Depth." From *Reason* magazine, November 2007. Copyright © 2007 Greg Beato. Reprinted by permission of *Reason* magazine and Reason.com.

Audrey Bilger. "On Language: You Guys." First posted on a university listserv, 2002. Later reprinted in *Bitchfest: Ten Years of Cultural Criticism from the Pages of Bitch Magazine*, edited by Lisa Jervis and Andi Zeisler. Reprinted by permission of the author.

Newman P. Birk and Genevieve B. Birk. "Selection, Slanting and Charged Language." From *Understanding and Using English*. Copyright © 1972 by Allyn & Bacon.

Sissela Bok. "The Burden of Deceit in Public Life." From *Commonwealth Humanities Lectures* (2006). Reprinted by permission of the author.

Bill Bryson. "The Hard Sell: Advertising in America." From *Made in America: An Informal History of the English Language in the United States* by Bill Bryson. Copyright © 1995 by Bill Bryson. Published by William Morrow. Reprinted by permission of HarperCollins.

Jeffrey Collins and Kristen Wyatt. "Whither the Southern Accent?" From *Associated Press*, November 23, 2005. Copyright © 2005 Associated Press. Reprinted by permission.

Greg Critser. "Let Them Eat Fat." From *Harper's* magazine, March 2000. Copyright © 2000 by Greg Critser. Reprinted by permission of *Harper's* magazine.

Donna Woolfolk Cross. "Propaganda: How Not to Be Bamboozled." From *Speaking of Words: A Language Reader*. Copyright © 1997. Reprinted by the permission of the author.

Annie Dillard. "Living Like Weasels." From *Teaching a Stone to Talk: Expeditions and Encounters* by Annie Dillard. Copyright © 1982 by Annie Dillard. Reprinted by permission of HarperCollins Publishers, Inc.

Sarah Federman. "What's Natural about Our Natural Products?" Copyright © 2000 by Sarah Federman. Reprinted by permission of the author.

Stanley Fish. "The Free-Speech Follies." First published in the *Chronicle of Higher Education*, June 13, 2003, Volume 40, Issue 40, page C3 Reprinted by permission of the author.

Linda Flower. "Writing for an Audience." From *Problem-Solving Strategies for Writing*, Fourth Edition, by Linda Flower. © 1993 Heinle/Arts & Sciences, a part of Cengage Learning, Inc. Reprinted by permission. www.cengage.com/permissions.

Grace Hsiang. "'FOBs' vs. 'Twinkies': The New Discrimination Is Intraracial." Pacific News Service, University of California, Irvine, April 15, 2005. Reprinted by permission of the author.

Caroline Hwang. "The Good Daughter." Copyright © 1988. First appeared in *Newsweek*. Reprinted by permission of the author and the Sandra Dijkstra Literary Agency.

Martha Irvine. "'Queer' Evolution: Word Goes Mainstream." From the *Burlington Free Press*, November 10, 2003. Copyright © 2008. Used with permission of the Associated Press. All rights reserved.

Andrew Keen. "Introduction." From *The Cult of the Amateur: How Today's Internet Is Killing Our Culture* by Andrew Keen. Copyright © 2007 by Andrew Keen. Used by permission of Doubleday, a division of Random House, Inc.

Jean Kilbourne. "Jesus Is a Brand of Jeans." First published in the *New Internationalist*, September 2006. Copyright © 2006 Jean Kilbourne. Reprinted by permission of the publisher.

Martin Luther King Jr. "I Have a Dream." Copyright © 1963 by Martin Luther King Jr., copyright renewed 1991 by Coretta Scott King. Reprinted by arrangement with the heirs to the Estate of Martin Luther King Jr., c/o Writer's House, Inc., as agent for the proprietor.

Robert D. King. "Should English Be the Law?" As appeared in the *Atlantic Monthly*. Copyright © 1997 by Robert D. King. Reprinted by permission of the author.

Barbara Kingsolver. "Called Home." From pages 9–22 (Chapter 1) in *Animal, Vegetable, Miracle* by Barbara Kingsolver and Steven Hopp & Camille Kingsolver. Copyright © 2007 by Barbara Kingsolver, Stephen L. Hopp, and Camille Kingsolver. Reprinted by permission of HarperCollins Publishers.

Naomi Klein. "Barricading the Branded Village." From *No Logo: Taking Aim at the Brand Bullies* by Naomi Klein. Copyright © 2000 by Naomi Klein. Reprinted by permission of St. Martin's Press, LLC and Knopf Canada.

Charles Krauthammer. "In Plain English: Let's Make It Official." From *Time* magazine, June 4, 2006. Copyright © 2006 Time, Inc. Reprinted with permission of Time, Inc. via Copyright Clearance Center.

Irving Kristol. "The Case for Censorship." Originally titled "Pornography, Obscenity, and the Case for Censorship" from the *New York Times Magazine*, May 28, 1971. Copyright © 1971. The New York Times. Reprinted by permission.

Anne Lamott. "Shitty First Drafts." From *Bird by Bird*. Copyright © 1994 by Anne Lamott. Used by permission of Pantheon Books, a division of Random House, Inc.

Ann Landers. "Refusal to Use Names Is the Ultimate Insult." From *Ann Landers* advice column, September 30, 1998. Copyright © 1998 by Ann Landers. Reprinted by permission of Creators Syndicate.

Susanne K. Langer. "Language and Thought." From *Ms.* magazine. Reprinted by permission of the publisher.

Charles R. Larson. "Its Academic, or Is It?" From *Newsweek*, November 6, 1995 issue, page 31. Copyright © 1995 Newsweek, Inc. All rights reserved. Used by permission and protected by the Copyright Laws of the United States. The printing, copying, redistribution, or retransmission of the material without express written permission is prohibited. www.newsweek.com.

Chang-rae Lee. "Mute in an English-Only World." From the *New York Times* op-ed, April 18, 1996. Copyright © 1996. The New York Times. Reprinted by permission.

Jennifer 8. Lee. "I Think, Therefore IM." From the *New York Times*, Technology section, September 19, 2002 issue, page G1. Copyright © 2002. The New York Times. Used by permission and protected by the Copyright Laws of the United States. The printing, copying, redistribution, or retransmission of the material without express written permission is prohibited. www.nytimes.com.

Richard Lederer. "Verbs with Verve." Originally appeared in *The Play of Words* by Richard Lederer. Copyright © 1990 by Richard Lederer. Reprinted with permission of the author.

Bonnie Liebman. "Claims Crazy: Which Can You Believe?" From the *Nutrition Action HealthLetter*, a publication of the Center for Science in the Public Interest, June 2003, Volume 30, No. 5. Copyright © 2003 by the Center for Science in the Public Interest. Reproduced with permission of the Center for Science in the Public Interest via Copyright Clearance Center.

Audre Lorde. "The Fourth of July." From *Zami: A New Spelling of My Name.* Copyright © 1982 by Audre Lorde. The Crossing Press, Freedom, CA. Reprinted by permission of Regula Noetzli, affiliate of the Charlotte Sheedy Literary Agency.

William Lutz. "The World of Doublespeak." From *The State of Language.* Copyright © 1989 William Lutz. "Weasel Words: The Art of Saying Nothing at All." From *Doublespeak: From Revenue Enhancement to Terminal Living.* Copyright © 1980 William Lutz. Reprinted by permission of Jeanne V. Nagger Literary Agency, on behalf of the author.

Robert MacNeil. "English Belongs to Everybody." (Chapter 8) From *Wordstruck* by Robert MacNeil. Copyright © 1989 by Neely Productions, Ltd. Used by permission of Viking Penguin, a division of Penguin Putnam (USA) Group, Inc.

PHOTO ACKNOWLEDGMENTS

6.8 © Robert Caplin/The New York Times/Redux Pictures

8.1 © 2007 Mike Lester, The Rome News-Tribune and Political-Cartoons.com

A.7 and A.8 Published by permission of the University of Vermont, Burlington VT 05405–0036.

INDEX OF AUTHORS AND TITLES

Instructor's Manual to Accompany

TENTH EDITION

Language Awareness

READINGS FOR COLLEGE WRITERS

Paul Eschholz • Alfred Rosa
Virginia Clark

Instructor's Manual to Accompany

TENTH EDITION

LANGUAGE AWARENESS

Readings for College Writers

Instructor's Manual to Accompany

TENTH EDITION

LANGUAGE
AWARENESS

Readings for College Writers

Paul Eschholz
Alfred Rosa
Virginia Clark
UNIVERSITY OF VERMONT

PREPARED BY

Betsy Eschholz

BEDFORD/ST. MARTIN'S   Boston • New York

Manufactured in the United States of America.

4   3   2   1   0   9
f   e   d   c   b   a

For information, write: Bedford/St. Martin's, 75 Arlington Street, Boston, MA 02116 (617-399-4000)

ISBN-10: 0–312–46342–1
ISBN-13: 978–0–312–46342–7

PREFACE

How an instructor uses a textbook is a highly individual matter. In this manual, we have indicated how we use the materials and ideas in *Language Awareness: Readings for College Writers* in our classes, and we hope that the manual suggests possibilities or alternatives that will be useful to you. Although *Language Awareness* might be assigned in various courses, we use it in a composition course; for such a purpose it can be easily complemented by a handbook or handbook/rhetoric.

In suggesting responses to the "Thinking Critically about the Reading" and "Language in Action" questions and suggestions, we tried to assist you by (1) indicating central themes or issues, (2) explaining and describing rhetorical strategies, (3) offering expected student responses to the questions, (4) anticipating problems that students might experience, (5) citing additional readings to enrich or develop a particular topic, and (6) providing additional questions when appropriate. The overall intent has been to save you time, not to indicate directions or answers. There are no substitutes for your own experience with the text and your sense of what will work most successfully for your students.

One of our most successful assignments (in addition to the prereading journal prompts in "Writing to Discover") has been to have our students keep a language journal, in which, in addition to making a daily record of their own responses to their language environment, they keep a scrapbook of newspaper and magazine articles about language. These may concern language issues, such as languages that are becoming extinct, the English-only movement, "Spanglish," political campaign metaphors, speech development in children, research on post-stroke speech therapy, linguistic imperialism, language as it is impacted by technologies such as instant and text messaging, and so forth. Or they may be examples of language in actual use, such as menu language, ad copy language, doublespeak, overheard speech, campus slang, rap-music slang, or new words formed out of Internet technology. It is truly amazing how many articles and examples of language in use students gather during a single semester, and most students seem to enjoy the project once they realize how much material there is around them and how quickly they are developing language awareness. Sometimes the materials they find reflect on issues already discussed in class and serve to reinforce earlier teaching points, while on other occasions these materials preview issues that are yet to be taken up in the course. In both cases students enjoy taking an active role in shaping classroom discussions and the emphasis given various issues. It is our belief that once the process of becoming language aware is initiated, a sensitivity to language, so essential in improving one's writing, rarely leaves the student.

Finally, if you have any suggestions or questions about the contents of either *Language Awareness: Readings for College Writers* or of this manual, we invite you to write the editors and authors of this text at Bedford/St. Martin's, 75 Arlington Street, 8th Floor, Boston, Massachusetts, 02116. We would enjoy hearing from you.

Contents

3. POLITICS, PROPAGANDA, AND DOUBLESPEAK

4. PREJUDICE, DISCRIMINATION, AND STEREOTYPES

5. EVERYDAY CONVERSATIONS

6. MEDIA AND ADVERTISING

7. LANGUAGE DEBATE: SHOULD LEARNING BE CENSORED?

8. LANGUAGE DEBATE: SHOULD ENGLISH BE THE LAW?

9. LANGUAGE DEBATE: WHAT'S ALL THE FUSS ABOUT NATURAL, ORGANIC, LOCAL FOODS?

Using "Reading Critically" and "Writing in College"

Language Awareness's structure is straightforward and uncomplicated: Two introductory chapters on reading and writing instruct students on each step of the process; nine chapters explore language-related themes, helping students to become more language aware and to use language more responsibly; a "Finding, Evaluating, and Documenting Sources" appendix helps students find reliable sources and execute them in MLA format; and a glossary defines key writing and language terms.

Our former "From Reading to Writing" introduction has been divided into two distinct sections: "Reading Critically" provides students with guidelines for critical reading, and "Writing in College" explores the world of academic writing. More detailed coverage of the use of outside sources is provided in the appendix. You may wish to discuss this material explicitly in class, adapting all or parts of it to your syllabus; or you may find it self-explanatory enough to ask students to read it on their own. Either way, these two sections and the "Sources" appendix provide a useful foundation for a writing course. They explain and illustrate the writing process, how to read a text critically, and how to write using one's reading and one's research.

1. Coming to an Awareness of Language

Discovering the Power of Language

Malcolm X

THINKING CRITICALLY ABOUT THE READING

1. Malcolm X wrote letters, first to the uneducated people he had known in the hustling world and later to the mayor of Boston, the governor of Massachusetts, and Harry S. Truman. None of these people answered his letters. Malcolm X's frustrations with his own inarticulateness and language dysfunction pushed him to acquire his homemade education.

2. The first-person narrator lends immediacy and believability to this very personal experience. A third-person narrator, either participant or omniscient, would sacrifice this personal tone.

3. Prior to his self-education, Malcolm X's vocabulary was ineffective because he could not extract the larger meaning from a text when reading or communicate his ideas in writing. An effective vocabulary should facilitate comprehension and communication. Malcolm X did not try to impress his readers with strange or multisyllabic words; rather, he chose words that would communicate his ideas most clearly. The clarity of his writing reflects his belief that writing and word use should be judged according to their ability to reach their audience.

4. Slang is appropriate in informal settings, such as conversations among friends and family members. In writing, slang can serve as a tool for creating realistic dialogue. However, for

all other formal writing, as well as conversation in a professional setting, Standard English is more appropriate.

5. When writing, the author is forced to communicate an idea in a form different from that used when speaking. Without intonation and facial expression, the author must express his or her idea using word choice alone. This requires a greater depth of understanding and the ability to organize ideas. By copying the words, rather than just memorizing their meaning, Malcolm X saw how they looked and were used in a written context and, therefore, retained them. Malcolm X writes, "I've never been one for inaction" (1). He wants to make things happen, and he sets the tone with this first sentence. He became "frustrated at not being able to express what I wanted to convey in letters," particularly to Elijah Muhammad (8), and he was going to do something about it. For Malcolm, being an articulate hustler meant "commanding attention" when he spoke. He describes being functional, on the other hand, as being able to speak or write in a plain manner merely to convey meaning. Unless we wish to recreate a realistic dialogue, we do not write as we speak, first, because the visual and audio component of speaking is lost and, second, because writing provides the author with an opportunity to express unspoken context and ideas.

6. While he may have been the most articulate hustler on the street, limited reading and writing abilities confined his prowess to his native environment; he only had words for what he had experienced. However, once introduced to the new ideas of Elijah Muhammed, he confronted his inability to express himself in the world at large. When no longer confined by the limits of his inadequate vocabulary, his ideas were free to speak for themselves.

    If students have trouble relating to the idea of being a prisoner of one's language on a personal level, ask them to think of characters in books or movies who have been trapped in or affected by language (for example, the high society New York families in Edith Wharton's *The Age of Innocence*).

LANGUAGE IN ACTION

Student answers will vary; some students may know very few vocabulary words and little about the *Reader's Digest* audience. You might ask who they think subscribes to the *Reader's Digest*. Have students seen the magazine? Would they be inclined to take the quiz if they glanced at it? Why or why not? Vocabulary building has always been associated with bettering oneself. Like Malcolm X (pp. 41–43), many people read vocabulary columns such as the one in *Reader's Digest*, do crosswords, or play popular word games such as Scrabble or Boggle for self-improvement. The public has the perception that a larger vocabulary somehow equates with power and upward mobility. Many people find learning new words fun, as well.

THE DAY LANGUAGE CAME INTO MY LIFE

HELEN KELLER

THINKING CRITICALLY ABOUT THE READING

1. By showing that the symbol for doll could be applied to more than one object, Sullivan shows Keller that language can be used to categorize the world around her. This teaches Keller that one idea or word is not limited to one object or circumstance, but can be applied to other similar objects or circumstances.

2. Not until paragraph 7, when Keller "discovers" language, can she begin to identify related ideas and concepts. She is pressed to connect water to its symbol in a different context so she is able to understand the nature of the symbol as a generalization rather than being specific to the water in the cup.

3. Giving names and context to the world around her brings order and a sense of coherence to Keller's previously dark world. Although still without sight and sound, Keller has a new tool with which to understand her world. Through language she can begin to make connections, see relationships, and develop more complex ideas. Naming things may enable abstraction, which is necessary to thinking.

4. At times the inability to communicate feels like trying to scream for help in a bad dream but not being able to make a sound or trying to row against a strong wind, pushing and struggling with each stroke but making little headway. Encourage students to think of specific occasions on which they have felt inarticulate.

5. Keller's first words were nouns and verbs. These words are the basic units of thought because they name the things in our world and the way they act. The building blocks of writing are the names we give to things we see in the world around us. A writer faces the same challenge Keller's teacher faced—to describe the world bluntly, in the simplest terms, and then to abstract it into meanings that cannot be named in one word. Even for the best of writers this is a challenging task; we can only wonder how Keller came to understand words such as beauty, goodness, and justice.

6. Abstractions are difficult to grasp if they are presented without context or illustration. The best writers evoke emotions by describing a context or by representing the abstraction in an image, which serves as a metaphor. Keller does this as well, when she describes her feeling of expectancy in the metaphor of an approaching ship (3).

LANGUAGE IN ACTION

Before discussing any of the sniglets presented in this exercise, make a list on the board of student examples of things that don't have names. What usually happens in this situation is that they discover that some of the things mentioned do in fact have names, names that they have never heard of. For those items that have no names, have the class make up a name and explain why it might be appropriate. At this point you can pursue an interesting discussion of the sniglets created by Rich Hall "and friends." Students soon discover that English is infinitely flexible and that by giving things in their environment names, they make them easier to talk about. You may want to bring up the concept of etymology and apply it to some of the sniglets. Students' views on the individual sniglets will vary; listen to see if any patterns emerge from their discussion.

ON BEING 17, BRIGHT, AND UNABLE TO READ

DAVID RAYMOND

THINKING CRITICALLY ABOUT THE READING

1. Dyslexia is a learning disability that affects comprehension of how to read and write. It is not essential to know more about dyslexia than Raymond tells us, but it is important to know that he has great difficulty reading and that a learning disability often leaves lasting psychological effects. The essay does raise questions about dyslexia—what causes it, what treatments are available, whether or not it can ever be overcome. David himself leaves the reader with questions about his future.

2. David Raymond is intelligent despite his learning disabilities. It is apparent from his story that he has had to work much harder than other students to achieve in school and that he has overcome many obstacles in his path. He has organized this story with the help of a typist and plans on pursuing higher education.

3. These early childhood experiences are important because of the lasting effects they have on self-esteem, one's perception of self-worth. Dyslexia often becomes apparent when a child is in school, since this syndrome has to do with difficulty with visual memory (learning to read and write). Damage to self-esteem in this setting is very harmful, since intelligence and ability are usually called into question.

4. The colloquial expressions are more striking when one realizes that Raymond is speaking, not writing, this essay (he probably dictated it). He also explicitly names a potential audience in his final paragraph—"kid[s] in the classroom" (16). He may choose a less formal diction in order to attract and engage that audience.

5. Raymond begins with an anecdote from the recent past and then begins his story in early childhood, when reading began to be a problem. He continues to tell his story chronologically, ending with a reflection on his first anecdote.

6. Raymond wants to express the profound effect dyslexia has had on him and to persuade the reader that he and others like him are not dumb.

LANGUAGE IN ACTION

Imagine trying to read the reflection of words backwards in a mirror. What if everything became jumbled and strange? What if, every time you tried to write a word, you came close to the correct spelling, but you just couldn't get it right. Words sound a certain way, and you know that these letters are in the word—but you just can't remember the right order.

Think about what it's like when you hear a foreign language and you try to spell the words, but there are different rules; the words are spelled differently from how they sound. Imagine if you were faced with new foreign words every day. How would that feel? These are important subjects to broach with your students. Pose to students that it would be especially confusing in school if you felt that you could do other subjects well (higher math or the recollection of historical information) but had trouble mastering your own language on paper. Would you begin to doubt your intelligence? Ask students to think about the frustration and helplessness that they might feel faced with this problem every day.

WHAT'S IN A NAME?

HENRY LOUIS GATES JR.

THINKING CRITICALLY ABOUT THE READING

1. Baldwin's quote means that, although race is a complicated topic, the real issue is one of identity and self. By turning a group of individuals into one generalized idea of a race, you hide the fact that they are individuals who cannot be effectively discussed as a whole. Gates's essay provides a concrete example with Mr. Wilson, who sees all African Americans as the same. Mr. Wilson treats "the question of color" by ignoring "the graver questions" presented by African American selfness.

2. Students may say they are embarrassed or angered by the list of bynames for African Americans. Some of the bynames will be incomprehensible, archaic, or unfamiliar to the students. Each of the slurs is offensive because it reduces an individual to a caricature, and because it is (usually) spoken with intent to humiliate. Some insult African American intelligence ("porch monkey," "spearchucker"), reduce them to a color ("darky," "schwarze") or assume an inappropriate level of familiarity ("brother," "homeboy") when coming from someone outside the black community.

3. The difference between the uses of racial terms is intent. Gates's parents were using words created by the white community to describe them. Both white and black people want to talk about black people as a group and use the same words. But the words originally were intended to insult or humiliate black people. When used by white people in that way, they retain their original hateful character. But when black people, who see each other as individuals with culture and values, use these words, they reclaim them for themselves. They may also represent some form of self-hatred.

4. Gates describes Mr. Wilson to show that he is a normal person in their town — Irish, like many others, and blue-collar, judging from his lunch pail. He is not a wealthy snob, nor is he poor and ignorant. Gates wants to show that Mr. Wilson was not so different from his own family, and that casual racism was not limited to a few particular types of people in his town.

5. "Those things" are habits, traditions, and aspects of society that Gates's family felt powerless to change. Gates tells this story to show how a casual, even innocuous-seeming, exchange can still be tinged with racism, and can be a life-changing moment for a child growing up in society. Gates could have several reasons for never looking Mr. Wilson in the eye — shame, that Mr. Wilson thinks him unworthy of a name; anger, that Mr. Wilson insulted his father; or revenge for the insult to his family.

6. Using dialogue separates the exchange between the two men from the rest of the narrative, and grabs the reader's attention. It also allows the reader to "hear" the two men speaking to each other, as Gates would have as a boy. When Mr. Gates says "Hello, Mr.

Wilson," it is surprising to read "Hello, George" as the reply. If Gates had simply described the exchange, that surprise, an the offensiveness of the moment, would have been less affecting. Instead, the reader better understands the surprise and chagrin that the young Henry Gates felt.

LANGUAGE IN ACTION

The Ann Landers column that accompanies Gates's essay reinforces the idea that a person's name has great significance. The letter writer complains that her mother-in-law refuses to address her by name, which the writer sees as a definite sign of hostility and disrespect. As the letter implies, using a person's name when interacting with him or her makes a person feel accepted as an individual. A person addressed as "Hey you" might develop an unwanted sense of anonymity. Landers, in her response, refers to Dr. Will Menninger's notion that the "sweetest sound in any language is the sound of your own name." There is an undeniable egocentrism at the heart of this idea, yet it seems to ring true. No words are more familiar to us than the words that make up our names.

Changing My Name after Sixty Years

Tom Rosenberg

THINKING CRITICALLY ABOUT THE READING

1. The title grabs the reader's attention because it is so direct. It causes the reader to wonder whether his name used to be Tom Rosenberg or whether it is now. The reader also may wonder why he chooses to change his name. Rosenberg answers these questions very effectively in his essay.

2. It isn't entirely clear why Rosenberg's parents changed their names when they immigrated to the United States from Germany in 1938. Rosenberg speculates that they made the change "out of fear, a desire to assimilate or a combination of both" (2). He does distinguish his parents from immigrants who entered the country through Ellis Island and "had their names changed by an immigration bureaucrat." His parents changed their name to Ross voluntarily.

3. On the whole, Rosenberg enjoyed few advantages as a result of the name change. As a small child growing up in the Bronx in the 1940s, he could not escape his heritage, even as he went by the name "Tom Ross." "I spent much of my youth denying my roots and vying for my peers' acceptance as 'Tom Ross'" (4). In college Rosenberg was able to pledge a predominantly Christian fraternity, and he eventually married a woman who was not Jewish. In his essay Rosenberg ponders whether these things would have happened if his name had been Rosenberg rather than Ross.

4. Rosenberg decides to change his first name as well as his last name for two reasons. First, he sees it as an opportunity to renew his commitment to Judaism. He also believes it to be a way of giving his children a sense of pride in their heritage.

5. Rosenberg's parents, who escaped from Nazi Germany, probably changed their name to Ross in part out of fear and in part out of a desire to assimilate. For the young Tom Ross,

this must have been confusing because he knew that he was Jewish, yet his parents were doing everything they could to deny this fact. Inevitably, he must have felt a strong desire to be accepted by others, but his own confusion and even perhaps loathing of his true identity likely made it difficult for him to accept himself.

6. The chronological structure of the essay is effective because it is important for the reader to have a sense of Rosenberg's background if he or she is to understand the author's reasoning for the name change. He foreshadows his conclusion early in the essay, when he refers to his parents' reasons for changing their name, mentioning that fear probably motivated them to make the change. In his conclusion, Rosenberg recalls what he said when he stood at the pulpit during the name-changing ceremony. He announces to his friends and family that he is changing his name now out of pride rather than fear.

LANGUAGE IN ACTION

Ask the students to say the names out loud. How do the first and last names sound together? Are they easy to pronounce and remember? Are the names long or difficult to spell? What images are created by the original names that change with the professional names? Are the professional names changed to cover up ethnicity? If so, what ethnic prejudices might the original name have encountered? Would the image created by the movie actor John Wayne work with the name Marion Michael Morrison? Finally, ask students for examples of current celebrities who have changed their names and discuss possible reasons for those changes. Are the reasons that people are changing their names today similar to the reasons people changed their names in years past?

ENGLISH BELONGS TO EVERYBODY

ROBERT MACNEIL

THINKING CRITICALLY ABOUT THE READING

1. The "killjoys" are people who are snobbish and intolerant, favoring a rigid and unchanging language. They "turn others away from an interest in the language, inhibit their use of it, and turn pleasure off" (2). MacNeil believes that part of the beauty of language is its ability to change in order to serve the needs of its people. Imposing rules alienates people and promotes elitism.

2. The anxiety of those who wish to "save" the language brings perverse side effects. Attempting to preserve the language through rules turns people away from, rather than toward, the language and stifles its growth. Using the word perverse emphasizes the point that the actions meant to preserve will do the exact opposite. Another word, such as negative or destructive, could logically replace perverse; however, it could not highlight this irony as successfully.

3. The expressions *turned on* and *turned off* were very "with it" at the time MacNeil wrote this article and are now acceptable in the English language. The terms were new, and people using them felt current or part of the mainstream of conversational speech. For most people "with it" means something new and may be used by those "in the know" or popu-

lar groups of young people hoping to sound in touch with current language. MacNeil makes his point by using one new term to describe another and illustrates how accepted and understandable our new language metaphors are.

4. Jespersen believes a language's ability to change reflects the culture from which it came. The grammatically inflexible French language developed out of a strict aristocracy, whereas the more flexible English language developed from a society based on individualism and freedom. MacNeil uses Jespersen's quote (5) to support his thesis that English "has prospered and grown because it was able to accept and absorb change" (3). Formal grammar was imposed on English in the seventeenth- and eighteenth-centuries when "critics thought the language was a mess, like an overgrown garden. They weeded it by imposing grammatical rules derived from tidier languages" (11). Equating the mess of language to an overgrown garden is a simile. MacNeil could have used another simile to express this idea; for example, language is like an unruly child who needs structure. Through rules, inappropriate behavior is controlled; this enables children to channel energy more productively. Ask students to comment on this alternative simile.

5. MacNeil quotes Jespersen who says that the English had been "great respecters of the liberties of each individual" and that everybody had been "free to strike out new paths" without having to fear a stern keeper enforcing rigorous regulations" (5). These roots "also nourished the great principles of freedom and rights of man in the modern world" (6), creating a climate that resisted authority. "The English-speaking peoples have defeated all efforts to build fences around their language, to defer to an academy on what was permissible English and what was not" (6). This resistance to authority is expressed in "errors" in common speech. MacNeil quotes Shakespeare's errors that have been around for at least four hundred years (8).

6. This is a wonderful opportunity to encourage students to share their own perceptions of the English language. Some may say that English intimidates them, that they can't understand the rules of Standard English, and others may say they feel comfortable speaking and writing in English. In any event, MacNeil's article should encourage the ownership students have in participating in its ongoing evolution.

7. MacNeil says that broadcasting's "dissemination of popular speech may easily give purists the idea that the language is suddenly going to hell in this generation, and may explain the new paranoia about it" (16). However, he argues that Americans also "hear more correct, even beautiful, English on television than was ever heard before . . . colloquial English, too, some awful, some creative" (17).

LANGUAGE IN ACTION

Here you must be careful, because student responses will vary depending on their background and life experience. Seize the opportunity to discuss these variations on language, finding out what terms students have heard, asking if they are familiar or understandable. Ask students how they might consider their audience when including such terms in their writing.

WORDS DON'T MEAN WHAT THEY MEAN

STEVEN PINKER

THINKING CRITICALLY ABOUT THE READING

1. The example illustrates that, although "we profess to long for the plain truth," blunt honesty is unacceptable in most social situations. Although Lange's character might be tired of come-ons and deceit, those who don't participate in the necessary social niceties are not rewarded.

2. Double entendres, veiled threats, ordinary politeness, and innuendo are among the categories that Pinker outlines. Students may find other categories, but should provide an example for each category they name. The categories overlap in that they are all ways people use language indirectly to get the result they want.

3. Pinker means that all cultures and societies have certain rules of politeness and formality that prevent us from speaking the plain truth all the time. Although this can make social interaction confusing and unnecessarily oblique, it also eases interactions by providing rules and allows communication to be more than just words. To speak the "plain truth," people would have to become much less touchy and use words in a more specific way. This also would mean discounting the influence of facial expression, tone of voice, and body language during speech.

4. Pinker explains that "every sentence has to do two things at once: convey a message and continue to negotiate [the speakers'] relationship." A conversation is more than an exchange of information; it's an experience that can strengthen or damage each person's interactions with the other. Modems transmit data that are understandable and quantifiable to both computers, whereas people have unique ways of understanding and interpreting what is said.

5. "Felicity conditions" are "the prerequisites to making a simple request." Although the request may be easy and convenient to fulfill, the speaker has to establish enough goodwill for the listener to fulfill it. Otherwise the listener will feel like "a flunky who can be bossed around at will." Students may provide examples of failing to establish "felicity conditions" from home, the workplace, or school. Examples should explain the interaction, the request, what was said, and what the reaction was.

6. Indirect speech requires making your meaning known to your listener without saying straight out what you mean. People resort to indirect speech when their request might be offensive if said plainly or when a third party might disapprove of what is going on. In politics and diplomacy, power and money are closely linked. In American society, making the wrong comment involving power and money can be offensive or embarrassing — even illegal.

LANGUAGE IN ACTION

The new words assigned to those items (*barnacle* for bed or couch) the servant already knew were arbitrary. They had no prior associations for the servant nor do they sound like anything familiar in relation to what they now mean. However, meaningful communication happens whenever two people agree. If everyone who reads this folktale carefully keeps track of the meanings that are assigned to each new word, he or she should be able to understand what is communicated in the last line. In the end, the person who masters the language, masters the situation.

Steven Pinker's first response to this fairy tale would, no doubt, be one of amusement. But, from an analytical standpoint, he would probably go back to the title of his essay: Words don't mean what they mean. In this story, the words themselves mean nothing outside of the context and meaning made up by the "Master of Masters." Once the girl and the old gentlemen agree on the words, they shared a complete understanding and their communication was unambiguous—if it hadn't been, she would not have been able to warn him about the "hot cockalorum."

LANGUAGE AND THOUGHT

SUSANNE K. LANGER

THINKING CRITICALLY ABOUT THE READING

1. Langer's thesis is the first sentence in her essay: "A symbol is not the same thing as a sign; that is a fact that psychologists and philosophers often overlook."

2. According to Langer, "a sign is anything that announces the existence or the imminence of some event, the presence of a thing or a person, or a change in the state of affairs" (3). A symbol, on the other hand, brings up the conception, or idea, of the object or condition. The significant difference between the two is that a sign is inexorably tied to concrete reality, whereas a symbol can act outside and independently of the immediate physical world. This frees thought from the conditions of the present.

3. In paragraph 1, Langer writes that signs are used by both humans and intelligent animals; "sounds and smells and motions are signs of food, danger, the presence of other beings, or of rain or storm." Dogs bark, rabbits thump, doves coo, and wolves growl. "We stop at red lights and go on green; we answer calls and bells, watch the sky for coming storms, read trouble or promise or anger in each other's eyes" (2). She also says, "There are signs of the weather, signs of danger, signs of future good or evil, signs of what the past has been" (3).

   A symbol "does not announce the presence of the object . . . but merely *brings this thing to mind*" (6). Examples are a person's name or, in religious experience, the Host which is a symbol and a Presence at the same time (6). A symbol can be "a mere idea, a figment, a dream" (7). A stream of thought consists of symbols like words, pictures, and memory images, "a complex of all their respective meanings" (7).

4. "Animals think . . . *of* and *at* things; men think primarily *about* things" (7). On an organic level, humans have an innate need to express symbolically that which they experience. In the face of challenging situations, this need for conceptualization causes them to act more indirectly than animals. Humans first conceptualize, then analyze, rather than act according to an instinctual impulse. Langer believes this distinction in mentality separates humans from other animals. This capacity of humans to think and communicate in symbols

has enabled us to conceptualize and create technologies and arts, which have in turn affected our biological evolution.

5. Langer prepares the reader for this abstract and bold statement by beginning with a discussion of signs, which are shared by humans and animals. She then moves on to show that humans have gone beyond sign-using and the biological cycle and use symbols; a symbol "does not announce the presence of the object . . . but merely *brings this thing to mind*" (6). "A sign is always imbedded in reality . . . but a symbol may be divorced from reality altogether" (7). Now we are liberated from the physically present world; "that liberation marks the essential difference between human and nonhuman mentality" (7). Now that experience is transformed into imagery, the human mind has "a dominant, organic need" (8). Our impressions are not only signs but symbols, "images representing our *ideas* of things; and the tendency to manipulate ideas, to combine and abstract . . ." (8). "Symbol mongering . . . seems to be instinctive, the fulfillment of an elementary need . . ." (9), a special power of the human mind that is different, a biological need and biological gift the animal world does not share.

6. In saying "In words or dreamlike image . . . we must *construe* the events of life" (13), Langer refers to humans' innate need to understand and communicate the world around them. Through language, humans can communicate a sense of order and develop an understanding of their perceptions. The perceptions can then be added to and manipulated to create new meanings. Language also enables conceptions to be communicated from one human to another.

LANGUAGE IN ACTION

From left to right the graphics are: AIDS, breast cancer, or hostages (symbol); target (sign); don't drink and drive (symbol); U.S. flag (symbol); right turn only (sign); recycling (symbol); caduceus (symbol of the medical profession); poison (symbol); handicap (sign); world peace (symbol); stop sign (sign); adultery (symbol); handle with care (sign); OK (sign).

A BRIEF HISTORY OF ENGLISH

PAUL ROBERTS

THINKING CRITICALLY ABOUT THE READING

1. Roberts's thesis is presented in the first sentence of his essay: "No understanding of the English language can be very satisfactory without a notion of the history of the language." Even though Roberts's history is by no means complete, his examples certainly convince most students of the need to know history to truly understand the English language. Ask students which parts of Roberts's history most surprised or interested them.

2 . Roberts emphasizes the connection between historical events and the development of the English language because the changes in language reflect the situations of the times. The following historical events or situations affected the English language:

a. The decline of the Roman Empire and the Romans' departure from England in the fifth century permitted the Anglo-Saxon invasion and the introduction of English.

b. Nomadic movement brought Angles, Saxons, and Jutes to England. Through combat and territorial disputes, tribes encountered various dialects.

c. Around the year 600, converts to Christianity learned the Latin alphabet.

d. The most famous king of the West Saxons, Alfred the Great, had a great love of learning and encouraged the spread and teaching of English and Latin texts.

e. In 866 Norsemen invaded England, injecting their language into English.

f. The Norman conquest of 1066 caused the shift from Old English to Middle English. This French-speaking group influenced grammar and vocabulary.

g. The printing press and the English Renaissance catalyzed the change from Middle to Modern English.

   Throughout history, commerce, religious conversion, conquest, and the invention of the printing press were factors that most affected the intermingling of languages.

3. The French-speaking Normans who came to England tended to be rulers and landlords. Therefore, the adopted French words reflect this highly educated ruling class. In paragraph 29, Roberts provides examples of words that were borrowed from French in the following areas: government, church, foods, colors, household, play, literature, education, and various commonly used terms from everyday speech.

4. In paragraphs 35 and 36, Roberts explains how the Great Vowel Shift systematically shifted the sounds of half a dozen vowels and diphthongs in stressed syllables. This shift affected thousands of words and gave us different symbols for vowel sounds.

5. Roberts's extensive use of examples helps to illustrate various points and establish him as an authority on the subject. Students should note how examples make the essay stronger and more credible. Ask students to imagine what the essay would have been like if he had used no historical examples, only generalizations.

6. Roberts's use of the words *savages, untamed tribes*, and *civilization* in the first ten paragraphs reflects the 1950s context in which the piece was written. Today, historians use words such as *indigenous* and *nomadic*, rather than savage or primitive. Roberts also assumes an audience of English speakers—"our linguistic ancestors" (2). Ask students to consider how these assumptions affect non-English readers. As writers, we need to be sensitive to the feelings of others and avoid words that contain a racial, ethnic, or gender prejudice.

7. Student opinions may be mixed concerning the significance of Roberts's essay. Understanding where words come from and the source of their connotations teaches us about our history and values. For example, the elitism associated with certain French words derives from the Norman Conquest. Students should note that language, like culture, cannot escape the influence of other civilizations. English, like other languages, is a product of its history.

LANGUAGE IN ACTION

Word origins are listed below:

barbecue — American Spanish, barbacoa

buffalo — Italian or Portuguese, bufalo; Latin, bufalus; Greek, boubalos casino — Italian, casa ("house")

decoy — Dutch, de kooi ("the cage")

ditto — Italian, dire ("to say")

fruit — Latin, fructus ("to enjoy")

hustle — Dutch, husselen ("to shake")

marmalade — French, marmelade; Portuguese, mamelada

orangutan — Malay, orang hutan (orang, "man" + hutan, "forest")

posse — Medieval Latin, posse comitatus ("power of the country")

raccoon — Algonquian (Virginia), arathkone

veranda — Hindi

2. WRITERS ON WRITING

WHAT HAPPENS WHEN PEOPLE WRITE?

MAXINE HAIRSTON

THINKING CRITICALLY ABOUT THE READING

1. Like a tennis coach, a writing teacher should help students by showing them "the strategies that experts use and by giving them criticism and reinforcement as they practice those strategies" (2). From this analogy, students see that improving writing requires time and effort by both parties in order to be successful.

2. Suggest that students add to the list of writing strategies that have worked well for them in the past. Ideas can be exchanged among students during a class discussion.

3. Hairston says that "explanatory writing *tends* to be about information; exploratory writing *tends* to be about ideas" (4). She uses a wide range of examples to demonstrate the spectrum of forms each kind of writing may take. Hairston explains that these distinctions matter because "there isn't *a* writing process" (15) but suggests that "you'll become a more proficient and relaxed writer if you develop the habit of analyzing before you start, whether you are going to be doing primarily explanatory or exploratory writing" (16). Hairston's essay is primarily a process analysis and, therefore, explanatory.

4. Hairston gives a complete discussion of explanatory writing before doing the same for exploratory writing. This type of organization is called block by block because each discussion is separate. Examples of explanatory writing are movie reviews, an explanation of new software, an analysis of historical causes, reports on political developments, and biographical sketches. Others are magazine articles and some nonfiction books or informative reports, both of which require a plan for finding and organizing information. In exploratory writing "the writer has only a partially formed idea of what he or she is going to write before starting" (8). Hairston's examples include a reflective personal essay, a profile of a homeless family, speculative essays about the future of the women's movement, and an essay on "why movies about the Mafia appeal so much to the American public" (8). Here the writer would expect some of the ideas to come while he or she wrote.

5. *Transitions*: words or phrases that link sentences, paragraphs, and larger units of a composition in order to achieve coherence.

   By answering the "so what?" question posed in paragraph 14, Hairston shifts her focus from the two different types of writing to the necessity to master both.

6. *Tone*: the manner in which a writer relates to an audience. Tone may be described as friendly, distant, angry, cheerful, and so on.

   Hairston writes in a straightforward, personal, and encouraging tone. She does not make the reader dig for meaning. She explains what she will discuss and provides a straightforward summation of strategies for writing. By addressing the reader as "you" and using examples applicable to the average college student, she brings a conversational tone to the piece. She encourages and supports the reader by immediately dispelling the myth that only gifted people can write.

7. Students can start by defining diction: the choice and use of words in speech and writing.

   Placing herself in the position of the coach, Hairston writes as a coach would speak to an athlete. With clarity and communication as her goal, she provides strategies used by professionals, dispels misconceptions, and gives encouragement needed to get started. Choosing words that most clearly and directly express the ideas to the reader recalls the reader recalls the style used by Malcolm X.

LANGUAGE IN ACTION

Students easily relate to the idea of sitting and staring at a blank piece of paper or a computer screen. After all, when we suffer from writer's block, we literally feel that we're not "plugged into" the writing process. Most students find it difficult to talk about the things they can't do well, so injecting a little humor into the situation lets us laugh at ourselves and move ahead with productive or helpful discussion.

WRITING FOR AN AUDIENCE

LINDA FLOWER

THINKING CRITICALLY ABOUT THE READING

1. A competent writer will look at the distance between him- or herself and the audience, a distance created by differences such as age or background, knowledge about the topic, attitudes toward it, and personal or professional needs. The writer must analyze those needs, clarify what the reader needs to know, and adapt that knowledge toward the reader.

2. Flower defines knowledge as "conscious awareness of explicit facts and clearly defined concepts "(4) . . . [that] can be easily . . . written down or told to someone else" (4). Attitude, on the other hand, is an "image" or "a loose cluster of associations" (4). The distinction is important because "a reader's image of a subject is often the source of attitudes and feelings that are unexpected and, at times, impervious to mere facts" (5). Once aware of this, writers can bridge the distance between themselves and the reader through word choice and examples.

3. Students' responses may vary, though Flower seems to make conscious attempts to direct her diction and examples at a college audience. The second paragraph asks the students to imagine themselves writing to their parents about a wilderness survival expedition they would like to join. The writers must bridge the gap between themselves and their New York City parents by communicating their desire to join this expedition in language their parents can understand. In her discussion of needs, for instance, Flower focuses on writing done on a job and in college courses—both examples of the kinds of writing that concern college students.

4. Students can begin by defining *connotation*: Word associations derived from personal experience, reading, and the influence of others, as opposed to denotation (the literal meaning of a word). Flower uses the word *lakes* to illustrate the clusters of associations that are connected with a word. Engage students in a discussion of the examples; for example, ask them how home differs from house.

5. Flower writes, "A good college paper doesn't just rehash the facts; it demonstrates what your reader, as a teacher, needs to know—that you are learning the thinking skills his or her course is trying to teach" (9). Ask students to discuss what thinking skills are and how they are demonstrated in a college paper. They may have other ideas about what goes into a good college paper, such as organization, clarity, or transitions. Some students may put a great deal of emphasis on grammar, punctuation, and mechanics.

6. When aware of the associations readers make with certain words, writers can use language more effectively to persuade, convey feeling or sentiment, and communicate ideas. Because readers will be emotionally affected by your words, you must be conscious of the associations they may bring to the words you use if you want to persuade them to your viewpoint in an argument. In a personal essay you can use associations to enhance the readers' understanding of the experience you are having. The informative piece seeks to explain in an objective way. If the language has the wrong connotations for the writer's purpose, it can backfire in any of these situations.

7. When the language used is too technical for the reader, he or she tunes out. Writers use definitions, meaningful examples, description, comparison and contrast, and tone to bridge the gap between themselves and the reader. When asking classmates, friends, or parents to help, their answers will vary depending on the education and background of these people so give students insight into which strategies might be most useful for a particular audience.

LANGUAGE IN ACTION

Students' responses will vary depending on their expertise. Have the students list the computer jargon in several columns, such as jargon I understand, jargon I think but am not sure I know, and jargon I don't have a clue about. Once they have compiled their lists, have them work in small groups to determine the audience for which the site was intended. The students will see how their own computer expertise is related to an understanding of the language.

Shitty First Drafts

Anne Lamott

THINKING CRITICALLY ABOUT THE READING

1. Lamott's thesis is in paragraph 2: "Very few writers really know what they are doing until they've done it." (Implied thesis: If you allow yourself to write badly at first, then you can begin to write well.)

2. When she speaks of the "fantasy of the uninitiated" (1) Lamott refers to the way people perceive the writing process. People who don't write often may think that writing comes easily and naturally to good writers, and they have not understood how difficult and lengthy the process can be for anyone who sits down with the blank page.

3. Lamott trusts the process "more or less" (7) because she, like most writers, must always fight the impulse to perfect the first draft. She indicates throughout the essay how difficult it is to turn off internal critics who, even when she allows herself to write freely, "comment like cartoon characters" (6) on her writing. Lamott draws a connection between her personal experience and that of other writers: "I know some very great writers, writers you love who write beautifully and have made a great deal of money, and not one of them sits down routinely feeling wildly enthusiastic and confident" (1).

4. The case can be made that writing a first draft is about *both* content and psychology—dealing with the psychological issues around the writing process (allowing oneself to write badly) helps the writer generate content (according to Lamott, any content in a first draft is preferable to no content).

5. Anne Lamott's attempts at humor add to the points she is making because she allows us to laugh at various inevitable unpleasant human emotions in her, and then laugh at ourselves. She casts the discomfort of the writing process into something familiar and funny. Examples:

   a. "Not one of them writes elegant first drafts. All right, one of them does, but we do not like her very much. We do not think that she has a rich inner life or that God likes her or can even stand her. (Although when I mentioned this to my priest friend Tom, he said you can safely assume you've created God in your own image when it turns out that God hates all the same people you do" (1).

   b. "I'd get up and study my teeth in the mirror for a while. Then I'd stop, remember to breathe, make a few phone calls, hit the kitchen and chow down. Eventually I'd go back and sit down at my desk, and *sigh* for the next ten minutes" (5).

   c. "They'd be pretending to snore, or rolling their eyes at my overwrought descriptions, no matter how hard I tried to tone those descriptions down, no matter how conscious I was of what a friend said to me gently in my early days of restaurant reviewing. Annie, she said, it is just a piece of *chicken*. It is just a bit of *cake*" (6).

   d. " . . . lots of quotes from my black-humored friends that made them sound more like the Manson girls than food lovers" (7).

6. By introducing her own behaviors into paragraph 5, Lamott shows that the reviewer experiences the same difficulties as the novice when writing. After listing the difficulties she encounters, she resolves the tension towards the end of the paragraph when she reminds

herself that all she needed was to write a "shitty first draft of, say, the opening paragraph." It is helpful, for the young writer especially, to know this information.

7. Lamott's piece is conversational and intimate with her readers. Because she is poking fun at her own bad writing, the use of the word "shitty" is less offensive. The *degree* of badness would be lost if she used a different word, and Lamott wants the writer to feel free to write as badly as possible. Keeping the colloquial tone also allows her to seem straightforward instead of melodramatic.

LANGUAGE IN ACTION

Answers to Verbs with Verve:

1. snapped—stamped
2. gurgled—crawled
3. boasted—strutted
4. minced or giggled—skipped, bounced, or pranced
5. giggled—bounced or skipped
6. mumbled—stumbled
7. drawled—sauntered
8. blubbered or sobbed—staggered lurched, or stumbled
9. slurred—lurched or staggered
10. apologized—bolted
11. jabbered or blurted—whirled
12. shrieked—darted or bolted
13. whooped—pranced
14. blurted—darted or bolted
15. murmured—hobbled
16. commanded—marched or strode
17. whispered—stole
18. murmured—tiptoed or stole
19. sighed—plodded
20. Cackled—flew

THE MAKER'S EYE: REVISING YOUR OWN MANUSCRIPTS

DONALD M. MURRAY

THINKING CRITICALLY ABOUT THE READING

1. Revision solves large structural problems of coherence and fluidity, whereas editing addresses more technical and small-scale issues like sentence structure and word choice.

2. Writers become concerned with word use only after the creation of a full first draft and preliminary editing. "As writers read and reread, write and rewrite, they move closer and closer to the page until they are doing line-by-line editing" (21).

3. The writer looks for information to be sure he or she has "specific, accurate, and interesting information" (13). The meaning is what the writer makes of the information. The distinction between information and meaning is important because accurate information is the building block that leads to greater meaning or, as Murray says, "The specifics must build to a pattern of significance. Each piece of specific information must carry the reader toward meaning" (14).

4. The "maker's eye," the writer's chief self-critical tool, "sees the need for variety and balance, for a firmer structure, for a more appropriate form" (26). Only the writer knows exactly what she or he wants to say and has an image of how it should be presented. Other readers provide outside perspectives; however, Murray warns that the writer should be suspicious of all criticism.

5. Murray says that a "piece of writing is never finished" (30), that it can always be improved or changed. Deadlines force this process to stop, to end the continual tinkering by the writer who reedits the work as long as time will allow.

6. Reading separates the writer from his or her ideas enough so that the editing process can begin. When reading a self-produced draft, the reader should view it as a work in progress, rather than the "finished" product in a newspaper or magazine.

7. The order of Murray's editing techniques—information, meaning, audience, form, structure, development, dimension, and voice—reflects the narrowing scope through which editing occurs. As the editing begins, writers concentrate on content and the accuracy and clarity of their information. Later, they focus on the more subtle qualities of dimension and voice.

8. When students read aloud, they often pick up their own errors, errors in grammar, style, or content. Does their writing make sense when read? Is it understandable? Have students read their own writing aloud, to themselves and to a partner. Often the writer will revise and change her or his own work effectively if the partner just sits quietly and listens, giving the writer time to revisit the work.

LANGUAGE IN ACTION

You may like to read Dillard's paragraphs aloud to your students before giving them instructions. In this way they can enjoy the entire passage before they start looking for parts of speech. Then you may want to review the concepts noun, verb, subordinate clause, and main sentence. This exercise offers you a chance to involve students in a grammar lesson without talking about grammar. Students will come to see that the strength of Dillard's prose is in her concrete nouns, strong action verbs, and varied sentence structure. One note of caution: some students will always underline gerunds (-ing forms of verbs) and infinitives (to + base verb), mistaking these for the main verb in a clause. A good follow-up to this exercise is to have students analyze a paragraph or two of their own prose in the same manner.

How to Write an Argument: What Students and Teachers Really Need to Know

Gerald Graff

THINKING CRITICALLY ABOUT THE READING

1. Graff is suggesting that, just as you would give your conversation partner some background information before you make your case, you give the reader an idea of the debate in which you are arguing. The participants in the conversation are the writer and the reader(s).

2. A debate is a conversation between two (or more) parties about the same issue. Each side must listen to the others' points and then respond to them in order to be effective. In the same way, people in conversation generally listen to each other and follow the thread of the conversation. The main difference is that, in a debate, the parties do not agree with each other, whereas in a conversation they may either agree or disagree.

3. When writing, readers bring more of their own ideas to the table. They have the time to think more about what is written and, since it is more concrete, it is easy to assume that anything left out was left out on purpose. And, because there is no opportunity for dialogue in a written argument, the writer must think of all possible objections—she has only one chance to convince.

4. Graff points out that critics can help to clarify an argument and are the reason the writer's argument is made in the first place: Without an opposing side, there is no argument.

5. A meta-text is a text within the essay which tells readers how and how not to read it. It is necessary to explain to the writer's rationale to the reader. If students have written with meta-texts, have them identify signal phrases such as the ones Graff mentions and discuss whether their meta-text was effective. If students have not used a meta-text, ask if this strategy would make sense for an argument paper they had written.

6. Restating a point in plain English will make the point clearer to the audience and to the writer. It can make the point with renewed fervor because of its clarity, but it can also reveal problems with the argument. And, it is a chance to repeat your idea so that it stays with the reader.

7. Student answers will vary. To stimulate discussion, ask students about times when they had to or wanted to make an argument, either in writing or orally. Would Graff's advice have been helpful in those situations? Did other obstacles come up that Graff does not address?

LANGUAGE IN ACTION

Graff's argument and "How to Dance the Tango" both explain a process in a series of numbered steps. By following them, a reader probably could write a draft of an argument and perform the steps of a basic tango. However, both pieces are merely skeletal instructions—a political writer used to writing position pieces or a professional tango dancer would perform these steps with more artistry and flair than can be expressed in a short how-to.

The writing style of the two documents is quite different. Graff addresses the writer directly ("you") in an informal, no-nonsense, instructional style. The tango instructions describe what "the lady" and "the gentleman" do in order to perform the steps of the tango. Although both documents are numbered lists, only the tango instructions need to be followed in order. Graff's list starts in order ("1. Enter a conversation . . . 2. Make a claim, the sooner the better") but soon becomes a list of recommendations that can be referred to many times while writing the argument.

Graff probably wrote a numbered list to make his advice easier to digest and less daunting to the novice writer than a long essay. Student opinions may vary; the numbered list is engaging and can be taken one step at a time, but following all the steps in order does not guarantee a well-written argument essay.

SIMPLICITY

WILLIAM ZINSSER

THINKING CRITICALLY ABOUT THE READING

1. Clutter is "unnecessary words, circular constructions, pompous frills, and meaningless jargon" (1). "Every word that serves no function, every long word that could be a short word, every adverb that carries the same meaning that's already in the verb, every passive construction that leaves the reader unsure of who is doing what" (3) contribute to clutter.

2. By *inflate*, Zinsser means trying to make ourselves sound larger and more important through excess verbiage. When inflated, a balloon rises, and our tendency is to revere those who appear higher and out of reach (for example, movie stars, academicians, scientists). Ask students if they witness similar "inflating" at their college or university.

3. In paragraph 9, Zinsser describes the following language-based obstacles:

   • Too much clutter disguises meaning.
   • A poorly constructed sentence allows the reader to make several different interpretations.
   • Switching pronouns midsentence causes the reader to lose track of who is talking or when the action took place.
   • The lack of a logical sequence between sentences forces the reader to focus on structure rather than on the ideas presented.
   • Misused words distract the reader.

   The reader tends to blame him- or herself for not understanding, and as a result he or she will have to spend too much time trying to understand the organization of the piece rather than its ideas. Eventually the reader will tire and "look for [a writer] who is better at the craft" (10).

4. Student answers may vary concerning the relationship between level of education and wordiness. Doctors, scientists, politicians, lawyers, and professors serve as a good testing ground. Discuss how wordiness has become associated with some professions. What are the effects of wordiness on the relationships these professionals have with clients, coworkers, and the general public?

5. Zinsser assumes that readers will blame themselves if they cannot understand what the writer is trying to say. If the reader is lost, the writer hasn't been careful enough. Ask students if they have tackled writing that doesn't seem to make sense and sends them back over sentences trying to figure out what they mean. Flower wants the writer to adapt her or his knowledge to the needs of the reader, to step back and consider the audience.

6. To cut down on clutter, Zinsser suggests that writers ask themselves: "What am I trying to say?", then "Have I said it?" and "Is it clear?" If authors know what they want to say while they are writing, chances are they will come close to saying it. If, however, they have only a vague or general idea of what they're trying to say, they will ramble on. And, as we all know, writing that rambles on is filled with clutter. Discuss ways students can improve clarity in thinking and how writing helps them do it.

7. In paragraph 3, Zinsser suggests ways to eliminate clutter. Ask students to review their own past papers or works in progress to find examples of clutter that weaken their sentences.

8. Students may pull a variety of sentences from the text which serve different purposes. In paragraphs 1, 6, 9, and 13, short sentences grab the attention of the reader, emphasize a point (for example, "Simplify, simplify"), and keep the piece moving.

LANGUAGE IN ACTION

Have one of your students read Zinsser's revised manuscript aloud while the rest follow along in their books. In this way the whole class will not only see how Zinsser's revisions tighten and strengthen the writing but also hear how they work. At this point have your students discuss specific examples of Zinsser's revision that they thought worked particularly well. They will recognize the importance of each word left after clutter is removed. They can then review their own paragraphs and see how much clutter they can remove to strengthen their own writing.

LET'S THINK OUTSIDE THE BOX OF BAD CLICHÉS

GREGORY PENCE

THINKING CRITICALLY ABOUT THE READING

1. Pence's thesis is that both students and professionals in many fields frequently use clichéd turns of phrase. He finds these clichés boring, and suggests that writers who rely on them are not thinking hard enough about what they mean. He supports his point with a long list of examples drawn from students, the news, medicine, business, and other areas.

2. Pence's list of clichés includes contradictory phrases, redundancies, illogical and meaningless phrases, confusing and silly expressions, improper use of the word *literally*, jargon, nouns acting as adjectival phrases, and phrases that convey the wrong visual images. He uses more vitriolic language—"one of the phrases I hate most is," "I also despise the phrase"—when he describes clichés that are used to soften an argument or protect the writer in some way. He seems less annoyed by redundancy, silliness, and jargon.

3. Calling a phrase a cliché is certainly not intended as praise. But there are some phrases used in everyday English that are standard but not banal. A bad cliché might be one that is particularly unnecessary, unnatural-sounding, or overused.

4. Pence gives examples from business that are particularly difficult to understand, with "strings of nouns acting as adjectival phrases." Although conversational clichés might be folksy or tired, they are more familiar and easier to understand than these newer phrases.

5. Pence's example from medicine seems to indicate that first the patient died, and much later, life support was removed. This could be confusing to non-medical readers—if the patient died, there is no reason to continue life support until the next day. His rewrite solves the problem by being more specific ("dead by neurological criteria" rather than "brain dead") and thus more understandable to readers.

6. Students may have different ideas and suggestions for their fellow students. Peer review is one way for students to check their writing for clichés; students may not notice if they use the same phrases repeatedly in their own writing.

LANGUAGE IN ACTION

when push comes to <u>shove</u>
fall between <u>the cracks</u>
scratch <u>the surface</u>
maintain the <u>status quo</u>
takes on a <u>whole new meaning</u>
paying lip <u>service</u>
put the <u>horse</u> before the <u>cart</u>
patience of a <u>saint</u>

Its Academic, or Is It?

Charles R. Larson

THINKING CRITICALLY ABOUT THE READING

1. Larson is exaggerating by citing only the examples that prove his point. He is, of course, leaving out examples of correct apostrophe use in advertising, newspapers, etc. He also deliberately and obviously misuses the apostrophe in many places in his essay. And, he uses strong language to describe his own reaction to punctuation problems: "Heaven knows I've tried to figure it out, agonized about it for years."

2. Larson writes, "The apostrophe is dead because reading is dead." He cites the poor quality of punctuation on the Internet and his inability to find a reading lamp as proof, concluding that "Everything pass'es too quickly." Although the Internet has done few favors for writing correctly, the popularity of blogs, Internet news sites, and other written online content today hardly supports his claim that "reading is dead."

3. Larson asks "why bother?" many times in this essay, but proves that he cares about apostrophes simply by continuing to write. His basic argument, particularly for "its" and "it's," is that it isn't so hard to know the difference: "How difficult is it to teach a sixth grader how to punctuate correctly?"

4. By the end of the essay, Larson has extrapolated from the public's disrespect for the apostrophe to a disrespect for punctuation and for grammar and language in general, in favor of television and other nonliterary entertainment. The lack of reading lamps does show a change in priorities for American consumers. Once, lamps were needed to facilitate reading, which might happen regularly in any household; now, they are mere backlighting for the ubiquitous television. And, if no one is reading, then no one will notice misuse of the apostrophe.

5. Larson is frustrated that, everywhere he looks, the simple apostrophe is misused. He asks questions throughout the essay because he is baffled: "How complicated can this be?" "If editors at publishing houses can't catch these errors, who can?" But he offers no hope and is resigned in the end: "Time to stop this grumbling. Thing's fall apart."

6. Larson spends most of the essay providing examples of apostrophe misuse and general disrespect for English. He starts to suggest better teaching as a solution—"How difficult is it

to teach a sixth grader how to punctuate correctly?"—but doesn't expand upon it. He also suggests "When in doubt, simply write out the full sentence, carefully avoiding all possessives and contradictions," but this is both impossible and a bitter reflection on how difficult it seems for anyone to write "too complex an alteration."

LANGUAGE IN ACTION

The apostrophes have been corrected as follows:

  a. ~~Its~~ It's not a matter of whether or not the residents in the area need the ~~cities~~ city's help.
  b. They're planning to build a new school but it needs to be approved by the ~~districts~~ district's voters.
  c. What's planned is a new elementary school in [the] old ~~ones²~~ one's location.
  d. ~~Wait'll~~ Wait until they see how hard it is to get the votes they'll need.
  e. The school system's not hearing ~~voters~~ voters' wishes; it's simply not open to suggestions.

LIKE I SAID, DON'T WORRY

PATRICIA T. O'CONNER

THINKING CRITICALLY ABOUT THE READING

1. O'Conner wants everyone to "relax" by moving away from the jargon associated with grammar and speaking clearly about it. She also wants to remove the negative stigma of bad grammar and allow people to ask questions without feeling judged. She would like everyone to know how to use proper grammar when it's called for, but doesn't see the need for everyone to know "the rules."

2. The rules of grammar can get in the way of "our natural love of words." The "intimidating terminology" used to teach grammar scares people away, and the purpose of those rules is lost.

3. O'Conner finds it ironic that grammar and punctuation, which are often perceived as old-fashioned or out of date, are becoming more important because so much writing is done on the Internet. Technology has made written communication faster and easier, and the amount of writing people do every day has increased significantly.

4. O'Conner has found by talking to people about grammar that, once they are in a non-judgmental environment, they are curious about and interested in correct grammar. Many "grammatically insecure people" nonetheless will argue over what is correct or simply like to talk about their use of language.

5. The Internet has provided a no-holds-barred environment for people to express themselves in writing, with no editing and no limits. Without a few restrictions, this feels like unmanageable chaos. Grammar provides a bit of structure, a few rules, and something like

a shared values system for everyone writing on the Internet. Having some kind of common ground is comforting in the vast ocean of cyberspace.

6. O'Conner's tone is friendly and relaxed, yet authoritative. As a "grammar maven," O'Conner could use her knowledge to intimidate, but instead uses it to share her love of language. She creates an environment in which mistakes can be made (It's only a grammatical error, not a drive-by shooting), no rule is infallible or infinitely applicable, and language is something to love, not fear. Her plain-speaking, casual tone is meant to be inclusive, giving the audience a new way of looking at their grammar angst.

7. O'Conner purposely commits a common grammatical mistake, one which she mentioned in her first paragraph. She is acknowledging her own occasional grammar mistakes and poking gentle fun at people who are always ready to jump on such (ultimately trivial) mistakes.

LANGUAGE IN ACTION

Voting data ~~was~~ were collected after the election. (data is plural; datum singular)

The ending of the movie was ~~climatic~~ climactic. (related to climax, not climate)

Sophia's lyrics complemented ~~his~~ her music. (gender agreement with female Sophia)

We could've (or could have) ~~of~~ gone to the football game, but it was too cold. (sounds like "of," but is a contraction of "could have.")

A huge ~~amount~~ number of students was gathered in the courtyard.

Liz's teacher made an ~~illusion~~ allusion to one of Shakespeare's sonnets. (wrong choice of words)

Jordan liked to reverse the old proverb by saying "It's not the ~~principal~~ principle but the money." (words sound the same, but their definitions differ)

The consensus ~~of opinion~~ was that the exam was very easy. ("of opinion" redundant)

~~Whose~~ Who's to say if it's the right answer. (contraction of "who is," not the possessive "whose," though they sound the same)

Gasoline prices are very ~~expensive~~ high now. (gasoline is "expensive"; prices are "high")

3. POLITICS, PROPAGANDA, AND DOUBLESPEAK

PROPAGANDA: HOW NOT TO BE BAMBOOZLED

DONNA WOOLFOLK CROSS

THINKING CRITICALLY ABOUT THE READING

1. According to Cross, propaganda is "a means of persuasion" (1) that can be used by anyone but is often used by politicians and advertisers to shape public attitudes on everything from toothpaste brands to public policy.

2. Cross believes that it is necessary for people in a democratic society to become aware of propaganda techniques so that they can be the informed questioning citizens a healthy

democracy requires (51). To counteract the influences of propaganda, people must overcome their indifference toward political affairs, raise their awareness of the techniques used by others to sway their opinions, and reflect thoughtfully on what they hear and read.

3. In paragraph 11, Cross says, "Another approach that propaganda uses is to create a distraction, a 'red herring,' that will make people forget or ignore the real issues. There are several different kinds of 'red herrings' that can be used to distract attention." Writers or speakers use red herrings to distract a reader's or listener's attention from the important issues or concerns. When "begging the question," "a person assumes as already established the very point that he is trying to prove" (37). Cross uses the example of Senator Yakalot who "announces that his opponent's plan won't work 'because it is unworkable'" when he should have been explaining *why* the plan was unworkable (37).

4. According to Cross, the most common propaganda trick is the testimonial device in which some loved or respected person endorses a particular product or idea (47). Around election time many candidates recruit famous movie stars and musicians to endorse their campaign (Arnold Schwarzenegger endorsed George Bush in the 1988 presidential election, and Barbra Streisand endorsed Bill Clinton in 1992). Basketball stars endorse everything from sneakers, to soda, to cereal.

5. Cross uses examples to clarify her definitions and to help readers identify phrases they hear every day as different propaganda devices. Students' reactions to Cross's use of examples will vary. Some may feel she relies too heavily on the fictitious examples of John Doe and Senator Yakalot when real quotes might be more effective. Cross seems to be having fun with the name "Yak-a-lot" and is more interested in talking about propaganda techniques than in skewering real politicians. Had she used real quotes, the reader's attention might have been diverted to the politics of the example and not the propaganda device being used. Some may feel that jumping from Mussolini to Joe Namath makes her essay seem scattered and less effective than if she stuck with quotes from two situations such as presidential campaigns and television advertisements. Others may comment that her broad range of examples proves how old and widespread the use of propaganda really is.

6. Cross uses the lemming analogy (pp. 154–155) because humans, like lemmings, have a tendency to follow everyone else without reflecting on why they are conforming or the possible effects of their actions. For lemmings, this leads to self-destruction. By drawing an analogy between the two, Cross suggests that the result might be the same for humans. Cross's analogy is not a false analogy because it compares two things that are similar in significant ways. History has shown that humans are prone to hop on the bandwagon. However, students may note that people may disagree about whether an analogy is valid. Through analogies, writers can explain certain aspects of a situation by showing how the same principles apply in similar situations.

LANGUAGE IN ACTION

In most cases students will respond positively to the advertisement for the breast cancer stamp and the campus flyer for student internships. This activity offers students the opportunity to analyze propaganda that is being used for accepted or worthwhile endeavors. In the ad for the breast cancer stamp, the propagandist tries to transfer the positive feelings (or glory by association) of helping, of fighting a disease, and of finding a cure to the reader. Because the cause is a good one, we readily embrace the ad's optimism and get in line to buy stamps. The writers of the internship flyer use glittering generalities (words and phrases with positive connotations) to persuade readers to apply for the advertised positions.

Have students identify words or phrases that were particularly powerful for them and explain, if they can, their reactions to these words. Engage students in a discussion of how these two examples of propaganda are different from the negative ones described in Cross's article.

POLITICS AND THE ENGLISH LANGUAGE

GEORGE ORWELL

THINKING CRITICALLY ABOUT THE READING

1. Students should base their summaries of Orwell's argument on the first two paragraphs of the essay. Basically Orwell argues that we disguise meaning from ourselves and our audience through bad writing; writing more clearly will force us to think more clearly, and thinking is, after all, the most basic building block of a healthy political state.

2. Published in 1946, "Politics and the English Language" seems to have been written originally for literate, thinking British citizens who had just come through the horrors of World War II. Orwell's references to "Fascism," "Americanisms," "hansom cabs," "aeroplanes," Greek, and Latin clearly help to identify his audience. Although his prose may be considered a little old fashioned by some contemporary readers, Orwell's message is still valuable, and this essay continues to be read by millions in the English-speaking world.

3. For Orwell, the mixing of incompatible metaphors is "a sure sign that the writer is not interested in what he is saying" (5); an engaged writer would demand consistency. This carelessness reflects and encourages the trend of thoughtless writing.

4. In paragraph 5, Orwell identifies newly invented metaphors that evoke visual images and dead metaphors that have "reverted to being an ordinary word and can generally be used without loss of vividness." In between these two extremes is a large group of metaphors that Orwell labels "dying"; these are "worn-out metaphors which have lost all evocative power and are merely used because they save people the trouble of inventing phrases for themselves." Orwell objects to their use because he believes they are a symptom of a lack of thinking on the part of writers.

5. Each of Orwell's metaphors and similes turns an abstraction into a concrete image, making his argument clearer to the reader. Each is vivid, memorable, and striking in its novelty. You may wish to ask students what figures of speech they would use to convey the same information.

6. Orwell lists the following four prewriting questions in paragraph 12:
   • "What am I trying to say?"
   • "What words will express it?"
   • "What image or idiom will make it clearer?"
   • "Is this image fresh enough to have an effect?"

   Orwell says that scrupulous writers will probably ask themselves two more questions as well:
   • "Could I put it more shortly?"
   • "Have I said anything that is avoidably ugly?"

7. Not all dictionaries will contain the term *question-begging*. In her essay "Propaganda: How Not to Be Bamboozled," Donna Woolfolk Cross says question-begging occurs when "a person assumes as already established the very point that he is trying to prove" (37, page 157). Cross's fictitious Senator Yakalot uses question-begging when he "announces that his opponent's plan won't work 'because it is unworkable'" (37, page 157). Orwell claims that the deterioration of political language contributes to the increasingly hostile and untrustworthy political atmosphere; "politics itself is a mass of lies, evasions, folly, hatred, and schizophrenia. When the general atmosphere is bad, language must suffer" (15). Students' answers concerning whether "the decadence of our language is probably curable" (17) will vary. Orwell claims that changing language over time may not be possible; however, smaller, short-term adjustments can be made by following the suggestions he gives in paragraph 18.

8. Orwell makes the transition from criticisms to proposals in paragraph 17: "I said earlier that the decadence of language is probably curable." By organizing his essay this way, Orwell helps the reader have a clear and complete understanding of the problem before he suggests solutions. Point out to students that William Lutz organizes his essay "The World of Doublespeak" (pages 177–187) in a similar format; he provides readers with a clear and complete definition of the term *doublespeak* before he discusses its uses and implications. Both authors want readers to be adequately equipped with the necessary information and understanding before they proceed.

LANGUAGE IN ACTION

Robert Yoakum's parody of contemporary political speech clearly illustrates what Orwell means when he talks about hackneyed speech: "prose consists less and less of *words* chosen for the sake of their meaning, and more and more of *phrases* tacked together like the sections of a prefabricated henhouse" (4). We can all recall hearing speeches like this one or sound bites on television that sound like they're saying something but are really saying nothing. Yoakum pokes fun at the way politicians try to befriend the voter, discredit opponents, show their support of U.S. values, be against taxes, and take a tough stand on crime and welfare, while at the same time managing not to say anything specific. If your students have read Cross's article "Propaganda: How Not to Be Bamboozled" (pages 149–159), have them analyze Yoakum's parody for the propaganda devices Cross enumerates.

THE WORLD OF DOUBLESPEAK

WILLIAM LUTZ

THINKING CRITICALLY ABOUT THE READING

1. The entire second paragraph describes doublespeak and outlines its characteristics, but the first sentence provides the basic definition: "Doublespeak is a blanket term for language which pretends to communicate but doesn't," which avoids responsibility, distorts meaning, and "conceals or prevents thought" (2).

2. According to Lutz, a euphemism is "an inoffensive or positive word or phrase designed to avoid a harsh, unpleasant, or distasteful reality" (5). Lutz categorizes euphemisms as doublespeak when used to mislead or deceive but as "the language of courtesy" (5) when used to express concern or to protect another's feelings.

3. Lutz means that North admits to being responsible for his actions (to having committed them) but that he does not hold himself accountable (or, accept the consequences) for them.

4. Lutz asserts that "doublespeak continues to spread as the official language of public discourse" (1) because it is effective; it separates perpetrators from their actions, emotionally detaches the public from the news it hears, and allows government branches such as the State Department and the Pentagon to avoid what Lutz calls "unpleasant realities" (6). Students' answers to the question of whether there has been an increase or decrease in the amount of doublespeak since the time Lutz wrote his article will vary, depending on their individual experiences with public doublespeak. While most observers would agree that the public is becoming aware of such language, doublespeak itself seems to be on the increase in such areas as politics, big business, international relations, advertising, and even education. Depending on their individual experience—what newspapers, magazines, and books they read, what television they watch, and their academic background or major—students are likely to provide a wide range of examples to back up their opinion.

5. Classification is a strategy of development that helps a writer simplify complicated material for readers by dividing a large subject (in this case doublespeak) into manageable categories (in this case euphemism, jargon, gobbledygook, and inflated language). This strategy enables Lutz to discuss one type of doublespeak at a time. In this way he can define each type, explain how it works, and provide examples to help us identify it in our own lives without confusing it with the other types of doublespeak.

6. Because Lutz's essay presents a concept unfamiliar to most readers, he needs a number of solid examples to make his terms and definitions clear in order to help the reader recognize doublespeak in its various forms and to show the implications of doublespeak to the reader. The variety and clarity of Lutz's examples show that he has done extensive research, has a good understanding of the subject, and has taken care to present his ideas thoughtfully.

7. He wants readers to recognize doublespeak as a way to "mislead, distort, deceive, inflate, circumvent, obfuscate" (2) and then to voice dissatisfaction with those who use it. For Lutz, this manipulation can only lead to negative results. "Serious doublespeak is highly strategic, and it breeds suspicion, cynicism, distrust, and, ultimately, hostility" (15). Lutz urges the U.S. public to demand higher standards and more accountability from their leaders rather than allow doublespeak and its inherent hazards to prevail.

LANGUAGE IN ACTION

Many students will find the list of acceptable expressions for teachers to use in parent-teacher conferences quite funny. Ask them if they remember similar expressions that were used by their teachers and school administrators to describe student behavior or performance. Engage students in a discussion of why such language is needed for teachers to discuss a child's performance or behavior with his or her parent. Who is being protected with such euphemistic language? Do these euphemisms really deceive parents? If not, does such language serve any useful purpose? What suggestions do your students have for promoting honest, thoughtful, and productive parent-teacher conferences?

THE BURDEN OF DECEIT IN PUBLIC LIFE

SISSELA BOK

THINKING CRITICALLY ABOUT THE READING

1. Bok includes deceit, secrecy, and lies among the variety of ways to mislead people. She defines "deceit" as intentionally misleading others. Lies are a form of deceit—statements known to be false to the speaker, intended to mislead. (Not all false statements are necessarily deceitful, however.) Secrecy is merely concealment; it does not necessarily involve the intention to mislead. Bok points out that "While all forms of deceit, all lies, involve keeping something secret, the reverse is not true." Lies and deceit involve keeping the truth a secret, but keeping a secret does not necessarily mean being deceitful.

2. The "burden of disease" is a useful parallel to what Bok intends to say about deceit. Most people understand how disease affects not only the sick, but the public as a whole. The influenza pandemic of 1918 is an example of both sickness and deceit harming the public. As influenza ravaged the country, President Wilson "took next to no public notice of the threat." Since laws were in place making it illegal to question the government, the public could not demand an effective response to the pandemic. Instead, the papers published useless advice, and citizens were left without guidance and with no faith in the government—"The pervasive distrust contributed to the burden of deceit and compounded the burden of disease, disability, and death."

3. Clear distinctions about deceit are necessary because the terms used mean different things to different people. For example, a politician can make a false statement, but it should not be called a lie if it was in fact a mistake. Bok feels that this accusative discourse contributes to the burden of deceit "by making it easier for people to conclude there is lying everywhere," which, in turn, "hampers the thoughtful national debate we ought to be having on the role of deceit in public life and the burden it imposes." When there is a blurring of definitions and distinctions in public debate, no one stops to think about whether there are times "when deceit might be considered excusable or even justifiable."

4. The "good lie" or the "just lie" is one we hear as adults from our leaders and as children from our parents. Behind this justification is the notion that the lie is meant to protect, not injure. Bok's procedure for weighing the potential impact of a lie is to first ask whether there are other ways to get the same result without lying. Then, think about the moral reasons to excuse the lie and the possible objections to those reasons. Finally, ask how other reasonable people would respond to these arguments. According to Bok, "most people value truthfulness more highly in others than when it comes to their own choices." We tend not to ask ourselves about our own motivations in deciding to lie or to calculate the pros and cons of the lie's effect on others, but when someone else tells us a lie, we feel angry and betrayed.

5. Lies have "corrosive and cumulative effects" not only on the credibility of the person who misleads with a lie, but on their profession, and on trust in general. "As lies spread, suspicions mount and trust erodes." Bok believes that "public servants, doctors, clergy, lawyers, bankers, journalists and other professionals" have a special responsibility not to deceive the public. When trust turns to mistrust, "it cuts at the roots of democracy," citizens lose confidence in their leaders, and people begin to see lies everywhere in govern-

ment. As a result, people are deprived of the truth and access to trustworthy sources of information. Disillusionment leads to a lack of participation, and without participation a democracy cannot serve the public good.

6. Bok's "hidden risks" are the risk to the liars themselves, risks to the liar's institution or profession, and the erosion of trust in general. People often fail to take into account the "hidden risks" of a lie because they can only see the immediate costs and benefits of a particular lie. The hidden risks are much less concrete and obvious, and harder to consider; they also add costs to the lie, and thus make it harder to justify.

7. False accusations and claims add to the burden of deceit not only because they are false, but because they deflect attention away from the truth. When everyone is distracted by replying to the false accusation, no one finds out the truth, and the result is only more deceit.

8. A debate is a two-way discussion in which each side must be heard. The shouting match that Bok refers to drowns out the discussion and "short-circuits reflection"; it substitutes simplified language and thinking for a thoughtful search for the truth. Truth is the loser; the winner is merely the one who can shout the loudest. Bok suggests slowing down the debate, looking at the true motivations of the people involved, and finding areas of agreement "even among those who hold such sharply discordant views."

LANGUAGE IN ACTION

In discussing these situations, you might remind students of one of the primary reasons that people (adults and children) lie: self-protection and protection of others, especially members of their own family. Ask them to think like a child who has no understanding of the unintended consequences of a lie, but who lies nonetheless. Remind students of Bok's recommendations for thoughtful, "adult" analysis, particularly in her procedure for weighing the potential impact of a lie, and in taking into account the "hidden risks" of a lie on themselves, their fellow-students, their profession, and their family. Ask students to think about their gut reaction to the situation and their reaction to the situation after weighing the potential hidden impact.

I HAVE A DREAM

MARTIN LUTHER KING JR.

THINKING CRITICALLY ABOUT THE READING

1. The Declaration of Independence states that all men are created equal and have the right to life, liberty, and the pursuit of happiness. The U.S. Constitution offers "we the people" certain rights and protections. Because the language of these documents feels inclusive, King accuses America of "defaulting" on promises of equal status and of privileges not given to African Americans.

2. While King spoke to supporters in the struggle for civil rights, his larger audience was not necessarily involved in the struggle. He wants to catch that wider audience's attention and

makes the point that recognizing racial injustice is important. The point is delivered by naming as many regions of the country as possible (which makes the wider audience feel implicated) and by invoking the American dream as the root of his "dream."

3. In order to be in the right, King states that he and his followers "must not be guilty of wrongful deeds" (7), meaning that they must not sink to the position of their enemies by replacing one injustice with another. The issue is important to him because his movement is heavily influenced by the writings in the New Testament; goals will be achieved not by punishment and power, but through a different method, by following a righteous path.

4. Because this is a speech, and King wants it to be memorable, he uses parallel constructions and repetitions throughout. Emphasized important words include "now," "dream," "let freedom ring," and "we cannot be satisfied." Repeated words, especially when they are emotionally charged, carry a stress that other words do not, and these words begin to carry the weight and meaning of the whole text.

5. *Examples of metaphor:*

The Emancipation Proclamation is "a great beacon light" (2) provides the reader with a visual image of relief and hope.

"We have come to cash a check" (4) allows one to imagine that something is *owed*.

"Veterans of creative suffering" (9) imbue the oppressed with honor and liken them to survivors in a war.

"Jangling discord . . . symphony of brotherhood" (14) uses sound as its association and indicates that there will be a transition in one's experience from chaos to pleasant order.

6. In the speech, King indicates that he will be satisfied in his quest for civil rights when the rights of the individual are recognized and when prejudice no longer exists.

7. King's dream is that everyone will enjoy the same freedoms, regardless of skin color. He envisions a time when race will no longer be a barrier for people.

LANGUAGE IN ACTION

Ask students if they have seen other advertising campaigns from Apple Computer of this sort, such as the one picturing John Lennon. How do your students feel about the use of major cultural icons in order to advertise computers? What does Martin Luther King Jr.'s tenets in his "I Have a Dream" speech have to do with the ideology behind computer use?

AND AIN'T I A WOMAN?

SOJOURNER TRUTH

THINKING CRITICALLY ABOUT THE READING

1. Truth means that with so much dialogue occurring around women's rights and around the rights of black Americans, there must be an imbalance of equality between white women and black women. She believes "white men will be in a fix" (1) because of the skewed treatment she and other women experience as a result of this inequality.

2. She points to her arm, which has accomplished women's work. She also cites her thirteen children as evidence of her womanhood, as well as her grief as a badge of her womanhood—for having had to give up her children to slavery. She wants to assert that her womanhood is the same in her experience as a black woman, as it would be if she were white, and she should be afforded the same respect as a woman, and as a human being.

3. She uses these terms to place herself outside the realm of men, and to question the validity of these men's authority to determine her inequality.

4. Truth uses repetition to hammer home her point, and to make obvious the answer that, yes, she is a woman, and should be afforded the same rights as other women. She also repeats the phrase "Where did your Christ come from?" (4) twice in order to drive home that women have had more of a part to play in the very creation of Christ than men. She may not provide answers to her question in paragraph 3 in order to allow for open interpretation and personal application of her question.

5. Truth's tone in this speech is one of indignation. Her repeated question of "And ain't I a woman?" and "Look at me!" (2) bear evidence to someone who is agitated, assertive, and forthright.

6. Truth asks where Christ came from, imlying that since Christ was born of woman, that women should have the same rights as men.

TIME TO MAKE PEACE WITH THE PLANET: 2007 NOBEL PRIZE FOR PEACE LECTURE

AL GORE

THINKING CRITICALLY ABOUT THE READING

1. Gore opens his lecture with the Alfred Nobel story, first to acknowledge the history of the creator of the Nobel Peace Prize, and second, to illustrate how people can be shocked into seeing a vision of the future so sudden and clear that it changes the course of their lives. Just as Nobel's premature obituary, with its condemnation of his deadly invention, caused him to choose the course of peace, so Gore's loss to George Bush in the disputed 2000 election (his "political obituary") caused him to choose another course for his public life; this epiphany led him to "seek new ways to serve my purpose." Gore also uses Nobel to talk about intent. Just as Nobel thought dynamite would promote human progress, not death and war, we never intended "to wage war on the earth itself" by ignoring the unintended consequences of our use of the earth's resources.

2. Among the unmistakable signs of the earth's "fever," according to Gore, are the melting of the North Polar ice cap; drought in South America, Asia, and Australia; unprecedented wildfires; and stronger and more frequent deadly storms—all resulting in migrations of millions of climate refugees. Gore's list of ways in which "we" are the cause of so many environmental problems include dumping seventy million tons of global-warming pollution into the atmosphere via the burning of coal, oil, and methane, "as if it were an open sewer"; and "recklessly burning and clearing forests."

3. Gore assumes that his audience has heard of global warming before, though they may not be as aware of its current effects and potential disastrous consequences. He assumes that they will be interested in and convinced by scientific evidence of global warming.

4. Carbon dioxide was seen as a culprit in the earth's rising temperature even in Nobel's time, when one of the first winners of the prize calculated that the earth's average temperature would increase as a result of CO_2 released in the atmosphere by the burning of coal. Seventy years later, scientists are still documenting the increasing CO_2 levels with alarm, and the effects of climate change are clear. CO_2 is easy to ignore because it is "invisible, tasteless, and odorless."

5. The truth can be inconvenient when it requires massive changes to solve the crisis the truth has revealed. The threat is unprecedented, Gore says, "and we often confuse the unprecedented with the improbable" and remain inert in the face of drastic and compelling evidence. In a sense, he is arguing that there is a dual failure of imagination on our part: We cannot imagine the scope of the crisis nor the solutions it requires. The truth about global warming is inconvenient because it asks so much of us; it calls for international cooperation and personal sacrifice. A large truth, such as global warming, is inconvenient because our cumulative actions have brought us to this crisis and it will take the entire world community to put the world right again.

6. The quotes Gore uses throughout his speech help illustrate the consequences of ignoring the signs of impending crisis or catastrophe. He wants to use the wisdom of people who came before him in order to have credibility in front of his audience. By quoting people from many fields, he is also saluting the Nobel tradition of honoring politicians, scientists, and artists. However, with some quotes, he is showing that the attitudes of the past are not sufficient to meet the challenge he describes. For example, Orwell wrote, "Sooner or later a false belief bumps up against solid reality, usually on a battlefield." The reality of global warming is more likely to destroy false beliefs with natural disasters, instead of war. And when citing an African proverb that says, "If you want to go quickly, go alone. If you want to go far, go together," Gore notes that neither option is sufficient: "We need to go far, quickly." Gore is also equating global warming with other international struggles for survival, in the urgent terms usually applied to war. "These prior struggles for survival were won when leaders found words at the eleventh hour that released a mighty surge of courage, hope and readiness to sacrifice for a protracted and mortal challenge."

7. Gore has managed an ironic juxtaposition: calling for us to "make peace with the planet" while asking that we mobilize "with the same urgency and resolve that has previously been seen only when nations mobilized for war," to engage in a "protracted and mortal challenge" in "defense of the common future." Students probably will offer ideas about what it will take to accomplish "peace with the planet" that revolve around international cooperation, the need for global action to solve global problems, and the links between political action in individual countries to global solutions. Among the "hard truths" that we must face are the connections between the climate crisis and the global crisis of "poverty, hunger, HIV-AIDS and other pandemics—the burden of disease—that will require global solutions. Gore calls upon all of us to "begin by making the common rescue of the global environment the central organizing principle of the world community." No one country can accomplish it; every country must cooperate and participate.

8. Gore is both pessimistic and optimistic; students will find a variety of examples and should write complete explanations of whether they found Gore convincing.

LANGUAGE IN ACTION

Rather than considering each label individually, ask students to weigh the impact of each label by comparing them. You might rank the labels based on their intensity, impact, and ability to jolt. Ask students to think of people—politicians, scientists, journalists, etc.—who would use each label, and why they would choose it rather than the others.

WHEN LANGUAGE DIES: 1993 NOBEL PRIZE FOR LITERATURE LECTURE

Toni Morrison

THINKING CRITICALLY ABOUT THE READING

1. The story is part of the lore of several cultures, Morrison says, and part of the story's significance lies in the fact that it speaks to people across all cultures. Young people, wanting to be clever and powerful, often challenge the wisdom of their elders. However, like the arrogant young people in Morrison's story, they are reprimanded because they are not as wise, because they underestimate someone with a physical disability, and because they take their power—to kill the bird, or not—for granted.

2. Statist language is the deadening language of bureaucracy and political systems, "content to admire its own paralysis." Morrison hates this language because it does not allow new ideas, thoughts, or stories. Instead, it only exists to perpetuate itself and the hollow systems of power which created it. It is static and dead, yet it "actively thwarts the intellect, stalls conscience, suppresses human potential"—the opposite of what Morrison aims to do with language.

3. Morrison lays the blame for the "looting of language" on multiple sources, all of which want control over people lives: the government's "obscuring state language," journalists and the "mindless media," academia with its calcified jargon, the commercially focused science community with its "arrogant pseudo-empirical language," and the language of the law that trades obfuscation for ethics.

4. According to the Biblical account (Genesis 11:1–9), Babel was the first city to be built after the Flood and was the center of all of humanity, with one common language among all. The citizens decided to build a grand tower that would reach to Heaven, but God did not look favorably on this hubris and arrogance. In order to stop the building of the tower he confused their languages so that the people could no longer understand each other, and dispersed them throughout the land. Morrison sees God's "punishment" of a confusion of languages as a blessing, not a curse. People were probably not ready to achieve Heaven if they were not ready to understand each other first, and the benefits of this "complicated, demanding" task would create "a view of heaven as life; not heaven as post-life."

5. Morrison means that language knows its limits, but that the limits are what make it sublime. Language cannot fully encompass lives or great events and it shouldn't want to. Its beauty comes from reaching toward what it cannot truly be.

6. For the old woman, the story emanates from the young people's desire for the truth. They were not around in the days of slavery, yet beg to know about it. The young people call her to task by asking her to cross the barrier of a generation gap to give them the wisdom they desire. They want her to explain and justify the world she, and the rest of the generations before, have made for the young people. "You are an adult. The old one, the wise one. Stop thinking about saving your face. Think of our lives and tell us your particularized world. Make up a story." Tell us the truth based on your experience and your wisdom. (30)

The story of the slaves' journey works in the same way as Lincoln's story of the Civil War; it seeks to describe the indescribable and, in doing so, keeps the story alive in memory. It is a creation of words that brings us all closer to the truth of slavery. The young people have proven their worthiness by admitting their inexperience and demanding the story. In doing so, they have helped create the story—there must be readers to have writers.

LANGUAGE IN ACTION

Students might begin their small group discussions with a consideration of what honesty means in everyday life, how it may or may not be a part of the way a person chooses to live, above and beyond writing. Consider the difference between fiction writing and non-fiction writing. Can a writer write fiction but still be honest?

A MODEST PROPOSAL

JONATHAN SWIFT

THINKING CRITICALLY ABOUT THE READING

1. Swift is addressing the problems of famine and poverty in Ireland, caused to a large degree by the English gentry who lived there and the English government abroad. He proposes that after the child stops nursing, that it stop consuming food and be turned into "a most nourishing and wholesome food." The proposal's advantages are many: No more charity will be required and the sins of poverty, such as prostitution, thievery, abortion, etc. will be no more. Rather than being a drag on society, children will "contribute to the feeding and partly to the clothing of many thousands," allowing the families that remain to flourish. By eliminating so many Catholics (Papists), "the principal breeders of the nation," more good English Protestants would remain in power; tenant farmers would have a means of making money to pay rent; they would have a homegrown and local source of delicious food; husbands would be more fond of their wives; the breeders who could bring "the fattest child to the market" would be less apt to beat them and damage the goods. There would be fewer mouths to feed and more money for families in poverty-stricken Ireland.

2. The "other expedients" (solutions that might right the wrongs of the English handling of the Irish) that he dismisses are taxing the English gentry; spurring local economies by investment in local Irish businesses and manufacturing; stopping cheating them in the stores; encouraging landlords to "have at least one degree of mercy towards their ten-

ants"; in general, to treat the Irish fairly and with humanity. Swift's purpose is to highlight realistic and rational solutions to a problem by putting these proposals side by side with a wholly irrational, unrealistic, and horrifying alternative.

3. The anonymous author is, as is Swift, a person of English decent, born in Ireland. He is dedicated to "the public good of his country" and wearied by so many years of trying to put forth solutions to the "Irish problem" of poverty. He describes himself in detail in the final paragraph as married, with children (too old to be butchered), and with no self-interest or money-making motivations in making his proposal. Swift's real voice comes out in paragraph 29, when he lists the "expedients" which he will not hear of (actually a list of reasonable, helpful ideas); in indicting the English at the end of paragraph 31; and in the description of his motives—including pleasing the rich—in the final paragraph.

4. There is nothing "modest" about a proposal that calls for the killing and eating of children; it is a proposal which would require revamping a society's entire moral code. The next statement is ironic because, usually, "useful members of the commonwealth" perform some service or job within society. The Irish children would be useful by literally nourishing other members of the commonwealth. Students should have no trouble finding ironic statements. You may wish to divide the piece into sections and assign a section to a group, so that the same phrase does not come up too often.

5. Swift's proposal is written in the brisk, no-nonsense style of a business proposition. It seems logical because the "factual" nature of statistics and numbers give the proposal the look and feel of a straightforward economic proposition. And, it makes Swift appear to have fully thought through his plan—he isn't just speculating.

6. Your students may already be familiar with "A Modest Proposal." If this is the case, you might suggest that they put themselves in the shoes of the audiences of the time. What would their expectation be? When might they catch on? The well-off, literate class is his audience, not the poverty-ridden, lower classes of Ireland. This audience was probably not expecting anything shocking, given the form of the proposal: a typical pamphlet, dealing dispassionately with the important issue of the Irish problem. Swift appears to be what he identifies himself to be in the final paragraph: a man doing his civic duty to provide for infants, relieve the poor, and advance the economy. He takes on the persona of the English gentry who find the poor to be abhorrent in their habits and a detriment to society (theirs, of course). It isn't until paragraph 9 that he reveals the nature of his proposal, and startles the reader.

7. At the core of Swift's proposal is his passionate call for the English masters to see the Irish people as human beings, not commodities or livestock, which can be bred and slaughtered at will, and to treat them with fairness and justice. The audience for this proposal is not the victims of hunger, but those who perpetrate poverty either by direct suppression or by ignoring the plight of the poor. Its outrageousness is what gives the piece power; its irony is a way to push a sophisticated audience to bring about the real changes Swift is proposing. He intended some humor, as in his final paragraph where he states that one of his purposes is to "give some pleasure to the rich." There is outrage throughout, especially in the asides set in italics. For example, at the end of paragraph 31, he alludes to the English who could eat up an entire nation (with or without salt). The humor lies in Swift's piling irony upon irony, culminating in his final paragraph in which he professes to have no hidden agenda and no self-gain in mind: After all, his children are too old and too tough for him to profit from this scheme.

LANGUAGE IN ACTION

Swift often uses words to summon an opposite meaning: The proposal is hardly "modest" in its scope or effect. Women are referred to as "breeders" in order to dehumanize them and to equate them with cattle. The words he chooses heighten the impact of the reality they reflect and bring forth the true horror of the treatment of the Irish people by the English. The words he chooses are tiny incendiary devices exploded throughout the essay. Write down the words that the students discover. Before discussing them in small groups, ask the students to consider the words as if they were applied to a contemporary group, such as an immigrant minority. This might intensify their meaning for a contemporary audience and show students how Swift's piece is relevant today.

My Amendment

George Saunders

THINKING CRITICALLY ABOUT THE READING

1. Although George Saunders writes in the first person, he is actually playing the role of "George," "an obscure, middle-aged, heterosexual short-story writer" who does not believe in Samish-Sex Marriage. Saunders reveals that he is playing a role through his use of humor (even as his tone remains serious) and the way that he writes about "himself."

2. This piece is aimed at opponents of same-sex marriage. At the beginning of the piece, the narrator gives his opinion on same-sex marriage: "Like any sane person, I am against Same-Sex Marriage, and in favor of a constitutional amendment to ban it." Then, using religious and moral arguments like those used by opponents of same-sex marriage, he proposes an insane extension of their policies.

3. The author is writing for people with political views similar to his own and for those who appreciate satirical humor. He shows this by writing silly things with a serious tone and by proposing an utterly unreasonable idea with absolute conviction.

4. "Samish-Sex Marriage" is marriage between two people who display similar gender traits, although one is male and one is female. For example, he mentions "K, a male friend of mine, of slight build, with a ponytail. K is married to S, a tall, stocky female with extremely short hair, almost a crew cut… I have wondered, Isn't it odd that this somewhat effeminate man should be married to this somewhat masculine woman?" How does it relate to "same-sex marriage"? The "-ish" is funny, because it is an informal, somewhat silly way to express what the narrator means (why not "Similar-Sex Marriage"?). But it also means that the concept is unclear and open to interpretation.

5. Few people are so bold as to claim to know exactly what God intends for humanity. Saunders is satirizing those who say they know that God only wants men and women to marry by taking that claim one step further into the realm of the ridiculous. He is showing that anyone who feels inclined to can make any argument about what God "has in mind," and those arguments should not be taken seriously.

6. The "Manly Scale of Absolute Gender" is the narrator's way to assign a number to a person's Manly- or Fem-ness. By naming it a "Manly" scale, the narrator is asserting his own

Manly-ness, as well as reinforcing the stereotype that men are more decisive and absolute. The scale satirizes our tendency to assign gender associations to activities, physical appearance, and personal traits.

7. The piece shifts in these paragraphs from a statement of opinion about a moral and political issue to a testimonial for the narrator's plan for gender-appropriate marriages. Although the narrator has shown he is very observant (and often critical) of his friends' Manly or Fem traits, he does not reveal much about himself until this section. The story of his past makes his radical proposition seem even more absurd. To conform to his strict beliefs about gender roles, he has turned himself from someone with a "strange constant feeling of being happy to be alive" to someone who "speak[s] in an extremely slow and manly and almost painfully deliberate way," and who never skips. After these "tremendous positive changes," the narrator has become more Manly, but less happy.

8. Although the narrator seems afraid of a society without strict rules about who is allowed to marry, the author actually wants to have a "nation of willful human hearts" finding love wherever they can.

LANGUAGE IN ACTION

The tone of this piece is at first friendly and innocent-sounding, presented as a story. As the tale takes on more and more reality, its true purpose surfaces and its tone is entirely serious. Some examples of phrases and sentences that impel the story forward and lend it its bitter tone are: "It needed to be saved"; "America was well-equipped for country-saving"; ". . . didn't foresee the result of their loving embrace on the small country"; "They bombed"; " . . . it was necessary to destroy the village in order to save it"; "sanctified." The tone is appropriate because it echoes America's attitude toward foreign affairs. At first the situation seems simple and America is the hero, coming to save a faraway country. However, things are always more complicated, more force is required, and the consequences are far graver than expected, given how nicely the story began.

4. Prejudice, Discrimination, and Stereotypes

WHAT'S SO BAD ABOUT HATE?

ANDREW SULLIVAN

THINKING CRITICALLY ABOUT THE READING

1. What Sullivan suggests is "hard-wired" is the human tendency to generalize about other groups of humans. Just as we like to form our own groups, in doing so we categorize everyone outside of our group as some form of "other." This tendency can lead to prejudice, which leads down the road to "something graver and darker."

2. The "-isms" identify the victims, but do not reveal the identities of the perpetrators or "what they think, or how they feel." Is it fear, contempt, power or powerlessness, or revenge that drives hate? The "isms" do not reveal motivations; thus, they are not useful in

treating the causes of "hate crimes." Adding to Sullivan's dislike of "isms" is that they are simplistic and impersonal and reveal nothing about the victims; in fact, he writes, "these 'isms' can exist without mentioning individuals at all."

3. Sullivan counters the notion that prejudice always is rooted in ignorance and can be overcome by familiarity with two examples: Southern whites' hatred of blacks under segregation, and the deadly hate between the Tutsis and the Hutus. In both these cases, the two groups had lived side by side for years. Rather than springing from ignorance or lack of experience with one another, theirs was a hatred "that sprang, for whatever reason, from experience."

4. Sullivan writes that all hate is not equal, that there is "reasonable hate" and "unreasonable hate." Using the genocide in Rwanda as one of his examples, he suggests that the victims of the genocide are justified in avenging the deaths caused by the perpetrators. "If the victims overcome this hate, it is a supreme moral achievement. But if they don't, the victims are not as culpable as the perpetrators." The victims, who actually suffered grievous physical and mental harm, are justified in hating; the perpetrators, who acted for irrational reasons, are not.

5. Young-Bruehl's typology of hate includes three distinct kinds: obsessive, hysterical, and narcissistic. Obsessive hate is based on a fantasized threat from a minority, whose very existence is threatening. It is accompanied by an almost physical aversion, as if the object of this hate is unclean, diseased, disgusting, and needs to be "cleansed" from the society. The source of hysterical hate, according to Young-Bruehl, is a kind of "love-hate" that emanates from repressed sexual envy and aggression. She uses a certain kind of white racist as an example: "He idealizes in 'blackness' a sexual freedom . . . that he detests but also longs for." Hysterical haters differ from obsessive haters in that they do not want to eradicate their victims, but rather to subjugate them "in order to indulge the attraction of their repulsion." Narcissist hate is sexism, according to Young-Bruehl, and is based on men's inability to imagine what it is to be a woman. It manifests itself not so much in hate as in condescension towards those who are not considered equals. Narcissism/sexism is also tinged with repressed erotic desire that creates a tension between deep longing and contempt.

Sullivan acknowledges that Young-Bruehl's typology does not cover all hate that exists, but "it's a beginning in any serious attempt to understand hate rather than merely declaring war on it." He later reaffirms his agreement with her typology because it deals more completely with both the victims and the perpetrators of hate. It seems to be more useful than the reductive "isms" mentioned earlier.

6. The core of Sullivan's argument is that "the distinction between a crime filled with personal hate and a crime filled with group hate is an essentially arbitrary one" and the laws against hate crimes are primarily a function of politics, and of special interest groups trying to carve out protections for themselves, "rather than a serious response to a serious criminal concern." Before the "invention of hate crimes," according to Sullivan, the seriousness of a crime of murder, for example, was not weighed by how much hate was involved—"A murder was a murder." Today, supporters of laws against hate crimes argue that such crimes should be punished more severely because they victimize more than the victim; they "spread fear, hatred and panic among whole populations, and therefore merit more concern." (40). Sullivan argues also that laws against hate crimes that target minority groups and others "with a history of persecution or intimidation" are condescending and "the kind of crude generalization the law is supposed to uproot in the first place."

(45). In paragraphs 47 and 48, Sullivan uses hard crime statistics to counter many of the claims of hate-crime-law advocates, such as the notion that society is experiencing an epidemic of hate crimes or that the crimes are becoming more vicious.

    Sullivan feels hate crime laws should be repealed, because the issues of prejudice, hate, opinion, criticism, and truth "are so complicated and blurred that any attempt to construct legal and political fire walls is a doomed and illiberal venture." He argues that laws will never eradicate hate, nor should they. What we should be working on is creating an environment of tolerance. He also argues that some expression of prejudice serves a useful social purpose by allowing people to let off steam, "to siphon off conflict through words, rather than actions." Sullivan concludes that hate can't be overcome when the haters are punished, but "when the hated are immune to the bigot's power."

7. In paragraph 40, Sullivan writes that the only "articulated passionate hate" he has ever experienced directly has been from other homosexuals. He does not feel victimized by this because he sees that much of it emanates from legitimate political differences, but it is nonetheless hateful and designed to hurt him personally. He feels that the intensity of the hatefulness is a result of exclusion, "of anger long restrained bubbling up and directing itself more aggressively toward an alleged traitor than an alleged enemy." He states that the hate of the hated is often "the most hateful hate of all."

LANGUAGE IN ACTION

    The Web site of the Anti-Defamation League (ADL) (http://www.adl.org/combating_hate) compiles a great deal of information on laws and legislation against hate-crimes of all kinds. There is also an interactive map of the United States from which you can find hate-crime legislation on a state-by-state basis. Ask students to compare the laws in a few states, and whether they see any loopholes or problems with the legislation.

THE LANGUAGE OF PREJUDICE

GORDON ALLPORT

THINKING CRITICALLY ABOUT THE READING

1. Allport's thesis is the first sentence in paragraph 5: "Most people are unaware of this basic law of language—that every label applied to a given person refers properly only to one aspect of his nature."

2. Allport writes that "in the empirical world of human beings there are some two and a half billion grains of sand corresponding to our category 'the human race'" (2). By equating the world's human population to individual grains of sand, Allport shows how difficult it is to consider individual features when confronted with such staggering numbers. To simplify matters, the grains of sand (people) are classified into categories according to one feature, overlooking all others. But what about the other classifications? Just because some grains of sand are clustered under one feature, must we forget that these grains fit other categories as well? Allport asks us to pause, think about what we are doing, and be aware

that this kind of classification "forces us to overlook all other features, many of which might offer a sounder basis than the rubric we select" (3).

3. Allport talks about emotionally toned labels, labels that can be insulting and lead to rejection. References to color bring about strong reactions, for example, black has "a preponderance of sinister connotations" (13), and he gives a number of examples to illustrate his point. In the section entitled "The Communist Label" (19) the need for an enemy was filled by a long list of symbols that served "as a focus for discontent and jitters" (22). These labels accelerated the hysteria surrounding the word communism (21). In times of unrest "a single identifiable enemy is wanted" (25), a word serving as a scapegoat for our social anxiety. He also writes about people who crave favorable labels and illustrates this need with the "Neighborly Endeavor" group that "banded together to force out a Negro family that had moved in" (32). These examples are diverse and effectively show us how people can use language to meet their own needs.

4. Nouns "cut slices" by presenting such narrow views of reality that they may "prevent alternative classification" (4). Allport says in paragraph 3 that "a noun *abstracts* from a concrete reality some one feature and assembles different concrete realities only with respect to this one feature." Nouns are therefore always "unfair" in that they must include and exclude. Refer your students to Allport's anecdote about the blind man (3), and ask them to comment on it. Can they recall similar instances of nouns "cutting slices"?

5. Allport says in paragraph 4 that "some labels, such as 'blind man,' are exceedingly salient and powerful. They tend to prevent alternative classification, or even cross-classification." These are "labels of primary potency" (4). Their tremendous power to control our perceptions of reality makes them very important. We can and should be wary of such labels even when they are favorable; since they are so emotionally charged, they may obscure the finer distinctions that should be made.

6. The photo experiment demonstrates that "a mere proper name leads to prejudgments of personal attributes" (8). The individual is "not judged in his own right" (8). Thus, labels are inaccurate and distort reality, because they are associatively laden with assumptions.

7. Allport says, "The common use of the orphaned pronoun *they* teaches us that people often want and need to designate out-groups (usually for the purpose of venting hostility) even when they have no clear conception of the out-group in question" (19). It is used so often because it depersonalizes and is nonspecific, and thus makes it easier for the speaker to be critical.

8. Because Allport does not explicitly define this term, students may wish to consult the dictionary.

   symbol phobia (33): fear of words; often characterized by the confusion of words with actual things.

   This concept illustrates the unfairness of labeling others because it shows how fearful each one of us becomes when others apply such labels to us. Allport believes any attempt to reduce prejudice must include semantic therapy because people cannot always say "whether it is the word or the thing that annoys them. . . . Hence to liberate a person from ethnic or political prejudice it is necessary at the same time to liberate him from *word fetishism*" (36). Allport captures the essential unfairness of symbol phobia when he says, "We are more inclined to [symbol phobia] when we ourselves are concerned, though we are much less critical when epithets of 'fascist,' 'communist,' 'blind man,' 'school marm' are applied to others" (33).

9. Allport's essay seems an obvious reaction to the McCarthyism of the 1950s and its preoccupation with the "red menace." Many of the associations attached to the label *communist* were established at that time and remain in place even today.

LANGUAGE IN ACTION

Arguments in favor of the UN action include the following: a) there's general agreement that these terms are offensive, b) precise language is preferable to general or vague language, and c) words charged with negative connotations are detrimental and should be changed to more neutral terms.

One argument against the UN action is changing vocabulary words does not necessarily change a person's racist attitudes or opinions.

While most students will agree with the UN action, they will also admit that it is difficult, if not impossible, to legislate tolerance and tone down prejudice by simply revising terminology.

SIGNS OF INFECTION

BOB HERBERT

THINKING CRITICALLY ABOUT THE READING

1. Power breeds power in part because that power can only be sustained at a cost to the less powerful. In a sense, the powerful define themselves by defining others in lesser terms. In Herbert's first example, Imus's "verbal bomb," drew upon gender and racial stereotypes to denigrate the team members and to keep "those girls" in their place. Because Imus is male, white, and "a very powerful radio personality," he has the power and position to define those in a lesser position: in this case, the team of young, female, black basketball players.

   Students will react differently toward this essay depending on their own sense of self and their "power" position in society. To stimulate discussion, it might be useful to ask students to define their place in their community as they see it; ask if there are times when they are the powerful and times when they are less powerful starting, perhaps, with their relative position within their own family.

2. Herbert's thesis is that we have replaced civility and civil discourse with the coarse, bigoted, socially destructive images and language of racism and misogyny which now permeate our culture. His evidence includes Imus, Michael Savage, and the "excesses of talk radio"; rap lyrics that reflect both self-hate and extreme sexism; and the ubiquity of this debased language across the racial, political, and cultural spectrum.

3. To debase someone or something is to reduce its value, "to lower in status, esteem, quality or character." "Bullying" and "the degradation of other human beings" goes back to his opening statement about power and power relationships in our society; each of these expressions relies on one person asserting their supposed power over the perceived weaker person— thereby violating that person's dignity and pride, personal sense of value, and value within the community.

4. Herbert identifies the "disease" as longstanding racial and gender bias and "the stereo-types they spawn." If these elements were not present, they would not have resulted in the offensive language heard today.

5. Herbert is taking a position similar to that of Andrew Sullivan. He is not asking for cen-sorship; he is asking, as Sullivan does, for more positive forces to assert their own power and, in doing so, replace the destructive stereotypes with a better way of viewing both women and blacks in our society.

6. Herbert's tone is mixed. He begins with hearty outrage at the treatment by Imus of the Rutgers' basketball players, and the stereotypes propagated by our "profoundly immature culture." But, he purposely "tones it down" in order to turn the situation into a thought-ful discussion of racism and sexism in this country, culminating with solutions rather than angry damnation of the "perpetrators."

LANGUAGE IN ACTION

The message is that foul language is now so prevalent in American audio culture that it's hard to tell one form from the other. The assumption in the cartoon is that the father would object to his son listening to rap. The joke is that, instead, the father would object to his son listening to Don Imus. Although talk radio might at one time have been considered "better" for the son to listen to, today, both rap and talk use streams of inappropriate speech. Herbert would agree with that, but while this cartoon seems bemused by the situation, Herbert is very concerned.

FROM THE DIXIE CHICKS TO THE ST. LOUIS RAMS: WHAT ANIMAL-BASED METAPHORS REVEAL ABOUT SEXISM

ALLEEN PACE NILSEN

THINKING CRITICALLY ABOUT THE READING

1. Nilsen reveals her thesis in the subtitle of the essay: *What Animal-based Metaphors Reveal about Sexism*. In the text, she builds up to the full scope of her thesis in steps. First Nilsen refers to the way "American English reflects our values," and later links the general "American English" with the specific "animal-based metaphors" from our agricultural past. In the final sentence of that paragraph, she states her intent: to discuss "what these metaphors reveal about our culture's sexist attitudes and values."

2. Metaphors, such as the animal-based metaphors of the past, reveal not only a rural her-itage, but the embedded meaning beneath the words themselves. These metaphors "pro-vide us with a glimpse of common beliefs and attitudes that reveal the attitudes of our cultural and linguistic ancestors and therefore the attitudes that we as a culture are likely to have inherited."

3. Nilsen equated Chicks with chicken, or coward, and challenged her students with the no-tion that the Dixie Chick's political problems sprang in part from their name. Her stu-dents saw neither the connection nor the cowardly subtext of the word "chicks." To her

students, "chick" was either a neutral term for a young woman, or a negative term which the Dixie Chicks were reclaiming. The students came up with alternative interpretations that were more related to "Dixie" and concepts of Southernness than to gender or cowardice.

4. Nilsen asked her students if the Dixie Chicks and the St. Louis Rams could switch names, and her students laughed at the idea. Not only would the gender of the group and the gender of the animal representing the group be reversed, but the behavior of those animals (and the behavior of their gender) would be backwards. By this inversion, the students realized that it was more than just the physical differences between men and women that are implied by the groups' names, but their behavior as well.

5. Archetypal metaphors are objects or beings (in this case, animals) which humans associate with "the archetypal images that people hold about important and permanent aspects of their lives including death, fear, love, the biological family, and the unknown." Nilsen argues that animals are used in these metaphors, particularly in fables and folk tales, and that they often represent traditional gender roles.

6. Nilsen argues that within common animal metaphors there are "mini-fables" which reveal truths about how American culture views gender roles. Nilsen brings these fables to light with four sets of examples and ends by urging us to question "both the usefulness and the truthfulness" of the stories behind everyday metaphors.

7. Nilsen sees in the "sexing of chickens" at the hatchery and the aborting of female fetuses in China an indication of "gender preference" and the perceived relative importance of one sex over the other. In the case of the chickens, the need for males is limited, so the males are discarded; females are saved because they are more valued for their unfertilized, edible eggs. In China, since the population is high and parents are encouraged to have only one child, it is the males who are saved. Both situations are unnatural, but created by humans based on a system of societal values.

8. In her summary, Nilsen is talking about the gender preferences that are embedded in our language, even to the extent that singular masculine pronouns are used whenever the gender of the person referred to is not known. If women are seen as a "subset" of male-oriented words such as "mankind," that reflects the notion of male superiority. If we use a gendered term to describe all instances of an animal (for example, referring to both bulls and cows as "cows") because one gender is more valuable, using male terms to describe women implies that men are valued more than women.

LANGUAGE IN ACTION

In addition to the discussion in class, it might be interesting to note and tabulate the words that participants selected for this exercise. Rank the words by the number of times they were selected and see if certain words came up more often than others. Also consider the intent of the word use—how many sentences were meant to be negative? Positive? Neutral? Was there any correlation between the intent of the sentence and the gender of the sentence's subject?

THE MEANINGS OF A WORD

GLORIA NAYLOR

THINKING CRITICALLY ABOUT THE READING

1. According to Naylor, "Words themselves are innocuous; it is the consensus that gives them true power" (2). In other words, people give words meaning by using them in various contexts.

2. The boy called Naylor a "nigger" because he was angry when she told him that "once again he had received a much lower mark" than she had received on a math test (3). She didn't know what a "nigger" was but knew it was something he shouldn't have called her.

3. *Girl* was "a token of respect for a woman" when used to describe a woman's commendable action or attitude (11): "G-i-r-l, stop. You mean you said that to his face?" (12). Because *girl* is used as a sign of respect, it would not be considered sexist language. Language is sexist when derogatory toward women. This supports Naylor's point that words are innocuous alone; only with context and tone are they given meaning.

4. In paragraph 14 Naylor says she doesn't agree "that the use of the word *nigger* . . . was an internalization of racism" because the "dynamics were the exact opposite"; "they transformed *nigger* to signify the varied and complex human beings they knew themselves to be."

5. Naylor's first two paragraphs present an abstract discussion of language and how words obtain meaning through the consensus of users. Naylor considers "the written word inferior to the spoken" word and says that the best passages in novels often fall "far short of the richness of life. Dialogue achieves its power in the dynamics of a fleeting moment of sight, sound, smell, and touch" (1). These opening paragraphs provide a nice lead into her concrete example of her family's use of the word *nigger*. In her discussion, Naylor writes a clear and detailed description of her family and its lifestyle, showing how this word is used when spoken, not written. Because of her introductory paragraphs, we understand the point Naylor is making about the clear power of dialogue and its meaning. When we agree on a meaning of a word, we have consensus. When Naylor says that it is the consensus that gives words true power, she means that words alone are harmless. In the article that follows ("An Essay on a Wickedly Powerful Word," pp. 295–296), consensus has given the word *nigger* two different meanings, one by the white and another by the black community. (See a folktale about agreement on word meaning in Chapter 1, in Language in Action from "Masters of All Masters.")

6. Although Naylor had heard the word *nigger* numerous times in her household growing up, the word she heard meant "man" or "person." She claims "context and inflections" shaped her perception of the word. Only when the word was displaced from its usual position and tone did she hear something else. The *nigger* she heard in her third-grade classroom was an entirely different word.

7. "In the singular, [nigger] was always applied to a man who had distinguished himself in some situation" (6); "when used with a possessive adjective by a woman—'my nigger'—it became a term of endearment" (9); and "in the plural, it became a description of some group within the community that had overstepped the bounds of decency" (10). Naylor

relies on the reader's familiarity with her classmate's meaning of the word. By trusting that the reader knows what she means, Naylor shows how widespread and deeply ingrained the negative stereotype has become. Sometimes in writing, suggestion can be stronger than definition or description because the reader's mind already has numerous ideas and images on which a talented author can draw.

8. Naylor's essay is fairly straightforward. By simply describing what happened in her classroom and her family life, she explains how words can become powerful weapons. Her simple and direct opening sentence, "Language is the subject," sets the tone of her essay. Other examples may vary.

LANGUAGE IN ACTION

This Language in Action activity includes four questions for the students to consider. It offers a perfect opportunity to break the class into small groups and give each group a single question to discuss and arrive at some consensus. After fifteen minutes of group work, have each group report its findings and entertain questions from classmates.

THE B-WORD? YOU BETCHA

ANDI ZEISLER

THINKING CRITICALLY ABOUT THE READING

1. Zeisler defines "bitch" as "a word we use culturally to describe any woman who is strong, angry, uncompromising and, often, uninterested in pleasing men." The cluster of meanings and words involving "bitch" are revealing in the dictionary, particularly in the way they reflect Zeisler's definition. For example, one definition is "a malicious, spiteful, or overbearing woman—sometimes used as a generalized term of abuse." The difference in the definitions is largely a matter of interpretation. Her strong could be the dictionary's "arrogant"; her uncompromising, their "overbearing"; her angry, their "unpleasant" and "malicious." In her definition, Zeisler turns potential negative and pejorative terms into compliments.

2. Zeisler and Jervis named their magazine *Bitch* because it's a word meant to upset and challenge the "tidy well-run world" in which powerful women are seen as scary, angry, and unfeminine. They endured the word in their growing up and wanted to turn it on its head, to reclaim the word for women like the gay community reclaimed "queer." For them it was the perfect word to describe a magazine whose purpose is to counter "sexism in consumer and popular culture." And, it was clearly an attention-getter, with name recognition and a cause wrapped up in one word.

3. "Bitch" remains an "incendiary" woman-hating word in most contexts, particularly when men apply it to other men (a use that springs from the prison world and has spread to mainstream culture). No matter how hard Zeisler tries to take charge of the word to empower women, the negative usage remains problematic and simply "won't go away."

4. McCain showed disrespect toward Hillary Clinton in laughing off the question: "How do we beat the bitch?" What annoys Zeisler the most, however, seems to be how frequently it is used against many women in politics, and it has nothing to do with their stance on political issues. Instead, she writes, "it's an expression of pure sexism—a hope that they can shut up not only one woman but every woman who dares to be assertive."

5. Zeisler advises men to read the magazine so they can see that the emphasis is not on hating men, but on discussing real issues that affect women. However, she feels that some people cannot tell the difference between being pro-woman and being anti-man.

6. For Zeisler, the word remains "simply another way to denigrate women," even if its use has become more common and less controversial. Talking about the use of the word isn't helpful, she writes, "if we don't also address the many unsaid words that follow in its wake."

LANGUAGE IN ACTION

Students probably will have no trouble seeing that mainstream rap usually uses "bitch" toward women and men in a degrading way, whereas Zeisler wants to use it to empower women. Ask students whether any rappers that they know of use "bitch" to mean a strong woman, don't use the term at all, or have questioned its use. How do female rappers use the word?

Snoop Dogg explains that he was "wrongfully taught" to call all women "bitch," but that his attitude changed after marrying and having a daughter. The Daily Intel blogger's tone is amused and disbelieving, both that a rapper with a reputation like Snoop's could give up "bitch," and that he suddenly seems to have developed a social conscience.

IN DEFENSE OF THE "CHICK FLICK"

GLORIA STEINEM

THINKING CRITICALLY ABOUT THE READING

1. Steinem's rhetorical advantage lies in her position as framer of the argument, and the only one with a voice. From a single comment by "the young man on the plane," she guides and controls the "discussion" in a conversational tone rather than preaching from a lectern—a more convincing, less threatening, format.

2. Steinem speculates that, whereas men are taken seriously when they write about women, "women aren't taken seriously when they write about themselves much less about men and male affairs." Although some of the classics she names have as much emotional drama, female-centered plots, and romance as "chick lit" today, they are considered classics because they were written by men. As long as most esteemed writers are men and women writers are immediately dismissed, "the list of Great Authors will be more about power than about talent."

3. Steinem argues that, though the label "chick flick" guides women to stereotypically female-oriented movies, the young man has no such guide for movies he might enjoy (and thus is "punished"). The bias she refers to is in the power structure of our society, where

there is a distinction between "movies" (for anyone to see) and "chick flicks" (for women only). "Whoever is in power takes over the noun—and the norm—while the less powerful get an adjective." This kind of bias in the language leaves the young man with only "half a guide" to discovering the movies (or literature) he might like.

4. Steinem guides the young man through the literature, commentary, and films for and by men that he might see using the single label "prick flicks": movies that glorify war; sadistic, masochistic movies that portray violence against women, movies that portray women as objects. By proposing a counterpart to "chick flicks" which is humorous, Steinem exposes how silly it is to have a gendered movie category. (We take it for granted with women's movies, yet proposing it for men's movies is ridiculous.) Despite the humorous tone of the essay, Steinem may be serious—after all, the examples of "prick flicks" that she cites certainly form a recognizable category.

5. By writing, "one simple label could guide you through diversity," Steinem insinuates that labels are limiting, and the young man will miss out on valuable "diversity," blinded by his preconceived notions. In this way, Steinem wraps up her argument first posed in the opening paragraph. Some students may find the final sentence weak, since she seems to have ended her argument by pleading with the young man on the plane to watch a chick flick. However, if they see the whole argument as somewhat facetious, they may conclude she intended the last sentence to mean that labels are ridiculous and that viewers shouldn't be guided (or limited) by them.

LANGUAGE IN ACTION

The father is telling the son to interrupt his mother's reading, not his, because she's "only" reading "chick lit"; his reading is important; hers is trite and superficial. The message is that male "lit" trumps female "lit," a message the father is passing down to his son. The split between the male and female world is well illustrated: The father is sitting in a wing chair, often seen in personal libraries; the mother is perched on a window seat. The effect is to show the "serious" nature of the father's position in the household, compared to the mother's more trivial interests.

"FOBs" vs. "Twinkies": The New Discrimination Is Intraracial

GRACE HSIANG

THINKING CRITICALLY ABOUT THE READING

1. Hsiang expected that her students would have stories of being harassed by white people for being Asian. Instead, the students responded by talking about the harassment and discrimination they come up against *within* their own ethnic group.

2. The early teenage years are often a time of self-discovery and identity crises. It is the time when young adults begin to form their own social groups and to date, and are most sensi-

tive to their peers. Some young adults choose to rebel against their parents' traditions, whether ethnic or not.

3. According to Hsiang, second generation Asian Americans face the most parental pressure because their parents hold traditional values and fear the negative impact of American culture on their children. The difficulty for the children is that, as Hsiang points out, "we cannot completely embody one culture when we are living in another." The pressure causes the split between groups within the culture as one group, the "FOBs," clings to their parent's culture, and another, the "Twinkies," rebels by assimilating into American culture.

4. In his essay, Andrew Sullivan posits that members of any minority group that has been marginalized by the larger society often directs their anger and frustration not at the society that discriminates against them, but at alleged traitors within their own group. Hsiang no doubt would agree with Sullivan, citing examples of clashes within the Asian-American community. But it is unclear whether she would agree that it is "the hate of the hated." Even as she writes about the difficulties of "living in a predominately white country with the face of a foreigner," she does not go so far as to use the word "hate." She also points out that not all Asian Americans buy into the "dichotomy between "FOBs" and "Twinkies"; instead, they try to forge a new identity which is both Asian and American.

5. Hsiang's solution is a recognition that Asian Americans are of two cultures that, despite some differences in opinion and life choices, form a "a new culture that should be fully celebrated."

LANGUAGE IN ACTION

Students will find reviews from a variety of different sources. Encourage them to look outside mainstream news and entertainment media to find a wider range of viewpoints, as well as opinions which are more strongly expressed. Ask students to consider the source of the review when they make a list of the criticisms raised, and ask whether their opinion of the treatment of race in the film changed after reading different reviews.

BLACK MEN AND PUBLIC SPACE

BRENT STAPLES

THINKING CRITICALLY ABOUT THE READING

1. Staples wants to let others share his experience of how, as a black male, he is perceived by others.

2. Because he wants to let the "other side" know what he's been through, Staples publishes in *Ms.* Magazine. This is an apt choice, since he wants to influence someone who may have an opposing viewpoint (someone who may feel threatened by black males, with or without reason).

3. Staples is surprised that he might cause fear because he does not experience himself as someone threatening or frightening. He explains that as an overworked student at the

University of Chicago, he suddenly comes face to face with the fact that he is "indistinguishable from the muggers" (2) simply because of his gender and race.

4. Staples offers anecdotal evidence to show that people are conditioned to react to him as a threat. He recounts the time when, as a rushed journalist, he was mistakenly pursued as a burglar (8). He also remembers a woman in a jewelry store protecting herself from his perceived threat by going to get her attack dog (9). His experiences help make his case because they amplify the disconnection between his motivations and their reactions.

5. If Staples blatantly discussed his situation as an example of racial prejudice, his essay would be less effective. He arrives at the power of his essay through description and implication. By focusing on the personal, the message is less accusatory and didactic, and he is ultimately more persuasive.

6. The beginning is a false start, and the reader's expectations are quickly turned on their head. The surprise and contrast generated by the first paragraph hold the reader's attention. Then there is an effective switch in direction and thought (an explanation of how Staples felt in the alley) that moves the reader from one frame of mind into another.

7. To deal with strangers in public places, Staples has taken to whistling classical music. He finds that this approach changes peoples' attitudes because it changes their perception of him.

LANGUAGE IN ACTION

You may want to split your students up into groups in order to re-enact these scenarios, or you could use these four points as journal prompts. Ask students what it is that compels them to feel territoriality about their possessions or their space. Does it have to do with geographical region? Gender? Whether or not a person has had to share space or material possessions with siblings or others? Make sure students link their reactions in some way with the points Staples makes about how we operate in space with others, regardless of race and gender.

THE FOURTH OF JULY

AUDRE LORDE

THINKING CRITICALLY ABOUT THE READING

1. Lorde's family ignores racism because they do not want to be affected by it. They wish to avoid, not confront it. Lorde is different because she wants to fight back. Her family's denial "made me even angrier. My fury was not going to be acknowledged by a like fury" (19).

2. Lorde disliked the Fourth of July as a child because she suffered from eye sensitivities. These sensitivities were worse in the summer (the sun is brighter, stronger in July). She dislikes the holiday as an adult because she feels excluded from it because of her race. She describes in detail the food her family takes on the train because the lunch is beautifully, carefully made. By describing the food in this way, she illustrates the difference between who her family is (how they conduct themselves, what they appreciate) and how they are perceived by the whites on the train.

3. Lorde believes that by being silent, her family does not impede the racism they experience. She notes that her mother doesn't speak of racism so that "perhaps it would go away" (5). Lorde knows that, although this method allows her mother to cope, it does nothing to stop the continuation of discrimination.

4. Lorde communicates her outrage by using words like *travesty* (10) to explain her experience of the Fourth of July holiday. She includes experiences of racism not her own by bringing in the example of Marian Anderson (8) who was not allowed to sing in a "Whites Only" auditorium. She repeats the word "white" again and again to emphasize how race colored her perceptions in 1947. The pain in her eyes is a metaphor for her experience of racism as a child.

5. The tone of Lorde's essay is angry, bitter, defiant. *Examples of tone*: "I viewed Julys through an agonizing corolla of dazzling whiteness and I always hated the Fourth of July, even before I came to realize the travesty such a celebration was for black people in this country" (10). "The waitress was white, and the counter was white, and the ice cream I never ate in Washington, D.C., that summer I left childhood was white, and the white heat and the white pavement and the white stone monuments of my first Washington summer made me sick to my stomach for the whole rest of that trip and it wasn't much of a graduation present after all" (20).

6. Lorde's title is ironic because blacks were still very much subjugated by discrimination in the United States in 1947. The Fourth of July holiday celebrates U.S. independence, but Lorde does not feel free or equal to other Americans because of racial discrimination.

LANGUAGE IN ACTION

After years of repressing her Italian culture, language, and heritage, Gillan's poem is her long overdue outcry against discrimination and stereotyping. Her rallying cry is that of Lorde's as well—finally finding the words to break the silence.

5. EVERYDAY CONVERSATIONS

SPEECH COMMUNITIES

PAUL ROBERTS

THINKING CRITICALLY ABOUT THE READING

1. Roberts is interested in the history of language and is writing in 1958, when the idea of a village was no doubt less remote to many of his readers. For these reasons, his reference to a "village" can be understood in some sense as literal. The concept of the village can, of course, as metaphorical, as a stand-in for communities of language users, however these communities are defined. His example of the "Old Village" and the "New Village" gestures toward the history of language development, but also serves as a parable to explain the ways in which language evolves when language users uproot themselves from their original communities and form new communities.

2. In discussing parents' roles in instilling the rules and norms of language in their children, Roberts raises the issue of "baby talk"—the imperfect imitations of adult speech (e.g., "muzzer" for "mother") that are often encouraged by admiring adults. According to Roberts, children learn to use language to make their basic needs known and to be admired. Baby talk begins as a straightforward attempt at communication, but often soon becomes primarily a means of evoking admiration.

3. The "forces" to which Roberts refers are the dynamics of the peer group. Children adopt the norms of the speech community they encounter at school in order to establish an identity independent of their role in the family and to be accepted by their peers.

4. In this passage, Roberts emphasizes the persistence of distinct speech communities based on shared linguistic heritage and geography. Although Roberts acknowledges the transformative effects on such communities of migration and contact with other speech communities, he says little about the homogenizing effect of mass media—an impact that is undoubtedly greater today than it was in 1958—and doesn't address the increasing mobility of the population at large. Taking these factors into account, one wonders whether the linguist Roberts speaks of as being able to "very clearly" trace the movements of the early settlers in the speech of their descendents would have as easy a time of it today.

5. Roberts assumes that class barriers in the United States are more permeable than they are in England, owing to historical, economic, and other cultural factors. For Roberts, this means that speech in the United States is less closely aligned with class status, and class status itself tends in the United States to be defined by education and occupation rather than by birth. These historical distinctions between England and the United States might still hold to an extent, though the impact of globalization and other changes in the intervening decades likely have diminished some of the disparity. As Roberts himself points out, "the whole trend of modern life is to reduce rather than accentuate these [class] differences" (34).

6. Roberts takes a wry view of this common (some would say, natural) prejudice, concluding that for most of us, the speech communities in which we feel most comfortable are "best." Roberts implicitly acknowledges the serious consequences such prejudices have in real terms—for example, in terms of class barriers in traditional societies.

LANGUAGE IN ACTION

Obama bridles at the stereotypes—the assumptions about his interests, abilities, and other qualities, based on his skin color—implicit in the comments of those he mentions toward the end of the passage. He starts the passage by reflecting on his belief that "black" and "white" speech codes were different, but could be bridged ("translated") by someone fluent in both. This celebration of his fluency is brought back to earth by his realization that the boundaries he viewed as permeable were viewed by some as impermeable—as "us" and "them." This interesting reflection from a public figure often identified by himself and others as representing the "future of race"—a mixed, not fixed proposition—should stimulate interesting class discussion.

WHITHER THE SOUTHERN ACCENT?

JEFFREY COLLINS AND KRISTEN WYATT

THINKING CRITICALLY ABOUT THE READING

1. These students don't want to be pigeonholed as "Southern," which they find limiting or even stigmatizing in some contexts, due to the persistence of prejudices against Southerners (as unsophisticated, "slow," "reactionary," etc.) that exist in some quarters. Prejudices against those with pronounced Boston or Brooklyn accents also exist, though these might be less extreme, depending on context.

2. The article describes Standard American Dialect as "the uninflected tone of TV news anchors that oozes authority and refinement" (2). In some contexts—for example, in politics or the media—any accent is viewed as potentially alienating to the desired widest possible audience and/or simply as unnecessary "baggage" (when it is irrelevant or undesirable to call attention to the specifics of the speaker's background). Standard American Dialect—a "neutral" (i.e., nonregional) accent—is considered more acceptable to the widest range of potential supporters/customers/adherents.

3. According to linguist Bill Kretzschmar, its disappearance can be traced to the late nineteenth-century decline in the cotton-based economy that supported plantation life: "'Blame it on the boll weevil,' he said, referring to the cotton pest. 'That accent from plantation areas, which was never the whole South, has been in decline for a long time. The economic basis of that culture started going away at the turn of the last century,' when the bugs nearly wiped out the South's cotton economy" (12). Its persistence in the media can be explained by the romantic associations evoked for some by the lifestyle and the era.

4. This milieu, for better or for worse, is considered to represent the likely direction of growth in the new South. Suburban Atlanta is described in the article as "the kind of transient place that leads to the death of indigenous dialects. It's packed with strip malls and subdivisions with no cotton patches or peach trees in sight" (15). Based on his studies of this area, linguist Kretzschmar says of the Southern accent, "It's not really disappearing, but the circumstances of living make it different." "People [in suburban areas like Roswell] don't have connections with their neighbors to maintain their way of speech. The circumstances of how people get together and talk in the cities have changed; they're not constantly talking to people who talk just like them. But in the South outside the cities, you have a lot of similarities" (24).

5. Unlike some other media figures (e.g., journalists), humorists/writers/entertainers whose appeal/persona is in part based on the specifics of their background could well profit from a colorful regional accent. Blount's point likely is meant in a broader sense—he seems to be arguing against the homogenization of accents (and, perhaps, by extension, the homogenization of so many other aspects of culture in our post-modern society) because their loss represents a loss of diversity in the culture at large.

6. Code switching is the ability to shift from one form of speech to another, based on the community one finds oneself addressing/interacting with. Politicians and others whose primary aim is to appeal to the widest possible group of people obviously would profit from such an ability. (As Paul Roberts points out, we all think our own codes the

"best"—for a politician, the ability to adhere to the "best" codes in any context could only be an advantage.)

LANGUAGE IN ACTION

Students likely will enjoy taking the survey. When they're finished, spend some time discussing where they fall in the "World Englishes" of which the survey is designed as a snapshot. Which, if any, of the results surprised them? Had they heard of most (or all) of the different usages? Ask them to take a look in particular at the map showing where English is spoken worldwide. Were they aware of how many different "Englishes" exist? What do they think of the survey's use of the plural "Englishes," as opposed to "English," to describe them?

MUTE IN AN ENGLISH-ONLY WORLD

CHANG-RAE LEE

THINKING CRITICALLY ABOUT THE READING

1. Many "English-only" movements provide an explicit rationale for keeping order in a community, which is deemed impossible if a significant part of the population deals exclusively or primarily in a language that is not the de facto language of government. Critics of such measures tend to emphasize xenophobia as the real root of the attempted reforms. Lee is sympathetic to the discomfort expressed by native English speakers in the New Jersey towns at the center of his article; at the same time, he does not ignore the bigotry that exists and informs the "English-only" efforts, at least in part.

2. She avoided contact with English-only speakers unless one of her children could interpret; she also studied English on her own. These strategies led to some painful early encounters, though Lee does indicate that his mother eventually became comfortable expressing herself in English.

3. Part of his hesitancy likely came from the hesitancy adolescents commonly have when enlisted to participate in public in activities with their parents. Part came from the sense that his mother was an outsider, and his fear of being similarly marginalized.

4. Both Lee's mother and the butcher felt frustration at not being able to communicate with another adult in what would normally be an ordinary transaction. The complicated economic relationship between Asian and non-Asian communities in the area—in particular, the butcher's sense that his livelihood was threatened by competition from outsiders who didn't normally do business with him—likely intensified this frustration.

5. Lee seems to have been surprised and struck by the poignancy of his mother's efforts, about which she was reticent. The question of whether the cover was meant to protect or hide the book likely will raise some interesting class discussion. Was she ashamed of not knowing English and of her attempts to learn it as an adult? Or was she determined and proud?

6. Lee wonders how those who complain about the Korean-only signs (and, implicitly, about those immigrants who "refuse" to use English) would react had they seen his mother hard at work studying English from her pocket workbook. He seems to suggest that greater understanding of the difficulties of those who struggle with English might alter the tone of the debate over signage in Palisades Park.

LANGUAGE IN ACTION

Students likely will express a variety of points of view on this topic. Ask them whether they've encountered similar situations in their lives. Do "English-only" (or 50/50) laws make sense to them? If so, why? If not, why not?

THE LOST ART OF THE RANT: HOW THE WEB REVIVED A STORIED TRADITION OF EXPLETIVE-LACED TIRADES

DANIEL SEIDEL

THINKING CRITICALLY ABOUT THE READING

1. Sports are a topic many of Seidel's readers know something about—whether or not they know anything about the history of the rant—and Seidel hopes by using it as an opening to draw readers in. Students will need to refer to his definition of a "rant" [writing that's "humorous, knowledgeable, a little angry, a little tongue-in-cheek, and sprinkled with expletives" (2)] in order to respond to the second part of this question. It's probably relevant to point out that sports journalism does have a reputation for being colorful and opinionated—some would say that the rules of "objective" journalism typically are more relaxed in this area than in others.

2. Seidel mentions some literary precursors (Dostoyevsky, Beckett, Roth), but emphasizes oral forms that he says were "perfected in taverns and street corners and smoke-filled comedy clubs." He then discusses the seventeenth-century "Ranters," a religious sect prone to public tirades against sin. The accessibility and wide readership of the Internet have, in Seidel's view, made it the natural inheritor of this tradition.

3. Students will have a variety of opinions on this topic. The Internet inarguably has provided an unprecedented opportunity for the wide dissemination of writing and other discourse (video, audio, etc.), and much of what is disseminated via the Internet is unedited. Whether this makes for more "bilious discourse" overall is debatable. The potential for dissemination is greater, but with more and more competition for readership/viewership, it's not clear exactly how much more discourse (sloppy or otherwise) actually reaches an attentive audience.

4. For Seidel, a *good* rant " expresses a real passion, and it is often a passion that has been enflamed by a feeling of powerlessness. . . . [Yet,] [d]espite their evident passion, most . . . have not simply been dashed off in the heat of the moment but have been crafted to harmonize outrage with decorum, anger with artfulness" (7–10).

5. According to Seidel, "The rant is an end in itself, an adrenaline-fueled literary catharsis. That's the paradox at the heart of ranting—its theatricality usually overwhelms all else, including the desire to change whatever outrage has elicited the rant in the first place" (11).

6. Seidel seems to be arguing specifically for an appreciation of the rant in its Internet variant; more generally, he seems to be praising the wide-open pluralism of writing culture on the Web. Although his piece is certainly knowledgeable and not without humor, it probably doesn't qualify as a "rant" according to Seidel's own definition—it seems less informed by passion than by reflection.

LANGUAGE IN ACTION

If you're using it for class discussion, it might be a good idea to examine the same prompt—ideally, after having it read aloud in class. If you have the facilities, you might also play the audio or video of a rant available online from Lewis Black, one of the best-known contemporary practitioners of the rant (www.lewisblack.com).

I Think, Therefore IM

JENNIFER 8. LEE

THINKING CRITICALLY ABOUT THE READING

1. At the heart of Lee's essay is the generalized cultural worry that "IM-speak" and the cluster of cultural trends surrounding it (the seeming decline in traditional reading and writing skills, overreliance on visuals as a means of conveying information, "multitasking," consumerism, and the triumph of pop culture) are doing away with traditional forms of knowledge and learning. A reference to Descartes, therefore, is an ironic gesture toward the high culture that IM, as an embodiment of pop or "low" culture, is thought to be in opposition.

2. Jacqueline Harding, presumably speaking for like-minded teachers, says that the use of IM-shorthand indicates that students don't know "where to draw the line between formal writing and conversational writing" (5). For her, IM-shorthand is the newest form of errors that have always plagued the writing of students unable to make this distinction. Others "see the creeping abbreviations as part of a continuing assault of technology on formal written English" (15)—presumably, these teachers are referring both to the bad habits students learn from the Internet, television, etc. and to the time they waste on them that could be more profitably spent studying and practicing writing.

3. Weaver seems to think that these represent sloppy thinking—the smiley faces stand in for a variety of complex ideas that students simply don't bother to express, leaving readers to guess their precise meaning. Weaver, like most traditionalists, deplores the shortcuts.

4. The wording of this complaint suggests a suspicion that students are speaking in codes that deliberately leave teachers and other adults in the dark. This raises the specter of loss of control, which is obviously uncomfortable for authority figures. This complaint puts

the criticism of IM-shorthand squarely in the context of perennial conflicts regarding the use of slang and, more broadly, the manners and morals of the "younger generation," when regarded by the older generation. As Lee writes, "Teenagers have long pushed the boundaries of spoken language, introducing words that then become passé with adult adoption. Now teenagers are taking charge and pushing the boundaries of written language" (28). The younger generation's "encroachment" on written language is, Lee suggests, a relatively new development.

5. Some teachers, Lee points out, "see it as an opportunity to teach students about the evolution of language" (31) or to "encourage students to use messaging shorthand to spark their thinking processes" (33) and creativity.

6. Lee quotes Jesse Sheidlower as saying, "Language is spread not because not anyone dictates any one thing to happen. The decisions are made by the language and the people who use the language" (28). Sheidlower's position, at its extreme, would seem to endorse an "anything goes" attitude—obviously not helpful, from the point of view of teachers who see it as their responsibility to teach standard written English. On the other hand, this perspective is consonant with the positions of teachers who use IM-speak as a means to an end, either of understanding language and its evolution or as a step towards conventional academic writing.

LANGUAGE IN ACTION

Students likely will have a variety of responses to this prompt. In general, sites like these that purport to record and explain slang or other trends are used by adults or others outside of the culture that generates them. Students likely will perceive much here that's out of date or inapplicable to them. They should be encouraged to suggest corrections, but, at the same time, reflect on the sites' audience and purpose. An interesting ancillary activity might be to ask students to design a site, by and for students, that purported to explain aspects of the adult world.

THE PLEASURES OF THE TEXT

CHARLES MCGRATH

THINKING CRITICALLY ABOUT THE READING

1. The obvious difference between an oral, firsthand declaration and text-messaging involves the physical presence of the complainant. What essential difference this presents is a matter of philosophical debate. (Left out of the equation here is what would seem an intermediate step—a phone call in which "I divorce you" is the substance of the message. You might ask students to discuss what the status of this declaration might be.) McGrath's point, however, seems to be that text-messaging strips human interaction of something essential—he seems to use the example of Malaysian divorce-by-text-message to signal a decline in authentic communication that he perceives as part of the text-messaging phenomenon.

2. McGrath points out some particular features (using "z" for "s," for example) that overlap; its general striving for efficiency/brevity; its "performative" aspect (i.e., "it's writing that aspires to the conditions of speech"); and its emphasis on bravura style and wit: "And sometimes when it makes abundant use of emoticons, it strives not for clarity so much as a kind of rebus-like cleverness, in which showing off is part of the point. A text-message version of 'Paradise Lost'—or of the prologue, anyway—that tries for a little more shniz-zle might go like this: "Sing hvnly mewz dat on d :X mtntp inspyrd dat shephrd hu 1st tot d chozn seed in d begnin hw d hvn n erth @{rcub};—outa chaos" (4).

3. McGrath uses the terms to mean "broad" (lateral) rather than "deep" (penetrative)—in other words, text-messaging can express many things, but none of them with much sub-tlety. As with virtually all of McGrath's discussion of text-messaging, this judgment is not favorable.

4. McGrath explains the distance by referring to technical reasons ["Because we don't have a single, national phone company, there are several competing and incompatible wireless technologies in use, and at the same time actual voice calls are far cheaper here than in most places, so there is less incentive for texting" (6)] and cultural reasons ["The Chinese language is particularly well-suited to the telephone keypad, because in Mandarin the names of the numbers are also close to the sounds of certain words; to say 'I love you,' for example, all you have to do is press 520. (For 'drop dead,' it's 748.) In China, moreover, many people believe that to leave voice mail is rude, and it's a loss of face to make a call to someone important and have it answered by an underling. Text messages preserve every-one's dignity by eliminating the human voice"(7)]. Although he does not say so outright, he seems to think it's only a matter of time before we achieve parity in this respect.

5. McGrath points out that many of us text-message in order to get the "credit" of commu-nicating without expending much effort. He writes, "it's a kind of avoidance mechanism that preserves the feeling of communication—the immediacy—without, for the most part, the burden of actual intimacy or substance" (8).

6. McGrath writes that "when at last we have succeeded in making it possible for anyone to reach anyone else anywhere and at any time, it turns out that we really don't have much we want to say" (9). In his view, a world where "we're all connected" technically provides a false promise of authentic connection, which continues to elude us. Although he stops short of saying so outright, the tenor of his essay seems to betray his conviction that ad-vances in technology in fact are actually increasing the true distance between individuals.

LANGUAGE IN ACTION

Speedwriting is commercial and, one would think, increasingly irrelevant in a world where technology has made person-to-person dictation virtually obsolete. Nevertheless, its emphasis on efficient written communication and even some of its conventions are strikingly similar to those of text-messaging.

You're Wearing That?: Understanding Mothers and Daughters in Conversation

Deborah Tannen

THINKING CRITICALLY ABOUT THE READING

1. According to Tannen, mothers and daughters have particularly intense relationships because "talk—particularly talk about personal topics—plays a larger and more complex role in girls' and women's social lives than in boys' and men's. For girls and women, talk is the glue that holds a relationship together—and the explosive that can blow it apart. That's why you can think you're having a perfectly amiable chat, then suddenly find yourself wounded by the shrapnel from an exploded conversation" (3).

2. Tannen interviewed "dozens of women of varied geographic, racial and cultural backgrounds, and. . . had informal conversations or e-mail exchanges with countless others" (9). She writes, "For each example, I begin by explaining the perspective that I understand immediately because I share it: in mother-daughter talk, the daughter's, because I'm a daughter but not a mother. Then I figure out the logic of the other's perspective. Writing this book forced me to look at conversations from my mother's point of view" (8). As a daughter, Tannen presumably would feel comfortable writing from her perspective alone. As a scientist, she is obligated to describe relationships as objectively as possible, from both the daughters' and the mothers' points of view.

3. Tannen reports that daughters' most frequent complaint was that their mothers were always criticizing them; from mothers, she most often heard that daughters took everything they said as criticism. [Tannen notes, "Both are right, but each sees only her perspective" (9).]

4. Tannen writes that daughters concede tremendous power to their mothers by caring so much about their mothers' opinions. Mothers, on the other hand, feel that their opinions, in which they invest so much, go unheeded. According to Tannen, both mothers and daughters shape their identities based in part on the extent of their closeness to and similarity to each other. This aspect of their relationship invests it with tremendous power.

5. Tannen calls this technique "reframing," which involves shifting the context in which one judges an action to a context appropriate to the actor. From her own experience, Tannen recounts her pain at her mother's seeming dismissal of her successful academic career, which in her mother's eyes came at the cost of Tannen's marriage: "She probably didn't know what to make of my life, which was so different from any she could have imagined for herself. I don't think she intended to denigrate what I had done and become, but the lens through which she viewed the world could not encompass the one I had chosen. Reframing how I look at it takes the sting out of this memory" (29).

6. Tannen refers here to "[c]aring about someone as much as you care about yourself, and the critical eye that comes with it" (33). For Tannen, this caring/critical stance is what makes the mother/daughter relationship uniquely powerful.

LANGUAGE IN ACTION

Most of your students should have some experience with mother/daughter relationships, even if at a distance (their mothers and grandmothers, for example; their sisters and their mother; a friend and her mother). Encourage them, however, to test Tannen's claims about the specificity of the mother/daughter relationship with their observations about different relationships within the family. Do they feel that Tannen's fraught relationship with her own mother, who was in her final illness as she wrote the book of which this essay forms a part, compromises her status as a scientist of language?

HE AND SHE: WHAT'S THE REAL DIFFERENCE?

CLIVE THOMPSON

THINKING CRITICALLY ABOUT THE READING

1. The group of computer scientists Thompson describes used a computer algorithm to examine 604 texts from the British National Corpus, a collection of documents put together by academics to study the use of modern language. Half of the texts were written by men, the other half by women. The scientists programmed the algorithm to search for words that were unique to each set. The experiment yielded fifty words that had predictive value. Using the algorithm in combination with these fifty elements, the scientists could predict the gender of an author more than 80 percent of the time.

2. The editors of *Proceedings of the National Academy of Sciences* rejected the paper "on ideological grounds" (2). They were concerned that the study sought to make a distinction between men and women and that it might be used to oppress women. When the researchers submitted their papers to other journals, they made certain to let editors know that one of their number was female.

3. Women are more likely to use personal pronouns like *I, you, she, myself,* and *yourself,* while men are more likely to use words like *a, the, that,* and *these,* as well as cardinal numbers and quantifiers like *more* and *some.* Thompson points out (7, 9) that it may surprise people that common words can provide so much information on gender.

4. Tannen had her students analyze articles that had appeared in men's and women's magazines. Their assignment was to guess which articles had appeared in which type of magazine. Basing their guesses on the style of writing in each article, they guessed correctly more often than not. The articles in the men's magazines tended to use the "male" style, while the ones from the women's magazines tended to use a "female" style. Tannen and her students took into account what Koppel and his associates perceived—that the intended audience of a piece of writing affects the type of language used.

5. Bing argues that the differences the researchers found may be cultural rather than innate or biological. She also wonders how well the algorithm would work if it analyzed books written by gays, lesbians, or transgendered people. (15)

6. Thompson likely decided to end his article with the quotation from Koppel in order to give the latter an opportunity to respond to the charges made by the critics of his study.

When Koppel says that "you can't be careful enough," he's referring to the dangers inherent in publishing a study that suggests that men and women differ in basic ways.

LANGUAGE IN ACTION

Using the methodology established by Koppel and his associates, one would guess that the author of the first selection is female. The piece is written in the first person, so the author uses the word *I* on several occasions. The author also uses the words *my* and *she*. The second selection refers primarily to things rather than people, which implies that it may have been written by a man. This author uses *a* and *the* a number of times, and there are several "*of* phrases" with post-head noun modifications: "signs of movement," "square of yellow," "baggage of chilly nights," and "season of leaves."

"QUEER" EVOLUTION: WORD GOES MAINSTREAM

MARTHA IRVINE

THINKING CRITICALLY ABOUT THE READING

1. There are many examples of words like *queer*, words which began as epithets only to be adopted or reclaimed in later years by the targets of the epithet. The use of the word *nigger* within the contemporary African American community is one such case, as is the casual use of the slur *mick* by Irish Americans. Inevitably language will be used against the members of an oppressed group, but when the members of that group become accepted and acquire a certain amount of power they are able to gain a measure of control over language. In many cases, as the examples above prove, this involves taking the words that have been used against them and changing their meaning and purpose.

   As for the flexibility of the English language, many English words accommodate more than one meaning. *Queer* is just one example. *Gay* also comes to mind. You might use this question as a way of opening a discussion about the development of language. Ask students to think about how words like *queer* or *gay* acquire slang or street definitions in addition to textbook definitions.

2. One of the reasons the word *queer* may have evolved more quickly than other words is that it has always been a slang word, whether its meaning was "strange," "perverted," or "gay." Naturally, since it has acquired a number of meanings over time, it must be of greater service today than it was years ago. As Irvine's article makes plain, the word *queer* can now be used in a variety of ways by a variety of individuals for a variety of purposes.

3. For perhaps twenty years the word *queer* has been used by the gay community to refer to itself. Increasingly the word has become a part of mainstream culture, to the point that it appears in the title of an extremely popular television show featuring five gay men (i.e., "Queer Eye for the Straight Guy"). Obviously, as the word become a more and more accepted part of mainstream culture, it becomes less and less effective as a slur.

4. Ward argues that people should take care in using the word *queer* because it is "very context-sensitive" (24). "It really matters who says it and why they're saying it" (25), he says.

5. When Irvine argues that *queer* is "taking on a hipster edge" (3), she means that it has become trendy to use the word. She provides evidence of the word's trendiness when she describes its apparently benign use by heterosexuals in conversation and mainstream publications.

6. Irvine is a newspaper reporter. She is not a columnist or essayist. She may have an opinion about the evolution of the word *queer*, but her purpose is to explain how the word's use and meaning have changed over time. She does so by interviewing several subjects and constructing an article around the information she receives from them.

LANGUAGE IN ACTION

If you have the facilities, you might do the search in front of the class and discuss the results of your search. (Seven of the first ten hits resulting from a search done as this material was written yielded references to "queer" used unambiguously in the sense Irvine defined as new in 2003.) Discuss with students whether Irvine's essay is dated. What other uses of the word "queer," if any, are they aware of?

MISSING THE NOSE ON OUR FACE:
PRONOUNS AND THE FEMINIST REVOLUTION

JOHN H. MCWHORTER

THINKING CRITICALLY ABOUT THE READING

1. Although the use of the phrase is laudable in its intent, according to McWhorter, its use has problems: First, it places the masculine "he" ahead of the feminine "she," thus partly replicating the problem (sexism) its use was meant to correct. Second, and most important, McWhorter considers the construction awkward—it's "cooked" or artificial, not spontaneous and vital, and therefore rarely used in any but the most self-conscious constructions of written English. In McWhorter's view, this makes it a failure as a linguistic construction.

2. Before the eighteenth century, the use of "he" as the default pronoun mirrored general acceptance of male preeminence in all areas that mattered. In the 1700s, according to McWhorter, an awareness of the injustice of this position arose, but the notion that "he" could and should be used as "gender-neutral" arose as well. McWhorter rejects the idea that "he" can be "gender neutral" because it is clearly and primarily used to denote the forty-nine percent of the population that is male.

3. The "gender-neutral" use of "he" was rejected as a reflection of a power imbalance that reinforced the status quo. Redress of the inequity was intended in part to reshape consciousness.

4. McWhorter seems to find little point in prescribing rules for language that will not be followed by native speakers in situations in which they are not constrained by context to be "correct." "Conscious," formal language is language that follows the rules prescribed by grammarians; McWhorter contends that such language is inauthentic compared to the language people speak when they are in a comfortable setting and are focused on the content,

rather than the form, of their speech. It might be argued that, for McWhorter, the ideal language would be one in which the binaries (conscious/unconscious, formal/casual, spoken/written) collapsed.

5. McWhorter finds that, apart from being highly self-conscious, awkward, and artificial, such usages are distracting to readers or listeners, calling unnecessary attention to themselves and detracting from the writer or speaker's intended meaning. Interestingly, he also considers the "s/he" construction "a disaster" because it's unpronounceable (therefore limited to writing) and aesthetically displeasing: "Even in writing, however, just look at it—it's too darned ugly to be used as frequently as a pronoun has to be. Imagine great literature splattered with s/he's!" (10).

6. McWhorter believes that language evolves naturally and that grammarians' concerns with correctness need to take a back seat to the wisdom of speakers, who, according to McWhorter, will devise ways to keep language appropriately reflective of cultural change.

LANGUAGE IN ACTION

Students' answers will vary here. You might want to ask them to provide examples of "politically correct" language they consider admirable or laughable and to explain why they view them the way they do.

ON LANGUAGE: YOU GUYS

AUDREY BILGER

THINKING CRITICALLY ABOUT THE READING

1. In much the same way that feminists and others sensitive to gender inequities object to the allegedly gender-neutral use of "he," Bilger objects to the use of "guys" as "gender neutral," because the word, in her view, clearly refers to males only, excluding fifty-one percent of the people its usage denotes. She points out that the ninth edition of *Webster's* did not include the "gender-neutral" definition of "guys," in part in order to call attention to the ways language inevitably changes over time, and in part to remind us that dictionaries both reflect and reinforce cultural values.

2. According to Bilger, Clancy's study concludes that "terms signifying maleness have been more readily perceived as signifying universals than those signifying femaleness. . . . And this should trouble us" (5). Why? Because "[c]alling women 'guys' makes femaleness invisible. It says that man—as in a male person—is still the measure of all things" (6).

3. When two female friends objected to Bilger's own use of the term "guys" to refer to them, they hit a nerve—and she realized that "guys" was as offensive as the allegedly gender-neutral use of "man," "he," and the like, which she (like nearly all feminists) had long since rejected. It was, in fact, a symptom of "internalized oppression" (8). It was difficult to purge because its usage was habitual, and its offensiveness previously invisible (as it remains for many people in the culture). Bilger has called openly for alternatives to the construction (which has yielded "folks," "people," etc., as possibilities).

4. "Internalized oppression" is a phenomenon in which the subordinate members of an unequal power relationship unconsciously (or sometimes even consciously) embrace their subordinate status, adopting the outlook and values of the dominant members, and even facilitating the oppression of others. In language, according to Bilger, such internalization is expressed through the adoption of language like "you guys."

5. Kleinman argues that male-based generics like "you guys" reinforce a system in which "'man' in the abstract and men in the flesh are privileged over women" (10). Kleinman and Bilger see language reform as part of the larger reform of an inequitable society.

6. Bilger quotes Walker as follows: "I see in its use some women's obsequious need to be accepted, at any cost, even at the cost of erasing their own femaleness, and that of other women" (11). Feminists who use the language themselves are replicating the values of the inequitable system they are committed to changing.

LANGUAGE IN ACTION

This card should generate a good deal of debate. Ask students to respond in particular to the card's question, "What if generics ended in 'white'"? Do they see the parallel, or do they reject this comparison between sexism and racism? You might want to challenge some of your braver/more motivated students to try printing up a card like this themselves, handing it to someone who uses the phrase "you guys," and reporting the results to the class.

6. MEDIA AND ADVERTISING

AMUSING OURSELVES TO DEPTH

GREG BEATO

THINKING CRITICALLY ABOUT THE READING

1. Keck wanted to find a medium for advertising aimed at fellow college students. His first story, about a monster allegedly "running amok at a local lake" (1), was, according to Beato, merely a means of distributing coupons for pizza and beer.

2. The paper's print circulation—even apart from its massive online presence—qualify it as one of the country's most successful newspapers, in an era when many long-established papers are struggling to remain economically viable. At many established newspapers, ad revenues are in decline and staff cutbacks are increasingly common; neither applies to *The Onion*, where, in 2007, major additions to staff were planned. Beato attributes its success to "low-tech attributes readily available to any paper but nevertheless in short supply: candor, irreverence, and a willingness to offend" (4).

3. In well-publicized scandals from 2003 and 2004, respectively, Blair and Kelley were charged with inventing sources and fabricating interviews, supporting evidence, and other elements of stories they submitted to their papers. Blair was also charged with plagiarism. Blair and Kelley both resigned from their papers under pressure. Beato is presumably

being tongue-in-cheek here—the *New York Times* and *USA Today*, unlike satirical (or "fake") news organizations like *The Onion*, are designed to publish the news "straight"—objectively and truthfully. In writing for these papers, Blair and Kelley implicitly accepted these constraints and violated them. Beato does not, however, appear to accept "straight" news organizations' claims to objectivity at face value—even when they play by the rules, he suggests, their "objectively" delivered news is at best news filtered through twin sieves designed to remove all possibility of offending either consumers and advertisers.

4. Beato seems to have real respect for *The Onion* and similar "fake news" outlets. Not only do they entertain, in his view, but they also convey real ideas about current issues and encourage critical perspectives on what's going on in the world. He admires the paper's willingness to offend in its attempts to express a "rude, blunt truth about the world" (11).

5. Unlike Postman, Beato doesn't see the trend toward "fake news" as necessarily a bad thing—as long, that is, as "fake news" encourages thought and discussion about what's really happening in the world. Presumably, Beato does, like Postman, disapprove of so-called news that ignores significant events, presents the trivial as significant, and/or blends hard news and opinion in such a way that the two are impossible to separate.

6. Beato maintains that, unlike traditional news outlets the "dance around" this "awfulness," *The Onion* bluntly expresses "the limits of our tolerance and compassion" (12) with its headlines satirizing perfunctory news coverage of disasters in faraway places and saccharine human interest stories.

7. He certainly does seem to respect the sophisticated humor and, most importantly, the ethic of honesty behind the fake news outlets he discusses (*The Onion, The Daily Show,* and *The Colbert Report*). More than simply praising such efforts however, Beato seems to be exhorting straight news outlets to imitate the "candor, irreverence, and the willingness to offend" that he considers key to their success.

LANGUAGE IN ACTION

"American Voices" installments clearly don't offer the detail mainstream news sources will offer on the topic. What they do tend to offer, however, is an array of off-the-cuff responses to the topic that likely will engender lively discussion among students in your class. Ask students to classify the range of responses to the topic represented in "American Voices." Are these perspectives reflected to any degree in the mainstream news treatment of the topic? Why or why not? Did reading about the topic and the satirical responses to it make them want to learn more about the topic?

SELECTION, SLANTING, AND CHARGED LANGUAGE

NEWMAN P. BIRK AND GENEVIEVE B. BIRK

THINKING CRITICALLY ABOUT THE READING

1. The Birks's purpose is to explain some of the linguistic processes involved in human communication rather than argue a certain position. For example, the Birks describe in para-

graph 24 the purpose and significance of charged language without passing judgment: "Charged language, then, is the natural and necessary medium for the communication of charged or attitudinal meaning. At times we have difficulty in living with it, but we would have even greater difficulty in living without it."

2. The Birks organized their essay in a logical order, beginning with what authors first see, the principle of selection, then how writers express this knowledge through slanting, and finally the different ways slanting occurs (emphasis, charged language, selection of facts). Most students should find this logical succession and the bold headings used to announce transitions a good organizational format for this essay.

3. In paragraph 6, the Birks say, "Slanting may be defined as the process of selecting (1) knowledge—factual and attitudinal; (2) words; and (3) emphasis, to achieve the intention of the communicator." Slanting "operates . . . to select certain facts and feelings from our store of knowledge, and to choose the words and emphasis that we shall use to communicate our meaning" (6). Slanting occurs after the principle of selection decides what we notice, affecting our communication rather than our observations. A writer can use emphasis, selection of facts, and charged language to give slant to a piece of writing.

4. Students' reactions to these examples may vary; however, had they not been included, the essay would have lacked the clear and concrete illustrations that help to clarify the meaning and purpose of the Birks's essay.

5. "Some of the difficulties in living with charged language are caused by its use in dishonest propaganda, in some editorials, in many political speeches, in most advertising, in certain kinds of effusive salesmanship, and in blatantly insincere, or exaggerated, or sentimental expressions of emotion. Other difficulties are caused by the misunderstandings and misinterpretations that charged language produces" (25). Because charged language "shapes our attitudes and values . . . gives purpose to, and guides, our actions" (26), as well as affects our relations with others, writers need to be conscious of the impact of their words on various types of readers. If writers use charged language unknowingly, they may convey sentiments they do not wish to convey or unintentionally offend readers.

6. The first examples the Birks use are a lumberjack, an artist, and a tree surgeon (2). The writers assume each is a man and use the pronoun his. The word *man* could be exchanged for the word *person*, and *he* could become *he* or *she*. A tree surgeon might be a woman. In paragraph 7, the Birks use the example of Socrates, a wise old man, and later in that same paragraph another example discusses whether a man is awkward and strong or is strong and awkward. In paragraph 9, the dog, Toddy, is a female and in that same example Mrs. Firmly is depicted negatively as she "slaps" the dog with a newspaper in the objective writing and later "hits" the dog in the slanted version. In some cases the pronouns can be changed, but more importantly, the examples chosen can create a better balance in male and female roles.

LANGUAGE IN ACTION

Ask students to clarify the distinction between slanted and charged language. The first letter contains the following slanted phrases: "ranks among the best magazines," "turbulent century," "genius of the issue," "truly inspired," "I will urge," "comprehend or appreciate," and "important social and political decisions." The second letter by Ames has some highly charged language: "touched my soul," "*my* loss," "pictures of the injured, dead, dying, and

crying," "God bless all of them," and "my sincere thanks for a free America." In the third letter Heichler opens with a number of facts. He was a refugee at fifteen, became a soldier at
nineteen and a U.S. Foreign Service Office at twenty-nine, and claims to be a witness to history. The letter concludes with some highly charged language about gender roles and the
women's movement. Though short, McGuire's letter is packed with feelings for the greatness
of "grunts." And finally, in the last letter, students will recognize the charged language
("painful," "bullet-riddled," "dear 85-year-old mother," and so on) among the verifiable facts
surrounding the photograph of the writer's younger brother.

One way to approach this activity is to break the class into small groups and assign each
group one of the letters to the editor for analysis. After about fifteen minutes, have each
group report their findings to the whole class, and end with a general discussion of slanting as
seen in the five letters.

TELEVISION NEWS: THE LANGUAGE OF PICTURES

NEIL POSTMAN AND STEVE POWERS

THINKING CRITICALLY ABOUT THE READING

1. Postman and Powers's attitude toward television news can best be described as wary or
   distrustful. In the opening paragraph, words such as *distorts, manufacturing, defenseless,
   vulnerable, attempts, armed, defend,* and *seductions* lead readers to this conclusion. Generally speaking, the diction throughout the essay supports this initial impression.

2. Postman and Powers state their thesis in the opening sentence: "When a television news
   show distorts the truth by altering or manufacturing facts (through re-creations), a television viewer is defenseless even if a re-creation is properly labeled." As a result of reading
   this article, Postman and Powers want readers and viewers to know what they're watching
   when they watch television news. They believe "the viewer must come with a prepared
   mind—information, opinions, a sense of proportion, an articulate value system. To the
   TV viewer lacking such mental equipment, a news program is only a kind of rousing light
   show" (21).

3. Postman and Powers use hypothetical examples to clarify many of the generalizations that
   they make. They use the example of Clint Eastwood to make clear the differences between television and the cinema (10). They quote NBC News executive Reuven Frank to
   make their point that television has to include everyone (19). Students' answers to the
   persuasiveness of these examples will vary. It is important to have them discuss what it is
   about each type of evidence that they find persuasive.

4. Postman and Powers delineate the differences between the language of pictures and the
   spoken and written language in paragraph 3. Pictures, according to Postman and Powers,
   "speak only in particularities. Their vocabulary is limited to concrete representation."
   Spoken and written language, on the other hand, deals with the world of ideas and concepts. "By itself, a picture cannot deal with the unseen, the remote, the internal, the abstract. . . . The picture documents and celebrates the particularities of the universe's
   infinite variety. Language makes them comprehensible."

5. Scenes of violence and dynamic destruction have appeal because they capture change—
"Something was here, now it's gone" (8). Viewers find such scenes exciting and in some
cases entertaining. Producers avoid "talking heads" because they know that the television
medium demands images that move. With talking heads, as Postman and Powers note,
"there is nothing to record or document, no change in process" (10). Television, with its
smaller screen and the distractions of home, must offer changes that are more extreme
and more dramatic than those of the movies. Postman and Powers make this point effectively with the example of Clint Eastwood, in paragraph 10.

6. In paragraphs 12–15 Postman and Powers describe television news as a "form of theater
in which the day's events are to be dramatized" (13). Everything on the set from the dramatic music that announces the show's beginning to the teletype machines, clocks, maps,
and busy staff in the background signal that we are watching a staged event. According to
Postman and Powers, the dominant theme of television news is "the imposition of an orderly world—called 'the news'—upon the disorderly flow of events" (15).

LANGUAGE IN ACTION

Start by asking your students some questions so that they can begin to think about the
possibilities that the picture suggests. What is happening here? What do the positions and arm
gestures, of the various soldiers tell you? What are your reactions to the artillery piece in the
picture? Students need to articulate the dominant emotional impression that this picture creates for them. Some may find a war image unsettling, disconcerting, or disgusting, while others may feel a certain patriotism or nationalism associated with the military. In light of all the
war images and other scenes of violence in the media that have bombarded Americans during
the last decade, some students may be numbed and have little or no emotional response.

Poll your students to find out what ideas this photograph conveys about war for them. As
Postman and Powers suggest, "pictures, especially single pictures, speak only in particularities" (3). While a picture can suggest ideas, "we use language itself to convert the image to
idea. By itself, a picture cannot deal with the unseen, the remote, the internal, the abstract"
(3).

THE CULT OF THE AMATEUR

ANDREW KEEN

THINKING CRITICALLY ABOUT THE READING

1. Writing in the nineteenth century, Huxley famously postulated that if an infinite number of
monkeys were supplied with an infinite number of typewriters, one of these monkeys eventually would type a masterpiece. Keen compares this scenario with today's real-world scenario, in which the vast number of people with access to the Internet produce a vast
amount of output—most of which, Keen writes, is appallingly mediocre.

2. Keen objects to the fact that the Web allows anyone to publish mediocre (or worse) material that appears to the casual user to be on par with skillfully produced material that pre-

sumably bears a closer relationship to truth and beauty: "These days, kids can't tell the difference between credible news by objective professional journalists and what they read on joeshmoe.blogspot.com" (11). He objects to what he sees as the resultant blurring of fact and fiction, truth and lies.

3. The sheer number of entries easily accessible online mean that Wikipedia is consulted more frequently than traditional sources of information, depite the fact that its entries are, according to Keen, not edited or vetted for accuracy. (There has been much debate about the latter claim, which Keen does not discuss in this piece. Some studies have concluded that the accuracy of the typical Wikipedia entry is on par with traditional sources.) As with the proliferation of blogs, Keen sees Wikipedia as contributing to the blurring of lines between fact and fiction and "perpetuating the cycle of misinformation and ignorance" he sees as central to our culture (12). He is also concerned about the accessibility of Wikipedia and sites like it to corporations and others "with an agenda" who aim to use the sites for the dissemination of propaganda (13).

4. According to Keen, "YouTube eclipses even the blogs in the inanity and absurdity of its content" (15). He argues that it appeals to our basest instincts, allowing us to entertain ourselves in unproductive ways, twenty-four hours a day, seven days a week.

5. Keen writes that Google's search engine "reflects the 'wisdom' of the crowd. In other words, the more people click on a link...the more likely that link will come up in subsequent searches. . . . [I]n other words, it just tells us what we already know" (16).

6. Keen doesn't appear to think much of the positive aims that MySpace and Facebook advertise for themselves: self-expression, self-discovery, and social connection. Instead, he sees them, like blogs, YouTube, and other manifestations of Web 2.0, as sheer self-indulgence, and their effect (ironically) ultimately as alienating rather than connecting individuals. He also gestures towards their more easily demonstrable negative effects by mentioning "anonymous sexual predators and pedophiles" (19) who are attracted to unedited displays of personal data.

7. Keen discusses financial crises in the newspaper, music, and film industries, which haven't been able thus far to cope with declining ad revenue, piracy, and competition from Internet news and entertainment. He sees these changes as contributing to the cultural decline made all but inevitable by the rise of Web 2.0.

LANGUAGE IN ACTION

If you choose to do this activity in class, you might make a list at the front of the room of students' most frequently visited sites. Depending on the composition of your class, there's likely to be considerable overlap. Ask students to talk about any changes in their Internet use over the past few years. Did their patterns change with their enrollment in college courses? If so, why and how?

WHAT HAPPENS WHEN BLOGS GO MAINSTREAM?

ANNALEE NEWITZ

THINKING CRITICALLY ABOUT THE READING

1. Newitz was writing her column in "old media," and, unlike the blogs she was reading then, she had to follow "old school rules," notably, submitting to editorial oversight, which meant citing only reputable, carefully documented sources and keeping purely personal perspectives in check. Six years later, she found most blogs had shifted to following the same rules, so that the gap between mainstream sources and "formerly alternative media" had narrowed considerably.

2. Newitz submits her blog posts to an editor, who checks them for both form and content; she carefully documents her sources; she does ample research on her subjects; and she refrains from publishing potentially libelous or inaccurate material. (She does point out that she sometimes writes while wearing pajamas.)

3. Newitz worries that, as blogs and other formerly alternative sources go mainstream, the self-editing will become self-censoring, and that inevitably will lead to the stifling of unconventional ideas and unpopular viewpoints.

4. According to Newitz, mainstream media self-censors by watering down or eliminating coverage of issues and ideas that might cause it legal or financial trouble: It "tiptoe[s] around hot-button issues like climate change and sex and delay[s] publishing stories that might upset the government" (7).

5. Newitz points to the "100-year histories" of newspapers like the *New York Times* that inhibit change and growth, employ huge staffs that depend on their survival, and have complex, long-established relationships with government, corporations, and influential public figures. She implies that these factors hamstring the mainstream publications' capacity to act freely and to take risks in what they report and how they report it.

6. Newitz seems to propose a happy medium between blogging as it was (unedited and sometimes irresponsible, but idea-rich) and mainstream media as they are (edited and responsible, but at the expense of new ideas and critical perspectives) as the ideal future for the media.

LANGUAGE IN ACTION

It's likely that the first post on today's Metafilter will not be something covered on the front page of the mainstream media. If you've discussed Andrew Keen's "The Cult of the Amateur" in class, you might want to ask students to consider how Keen might respond to this likelihood and contrast it with how Newitz might respond. What do students think of the top postings on Metafilter.com? Are they important? What about today's top stories on CNN.com and other mainstream outlets? How do they suppose decisions are made about what to cover at the mainstream outlets?

THE HARD SELL: ADVERTISING IN AMERICA

BILL BRYSON

THINKING CRITICALLY ABOUT THE READING

1. The story about Eastman eases the reader into the topic, but more importantly, it shows readers what advertising has done for products in their daily lives. Starting off as a junior clerk in 1885, Eastman proved how quality and high-volume advertising propelled the meaningless Kodak through the end of the nineteenth century and set a precedent for businesses to come.

2. Bryson's purpose in this essay is to inform—to give his readers a historical perspective on advertising in the United States and to explore some of the trends that have appeared over the years. Bryson's numerous examples seem geared to illustrate the United States's advertising history and not to persuade readers to one point of view or another.

3. Students' responses to Bryson's examples will vary considerably depending on their familiarity with the products being discussed and their interest in history. Many students will find the extensive example of Eastman and Kodak fascinating while others will be drawn to the examples of more modern products. Encourage students to discuss why they find some examples more effective than the others.

4. "A *trademark* is effectively the name of a product, its *brand name*" (24). Other examples of trademarks that have or will become household words are Pampers, Walkman, Polo, Birkenstock, and Rollerblade.

5. Bryson refers to "creeping illiteracy" as "grammatical manglings" in advertising that misuse adverbs, misspell words, or make any number of other grammatical errors. Slogans like "comb it handsome" incorporate errors to shorten phrases and attract consumer attention (37).

6. Bryson uses commercial manipulation to refer to the way advertising copywriters manipulate language to manipulate consumers. The hand cream with oxygenating moisturizers (38) sounds more exciting and healthful than perhaps the product actually is. Through verbal hypnosis, advertisers create the illusion of a premium or higher quality product when in fact the item may be an equal alternative to similar products. The fur coat renamed Hudson seal was supposed to create a more dignified image than the original dyed muskrat (39). This method produces results because consumers willingly submit to the hypnosis; they want to buy the image as well as the product. When buying sneakers most children want more than a sturdy shoe; they want to feel like champions. Sure, kids know that they will not play like Michael Jordan after putting on his sneakers, but they want the image anyway. (Note: Adults are equally affected by such hypnosis.) People can guard against commercial manipulation and verbal hypnosis by stopping to ask what a product or hyped up feature actually is before being swept up by the sound or idea of the words advertising the product.

7. In paragraphs 43 and 44 Bryson discusses the challenge of trying to sell products in an increasingly multicultural society. His examples of what can happen with Spanish highlight the problems that occur when many words can be used to communicate a single idea (brown sugar) and the humorous situations that are encountered when translating from one language to another.

LANGUAGE IN ACTION

After discussing Hugh Rank's "Intensify/Downplay" schema so that students understand the techniques public persuaders use, divide the class into six groups, giving each of the groups one of the Navy advertisements for analysis. Students should pay particular attention to the interplay between the verbal and the visual messages in each ad, and compare the World War I posters to today's advertisements. After ten to fifteen minutes of group analysis, have each group report its findings to the whole class. Conclude with a general discussion of the ads, drawing connections among the ads of how they intensify or downplay.

Weasel Words: The Art of Saying Nothing at All

William Lutz

THINKING CRITICALLY ABOUT THE READING

1. In paragraph 2 Lutz says, "Advertisers use weasel words to appear to be making a claim for a product when in fact they are making no claim at all . . . Weasel words appear to say one thing when in fact they say the opposite, or nothing at all." As Lutz explains, weasel words get their name from the weasel, an animal that is able to suck out the insides of birds' eggs, leaving hollow eggs for the unsuspecting birds. Like these hollow eggs, weasel words are themselves hollow.

2. Lutz's many examples not only illustrate each of the various kinds of weasel words and differentiate them from the others but also clearly establish Lutz as an authority on the subject. Because their answers are likely to vary, encourage students to explain why they find certain examples more effective than others.

3. Advertisers use the word *help* because consumers add positive connotations to the word: "Now 'help' only means to aid or assist, nothing more. It does not mean to conquer, stop, eliminate, end, solve, heal, cure or anything else" (3). Advertisers encourage this misreading by distracting the reader from the word help to other words in the slogan: "The trick is that the claim that comes after the weasel word is usually so strong and so dramatic that you forget the word 'help' and concentrate only on the dramatic claim" (3).

4. "'Virtually' means *not in fact*. It does *not* mean 'almost' or 'just about the same as'" (10), but because consumers misread the word's meaning to the point of complete inversion, advertisers can easily deceive us without actually lying.

5. On the basis of Lutz's arguments, we can see "works like liquid ball bearings" uses two techniques that render the slogan meaningless. The word *works* only suggests that the product will perform some task without explaining the exact nature of the task and whether this action will benefit our cars. "Like liquid ball bearings" serves to distract the reader; "'like' gets you to ignore the product and concentrate on the claim the advertiser is making about it" (22). So, instead of thinking about what the motor oil will do for our cars, we imagine how well liquid ball bearings might lubricate our engine and connect that feeling to the advertised product.

6. Lutz's "unfinished words" category includes such claims as "lasts 'up to twice as long'" (29), "has more flavor," and "has fifty percent less fat." Such claims imply a comparison.

For each claim we want to ask, "Than what?" Advertisers leave it to consumers to complete the comparisons. As Lutz says, "Since each of us fills in the claim differently, the ad and the product can become all things to all people, and not promise a single thing" (30).

7. Lutz uses the strategy of division and classification to develop his essay because it helps him simplify what might otherwise be a complex subject. He takes the large subject of weasel words and divides it into various categories like "help," "virtually," "new and improved," and so on. He then classifies specific ads into these categories. Because of this categorization, we come to understand how each category works and how it is different from the others. Most students find the headings in Lutz's essay helpful. Finally, because some ads don't fall neatly into one or another of Lutz's categories, he felt that it was necessary to establish the category "combining weasel words" for those ads that use more than one type of weasel word.

LANGUAGE IN ACTION

In analyzing their chosen ad, students will discover a number of the weasel words discussed by Lutz. You might find it useful to do this exercise yourself and analyze your results along with the class. Talk about what the ads seem to suggest about their product and what the products probably achieve. Adbusters, a Canadian anti-consumerist group, over the years has spoofed many well-known advertisements. These spoofs expose the lies behind advertisements using humor (often black humor) to make their point, and could be a useful teaching tool.

Lead Us into Temptation

James B. Twitchell

THINKING CRITICALLY ABOUT THE READING

1. One of Twitchell's central points is that consumers are complicit in the cult of consumerism: Far from being unwitting dupes of a menacing "industrial complex," we foster the spread of consumer culture by avidly pursuing a life that consists largely of getting and spending.

2. "Mallcondo" culture is Twitchell's term for where he sees U.S. culture headed: as a cocoon—a closed system "based on principles of enclosure, control, and consumption" (4)—with the mall at its center. According to Twitchell, entrance into this culture, with its built-in system of desire and its fulfillment, is "the goal of middle-class life" (5). The central place of the mall constitutes the essential difference between our "pleasure dome" and the one decreed by Kubla Khan in Shelley's poem, which had the natural world at its center.

3. Twitchell believes that "We live through things. We create ourselves through things. And we change ourselves by changing our things. We often depend on such material for meaning" (10). Consumer culture, according to Twitchell, provides meaning and purpose to people living without deeply held beliefs in any system of values other than that governing

economic exchange.

4. Twitchell reminds his readers that humans created consumer culture and that we can and should strive to understand (and, presumably, to control) it: "That we demonize it, that we see ourselves as helpless and innocent victims of its overpowering force, tells far more about our eagerness to be passive in the face of complexity than about our understanding of how it does its work" (15).

5. In this passage in paragraph 30, Twitchell focuses on the commodification of museums: "Not only are all major museum shows sponsored by corporate interests, but they all end in the same spot: the gift shop." In paragraph 24, he explains the general plight of High Culture in the United States as follows: "[B]uying stuff is not just our current popular culture, it is how we understand the world. High culture has pretty much disappeared, desperately needing such infusions of life-preserving monies from taxpayer-supported endowments and tax-free foundations to keep it from gasping away."

6. "Mollie" was described wryly in a regular *New York Times* feature as enjoying The Nutcracker at Lincoln Center for the costumes and for the shopping break (or intermission) in the middle. Twitchell uses Mollie as emblematic of the denizen of "mallcondo" culture.

7. Twitchell briefly discusses carnival's role in the pre-industrial West, as a brief period of excess and consumption (e.g., Mardi Gras) balanced by restraint (Lent). He contends that religion/the church as a force of restraint has all but disappeared from our culture, with the result that "carnivalesque" consumption occupies more and more of our time, attention, and resources.

LANGUAGE IN ACTION

Your students likely will have different responses to this cartoon. Most will agree it's a satirical look at the omnipresence (and, some would say, omnipotence) of advertising in our daily lives. You might start the discussion by asking whether the "he" of the cartoon is meant to be representative or exceptional. If the former, what does he represent? If the latter, what message should we take away from the cartoon—or does it have a message? Your students might also have interesting things to say about the medium, particularly with the relatively recent but seemingly enduring vogue for graphic novels. How does the information conveyed by this relatively short series of panels compare to that conveyed by the essay it follows? Should we take it as seriously as we take the essay? Yet another way to approach the piece might be to ask what the "tropical island" represents: Is there any escape from advertising and our consumer culture?

Jesus Is a Brand of Jeans

Jean Kilbourne

THINKING CRITICALLY ABOUT THE READING

1. In order to illustrate her contention that "the product is [now] not so much a means to an end, as the end itself" (3), Kilbourne points to two ads: one for sports gear, in which the gear is lovingly packed into a child-seat from which the child seated next to it presumably

was displaced; and one for a car, in which a man makes love to a woman whose face is obscured by an image of the car. Kilbourne explains the shift from advertising's time-tested promise that products would bring love from other people by noting, "After all, it is easier to love a product than a person" (4).

2. Kilbourne writes that advertising "promotes a bankrupt concept of *relationship*. . . . [W]e are surrounded by advertising that yokes our needs with products and promises us that *things* will deliver what in fact they never can" (6). She suggests that the relentless onslaught of ads that promote this fantasy actually distorts our concept of what relationships with other people can and should be. In paragraphs 4 and 5, she provides examples of ads that prey on our desire for connection, our concern for our children, our desire to maintain long-term relationships, and our longing to repair damaged relationships.

3. This "climate of cynicism" is, according to Kilbourne, the inevitable result of advertising's campaign to portray human relationships as undesirable compared to relationships with products and brands.

4. Kilbourne quotes Goebbels (10) in support of her contention that propaganda is most dangerous when its targets consider themselves unaffected by it. Her association of the strategies of advertisers with those of a notorious Nazi most forcibly underlines Kilbourne's view of advertising as a potent force for evil in our culture.

5. According to Kilbourne, objectification leads to low self-esteem (particularly in girls, since girls/women still are most often objectified in advertising) and to the inability to form meaningful relationships. Advertising's promotion of relationships with products rather than people creates unhealthy addictions in consumers, particularly when the products are themselves chemically addictive, as in the case of tobacco and alcohol.

6. By transformation, Kilbourne is referring to the enlightenment—usually interpreted as self-knowledge and acceptance—that comes, in most religions, through suffering and sacrifice. According to Kilbourne, in consumerism, "the religion of our time (with advertising its holy text) . . . enlightenment is achieved instantly by purchasing material goods" (20). Kilbourne believes that such cheaply bought enlightenment is fool's gold—worth nothing at base, and ultimately harmful in making us believe that we possess something worthwhile.

7. The Gwich'in got television, along with its commercials, in 1980. Observers report that within ten years, tradition (including the language of the tribe, hunting methods, and oral history) were largely abandoned in favor of *Beverly Hills 90210* and Nike sneakers. Kilbourne uses the example to stress the enormous transformative power of advertising and to emphasize how much can be lost, more quickly than many of us think.

LANGUAGE IN ACTION

Although the *New York Times* makes no explicit comment, the photograph's juxtaposition of these two elements underlines the hypocrisy of our culture's rules regarding the promotion and consumption of sex. Kilbourne likely would have much to say about the phenomenon that is *America's Next Top Model*, in addition to the cult of the "super model" that gave rise to it. You might ask your students to use the show to test one or more of Kilbourne's ideas.

BARRICADING THE BRANDED VILLAGE

NAOMI KLEIN

THINKING CRITICALLY ABOUT THE READING

1. According to Klein, so-called "big box" chains like Wal-Mart, Kmart, and Blockbuster increasingly determine what the culture industry produces by refusing to sell what they don't like. This "corporate censorship" is, according to Klein, worse in some ways than government or pressure-group censorship, because its ideological motivation often is assumed to be purely economic in nature.

2. According to Klein, the explicit primary motivation is economic: The chains want their stores to be "one-stop shopping" for families, so they avoid stocking any product that parents might not want their children to see. Klein suggests, however, that this censorship ultimately springs from a conservative Christian ideology suspiciously close to the one the chains ascribe to parents who shop in their stores.

3. Klein seems most worried about the significant cultural impact such decisions can have: A group of executives at Wal-Mart, Kmart, and similar corporations is effectively determining what music we can listen to, what articles we can read, what images we can see, and what movies we can watch.

4. Rather than allowing its customers to see what's available and make their own decisions, the big-box chains are vetting magazines, films, books, and music, and, depending on whether they pass muster, either refusing to make them available to their customers or (perhaps more alarmingly) demanding changes in them before doing so. In cases where, as the spokesperson for Warner Brothers Records says, these chains are "the only game in town" (10), refusal to carry certain books, CDs, etc., effectively restricts entire segments of the population from access to them. If producers knuckle under to big-box pressure to alter products before they sell them, then censorship is built into the production process—increasing, in Klein's view, its insidious impact on the culture at large.

5. Klein writes that some of the complacency surrounding the censorship exercised by big-box retailers can be attributed to the fact that producers of culture and the retailers are in some cases owned by the same companies. One example Klein provides is the global conglomerate Viacom, which owns both Paramount Films and Blockbuster Video.

6. Klein considers this situation even more disturbing: "When newspapers, magazines, books, and television stations are but one arm of a conglomerate. . . there is obvious potential for the conglomerate's myriad financial interests to influence the kind of journalism that is produced" (13). Klein cites two examples of conglomerates' attempts to unduly influence reporting by their media holdings—one involving reporters for ABC news (owned by Disney), and another involving *Court TV* and *American Lawyer* (owned by Time-Warner).

7. Klein worries about instances where media outlets either inappropriately modify or don't publish stories that might be perceived as critical of their parent companies.

LANGUAGE IN ACTION

If you are treating this as a class activity, you might start by asking students for the categories—government; religious; political; corporate; school?—into which their experience of censorship falls. Do they agree with Klein that corporate censorship is a growing concern? Does censorship in *any* area concern them? Why or why not? Be sure to refer to Chapter 7's debate on censorship for further reading on the topic.

7. LANGUAGE DEBATE: SHOULD LEARNING BE CENSORED?

WE ARE FREE TO BE YOU, ME, STUPID, AND DEAD

ROGER ROSENBLATT

THINKING CRITICALLY ABOUT THE READING

1. Rosenblatt is saying that most of us are more comfortable with free speech in theory than in practice, particularly when someone's exercise of speech violates our cherished notions of right and wrong. He illustrates this contention with examples from the world of sports. Mahmoud Abdul-Rauf's refusal to stand for the national anthem is a form of expression likely to anger conservatives; John Rocker's comments about subway riders is more likely to rile liberals. Rosenblatt thinks the resulting suspensions were equally wrongheaded.

2. Rosenblatt wants his readers to reject gut-level responses to speech or other forms of expression that might offend us. In saying we "think" we know what we'll tolerate, he seems both to acknowledge the humanness of the gut-level response and to assume that, on further reflection, a reasonable person would put that response aside, allowing one's mind to "expand."

3. "Wild" implies a certain degree of recklessness, but paired with "courage," it seems to convey a more moderate sense of risk-taking. The phrase evokes a degree of youthfulness and "cool," attributes Rosenblatt might want to associate with the Founding Fathers in order to encourage his readers to take a fresh look at their achievement. The phrase also echoes Rosenblatt's characterization of American freedom in paragraph 3: "The beauty of American freedom is that it is ungovernable, that it always runs slightly ahead of human temperament."

4. These executives defended their promotion of cigarettes as a freedom-of-choice issue. Rosenblatt seems to agree with the position, despite the lawsuits that have criminalized some tobacco companies' activities and the murkiness surrounding the notion of "choice" in the use of a chemically addictive substance.

5. Apart from surreptitiously published or performed materials (books, music, poetry) protesting the regime, Rosenblatt reports that people used double-edged humor to express themselves. The desk clerk used a conventionally professional speech pattern ("Mr. Rosenblatt, would you mind coming back . . ."), subverting it with absurd detail ("in 15 years?") that highlighted the inadequacies of the current system.

6. Judging from this essay, it seems that Rosenblatt does object to any curtailing of speech that can't be likened to crying "fire" in a crowded theater. Using examples from sports, politics, art, commerce, repressive regimes, and education, he calls those whose expression has the strong potential to offend "jackasses" and "sons of bitches," but implies that those who illegitimately curtail such expression are guilty of "stupidities." Underlying this attitude is his belief that free expression, "like a legal drug," expands the mind, and that this expansion of mind in individuals is necessary for a vigorous society.

PORNOGRAPHY, OBSCENITY, AND THE CASE FOR CENSORSHIP

IRVING KRISTOL

THINKING CRITICALLY ABOUT THE READING

1. Kristol claims that he perceives "a rapidly growing unease and disquiet" (2) with the changes wrought by the successful (and, in Kristol's view, misguided) fight against censorship. He claims that liberals' "dogmatic resistance to the idea of censorship" disallows necessary distinctions, putting *Lady Chatterley's Lover* on the same level as the tawdriest pornography—thus exposing all and sundry to what Kristol considers the morally corrupting effects of the latter.

2. Kristol believes that art certainly can improve and corrupt, and that the aim of education is improvement (as well as the ability to tell the difference between the improving and the corrupting). Students will have varying opinions on this. Ask them to provide examples both of books and of their real or alleged corrupting effects. (Be sure to insist that these effects if claimed as real, have to be demonstrable.)

3. In order to bolster his argument that all of us, when pressed, would draw the line of the "permissible" somewhere, Kristol suggests in paragraph 6 that virtually no one would endorse onstage suicide, torture, or gladiatorial contests in today's society, even if the stated aim was "artistic" and all involved were consenting adults.

4. Kristol believes that pornography (which treats "sex as a public spectacle") is distinct from "erotic art" in that "its purpose is to treat human beings obscenely, to deprive human beings of their specifically human dimension." For his reason, Kristol believes it has the potential to "brutalize and debase" the society that produces and consumes it.

5. Kristol claims that radical proponents of pornography who believe that "everything is permitted" are essentially nihilists, believers in nothing, and that they are therefore the enemies of civilization. Pornography itself, he writes, is "inherently and purposefully subversive of civilization." In his view, this makes censorship of pornography a political question, in the deepest sense. More specifically, he writes, obscenity/pornography is a threat to democracy because it disrupts "the way the citizen in a democracy views himself" and thus the "quality of public life" that in Kristol's view is essential to a democracy.

6. By "quality of life," Kristol refers not to mundane factors such as income vs. cost-of-living, but to the quality of *moral* life, measured in terms of self-knowledge, self-control, and right conduct, which for Kristol are important constituents of virtue. Democratic society, according to Kristol, is most importantly a form of self-government. As such, its

quality depends on the quality of the citizenry that makes it up. Kristol argues that the democratic society, if it is to remain uncorrupted, needs to ensure that the individual citizens who make it up are uncorrupted. For these reasons, Kristol argues, a healthy democracy would unhesitatingly censor pornography for the good of the society.

THE FREE-SPEECH FOLLIES

STANLEY FISH

THINKING CRITICALLY ABOUT THE READING

1. Fish argues that many claims of "First Amendment" rights, especially in academia, reflect a misunderstanding of what the First Amendment actually protects: "[The student] was alluding to the old saw that the First Amendment protects unpopular as well as popular speech. But what it protects unpopular speech *from* is abridgment by the government of its free expression; it does not protect unpopular speech from being rejected by a newspaper, and it confers no positive obligation to give your pages over to unpopular speech, or popular speech, or any speech." Fish alludes to examples of illegitimate claims to First Amendment protection outside academia in his first paragraph, but the extended examples he provides in his argument all come from academia: campus newspapers at the University of Illinois and Santa Rosa Junior College, the Harvard University English department, and U.C. Berkeley. These claims, and others like them, constitute the "free-speech follies" he refers to in his title.

2. The editor claimed that 1) the paper was "committed to giving all people a voice"; 2) it printed the opinions of those with whom it did not agree; 3) it did so in the name of avoiding "silencing" and "self-censorship"; and 4) "hate speech" and "free speech" are relative terms. Fish takes each of these claims in turn, calling them flat wrong. He insists that the paper, like all papers, would exclude some voices (he gives the example of the KKK) widely considered objectionable; that they clearly apply judgment in deciding which articles to print; and that the paper, like all papers, has the responsibility to exercise this judgment. Fish argues that the decision to print the piece had nothing to do with the First Amendment.

3. In paragraphs 7 and 8, Fish writes that what the editor of the *Daily Illini* refers to as "self-censorship" is actually judgment, which is a necessary constituent of responsible and effective expression. He contends that we all "censor" ourselves appropriately "whenever we decide not to say something or cut a sentence that went just a little bit too far or leave a manuscript in the bottom drawer because it is not yet ready."

4. Fish interprets the First Amendment strictly, as prohibiting the government from restricting speech: "It does not protect unpopular speech from being rejected by a newspaper, and it confers no positive obligation to give your pages over to . . . any speech."

5. In Fish's view, the department's invitation to the poet to speak on campus was a judgment call, not a question of the First Amendment. As with the decisions of campus newspapers to publish controversial pieces, the question was not one of rights (in this case, the right of the poet to speak at this particular forum) or obligations (of the department to provide the forum): ". . . At each stage, whatever they did or didn't do would have had no relationship whatsoever to any First Amendment right."

6. As with the other examples Fish provides, this example illustrates a case where judgment and responsibility were at issue, not First Amendment rights. The chancellor's edits were, in Fish's view, appropriate: "Goldman still speaks freely through her words. The project director can still make her political opinions known by writing letters to the editor or to everyone in the country, even if she cannot use the vehicle of a university flier to do so. . . . The project goes on unimpeded, and the university goes about its proper academic business."

7. In turning her back to the flag during the national anthem, Fish says, Toni Smith was "truly exercising her First Amendment rights, rights that ensure that she cannot be compelled to an affirmation she does not endorse."

HOW CAMPUS CENSORS SQUELCH FREEDOM OF SPEECH

STUART TAYLOR JR.

THINKING CRITICALLY ABOUT THE READING

1. The facts of the case are disputed, but Taylor contends that the conservative—some would say offensive—message of Hinkle's flyer was the source of the African-American students' call to campus police. The university contends that Hinkle disrupted the students' Bible study meeting and ordered him to apologize to the students in writing or face penalties.

2. Based on research done by the Foundation for Individual Rights in Education (FIRE), Taylor reports that there appear to be "vague rules against racial or sexual 'harassment'" at Georgetown, the University of Massachusetts, Brown, Dartmouth, and the University of Maryland. Although most of these rules regulate speech, Taylor points out that "[m]any campuses define 'leering' as a form of harassment. A training document once used at the University of Maryland even warned against 'holding or eating food provocatively.'"

3. Taylor writes of the rules: "Their vagueness and overbreadth violate students' First Amendment rights in the case of public universities and may violate their contractual rights in the case of those private universities that advertise themselves as devoted to free and open debate."

4. In addition to offering legal assistance to students who, like Hinkle, run afoul of speech code rules, FIRE "employs the threat of public exposure to persuade campus administrators to back off in individual censorship-through-discipline cases. It has also produced pamphlets informing students in detail of their legal rights. And in the past few months, FIRE has helped launch a litigation offensive against speech codes."

5. Texas Tech confines "free speech activities" to a designated twenty-foot-wide gazebo, unless students seek and receive official approval six days in advance to engage in such activities elsewhere on campus. Considering these policies a clear infringement of students' right to free speech, FIRE has taken the school to court. [According to FIRE's Web site (thefire.org), a federal judge struck down the university's speech code in 2004.]

6. According to *American Enterprise*, faculty in most academic departments at top schools are disproportionately "registered in parties of the left (including Democrats)"; Taylor cites this finding, following it with the assertion that "[d]espite the cries of 'McCarthyism'

raised by the left since September 11, there has been only a smattering of unwarranted attacks on leftist or anti-American speech." He supports the latter claim with a single example of an Ethiopian student at San Diego State University who was disciplined for reproaching students who were (according to Taylor) "gleefully celebrating" the 9/11 attacks shortly after they occurred.

THE LANGUAGE POLICE

DIANE RAVITCH

THINKING CRITICALLY ABOUT THE READING

1. Ravitch cites examples of censorship promoted by the political right and left, listing as many different situations and motivations as she can. Her analysis is less abstract and equally important as those that so often make the news because the decisions she chooses to look at affect everyone in the educational system—children, parents, educators, and administrators. Her analysis is important because the books in question are used for educational purposes, presumably to encourage and help shape individual thought.

2. According to Ravitch, the New Right defined secular humanism as "a New Age religion that ignored biblical teachings and shunned moral absolutes." As a religion, they reasoned, it should either be banned from public schools (as secular humanists argued Christian teaching should be) or taught alongside Christian doctrine. Examples of "secular humanist" content the New Right wanted banned from textbooks are discussions of "abortion, out-of-wedlock pregnancy, homosexuality, suicide, drug use, foul language" and the teaching of evolution.

3. Ravitch claims that left-leaning groups, the most active of which she identifies as "militantly feminist" and "militantly liberal," have had extraordinary influence over the educational publishing industry that produces textbooks. Ravitch ascribes this influence in large part to the activities of the Council on Interracial Books for Children (CIBC), which from its inception in 1966 became increasingly radical in its demands for "fairness" in educational materials, subjecting all such materials to stringent "bias checklists" which, according to critic Nat Hentoff, amounted to "righteous vigilantism."

4. The checklist judged whether a given book exhibits racism, sexism, elitism, materialism, ageism, conformism, escapism, and individualism; whether it promotes positive or negative images of females/minorities; whether it "inspires action versus oppression"; and whether it is "culturally authentic." According to Hentoff, use of the checklist inhibited freedom of expression and artistic creativity.

5. Ravitch points out that the culture at many publishing companies was left-leaning in the first place, "which helps to explain why the major publishing companies swiftly accepted the sweeping linguistic claims of feminist critics and willingly yielded to a code of censorship." She writes that some companies such as Holt fought attempts at censorship by right-wing groups. On the other hand, she reports, by the end of the 1980s, because offending any groups raised the specter of a loss of revenue, "every publisher had complied with the demands of critics, both from the left and right." Although Ravitch attempts to present a balanced account of the activities of right and left, she does seem to be more

sympathetic to the left-leaning groups, which she represents as having taken a good thing too far, as in the following passage: "CIBC's critiques of racial and gender stereotyping undoubtedly raised the consciousness of textbook publishers about the white-only world of their products and prompted necessary revisions."

6. It is difficult to know whether or not a text has undergone censorship, since no one slaps a label that says "censored" on such books. However, tone and a consistent general subject matter can indicate whether or not a book has been censored. The difficulty knowing whether or not a book has been censored makes the issue more important because people often think they have freedom to information, freedom to enjoy whatever literature they choose—it is hard to believe that this is not always the case.

7. Ravitch indicates that the work of the language police is often felt when the publishing industry changes its "bottom line" because of complaints, boycotts, or lawsuits. Textbook censorship becomes "invisible" because even when the language police's outcry has died down, publications continue to be affected. The public is made up of the right, the left, and the middle, all of whom want textbooks with a bias in this direction, that direction, or no bias at all. It is impossible to set up a group in charge of guaranteeing bias-free textbooks. A watch-dog oversight group would limit choices (much like the censors) and ultimately offer the same "thin gruel" that Ravitch bemoans at the end of her essay.

WITH A NO. 2 PENCIL, DELETE: THE DESTRUCTION OF LITERATURE IN THE NAME OF CHILDREN

ANNA QUINDLEN

THINKING CRITICALLY ABOUT THE READING

1. Her tone in the opening paragraph is sarcastic: She reports being "honored" that her work "was going to be mangled for the sake of standardized testing" in Georgia, and "disappointed" that she was left out of New York State's test, which "included excerpts from literary writers edited so nonsensically that the work had essentially lost all meaning."

2. According to the editor of Quindlen's piece, "The words 'slave' and 'pornography' deal with controversial issues that could cause an emotional reaction in some students that could distract them from the test and affect their performance." It seems likely that the fear of offending parents (however unlikely) also played a role. Students will have varying opinions on whether the edits could or should be defended.

3. According to Quindlen, all references to Jews and Poles were taken out of Singer's excerpt, and all references to race removed from Dillard's piece about being the only white child in a library in a black neighborhood. The New York State Education Department's guidelines require the removal of any material that might conflict with the beliefs, values, or experiences of any parent, teacher, or examinee. Quindlen writes that the guidelines would seem to exclude anything "except the most homogenized piece of pap about Cape Cod tide pools."

4. Quindlen claims that educators are withholding quality literature from students, inflicting dull textbooks on them, and leaving them intellectually stifled by "incessant testing." Stu-

dents will have varying opinions on this (depending in large part, presumably, on their own educational experiences).

5. In response to the New York state guideline that stipulates the avoidance of material that "assumes values not shared by all test takers," Quindlen writes that "[t]here is no book worth reading, no poem worth writing, no essay worth analyzing, that assumes the same values for all." She implies that all good writing challenges readers' assumptions and stimulates them to test their own ideas—and bemoans the fact that good writing is explicitly excluded by the New York state guidelines.

6. Quindlen asserts that students learn "[t]hat the written word doesn't really matter much, that it can be weakened at will. That no one trusts a student to understand that variations in opinion and background are both objectively interesting and intellectually challenging." It's unlikely that many students actually will be aware of the "cut-and-paste" practices as such, weakening her claim that they will learn disrespect for the integrity of the written word. Her point that the resulting "pabulum" will not challenge students is easier to defend.

7. Quindlen is acknowledging a possible objection from her reader—that she must be comfortable with being edited, since she writes for a magazine with limited space. She admits that she edits herself sometimes, but she explains that she is not arguing against changing a piece for length or clarity. By refuting this possible argument, she effectively refocuses on her point.

8. LANGUAGE DEBATE: SHOULD ENGLISH BE THE LAW?

SHOULD ENGLISH BE THE LAW?

ROBERT D. KING

THINKING CRITICALLY ABOUT THE READING

1. The issue of language in the United States became politicized in the 1980s and 1990s when several states passed laws requiring that all government business be conducted in English. In 1996 the U.S. House of Representatives followed suit, passing a bill that would have made English the nation's official language. The trend arose in response to the increasing presence of Spanish-speaking immigrants in the United States.

2. To be politically correct is to act or speak in ways designed not to offend. The leaders of the Official English movement have no interest in being politically correct. King makes this statement—"Official English is politically very incorrect" (8)—in the context of a discussion of the political leanings of those who support making English the nation's official language. Although the majority of the proponents of Official English are now politically conservative, King points out that in an earlier era many people with more liberal views supported the notion.

3. King argues that Official English is controversial because it intersects with a number of other important issues, including "immigration (above all), the rights of minorities (Span-

ish-speaking minorities in particular), the pros and cons of bilingual education, tolerance, how best to educate the children of immigrants, and the place of cultural diversity in school curricula and in American society in general" (12).

4. King explores the relationship between language and nationality in order to dispel the notion that a country without a single, official language is necessarily a country rife with tension and problems. He cites the examples of Switzerland and India, both of which have several official languages and also enjoy relative prosperity. (King acknowledges that India does face some serious challenges as a result of internal problems but contends that language is not at the root of these problems.) The thrust of his argument is that many things besides language—religion, culture, shared history—tie people of a nation together. On this basis, King draws the conclusion that the existence and use of languages besides English in the United States does not threaten the nation's unity.

5. By *unique otherness* King means that the people of a country have certain things in common that bind them together. In the case of the United States, King argues, Americans have a shared history that includes the Civil War, the frontier tradition, a love affair with the automobile, and sports. All of these things, and others, constitute Americans' *unique otherness*. Students' opinions may differ about whether Americans' unique otherness will allow the country to rise above conflicts over issues of language. King's piece offers an opportunity for discussion about what Americans have in common and whether those commonalities are enough to hold the nation together in the face of divisions caused by language, religious, or cultural differences.

6. Students may have different feelings about this issue. Ask them about their experiences in places in the United States where the majority of people do not speak English. Point out that this essay was published in 1997 and that King wrote, "we are not even close to the danger point." Has the situation changed since then? What would constitute "the danger point"?

IN PLAIN ENGLISH: LET'S MAKE IT OFFICIAL

CHARLES KRAUTHAMMER

THINKING CRITICALLY ABOUT THE READING

1. "One of the major reasons for America's great success as the world's first 'universal nation,' for its astonishing and unmatched capacity for assimilating immigrants, has been that an automatic part of acculturation was the acquisition of English" (paragraph 3). In other words, America's great success came in large part from the fact that immigrants had to learn English.

2. He argues that immigrants who speak only their native language are a real threat to the culture and population. There is a need for an official language. In the past, the multitudes of immigrants spoke myriad languages, so no one language could dominate the country. Now, however, Spanish is in a position to cause unrest and social division.

3. Monoclonal immigration is the movement of a singular type of people from one country to another. Rather than having many people from many countries immigrating, one culture's movement dominates and challenges the norms of the chosen country. Because people

from that culture are so heavily represented in the new country, they don't feel the need to assimilate to the ways of the country they've immigrated to and this threatens national identity.

4. The great worry about Spanish is that the language and culture will serve to divide the United States in two. The culture will experience unrest, and a battle between the English- and Spanish-speaking portions of the culture will ensue, just as occurred in Quebec between its French- and English-speaking counterparts. He is afraid the country will be caught in an endless and unnecessary struggle between the two groups.

5. Krauthammer believes that "linguistic unity" at the very least will send the message that the United States is one country. This will help prevent two separate dominant cultures. You may want to ask students if they think that making English official is enough to prevent the social unrest and divisiveness Krauthammer warns about. You may also ask them to name examples of current social unrest in the United States and whether Krauthammer mentions them.

6. He believes that unless the U.S. government can truly instill English as the official language—meaning "the language of the government and its institutions"—the country will be vulnerable to divisiveness. If the government cannot do so now, it will have a hard time unifying the country in the future. Fear of sounding "racist" is preventing the government from taking a stand on the issue that would instill continuity and social rest. It is the government's job to keep the peace, and making English the official language would help achieve this end, according to Krauthammer.

WHY AND WHEN WE SPEAK SPANISH IN PUBLIC

MYRIAM MARQUEZ

THINKING CRITICALLY ABOUT THE READING

1. Marquez indicates in paragraph 5 that she speaks Spanish in certain situations as a matter of respect for her parents and comfort with her original culture (her roots). If they were speaking Spanish together it would not be rude, unless a non-Spanish speaker was trying to understand or communicate with them.

2. The U.S. government has not made English the official language of the country because "being an American has very little to do with what language we use during our free time in a free country" (7). Government tries to leave individuals (and their rights) alone. Given Marquez's argument, it is unclear why such legislation is needed now.

3. The English-only debate gets muddied when people see language as "some sort of litmus test used to gauge American patriotism" (9). Marquez explains that some "American" values are "defined by English speakers from North America" (6). In those cases, what it means to be "American" is unreasonably narrowed to one type of person.

4. Marquez would stop speaking Spanish and use English if she was in a group with two bilingual and one non-Spanish speaker. This is interesting, given that most people in the United States would not be able to accommodate a non-English speaker. Marquez knows that her action would include the person who could not understand, and one would hope that other bilingual speakers would behave in the same way.

Saying "Adios" to Spanglish

Leticia Salais

THINKING CRITICALLY ABOUT THE READING

1. Salais believes that being bilingual is a gift, allowing one to help others and to appreciate the richness of other cultures.

2. Salais begins her essay with a sentence in Spanish that she does not immediately translate, inviting the reader to discover the meaning on his/her own. In doing so, she illustrates her position that fluency in both languages is an asset. She repeats the strategy in the closing of her essay, where she celebrates her older son's use of Spanish (also not immediately translated) in preference to English.

3. Salais saw her Latina background as a disadvantage growing up, because she associated it with the poverty in which she was raised: "I did everything I could to escape the poverty and the color of my skin." Rejecting the Spanish language was her way of entering the mainstream where, she hoped, she would find an easier path to success and happiness.

4. After initially rejecting bilingualism for herself and her oldest son, Salais began to experience its advantages, specifically in terms of communicating with Spanish speakers from many countries with whom she came in contact through her work in a nursing home. She began to realize that speaking Spanish opened up new worlds to her and worked in earnest to improve her proficiency.

5. She realized that in keeping her firstborn son from speaking Spanish, she was depriving him of the practical, emotional, and aesthetic advantages it could bring. She corrected her mistake with her second-born son, writing, "I am proud to say that his first language was Spanish."

6. Salais likely is attempting to underline yet another practical advantage of bilingualism; however, some readers might feel that her emphasis on the power bilingualism gives her to exclude others contradicts her implicit claim that bilingualism opens doors.

From Outside, In

Barbara Mellix

THINKING CRITICALLY ABOUT THE READING

1. Mellix is somehow limited at first by her "native tongue." Through her narrative she comes to master the "proper" English, which feels foreign. Only by making the entire range of English her own does she fully enter the language.

2. Mellix learns that Black English is all right for use within the family but not for social occasions. Black English is preferred in the family because it doesn't imply the superiority associated with "proper" English. This "doubleness" creates a split in Mellix, and she feels somehow removed from Standard English even though it, too, is part of her experience.

3. There is a sense of inferiority associated with the use of Black English amongst whites and a "putting on of airs" associated with the use of Standard English speaking with her fellow Blacks. Using Standard English, for Mellix, meant moving outside the familiar, the family, the known.

4. Mellix's father told stories that illustrated the limits of Black English and her mother punished the use of Black English in the presence of company. The "power" of language lies in how it shapes relationships between people. People relate to each other and make choices of what language to use based on the way they wish to present themselves to the world.

5. In her college composition class, Mellix realized that she is behind the words she writes no matter which version of English she chooses. The words she selects and matches to her internal experience allow her to take control of English "venturing into new territory" (28) with each use of the language.

THE GOOD DAUGHTER

CAROLINE HWANG

THINKING CRITICALLY ABOUT THE READING

1. At the point in her life she describes in the opening of her essay, Hwang was particularly concerned about her identity, having just dropped out of graduate school and not decided yet where she was headed. Clearly, this uncertainty extended to how her Korean background fit into her life in America. Suddenly learning that she had mispronounced her Korean last name all her life must have been unsettling under these circumstances.

2. Hwang's parents are immigrants who came to America seeking opportunities not available to them or to their offspring in Korea. Their high hopes and ambitions for her ("They told me often, while I was growing up, that, if I wanted to, I could be president some day"), along with "the sacrifices they made in leaving Korea—including my mispronounced name" made success a high priority for Hwang. As she writes in paragraph 15, "By making the biggest move of their lives for me, my parents indentured me to the largest debt imaginable—I owe them the fulfillment of their hopes for me."

3. Torn between following her own dreams of being a writer and fulfilling her parents' expectations that she find a stable, remunerative career, Hwang compromises by entering a Ph.D. program in English literature. When she leaves the program, for which she feels no passion, she writes, "I . . . felt I was staring at the bottom of the abyss." The "halfwayness" she perceives in her life choices mirrors her sense that she is caught between two cultures, Korean and American: ". . . I feel displaced in the only country I know. I identify with Americans, but Americans do not identify with me."

4. The English-only debate, on some level, is a debate about assimilation. Hwang's parents wanted her to become fully assimilated in order to ensure her success in America; for this reason, presumably, they taught her little about the Korean language (including its correct pronunciation). Advocates of "English-only" measures insist that immigrants (and the children of immigrants) adopt English as their primary means of communication outside the home; in the view of some such advocates, this can most readily be achieved by making

English the primary means of communication within the home as well. This model of assimilation seems to be the one adopted by Hwang's parents; Hwang's essay acknowledges their good intentions, but emphasizes what can be lost along the way.

5. Students will have varying perspectives on this question. Language facility, though a crucial ingredient in cultural identity, is by no means the only one. Hwang's ancestry and some of her parents' expectations (as, for example, their insistence that she marry a man of Korean extraction) certainly complicate her "all-American" identity.

6. As with question 5, students will have different responses to this question. Hwang would probably not argue with her designation as "American," but the question remains: Is that the whole of her identity? What role does—or should—the culture of the country her parents left behind have in this identity? What, in the end, does it mean to be an "American"? Is there such a thing as a truly "all-American" identity?

9. Language Debate: What's All the Fuss About Natural, Organic, Local Foods?

Putting It Back Together Again: Processed Foods

Michael Pollan

THINKING CRITICALLY ABOUT THE READING

1. The first age comprised salting, drying, curing, and pickling foods; the second added canning, freezing, and vacuum-packing; the third age, which Pollan dates from the end of World War II, aims to "improve on nature" with highly processed foods (like margarine, Cheez Whiz, and the like) intended to replace their natural equivalents. As Pollan points out, this third age depended not just on technology, but on marketing and a culture that prizes convenience.

2. Students' responses likely will vary widely. The Institute of Cereal Technology is the place where new kinds of cereal, which constitute General Mills' most profitable line of products, are invented. Pollan describes an extremely secretive, high-stakes, high-tech corporate environment likely at odds (at least to some extent) with the way most of us imagine the places responsible for making our morning cornflakes. Some students likely will express surprise at the vast difference between the cost of raw ingredients and the cost of the final product.

3. Pollan suggests that the term "food system," increasingly in use in the food industry, is a euphemism for "processed food," which has negative connotations. He does imply that the level of processing is more extreme than ever, which might in itself justify the need for a new term: "It's probably as good a term as any when you're describing . . . a nutraceutical breakfast cereal so fortified with green tea, grape seed extract, and antioxidants that it's not even called a cereal but a 'healthy heart system.'" Students will have different responses to this use of language. As Pollan points out, it does seem to indicate a real change in the way we prepare and consume food, but it also puts a positive spin on what, for Pollan, is clearly a negative development.

4. The primary problem Pollan cites is the biological limit on how much food consumers can consume, called the problem of the "fixed stomach" in the food industry: "What this means for the food industry is that its natural rate of growth is somewhere around one percent per year—one percent being the annual growth rate of the American population. The problem is that Wall Street won't tolerate such an anemic rate of growth." The solution the industry has found is twofold: They charge more for food by "adding value" (i.e., processing, branding, and marketing it) and they have developed at least one means of overcoming the "fixed stomach" in the form of indigestible starch, which "slips through the digestive tract without ever turning into calories." Pollan predicts that fake sugars, fats, and starches will achieve one of the food industry's key aims: "the ultimate—the utterly elastic!—industrial eater."

5. Because the availability and price of raw goods depends on nature, which is (still) beyond the food industry's control, it's in their interest to devise highly processed foods in which ingredients can be substituted without affecting the product's salability. Essentially, the management consultant's observation means that American consumers can expect to encounter ever more elaborately processed foods, since the food industry's bottom line depends upon them.

6. Chicken, relatively inexpensive as a whole, unbranded food, generates far more profit for a producer when sold in a highly processed, branded form such as chicken nuggets. Students likely consume "high-value-added products" every day—in fact, it might be more challenging for them to list the *un*processed foods they typically eat. According to Pollan, farmers see little or none of the profit generated by "value-added" products: "Of a dollar spent on a whole food such as eggs, $0.40 finds its way back to the farmer. By comparison, [farmer] George Naylor will see only $0.04 of every dollar spent on corn sweeteners" (16). Consumers, enticed by convenience and beguiled by marketing strategies, end up paying more for food that is less healthy than whole foods. In the end, the food processor is the party that gains from the "value" added to highly processed foods, in the form of fat year-end profits.

7. The "dilemma" is a problem for food producers. Although food production can continue to expand, the amount of food people can eat will stay essentially fixed. There is not a lot of room for a business to grow once people can buy enough food so they do not go hungry. Pollan explains that food companies have two choices: to convince people to pay more for the food they eat or to convince them to eat more (or, a combination of the two strategies). The increasing number of "premium" products and rising obesity levels in the United States, seem to indicate that these strategies are in effect.

CALLED HOME

BARBARA KINGSOLVER

THINKING CRITICALLY ABOUT THE READING

1. Kingsolver describes "agricultural basics" as knowing such things as "what animals and vegetables thrive in one's immediate region and how to live well on those." Kingsolver claims that the loss of this knowledge causes problems "as diverse as overdependence on petroleum, and an epidemic of diet-related diseases."

2. Students will have a variety of opinions on this. You might ask them whether Kingsolver's examples in paragraphs 8–13 ring true to them. How well do they understand the growth of pineapples, potatoes, or other of the fruits and vegetables we eat? Do they, in fact, know what animals and vegetables thrive in the region in which they live?

3. Kingsolver writes about the post-World War II explosion in corn and soybean production, which was fueled by the use of chemical fertilizers manufactured from wartime surpluses of ammonium nitrate (formerly used to make explosives). Pressure from the burgeoning food industry convinced government to withdraw economic safeguards that formerly protected independent farmers growing other crops and instead to subsidize further production of corn and soybeans, which were used to produce the industry's increasingly highly processed foods. These foods yield less profit for the farmer, but more for the processors, marketers, and distributors. Perhaps most importantly for Kingsolver, they represent less nutritious food for Americans increasingly beset by diet-related illnesses.

4. According to Kingsolver, "[f]ood cultures concentrate a population's collective wisdom about the plants and animals that grow in a place, and the complex ways of rendering them tasty. These are mores of survival, good health, and control of excess." She asserts that a food culture like that of Italy or France, where food is recognizably Italian or French and predictable rules govern its consumption, has never taken root in the United States: "We have yet to come up with a strong set of generalized norms, passed down through families, for savoring and sensibly consuming what our land and climate give us."

5. Kingsolver points to the "string of fad diets convulsing our bookstores and bellies" (25) as a sign of something deeply wrong in our relation to food. She implies that our lack of a food culture can be ascribed in large part to "a profit-driven food industry [that] has exploded and nutritionally bankrupted our caloric supply" (25). She sees a glimmer of hope for resistance to this all-but-overwhelming force in the fact that "[b]etter food—more local, more healthy, more sensible—is a powerful new topic of the American conversation" (28).

6. In paragraph 32, she suggests that we strive to eat food that comes from the region in which we live; that we learn and come to terms with the natural facts of how food is grown; and that we start learning about where all of the food we eat currently comes from. She writes that even these small steps undertaken by individual families will make a difference.

WHAT'S NATURAL ABOUT OUR NATURAL PRODUCTS?

SARAH FEDERMAN

THINKING CRITICALLY ABOUT THE READING

1. In paragraph 5 Federman gives the dictionary definition of natural: "1) determined by nature, 2) of or relating to nature, 3) having normal or usual character, 4) grown without human care, 5) not artificial, 6) present in or produced by nature." In the same paragraph Federman lists a number of the connotations that consumers bring to this word: wholesome, pure, vegetarian, environmentally friendly, healthy, organic, pure, and better. Have your students talk about the associations they have for the word.

2. The Nutrition Labeling and Education Act of 1990 restricts the use of the following terms: "low fat, low sodium, low cholesterol, low calorie, lean, extra lean, reduced, good source, less, fewer, light, and more" (6). *Organic* products must align themselves with the standards established by such acts as the California Organic Foods Act of 1990. At this point, *natural* is an unregulated word.

3. Manufacturers use the word *natural* to create an appeal or image for their products and to promote a new product line without knocking the standard product. When Federman says "they use the word and 'we' create the aura" (7), she means that manufacturers use the word *natural* (or one of its variants) and that the consumers bring the positive associations, or aura, to the product.

4. Federman uses the examples of Kraft's Natural Shredded Non-Fat Cheese (4) and Lays "Naturally Baked" Potato Chips (7) for several reasons. First and most obvious is the fact that most readers are familiar with these products. Second, she's asking readers to take a critical look at how the words *natural* and *naturally* are being used—something that most consumers haven't paid any attention to. Encourage students to provide other examples of products that use these words in similar ways. Like Federman, they might point to both national brands and products that are limited to a particular region of the country (in Federman's case, the West Coast).

5. Students may come up with a variety of reasons why manufacturers often charge more for their "natural" products. Our students have suggested that a) with a high price, the product must be better (or better products are higher priced); b) natural ingredients cost more to produce; and c) with a small market, production costs may in fact be higher.

CLAIMS CRAZY: WHICH CAN YOU BELIEVE?

BONNIE LIEBMAN

THINKING CRITICALLY ABOUT THE READING

1. Structure/function claims relate to how food affects the body's structure or function. Such claims do not mean that a food cures any particular kind of illness.

2. A supplement becomes a drug if it can accurately claim to "diagnose, cure, mitigate, treat, or prevent" disease (11).

3. Preliminary health claims are based on preliminary (as yet inconclusive) studies. The food industry is allowed to make structure/function claims, while adhering to very few restrictions, on many different foods. It is fairly easy for the industry to make structure/function claims. Solid health claims are based on actual scientific fact and evidence.

4. Food companies are competing with each other to sell their products, and there is an element of deceit in using easily made claims to promote their foods. Claims put customers at risk if they think that a structure/function claim means a food prevents or cures disease. Because the wording of structure/function claims is vague, it might be construed as a disease claim.

Is Whole Foods Wholesome?

Field Maloney

THINKING CRITICALLY ABOUT THE READING

1. The chain has a largely positive public image, based on its commitment to organic products, its fair treatment of its staff, and other seemingly progressive practices, such as its purchase of wind power from a Wyoming utility.

2. The first reason to buy organic offered by the chain on its banner is that buying organic saves energy. Maloney takes issue with this, claiming Whole Foods doesn't factor in energy expended in transporting organic produce over long distances. According to Maloney, its claim that buying organic helps the small farmer is "semantic sleight of hand. . . . There are a lot of small, family-run organic farmers, but their share of the organic crop in this country, and of the produce sold at Whole Foods, is miniscule." Maloney also claims that the chain's vaunted "Commitment to the Local Farmer" is largely invisible outside of marketing materials: The vast majority of produce in the store, according to Maloney, is non-local, as one would expect from a multinational corporation. Maloney concludes his critique of these marketing claims by asserting the following: "If Whole Foods marketing didn't revolve so much around explicit (as well as subtly suggestive) appeals to food ethics, it'd be easier to forgive some exaggerations and distortions." Students will differ in their responses to Maloney's claims. You might ask students what their experience of Whole Foods has been. Do they believe that Maloney's claims represent current practices at the store? Are his examples of how Whole Foods promotes its produce representative or exceptional?

3. If Maloney's contention that selling local foods is not compatible with the model of a multinational corporation, the existence of a local foods movement representing significant buying power obviously would present it with a quandary. It might be interesting to ask students to anticipate ways in which a corporation like Whole Foods might attempt to solve such a dilemma: By attempting to discredit the local foods movement? By adjusting their model to allow for more flexibility in offerings at different branches? By supporting local producers in a mutually beneficial arrangement (for example, by subsidizing farmers' markets)?

4. Elitism is a fairly common charge against Whole Foods (nicknamed "Whole Paycheck" by critics) and those who shop there. Maloney argues that the "organic-food movement is in danger of exacerbating the growing gap between rich and poor in this country by contributing to a two-tiered national food supply, with healthy food for the rich." Whole Foods and other suppliers of organic foods likely would argue that organic foods simply are more expensive to produce and distribute, and that their markups are comparable to those of sellers of conventional produce. They also might argue that it's appropriate for Americans to spend more, proportionately, on food than they do currently, if that means eating better in terms of nutrition and safety—in other words, they should adjust their priorities. Your students are likely to have fairly pronounced opinions on this subject. You might ask them whether, in their opinion, the problem lies with Whole Foods or with the larger system of food production and distribution in the United States—particularly if they have read the essays by Pollan or Kingsolver in this section.

5. Maloney, essentially espousing the populist argument about the elitism of Whole Foods, seems to believe that Wal-Mart's entry into the organic foods market will be a good thing in terms of making organic food available to those with limited budgets—and that this will be a good thing for the country's health. His use of the word "sustainable" in this passage recalls his description in paragraph 2 of Whole Foods' progressive policies regarding staff compensation, with an implied contrast to Wal-Mart's less-than-stellar record in this area. He seems to imply, however, that the trade-off is worth it. Your students likely will have a variety of responses to this. Are they Wal-Mart customers? Do they know anything about the controversy over its treatment of its employees? How much, if at all, does such controversy affect their buying decisions?

THE POOR GET DIABETES, THE RICH GET LOCAL AND ORGANIC

MARK WINNE

THINKING CRITICALLY ABOUT THE READING

1. Like Field Maloney, Mark Winne is deeply worried about the fact that lower-income people have so little access to healthy food. He blames the "anti-poor policies" of Ronald Reagan's administration in the 1980s with giving rise to more widespread hunger, minimally addressed by soup kitchens and food banks. He suggests that inadequate access to fresh, healthy foods is directly related to the nationwide rise in rates of obesity and diabetes, which disproportionately affect those with lower incomes. Sadly, according to Winne, only the wealthy have the leisure to contemplate "how to bestow style and grace on something as ordinary as a local tomato"; those with lower incomes have to cope with "getting to a food store where the bananas weren't black."

2. Supermarkets in lower-income neighborhoods close when the costs of maintaining them are no longer offset by acceptable profits; this tends to happen when nearby residents have too little disposable income to spend more than the bare minimum on food. The inconvenience of having to travel outside of the neighborhood for fresh food predisposes even those who have the money and time to travel to fall back on what remains: in many cases, fast food. The impact on health can be seen in disproportionately high rates of obesity and diabetes in these neighborhoods. The question of whether Whole Foods (for example) will open a branch in East Harlem should generate some interesting discussion. If you have Internet access in your classroom, you might start with a search verifying that in fact Whole Foods has *not* opened a store in East Harlem. Assuming it has not, ask students to speculate on what would have to change in order to make Whole Foods do so. What factors are at play? What variables determine the outcome?

3. According to Winne, many people believe that lower-income consumers either are unaware of the existence of organic foods or uninterested in buying them, given the chance. Based on interviews he conducted as the director of the non-profit Hartford Food System, Winne concluded that both notions are myths. In asking students about their own assumptions, you might want to ask them about their own views on organic food. Do they buy it? Can they? Why or why not?

4. Winne concluded that "Their awareness of the benefits of local and organic food was very high. For the elderly, there was the nostalgic association with tastes, places, and times gone by. For those with young children, there was an apprehension that nearly everything associated with their external environment, including food, was a threat." Unfortunately, Winne also found that their access to such foods was very poor, for reasons of cost and convenience.

5. Winne points to two means of closing the food gap: private initiatives and public policy. According to Winne, private nonprofits can help coordinate the entry of Community Supported Agriculture (CSA) ventures and supermarkets into low-income neighborhoods: Presumably, once assured there is a market for their products in these underserved neighborhoods, CSAs and markets would flourish there. Additionally, their presence would provide employment opportunities and strengthen the local tax base. Winne also praises recent public policy initiatives, which include federal and state funding for farmers' market vouchers and changes to the national Woman, Infant, and Children Program (WIC) that subsidizes the purchase of local fruits and vegetables. Ask students whether they agree that government should play a larger role in ensuring that low-income residents have better access to healthy foods. Are there solutions other than the ones Winne proposes?